Tree kangaroos shown in their natural surroundings in a New Guinea forest

THE UNIVERSAL
STANDARD
ENCYCLOPEDIA

THE UNIVERSAL STANDARD ENCYCLOPEDIA

VOLUME 23

TECHNICAL—ULTRASONICS

*An abridgment of The New Funk & Wagnalls Encyclopedia
prepared under the editorial direction of*
JOSEPH LAFFAN MORSE, Sc.B., LL.B., LL.D.
Editor in Chief

STANDARD REFERENCE WORKS
PUBLISHING COMPANY, INC., NEW YORK

THE UNIVERSAL
STANDARD
ENCYCLOPEDIA

LIST OF ABBREVIATIONS USED

abbr., abbreviated
A.D., Anno Domini
alt., altitude
A.M., ante meridiem
anc., ancient
approx., approximately
Ar., Arabic
AS., Anglo-Saxon
A.S.S.R., Autonomous Soviet Socialist Republic
at.no., atomic number
at.wt., atomic weight
b., born
B.C., before Christ
b.p., boiling point
B.T.U., British Thermal Unit
Bulg., Bulgarian
C., centigrade, syn. Celsius
cent., century
Chin., Chinese
cm., centimeter
Co., County
colloq., colloquial
cu., cubic
Czech., Czechoslovakian
d., died
Dan., Danish
Du., Dutch
E., east, easterly, eastern
ed., edition
e.g., for example
Egypt., Egyptian
Eng., English
est., estimated
et seq., and following
F., Fahrenheit
fl., flourished
fr., from
Fr., French
ft., foot

Gael., Gaelic
Gen., General
Ger., German
Gr., Greek
Heb., Hebrew
Hind., Hindustani
Hon., Honorable
h.p., horsepower
hr., hour
Hung., Hungarian
I., Island
i.e., that is
in., inch
Ind., Indian
Ir., Irish
It., Italian
Jr., junior
kg., kilogram
km., kilometer
lat., latitude
Lat., Latin
lb., pound
lit., literally
long., longitude
m., mile
M., Middle
min., minute
M.L., Medieval Latin
mm., millimeter
mod., modern
m.p., melting point
M.P., Member of Parliament
m.p.h., miles per hour
Mt., Mount, Mountain
N., north, northerly, northern
N.T., New Testament
OE., Old English
OF., Old French
OHG., Old High German
ON., Old Norse

ONF., Old Norman French
O.T., Old Testament
oz., ounce
Phil., Philippine
P.M., post meridiem
Pol., Polish
pop., population
Port., Portuguese
prelim., preliminary
pron., pronounced
q.v., which see
R., River
rev., revised, revision
Rev., Reverend
Rom., Romanian
Russ., Russian
S., south, southerly, southern
sec., second
Skr., Sanskrit
Sp., Spanish
sp.gr., specific gravity
sq., square
S.S.R., Soviet Socialist Republic
Sum., Sumerian
Sw., Swedish
syn., synonym
temp., temperature
trans., translation, translated
Turk., Turkish
U.K., United Kingdom
U.N., United Nations
U.S., United States
U.S.A., United States of America
U.S.S.R., Union of Soviet Socialist Republics
var., variety
W., west, westerly, western
yd., yard

Note.—The official abbreviations for the States of the Union are used throughout. For academic degrees, see article DEGREE, ACADEMIC. Other abbreviations or contractions are self-explanatory.

TECHNICAL EDUCATION, all instruction that has for its object the direct preparation for a career or vocation. In common use, the designation is applied to such instruction as bears directly upon the industrial arts. The field of such education ranges from instruction in the arts and sciences that underlie industrial practice in its broadest and most complex relations to the simple training in manipulation needed for the prosecution of some productive trade. This wide province naturally calls for numerous and widely divergent types of schools.

Technical schools may conveniently be divided into three classes. (1) Institutions of a collegiate or university grade, to which the titles engineering schools, institutes of technology, polytechnic institutes, and schools of applied sciences are variously given, and which are devoted to instruction in advanced mathematics and science, and the theory and practice of industrial operations. (2) Schools in which the purpose is to prepare for practical work in some particular field of industry and which afford instruction in those branches of science and art that underlie its special problems. This class is represented by schools of weaving, dyeing, building, and machine construction and drafting. Evening continuation schools which afford instruction in science, art, and technical methods may also be considered in this group. (3) Trade schools which supply a training in the practice of some productive trade. The function of the first type of school is to educate its students for managers and superintendents of industrial establishments, consulting and designing engineers and architects.

Engineering Schools, Schools of Applied Science, and *Institutes of Technology.* The earliest establishment of this type of school occurred in France and Germany. In France the École des Ponts et Chaussées, originally started in 1747 as a drawing school, was organized in 1760 for the training of engineers for the government service. In 1794 the celebrated École Polytechnique was founded primarily to fit men for the engineer and artillery corps of the French army.

Later in the century came the great development of pure science in the German universities, and following this came an era of equal activity in the field of applied science, which quickly resulted in the widespread establishment of polytechnics or *Technische Hochschulen.* Rivalry between the various states played a part in the spread of these schools, each striving to outdo the others in magnificence of buildings and completeness of equipment. These institutions, which often had their beginnings in secondary technical or trade schools, have now become foundations co-ordinate with the universities, requiring equal academic preparation for admission, and representing specialized courses in engineering, architecture, industrial chemistry, and agriculture.

The splendid Technische Hochschule in Charlottenburg, and similar institutions in Munich, Dresden, Darmstadt, Hanover, Cassel, Aachen, and Breslau are foremost examples of this class. Engineering schools of a high grade are maintained also by the governments of Austria, Italy, Switzerland, Sweden, and the U.S.S.R. Great Britain awakened more slowly to the need of technical education than other European countries, the chief stimulus being interest aroused by the Exhibition of 1851. In 1881 a Royal Commission on Technical Instruction was appointed to investigate the entire subject. Among other results of this awakening was the foundation of the City and Guilds of London Institute, formed by a union of many of the wealthy corporations of the old London guilds. The scope of the Institute activities includes the support and management of three institutions and the support of several others in the city of London, and the direction of a system of examinations dealing with the work of technical classes throughout England and Wales, and represents a system that touches all the important phases of technical instruction with the single exception of the trade school.

The most important of the three schools established in London, the Central Institution of the City and Guilds of London Institute, a well-organized school of technology, now forms a part of the Imperial College of Science and Technology, and is recognized as a school of the University of London in the faculty of engineering. Courses are provided for training engineers, architects, industrial chemists, and technical teachers. Other schools of an advanced character and several university departments of applied science have come to the front in Great Britain, prominent among which are the University of Manchester, the Manchester School of Technology, the University of Birmingham, the University of Leeds, the University of Sheffield, Armstrong College, and a number of others. Schools of engineering are maintained at the University of Glasgow, the University of Edinburgh, University College of Dundee, and the Glasgow and West of Scotland Technical College.

In the United States the development of the school of technology has been exceedingly rapid, and has resulted in a type of institution that in some respects is the superior of anything to be found abroad. The Rensselaer Polytechnic Institute founded in 1824 by Stephen Van Rensselaer as a school of theoretical and applied science, was the first establishment in this field. The work of this school has been almost exclusively devoted to the training of civil engineers. In response to the growing demand for scientific instruction, the Sheffield Scientific School (1847) at Yale and the Lawrence Scientific School (1848) at Harvard were founded. Most of the technical schools, however, date from the later years of the Civil War. In 1861 the charter of the Massachusetts Institute of Technology was granted, and in 1865 the first classes were organized.

The Worcester Polytechnic Institute was opened to students in 1867. This was the first school of technology in the United States to provide systematic instruction in workshop practice as an element of the course in mechanical engineering. In 1864 the first courses in the School of Mines, Columbia University, were organized, and from this have developed the several schools of applied science of that institution. In 1871 the Stevens Institute of Technology at Hoboken was opened. The beginnings of the Sibley College of Mechanical Engineering and the Mechanic Arts were made at Cornell University in 1872, and other courses in applied science were soon established there. In the next twenty years a large number of schools of the first rank were founded either as separate institutions or as departments of universities. Notable among those of the first kind are Purdue University, Lafayette, Ind.; Rose Polytechnic Institute, Terre Haute, Ind.; the Michigan School of Mines, Houghton, Mich.; the Case School of Applied Science, Cleveland, Ohio; and the Armour Institute of Technology in Chicago, Ill.

Prominent among the second group are the engineering departments of Lehigh University, the Ohio State University, Washington University (St. Louis), and the universities of Michigan, Wisconsin, Minnesota, Pennsylvania, and California. The State land-grant colleges established under the Morrill Act of 1862 also gave a great impetus to the study of engineering and mechanic arts. See LAND-GRANT COLLEGES.

Technical and Applied Art Schools and *Continuation Schools.* All the types of this group of institutions have reached a high point of organization on the continent of Europe. Technical schools, in which to practical training in the methods of a special craft is added instruction in the scientific principles upon which they are based, appear in greatest numbers in Austria, Germany, and France. Some have been established by guilds or masters' societies, some by a union of manufacturers of a town or city wishing to improve the efficiency of their establishments, and others by action of the local authorities or by the government. A steady tendency toward government control and support is apparent in all the continental countries. Prominent among schools of this type are the special schools for weaving and dyeing, of which frequent examples are found in various parts of Germany. The most famous institution of the kind is located at Krefeld, West Germany. In this model institution thorough study is made of the chemistry and technology of dyeing, and of the mechanism and pattern designing involved in weaving. The Advanced School of Weaving in Lyons, France, the School of Silk Weaving near Zurich, Switzerland, the School of Weaving and Dyeing at the University of Leeds, and the textile departments of the Manchester School of Technology and of the Bradford Technical College, are other examples of this type of school. In the United States similar schools are the textile and dyeing schools of the School of Industrial Art of the Pennsylvania Museum in Philadelphia and the textile schools in Lowell and New Bedford, Mass.

France has a very important and highly organized system of state schools for the training of foremen and superintendents in mechanical industries in Chalons, Aix, Angers, Cluny, and Lille. The courses are three years in length. The instruction, both practical and theoretical, given in these schools, has been of so thorough a character that the result in large part has been to train managers and mechanical engineers rather than foremen. Other technical schools of an advanced character are the Industrial Institute of the North of France, in Lille, and the Institution Livet, a private foundation in Nantes. The Écoles La Martinière in Lyons offer training in industrial art and science.

In the United States schools of applied art are fairly numerous, and those in large cities generally offer training in applied art and design. The prominent institutions in this field include Rhode Island School of Design, Providence, R.I.; The Cooper Union, Parsons School of Design, and Pratt Institute, all in New York City; Philadelphia Museum School of Industrial Art and Drexel Institute, both in Philadelphia, Pa.; Maryland Art Institute, Baltimore, Md.; Cleveland School of Art, Cleveland, Ohio; Chicago Art Institute, Chicago, Ill.; Kansas City Art Institute, Kansas City, Mo.; Chouinard Art Institute and Art Center School, both in Los Angeles, Calif.

The American public-school system offers both day and evening instruction in technical subjects at special vocational high schools.

TECHNICOLOR. See COLOR PHOTOGRAPHY.

TECHNOCRACY, a nonprofit, nonsectarian membership organization of American citizens, until 1930 the Technical Alliance of North America, a research organization founded in New York City in 1920 by engineers, scientists, and economists. In 1933 the Technocracy group became incorporated under the laws of the State of New York and its later growth as a nationwide membership followed. The social analysis of Technocracy is founded on what is described as "a new technique of mensuration", first devised and applied to the physical operation of a geographical area by Howard Scott. This technique of social analysis and operations is described as an engineering or technological method as contrasted to the political, economic, or social methods of the politician, businessman, or humanitarian. Technocracy is not a moral political philosophy but is the statistical mechanics of area operation. The activities of Technocracy are of an educational nature; the organization conducts study classes among its members.

TECK, ALEXANDER, PRINCE OF TECK and 1st EARL OF ATHLONE (1874–1957), British soldier, born in Kensington Palace, London, the third son of the Duke of Teck and Princess Mary Adelaide, and a brother of Queen Mary, consort of George V. Educated at Eton and at the Royal Military College, Sandhurst, he became successively a captain in the Seventh Hussars and in the Royal Horse Guards, and later was brevetted lieutenant colonel in the Second Life Guards. He served in Matabeleland in 1896, in the South African War in 1899–1900, and in the European War in 1914–15, being mentioned in the dispatches in each. For services in the South African War he also gained the queen's medal with five clasps and was made a member of the Distinguished Service Order. He was governor-general of the Union of South Africa (1923–31). He was appointed governor of Windsor Castle (1931), chancellor of London University (1932), great master of Order of St. Michael and St. George (1936), and was governor-general of Canada (1940–46). He married in 1904 Princess Alice, daughter of the Duke of Albany and granddaughter of Queen Victoria.

TEDDER, ARTHUR WILLIAM, 1st BARON TEDDER OF GLENGUIN (1890–   ), British aviation officer, born in Glenguin, Sterlingshire, Scotland, and educated at Magdalene College, Cambridge University. At the outbreak of World War I Tedder received a commission in the British army, and subsequently served in France. In 1916 he was transferred to the Royal Flying Corps. He continued to serve in the aviation arm after the Armistice, and in 1919 was transferred to the Royal Air Force (created in 1918). Tedder later served in the Middle and Far East, and occupied several administrative positions in England. He was commander in chief of the R.A.F. in the Far East from 1936 to 1938, was deputy commander in chief of the R.A.F. in the Middle East in 1940, and a year later was made commander in chief. Tedder is credited with the effective co-ordination of British air and ground forces during the El Alamein offensive which helped drive the German forces from North Africa in World War II. In July, 1942, he was promoted to the rank of air chief marshal, and he was knighted in the same year. On Nov. 27, 1942, he was appointed vice chief of staff of the R.A.F. and on Feb. 11, 1943, Allied commander in chief of the Mediterranean air forces. In December of the latter year he was named deputy commander in chief of the Allied expeditionary forces, under General Dwight Eisenhower, and in October, 1944, assumed in addition the post of chief of Allied air operations in w. Europe. In 1946 Tedder became chief of the air staff (a position which he held until 1950) and was raised to the peerage. He was appointed chancellor of Cambridge University in 1950. In 1950–51 he represented Great Britain on the standing group of the Military Committee of the North Atlantic Treaty Organization. His works include *Air Power in War* (1948).

TE DEUM, a majestic Latin hymn of the Western Church, so called from its first words. It is ascribed by some to St. Ambrose and St. Augustine, and by others to Hilary of Arles. In its modern form it was used by Hincmar of Reims in the 9th century. The hymn consists of twenty-nine verses; the first twenty-one are uniform in the four oldest versions current, and it seems probable that verses one to ten were a Greek hymn of the 2nd century.

TEETH, hard bodies in the mouth, attached to the skeleton, but not forming part of it, and developed from the dermis or true skin. A tooth consists of three calcified tissues, the enamel covering the crown of the tooth, the dentine which forms its essential substance, and the cementum investing the root or fang. The enamel consists of fine prismatic cells in which the original protoplasm has been replaced practically entirely by lime salts, rendering it excessively hard and resistant to wear. The dentine resembles bone but contains a vast number of fine canals or tubules containing the processes of cells lying in the central or pulp cavity of the tooth. The cementum is a layer of very dense bone which gives attachment to a large number of fibers, called Sharpey's fibers, which firmly fix the tooth in its socket. In the pulp cavity lie blood vessels, numerous nerves and many cells, the odontoblasts, largely concerned in the development of the dentine.

The number of teeth, thirty-two, which characterizes man, the apes of the Old World, and the true ruminants, is the average one of the mammals. The *incisors,* or cutting teeth, are situated in front, and possess a single conical root or fang, and a vertical crown bevelled behind, so as to terminate in a sharp cutting edge. These teeth are especially fitted, as their name implies, for cutting the food. In man there are two of these incisors in each side of each jaw (in the premaxilla).

The *canines* (so called from their prominence in the dog) come next to the incisors. Their crown is rather conical than wedge-shaped, and their fang sinks more deeply into the jaw than in the case of the incisors. In all carnivorous animals they are largely developed, being obviously formed for tearing the flesh of their prey. The *pre-*

molars (known also as bicuspids and false molars) come next in order to the canines; they are smaller than the latter, and their crown presents two pyramidal eminences.

The *true molars* (or multicuspids) are placed most posteriorly. They are remarkable for their comparatively great size, the square form of the upper surface, on which are from three to five elevations or cusps, and for their short root, which is divided into from two to five branches, each of which is perforated at its extremity. They appear first in the permanent set.

In the primary or milk dentition we have only twenty teeth, the twelve adult molars not being represented.

Decay is by far the most common of the diseases which affect the teeth, and consists in a gradual and progressive disintegration of the tooth substance. The exciting cause consists in the decalcification of the tissues of the teeth by acids which are for the greater part generated in the mouth by fermentation. Many of the diseases of the teeth and gums might be prevented or greatly retarded by proper attention to the cleansing of these organs. The teeth should be brushed twice daily, in the morning and in the evening. See DENTISTRY.

TEGNÉR, ESAIAS (1782–1846), one of the most prominent of Swedish poets, born in Kyrkerud, in the province of Vermland. It was not until 1808 that he attracted any attention as a poet; but the stirring *War-song for the Militia of Scania* made his name known, and the patriotic appeal, *Svea* (1811), made it famous. In the following year he was chosen professor of Greek. The best creations of his poetic genius all belong to a comparatively short period of time (1817–25)—*Song to the Sun* (1817), *Epilogue on the Degree Day at Lund* (1820), *The Candidate for Confirmation* (1820), and *Axel* (1821). *Frithiof's Saga* (1825), a cycle of epics treating of old Scandinavian days, is his masterpiece. He is probably best known to the English-speaking world by Longfellow's translation, *The Children of the Lord's Supper,* which appeared in 1841. Tegnér's collected works were published in 1847–50 (7 vols., Stockholm), and again in 1882–85 (8 vols.).

TEGUCIGALPA (Ind., "silver hills"), capital of the republic of Honduras, situated about 3200 ft. above sea level, on the Choluteca R., 60 miles N.E. of the Gulf of Fonseca in the Pacific Ocean. The city is one of the two capitals on the American

Joseph Covello, from Black Star

Rival political parties demonstrating on Ferdowsi Street in Teheran, Iran

continent which is not served by a railroad (Asunción, Paraguay, being the other). Administratively, Tegucigalpa has been amalgamated with the suburb of Comayagüela, with which it is connected by bridge. The city is in the center of an agricultural and gold and silver mining district. Tegucigalpa is the site of the National University. The chief buildings include a cathedral, a presidential palace, a place of justice, a National Theater, a mint, and the Bank of Honduras. The city was founded in the 16th century. During the 18th century, large quantities of gold, silver, and marble were mined and quarried, but the value of the minerals has declined in modern times. In 1880 the city became the capital of the republic, after having been co-capital with Comayagua (q.v.). Pop. (1950) 92,951.

TEHERAN, or TEHRAN, the capital and largest city of Iran (q.v.), situated on a sandy plateau, 3800 ft. above sea level, 70 miles s. of the Caspian Sea. To the N. of the city is the Shemran district, used for govern-

mental and private summer residences; in the s. are the ruins of Rhages, birthplace of the famous caliph Harun al-Rashid. The center of Teheran is a square, the Meidan Sepah, in which are the important government buildings. To the s. of the square is the old Ark, or fortified palace, of the shahs, containing, among other celebrated art and historical objects, the jeweled Peacock Throne of Persia. A new palace has been constructed in the w. part of the city. Among the educational facilities is Teheran University. Industrial establishments include factories for cotton spinning and the manufacture of tobacco products, cement, beet sugar, glass, and soap. The city was founded in the 12th century, but remained a small trading center until about 1788, when it was made the capital of Persia. After the establishment of the Kajar dynasty, in 1794, the city rose to importance. Under the present Pahlavi dynasty, Teheran has been modernized, industrialized, and considerably rebuilt. In 1943, during the World War II, it was the site of an important conference between the U.K., U.S., and U.S.S.R. (see TEHERAN CONFERENCE). Pop. (1949) 1,010,000.

TEHERAN, or TEHRAN, CONFERENCE, a conference concerning war strategy and postwar settlements between President Franklin D. Roosevelt of the United States, Prime Minister Winston Churchill of the United Kingdom, and Marshal Joseph Stalin of the Soviet Union, held at Teheran, Iran, from Nov. 28 to Dec. 1, 1943, during World War II. During the discussions, the three leaders and their aides formulated plans for a concerted attack on w. Europe, then entirely German-held, and also stated their responsibility, following victory, of establishing an enduring peace and of setting up a world family of democratic nations. The aid of Iran to the Allied cause was recognized, and economic aid was promised that country for its resistance to threats by the Axis powers. The declaration concerning Iran, assuring the "independence, sovereignty, and territorial integrity" of the kingdom, was significant in view of the rivalry for dominance in that area between the U.K. and the U.S.S.R. See CAIRO CONFERENCE.

TEHUANTEPEC, an isthmus in Mexico, between the Pacific and the Gulf of Mexico. The soil is rich, forests are extensive and yield fustic and logwood, and there are large pasturages. Suggestions have frequently been made since the days of Cortes (1520) to construct here an inter-oceanic canal, and the American Eads proposed to build a ship railroad. The Tehuantepec National Railroad (189 m. long), connects the ports of Puerto Mexico (Coatzacoalcos), on the Gulf of Mexico and Salina Cruz on the Pacific.

TEHUELCHE, a general term for several different Patagonian tribes. There is evidence that the Tehuelches are immigrants from more northern portions of South America, but their origin is doubtful. They occupy a relatively small territory between the Strait of Magellan and the Santa Cruz River. They are considered the tallest of human races. Accurate observations on this point are few, but the average stature of male Tehuelches is about 1.75 meter (5.74 ft.). They are also very brachycephalic in head form. In culture they are low.

TEJU, JACUARU, or TEGU, common name applied to any of three species of lizards constituting the genus *Tupinambis* of the family Teiidae, and inhabiting tropical America. The lizards, which attain a total length

of about 4 feet, are usually black in color, with white or yellow spots or bands crossing the back. The head is massive, about 6 inches in width in an adult specimen, and is covered with large, bony shields; the jaws are powerful and contain strong teeth. The teju is carnivorous, eating lizards, rats, and small chickens. The heavy body is covered with small, square scales arranged in transverse arcs over the back and sides. The tail is long and slender, making up more than half the total body length. In South America, tejus are hunted with dogs for their flesh. The common teju is *Tupinambis teguixin*.

TELAMON, in Greek legend, the son of Æacus, King of Ægina, and the brother of Peleus (q.v.). Having assisted Peleus in murdering their half-brother Phocus, he was expelled from Ægina by his father. He was received by the king of Salamis, whose daughter Glauce he married. Telamon succeeded to the throne, and by his second wife, Periboea, was the father of the famous warrior Ajax (q.v.). Telamon joined in the Calydonian hunt (see CALYDONIAN BOAR) and in the expedition of the Argonauts (q.v.), and was the first to scale the walls of Troy when that city was attacked by Hercules. Upon the capture of the city Hercules gave to Telamon, as part of the spoils, Hesione, the daughter of King Laomedon, and by her Telamon was the father of Teucer (q.v.), who later fought against the Trojans with his half-brother Ajax.

TEL AVIV, chief city and a seaport of Israel (q.v.), situated on the Mediterranean Sea. The city has wide avenues, lined with trees, and is almost entirely occupied by modern apartment houses. A broad beach and promenade fronts the Mediterranean. Tel Aviv is the center of Israeli cultural life. Its facilities include a municipal museum, and music and art centers, and many newspapers and periodicals are published there. Its population is almost entirely Jewish, but because the majority are recent immigrants Tel Aviv is exceedingly cosmopolitan in languages, customs, and folkways. The city is the center of a large and diversified industry, including chiefly food, textile, and chemical manufacturing, and the building trades. In 1936 the city established its own port (the facilities of Jaffa having been formerly used) at the mouth of the Yarkon R., consisting of a lighter basin 14,000 sq. meters in area.

Tel Aviv was founded in 1909 as a suburb of Jaffa, on a sand dune N. of that city, and

Joseph Covello, from Black Star

Theater building on Mograbi Square in the city of Tel Aviv

was financed in part by a loan from the Jewish National Fund. The city grew slowly and in 1916, during World War I, was completely evacuated by Turkey, then in control of Palestine, because of the pro-Allied sentiments of its inhabitants. After the anti-Jewish riots in Jaffa in 1921, the Jews of Jaffa emigrated to Tel Aviv, thereby considerably increasing its population. By 1931 the citizens of Tel Aviv numbered 45,000, a number which increased to 145,000 in 1936 because of large-scale immigrations of Jews from fascist-controlled sections of Europe. During World War II Tel Aviv was raided several times by Axis planes, resulting in many casualties. In the war which followed the establishment of the state of Israel in 1948 the city, made the provisional capital, was bombed several times by Egyptian planes. In 1949 the Arab city of Jaffa was incorporated into Tel Aviv. Pop. (1951 est.) 370,000.

TELEDU, STINKING BADGER, or JAVANESE SKUNK, common name applied to a small, mustelid mammal, *mydaus meliceps*, which lives in burrows in the mountains of Java, Borneo, and Sumatra. The animal is slightly smaller than the true badgers (q.v.), to which it is closely related. It differs from the true badgers in having a short tail, small ears, united toe pads, and a split upper lip. Its most conspicuous difference, however, is the skunklike elaboration and ejection of an offensively smelling fluid. In coloration, the teledu somewhat resembles the common American skunk, being blackish brown with a white or yellow stripe running longitudinally down the center of its back.

TELEGRAPH, any system of communication employing nonverbal electric signals which pass over wires. Originally any form of communication over long distances in which messages were transmitted by signs or sounds was called telegraphy. According

Western Union Telegraph Co.

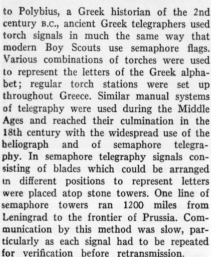

Left: Telegraph-recording instrument invented by Samuel F. B. Morse, completed in 1836. Above: Morse's improved telegraph-recording instrument of 1844.

to Polybius, a Greek historian of the 2nd century B.C., ancient Greek telegraphers used torch signals in much the same way that modern Boy Scouts use semaphore flags. Various combinations of torches were used to represent the letters of the Greek alphabet; regular torch stations were set up throughout Greece. Similar manual systems of telegraphy were used during the Middle Ages and reached their culmination in the 18th century with the widespread use of the heliograph and of semaphore telegraphy. In semaphore telegraphy signals consisting of blades which could be arranged in different positions to represent letters were placed atop stone towers. One line of semaphore towers ran 1200 miles from Leningrad to the frontier of Prussia. Communication by this method was slow, particularly as each signal had to be repeated for verification before retransmission.

Attempts to use phenomena associated with electricity in communication began long before the nineteenth century. In 1558 the Italian physicist Giambattista della Porta described a "sympathetic telegraph" which was to consist of two needles mounted on dials so that they pointed to the various letters of the alphabet in turning. Both needles were to be magnetized by rubbing with a lodestone, and it was thought that movement of one needle would cause similar movement of the other needle even though placed far away. The first practical suggestion for construction of an electric telegraph did not come until 1753. In that year a Scottish surgeon, Charles Morrison, wrote anonymously to the *Scots Magazine* suggesting an instrument which would employ electricity sent over wires for a great distance, with the earth completing the circuit between two points. Morrison advocated a cumbersome system in which many wires were to carry signals, one wire for each letter in the alphabet. The receiver at the other end of each wire was to consist of a pithball hung over a piece of paper marked with a letter of the alphabet. A charge sent to the ball by wire would attract the paper, and messages could be read by horizontal movement of the paper sheets. Systems of this type were actually built a few decades later, and in the years before 1835, when the American inventor Samuel Finley Breese Morse began developing his apparatus, other telegraphy techniques were tested.

Morse is credited with being the first man to invent a recording telegraph. His system employed a simple code in which messages were transmitted by electric pulses passing over a single wire; see MORSE CODE. Morse's apparatus, completed in 1836, resembled a simple electric switch. It allowed current to pass for a prescribed length of time and then shut it off, all at the pressure of a finger. The Morse telegraph receiver had an electromagnetically controlled pencil which made marks on a clockwork-operated cylinder of paper revolving beneath it. The marks varied with the duration of the electric current passing through the wires of the electric magnet and took the written form of dots and dashes. The pencil was so arranged that when current passed through the electromagnet it was attracted to the paper. The Morse receiver was the first practical means ever devised for recording incoming signals.

While experimenting with his instrument, Morse found that signals could be transmitted successfully for only twenty miles. Beyond that distance the signals grew too weak to be recorded. Morse and his associates therefore developed an apparatus called a relay which could be attached to the telegraph line twenty miles from the signal station to repeat signals automatically and send them an additional twenty miles. The relay consisted of a switch operated by an electro-magnet. An impulse entering the magnet's coil caused an armature to rotate and close an independent circuit actuated by a battery. This action sent a fresh pulse of current into the line and in turn this pulse activated successive relays until the receiver was reached.

A few years after Morse developed his receiving instrument and demonstrated it successfully before the President of the United States, one of his associates, Alfred Vail, discovered that it was possible to distinguish dots and dashes by sound alone. The Morse recording apparatus therefore became unnecessary and was discarded. But the other fundamental principles of the Morse system are still used today in many telegraph circuits; and some devices for recording signals in modern times were patterned after the Morse recorder.

A simple Morse telegraph circuit as still used on some railroads in America and Europe consists essentially of the key or switch for turning current on and off and a connecting wire running between stations. The circuit is completed by return of current through the earth, thus making necessary the proper grounding of each end of the telegraph line. The receiving apparatus consists mainly of an electromagnet arranged so that when it is magnetized an armature is drawn with a click against an anvil. Batteries or generators supplying current for the signals may be located at each receiving station or the circuit may be arranged so that only the main station on the line has a direct source of current. In some systems the current flows constantly except when turned off for prescribed lengths of time by contact with the signal key; in others the current is turned on only during signalling.

Early telegraphy was too expensive for widespread use, and so several means of sending several messages simultaneously over a single line were developed. In duplex telegraphy, the earliest advance of this kind, two stations could exchange single messages simultaneously. In quadruplex telegraphy, invented by Thomas Edison in 1874, two stations could exchange two messages simultaneously. In multiplex telegraphy, the system used today on lines between important stations where traffic is heavy, as many as four sending and four receiving telegraph machines can use a line at the same time.

Automatic Telegraphy. In commercial operation the simple, hand-operated telegraph key and sounder have been replaced almost entirely by automatic sending and receiving machinery, cutting costs by increasing the speed and accuracy of communication. Three common automatic-telegraphy systems exist: the "recording system", in which signals are sent and received on a recording device in code; the "facsimile system", in which an exact copy of the original message is reproduced just as it was written, drawn, or typed; and the "printing system", in which code signals are reproduced in a printed message at the receiver. Most recording-system transmitters are controlled by a perforated tape, and send dot-and-dash signals. Special typewriters are used to prepare the perforated tape. These have keyboards similar to those of standard typewriters; the keys operate cutting devices which punch various patterns of perforations in the paper tape. The signal is generated by completion of a circuit, which occurs when the holes in the moving tape permit the contact of two metal surfaces. Recording-system receivers are modifications of Morse's original magnetic recording device, having a stylus or an inked wheel recording dots and dashes on a moving strip of paper. Recording-system equipment is used much less often, however, than other systems of automatic telegraphy.

Modern facsimile telegraphs are essentially like telephoto devices which are employed to send newspaper pictures over wires. The message or picture to be sent is placed on a slowly revolving cylinder. An electric eye in the machine scans the picture, one linear segment at a time, and controls the transmission of current impulses which vary with the degree of shading in the exposed area. In turn this current controls operation of a receiver at the other end of the line, where a sheet of sensitized paper is darkened in a pattern corresponding, segment by segment, to the original. Facsimile telegraphs

Western Union Telegraph Co.

Top: Telegraph operator typing a message on a recording transmitter, which sends signals in code. Bottom: Equipment in the message center of an automatic-telegraphy system.

Western Union Telegraph Co.

Top: At an automatic-telegraphy terminal a telegram is transmitted to office of delivery by push of a button. Bottom: Receiving message, printed on tape, at its destination.

Western Union Telegraph Co.

*Above: Sending a message on a desk-type fac-
simile-telegraph instrument. An electric eye
scans message as paper revolves on cylinder,
and converts letters into electric impulses.
Left: Message is received on an identical machine at destination by reversal of process.
A special, chemically-treated paper is used.*

are employed extensively for communication
between branch telegraph offices and the
main office and for transmission of messages
from the headquarters of large firms to the
main station of telegraph companies. In
addition, private subscribers use facsimile
devices small enough to be placed in a corner of a desk. Facsimile telegraphy greatly
increases the speed of service by eliminating
the need for messengers to carry telegraph
messages to and from the subscriber's office.
The bulk of telegraph messages, however, are
still delivered by messengers who walk or
ride bicycles to their destination.

In the printing system of automatic
telegraphy, which is the system now most
extensively used, the code used to control the
transmitter differs from Morse dot-and-dash
signaling. It is based on the thirty-one
combinations possible with a five-unit series
of impulses. As in the recording system

described above, the transmitter is usually
controlled by a specially perforated tape.
The receiver used may type out the message
on a sheet of paper in final form or on
gummed strips of paper which are later
pasted to a telegraph blank.

Some printing automatic telegraphs do
away with tape control of the transmitting
machine. Teleprinters as developed in the
1920's for the Western Union Telegraph Company are operated like typewriters. As the
telegrapher strikes keys, the machine at
another office to which it is connected writes
the message out. Newspapers and other
business offices use such machines for instantaneous reception of messages.

Signals traveling over a length of wire
tend to weaken for various reasons. Among
these are the line's inherent resistance to the
flow of current and the tendency of current
to leak from the line because of imperfect
insulation. Signals are also distorted in form
as they travel over the line, because of
interference by various types of stray cur

rent which may be generated on the line by nearby power lines or other telegraph circuits. It is therefore necessary to divide a long telegraph circuit into sections. These sections can be connected together successively by devices called repeaters which receive signals from one section and pass them on to the next with renewed power. Modern repeaters not only repeat signals but also correct the form of the signal, restoring its original characteristics.

A single pair of wires can simultaneously transmit hundreds of messages, which are separated at the receiving end by electronic filters. One wire of each such pair serves as a "ground" and the other is activated by alternating currents, called carrier currents, of differing frequencies. For each frequency or "channel" there is a filter at the other end of the line which provides passage for only that frequency. As many as 288 messages can travel together in this way on a single pair of wires. Telegraph messages are frequently sent on wires simultaneously carrying spoken telephone conversations. Relatively high-frequency currents carry the telephone conversations while much lower frequencies carry the telegraph message. A filter can be used at the end of the line to separate these frequencies and direct signals to either a telephone or a telegraph receiver. Most telegraph lines are strung on high wooden poles in rural and suburban areas and are carried by lines extended underground and sheathed in heavy insulation in cities.

All communications transmitted by telegraph can also be transmitted by wireless methods; see RADIO; FACSIMILE.

Almost all telegraphic messages in America are transmitted by the Western Union Telegraph Company. In a recent year the company had about 1,338,000 miles of wire in operation; approximately 16,200 offices handled about 180,000,000 revenue messages the same year.

TELEGRAPH PLANT (*Desmodium gyranes*), an Indian leguminous plant. The small lateral leaflets of its trifoliate leaves have, especially in a warm, moist atmosphere, a strange spontaneous motion; they jerk up and down (sometimes 180 times in a minute), as if signaling, and also rotate on their axes.

TELEMACHUS, in Greek legend, the son of the hero Ulysses and his wife Penelope (qq.v.). Ulysses feigned madness to avoid going to Troy, but his strategem was dis-

covered when Palamedes (q.v.) placed the infant Telemachus in front of his father's plow. Telemachus plays a prominent part in the *Odyssey* of Homer, the scene of which is laid about twenty years after the close of the Trojan War. Under the guidance of the goddess Athena, he sets out in search of his father, who has not returned from Troy, after having vainly endeavored to eject his mother's troublesome suitors from the house. After visiting Pylos and Sparta, Telemachus returns to Ithaca, where he finds his father in the guise of a beggar and assists him in slaying the suitors. According to later legends, Telemachus married the sorceress Circe, or one of her daughters, and was said to have founded Clusium in Etruria.

TELEMANN, GEORG PHILIPP (1681–1767), German composer, born in Magdeburg, Prussia, and educated at Magdeburg, Hildesheim, and Leipzig. At the University of Leipzig, Telemann organized a student music society soon after his matriculation in 1701. About this time, he wrote a number of operas for the Leipzig Theater and undertook to produce a composition of ecclesiastical character for the Thomaskirche in Leipzig at biweekly intervals. In 1704 he received the post of organist in the Neukirche, and became conductor of the private orchestra maintained by a wealthy nobleman at Sorau. Several years later he became orchestral conductor at Eisenach, in Thuringia, where he made the acquaintance of his illustrious compatriot, the composer Johann Sebastian Bach. Thereafter, Telemann successively held the posts of music director of the Katharinenkirche in Frankfurt am Main, choral conductor in the Barfüsserkirche, and orchestral conductor at the court of the Prince of Bayreuth. From 1721 until his death he served both as cantor of the Johanneum and as music director at Hamburg. The numerous compositions of Telemann include the oratorios *Die Tageszeiten, Die Auferstehung Christi, Der Tag des Gerichts,* and *Der Tod Jesu;* about six hundred overtures; forty operas; twelve violin sonatas; six trios; and six suites for violin, oboe, and piano.

TELEOLOGY, the doctrine of final causes (see CAUSALITY), usually limited to the argument for a creator and for the existence of God derived from the existence, beauty, and perfection of the world. See also THEISM.

TELEOSTEI. See FISH: *Classification.*

TELEPATHY, word coined about 1886 from the Greek to express the supposed power of communication between one mind and another by means unknown to the ordinary sense organs. See PSYCHICAL RESEARCH.

TELEPHONE, an instrument designed to reproduce sounds at a distance by means of electricity. A sounding body is always vibrating, and the more rapid the vibration the higher is the note produced. The problem of telephony is to reproduce in the receiver the same vibrations as the voice sets up in the transmitter.

Early Forms. In England in 1667 Robert Hooke conveyed sounds to a distance over an extended wire, but two hundred years passed before Wheatstone was able to transmit sounds from a musical box in a cellar to the upper rooms of a two-story dwelling and this he did by means of an "enchanted lyre" or a wooden rod. These early experiments were acoustical telephones, the sound vibrations themselves being transmitted over the conductor.

The first person able to indicate clearly the possibility of electric telephony was Charles Bourseul, who, in 1854, put forward the suggestion that the vibrations imparted to a movable disk or diaphragm, by speaking in front of it, might be employed to make and break an electric circuit, and thereby to produce similar vibrations in a second diaphragm elsewhere in the circuit, and so reproduce the original sound. Six years later Reis of Frankfort invented an instrument based on this suggestion, in which a collodion membrane, vibrating under the influence of the sound waves produced by the voice, alternately made and broke a battery circuit. In 1876 an American inventor, Alexander Graham Bell, was granted a patent for an electric speaking telephone and early in 1877 produced the first telephones to transmit and receive the human voice with all its quality and timbre.

Bell's Magnetic Telephone. No battery or other generator was used in the circuit, which consisted simply of a transmitter, a receiver, and a single connecting wire, the return circuit being made through ground. The transmitter and receiver were exactly similar instruments. Each contained a long horseshoe magnet, supplied with soft iron pole pieces. Round about these were wound bobbins of fine wire, the two coils being joined together, and their free ends being connected to the wires leading to the distant receiving

station. In front of the pole pieces was a diaphragm of thin sheet iron which was secured firmly around its edge to the mouthpiece frame. Adjustment between the diaphragm and pole pieces was by means of a thumb screw. When the sound waves produced by the voice impinge on the disk they cause it to vibrate in consonance with themselves. Further, this vibration causes the center of the disk alternately to approach to, and to recede from, the magnet poles, and thereby induces corresponding currents in the coils round the pole pieces. At the receiving station these currents act on the magnet field in the receiver, strengthening or weakening it according to their direction, and so increasing or diminishing its attraction on the disk, with the result that disk reproduces the vibrations of the disk in the transmitter, and the original sound is reproduced.

Circuits and Instruments. The currents produced in Bell's magnetic circuit were very weak. It has been found that much better effects are produced by varying the strength of a current from a generator. All modern telephone circuits, therefore, with few exceptions, include a *battery*.

Instruments of the Bell type are now mainly used as *receivers* only. In the modern Bell receiver itself the magnet is greatly shortened, and the instrument is flattened down into the form of a watch. In the Ader receiver the magnetic field acting on the ferrotype iron diaphragm is rendered more intense and more uniform by a ring of soft iron placed outside the diaphragm.

In actual practice the telephone *transmitter* consists of an outer case for protection. Behind a perforated grill is mounted a thin aluminum diaphragm radially corrugated. In the center is a dome about the size of a pea. Back of this and attached to the case is a brass cup. A pile of tissue paper rings forms a flexible seal between them. The enclosed space is filled with carbon granules, highly polished. When the dome, which is part of the diaphragm, is vibrated by speech waves from the grill, the carbon granules are gently agitated, varying the pressure. The increasing pressure decreases resistance, hence increasing the flow of electric current through the granules and vice versa. Thus the speech waves modulate electric current into a copy of themselves.

Since the unmodulated direct current carries no intelligence, no useful purpose is served in transmitting it over the line. In

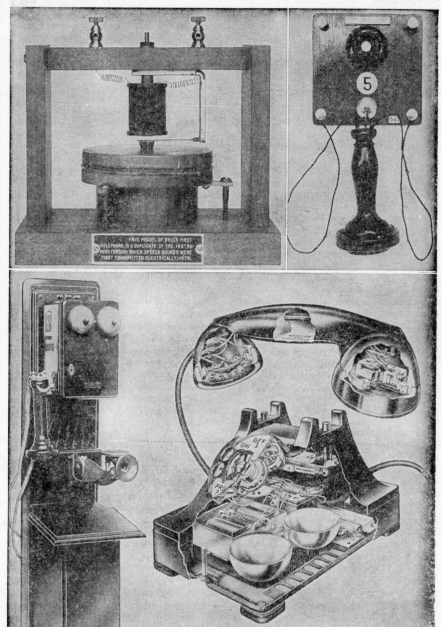

American Telephone & Telegraph Co.

THE TELEPHONE, EARLY AND MODERN. *Top, left: Model of the first telephone invented by Alexander Graham Bell, 1875. Top, right: Subscriber's-telephone set of 1878. Bottom, left: Long-distance wall-telephone set of 1886. Bottom, right: Cutaway drawing of a modern desk-type dial telephone. This complex instrument contains 433 parts made of 48 materials.*

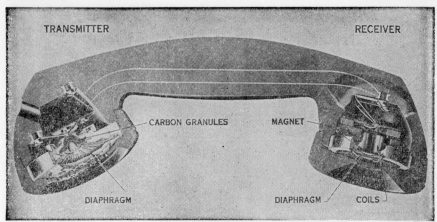

TRANSMITTER RECEIVER

CARBON GRANULES MAGNET

DIAPHRAGM DIAPHRAGM COILS

American Telephone & Telegraph Co.

Cross section of the handset of a modern desk-type telephone

early telephones, direct current was battery generated. The local circuit included, in addition to battery and transmitter, one winding of a transformer called an *induction coil*, the other winding, connected to the line, being so proportioned as to step up the speech wave voltage, before applying it to the telephone. Modern telephones receive the battery supply over the line from the central office but the induction coil remains to play much the same part.

The use of the *induction coil* with the transmitter dates back almost to the beginning of telephony. By connecting the transmitter and its battery to the primary and the line and receiver to the secondary of the coil, great changes in the strength of the variable current on the line are produced, enabling better reception at the distant station. For long lines, amplifiers are used. Modern amplifiers consist of vacuum tubes and auxiliary apparatus enabling the voice and signaling currents to be transmitted over long distances.

Automatic Telephone Exchanges had been in service in isolated installations of moderate size for some years, but in the interval since 1920 their development and increased use has been remarkable. The earlier installations by independent companies were of the so-called step-by-step system and this system is still in use. For very large telephone districts the panel type became the standard of the Bell System. This type in turn has been superseded for many new installations by the crossbar system.

The *crossbar system* accomplishes required connections with a much simpler mechanism. All motion is avoided and a direct method of switching is employed. The only movement required is that of a mechanical link to close the required set of contacts.

An outstanding feature of any of the systems is a device on the subscriber's instrument for transmitting a series of a definite number of successive impulses of current corresponding to the number of the party called. A line finder, at the central station called, is a selector whose function is to find a terminal of a particular line on which a call originates out of a group with which it is associated, and to connect a "sender" to that line. A comparatively large number of subscribers' lines may be served by a comparatively small number of line finders. The line finder finds the calling line and connects the selector and sender thereto. The sender switch receives the electrical impulses from a subscriber's dial on a decimal basis, stores them, and translates them to a nondecimal basis corresponding to the particular group of lines and trunks involved in the path of the call. The sender replaces the intelligence of the operator. The district selectors controlled by the sender, have the duty of selecting a particular group of trunks and one trunk of that group. They have the same function as the switchboard plug and cord, which in a manual station can be plugged by the operator into any one of a number of jacks which are the terminals of trunks or lines. There are "district selectors", incoming selectors", and "final selectors" in the circuit, in the order named, from the calling

American Telephone & Telegraph Co.

Top: Long-distance operator completing a call by manipulating keys at a switchboard.
Bottom: Rows of crossbar-dial switches in a long-distance telephone center.

line to the called line. The district selector selects a trunk to the proper exchange, either the home or a distant exchange. The incoming selector selects a trunk to the final selectors of the same exchange. The final selector selects the terminals of the line of the called party.

Transoceanic Telephony. Overseas radiotelephone service, introduced commercially in 1927, is available between the United States and over 80 countries, as well as to ships at sea. Because the low-frequency waves employed in transmissions are reflected from the ionosphere, the service is subject to disruption by magnetic storms. In 1955 work was begun on the laying of the world's first transoceanic submarine telephone cable, extending between Newfoundland and Scotland. The cable will provide 36 circuits linking North America and Europe.

Carrier-current Telephony. This name was given to the method of sending telephone messages by means of frequencies above the voice range, extending from about 4000 to several million cycles a second. By this means it is possible with present methods to send as many as 600 telephone messages simultaneously over a single conducting medium. Carrier-current telephony techniques are also being used to send telephone messages over power distribution lines without interfering with the usual service of the lines.

Amplifiers. With the increasing distance covered and increasing complexity of systems, it becomes necessary to amplify the messages at intervals of five to two hundred miles, depending upon the type of line structure and communication system. For this purpose, the electron tube has been most satisfactory.

Coaxial Cable. A further advance in obtaining a number of circuits from cable conductors by carrier means is the development of the coaxial cable. The cable is merely a pair of conductors, one a small tube, the other a wire held at the center of the tube, by which a large number of messages can be transmitted simultaneously. An experimental installation of this cable was begun in 1936. Today two of these coaxial units provide as many as 600 two-way telephone message circuits. See ELECTRIC CABLE.

Telephone and Broadcasting. Long distance telephone lines have made possible the simultaneous transmission of radio programs from widely scattered broadcasting stations. To provide a wire system that could transmit the wide range of frequencies inherent in

music, cable systems have been equipped with special loading coils about every half mile. The system of special telephone circuits set aside for broadcasting purposes comprises a total of about 155,000 miles of wire lines. Of these, about 115,000 miles are in regular full-time use for chain broadcasting while the rest are held in reserve for frequent use in special broadcasts and for assuring continuity of service. Thus it is possible for multiple stations to be grouped for the broadcasting of events of national interest.

TELESCOPE, essentially a lens or mirror to form an image of a distant object, together with a microscope to enable the observer to examine this image in detail, or a photographic camera or some form of spectroscopic apparatus.

The invention of the telescope was doubtless accomplished in Holland, but there is some confusion and controversy to be encountered in attempting to determine the original inventor. It seems certain that the instrument was known more or less about Europe, but the honor of its invention is usually given to Galileo, who was the first to describe it and exhibit it in a complete form (May, 1609). To Kepler we owe the discovery of the principle of the astronomical telescope with two convex lenses. This idea was actually employed in a telescope constructed by Father Scheiner (*Rosa Ursina*, 1630). The difficulties due to spherical aberration were early experienced by opticians and astronomers, and in an attempt to obviate them astronomical telescopes were constructed of considerable focal length and power.

The invention of the achromatic object glass by Dollond in 1757–58 and the improvement of optical flint glass, which commenced in 1754, soon made possible the construction of improved telescopes; but these were all of modest dimensions, and until well into the nineteenth century few if any object glasses were constructed greater than 12 inches in diameter. The discovery of methods of making large disks of flint glass was made by Guinand, a Swiss mechanic, who then became associated with Fraunhofer, and telescopes as large as 10 inches aperture were readily made. His successors made instruments with object glasses 15 inches across.

The next successful manufacturer of telescope lenses was Alvan Clark of Cambridgeport, Mass., who, from the time when an object glass manufactured in his shop was purchased by the Rev. W.R. Dawes of Eng-

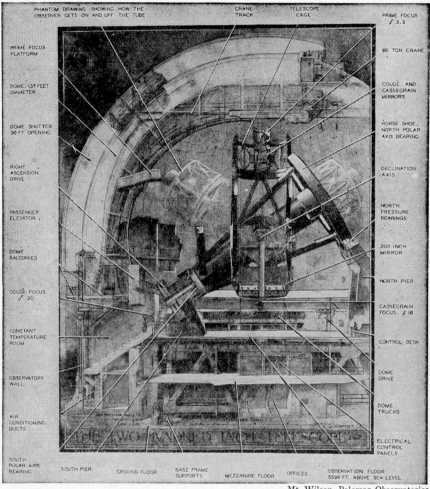

PHANTOM DRAWING SHOWING HOW THE OBSERVER GETS ON AND OFF THE TUBE

CRANE TRACK

TELESCOPE CAGE

PRIME FOCUS *f* 3.3

PRIME FOCUS PLATFORM

60 TON CRANE

DOME, 137 FEET DIAMETER

COUDÉ AND CASSEGRAIN MIRRORS

DOME SHUTTER 30 FT OPENING

HORSE SHOE, NORTH POLAR AXIS BEARING

RIGHT ASCENSION DRIVE

DECLINATION AXIS

PASSENGER ELEVATOR

NORTH PRESSURE BEARINGS

DOME BALCONIES

200 INCH MIRROR

COUDÉ FOCUS *f* 30

NORTH PIER

CONSTANT TEMPERATURE ROOM

CASSEGRAIN FOCUS *f* 16

CONTROL DESK

OBSERVATORY WALL

DOME DRIVE

AIR CONDITIONING DUCTS

DOME TRUCKS

ELECTRICAL CONTROL PANELS

SOUTH POLAR AXIS BEARING — SOUTH PIER — GROUND FLOOR — BASE FRAME SUPPORTS — MEZZANINE FLOOR — OFFICES — OBSERVATION FLOOR 5598 FT. ABOVE SEA LEVEL

Mt. Wilson, Palomar Observatories

Drawing showing parts and operation of 200-inch telescope at Mt. Palomar, California

land, gradually achieved the highest rank as a maker of telescope lenses. With him was associated his son Alvan G. Clark. At the Cambridgeport works were constructed the lenses not only for the leading American observatories, but also for the Imperial Russian Observatory in Pulkova and other European institutions. Other makers of refracting telescopes in the United States have been Brashear in Pittsburgh, Pa., who was succeeded by J.W. Fecker, Warner, and Swazey, while in Europe, Grubb of Dublin, Henry Brothers of Paris, and Steinheil in Germany were notable for their work.

The formation of an image by a concave mirror has been employed in the reflecting telescope, of which numerous varieties have been devised and with which many of the most important astronomical discoveries have been made. Father Zucchi, an Italian Jesuit, was the first to use an eye lens to view the image produced by a concave mirror (1616–52), but to Gregory is due the first description of a telescope with a reflecting mirror, and the instrument has since been known by his name. An actual working instrument based on this principle was devised and constructed by Isaac Newton. In these telescopes the great difficulty was viewing the image, as the eyepiece and the head of the observer

Yerkes Obs.; Mt. Wilson, Palomar Observs.

OBSERVATORY TELESCOPES. *Left: 40-inch refracting telescope at Yerkes Observatory, Wisconsin. Above: Observer seated in prime focus of 200-inch reflecting telescope at Mt. Palomar, California. Below: Side view of the 200-inch telescope at Mt. Palomar.*

Allen B. Du Mont Laboratories

Left: Transmitting antenna of television station, atop a building in New York City. Right: Top view of chassis of television-receiving set with 12½-inch picture tube.

would cut off a large portion of the incident rays. In the Gregorian telescope this was obviated by the interposition of a second concave mirror, which reflected the rays to the eyepiece. Draper used a total reflection prism instead of the plane mirror with considerable success, being one of the few astronomers in the United States to construct a reflecting mirror.

Cassegrain employed a convex mirror instead of a concave one. Herschel obtained satisfactory results by tilting his mirror and placing the eyepiece below the axis of the instrument, so that it was not in the way of the incident rays. Herschel's mirrors were as large as 4 feet in diameter, with a tube 40 feet in length. The mirrors for reflecting telescopes were usually made of speculum metal, which is composed of a mixture of copper and tin, until Liebig discovered the method of depositing a film of silver on a glass surface. The use of silvered glass for mirrors was suggested by Steinheil, and later by Foucault, and finally met with general adoption as it not only facilitates the construction of the mirror, but makes possible its resilvering at any time without the destruction of its configuration. Silvering the mirror has been superseded by coating the mirror with aluminum, which lasts much longer.

The first equatorial mounting (q.v.) is

ascribed to Lassel. In England telecopes were mounted by having the polar axis supported at each end, but the German system, where the mounting is in the center and the weight of the telescope is balanced by counterpoises, is now generally used for large refractors, and a modified form is employed for reflectors. The great telescope of the Yerkes Observatory of the University of Chicago at Williams Bay, Lake Geneva, Wisconsin, is the largest refracting telescope with an equatorial mounting. At present, the list of great reflectors (reflecting telescopes) includes:

200-inch at Mt. Palomar, California;

100-inch at Mt. Wilson Observatory, Pasadena, California;

82-inch at the McDonald Observatory on Mt. Locke in Texas;

74-inch at the Dunlap Observatory, Toronto, Canada;

72-inch at the Dominion Astrophysical Observatory, Victoria, B.C.;

69-inch at the Perkins Observatory at Delaware, Ohio;

61-inch at the Harvard Observatory, Harvard, Mass.;

60-inch at Bloemfontein Observatory, Bloemfontein, Union of South Africa.

TELEVISION, the instantaneous transmission of images, such as scenes or pictures, either fixed or moving, by electronic means over electrical transmission lines or by radio

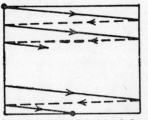

From *Basic Television—Principles & Servicing,*
by Bernard Grob, McGraw Hill

Fig. 1

broadcasting stations. It resembles in many of its fundamental principles the process of facsimile transmission (see FACSIMILE), which has been widely used for many years as a means of communicating news pictures, maps, and legal documents. Unlike television, however, facsimile is not instantaneous and does not permit the transmission of a continuously changing picture.

Formation of Television Pictures. Both television and facsimile depend upon the reduction of the image to a large number of individual small components. Although each tiny section is a separate light or dark spot, the sections are so small and so numerous that the picture appears to the eye of the observer as a smooth grading of tones in an integrated pattern. By such a division into parts ordinary photoengraving, such as used in the half-tone illustrations in this encyclopedia, is characterized; under a magnifying glass individual black dots of varying size are visible.

Television and facsimile pictures are similarly formed of a pattern of tone elements which blend to form a complete picture. The dots of a half-tone engraving are all present simultaneously on the paper surface, but the individual tone elements of the facsimile and the television image appear on the receiving surface one after another in temporal succession. In facsimile these elements are printed or photographed and accumulate to form a whole image as the area is traced out; in television they accumulate to form an image because the character of the chemical coating on the television screen retains each element for a short time, and because of the phenomenon of persistence of vision in the viewer.

Scanning. Breaking up an image into a sequence of individual elements which can later be reassembled into the proper positions to recreate the picture is accomplished by a

technique known as scanning. The eye of the scanner sweeps over the entire picture in much the same way as the eye of a reader sweeps over a page of print, word by word and line by line. Facsimile scanning is usually done by a moving photoelectric cell (q.v.) which passes over an illuminated picture. The variations of intensity of each particular portion of the picture as registered by the electric eye are transmitted ultimately to a beam of light which travels over a photosensitive film, the position of the light being exactly synchronized with the position of the receiving eye with respect to the picture area. Thus, when the entire area of the original picture has been traversed, the picture has been *scanned*, and the signal generated in the course of the process may be used to create a duplicate at the site of the receiving apparatus.

Various means of scanning mechanically and electrically have been devised, some of which are described below under *History*. Almost all modern television systems, however, rely upon the motion of a beam of electrons which sweeps across the screens of camera tubes or receiving tubes by electrical means. The advantage of scanning with an electron beam is that the beam can be moved with great speed and can scan an entire picture in a small fraction of a second.

Fig. 1 shows in simplified form the path followed by an electron beam in scanning the entire area of a picture or image. The solid lines represent the path of the beam over the image surface and the dotted lines the flyback or retrace periods. During these periods, which are necessary to bring the beam back to the starting point of the next line or the next entire scanning operation, the beam is arranged to be ineffective for scanning. The illustration shows a simple scanning pattern composed of comparatively few lines and a simple repetition of the scanning pattern. In actual television scanning a large number of lines are used and the pattern is scanned in two interlaced parts.

A complete individual scanning pattern such as that shown produces a single static picture similar to a single frame of motion picture film. As the pattern is repeated a number of times per second, changes in a moving image are recorded and these changes blend into continuous motion for the observer just as do the changes recorded in successive frames of motion picture film.

The greater the number of lines scanned from top to bottom of an image and the greater the number of elements recorded on each line as it is scanned from left to right, the greater is the "definition" of the image reproduced. Definition is the capacity of the image to show fine details or small objects, and in general is equivalent to the clarity of the picture. In television the frequency of repetition of the pattern, the number of scanning lines used, and the number of elements reproduced in the scanned lines must be standardized for any given system in order that the television transmitter and receiver can operate in synchronism. As a practical matter these so-called television standards are set up for all transmitters and all receivers used in the entire country. In the United States broadcasters and receiver manufacturers have agreed on a standard of 525 horizontal lines per frame and a frequency of 30 frames per second. Similarly the number of "picture elements" in each line has been limited for technical reasons to 426 elements per line. The result is an image that consists of 223,650 individual elements for the entire frame; these elements are repeated 30 times per second to give a total of 6,709,500 transmitted in each second.

Clearer television pictures can be obtained and have been obtained experimentally by increasing the number of lines and elements. The system used at present is the best that is technically obtainable for present transmission frequencies. For purposes of comparison, the best theoretical definition obtainable with a television image on the present standards is equivalent to that found in a half-tone engraving 3 in. by 5 in. using a screen of the type used in illustrating this encyclopedia. Compared to the definition of standard 35 mm. motion picture film of the type shown in theaters, the television image contains about ⅓ as many elements and thus is far less detailed.

The Television Signal. The television signal is a complex electric wave of voltage or current variation which is composed of the following parts: a series of fluctuations which correspond to the fluctuations in light intensity of the picture elements being scanned, a series of synchronizing pulses which lock the receiver to the same scanning rate as the transmitter, an additional series of "blanking pulses", and a frequency-modulated signal carrying the sound which accompanies the image. The first three of these elements make up the "video signal" and are discussed below. The sound signal is of the

type discussed in the article FREQUENCY MODULATION.

Fluctuations of current or voltage corresponding to the variations in light intensity are often termed the camera signal. The frequency of this signal is about 4 million cycles per second, varying for each individual picture element. The method of producing the camera signal is dealt with in the section *Television Cameras* below and its reproduction at the receiver in the section on *Kinescopes.*

Synchronizing pulses are short bursts of electrical energy generated by appropriate oscillators (see ELECTRONICS) at the transmitting station. These pulses control the rate of horizontal and vertical scanning of both camera and receiver. The horizontal synchronizing pulses occur at intervals of $\frac{1}{15,750}$ of a second and last for approximately $\frac{1}{200,000}$ of a second. The vertical synchronizing pulses recur at intervals of $\frac{1}{60}$ of a second and last approximately $\frac{1}{5000}$ of a second.

Blanking pulses make the electron beam inoperative in the camera and the receiver during the time which it takes the electron beam to "fly back" from the end of one horizontal line to the beginning of the next and from the bottom of the vertical pattern to the top. The timing and structure of these pulses is highly complex.

Television Cameras. The television camera resembles ordinary cameras in being equipped with a lens or lenses and a means of focusing the image formed by the lens on a sensitive surface. The sensitive surfaces used are electronic tubes called camera tubes which have the ability to transform variations in light intensity into variations in electrical charge or current. The original camera tube was the iconoscope, a type still used for televising films. For televising scenes where the light level is low, as in normally lighted halls or rooms, the newer, highly sensitive image orthicon is used.

The operation of the iconoscope can be understood by referring to Fig. 2. Light from the camera lens enters the tube from the left and falls in focus upon the signal plate. The front of this plate, which is made of an extremely thin sheet of mica, is covered with a very fine mosaic pattern made up of globules of silver coated with cesium or some other light-sensitive material. Each

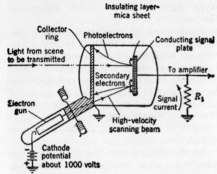

Insulating layer-mica sheet

Collector ring
Photoelectrons
Conducting signal plate
Light from scene to be transmitted
Secondary electrons
To amplifier
Signal current
R_s
Electron gun
High-velocity scanning beam
Cathode potential about 1000 volts

From *Basic Television—Principles & Servicing,*
by Bernard Grob, McGraw Hill

Fig. 2

individual globule is separated from the others by a small space and is therefore insulated electrically from them. The back of the signal plate is coated with graphite, which conducts electricity. In the neck of the iconoscope is an electron gun, a source of an electron beam which is directed toward the mosaic. When light strikes one of the silver-cesium globules, this globule emits a number of electrons proportional to the intensity of the light because of its photosensitive properties. As a result the globule becomes positively charged. The total effect of the lens image on the mosaic plate is to create a pattern of individual positive charges which correspond in position and intensity to the light image thrown on the plate by the lens. By electrostatic induction, this pattern of charges causes a similar pattern of negative charges to appear on the back of the plate.

The beam of electrons from the gun traces a scanning pattern across the front of the mosaic under the influence of electrical impulses supplied by the synchronizing generators to two pairs of magnet coils at the neck of the iconoscope. One pair of these coils deflects the beam horizontally, and the other, placed at right angles to the first, deflects the beam vertically. As the electron beam strikes each positively charged globule of the mosaic, it releases the charge of the globule (by supplying the missing electrons which were driven off by the influence of light) and at the same time varies the induced charge on the back of the signal plate. The result is a constantly varying charge on the signal plate. This fluctuation is the camera signal and its intensity varies in exact proportion to the light image on the mosaic as the electron beam scans the mosaic.

(This description of the operation of the iconoscope has been somewhat simplified by omitting a description of the emission of secondary electrons from the mosaic under the influence of the scanning beam. These electrons are "collected" by a metal coating at the front of the tube, called the collecting ring, which is connected to ground and which completes the signal circuit.)

As a camera tube the iconoscope has several disadvantages. One of the most important is that it requires extremely strong illumination of the subject to produce a usable signal. When television cameras are used in the studio under controlled light conditions, this disadvantage is not serious, but the iconoscope is unsuitable for use in the televising of news events under adverse light conditions. A number of other camera tubes have been invented to overcome this difficulty. The most successful of these is the image orthicon. The sensitivity of this tube is such that it will produce a camera signal under any lighting conditions which are suitable for viewing with the naked eye; in demonstrations, the image orthicon has produced adequate television images of scenes lit only by candles. An added advantage of the image orthicon is that it uses a comparatively small screen and can thus be incorporated into a camera of small size.

The image orthicon tube, as shown in Fig. 3, has a flat glass window at one end which serves as its screen. The inner side of the plate is coated with a continuous layer of silver-cesium to form a sensitive photoelectric surface. Spaced close behind this layer and parallel to it is a target made of glass having low electrical sensitivity. In front of the target is a screen of wire mesh having as many as 1000 openings per square inch. Back of the target a concentric metallic ring coated on the inside of the tube forms a decelerating element, and behind this ring is a concentric cylindrical coating within the neck of the tube which serves as a positive plate or anode. At the end of the tube is an electron gun to provide a beam of electrons and a structure called an electron multiplier.

When light strikes the sensitive coating of the tube, electrons are emitted. These electrons move in the direction of the target, which is kept at a positive potential with respect to the sensitive surface. Before reaching the target the electrons pass through the openings, which comprise about 60 percent of the total surface of the wire mesh. The electrons travel in straight lines from photoelectric surface to target and are prevented from scattering by the action of a magnetic field imposed by a magnet (not shown in the figure) which surrounds the image section of the tube.

The electrons which strike the target cause the emission of "secondary" electrons in the proportion of several electrons to each individual electron which reaches the target from the photo surface. This secondary emission builds up a pattern of positive charges on the target plate corresponding to the light image on the photo surface. Light areas are more positive and dark areas less positive in this charge image. The secondary electrons from the front of the target are picked up by the mesh screen.

The electrical properties of the glass used for the target screen are such that its resistance to flow of an electrical charge or current is much greater along the surface of the screen than through the screen. As a result, the various positive charges on the outer side of the target do not equalize themselves over the surface but pass through to the inner side of the target, reproducing the charge pattern on the inner as well as the outer side of the target.

The scanning mechanism of the tube consists of the electron gun and the cylindrical anode in the neck of the tube, which act together as a source of an electron beam, and a set of deflecting coils (not shown) mounted outside the neck of the tube like the deflecting coils of the iconoscope. The scanning beam is slowed, just before it strikes the target, by the action of the positively charged decelerating ring and reaches the target without sufficient energy to knock out secondary electrons. As the beam strikes each portion of the positive electrical charge pattern on the target, it gives up enough electrons to neutralize the positive charge at that point on the target. The remaining electrons are reflected back toward the electron gun and its associated electron multiplier. In areas with a strong positive charge, corresponding to light areas of the image, more electrons are needed to neutralize the charge and, as a result, fewer electrons are reflected.

The electron multiplier, which consists of a disk surrounding the aperture through which the electron gun "fires" followed by a succession of symmetrical elements behind this disk, acts as an amplifying device by secondary electron emission. The first disk in a typical image orthicon is held at a positive potential of about 200 volts, and the succeeding elements or dynodes are held at higher positive potentials. Electrons striking the disk knock off a greater number of secondary electrons, which, in turn, knock off still more electrons as they pass from dynode to dynode. As a result the camera signal is "multiplied" as it passes from element to element.

Several other types of camera tubes are sometimes used in modern television transmission; among them is the *image dissector* in which the entire electrical image is moved past an aperture to accomplish the scanning action.

Television Transmitters. Except for the special circuits required to produce the synchronizing and blanking pulses required for scanning, and the various types of special equipment used to examine or monitor the signals from the television camera, the re-

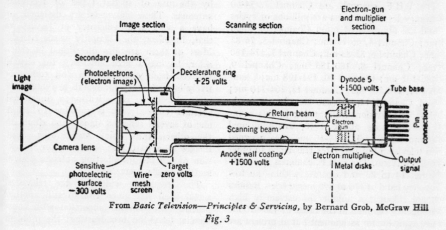

From *Basic Television—Principles & Servicing,* by Bernard Grob, McGraw Hill

Fig. 3

mainder of a television transmitting system resembles that of an ordinary amplitude-modulated broadcasting station. The sound equipment is in no way different from that used in ordinary F.M. broadcasting and the sound signal is sometimes broadcast from its own separate antenna, forming in effect a completely separate broadcasting unit.

Television broadcasting, however, has a number of special problems which are not encountered in ordinary sound broadcasting. The chief of these is that of "band width". The process of modulating an electromagnetic wave (see MODULATION) involves the generation of a series of frequencies called sidebands which correspond to the difference in frequencies between the radio of "carrier" frequency and the modulating frequencies. In ordinary broadcasting in which the signal employs only frequencies up to 10,000 cycles (10 kilocycles) per second, the sidebands occupy little space in the spectrum of frequencies and different stations can be assigned carrier frequencies as little as 5 kilocycles apart without interference. The frequency range of a single television signal, however, is about 4,000,000 cycles or 4000 kilocycles and such signals therefore occupy about 40 times as much space as the entire frequency band used for standard broadcasting. In order to provide sufficient channels to accommodate a number of television stations serving the same area, it is necessary to utilize comparatively high transmission frequencies for the television carriers. The channels assigned to television broadcasting in the U.S. number 82. This total is composed of 12 channels in the very-high-frequency band and 70 in the ultra-high-frequency band. The V.H.F. channels are Channel 2, 54-60 megacycles (megacycles are millions of cycles and are abbreviated mc); Channel 3, 60-66 mc; Channel 4, 66-72 mc; Channel 5, 76-82 mc; Channel 6, 82-88 mc; Channel 7, 174-180 mc; Channel 8, 180-186 mc; Channel 9, 186-192 mc; Channel 10, 192-198 mc; Channel 11, 198-204 mc; Channel 12, 204-210 mc; and Channel 13, 210-216 mc. In the early days of television broadcasting in this country, beginning about 1940, an additional channel, Channel 1, 44-50 mc, was assigned to television but was later reassigned to other radio services. The U.H.F. channels are numbered 14 to 83 and operate within the frequency band of 470 to 890 megacycles. Besides these channels a number of extremely high frequency channels in the range of 480-920 mc are available for assignment but at present are employed only for experimental purposes.

The use of high frequencies for television broadcasting has introduced a number of problems which are quite different from those of conventional sound broadcasting. The range of low-frequency radio signals is quite extensive, reaching to hundreds and even thousands of miles. High-frequency signals, on the other hand, are comparatively limited in range and often do not extend beyond the actual line of sight from place to place as determined by the curvature of the earth. Thus, while the service area of a standard broadcasting station may have a radius of well over 100 miles, that of a television station is usually limited to about 35 miles or even less, depending upon the height of the transmitting and receiving antennas. Provision of complete television coverage for a country as large as the U.S. therefore requires a much greater number of television stations than are employed for standard broadcasting.

Another problem encountered in the use of high frequencies for television broadcasting is that radio waves of such frequencies behave very much like light waves and are reflected from solid objects such as hills or buildings. Often several such reflections from a single station will be received simultaneously at a given receiver location, giving rise to multiple or "ghost" images on the receiver screen because the reflected signals have traveled different distances and therefore arrive at the receiver at slightly different times. The problem of reflected signals as well as the problem of receiving television signals at distances beyond the normal service range have been solved to a great extent by the use of special types of receiving antennas. These antennas are designed to have a very high efficiency or "gain" so that, in effect, they amplify weak signals. Most of them are also directional in character, having a high efficiency for signals received from one direction and comparatively low efficiency for signals arriving from other directions. By orienting a directional antenna correctly, it is possible to select one of several reflected signals and eliminate the others, thus doing away with ghost images at a particular location. For discussion of the factors affecting antenna design, see the article ANTENNA.

The frequency width of the television signal itself has given rise to still another practical problem in connection with commercial television broadcasting: the problem

NBC Photos; Allen B. Du Mont Laboratories

Above: Television cameras on an indoor set.
Right: Mobile-television unit for televising
spot-news events and features. Below: En-
gineer at control panel during broadcast.

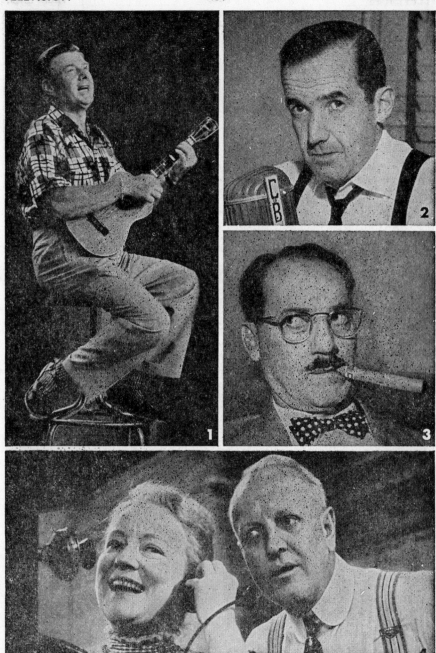

AMERICAN TV PERSONALITIES. *1. Arthur Godfrey, master of ceremonies; 2. Edward R. Murrow, news analyst; 3. Groucho Marx, comedian; 4. Peggy Wood and Judson Laire, dramatic stars;*

5. *Lucille Ball, comedienne; 6. Walter Winchell, news commentator; 7. Perry Como, singer;*
8. Douglas Edwards, news commentator; and 9. Jackie Gleason, comedian.

C.B.S.; Wide World; United Press

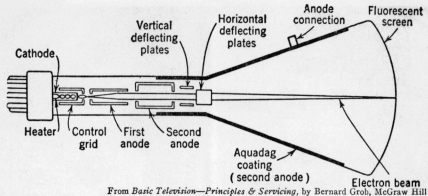

Cathode

Vertical deflecting plates

Horizontal deflecting plates

Anode connection

Fluorescent screen

Heater Control grid First anode Second anode

Aquadag coating (second anode)

Electron beam

From *Basic Television—Principles & Servicing,* by Bernard Grob, McGraw Hill

Fig. 4

of relaying television programs from one station to another for network broadcasting. In ordinary sound broadcasting practice, programs are relayed over ordinary telephone lines from city to city. Many of these lines are available and make it easy to distribute a single program to stations in every part of the country. Ordinary wire lines, however, will not carry the broad band of frequencies necessary for television. The only type of land line suitable for such transmission is the *coaxial cable,* a line consisting of a cylindrical outer conductor with a second conductor in the form of a wire running coaxially through it. Coaxial cables are expensive to construct and maintain. A simpler answer to the question of relaying television programs has been found in the use of radio relay stations. These stations receive the television signal by radio, amplify it, and retransmit it automatically. By stringing a chain of such relay stations between two cities, a program originating in one city may be transmitted and rebroadcast in the other. One typical chain between New York and Boston employs seven such relay or repeater stations spaced about 30 miles apart. A total of 107 relay stations are used in transmitting programs between New York and Los Angeles.

Kinescopes. The heart of the television receiver is the picture tube or kinescope, which translates the electrical impulses of the television signal into visible light. The kinescope stands in the same relation to the receiver as the camera tube does to the television transmitter. In its actual structure the kinescope is a cathode-ray tube, so called because it generates a beam of electrons originating at the cathode of negative electrode.

Fig. 4 shows diagrammatically the action of a typical kinescope. Housed in the narrow neck of a funnel-shaped tube is the electron gun, consisting of a heated cathode filament, a control grid, and two anodes. Electrons emitted from the cathode are focused into a narrow beam by passing through a narrow opening in the control grid, which is held at a negative electrical potential with respect to the cathode. This slight negative "bias" on the grid has the effect of driving some of the electrons back to the cathode and allowing only those electrons to pass which travel in a beam toward the opening. The two anodes are both at positive potentials with respect to the cathode and thus attract electrons. The combined effect of the positive fields of the two anodes is to focus the electrons flowing through the tube so that they all strike a single point on the screen at the large end of the tube, and provision is usually made to vary the relative strength of the fields to focus this spot exactly on the screen. Occasionally a magnetic focusing coil is substituted for the two focusing anodes.

The screen is formed by coating the inner end of the tube with any one of several types of chemicals known as phosphors, which have the property of glowing when subjected to an electric charge such as a beam of electrons. When the tube is operative the electron beam is visible on the face of the tube as a small luminous spot.

In the kinescope shown the electron beam is moved for scanning by means of two pairs of deflection plates. When a positive charge is placed on one of these pairs and a negative charge on the other, the beam is deflected away from the positively charged

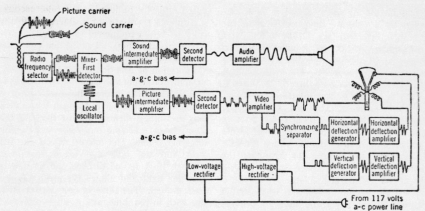

From *Basic Television—Principles & Servicing,* by Bernard Grob, McGraw Hill

Fig. 5

plate and toward the negatively charged one. The first of the pairs of plates in the tube diagrammed here deflect the beam up and down and the second pair deflect it from side to side. Oscillating scanning voltages are generated in the receiver and are exactly synchronized to those of the transmitter by means of the synchronization pulses from the transmitter. Thus when a station is tuned in on the receiver, the scanning rate and sequence of the kinescope are automatically locked to those of the camera tube at the transmitter.

The camera signal from the transmitter is amplified by the television receiver and applied to the control grid of the kinescope. When this grid is driven negative by the signal, the grid repels electrons and, when the negative signal is strong enough, no electrons pass the grid and the screen is dark. In the event that the grid is driven moderately negative, some electrons pass the grid and the screen shows a faintly luminous spot corresponding to gray in the original image. When the grid is not driven negative by the signal or is made more positive by it, the screen shows a brilliant spot, corresponding to white in the original image. By means of the combined action of the scanning voltage and the camera signal voltage, the electron beam traces out a luminous pattern on the screen which is an exact reproduction of the original scene. The phosphors used on the screen continue to glow for a short time after they have been activated by the electron beam, so that the individual spots blend into one another to form a continuous picture.

The size of the end of the ordinary kinescope tube determines the size of the picture on the screen. Kinescopes are manufactured with screens having diameters between 5 and 27 inches. The larger sizes are more desirable as the images may be viewed simultaneously by more people. The construction of large-diameter tubes is costly and difficult, and such tubes are more subject to breakage. To achieve a very large image, using comparatively small tubes, receivers may be equipped to project the image on translucent or opaque screens. This technique is employed in theatre television. Projection kinescopes must be operated at high voltages in order to provide images that are considerably brighter than those delivered by direct-view tubes.

Television Receivers. The circuits of modern television receivers are necessarily complex but the general scheme of their operation is easily understood by reference to Fig. 5. The signal received by the antenna is tuned and amplified in the radio frequency-selector stage. Passing on to the mixer stage the signal is combined with the output of a local oscillator in the receiver which generates a steady frequency. This combination or mixing produces beat frequencies corresponding to the picture signal and the sound signal. Separated by selective filter circuits which pass one band of frequencies and reject all others, the two signals are then separately amplified. The sound signal is amplified by an intermediate amplifier, demodulated, and amplified again by an audio amplifier as in a conventional frequency-modulation receiver of the type described under FREQUENCY MODULATION.

The picture or video signal is also amplified by a separate intermediate amplifier and then detected (see DETECTION). After further amplification by a video amplifier, the signal is divided by filter circuits into two separate components. The camera signal and blanking pulses pass directly to the grid of the kinescope to control the intensity of the electron beam. The two sets of synchronizing pulses are separated by filtering into the vertical and horizontal components and are applied to oscillators which generate the voltages to be used for deflecting the electron beam. The outputs of the vertical end of the horizontal oscillator are amplified and led to the appropriate sets of deflecting magnets at the kinescope tube to provide the proper scanning pattern.

Color Television. In 1950 the Federal Communications Commission adopted rules and engineering standards for a color television system. In judging several proposed methods for transmitting color, the Commission held that the only suitable method at that time was one developed by the Columbia Broadcasting System. The C.B.S. color method was, however, incompatible in the sense that existing receiving sets could not receive color transmissions even in monochrome without adaptation. In 1953 the Commission superseded its earlier decision by adopting a compatible color system that had been proposed by the National Television System Committee, an all-industry group (including C.B.S.), whose engineers co-operated in the development of necessary engineering standards. By means of this system all monochrome receivers can, without adaptation, pick up color signals in black and white.

In the new engineering standards adopted by the Federal Communications Commission, color television is brought about in much the same way as black-and-white television, except that each picture is transmitted three times, once in each of the three additive primary colors, red, green, and blue. The monochrome television transmitter is required to send only one type of picture information, namely brightness, but the color transmitter must add hue and saturation. For hue and saturation definition the picture must be separated into three color images, each requiring a different signal. These three signals, added to the brightness signal, are then converted into electrical energy for transmission. The transmitted signals are reconverted by the receiving set into the three separate color images, and the three images are then superim-

posed optically to form a full color picture.

Although there are some differences in the color-television equipment turned out by different manufacturers, all equipment conforms to the same engineering standards. The Radio Corporation of America, a pioneer in the development of compatible color, designed a system which works in the following manner.

The color image passes through the camera lens and hits a dichroic mirror that has the property of reflecting one color and passing all other colors. The mirror reflects the red light and the blue and green rays pass through it. A second dichroic mirror reflects the blue light and allows the green rays to pass through. The three images thus created, one each in red, blue, and green, are focused on the faces of three camera tubes (image orthicons). In front of the tubes are color filters which assure that the color quality of each primary color has the precise value for the system. The electron beam in each tube scans the image pattern and produces a primary color signal. Samples of these three color signals then go to an electronic adder which combines them to make the brightness, or black-and-white signal. Signal samples also are fed to another unit which encodes or combines them to produce a signal carrying the hue and saturation information. The color signal is then combined with the brightness signal to form the complete color-television signal that goes out on the air.

For its color-television receiver, R.C.A. designed a tri-color picture tube that has three electron guns, one for each primary color, which scan and stimulate color phosphor dots on the viewing screen. The tiny dots, which may number 600,000 or more, are arranged in clusters of three, a red, green, and blue phosphor in each cluster. A shadow mask between the electron guns and the viewing screen has tiny perforations, so placed that the stream of electrons from each gun can fall only on its appropriate color phosphor. The beam that "paints" red information will strike only the red phosphors, etc. When the incoming color signal reaches a color-television receiver, it passes through a separator that splits the color from the brightness. The color information is then decoded. When it is recombined with the brightness information, a series of primary color signals are produced and applied to the tri-color tube, thus recreating the image seen by the color camera. If a color-television signal reaches a black-and-white receiver, the electronic data pertaining to hue and saturation are ignored by the

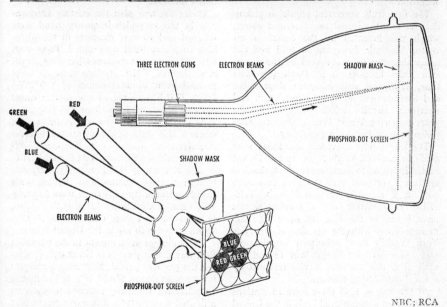

THREE ELECTRON GUNS ELECTRON BEAMS SHADOW MASK

PHOSPHOR-DOT SCREEN

GREEN RED

BLUE

SHADOW MASK

ELECTRON BEAMS

BLUE
RED GREEN

PHOSPHOR-DOT SCREEN

NBC; RCA

Top: Color-television camera with cover removed. Two dichroic mirrors allow green rays to pass to center lens while silvered mirrors reflect blue and red rays to lenses at left and right. Bottom: Drawing of the RCA tri-color tube.

receiver's circuits and only the brightness signal remains effective. Unless the viewer is informed in advance, he probably will not realize that the picture on his black-and-white viewing screen originated at the studio in full color.

History. The history of the development of television has been basically the history of a search for an adequate device for scanning the image. The first such device was the so-called *Nipkow disk,* patented by the German inventor Paul Nipkow in 1884. This was a flat, circular disk which was perforated with a series of small holes arranged in a spiral radiating from the center to the rim. As the disk was revolved in front of the eye, the outermost hole scanned a strip across the top of the image, and the succeeding holes scanned strips lower down until the entire image had been scanned. With suitable lens systems, and by using photoelectric cells as transmission elements and electric lamps which could be varied in intensity as receiving elements, a number of wired and later wireless television systems were constructed. Because of its mechanical nature, however, the Nipkow disk failed to operate efficiently when made in large sizes and revolved at high speeds to obtain better definition.

The first truly successful television pickup devices were the iconoscope described above, which was invented by the American inventor Vladimir Zworykin in 1933 and the image dissector tube, invented by the American Philo Farnsworth at about the same time. With the availability of these tubes and the advances in radio transmission and electronic circuits which occurred in the years following World War I, practical television systems became a possibility.

The first public television broadcasts were made in England in 1927 and in the United States in 1930. In both instances mechanical systems were used and the programs were not on a regularly scheduled basis. Television broadcasting on a regular service basis began in the U.S. on April 30, 1939 in connection with the opening of the New York World's Fair. Scheduled broadcasting was interrupted by World War II and not until after the war was service resumed by a few broadcasting stations.

At the end of 1946 there were 12 stations operating on a commercial basis in the United States. With the growth of the television audience, broadcasting companies gave increased attention to program techniques. Telecasts of

sporting events became especially popular. Advertisers entered the field on a large scale, sponsoring a wide variety of programs. By 1948 the number of stations had increased to 46, construction had begun on 78 more, and over 300 applications had been submitted to the Federal Communications Commission for permits to build new stations. The boom forced the Commission to recognize that the existing plan allocating the very-high-frequency band for about 400 stations operating on 12 channels was obviously inadequate to serve the entire country. Late in 1948 the Commission halted the licensing of new stations until a new plan could be drawn up.

Sales of receiving sets mounted steadily during the next few years. As additional millions joined the TV audience other entertainment industries suffered severe declines of patronage. The motion-picture industry, which experienced the most serious reverses, closed thousands of theaters.

The moratorium on new construction ended in 1952, when the Commission announced a plan providing for a total of 2053 stations in 1291 communities in the United States and its territories and possessions. Channel assignments in 242 communities were set aside exclusively for use by noncommercial, educational interests.

Under the new plan the existing 12 channels in the very-high-frequency band were retained and 70 new channels in the ultra-high-frequency band were added. To prevent interference among stations telecasting on the same channel, V.H.F. stations using the same channel must be a minimum of 170 miles apart. U.H.F. stations on the same channel must be separated by at least 155 miles.

As U.H.F. stations went on the air in areas where V.H.F. stations already existed, receiver manufacturers turned out dual-band sets which would receive both V.H.F. and U.H.F. signals. Exclusively U.H.F. receivers were also built for those communities having only U.H.F. stations. By 1954 there were 360 television stations, including 125 U.H.F. stations, in operation and more than 27,660,000 television receivers in use in the United States.

The tempo of development in the television field was similarly rapid in Great Britain during the postwar period. Following a six-year interruption due to World War II the British Broadcasting Company resumed telecasts on a limited scale in 1946. The company, as part of a plan to make TV broadcasts available to at least 80 percent of the population, completed construction in 1949 of the most powerful transmitting station in the world. The plan, which entailed the expenditure of £10,-000,000 and the construction of eight additional stations, was fulfilled in 1952. In that year TV receiving sets produced in Great Britain totaled more than 720,000.

Experiments with various television systems were conducted in several European countries, including France and the Netherlands, during the immediate postwar period, but the Soviet Union, which began regular telecasts from Moscow in 1948, was the first continental country to initiate operations as a public service. No information was available, then or later, on the number of receiving sets in use.

Two French TV stations, one in Paris, the other in Lille, were in operation by the end of 1950, but the audience was small, receiving sets in the country numbering less than 20,-000. In 1951 West Germany, Denmark, and the Netherlands began public-service telecasts on a limited basis. Experimental telecasts were carried on in Spain, Switzerland, Belgium, and Sweden during the year. Italy initiated television service on a limited scale in 1952; plans were announced for establishment of a nationwide broadcasting network within the next five years. Both West Germany and the Netherlands substantially expanded broadcasting facilities in 1952–53. In 1953 regular telecasts were begun in Belgium. Meanwhile, in the Western Hemisphere, a number of Canadian TV stations had begun operations in 1952.

TELFORD, THOMAS (1757–1834), Scottish civil engineer, born in Eskdale, Dumfriesshire. During his youth he was a stonemason and supervised the construction of numerous homes in London. He then turned to the designing and construction of canals, for which he is best known. Among the most famous of the canals which he designed are the Ellesmere Canal connecting the Severn, Dee, and Mersey rivers in England, begun in 1793 and finished in 1805; the famous system of artificial canals connecting a chain of natural Scottish lakes known as the Caledonian Canal (q.v.), begun in 1803 and completed in 1823; and the Gotha Canal connecting the Baltic and North seas, begun in 1808 and opened to seagoing traffic two years later. Among Telford's other construction projects are numerous roads and bridges in northern Scotland. In 1818 he was elected president of the newly founded Institution of Civil Engineers. He was the author of *The Life of Thomas Telford, Civil Engineer, Written by Himself* (published posthumously in 1838).

TELL, WILLIAM, a legendary Swiss patriot of the 14th century. According to tradition, he was the leader of an uprising of the Swiss peasantry against their Austrian rulers, a revolt which purportedly resulted in the unification and independence of the Swiss nation. Tell is said to have won the freedom of the Swiss by successfully meeting the challenge of the Austrian bailiff Gessler, who offered to grant the demands of the populace if Tell, using a bow and arrow would shoot an apple from the head of his young son. The legend of William Tell first appeared in literary form in a ballad written probably in the 15th century; it later served as the basis for the famous drama *Wilhelm Tell* (1804) by the German playwright Johann von Schiller (q.v.), and for the opera *Guillaume Tell* (1829) by the Italian composer Gioacchino Rossini (q.v.).

TELLER, EDWARD (1908–), Hungarian-American physicist, born in Budapest, and educated at the Karlsruhe Institute of Technology and at the universities of Munich and Leipzig. He taught successively at Göttingen, London, and George Washington universities from 1931 to 1941, when the U.S. Government recruited him for the atomic-bomb project. After World War II he joined the staff of the Institute for Nuclear Studies and was appointed (1946) professor of physics at the University of Chicago. In 1952 he became director of the newly established U.S. Atomic Energy Commission laboratory at Livermore, Calif. Teller is best known for his contributions to the development of the hydrogen bomb. He is coauthor of *The Structure of Matter* (1948).

TELLURIUM (from Lat. *tellus*, "the earth"), a brittle, silver-white, semimetallic element, of atomic number 52, atomic weight 127.6 and symbol Te, belonging to the sulfur-selenium family. Tellurium was recognized as an element and given its name in 1792 by the German chemist Martin Klaproth. Tellurium occurs in the pure state, or is found in combination with gold, silver, copper, lead, and nickel in such minerals as sylvanite, petzite, and tetradymite. Occasionally it is found in rocks as tellurite, or tellurium dioxide, TeO_2. The slimes from lead and copper refineries and the flue dusts from telluride-gold deposits are the principal commercial sources. Deposits occur in Mexico, Germany, South America, western Australia, and Ontario, Canada. In the United States, small amounts of the element are obtained from rocks in Colorado and California.

Tellurium is a comparatively stable element, insoluble in water and hydrochloric acid but soluble in nitric acid and aqua regia. It has a melting point of 452°C. (845.6°F.), a boiling point of 1390°C. (2534° F.), and a specific gravity of 6.24. Three isotopes are known, each having valences of two, four, or six. Commercially, tellurium is often obtained as a sludge formed during the electrolysis of copper and lead. It is also prepared by the reduction of telluric oxide, forming a grayish-white, metal-like powder.

Tellurium reacts with an excess of chlorine to form tellurium dichloride, $TeCl_2$, and tellurium tetrachloride, $TeCl_4$. It is oxidized by nitric acid to produce tellurium dioxide, TeO_2, and by chromic acid to produce telluric acid, H_2TeO_4. In combination with hydrogen or metals of the sulfur group it forms tellurides such as hydrogen telluride, H_2Te, and silver telluride, $AgTe_2$. Tellurium is used in the manufacture of rectifiers and crystal detectors in various forms of wireless equipment, and together with other organic substances, is employed in antiknock compounds for gasoline. It is also used to a limited extent for imparting a blue color to glass.

TELUGUS, or TELINGAS, the northeastern division of the Dravidian family in southern India, numbering over 23,000,000. The Yanadis of Nellore, considered by some authorities to be the primitive Telugus, both with respect to physical characteristics and general culture status, are markedly dolichocephalic, broad-nosed, short-statured, and dark-skinned. The castes of the Telugus, adopted through Hindu influence, run down from the Brahmans to the despised Madigas, who are leather workers.

TEMPER. See IRON, METALLURGY OF: *Heat Treatment of Steel.*

TEMPERANCE, primarily, a moderate use and enjoyment of all good things. In modern days the word is often used to designate great moderation in using alcoholic beverages, or even total abstinence from them.

Organized temperance sentiment, as it is understood today, had its origin in the United States and in Great Britain early in the 19th century. By 1830, organizations in the former country numbered over 100,000 members, and in the latter some 3500 members. Numerous societies having a common aim had developed in the United States by 1865, and at that time a movement spread toward their consolidation into the National Temperance Society and Publication House, a nonsectarian and nonpartisan society, advocating total abstinence. This society published and distributed pamphlets, textbooks, and papers, held public meetings, and called national and international conferences. In 1868 political parties were organized in Illinois and in Michigan, and these led, in 1869, to the organization of the National Prohibition Party. In 1874 the Woman's Christian Temperance Union, one of the strongest factors in the development of the total abstinence movement was organized as a result of the Women's Crusade.

Sentiment spread with rapidity. Although the Prohibition Party never acquired much numerical strength, its influence was felt by both major political parties, necessitating more careful scrutiny of the characters of their respective candidates, especially in local elections. But the greater accomplishment of the several temperance organizations was in the collection of economic facts regarding overindulgence in alcoholic beverages. As a result of the latter, plus individual independent research, by 1917 many of the railroads had followed the lead of the Pennsylvania System in adopting ironclad regulations prohibiting the use of intoxicating liquors by employees under penalty of discharge; and a large and influential group of industrial concerns had adopted similar rigid rules. Mercantile and business houses found that many transactions, such as wholesale selling, which hitherto had been accompanied by excessive drinking, could be conducted on a temperance basis. For developments since 1918, see PROHIBITION.

TEMPERANCE LEAGUE OF AMERICA. See ANTI-SALOON LEAGUE OF AMERICA.

TEMPERA PAINTING, in art, a method of painting in which the pigment is carried in an egg, casein, gum, or glycerine solution in water. The process of painting in tempera is the oldest method of painting known to mankind; the wall paintings of ancient Egypt and Babylon, and of the Mycenæan period in Greece were probably executed in tempera with a medium of yolk of egg, to which, sometimes, a little vinegar was added. The use of tempera subsequently became widespread throughout Europe and reached its height in Italy. The ground upon which the 13th-century Florentine painters Giotto, Cimabue, and their contemporaries painted was usually plaster of Paris, known as "gesso". The method of preparing a panel was first to fill all the cracks and crevices in a poplar, lime, or willow panel with a mixture of size and sawdust. The panel was then covered with a piece of fine linen cloth, which was kept in place with size, and this surface was coated with heavy gesso, known as *gesso grasso*. Finally, a lighter gesso coating called *gesso sottile*, which provided the painting surface, was laid on with a brush.

As the surface was very absorbent, the painter was forced to work with great rapidity and sureness. The Italian painters of the Renaissance ground their colors by hand and mixed the powdered colors with the medium. Today, however, tempera paints are prepared in tubes and pots, requiring only the addition of water or of some other medium, usually casein. Owing to the fact that the colors are opaque, tempera paints may be applied to a dark ground with great effectiveness. The tempera medium has always proved attractive to artists. It is now frequently employed in commercial art, because it produces colors which are more vivid than those obtainable in either oil or water color, and provides a "mat" or flat surface, without prominent highlights, which lends itself well to photographic reproduction.

TEMPERATURE, the thermal condition of a body which determines the interchange of heat between it and other bodies. Our first ideas of temperature are derived from our sensations of hot and cold. The effect of adding heat to a body is to make it hotter, unless it is at its melting or boiling point (see HEAT). This rise of temperature is accompanied by volume changes, on which the more usual methods of measuring temperature depend (see THERMOMETER). A scientific measure of temperature should be independent of any particular substance, and should depend solely upon the fundamental properties of heat itself. This absolute measure of temperature was first given by Lord Kelvin (Sir W. Thomson), who based his system on Carnot's thermodynamic cycle (see THERMODYNAMICS).

In meteorology, the distribution of land and sea influences the distribution of temperature to a very great extent. In January the great land areas in the Northern Hemisphere are much colder than the ocean areas at the same latitude; in July this relation is reversed. The earth's surface temperature must be an important factor in determining the mean temperature of the air. The periodic changes in the atmospheric air are due mainly to the sun's radiation heating up the solid parts of the earth. Consequently the temperature falls as we ascend in height. Up to the highest accessible altitudes the fall in temperature is fairly steady as the height increases.

TEMPERATURE OF THE BODY. The temperature in the healthy human adult averages from 98.4° to 98.6° F., but 97.5° and 99° F. are within normal limits. In the newborn child the temperature is slightly above the average, as it is in old age. Race has but a slight influence, a difference of 0.29° F. being observed between the nations of southern Europe and those of the northern part. The temperature rises slightly after a meal and during exercise. During the day the body heat varies about half a degree, being highest between 5 and 8 P.M., and lowest between 2 and 6 A.M.

TEMPLE, a building consecrated to religious worship, especially among pagan peoples. The term is also applied to the chief sanctuary of the Jews (see TEMPLE AT JERUSALEM), to Christian churches belonging to the Knights Templar, and in France to Protestant places of worship. It is also applied to the meeting places of certain Masonic bodies, and to buildings having the form or character of an antique temple. A temple was usually dedicated to some deity, whose image it contained; the interior was accessible to priests, but not to the general body of worshipers. Among most ancient peoples the temple was the principal architectural feature, as in Greece, where the history of temple construction is practically the history of architecture. The subject is therefore best treated under the general title ARCHITECTURE, and in the articles on the several countries. In general, it may be observed that the ancient temples (excepting those of Chaldea-Assyria) had these elements in common: a sanctuary containing the effigy or some other sacred symbol of the deity or deities worshiped; colonnades to shelter worshipers outside the sanctuary; one or more courts or enclosures with important gateways; and sometimes such adjuncts as a lake, grove, fountain, or well sacred to the deity. The Pantheon in Rome was dedicated "to all the gods". Temples of fame are a modern product; these include the Walhalla near Ratisbon, the Ruhmeshalle at Munich, and the Temple of Fame of the University of New York, which is really an open colonnade. See HALL OF FAME.

TEMPLE, a city of Bell Co., Tex., situated 72 miles N.N.E. of Austin. It is an important shipping and manufacturing center, with a large wholesale trade in cereal grains. Industrial establishments include railroad repair shops, cotton gins, flour mills, and plants producing rock-wool insulation, tools, toys, and cotton goods. Temple Junior College (1926) and McCloskey Veterans Hospital are located in the city. Temple was founded in 1881 and chartered as a city in 1884. Pop. (1950) 25,467.

TEMPLE, SIR WILLIAM (1628–99), English diplomatist, statesman, and essayist. He married Dorothy Osborne in January, 1655, and was returned for Carlow to the convention parliament at Dublin in 1660. In 1665 he was made resident at the court of Brussels. His most important success was the treaty of 1668, known as the Triple Alliance, by which England, Holland and Sweden united to curb the schemes of France. Temple also took part in the Congress of Aix-la-Chapelle (May, 1668), and was appointed ambassador at The Hague. In 1677 he assisted in bringing about the marriage of the Prince of Orange with Princess Mary. Charles II accepted his constitutional remedy of a reformed privy council of thirty persons.

The remainder of his days Temple devoted to letters and to gardening. The king occasionally consulted him, and for a time Jonathan Swift was his secretary.

TEMPLE AT JERUSALEM, the sanctuary erected by Solomon (about 993–953 B.C.) on the eastern hill, between the Tyropæon and Kidron valleys, N. of the original city of David on the Ophel hill, and opposite the Mount of Olives. According to 2 Chron. 3:1 it was built on the threshing floor which David had bought from Ornan the Jebusite.

Solomon's temple was destroyed by Nebuchadrezzar in 586 B.C. and was rebuilt by 516 B.C., with the permission of Darius Hystaspis, desecrated by Antiochus IV Epiphanes, dedicated to Zeus in 168 B.C., but rededicated to Yahwe in 165 B.C. Both the first and second edifices, were, however, surpassed in architectural splendor by the third temple, begun by Herod in 20 B.C. and completed in 64 A.D.

The area of the temple terrace was greatly enlarged by new substructures built with masonry of colossal magnitude. Marble was profusely used for colonades, gates, and walls, and the magnificence of Roman carved decoration and architectural detail was blended with the Oriental arrangement essentially

like the two preceding structures. This temple, from which Jesus expelled the money changers and merchants, was destroyed during the pillage of the city by Titus in 70 A.D., but contrary to his orders. After the insurrection of Simon Bar Cocheba (q.v.) had been quelled, an altar or shrine seems to have been erected in its place to Jupiter Capitolinus by Hadrian, in front of which were two statues of the emperor, at least one of them equestrian. On the temple area, Abd el Melek, who reigned from 685 to 705, ordered that a splendid mosque, the *Kubbet el Sakhrah,* or Dome of the Rock, be erected. This is commonly known as the Mosque of Omar.

TEMPLE UNIVERSITY, a coeducational, nonsectarian institution of higher learning, situated at Philadelphia, Pa. It was founded in 1884 as Temple College by the Baptist Temple in Philadelphia; the present name was adopted in 1907. During its first seven years the College offered only evening classes for men, and was intended primarily for those whose occupations prevented them from attending regular daytime schools. Evening classes are still held in all departments except medicine and dentistry. Courses leading to bachelor's, master's, and doctor's degrees are offered in the liberal and fine arts, sciences, theology, law, medicine, pharmacy, dentistry, music, chiropody, commerce, education, and nursing. An accelerated program of two years and six months, leading to the bachelor's degree, is also available. In 1947–48 a Community College and Technical Institute were added to the University to provide two-year training programs in management and labor service. In a recent year the enrollment was nearly 17,500 and the faculty numbered about 970; the library included about 323,000 volumes.

TEMUCO, capital of Cautin Province, Chile, on the Cautin River, in the S. of the State, 80 miles N.N.E. of Valdiva. It has tanneries and breweries. Pop., about 42,000.

TENACITY. See TENSILE STRENGTH.

TENANT. See LANDLORD AND TENANT.

TENASSERIM, the southernmost division of Burma. It is a long narrow strip of territory, 500 m. long by 40 to 80 m. broad between the sea and the mountains of the Siamese frontier. Area, 37,614 sq.m.; pop., about 1,800,000.

TENCH, a genus of fishes found in continental Europe, of the Carp family, Cyprinidae, represented by a single species, *Tinca* *vulgaris.* The thick body is covered with small scales and abundant mucus.

TEN COMMANDMENTS. See DECALOGUE.

TENERIFE or **TENERIFFE** (anc. *Pintuaria*), the largest of the Canary Islands, situated in the Atlantic Ocean about 175 miles N.W. of Cape Bojador, Africa, and forming part of Santa Cruz de Tenerife Province, Spain. The island extends about 60 m. in a north-east-southwest direction and ranges between 30 m. and 10 m. in width. Massive Pico de Tenerife, also known as Teyde or Teide, occupies the main portion of the island. A dormant, cone-shaped volcano which attains a height of 12,192 ft., Pico de Tenerife is surmounted by two craters. Chahorra, the largest of craters, has a diameter of 4000 ft. and a depth of about 150 ft. On the N.W., N., and N.E., the base of the uplift consists of generally level uplands. A rugged ridge, with elevations up to 8900 ft., extends around the remainder of the base. Much of the terrain between the ridge and the sea is composed of tablelands. The narrow, peninsular section of Tenerife is occupied by a range of mountains, of which Izana (7374 ft.) and Perejil (6027 ft.) are the highest peaks.

Excluding the more elevated areas, Tenerife possesses a dry, subtropical climate, which is modified by oceanic influences. Temperate conditions prevail on the higher mountain slopes, and during the winter months the summit of Pico de Tenerife is snow-covered. The vegetation, especially below 4000 ft., is luxuriant and diversified. Many tropical plants, including the date palm, coffee plant, and banana tree, flourish between sea level and the 1300-ft. level. Noteworthy among the indigenous trees of this belt is the Dragon Tree (q.v.). Various species of laurel, oak, olive, myrtle, and buckthorn are found between the 2800-ft. and 4000-ft. levels. The belt between 4000 ft. and 6400 ft. abounds with pine trees. Species of wild flowering plants on the island total more than 800.

Agriculture and fishing are the chief industries of Tenerife. In terms of value, bananas are the leading crop. Besides coffee and dates, other major crops include sugar cane, oranges, onions, potatoes, tomatoes, cotton, and grain. Because of the general aridity, farming enterprises are largely dependent on irrigation.

Santa Cruz de Tenerife (q.v.), the administrative center of the province, is the largest town and principal seaport of Tenerife. The next-largest town is Laguna. (For additional information concerning Ten-

erife, see CANARY ISLANDS.) Area of island, 795 sq.m.; pop. (1950) 442,380.

TENIERS, DAVID, known as THE ELDER (1582–1649), Flemish painter, born in Antwerp. His subjects are homely, the interiors of public houses, rustic games, weddings, and the like.

TENIERS, DAVID, known as THE YOUNGER (1610–90), son of the preceding, born in Antwerp. He had the favor and friendship of the archduke Leopold William, Don Juan, natural son of Philip IV of Austria, the Prince of Orange, the Bishop of Ghent, and other dignitaries. He was admitted "master" of the guild of St. Luke in 1632, and in 1644 was elected its president.

TENNANTITE. See TETRAHEDRITE.

TENNESSEE, one of the East South Central States of the United States, bounded on the N. by Kentucky and Virginia, on the E. by North Carolina, on the S. by Georgia, Alabama, and Mississippi, and on the W. by the Mississippi R., which separates the State from Arkansas and Missouri. Tennessee ranks as the 33rd State in the Union in area, 16th in the order of population (1950), and 16th in the order of admission, having entered the Union on June 1, 1796. The capital is Nashville. In the order of population (1950) the principal cities are Memphis, Nashville, Chattanooga, and Knoxville (qq.v.). From E. to W. the extreme length of Tennessee is 432 m., and from N. to S. the extreme width is 115 m. Area of the State, 42,246 sq.m., including 285 sq.m. of inland water surface. The population (1950) is 3,291,718.

The surface of the State is divided into a number of well-marked topographical provinces which tend to decrease in height from E. to W. The easternmost part of the State consists of the Appalachian belt of mountains, with a width of from 10 to 15 m. The belt is formed by the Great Smoky and Unaka mountains, the main ridges of which average 5000 ft. in elevation and in places exceed 6000 ft. The highest point in the State, Clingman's Dome, is in the portion of the range which is located in Sevier Co., and is 6642 ft. above sea level. Immediately to the W. of the mountain belt is the Great Valley of E. Tennessee, a depression 30 to 60 m. wide, consisting of an alternate succession of parallel ridges and valleys. It is bordered on the W. by the Cumberland Plateau, which possesses an average elevation of over 1800 ft. above sea level and an extreme elevation of 3550 ft. The eastern edge of the plateau is a straight, abrupt scarp, but its

Paul A. Moore, Tennessee Conservation Dept.

Tennessee State Capitol in Nashville

western edge has been deeply eroded by headwater streams. Next toward the w. is the Highland Rim Plateau, a plain which possesses an elevation of about 1000 ft. along its eastern border, and between 600 and 800 ft. along its western margin, and which lies, for the most part, a few miles w. of the Tennessee R. in its northern course across the State. Within the highland plain and 300 to 400 ft. below its level, in central Tennessee, is an oval depression about 125 m. long and 60 m. wide, known as the Central Basin. West of the Highland Plateau is the West Tennessee Plain, 600 to 800 ft. high on its eastern border, with a westward slope to 300 or 400 ft. Bordering the West Tennessee Plain is the alluvial plain of the Mississippi R. The latter is a narrow belt, largely swampy, with a depressed area containing Reelfoot Lake, in the northern portion of the State. The lowest point in the State is situated along the Mississippi R. in Shelby Co., and is 182 ft. above sea level. The average elevation is about 900 ft. above sea level.

The climate of Tennessee is generally mild and equable. The mean annual temperature is 58°F., and the variation from this is not over 2 or 3 degrees in any section, except that of the Appalachian region. July is usually the hottest month and January the coldest. The annual rainfall averages about 50 inches and is well distributed geographically. The average annual snowfall is about 8 inches. The prevailing winds are from the s. and the s.w.

The drainage of the entire State reaches the Mississippi R. The eastern portion is drained by the Tennessee R., which flows s.w. into Alabama and then w.n.w. to the Mississippi. The Cumberland R. flows southwestward into the Tennessee Central Basin, turns and flows w., and then turns n. into Kentucky to the Mississippi. The West Tennessee Plain is drained directly into the Mississippi through the Wolf, Hatchie, Forked Deer, and Obion rivers. The Cumberland and the Tennessee, and a few of the larger tributaries of the latter in E. Tennessee are navigable.

The Tennessee Valley Authority, an independent corporate agency of the Federal government created in 1933 to provide for the unified development of all the resources of the 40,910-sq.m. watershed of the Tennessee R. and its tributaries, has created approximately 600,000 acres of water in a series of lakes as a result of the construction of numerous dams in the State. One of the most important of the lakes, that created by the Norris Dam (see DAMS), possesses an area of over 80 sq.m. and a shore line of more than 800 m. In addition, the TVA has created three parks which are similar in facilities to the State parks. Tennessee possesses sixteen State parks covering an area of more than 68,000 acres, eleven State forests covering more than 120,000 acres, and fifteen fish hatcheries, lakes, and game preserves, which cover a total area of about 236,000 acres. In addition, the State contains a number of national monuments, military parks, and the Great Smoky Mountains National Park (q.v.), half of which is located in North Carolina and half in Tennessee. Game, such as foxes, rabbits, opossums, and ducks, is plentiful, and the streams contain bass and trout. The Cherokee National Forest is the home of numbers of Prussian boars, which were originally imported from Germany; in November of each year the forest is the scene of a wild-boar hunt. There are approximately 19,000 sq.m. of forests, of which the Federal government controls more than 1200 sq.m. The chief trees include yellow pine, yellow poplar, oak, chestnut, gum, and hemlock. The forests

yield an average of 500,000,000 board ft. of lumber a year.

Mining is an important industry in the State and the principal mineral is coal. Approximately 5000 sq.m. of Tennessee is underlaid with coal and in a recent year more than 5,000,000 short tons of coal were mined. The State leads the nation in the production of iron pyrites and is the only source of sinter iron. Other minerals are zinc, copper, silver, gold, cement rock, marble, phosphate, and manganese ore. Recently the total annual value of mineral products in the State exceeded $90,000,000.

Manufacturing is the most important industry in value of products. In a recent year about 3300 manufacturing establishments employed more than 221,000 wage earners; value added to products by manufacture totaled about $957,500,000. The principal products are cotton cloth, knitted goods, rayon, silk, woolen, and worsted goods, celluloid, footwear, aluminum, and plastics. Meat packing, food processing, printing and publishing, and lumbering are also important.

Agriculture supports more people than any other industry. In a recent year more than 231,500 farms, embracing a total area of almost 18,600,000 acres, were valued at (land and buildings) approximately $1,432,000,000. The chief crop is corn, of which about 60,-360,000 bushels were produced in a recent year. Other crops are tobacco (143,214,000 pounds), cotton (534,000 bales), winter wheat, oats, hay, Irish potatoes, sweet potatoes, peanuts, barley, peas, tomatoes, apples, peaches, and strawberries. Livestock

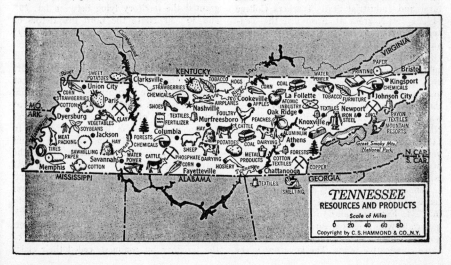

TENNESSEE
RESOURCES AND PRODUCTS
Scale of Miles
0   20   40   60   80
Copyright by C. S. HAMMOND & CO., N.Y.

raising, dairying, and beekeeping are also important agricultural industries. In a recent year the State ranked seventh in the nation in the production of honey. Livestock in the State recently numbered 1,550,000 cattle (including 640,000 milch cows), 270,000 sheep, 197,000 mules, and 113,000 horses.

Transportation facilities in Tennessee include about 3500 m. of main-track railway, 7800 m. of State highways, and 61 airports, of which 26 are municipal and 20 are equipped for night flying.

Attendance at the elementary and secondary schools of Tennessee is free for all children more than six years old, and compulsory throughout the full school year for all children between the ages of seven and sixteen except for those who have completed high school. In a recent year more than 4700 public elementary and secondary schools were attended by more than 659,000 students and staffed by about 22,000 teachers. Separate schools are maintained for white and Negro students. Since the adoption of a uniform school code in 1925 Tennessee has prohibited the teaching of the theory of evolution (see BRYAN, WILLIAM JENNINGS; DARROW, CLARENCE) in all schools partially or wholly supported by the State. In addition, the State demands that white children be taught only by white persons who have been born in the U.S. and whose parents could speak English, and who themselves have spoken English since childhood. Institutions of higher learning which the State supports include the University of Tennessee at Knoxville, founded in 1794, the Agricultural and Industrial State Teachers College (1912) for Negroes at Nashville, the Tennessee Polytechnic Institute (1916) at Cookeville, the Alvin C. York Agricultural Institute at Jamestown, and a number of teachers colleges. Among the private institutions of higher learning in the State are Fisk University (1866), for Negroes, at Nashville, the University of the South (1857) at Sewanee, Vanderbilt University (1873) at Nashville, the University of Chattanooga (1867) at Chattanooga, Cumberland University (1842) at Lebanon, and the Meharry Medical College (1876), for Negroes, at Nashville.

Tennessee is governed according to the terms of the constitution of 1870, as amended in 1953. Executive authority is vested in a governor, who is elected for a two-year term, and who may not hold office for more than three consecutive terms. The governor is the only elected official in the executive department. There is no lieutenant governor; in the event of a vacancy in the governor's chair, the speaker of the senate becomes the acting governor. A comptroller of the treasury and a secretary of state are chosen by a joint ballot of the senate and house of representatives for two-year terms, and an attorney general is appointed for an eight-year term by the justices of the supreme court. Legislative authority is vested in a general assembly which consists of a senate of 33 members and a house of representatives of 99 members, all elected for two-year terms. Judicial authority is vested in a supreme court of 5 justices elected for eight-year terms, a court of civil appeals, chancery courts, circuit courts, county courts, criminal courts, justices of the peace, and recorder's courts. Qualified voters are all U.S. citizens who have passed the age of twenty-one and have resided in the State a minimum of one year, the county a minimum of six months, and the voting district a minimum of thirty days. Chiefly because of the poll tax, which was abolished in 1953, the voting disfranchisement in the past was great; in the 1952 Presidential election approximately 45 percent of the potential voters of the State cast ballots. Tennessee is divided into 95 counties and is represented in the Congress of the U.S. by 2 senators and 9 representatives.

History. The first European to explore the region was probably the Spanish explorer Hernando de Soto, in 1541. In 1584 the territory was a part of an English grant to Sir Walter Raleigh, and in 1665 Charles II granted the territory lying between lat. 29° and 36° 30′ N. to the Lord Proprietors of Carolina (see NORTH CAROLINA: *History*; SOUTH CAROLINA: *History*). The French explorer La Salle built a fort near the present site of Memphis in 1682 and called it Fort Prud'homme. The first English settlement established in the territory was Fort Loudon, which was built in 1756 at the suggestion of the governor of Virginia. The fort was garrisoned by English Royal troops, but in 1760 the Cherokee Indians captured it and massacred the soldiers and the settlers in the surrounding region. The region, which was then regarded as a common hunting ground by the Cherokees, Chickasaws, Chocktaws, Creeks, and Miamis (qq.v.), was opened to the colonists by explorers and hunters such as Daniel Boone (q.v.). In 1768 the Iroquois (q.v.) Indians, who claimed sovereignty of the territory by conquest, ceded their claim

Tenn. Cons. Dept.; Chatt. C. of C.

IN TENNESSEE. *Above: Aerial view of the city of Memphis, on the Mississippi River. At right: "The Hermitage," home of Andrew Jackson near Nashville. Below: Moccasin Bend, meander of the Tennessee River. Chattanooga is at right.*

Tenn. Cons. Dept.; A.E.C. Photo, Oak Ridge C. of C.

IN TENNESSEE. *Above: Norris Dam, built by the Tennessee Valley Authority. Left: Aerial view of atomic-energy laboratories and other installations at Oak Ridge.*

to the English. Settlements were established in Tennessee soon afterward and in 1771, after the defeat of the Regulators (q.v.) in North Carolina, a number of the Regulators traveled to the region, supposing the territory to be Virginia soil. When the territory was found to be within North Carolina, which did not, however, assert jurisdiction or protect settlers from Indian attacks, the inhabitants of two of the settlements in Tennessee met in 1772 and formed the Watauga Association (q.v.), which served as a form of government for several years. The Watauga settlers gave the name Washington District to their colony, and in 1776 it was annexed to North Carolina.

The number of settlers increased rapidly, and nearly 500 men under John Sevier and Isaac Shelby crossed the mountains and participated in an attack on the British in 1780 during the American Revolution. In 1784 North Carolina ceded to the U.S. government the western lands which had originally been constituted as the Watauga Association. The cession was to be accepted within two years, North Carolina maintaining sovereignty over the lands in the interim. The inhabitants, indignant at being transferred without their consent, formed the State of Franklin or Frankland (see FRANKLIN, STATE OF), and elected John Sevier as their governor. Congress ignored the request of the State of Franklin to be recognized as a State of the Union, and North Carolina promptly repealed the act of cession and asserted its jurisdiction. In 1788 North Carolina legislated the State of Franklin out of existence and imprisoned Sevier, charging him with high treason; however, he escaped.

In 1790, North Carolina again ceded the region, called the Territory South of the River Ohio, to the U.S. government, and a Territorial government was established. In 1796 the Territory was admitted to the Union as the State of Tennessee, with the addition of the region extending w. from the original State of Franklin to the Mississippi. Sevier, pardoned, served as the first governor of the new State.

A strong Union party existed in Tennessee at the outbreak of the Civil War, and in February, 1861, the people refused to hold a convention to consider secession; but when President Abraham Lincoln issued his call for troops, sentiment changed and the State voted itself out of the Union in June. During the Civil War the State furnished the Confederacy with about 115,000 soldiers; more than 30,000 men from Tennessee served with the Union army. Andrew Johnson (q.v.) who later became the seventeenth President of the U.S., had refused to resign his seat in Congress as the senator from Tennessee, and when Union troops drove the Confederate governor from the State, Johnson was appointed military governor, a position he held until his election to the Vice-Presidency of the U.S. The State was readmitted to the Union after the close of the war, on July 23, 1866. The Reconstruction (q.v.) period proved difficult for the State, but Tennessee was not subject to government by carpetbaggers (q.v.). During the latter part of the 19th century, the exploitation of the State's natural resources, and the growth of the cotton industry aided economic recovery. In 1942, during World War II, the town of Oak Ridge (q.v.), Tennessee, was established near Knoxville to provide a residence community for personnel working in the various Oak Ridge plants of the atomic-energy project.

From 1872 through 1952, the voters of Tennessee have cast a majority of their ballots for the Democratic Presidential candidate in every election except those of 1920, 1928, and 1952, when the Republican candidates received a majority or plurality of the votes. In the 1952 Presidential election General Dwight D. Eisenhower, the Republican candidate, received 446,147 votes; the Democratic candidate Adlai Ewing Stevenson received 443,710 votes; and minor-party candidates received an aggregate of 2696 votes.

TENNESSEE RIVER, the largest tributary of the Ohio River. It is formed by the confluence of the Holsten and the French Broad rivers, about 4 miles E. of Knoxville. Including the Holston, its length is about 1200 m. Its drainage basin includes about 39,000 sq.m. The main stream is navigable for 673 m. from its mouth.

TENNESSEE, UNIVERSITY OF, a coeducational, State-controlled institution of higher learning, situated at Knoxville, Tenn. It was established in 1794 as Blount College; it became a State institution and adopted the present name in 1879. At Knoxville courses are offered in the liberal arts, engineering, home economics, education, law, agriculture, and business administration, leading to undergraduate and graduate degrees. Schools of medicine, dentistry, pharmacy, nursing, public health, and biological sciences are located at Memphis, Tenn. In 1947 the university opened a branch of its graduate school in Oak Ridge, Tenn., as a part of the Nuclear Studies Institute, which is attended chiefly by persons employed in the atomic-energy plants of Oak Ridge who are studying for graduate degrees. In 1953 there were 6820 full-time students enrolled; the faculty numbered 1154; the library contained 290,000 volumes. The endowment of the university totaled $770,717.

TENNESSEE VALLEY AUTHORITY. See TENNESSEE.

TENNIEL, SIR JOHN (1820–1914), English cartoonist and illustrator. From 1851 to 1901 he was cartoonist for *Punch*, executing about 2300 cartoons, including the famous political cartoon "Dropping the Pilot" in March, 1890, when the kaiser dismissed Bismarck, and also innumerable small drawings and designs for Punch's *Almanac* and Punch's *Pocket-books*. He was knighted in 1893. Among his principal book illustrations are those for *Æsop's Fables* (1848) and Lewis Carroll's *Alice's Adventures in Wonderland* (1866) and *Through the Looking Glass* (1870).

TENNIS, a term principally applied to the game of lawn tennis, but also applied to court (or royal) tennis, a much different game (see COURT TENNIS). Tennis, or lawn tennis, is played either outdoors or indoors, but usually outdoors, with rackets and balls, by two or four people, on a court of turf or of some hard, even substance such as clay, concrete, or wood. The game when played by two contestants is known as "singles", and by four, as "doubles".

The court for singles is 78 ft. long and 27 ft. wide. For doubles the court is the same length, but the width is extended by

Playing a game of tennis in 17th-century France

the addition on either side of an alley 4½ ft. wide, making the entire width of the court for doubles 36 ft. A single court on which either game may be played is generally used; it is marked out with white lines to indicate the different dimensions for singles and doubles, and the various divisions of the court necessary for the game (see diagram). For the doubles court, two lines known as side lines are marked longitudinally from one end of the court to the other 36 ft. apart; for the singles court the side lines are 27 ft. apart. At either end of the court a line known as the base line is marked across the entire width of the court, 36 ft.; the base lines serve for both doubles and singles. Eighteen ft. in longitudinally from each base line, a line known as the service line is marked from one singles-court side line to the other, a distance of 27 ft. The areas between the base lines and service lines are known as the back courts. Across the exact center of the court from one side to the other a net is stretched between posts 3½ ft. high and staked into the ground 3 ft. outside the court; the net must be exactly 3 ft. high at the center. Lines known as center service lines are marked on the court longitudinally from the center of each service line to the center of the net. The area of each court from service line to net is thus divided into two equal parts, each known as a service court; each service court is 21 ft. long and 13½ ft. wide. The ball used in tennis is made of inflated rubber coated with flannel;

it is between 2½ and 2⅝ inches in diameter and weighs between 2 and 2¹/₁₆ ounces. The racket is usually made of wood and consists of an oval-shaped head strung usually with gut or nylon, and a handle; the racket weighs from 14 to 16 ounces.

The game is begun by a player serving the ball, i.e., striking it across the net to the opponent's side according to the rules described below; the player who begins the game is called the "server" and the one who receives the ball the "receiver". The side to serve first is determined by the toss of a coin or of a racket. The server delivers the ball from behind the base line and within the center mark and side line of his right-hand service court into the diagonally opposite or right-hand service court of his opponent. The server must maintain contact with the ground; after tossing the ball into the air or letting it fall, he must strike the ball before it touches the ground. He is permitted two tries in which to hit the ball into the diagonally opposite service court of his opponent. If a try results in the ball hitting the net, striking any part of the opponent's court except the diagonally opposite service court, or going out of the court altogether, it is called a "fault". If both tries result in faults, the opponent scores a point. Faults are also called if the server breaks contact with the ground before service is completed, or if he steps over the base line. If the ball, on either try, strikes the top of the net and falls into the diagonally opposite service court, it is called a "let" and the server is permitted to make the try over.

After the ball is successfully served, the receiver endeavors to return it over the net to any part of the server's court; if he succeeds in so doing, the server then endeavors to hit the ball back over the net into any part of the receiver's court. A player may strike the ball after service before it bounces or after it has bounced once. The ball is kept in play until either player or side has failed to hit the ball before it has bounced twice, or has driven it into the net, or has hit it out of the court. In each case the opponent scores a point. After the first point has been played, the server puts the ball into play from the base line of his left-hand service court into his opponent's diagonally opposite or left-hand court; the server continues serving alternately from the base line of each service court until an entire game (see below) has been played, and then his opponent serves for a game. In doubles each of the two players serves a game in turn, one of the opponents serving between each turn.

The player or side winning the first point scores 15; the opponent at this juncture has a score of zero or "love". The second winning point counts 15 additional making a total of 30; the winning of the third point brings 10 more, making 40. The winning of the fourth point gives the player or side the game, on condition that the opponent has not scored more than 2 points. If both sides have won three points, making the score "40-all", the score is said to be at "deuce", equivalent to 30 against 30, and the game thus is carried on until one of the sides wins by two points. When the score is deuce, the players or side scoring the next point is said to have the "advantage". The player or side first winning 6 games while the opponent has won 4 or fewer, wins the "set". If when one player or side has won 6 games, the opponent has won 5, the game goes on until one of the sides has won 2 more games than the other. In championship matches for women the victor is the side which wins the first 2 sets out of a possible 3, and for men the first 3 out of a possible 5. Championship matches are judged by fifteen officials: one umpire, one referee, one net judge, two foot-fault judges, and ten linesmen.

The modern game of lawn tennis was invented in England in 1873 by Major

Walter C. Wingfield, a British army officer, for use at lawn parties. Major Wingfield claimed that he modeled the game, which he called "spharistike", after an ancient Greek game; authorities believe, however, that in reality he adapted to outdoor play the principles of the widely popular English game of court tennis. The early participants in the game preferred to call it "tennis-on-the-lawn" or "lawn tennis" The game was introduced into Bermuda the same year, and from Bermuda was brought to the United States by an American girl, Miss Mary Ewing Outerbridge, of Staten Island, N.Y. The first game of lawn tennis played in this country took place on the grounds of the Staten Island Cricket and Baseball Club in the spring of 1874. By the last decade of the 19th century, lawn tennis had been introduced into British colonies all over the world and into many other parts

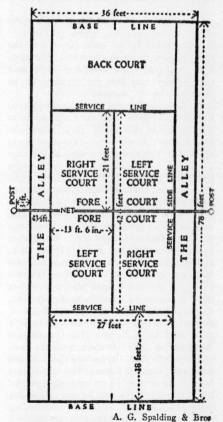

A. G. Spalding & Bros

Diagram of a tennis court for doubles

'Acme Photo

A Davis Cup tennis match in Brussels, Belgium

of the world. Tennis today is one of the most popular games in the world. The game can be played from childhood until well into middle age, and the number of its players is in the millions.

In the United States the rules and standards for the game fluctuated widely from locality to locality until 1881, when the United States Lawn Tennis Association was organized to standardize rules and equipment; the Association is still the governing body for amateur tennis in this country. Play for the annual United States singles championships for men began in Newport, R.I., in 1881; the national men's singles championships continued to take place annually in that city until 1915, when they were transferred to Forest Hills, N.Y. Matches for the national women's singles began in 1887, at the Philadelphia Cricket Club, and continued there until 1921, when they were likewise brought to Forest Hills. In addition to the above-mentioned championships, annual tournaments are held in the United States to determine the national champions in men's doubles, women's doubles, intercollegiate singles and doubles, and other categories. Of international importance are the Davis Cup (q.v.) amateur matches held annually to determine the champion national tennis team of the world. Among other important championships are the annual Wightman matches played between

teams of women from the United States and Great Britain; and the British amateur championships for men and women played annually at Wimbledon, England. Since the best amateur players in the world generally participate in the British tournament, the winners have a good claim to the world championships for the year in which they win the various titles.

Professional tennis has flourished in the United States since 1926, when the sports promoter Charles C. Pyle organized a professional tour of the United States for a group of leading players of the United States and France, including Suzanne Lenglen, Mary K. Browne, Vincent Richards, and Howard O. Kinsey. Since that time many groups of players have made profitable tours of the United States and other countries. Many of the best amateur players of the United States and other countries become professional players at the height of their amateur careers. The governing body for professional tennis in this country is the United States Professional Lawn Tennis Association, organized in 1927. Until 1952, the association held an annual tournament to determine the U.S. professional championships.

Following are tables of the winners in the important American amateur championships, the British amateur singles championship, and the United States professional singles championship.

WINNERS OF UNITED STATES NATIONAL TENNIS CHAMPIONSHIP

MEN'S SINGLES

Player	Year	Player	Year
Richard D. Sears	1881–1887	William T. Tilden, 2nd	1929
Henry W. Slocum, **Jr.**	1888–1889	John H. Doeg	1930
Oliver S. Campbell	1890–1892	H. Ellsworth Vines, Jr.	1931–1932
Robert D. Wrenn	1893–1894	Fred J. Perry (Eng.)	1933–1934
Fred H. Hovey	1895	Wilmer Allison	1935
Robert D. Wrenn	1896–1897	Fred J. Perry (Eng.)	1936
Malcolm D. Whitman	1898–1900	J. Donald Budge	1937–1938
William A. Larned	1901–1902	Robert L. Riggs	1939
Hugh L. Doherty (**Eng.**)	1903	Donald McNeill	1940
Holcombe Ward	1904	Robert L. Riggs	1941
Beals C. Wright	1905	Frederick R. Schroeder, Jr.	1942
William J. Clothier	1906	Joseph R. Hunt	1943
William A. Larned	1907–1911	Frank A. Parker	1944–1945
Maurice E. McLoughlin	1912–1913	Jack A. Kramer	1946–1947
Richard N. Williams, 2nd	1914	Richard Gonzales	1948–1949
William Johnston	1915	Arthur Larsen	1950
Richard N. Williams, 2nd	1916	Frank Sedgman (Australia)	1951–1952
R. Lindley Murray	1917–1918	Anthony Trabert	1953
William Johnston	1919	E. Victor Seixas, Jr.	1954
William T. Tilden, 2nd	1920–1925	Anthony Trabert	1955
Jean R. Lacoste (Fr.)	1926–1927	Kenneth R. Rosewall (Australia)	1956
Henri Cochet (Fr.)	1927		

WOMEN'S SINGLES

Player	Year	Player	Year
Ellen F. Hansell	1887	Mrs. Franklin I. Mallory	1920–1922
Bertha L. Townsend	1888–1889	(Bjurstedt)	
Ellen C. Roosevelt	1890	Helen N. Wills	1923–1925
Mabel E. Cahill	1891–1892	Mrs. Franklin I. Mallory	1926
Aline M. Terry	1893	Helen N. Wills	1927–1929
Helen R. Helwig	1894	Betty Nuthall	1930
Juliette P. Atkinson	1895	Mrs. Helen Wills Moody	1931
Elisabeth H. Moore	1896	Helen Jacobs	1932–1935
Juliette P. Atkinson	1897–1898	Alice Marble	1936
Marion Jones	1899	Anita Lizana (Chile)	1937
Myrtle McAteer	1900	Alice Marble	1938–1940
Elisabeth H. Moore	1901	Mrs. Sarah P. Cooke	1941
Marion Jones	1902	Pauline M. Betz	1942–1944
Elisabeth H. Moore	1903	Mrs. Sarah P. Cooke	1945
May G. Sutton	1904	Pauline M. Betz	1946
Elisabeth H. Moore	1905	A. Louise Brough	1947
Helen H. Homans	1906	Mrs. Margaret O. du Pont	1948–1950
Evelyn Sears	1907	Maureen Connolly	1951–1953
Mrs. Maud Barger-Wallach	1908	Doris Hart	1954–1955
Hazel V. Hotchkiss	1909–1911	Shirley Fry	1956
Mary K. Browne	1912–1914		
Molla Bjurstedt	1915–1918		
Mrs. George W. Wightman	1919		
(Hotchkiss)			

Men's Doubles

Players	Year
Richard D. Sears and James Dwight	1886–1887
Oliver S. Campbell and V.G. Hall	1888
Henry W. Slocum, Jr. and H.A. Taylor	1889
V.G. Hall and Clarence Hobart	1890
Oliver S. Campbell and R.P. Huntington, Jr.	1891–1892
Clarence Hobart and Fred H. Hovey	1893–1894
M.G. Chace and Robert D. Wrenn	1895
C.B. Neel and S.R. Neel	1896
L.E. Ware and G.P. Sheldon, Jr.	1897–1898
Holcombe Ward and Dwight F. Davis	1899–1901
Reginald F. Doherty and Hugh L. Doherty	1902–1903
Holcombe Ward and Beals C. Wright	1904–1906
Fred B. Alexander and H.H. Hackett	1907–1910
Ray D. Little and Gus F. Touchard	1911
Maurice E. McLoughlin and Thomas C. Bundy	1912–1914
William Johnston and Clarence J. Griffin	1915–1916
Fred B. Alexander and H.A. Throckmorton	1917
William T. Tilden, 2nd, and Vincent Richards	1918
Norman E. Brookes and Gerald L. Patterson (Australia)	1919
William Johnston and Clarence J. Griffin	1920
William T. Tilden, 2nd, and Vincent Richards	1921–1922
William T. Tilden, 2nd, and B.I.C. Norton	1923
Howard O. Kinsey and Robert G. Kinsey	1924
Richard N. Williams, 2nd, and Vincent Richards	1925–1926
William T. Tilden, 2nd, and Francis T. Hunter	1927
George M. Lott, Jr., and John F. Hennessey	1928
George M. Lott, Jr., and John H. Doeg	1929–1930
Wilmer L. Allison and John Van Ryn	1931
H. Ellsworth Vines, Jr., and Keith Gledhill	1932
George M. Lott, Jr., and Lester R. Stoefen	1933–1934
Wilmer L. Allison and John Van Ryn	1935
J. Donald Budge and C. Gene Mako	1936
Gottfried von Cramm and Henner Henkel (Ger.)	1937
J. Donald Budge and C. Gene Mako	1938
Adrian K. Quist and John Bromwich (Australia)	1939
John A. Kramer and Frederick R. Schroeder, Jr.	1940–1941
Gardnar Mulloy and William F. Talbert	1942
Jack A. Kramer and Frank A. Parker	1943
Robert Falkenburg and W.D. McNeill	1944
Gardnar Mulloy and William F. Talbert	1945–1946
Jack A. Kramer and Frederick R. Schroeder, Jr.	1947
Gardnar Mulloy and William F. Talbert	1948
John Bromwich and William Sidwell (Australia)	1949
John Bromwich and Frank Sedgman (Australia)	1950
Frank Sedgman and Ken McGregor (Australia)	1951
Mervyn Rose and E. Victor Seixas, Jr.	1952
Mervyn Rose and Rex Hartwig (Australia)	1953
Anthony Trabert and E. Victor Seixas, Jr.	1954
Kosei Kamo and Atsushi Miyagi (Japan)	1955
Lew Hoad and Kenneth R. Rosewall (Australia)	1956

WOMEN'S DOUBLES

Players	Year
Ellen C. Roosevelt and Grace W. Roosevelt	1890
Mabel E. Cahill and Mrs. W.F. Morgan	1891
Mabel E. Cahill and A.M. McKinley	1892
Aline M. Terry and Hattie Butler	1893
Helen R. Helwig and Juliette P. Atkinson	1894–1895
Elisabeth H. Moore and Juliette P. Atkinson	1896
Juliette P. Atkinson and Kathleen Atkinson	1897–1898
Myrtle McAteer and Jane W. Craven	1899
Edith Parker and Hallie Champlin	1900
Juliette P. Atkinson and Myrtle McAteer	1901
Juliette P. Atkinson and Marion Jones	1902
Elisabeth H. Moore and Carrie B. Neely	1903
May G. Sutton and Miriam Hall	1904
Helen Homans and Carrie B. Neely	1905
Mrs. L.S. Coe and Mrs. D.S. Platt	1906
Carrie B. Neely and Marie Weimer	1907
Evelyn Sears and Margaret Curtis	1908
Hazel V. Hotchkiss and Edith E. Rotch	1909–1910
Hazel V. Hotchkiss and Eleanora Sears	1911
Mary K. Browne and Dorothy Green	1912
Mary K. Browne and Mrs. R.H. Williams	1913–1914
Mrs. George W. Wightman (Hotchkiss) and Eleanora Sears	1915
Molla Bjurstedt and Eleanora Sears	1916–1917
Eleanor Goss and Marion Zinderstein	1918–1920
Mary K. Browne and Mrs. R.H. Williams	1921
Helen N. Wills and Mrs. J.B. Jessup	1922
Kathleen McKane and Mrs. B.C. Covell	1923
Helen N. Wills and Mrs. George W. Wightman	1924
Helen N. Wills and Mary K. Browne	1925
Elizabeth Ryan and Eleanor Goss	1926
Mrs. L.A. Godfree and Ermyntrude Harvey	1927
Helen N. Wills and Mrs. George W. Wightman	1928
Mrs. Phoebe Watson and Mrs. L.R.C. Michell	1929
Betty Nuthall and Sarah Palfrey	1930
Mrs. E.B. Whittingstall and Betty Nuthall (Eng.)	1931
Helen Jacobs and Sarah Palfrey	1932
Betty Nuthall and Freda James (Eng.)	1933
Helen Jacobs and Sarah Palfrey	1934
Helen Jacobs and Mrs. Sarah Palfrey Fabyan	1935
Carolin Babcock and Mrs. M.G. Van Ryn	1936
Alice Marble and Mrs. Sarah P. Fabyan	1937–1940
Mrs. Sarah P. Cooke and Margaret Osborne	1941
A. Louise Brough and Margaret Osborne	1942–1947
A. Louise Brough and Margaret Osborne du Pont	1948–1950
Doris Hart and Shirley Fry	1951–1954
A. Louise Brough and Margaret Osborne du Pont	1955–1956

Wide World Photos

TENNIS. *Top: United States team (foreground) against Australian team in Davis Cup match.*
Bottom: Wayne Sabin (foreground) and Don Budge in a National Championship match.

BRITISH AMATEUR (WIMBLEDON) SINGLES CHAMPIONS

Players	Year	Players	Year
William T. Tilden, 2nd (U.S.)	1920–1921	No Matches	1940–1945
Gerald L. Patterson (Australia)	1922	Yvon Petra (France)	1946
William M. Johnston (U.S.)	1923	Jack A. Kramer (U.S.)	1947
Jean Borotra (France)	1924	Robert Falkenburg (U.S.)	1948
Réné Lacoste (France)	1925	Frederick R. Shroeder, Jr. (U.S.)	1949
Jean Borotra (France)	1926	Budge Patty (U.S.)	1950
Henri Cochet (France)	1927	Dick Savitt (U.S.)	1951
Réné Lacoste (France)	1928	Frank Sedgman (Australia)	1952
Henri Cochet (France)	1929	E. Victor Seixas, Jr. (U.S.)	1953
William T. Tilden, 2nd (U.S.)	1930	Jarslav Drobny (Egypt)	1954
Sidney B. Wood, Jr. (U.S.)	1931	Anthony Trabert (U.S.)	1955
H. Ellsworth Vines (U.S.)	1932	Lew Hoad (Australia)	1956–1957
John H. Crawford (Australia)	1933		
Frederick J. Perry (England)	1934–1936		
J. Donald Budge (U.S.)	1937–1938		
Robert L. Riggs (U.S.)	1939		

UNITED STATES PROFESSIONAL SINGLES CHAMPIONS

Players	Year	Players	Year
Vincent Richards	1927–1928	Ellsworth Vines	1939
Karel Kozeluh	1929	J. Donald Budge	1940 and 1942
Vincent Richards	1930 and 1933	Bruce Barnes	1943
William T. Tilden, 2nd	1931 and 1935	No Title Play	1944
Karel Kozeluh	1932 and 1937	Welby Van Horn	1945
Hans Nusslein	1934	Robert L. Riggs	1946, 1947, and 1949
Joseph Whalen	1936	Jack A. Kramer	1948
Frederick J. Perry	1938 and 1941	Pancho Segura	1950 and 1951

TENNYSON, ALFRED, 1st BARON TENNYSON (1809–92), English poet, born in Somersby, Lincolnshire, and educated at Trinity College, Cambridge University. In 1829, while at Cambridge, Tennyson wrote the spirited blank-verse poem *Timbuctoo*, for which he received the chancellor's gold medal, and in the following year appeared his first published book, *Poems, Chiefly Lyrical*. In 1831 he left Cambridge without taking a degree, and with his close friend Arthur Henry Hallam, son of the eminent British historian Henry Hallam, joined a Spanish revolutionary army in the insurrection against the despotic rule of King Ferdinand VII of Spain. The young men saw active service for a time in the Pyrenees, but participated in no military engagements. Tennyson's second volume, *Poems* (1832), contained such familiar verses as "The Lady of Shalott", "The Miller's Daughter", "The Palace of Art", "The Lotos-Eaters", and "A Dream of Fair Women". The sudden death of his friend Hallam in September of the following year produced in Tennyson a profound spiritual depression, and he vowed to refrain from issuing any more of his verse for a period of ten years. During this time he devoted himself to reading and meditation, and wrote *The Two Voices* (1834), a philosophical poem on death and immortality.

In 1842, at the expiration of his self-imposed period of silence, Tennyson won wide acclaim with the publication of his *Poems*, in two volumes, which contained such works as "Morte d'Arthur", "Ulysses", "Locksley Hall", "Godiva", and the poignant lyric "Break, Break, Break". This work firmly established Tennyson's position as the foremost poet of his day, and served to bring him in contact with such distinguished literary figures as the essayist Thomas Carlyle, the novelist Charles Dickens, and the poets Samuel Rogers and Elizabeth Barrett Browning. In consequence of an improvident investment, Tennyson lost his modest fortune,

Alfred, Lord Tennyson

and would have been reduced to extreme poverty had not the elder Hallam prevailed upon the British prime minister Sir Robert Peel in 1845 to grant the poet an annual government pension of 200 pounds for life. *The Princess*, a romantic treatment in musical blank verse of the question of women's rights, was published in 1847. The third edition of the poem (1850) contains a number of exquisite short lyrics.

Perhaps the most important year in Tennyson's literary and personal life was 1850. In June appeared his *In Memoriam*, a tribute to the memory of Arthur Hallam. Both the loose organization and intensely personal character of this poem perplexed many of the readers of Tennyson's day, but the work has since taken its place with John Milton's *Lycidas*, Percy Bysshe Shelley's *Adonais*, and Matthew Arnold's *Thyrsis* as one of the great elegies in English literature. In the same month Tennyson married Emily Sarah Sellwood, and in November was appointed poet laureate, succeeding William Wordsworth. He settled with his bride at Twickenham, in Middlesex, whence he moved three years later to his estate, Farringford, near Freshwater, in the Isle of Wight. There he resided for at least a part of each year for the remainder of his life.

In 1854 appeared "Charge of the Light Brigade", celebrating a memorable action by British cavalry in the Crimean War, and in the following year was published *Maud, and Other Poems*. With the first series of *Idylls of the King* (1859), Tennyson returned to the subject of the Arthurian cycle (q.v.), which he had already essayed in his "Morte d'Arthur". The book was enthusiastically received, more than ten thousand copies being sold in the first month of publication. *Enoch Arden* (1864), however, was the most immediately popular of all his volumes of poetry; in the first year after publication sixty thousand copies were sold, and the title poem was translated into eight languages. Tennyson next produced the historical dramas *Queen Mary* (1875), *Harold* (1876), and *Becket* (1884). In 1884 he was created a peer, taking his seat in the House of Lords as Baron Tennyson of Freshwater and Aldworth. His other notable works include *Ballads and Other Poems* (1880), *Tiresias and Other Poems* (1885), *The Idylls of the King* (complete edition, 1885), *Demeter and Other Poems* (1889), and *The Death of Œnone and Other Poems* (published posthumously, 1892).

No English poet has produced acknowledged masterpieces in so many different literary genres as Tennyson. The consummate artistic excellence of his verse, resembling in many of its qualities the stately and heroic measures of the ancient Roman poet Vergil, has secured for him an enduring place in literature. He furnished perhaps the most notable example in English letters of the eclectic style, made up of elements derived from the styles of many of his distinguished predecessors; and he expressed a consoling, readily comprehensible philosophy.

TENOCHTITLÁN, the ancient capital of the Aztecs, occupying the site of present-day Mexico City.

TENOR (From Lat. *tenere*, "to hold"), in music, the highest adult male voice (with the exception of the falsetto), having an approximate range from C to C". Two classes of tenors are recognized, namely, the *dramatic* tenor (*tenore robusto*) and the higher *lyric* tenor (*tenore de grazia*). In its lower register, the quality of the dramatic tenor resembles that of the baritone (q.v.). The term "tenor" is derived from the fact that in the polyphonic (see POLYPHONY) music of medieval times the tenor voice "held" the melodic line, known as the *cantus firmus* or plain song, to which the the the altos (see CONTRALTO) above, and the baritones and basses below, furnished a harmony. "Tenor" is also used to designate the register of various musical instruments, such as the banjo, bassoon, horn, and viola. See also HARMONY; SINGING; VOICE AND SPEECH.

TENREC, or TANREC, common name applied to any of the burrowing insectivores constituting the family Tenrecidae, found only on the island of Madagascar. Tenrecs are the largest of the insectivores, attaining a length, including tail, of about 16 inches. They have robust bodies, short legs, and sharp, pointed snouts, and are often coated with spines, bristles, or hairs; some species are commonly called "hedgehogs" in Madagascar. The animals forage at night for earthworms, which constitute their chief article of diet, and live in burrows in the ground; they hibernate during the winter. Tenrecs are extremely prolific, producing as many as

The common tenrec

twenty-one young in a litter. Their flesh is edible. The common tenrec, *Tenrec ecaudatus*, differs from other species of the family in lacking a tail.

TENSILE STRENGTH, or TENACITY, in physics, the degree of resistance to rupture possessed by all kinds of solid matter. In technical terms, the tensile strength of a substance is the greatest longitudinal stress which the substance can withstand without being torn asunder, such as the force required to break a wire by pulling at both ends. The tensile property may be compared with other material properties of resistance to applied force, such as resistance to crushing, shearing, or torsion. The absolute force required to pull apart a particular material depends both on the thickness or cross-sectional area at right angles to the stress, and the inherent tenacity of the material in question. Hence tenacity is usually expressed numerically with reference to a unit area of cross section: for example, number of pounds or tons per square inch, or kilograms per square centimeter necessary to produce rupture. The accompanying table gives the tensile strength of some of the more

important materials used in commerce and industry.

TENSILE STRENGTH OF MATERIAL

MATERIALS	LBS. PER SQ. IN.
Metals	
Aluminum	15,000
Aluminum bars (extruded)	28,000
Nickel aluminum	40,000
Aluminum wire	50,000
Brass (cast)	24,000
Bronze gun metal	35,000
Phosphor bronze	46,000
Manganese bronze	60,000
Aluminum bronze	70,000
Gold (cast)	20,000
Lead	2,000
Platinum wire	32,000
Silver (cast)	40,000
Tin	3,500
Zinc	5,400
Copper (cast)	24,000
Soft copper wire	35,000
Hard copper wire	60,000
Cast iron	20,000
Wrought iron	50,000
Carbon steel	60,000
Vanadium steel	70,000
Nickel steel	80,000
Manganese steel (cast)	90,000
Chrome-vanadium steel	100,000
Chrome-nickel-vanadium steel	129,100
Manganese steel (quenched)	140,000
Steel piano wire (.033 in. diameter)	370,000
Woods	
Ash	14,000
Black walnut	12,000
Beech	14,500
Cedar	10,000
Chestnut	10,000
Elm	13,400
Hemlock	8,700
Hickory	15,000
Locust	22,000
Maple	10,500
White oak	14,500
Poplar	7,000
Redwood	8,500
Spruce	14,500
White pine	12,000
Yellow pine	11,000
Red fir	10,000
Yellow fir	12,000
Teak	14,000

TENSING NORKAY (1914–   ), Nepalese Sherpa mountain climber, born in Tama, Sola Khumbo. He tended livestock in his youth, acquiring considerable experience in mountain climbing. Ambitious to become a professional mountaineer, he emigrated (1933) to India, settling in Darjeeling. There, in 1935, he obtained employment as a porter with an expedition to Mt. Everest (see EVEREST, MOUNT), the highest known mountain in the world. He subsequently participated in numerous attempts to reach the summit of that peak. In October, 1952, he was selected as a chief climber and the head porter of a British expedition then being assembled for an attempt to scale Mt. Everest. Together with the New Zealand mountaineer Edmond P. Hillary, Tensing reached the summit on May 29, 1953. He was later decorated by the British and Nepalese governments for his achievement. Tensing wrote *Tiger of the Snows* (autobiography, with James Ramsey Ullman, 1955).

TENT CATERPILLAR, the larvae of four species of silk-spinning moths of the genus *Malacosoma* (formerly *Clisiocampa*). The female of the apple-tree tent caterpillar, *Malacosoma americana*, a dull reddish-brown moth, lays eggs in ringlike masses fastened to small twigs of apple, cherry, or thorn. The caterpillars hatch in early spring in the nearest fork of the twigs and spin a web or tent in which they live in company, but which they leave when hungry, to feed upon leaves. The eggs are easily seen in the winter and may be destroyed and the caterpillars killed just at nightfall within the tents by burning or spraying with kerosene. An incredible amount of damage is done by these larvae every year to forest and fruit trees in America.

TENTYRA. See DENDERA.

TENURE, in the law of real property of feudal England, the manner in which a person held or owned real property. Under the feudal system the king owned all the land, and his vassals, as tenants, were entitled to hold only those portions of the land allotted by him and only under conditions imposed by him. The vassals or tenants in turn divided their lands among others, who became their vassals; this process was known as subinfeudation. Various forms of tenure were developed for the specific services required of the person holding the land. Feudal tenures were classified either as being *free*, by which the tenants held land as freeholders; or as being *base* or *nonfree*, by which the tenants

held land as villeins. The earliest form of the free tenure was that by knight's service, involving allegiance and military service to the overlord and through him to the king. Later, in lieu of rendering military service, freehold tenants were permitted to make money payments known as *scutage* to the overlord. Such payments were levied at irregular intervals. Scutage payments were abolished by statute in the reign of Charles II, and were succeeded by payments annually of a fixed sum, or a certain amount of produce, as rent. Tenants making such payments were then said to hold their land by free and common socage tenure; such tenants took the oath of loyalty to the overlord but were relieved of any military obligations. An infant heir to lands held in socage tenure had to account when he became of age for the rents of the lands; the oldest male relative was termed the *guardian in socage* of the infant. Tenants holding lands by socage tenure in towns were called burgage tenants.

During the Norman era there had existed in England a class of tenants, known as villeins, who were virtually serfs, and were required to perform menial services for the lord of the manor in return for their holdings. The villein was considered as attached to the manor, could be punished at will by the lord, and could not leave the manor (see MANORIAL SYSTEM). Such tenure was known as the tenure of villeinage. Subsequently the payment of rent in some form was substituted for menial services, and the rights of the tenant in the land were evidenced by a record made on the rolls of the court of the manor. Such tenants were then called copyhold tenants or copyholders. Copyhold tenure eventually took on the characteristics of freehold estates. The feudal control, by the overlord, of transfers of property by tenants was ended in 1290 by the Statute of Quia Emptores. See FEUDALISM.

TEN YEARS' WAR, a Cuban insurrection fought between 1868 and 1878 against Spain. The insurrection, caused chiefly by the failure of the Spanish to grant various promised reforms to Cuba, broke out in Oct., 1868, when Carlos Manuel de Céspedes, a wealthy planter and political leader who favored the independence of Cuba, the gradual emancipation of slaves, and universal suffrage, proclaimed a revolution against Spain. All of the Cuban insurrectionists were not in favor of independence, some desiring annexation by the United States and others asking for governmental and social reforms but preferring to remain in the Spanish empire. A republican government was organized on April 20, 1869. The insurrection was characterized by guerrilla warfare, which became increasingly brutal as it progressed. Skirmishes were almost entirely limited to E. Cuba. Anticipated intervention by the U.S. never became a reality, and in 1878 the Cuban rebels were brought to submission by the Spanish and the insurrection was ended by the signing on Oct. 10, in that year, of the Convention of El Zanjón, which stipulated that slavery would be abolished in Cuba and that governmental reforms would be instituted. However, the liberal spirit of the Convention was not fulfilled. See CUBA: *History*; SPAIN: *History*.

TEOSINTE, Mexican name for *Euchlaena mexicana*, a tall, spreading, leafy annual grass, closely related to maize or Indian corn. It is a native of the warmer parts of Mexico and Central America. The plant requires a rich, moist soil and a long, hot season. In its native habitat it grows rapidly, often attaining a height of 10 to 15 feet in a few months. The stalks bear tassels of staminate flowers and a number of small, flattened, poorly filled ears, the grain of which seldom matures farther north than lat. 30°. On account of its extensive tillering (30 to 50 stalks often springing from a single root) and its very leafy habit, teosinte produces as much green fodder upon a given area of land as any other grass. The stalks are tender, and the whole plant is readily eaten by livestock. The plants may be cut several times during the season, but a single cutting just before the autumn frosts is said to yield about as much forage as the more frequent cuttings. Teosinte grows best in the United States in the region of the Gulf coast. In Texas, where it is grown for green forage and hay, it produces three crops a year, but matures seed only in the extreme southern part of the State.

TEPEHUAN, a brave and warlike tribe of Piman stock. They are now restricted to the mountainous region in the extreme northwestern portion of Durango, with adjoining portions of Chihuahua and Sinaloa, Mexico. They are an industrious, agricultural people, living in houses of logs or stone set in clay mortar, or frequently utilizing the mountain caves for shelter. They cultivate cotton, which they weave into fabrics of beautiful texture and colors. They are now reduced to a mere remnant.

TEPIC. See NAYARIT.

TEPLICE-ŠANOV (Ger. *Teplitz*), a town of Czechoslovakia, formerly belonging to Austria, 46 miles N.W. of Praha (Prague), in the valley of the Biela, between the Erzgebirge and the Mittelgebirge ranges. It is a favorite watering place, famous for its hot springs. It has important manufactures of machinery, hardware, buttons, cotton and india-rubber goods, chemicals, glass, pottery, and sugar. The town is known for the treaty of alliance signed there on Sept. 9, 1813, by the monarchs of Russia, Prussia, and Austria against Napoleon. Pop. (1947) 45,301.

TERAMO (anc. *Interamna*), a town of Italy, capital of the province of Teramo, on the Tordino, 84 miles S. of Ancona. Its cathedral (1355) has been modernized. Straw hats, pottery, and leather are manufactured, and silk is spun. Area of province, 750 sq.m.; pop. (about 225,000). Pop. of town, about 31,000.

TERATOLOGY (Gr. *teratologia*, "a telling of wonders"), the branch of biological science dealing with abnormalities in fetal or embryonic development. Teratology unites the study of embryology with the techniques of pathology, and is sometimes called *pathological embryology*. Individual human beings are never completely alike at birth. The prenatal developmental differences between human beings are only slight and are known as *normal variations*. Teratology does not deal with such normal variations but with developmental abnormalities which exceed the normal range. Congenital abnormalities, such as club foot, harelip, and cleft palate, are scientifically known as *anomalies* or *terata*: typical anomalies include *agenesis* or failure of development of an organ or other part, partial but incomplete development of an organ or part, exaggerated development, displacement of organs to abnormal locations, and fusion or splitting of organs normally split or fused, respectively. About 1 out of every 165 newborn children have major anomalies; a far greater number of fetuses and embryos which die before birth have such abnormalities.

Individuals possessing externally visible anomalies have, since ancient times, been known as "monsters" (Lat. *monstrum*, "omen of calamity") because the ancients believed that deformed infants were born to warn mankind of misfortune. Babylonian cuneiform inscriptions, dating from about 2000 B.C., list terata and the events that such abnormalities supposedly indicated. The ancient Romans and Hebrews believed that monsters were conceived by women during the menstrual periods. The ancient Greeks believed that anomalies were created by the gods to amuse themselves and to bewilder mankind; evidences of this concept exist in the English phrases "freak of nature" and "sport", which are often used to describe monsters. Modern superstitions regarding the cause of monsters emphasize external influences exerted upon the mother during the gestation period; for example, illness of or injury to a part or organ of the mother supposedly results in malformation of the corresponding part of the embryo.

The true causes of anomalies are numerous and may be classified according to whether the developmental disturbance is *internal* to the fertilized ovum, fetus, or embryo, or is produced by *external* forces. Among the internal causes of anomaly formation are: heredity, which governs the production of supernumerary fingers and of identical twins; inferior or superior quality of the protoplasm of the fertilized egg, resulting in arrested or accelerated development; physiological imbalance in the fetus which may produce mechanical distortions by oversecretion of fluid; and influence of the development of one organ upon another whereby a slight malformation of one organ may cause more extensive abnormalities in other organs developing at the same time. Among the external causes of anomaly formation are changes in external temperature, radiation, oxygen deficiency, maternal disease such as syphilis, delayed implantation of the fertilized egg in the uterus, and nutritional deficiency. Many scientists believe that harmful drugs, such as alcohol, narcotics, and lead, pass to the fetus from the mother and result in developmental disturbances.

Twinning. The development of identical twins is the best-known example of anomaly formation; twins are not, however, popularly regarded as monsters. In three out of every four pairs of twins produced, the infants result from the fertilization of two ova; such pairs are known as *ordinary* or *fraternal twins*, and may contain two males, two females, or one male and one female. In one out of every four pairs of twins, the infants result from a developmental disturbance within the fertilized egg which splits into two parts, each of which continues to develop. Such a developmental disturbance is usually caused by hereditary factors and occurs in one out of every 88 human pregnancies. The twins, known as *identical twins*,

are of the same sex and resemble each other closely, having the same genetic constitution. Triplets, quadruplets, and quintuplets are developed in the same manner and are produced in one out of 7700 (roughly 88^2) pregnancies, one out of 681,500 (88^3) pregnancies, and one out of 60,200,000 (88^4) pregnancies respectively.

The abnormal nature of the development of identical twins becomes evident when the fertilized ovum does not split completely, and results in the development of "freaks" such as the Siamese twins, which are partially joined together. The Siamese twins, Eng and Chang (1811–74), were two brothers, born with a fleshy connection between them. The connection extended from the navel to the bottom of the breastbone of each; it was about $1\frac{1}{2}$ inches wide on top and 3 inches wide on the bottom. The brothers were exhibited in sideshows in the United States and England and became wealthy; they married and had twenty-two children between them. Chang, having contracted pneumonia, died of this disease, and Eng expired two hours later. Many cases of joined identical twins have been observed but few have survived long after birth. Such twins may be joined at the chest, back, side, or rump; cases of twins joined at the head are also known. The degree of separation of joined twins varies; the bond connecting Siamese twins may be slight, and in several similar recent cases successful operations have been performed to separate such twins; however, conjoined twins often share several essential organs, and separation cannot be performed without the death of at least one of the twins.

The nature of the twinning process also throws light on the occasional birth of children which have parasitic monsters attached to them. Such births are actually the result of incomplete twinning in which one twin develops normally, and the other twin, partially joined to its sibling, fails to develop completely. The fully developed child is scientifically known as the *autosite*; the incompletely developed twin is known as the *parasite*. Operations for the removal of the parasite from the autosite are often successful.

External Anomalies. Superficial anomalies, although often not as serious as malformations of the internal organs, are popularly best known and were responsible for the superstitions about "monsters" held by the ancients. Anomalies of the skull include:

cranioschisis, or "open-roofed skull", in which the bones forming the roof of the braincase do not develop, and the brain is extremely reduced in size; *microcephalus*, in which the skull and braincase are abnormally small; *hydrocephalus* or *macrocephalus*, in which the brain swells during the accumulation of excessive cerebrospinal fluid, causing unusual enlargement of the skull; *scaphocephaly*, in which the skull becomes wedge-shaped because of premature suturation of some of the skull bones while others continue to grow; *acrocephaly*, or pointed skull; and *plagiocephaly*, or twisted skull.

Anomalies of the face include: *aprosopus*, in which the features never develop; *synotus*, in which the ears are located close together in the neck region (usually associated with *agnathus*, in which the chin is absent); *anophthalmia*, in which the eyes are absent; *cyclopia*, in which only one eye is present, usually in the middle of the forehead; an anomaly of the nose associated with cyclopia, in which the nose becomes a tubular proboscis located above the central eye; *harelip*, in which the upper lip is cleft; *cleft palate*, in which the upper jaw is split; abnormalities in the size, number, shape, and location of the teeth; absence of the tongue or division of the tongue into two or three lobes; *macrostomus*, in which the mouth slit is too large; *microstomus*, in which the mouth slit is abnormally small; *astomus*, in which the mouth opening is completely closed; and *micrognathus*, in which the lower jaw is abnormally small.

The major external anomalies of the trunk are *gastroschisis*, in which the abdominal wall does not close, often accompanied by herniation of the internal organs, and *rachischisis* or cleft spine, a similar condition of the spinal column. Anomalies of the breasts include *amastia*, or absence of breasts, *hypermastia*, in which additional breasts are present, *hyperthelia*, in which only additional nipples are present, and *gynecomastia*, occurring in males, in which the breast is of a female type. Embryonic tails as large as 3 inches in length have been observed on new-born infants.

The best-known anomalies of the limbs are *clubfoot* and *clubhand*. In *amelus*, the limbs fail to develop or appear as short stubs; in *hemimelus* the upper portion of the limb is normal, but the lower portion is a stump. In an analogous condition, *phocomelus*, the upper portion of the limb does not develop, the complete lower portion of the limb arising directly from the trunk like the flipper of a seal. Other anomalies of the limbs include: *sympodia*, in which the legs are united; *polydactyly* and *dichirus*, in which one or more additional digits appear on the hands or feet; *syndactyly*, in which the digits are united by a connection of bone or a webbing of flesh; *brachydactyly*, in which the digits are abnormally short; and *hyperphalangism*, in which the digits are abnormally long.

Excessive congenital hairiness is known as *hypertrichosis*; congenital absence of hair is known as *hypotrichosis*. *Anonychia*, or the congenital absence of nails, has also been observed. Deficiency of skin pigmentation, or *albinism*, and excess of pigment, or *melanism*, are well-known skin anomalies.

Internal Anomalies. Anomalies of the internal organs are often much more dangerous to life than external malformations. Physicians are learning to recognize the outward signs of visceral malformation prejudicial to health, and are just beginning to develop operative techniques to correct such malformations. The "blue-baby" operation, devised toward the close of the first half of the 20th century, corrects one such malformation: a persistent connection between the artery leading from the heart to the lungs and the artery leading from the heart to the body, resulting in the circulation of stale blood through the body of the infant. Malformations of internal organs are discussed below in relation to the systems these organs comprise.

Malformation of the brain is usually associated with anomaly of the skull; virtual absence of the brain, or *anencephaly*, herniation of the brain, or *encephalocele*, and herniation of the brain membranes, or *meningocele*, are usually associated with deficient closure of the roof of the skull. The brain may be unusually small or unusually large. The spinal cord is sometimes absent (*amyelus*) or may protrude through a cleft spine as in *spina bifida*. The peripheral nerves often show anomalies in number and position, but few of these anomalies are serious.

Anomalies of the endocrine system are frequent; accessory thyroid, parathyroid, and suprarenal glands often occur in the human. The ovaries and testes are discussed below in the paragraph on anomalies of the reproductive system.

The digestive system is very subject to malformation. One of the commonest anomalies of the digestive system is *situs inversus*, in which organs normally placed on the right side of the body occur on the left side and organs normally occurring on the left side of the body are located on the right side. Organs in the thoracic cavity are often affected by this reversal in the abdominal cavity. *Stenosis*, or narrowing of the opening, and *atresia*, or complete closure of the opening, occasionally affect the esophagus, stomach, or intestines, and must be treated surgically. A fistula, known as *Meckel's diverticulum*, occurs as a blind sac leading from the ileum toward the navel in about two percent of all adults. In some cases the fistula penetrates the body wall, opening to the outside, and is then called an umbilical fecal fistula. An imperforate or closed anus occurs in a small number of infants; provision for excretion must be made surgically. Absence o duplication of the gall bladder sometimes occurs, and accessory pancreases and split pancreases are well known.

The lung is subject to wide variations in the number and size of its lobes. The most serious respiratory anomaly is the presence of a fistula or open connection between the windpipe and the esophagus. The diaphragm is occasionally pierced by a hole, resulting in herniation of the abdominal organs into the pleural cavity.

The condition producing "blue babies" is the most common anomaly of the heart and blood vessels, occurring in about 1 out of every 4 infants; the degree of severity of this condition is only rarely great enough to produce serious symptoms. Anomalies of the arteries and veins are common, but rarely interfere with the life processes. The spleen is occasionally split or duplicate.

The kidneys are subject to several serious terata. Occasionally a kidney fails to develop altogether or is hypoplastic, that is, excessively dwarfed in size; rarely, excess kidney tissue is present. The two kidneys are sometimes joined at their lower ends, and are then known as "horseshoe kidney". Sometimes a kidney fails to descend and remains in the pelvis; such a kidney is called an ectopic or pelvic kidney. *Polycystic kidneys* are usually congenital, and produce painful symptoms resulting from enlargement of cysts and compression of neighboring kidney tissue. The ureters may not open into the bladder but lead directly into the urethra, rectum, uterus, or vagina.

Anomalies of the reproductive system are **extremely** important because of their psychological effect on the afflicted individual.

Every case of mammalian "hermaphroditism" (see HERMAPHRODITISM) is produced by developmental failure. Until the fifth to the sixth weeks of embryonic life, the sex organs of the embryo give no indication as to the future sex of the embryo; the gonads are generalized in structure, and both male and female sex ducts are present. In the development of a normal individual of a specific sex, the gonads and secondary sex organs predominant in that sex develop, and the secondary sex organs of the other sex degenerate In anomalous development, secondary sex organs of both sexes develop almost equally, or sufficiently so that primitive organic characteristics of the usually suppressed sex are recognizable, a condition called pseudohermaphroditism. The presence of male or female gonads determines whether the individual is a male or female pseudohermaphrodite, respectively. In lower mammals, hermaphrodites possessing both testicular and ovarian tissue have been known to occur; true hermaphroditism of this sort almost never occurs in man. Congenital absence of gonads or duplication of gonads is also rare. *Cryptorchism*, or failure of the testes to descend into the scrotum from the abdominal cavity, is a common anomaly and may accompany malformation of the male external genitalia.

Common anomalies of the internal female reproductive system include duplication of the uterus and vagina, presence of a partitioned uterus, and narrowing or closure of the vaginal canal, often accompanied by an imperforate hymen. Complete absence of one or both Fallopian tubes, of the uterus, or of the vagina occurs rarely, usually accompanying malformation of the external genitals.

Although anomalies of the genitalia are externally visible, they are discussed here, rather than in the section on external anomalies, because of their close association with the internal development of the reproductive system. In extreme cases, the external genitalia and other secondary sexual characteristics completely resemble those of one sex, and the gonads are those of the other sex. Such false hermaphroditism or pseudohermaphroditism occurs much more frequently in males than in females. The penis is rarely absent, but is often rudimentary, resembling a clitoris. Often, the urethral canal fails to fuse on the underside of the penis, causing a condition known as *hypospadias*; when this condition is accompanied by failure of fusion of the two halves of the scrotum, the appearance of the genitals is typically feminine.

Sometimes, the urethral canal is open on the upper side of the penis, a condition known as *epispadias*. In female pseudohermaphroditism, the labiae may be large or fused and the clitoris overdeveloped. See REPRODUCTIVE SYSTEM.

TERBIUM, a metallic element of atomic number 65, atomic weight 159.2, and symbol Tb, the least abundant member of the group of elements called rare earths (q.v.). It was discovered in 1843 by the Swedish chemist Carl G. Mosander, but has not yet been isolated in pure form. Terbium ranks 54th in order of abundance among the elements of the earth's crust, and is found in small quantities combined with cerite, gadolinite, and other rare earth minerals. It yields several colorless or white salts and a white oxide known as terbia, Tb_2O_3.

TERBORCH, or **TER BORCH,** GERARD (1617–81), Dutch painter, born in Zwolle. The influence of Frans Hals is noticeable in his first dated picture, "Consultation" (1635, Berlin Museum). To the same period may be assigned the "Knife-Grinder's Family" and "Boy with a Dog" (Pinakothek, Munich). In 1635 he went to England, where he painted several portraits of William III. In 1646 he went to Münster, Westphalia, where he painted his most celebrated work, the "Peace Congress of Münster" (1648, National Gallery, London), containing sixty likenesses, a perfect specimen of miniature portrait painting, and one of the most imposing historical works in Dutch art. From 1651 till 1680, having returned to Holland, he painted a series of genre and small portrait subjects, considered unexcelled in Dutch or any other art.

TERCEIRA, the second-largest island of the Azores. See AZORES.

TEREDO. See SHIPWORM.

TEREK, a river of S.E. Russia, one of the chief streams flowing from the Caucasus. It rises in a glacier near the summit of Mount Kazbec at an altitude of nearly 14,000 ft. and descends the N. slope of the Caucasus in a tumultuous course through deep and narrow gorges. It then turns E. and after a flow of 400 m. enters the Caspian Sea through a large delta. The river is navigable 254 m. for small vessels.

TERENCE, or (Lat.) PUBLIUS TERENTIUS AFER (190?–159? B.C.), Roman playwright, born in Carthage. He was taken to Rome as the slave of the senator Publius Terentius Lucanus, who educated him and later manumitted him. On gaining his freedom he assumed his patron's *nomen,* Terentius. His first play was the *Andria,* produced in 166 B.C. Its success was immediate, and Terence, who had an engaging personality, soon became a favorite among Roman literary circles. He is said to have been an intimate friend of Publius Cornelius Scipio (q.v.) Æmilianus, in whose circle were statesmen and men of letters concerned with improving and refining the Latin language. Terence's six comedies, produced between 166 and 160 B.C., are all *fabulæ palliatæ,* or comedies based upon Greek originals (see DRAMA: *Roman Drama*). Of these, the *Andria, Heautontimorumenos, Eunuchus,* and *Adelphœ* are derived from comedies by the Greek dramatist Menander (q.v.), and the *Phormio* and the *Hecyra* are modeled upon originals by the Athenian playwright Apollodorus of Carystus (300–260 B.C.). In 160 B.C. Terence made a journey to Greece, to search for additional plays by Menander, and died the following year on his way home.

Terence's comedies, unlike those of his famous predecessor Titus Maccius Plautus (q.v.), contain little song and dance; they lack the broad farce inherent in the works of Plautus, and their humor, rather than being derived from puns and wordplay, exaggerated characterization, and laughable situations, arises out of a subtle handling of both plot and character. There is less use of trickery than in the works of Plautus, and more of mistaken identity and recognition; with the exception of the *Hecyra,* the plot is always double, with two love affairs being interwoven and the happy solution of one usually dependent upon the outcome of the other. Terence introduced greater suspense into ancient comedy, resulting in part from his abandoning the customary use of the prologue to disclose the plot, and instead utilizing it as a defense against unfavorable criticism. His work is more Greek than Roman in quality, and the plays include no allusions to Roman localities or events. Terence had high ideals of artistic perfection, bringing elegance and restraint to the Latin language, and was praised later by Gaius Julius Cæsar as "a lover of faultless speech". Although less a master of comic devices and techniques than Plautus, Terence had a great influence upon Renaissance comedy; the French dramatist Molière made adaptations of the *Phormio* and the *Adelphœ,* and through him Terence's comedies influenced English playwrights of the 17th and 18th centuries.

TERESA, SAINT (1515–82), famous Carmelite nun and mystical writer, born in

Ecstasy of Saint Teresa (sculpture by Lorenzo Bernini in Santa Maria church in Rome)

Avila, in Old Castile. In her eighteenth year she entered a convent of the Carmelite Order. After a time her religious exercises reached a most extraordinary degree of asceticism. She began her work of reforming the Carmelite Order in Avila, Spain, but afterward removed with her little community to St. Joseph's, where she established in its full rigor the ancient Carmelite rule (1562). The general of the Carmelite Order, J.B. Rossi, was so struck with the condition of the convent that he urged upon her the duty of extending throughout the Order the reforms thus successfully initiated. Teresa entered upon the work with great energy, and succeeded in carrying out her reforms. (See CARMELITES.) She was canonized by Gregory XV in 1622, her feast day being fixed on October 15. Her works consist, besides her famous letters, mainly of ascetical and mystical treatises.

TERHUNE, ALBERT PAYSON (1872–1942), American writer, born in Newark, New Jersey, and educated at Columbia University. In 1893–94 he made an extensive tour on horseback through Syria and Egypt, living for a time among the nomadic Bedouins of the Syrian desert. From 1894 to 1916 he served on the editorial staff of the New York *Evening World*. Terhune is remembered principally for his stories about dogs. His works include *The Fighter* (1909), *Lad: A Dog* (1919), *Bruce* (1920), *Buff: A Collie* (1921), *His Dog* (1922), *The Heart of A Dog* (1926), *Lad of Sunnybank* (1928), *The Way of A Dog* (1934), and *A Book of Famous Dogs* (1937).

TERMINUS, in Roman religion, a divinity presiding over public and private boundaries, and represented by a stone or post set in the ground. His only sanctuary was in the Temple of Jupiter on the Capitoline Hill, at which he was honored in the form of a boundary stone, set under an opening in the roof so that his rites might be considered to be performed in the open air, as the ritual required. Originally Terminus seems to have been identified with Jupiter, but gradually he came to be considered a separate and distinct god. The *Terminalia*, celebrated on February 23, appears to have been simply a festival of neighbors at their common boundary lines.

TERMITES (*Termitidae*), any one of the insects of the order Isoptera, comprising those forms known as white ants. They are not at all related to the true ants, but their general appearance and the fact that they live in societies have given them the popular name. Like the ants, the termites are social insects, living in colonies and building nests or hills. They are widely distributed in tropical countries, but they also occur in the temperate parts of North and South America, and a few have established themselves in Europe.

The termite society consists for the most part of wingless, sexually immature workers, and a less numerous caste of large-headed strong-jawed soldiers. The workers collect food, form burrows and tunnels, build hills, and care for the males, females, eggs, and larvae. The males and females have wings, which the latter lose after impregnation.

In general appearance and size a wingless termite is antlike, but the winged forms are much larger and flatter, and their wings are quite different.

The nests, often built of earth, are hard and persistent, and sometimes more than 12 ft. high. These ant hills are divided into chambers and galleries, and there are generally two or three roofs within the dome-shaped interior. The thick walls are perforated by passages leading to the nurseries and storehouses. Termites sometimes attack the woodwork of houses and soon reduce the thickest timbers to a mere shell. Those species which live in trees sometimes construct nests of great size, like sugar casks, of particles of gnawed wood cemented together and very strongly attached to the branches.

In the United States there are comparatively few species, and only one, *Termes flavipes,* which has a northward range. This is the common white ant found frequently living in the joists and other large timbers of houses. The most remarkable termitaries are those of *Termes bellicosus,* abundant on the w. coast of Africa. They are sugar-loaflike in shape, 10 to 20 ft. in height, and, though built of cemented particles of earth, are strong enough to bear a man's weight.

TERN, one of a group, the Sterninae, of small shore birds, found in most parts of the world, resembling gulls in habits and appearance. About 75 species are known, varying in size from the Caspian tern, *Sterna tschegrava* or *caspia,* which is nearly 2 ft. long and 4½ ft. across the wings, down to the dainty least tern, *S. antillarum,* which is

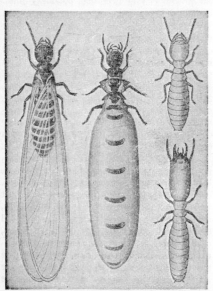

THE TERMITE. *Left: Male. Middle: Female after impregnation. Right, top: Worker. Right, bottom: Soldier.*

Arctic tern (Sterna paradisaea)

only 9 in. long. The typical color of the terns is blue gray above, white beneath, and black on the crown, but one or two species are pure white, some are black and white, some sooty brown, and some almost wholly black. The common tern is *S. hirundo,* abundant on the coasts of the whole Northern Hemisphere and of Africa. It breeds locally on the coast and in the Mississippi Valley from the Gulf States to Greenland, but, owing to incessant persecution, it selects only unoccupied sandy islets for its breeding places. The sooty tern, or egg bird, of the West Indies, *S. fuliginosa* or *fuscata,* and the elegant tern, *S. elegans,* of the Pacific coast, are among the most interesting of the 15 or 16 other North American species. See GULL.

TERNATE, a small island of the Moluccas. Area, about 25 sq.m. See MOLUCCAS.

TERNI, a cathedral city in the province of Perugia, Italy, 70 miles N.E. of Rome. It has large iron and steel works. About 2 m. away is the famous cataract of Velino, 650 ft. high, celebrated by Byron in his *Childe Harold.* Terni is the ancient *Interamna Umbrica,* perhaps the birthplace of Tacitus, and has many interesting Roman remains. Pop., about 63,000.

TERNSTROEMIACEAE, a family of polypetalous plants, consisting of trees and shrubs, natives of warm and temperate countries. They are most abundant in South America; a few are found in North America; some in India, China, and the Indian Archipelago. The leaves are alternate, leathery, in many species evergreen, generally undivided, and sometimes dotted. This order is very important as containing the tea (q.v.) shrubs. It is also interesting because of the great beauty both of the foliage and flowers of many of the species, of which the genus *Camellia* (q.v.) affords the best-known examples.

TERPANDER (fl. 7th century B.C.), Greek musician and poet, born in Antissa, on the island of Lesbos. He went to Sparta and in 676 B.C. was crowned victor in the first musical contest at the *Carnea*, a Spartan festival in honor of the god Apollo. Terpander established the first music school in Greece and is credited with increasing the number of strings of the lyre from four to seven (see LYRE). He was also probably the first to set poetry regularly to music and is hence regarded as the father of Greek lyric poetry.

TERPSICHORE, in Greek mythology, one of the nine Muses (q.v.). She presided over choral dance and song. In a latter assignment of functions to the Muses, she was regarded as the muse of the lesser lyric poetry, and her symbol was the lyre. From her name is derived the modern term for a dancer, "terpsichorean".

TERRA-COTTA, an Italian term for earthenware. Statues, statuettes, bas-reliefs, and architectural members such as columns, cornices, friezes, consoles, and the like made of burnt clay are said to be executed in terracotta whether they are ancient or modern. The color is either buff yellow or red. Many masterpieces of ancient Greek and Roman sculpture are executed in this material, and many works in burnt clay, by Italians of the Middle Ages and early Renaissance periods, are exquisite productions.

Some of the best terra-cotta for buildings is made in the United States; and here also color has been sparingly used. Among its advantages as a building material are the ease with which it may be molded to any desired architectural or sculptural form and indefinitely repeated, its durability, lightness, strength, and cheapness. It may be made in almost any desired color, but is usually dark red.

TERRAPIN, the popular name of many species of fresh-water and tidal-water tortoises of the family Emyidae, natives of tropical and the warmer temperate countries. The family is represented in the United States by about twenty species. The word "terrapin" has no exact scientific significance, but in the United States it is most commonly applied to the diamond-back terrapin, *Malacolemmys centrata* or *palustris*. This species is found in salt marshes from New York to Texas, and is gray with black markings. Its flesh is highly esteemed as a table delicacy, and in some places along the southern coast large numbers of these turtles are reared for market in inclosures.

TERRE HAUTE, county seat of Vigo Co., Ind., situated on the Wabash R., 73 miles w.s.w. of Indianapolis. It is served by four railroads, and maintains a municipal airport. Terre Haute is an important railroad and manufacturing center, and the commercial center of an area noted for farming and the production of coal, oil, and clay. Among the industrial establishments in the city are extensive railroad shops, rolling mills, printing and engraving plants, paper mills, distilleries, breweries, food and meat packing plants, and factories manufacturing chemicals, paints and varnishes, brick, drain tile and other clay products, glass, tin cans, coke by-products, wooden boxes, iron and steel products, metal stampings, bronze and brassware, machinery, and food products. Terre Haute is the site of Indiana State Teachers College, established in 1870; Rose Polytechnic Institute (1874), the oldest engineering college w. of the Allegheny Mts.; St. Mary-of-the-Woods College (1840), for women; and a Federal penitentiary. The municipal park system comprises eighteen parks, including swimming pools, golf courses, a zoo, a fish hatchery, and a stadium with a seating capacity of 20,000 persons.

Fort Harrison, named in honor of Gen. William Henry Harrison, first Territorial governor of Indiana, was built on the site of the present city in 1811. The following year, while under the command of Captain Zachary Taylor, the fort was successfully defended against an attack led by the Indian chief Tecumseh. The settlement which developed around the fort was incorporated as a town in 1838 and as a city in 1853. It was the birthplace of Eugene V. Debs, noted Socialist leader, of the writer and editor Theodore Dreiser, and of Paul Dreiser, brother of Theodore Dreiser and writer of the song *On the Banks of the Wabash*. Pop. (1950) 64,214.

TERRESTRIAL ELECTRICITY, the science pertaining to electrical phenomena exhibited by the earth and atmosphere. Under normal conditions the surface of the earth is everywhere negatively charged, and the magnitude of the charge density is such that the potential gradient, or increase of electrical potential per meter increase of altitude above the surface, amounts to about 150 volts per meter. The potential gradient shows annual and diurnal variations of very considerable amount. It diminishes with increase of altitude, and probably becomes sensibly zero at altitudes of little more than 10 kilometers. The atmosphere possesses the power of conducting electricity to an extent which, though extremely small, is nevertheless sufficient to insure that nine tenths of the charge on the earth would disappear in 10 minutes if there were no means of replenishing the loss. Although many attempts have been made to account for the permanent existence of an electrical field in a conducting atmosphere, no completely satisfactory theory has yet been evolved. Instruments used in the measurement of earth currents include the declinometer, the dipping needle, and the electrometer.

TERRESTRIAL MAGNETISM. See MAG-NETISM, TERRESTRIAL.

TERRIER, any of several breeds of small dogs originally employed for hunting small, furred game. Terriers hunt by digging into the ground at the hiding place of the game and then fighting the game underground or driving it out of its place of concealment. They are now kept principally as pets. The principal breeds of terrier are the Airedale, Bedlington, Boston, Bull, Dandie Dinmont, Fox, Irish, Kerry Blue, Manchester, Norwich, Schnauzer, Scottish, Sealyham, Skye, Staffordshire, Welsh, and Yorkshire (qq.v.).

TERRITORIAL WATERS, in international law, waters subject to the jurisdiction of a sovereign state, as distinguished from high seas (q.v.), and consisting of waters lying within the state, waters which are boundaries between states, and coastal waters. Jurisdiction over boundary waters, such as lakes or rivers, is fixed by treaties; the limit of each state's jurisdiction is usually an imaginary line drawn through the center of such waters. In the United States each State exercises jurisdiction over waters lying wholly within the State; such streams which form part of the system of interstate waterways are, however, subject to the control of the Federal government. With respect to territorial waters on the coast of a state, the theory of international law formerly was that the jurisdiction of such a state extended along its coast for three miles from low-water mark. The theory was based on the cannon shot of the period; since such an area was within the range of a cannon it was deemed subject to control from the shore. Though conditions of warfare have changed, the three-mile limit is still the accepted limit of territorial jurisdiction; however, for revenue purposes, especially for the protection of special industries, such as fishing, various limits beyond the three-mile limit have been claimed from time to time. Thus, during the early 1930's, in connection with prohibition enforcement, the jurisdiction of the United States over coastal waters was extended by international treaties to twelve miles from the coast. The general rule is that arms of the sea which are not more than ten miles wide are considered territorial waters; greater widths have, however, been so considered, as the waters of Conception Bay, Newfoundland, where the headlands are twenty miles apart.

The concept of jurisdiction by a state over its territorial waters implies that no other state can exercise any rights there, as of fishing, except by permission. A state has the right to refuse access to armed vessels of other states; merchant vessels of belligerent nations entering such territorial waters become subject to the jurisdiction of that state. As a general rule, all nations possess a common right of navigation on territorial waters. The regulation of navigation over territorial waters which serve as means of communication between two portions of the high seas, including such straits as the Dardanelles and the Bosporus, and such passages as the Suez and Panama canals, is fixed by international treaties.

TERRITORIES, the name given in the United States to certain parts of the national domain which have not been erected into States. They are the District of Columbia and Alaska on the continent, and Hawaii, the Samoan Islands, and Guam in the Pacific. Puerto Rico, now a Commonwealth, was a U.S. Territory until 1952. They may be classified, under their present status as political bodies, as (1) unorganized Territories; (2) the Federal District; and (3) the insular possessions. The Territories are not regularly represented in Congress, but are allowed to send a delegate, who is given a seat in the House of Representatives with a right to take part in the debates, but not to vote. For the government of Alaska, Hawaii, the District of Columbia, and the Samoan Islands, see separate articles under these titles. The Virgin Islands, a dependency in the West Indies, and the Panama Canal Zone, a military reservation, are not classed as Territories.

By the United States Constitution the national Congress is given power "to make all needful rules and regulations respecting the territory or other property belonging to the United States". From the beginning this clause was construed as giving the powers incident to jurisdiction as well as to ownership, and even before the adoption of the

Constitution the Northwest Territory was regularly organized by the old Confederation Congress, which for this purpose passed the famous Ordinance of 1787. This ordinance served as the model for much of the subsequent legislation in the same field, though there were a number of important variations.

TERRITORIES, OFFICE OF, agency of the U.S. Department of the Interior, established in 1950, and vested with responsibility for all departmental matters pertaining to Territorial affairs. The agency has jurisdiction in matters relating to Territories, island possessions, trusteeship areas, and dependent areas under U.S. sovereignty. Prior to 1950 the functions of the agency were performed by the Division of Territories and Island Possessions, created in 1934. The Office of Territories assists the Territorial governments in working out plans and policies for the establishment of sound economic conditions and of political relationships with the United States satisfactory to the local populations of the Territories. The office also acts as a liaison agency between the Federal government and Territorial governments. Among the functions specifically assigned to the office are supervision of the operation of the Alaska Railroad, the Alaska Road Commission, and the Puerto Rico Reconstruction Administration. The office is administered by a director appointed by the President with the approval of the Senate.

TERROR, REIGN OF. See REIGN OF TERROR.

TERRY, DAME ELLEN (ALICE) (1848–1928), English actress, born in Coventry. Her first appearance on the stage was as the boy Mamillius in Charles Kean's revival of *A Winter's Tale*, at the Princess's Theatre in 1856. In 1863 she made her appearance at the Haymarket in London. In 1875 she joined the Bancrofts at the Prince of Wales's Theatre. In 1878 she began her long association (24 years) with Henry (later Sir Henry) Irving (q.v.) at the Lyceum, as Ophelia to his Hamlet. Her most notable roles were Portia in *The Merchant of Venice* (1879), Juliet in *Romeo and Juliet* (1882), Viola in *Twelfth Night* (1884), Marguerite in *Faust* (1885), Mistress Page in *The Merry Wives of Windsor* (1902), Alice Grey in Barrie's *Alice Sit-by-the-Fire* (1905), Lady Cecily Waynflete in Shaw's *Captain Brassbound's Conversion* (1906), and Hermione in *A Winter's Tale* (1906). Her first visit to the United States as an actress was made with Irving in 1883, when she won a welcome that was repeated on eight subsequent occasions. Her last regular stage appearance was made in June, 1919, when she played the nurse in *Romeo and Juliet* at the Lyric Theatre in London. In 1925 King George of England conferred on Ellen Terry the high distinction of Dame Grand Cross of the Most Excellent Order of the British Empire. In 1913 she wrote *The Russian Ballet*.

TERTIAN FEVER. See MALARIA.

TERTIARY PERIOD, in geology, a division of time including the beginning of the Cenozoic era, immediately following the Cretaceous period of the Mesozoic era (formerly known as the Secondary period), and preceding the Pleistocene epoch of the Quaternary period; see GEOLOGY, SYSTEMATIC. According to an older classification, the Tertiary period is the third of four major geologic time periods; compare QUATERNARY PERIOD. The Tertiary period began about 60 million years ago and ended about 1 million years ago. The Tertiary period is now generally divided into four major epochs: Eocene, Oligocene, Miocene, and Pliocene. For information on the physiographic changes, flora, and fauna of the Tertiary period, see separate articles on the epochs mentioned above.

TERTULLIAN, or (Lat.) QUINTUS SEPTIMIUS FLORENS TERTULLIANUS (about 160–about 230 A.D.), Latin ecclesiastical writer, born in Carthage, one of the greatest of the Latin Church fathers, and the creator of Christian-Latin literature. He was trained for the profession of law, practiced in Rome, and became a convert to Christianity about 190 A.D. After his conversion he returned to Carthage, where he was made presbyter and spent the rest of his life. About 203 A.D. Tertullian became a member of the heretical Montanistic sect, which by his day had lost some of its original unorthodoxy but was violently opposed to secularism in the Church. About 207 A.D. he abandoned orthodox Christianity and was thenceforth unsparingly severe in his views of ecclesiastical discipline and in his judgment upon the alleged moral laxity of the "psychics", as he called the members of the Church. He retained, however, the deepest respect for the authorities upon which the Church was founded, his only quarrel being with the development of ecclesiastical hierarchy, which he feared would become a political organization. His writings are notable for their blunt manner, keen satire, skillful dialectic, moral strength, and bitter partisanship. As a result of his legal training he expressed his views in a form which imprinted upon Western theology a legalistic character which it has never lost. Tertullian was the first theologian to formulate in Latin the principles on which Catholic orthodoxy came to be based.

Among his many extant writings the best known is the *Apology*, composed probably in 197 A.D. It is a vigorous vindication of the Christians against the attacks and false charges of the heathen world. His polemical zeal was further directed against Jews and heretics, as in his *To the Nations, Against the Jews, Against Marcion, Against the Valentinians,* and *Against Praxeas.* He wrote many tracts on subjects connected with morals and Church discipline, including *On Baptism, On Penance, On Prayer, On Patience, On Idolatry,* and *On Shows.* His characteristic strictness appears even more strikingly in the works written after he became a Montanist; these include, in addition to many of the polemical works already mentioned, *On Women's Apparel, On the Veiling of Virgins, On Monogamy, On the Exhortation to Chastity,* and *On Fasting.*

TERUEL, capital of the province of the same name, Spain. The city lies at the confluence of the Guadalaviar and Alfambra rivers, about 72 miles N.W. of Valencia. It is a commercial center, served by the Sagunto-Calatayud railway line. Among the noteworthy points of interest in Teruel are the 16th-century cathedral, an aqueduct completed in 1560, and the old quarter, a section retaining many medieval features. Teruel was the scene of considerable fighting during the Spanish civil war (1936-39). Early in the winter of 1937-38, a Loyalist army stormed and captured the city, but it was subsequently recaptured by the insurgents.

The province of Teruel is situated in N.E. Spain. Several mountain ranges traverse the province. Javalambre (6568 ft.) is the highest summit. The chief river is the Tagus (q.v.). Besides the Guadalaviar, other important rivers are the Jiloca and the Jalón. The economy of the province is predominantly agrarian. Livestock raising is a leading industry, and the major crops include corn, olives, fruits, wine grapes, hemp, and flax. The province contains a variety of mineral deposits, notably iron, coal, sulfur, and lead. Area, 5721 sq.m.; pop. (1950 prelim.) 236,002. Pop. of city, about 14,000.

TERZA RIMA, an Italian verse form, of which the first and most notable use was made by Dante in the *Divina Commedia.*

Each stanza consists of three hendecasyllabic lines with two rhymes; lines 1 and 3 repeat the middle rhyme of the preceding stanza, and thus the stanzas are closely interwoven. The series or canto necessarily begins and ends with an alternating couplet: aba, bcb, cdc . . . yzyz. The end of a stanza tends to coincide with a pause in the thought. See RHYME.

TESHU LAMA. See LAMAISM; TIBET: *History.*

TESLA, NIKOLA (1857–1943), American inventor and electrician, born in Smitjan, Lika, Austria-Hungary. He worked in the telegraphic engineering department of the Austrian government until 1881, when he became engineer to an electric company in Budapest. In 1884 he came to America, where he was naturalized and at first was employed in the Edison plant in Orange, N.J. Subsequently working in Pittsburgh and elsewhere, he devoted himself to experimental research and invention. He discovered the principle of the rotary magnetic field, applying it in a practical form to the induction motor. Tesla's discovery made possible the alternating current motor and the transmission of power by such current, employing what became known as 2-phase, 3-phase, multiphase or polyphase systems, particularly on long-distance lines, later used extensively. Tesla invented many electrical appliances, including dynamos, transformers, induction coils, oscillators, and arc and incandescent lamps, and is principally known for his researches in alternating currents of high frequency and high potential. Tesla's later work dealt with the application of such currents to wireless telegraphy, the transmission of power without wires, and many similar problems.

TEST ACTS, in English history, a series of Parliamentary enactments, passed after the Reformation (q.v.), and requiring public officials to qualify for office by passing a religious test. The most notable of these enactments was that adopted in 1672, and designed to disqualify Roman Catholics from holding office. Among other provisions, the test act of 1672 required civil and military officers to take an oath of allegiance to the king, and an oath, called the oath of supremacy, acknowledging the supremacy of the sovereign in ecclesiastical, as well as temporal, affairs (see SUPREMACY, ROYAL); to renounce the dogma of transubstantiation (see MASS); and to receive communion in accordance with the rite of the established Church of England. In 1678 the provisions of the act of 1672 were extended to the peers of the realm, who comprised the House of Lords, and to the members of the House of Commons. In their essential provisions, the later test acts were identical with the enactment of 1672. A test act intended to disqualify Protestant nonconformists was enacted against Presbyterians in 1681; ten years later Parliament enacted another test act intended to perpetuate Protestant supremacy in Ireland.

After 1689 the provisions of the test acts were nullified in the case of Protestant dissenters as a result of the enactment of various laws, including measures legalizing the acts of magistrates who did not conform to the provisions of the test acts. In later years the test acts were modified by amendatory legislation in the case of Catholics and were repealed in 1828; see CATHOLIC EMANCIPATION ACT. Deep-rooted traditions of religious liberty led the Founding Fathers of the United States to prohibit the establishment of religious qualifications for public office. Article VI of the U.S. Constitution provides that "no religious test shall ever be required as a qualification to any office or public trust under the United States". The State constitutions contain similar provisions.

TESTAMENT. See BIBLE; WILL.

TESTES. See REPRODUCTIVE SYSTEM.

TESTIMONY. See EVIDENCE.

TESTOSTERONE, crystalline male sex hormone, $C_{19}H_{28}O_2$, normally present in the tissue of mammalian testes. It melts at 154° C. (309° F.), and is insoluble in water but soluble in alcohol and other organic solvents. Testosterone was originally extracted from testes, but in 1934 Leopold Ružička and Adolph Butenandt (qq.v.) developed a method of breaking down sterols which enabled them to synthesize testosterone from cholesterol. The method made a series of testosterone compounds easily accessible, so the hormone is now available as pure testosterone, testosterone propionate, and methyl testosterone.

Human males suffering from testosterone deficiency do not have well-developed masculine characteristics. They have little or no sexual desire, scanty development of body hair, and fat layers distributed much as in females. Administration of testosterone compounds is becoming increasingly successful in remedying these defects, and in alleviating prostatic enlargement in older males. Testosterone does not increase virility in normal males; on the contrary, administration of testosterone to normal males causes a decrease in sexual desire and may lead to impotency. See HORMONES.

TETANUS, or LOCKJAW, one of the most formidable diseases of the nervous system, characterized by an involuntary, persistent, intense, and painful contraction or cramp (see SPASM) of more or less extensive groups of the voluntary muscles, nearly the whole of the body being sometimes affected. The muscles of the neck, jaws, and throat are almost always the first to give evidence of the presence of the disease. The neck feels stiff, the jaws are opened with difficulty, and often become tightly clenched, and the face has a peculiar fixed smile (*risus sardonicus*). The disease spreads to the muscles of the trunk and the larger muscles of the limbs, with imminent danger of death.

The disease is dependent on a bacillus, *Clostridium tetani*, discovered by Nicolaier in 1884, and cultivated by Kitasato in 1889. The bacillus is a slender rod, with one rounded end containing a spore, and exists in the feces of the herbivora and man, and under favorable conditions the spores remain virulent for years. It is found especially in well-manured soil and in dust and surface soil. This accounts for the fact that wounds infected by dust are often followed by tetanus. The organism often enters the tissues through wounds so slight as to be overlooked.

The preventive treatment of tetanus is most important. Wounds likely to be contaminated with earth should be opened freely, disinfected thoroughly, and well drained, and a dose of antitetanic serum administered. When these precautions have not been taken and lockjaw sets in, the serum should be promptly injected either into the muscles or spinal canal. No wound is too small to be neglected, and upon the first suspicion of possible infection, medical aid should be immediately consulted. In Germany, upon a death from this cause, neglect is inferred unless an antitetanic serum has been administered.

TETHYS, in Greek mythology, a Titaness (see TITANS), daughter of Uranus, god of heaven, and Gæa, goddess of earth. Tethys was the wife of her brother Oceanus (q.v.) and by him mother of the 3000 Oceanids, or ocean nymphs, and of all the river gods.

TETRACHORD, in music, originally, a lyrelike, four-stringed instrument of ancient Greece. From this instrument was derived a series of four notes, also called a tetrachord, which formed the basis of all Greek music.

The four notes of the tetrachord, counting downward from the first, comprise the interval of the so-called perfect fourth. Two such tetrachords constituted a scale. When the lowest tone of a tetrachord was the highest tone of another the tetrachords were said to be *conjunct*. When these tones were one tone apart, the tetrachords were said to be *disjunct*, and the tone between the two tetrachords was called the *diazeuctic* (disjunctive) tone. Three types of tetrachord existed in ancient Greek music, namely, the Dorian, Phrygian, and Lydian, each deriving its name from the region of ancient Greece or Asia Minor in which it originated. From each tetrachord a separate scale was developed, named after the tetrachord basic to it. The Greeks also distinguished between *chromatic* and *enharmonic* tetrachords. The first two intervals of the former are semitones, and the third a minor third; the first two intervals of the latter are quarter tones, and the third a major third. The early Greek modes (see MODE) were arranged in descending groups of tetrachords; these were adopted and later transformed by the Christian Church into ascending groups of pentachords and tetrachords. See also GREEK MUSIC; RELIGIOUS MUSIC.

TETRAGRAMMATON, a term used to designate the name of Israel's God, consisting of the four letters JHVH or JHWH. In the Masoretic text it occurs 6823 times and is written with the vowels of Adonai, Lord (originally, my Lord), or with those of Elohim, God. By these vowels the reader was warned not to pronounce the divine name, but to substitute for it Adonai or Elohim. See JEHOVAH.

TETRAHEDRITE, or GRAY COPPER, an opaque, brown or black-streaked mineral, consisting of copper sulphantimonite, Cu_3SbS_3, and varying amounts of silver, and crystallizing in the hextetrahedral class of the cubic system. It has a hardness ranging from 3 to 4.5, a specific gravity of 4.6 to 5.1, and shines with a brilliant metallic luster. The color ranges from grayish black to black. In many deposits the copper is replaced by various amounts of iron, zinc, silver, lead, and mercury, and the antimony by arsenic or bismuth. The arsenic compound forms a complete series, and is known as *tennantite*, after the English chemist Smithson Tennant (1761–1815). The silver-containing variety is known as *freibergite*. Tetrahedrite is commonly found associated with minerals of copper and silver which were formed and de-

posited by the action of hot water. It may also occur as small crystals in various dolomite deposits, and is often combined with minerals such as pyrites, sphalerite, galena, and other silver, lead, and copper ores. Principal European deposits are found in Cornwall, England, in the Harz Mountains of Germany, and in Transylvania, Romania. In the United States it is excavated in various silver and copper mines of Colorado, Montana, Arizona, Nevada, and Utah, and, in the remainder of the Western Hemisphere, in Mexico, Peru, and Bolivia. It is used chiefly as an ore of silver (q.v.). See separate articles on most of the minerals named.

TETRAZZINI, LUISA (1874–1940), Italian coloratura soprano, born in Florence. After only three months' regular study under Ceccherini at the Liceo Musicale of Florence she made her debut as Inez in *L'Africaine* (1895), and then sang in Rome and other Italian cities. Her successes in Russia and Spain secured an engagement for Buenos Aires. From there she went through Mexico to California, whence her fame as a second Patti began to spread (1906). In 1908 Oscar Hammerstein engaged her for his Manhattan Opera House in New York. She later sang as guest with the Metropolitan, Boston, and Chicago companies. She wrote *My Life of Song* (1921).

TETUÁN, administrative center and seaport of the Spanish Zone, Morocco, situated on the Mediterranean Sea about 33 miles S.E. of Tangiers and about 25 miles S. of Ceuta. The city lies in a fertile agricultural district and is linked to Ceuta and points S. by a narrow gauge railway. Among noteworthy points of interest are the Moorish quarter and the old encircling fortifications. The principal exports are leather, fruit, wool, silk, cotton, and livestock. Tetuán was founded in the 16th century by Moors who had been driven from Spain. Pop., about 94,000.

TETZEL or **TEZEL,** JOHANN (1465?–1519), German Catholic monk of the Dominican order (see DOMINICANS), born in Pirna, Saxony, and educated at the University of Leipzig. A popular and effective preacher, Tetzel was entrusted by the Church with the proclamation of indulgence (see INDULGENCE), the most notable of which was in support of the building of St. Peter's Church, at Rome. In opposition to the preaching of Tetzel, the great religious reformer (see REFORMATION) Martin Luther (q.v.) issued his celebrated ninety-five theses, on October 31, 1517. Tetzel responded with a series of 106 countertheses in the following January, and in April set forth a reply to Luther's sermon on indulgences. Despite his vigorous denunciation of the Protestant heresy, however, Tetzel was severely rebuked by the papal legate Karl von Militz (1490?-1529) for exceptionable language and improper procedure in the presentation of his theses.

TEUCER, in Greek legend, the name of two heroes, one Trojan and the other Greek. **1.** The son of the river god Scamander and the nymph Idæa, and the first king of Troy. He is said to have given his daughter Bateia in marriage to Dardinus, who later succeeded him as king. Teucer is thought to be an eponymous hero invented by the Teucrians, the earliest inhabitants of the Trojan plain and the founders of the city of Troy. **2.** The son of Telamon (q.v.), King of Salamis, and of Hesione, daughter of King Laomedon of Troy. He accompanied his half-brother Ajax (q.v.) to the Trojan War, in which he distinguished himself by his archery. After the war he was banished by his father because he had not avenged the death of Ajax, whereupon he sailed to the island of Cyprus and there founded another Salamis.

TEUTOBURGER WALD, a mountain range in West Germany, situated in the State of North Rhine-Westphalia, and extending for about 70 m., from near Osnabräck to near Paderborn. Its highest summit is Völmers-od (1536 ft.). In 9 A.D. the Teutoburger Wald was the scene of an important battle in which Arminius, or Hermann, the leader of the Cherusci, destroyed three Roman legions under the general Publius Quintilius Varus. As a result of the battle Rome lost all possessions E. of the Rhine River, which became the N.E. boundary of the Roman Empire. The exact location of the battle is not known.

TEUTONES, a powerful tribe of Germany in ancient times, dwelling originally at the mouth of the Elbe R. About 120 B.C. the Teutones joined the Cimbri (q.v.) in their migration southward, the two peoples invading Gaul and the territory of the Romans. The Teutones remained in Gaul from 104 to 102 B.C., when they were annihilated by the Roman general Gaius Marius (q.v.) at Aquæ Sextiæ (modern Aix-en-Provence).

TEUTONIC KNIGHTS (The Teutonic Knights of St. Mary's Hospital at Jerusalem), an order of knighthood which originated in a brotherhood formed by German knights in 1190 during the siege of Acre by the Crusaders and recognized by Pope Clement III

in 1191. In 1198 this association was changed into an order of knighthood as a balance to the political influence of the Templars and Hospitalers. Hermann von Salza, grand master from 1210 to 1239, saw no future in Palestine, and the order engaged in the conquest of the heathen Prussians, inhabiting the Baltic regions to the northeast of Germany. After a fierce struggle of half a century they completed their subjugation in 1283. Christianity was planted with fire and sword, cities were founded, and the land was colonized by Germans. In 1237 the Teutonic Knights absorbed the order of the Brothers of the Sword, and so acquired Livonia and Kurland. They waged long wars with the Lithuanians for the possession of the territory intervening between these regions and the Prussian country. Early in the fourteenth century they extended their dominion westward, making themselves masters of Danzig and Little Pomerania (Pomerellen). In 1410 the order began to decline. In 1809 it was entirely suppressed by Napoleon in all the German States. It was revived in 1834 as an Austrian order.

TEUTONIC MYTHOLOGY. See SCANDINAVIAN MYTHOLOGY.

TEUTONS, a group of peoples speaking Teutonic tongues, an important division of the Aryan family of languages. The name is from Latin *Teutones* (q.v.), *Teutoni*; Gothic *thiuda*, a nation. The Teutonic stock is subdivided into the Scandinavian and the Germanic, the latter including Germany and Switzerland, and the Dutch, the Flemings of Belgium, and the descendants of the Angles, Saxons, and Jutes.

TEXARKANA, two cities forming a single community situated on the boundary between Arkansas and Texas, 187 miles S.E. of Dallas, Tex., and 147 miles S.W. of Little Rock, Ark. Texarkana, Ark., is the county seat of Miller Co., and Texarkana, Tex., is in Bowie Co. The community is served by five railroads, and maintains a municipal airport. Texarkana is the trading center and shipping point of a wide area in both States, and an important lumbering and manufacturing center. Among the industrial establishments there are railroad repair shops and yards, lumber mills, planing mills, creosoting plants, cottonseed-oil mills, cotton gins and compresses, and factories producing structural lumber, caskets, furniture, vegetable crates, railroad tank cars, concrete blocks, clay and tile products, toys, paint, mattresses, cotton textiles, processed foods, and pickles

Texas State Capitol in Austin

Texarkana is the site of Texarkana Junior College, established in 1927, and of four annual State fairs. Most notable of the various parks in Texarkana is Spring Lake Park, covering more than 170 acres. The Texas-Arkansas boundary passes through the U.S. Courthouse and Post Office Building and the Union Railroad Station. The two cities have separate municipal governments, although in all other respects they are operated as one city. Texarkana was settled in 1874. Pop. (1950) of Texarkana, Ark., 15,875, and of Texarkana, Tex., 24,753.

TEXAS, one of the West South Central States of the United States, bounded on the N. by New Mexico, Oklahoma, and Arkansas, on the E. by Oklahoma, Arkansas, Louisiana, and the Gulf of Mexico, on the S. by the Gulf and Mexico, and on the W. by Mexico and New Mexico. Texas ranks as the 1st State in the Union in area, 6th in order of population (1950), and the 28th in order of admission to the Union, having entered on Dec. 29, 1845. The capital is Austin. In descending order of population (1950), the principal cities of the State are Houston, Dallas, San Antonio, Fort Worth, Austin, El Paso, Corpus Christi, Beaumont, Waco, Amarillo (qq.v.), and Lubbock. The area of Texas comprises about one twelfth of the total area of the United States and the State is longer and wider at its extreme points than any other State. The maximum length of the State is about 800 m., and the maximum width is about 770 m. The distance from El Paso, which is situated in the westernmost part of Texas, to Beaumont, which is located near Louisiana and the Gulf of Mexico, is greater than the distance between New York and Chicago. Although the general coastline of Texas measures only 367 m., the over-all coastline, measured around bays, inlets, and estuaries reached by tidal water, is 2982 m. Area of Texas, 267,339 sq.m., including 3695 sq.m. of inland water surface. Population (1950) 7,711,194.

Texas possesses an irregular triangular shape with the apex pointed s.; a rectangular, handlelike projection called the "Panhandle" extends northward. In general, the surface rises gradually from E. to W. in a succession of broad and more or less terraced slopes running parallel with the Gulf coast. A number of well-marked topographical regions may be distinguished. The first is the coastal plain, a continuation of the same formation in the other Gulf States (see LOUISIANA; MISSISSIPPI); it rises gradually from sea level to an altitude of 500 ft. about 150 m. inland, and it is level in its lower portion and somewhat hilly near its inner border. The coast itself is lined almost throughout its length by lagoons cut off from the sea by long, narrow sand islands. The northern lagoons generally extend some distance inland in large, irregular bays and estuaries, lined partly by low, marshy shores, and partly by high bluffs. The principal bays are those of Galveston, Matagordo, San Antonio, and Corpus Christi. The longest island, Padre, is at the s.e. extremity of Texas, and extends for more than 100 m. from the mouth of the Rio Grande to Corpus Christi Bay. Padre Island encloses the largest lagoon along the Texas Gulf coast, the Lagoon de la Madre.

The western portion of the coastal plain is a belt of rolling country known as the Black Prairie, which is about 100 m. wide in the n. and s., but extremely narrow in the middle. It is succeeded on the n.w. by a very broad belt of country, the North Central Plains, called by geologists the central denuded region. It rises from a height of 600 ft. in the e. to over 2000 ft. in the w., and is a rugged and much eroded, though not mountainous,

region, possessing ridges, prairie valleys, isolated tablelands, and irregular depressions. The North Central Plains are bounded on the w. and s.w. by the Plateau region, a continuation of the continental Great Plains. South of the Panhandle, the Plateau region forms a large, flat-topped tableland, the Llano Estacado, which, from an elevation of 4000 ft., falls on the e. into the North Central Plains in a high, steep, and ragged escarpment cut back by several large river valleys. On the s.e. the Great Plains run out into a lower plateau of different formations known as the Grand Prairie, which sweeps around the southern end of the central denuded plateau and runs northward between the latter region and the Black Prairie, where its elevation decreases. The southern portion of the Great Plains in Texas is known as Edwards Plateau. The Plateau region of the Great Plains extends southward to the Rio

TEXAS
RESOURCES AND PRODUCTS
Scale of Miles
0   25 50   100   150
Copyright by C.S. HAMMOND & Co., N.Y.

Dallas Chamber of Commerce

Above: Skyline view of downtown Dallas, Texas. Three tallest of buildings seen are, from left to right, Medical Arts Hospital, Mercantile National Bank Building, and Magnolia Building. Right: The Alamo, famous historical landmark in San Antonio, Texas.

Grande Valley, and is bounded on the s.e. by the Balcones Escarpment.

The last topographical region, the portion of the State lying in the s.w. and called the Trans-Pecos province, is a mountainous country containing a number of high, isolated, and barren ridges alternating with broad and arid plains. The principal divisions of this region are the Stockton and Diablo plateaus, and a number of isolated, block mountain ranges including the Guadalupe and the Davis mountains. The highest point in the State is Guadalupe Peak (8751 ft. above sea level), situated in Culberson Co., just s. of New Mexico. The lowest point is at sea level along the Gulf of Mexico. The average elevation of Texas is 1700 ft. above sea level.

The principal rivers are the Rio Grande, Red River, and the Canadian, Pecos, Brazos, Sabine, Trinity, Colorado (qq.v.), San Antonio, Neches, Guadalupe, and Nueces. Almost all the rivers flow southeastward. With the exception of the Canadian R. in the n., and the Rio Grande and Pecos in the s., which rise in the Rocky Mountains, all the larger rivers rise on the e. edge of the Great Plains, the Llano Estacado, and the Grand Prairie. The extreme northern portion of Texas is part of the Mississippi Basin. The Canadian

R. flows eastward across the Panhandle to join the Arkansas R., while the Red R., which rises on the escarpment of the Llano Estacado, forms a portion of the State's northern boundary as it flows e. and then s.e. to the Mississippi R. The independent rivers flow directly to the Gulf of Mexico, and all, except the Brazos and the Rio Grande, empty through estuaries into the coast lagoons. The Sabine R. flows s.e. to the

Louisiana boundary, and then s., forming the border, to the Gulf. The Rio Grande, flowing southeastward, separates Texas from Mexico. Several of the rivers are navigable for considerable distances at high water, but their mouths are generally obstructed by bars.

Texas reaches within two and a half degrees of the tropical zone, but the great range in latitude, and to some extent in altitude, produces a considerable range in climatic conditions. Although warm, the climate is drier than that of the other Gulf States. The mean annual temperature in the Panhandle is 55°F., and that in the southernmost part of Texas is 72°F. On the coast the temperature seldom falls below the freezing point, while in the N. and N.W. it may fall several degrees below zero. In the winter the State is subject to severe winds, known as northers, which often lower the temperature as much as 50 degrees in a few hours. In the fall, the Gulf coast portion of the State is subject to tropical hurricanes. Rainfall is abundant in the s.e., but the amount decreases toward the w. Galveston receives an average of 46 inches a year and El Paso receives an average of 9 inches a year. There is little or no snowfall along the lower Rio Grande and the coast, but parts of the Panhandle receive as much as 19 inches a year. The average snowfall for the State as a whole is 5 inches a year.

The fauna of Texas includes deer, coyotes, prairie dogs, jack rabbits, bears, mountain lions, raccoons, skunks, opossums, muskrats, foxes, minks, game birds, alligators, snakes, and toads. Among the trees in the State are the pine, ash, magnolia, oak, gum, hickory, and cypress. Well over 10,000,000 acres of forest land are in Texas, and there are numerous State parks and the Big Bend National Park (q.v.).

Texas is the ranking State of the U.S. in the production of minerals; it is first in petroleum, helium, natural gas, and sulfur. In a recent year Texas produced more than 829,280,000 barrels of petroleum (about 42% of the total production in the U.S.), 3,519,-173,000,000 cu.ft. of natural gas, 3,678,000 tons of sulfur (about 76% of the total U.S. production), and over 55,000,000 cu.ft. of helium (Texas is the only source of the gas in the U.S.). Other mineral products of the State include natural gasoline, liquefied petroleum gases, salt, lignite, gypsum, asphalt, sandstone, granite, mercury, potash, limestone, coal, silver, copper, lead, graphite, zinc, gold, manganese, and marble.

Although less than 20% of the total area of Texas is under cultivation, the State ranks second in the U.S. (after California) in value of its crops. Texas leads the nation in the production of cotton, pecans, and grain sorghum. In a recent year about 4,074,000 bales of cotton, 33,000,000 pounds of pecans, and 42,143,000 bushels of grain sorghum were produced. Approximately 120 crops are cultivated; cotton, which represents nearly 50% of the total value of crops produced, is the most important. Other crops include winter wheat, onions, corn, rice, oats, potatoes, sweet potatoes, peanuts, oranges, peaches, grapefruit, vegetables, barley, rye, apples, cantaloupes, figs, dates, blackberries, and strawberries. In a recent year there were about 331,500 farms, covering more than 145,389,000 acres and valued at (land and buildings) approximately $6,718,000,000; the cash income from crops exceeded $1,267,000,-000, and the cash income from the sale of livestock was approximately $879,700,000. Texas leads all States in cattle, which recently numbered over 8,940,000 (including 1,053,000 milch cows). In addition, there were about 6,176,000 sheep, 96,000 mules, 549,000 turkeys, 22,992,000 chickens, 2,099,000 goats, 321,000 horses, and 1,645,000 hogs. Texas also leads the nation in wool and mohair production. In a recent year the wool clip from 6,555,000 sheep totaled about 51,-569,000 pounds, and the mohair clip from 2,675,000 goats was approximately 13,900,-000 pounds.

Texas is the foremost manufacturing State of the Southwest. In a recent year over 7100 manufacturing establishments employed almost 329,000 persons; value added by manufacture totaled more than $2,268,000,000. Only seven States possess more manufacturing plants than Texas. The State's manufacturing industries are almost completely based upon the local agricultural and mining industries. Petroleum refining accounts for approximately 40% of the total value of the manufacturing output. Slaughtering and meat packing; the manufacture of cottonseed oil, cake, and meal; flour and grist milling; and the manufacture of foundry and machine-shop products, leather goods, and lumber and wood products are other important industries. Fishing is also important; shrimp, oysters, and red snappers are caught.

Transportation includes more than 15,000 m. of main-track railway and approximately 47,000 m. of State highways, in addition to Federal and county highways and roads. Over

Tex. Highway Dept.; Stand. Oil

SCENES IN TEXAS. *Above: Lonely stretch of highway crossing a vast plain. Right: Highway at a small town. Below: View from the shore of Galveston Bay.*

640 airports are in the State, of which more than 165 are commercial, more than 150 municipal, and 100 equipped for night flying. Eleven commercial air lines operate in the State.

Attendance at the elementary and secondary schools of Texas is free and compulsory during 100 days of the school year for all students between the ages of seven and sixteen. In a recent year more than 2800 public elementary and secondary schools were attended by more than 1,307,000 students and were staffed by more than 49,000 teachers. Segregation of white and Negro children is practiced. There are 95 institutions of higher learning, of which 21 are maintained by the State. The University of Texas (see TEXAS, UNIVERSITY OF) at Austin is the largest of the State-supported schools. Other institutions of higher learning include Baylor University at Waco, Texas Christian University at Fort Worth, Southern Methodist University at Dallas, Rice Institute at Houston, Hardin-Simmons University at Abilene, Texas Technological College at Lubbock, Texas Agricultural and Mechanical College at College Station, Howard Payne College at Brownwood, Southwestern University at Georgetown, Incarnate Word College at San Antonio, Trinity University at San Antonio, and Texas Wesleyan at Fort Worth.

Texas is governed according to the terms of the constitution of 1876, as amended. Executive authority is vested in a governor, lieutenant governor, comptroller of public accounts, treasurer, superintendent of public education, attorney general, and commissioner of agriculture, all of whom are elected for two-year terms; three railroad commissioners, who are elected for six-year terms; and a secretary of state, who is appointed by the governor. Legislative authority is vested in a senate consisting of 31 members, of whom half are elected for four-year terms every two years, and a house of representatives consisting of 150 members, all elected for two-year terms. Judicial authority is vested in a supreme court, 11 civil appellate courts, and a court of criminal appeals, all consisting of 3 justices apiece elected for six-year terms; more than 100 district courts; county courts; and justices of the peace. Electors are all U.S. citizens who have reached the age of twenty-one, resided in the State at least one year, the county at least six months, and have paid a poll tax prior to Feb 1 of the year in which they wish to vote. Texas is divided into 254 counties, and is represented in the Congress of the U.S. by 2 senators and 22 representatives.

History. The first European to penetrate the region which is now Texas was Cabeza de Vaca (see CABEZA DE VACA, ÁLVAR NÚÑEZ) in 1528. In 1540 Francisco Vásquez de Coronado (q.v.) explored the region. During the following century numerous other Spanish expeditions crossed the territory and in 1682 the first settlement in Texas was founded at Isleta, near El Paso. In 1685 Robert Cavelier, Sieur de La Salle, established a French colony at Matagorda Bay. Although the French colony soon ended in failure, the settlement being abandoned, the Spanish took steps to strengthen their claim to Texas against possible future encroachments by the neighboring French in Louisiana. From 1690, the Spanish established numerous missions, towns, and military posts in Texas. The region, which the Spanish had named after the Texas Indians, an intertribal confederacy of Caddo Indians, underwent its first American invasion in 1799 when a small party of Americans, led by a trader named Philip Nolan, penetrated the region ostensibly to capture wild horses. Two years later, on a second expedition, the adventurers were attacked by the Spanish, who killed some and imprisoned the survivors.

After the purchase of Louisiana (see LOUISIANA PURCHASE) in 1803, the people of the U.S., particularly the inhabitants of the Southwest, considered Texas a part of the destined dominion of the Republic and never lost an opportunity to strike at the Spanish power. An American invasion occurred in 1812 when Augustus Magee, a former U.S. Army officer, and Bernardo Gutiérrez, a Mexican patriot who was fighting for the independence of Mexico from Spain, led an expedition into Texas, captured San Antonio, and defeated several Spanish-Mexican forces before they themselves met defeat (see MEXICO: *History*). In 1819 and 1821 James Long, a Mississippian, led expeditions into Texas for the purpose of making the region an independent state, but he also met with defeat. In the latter year Moses Austin, an American, secured from the Spanish government the right to establish a colony in Texas. He died soon after, but his son Stephen (see AUSTIN, STEPHEN FULLER) took up his work. In this period Mexico succeeded in securing its independence from Spain, and in 1823 Austin concluded a new agreement confirming his father's grant. The new Mexican government then authorized empresarios, or agents, to

Herding cattle on a grazing range in Texas

attract American settlers to Texas. Austin was the most successful of the empresarios, and the system was responsible for the rapid growth of the American colonies in Texas. In a few years American grants covered the region between the Sabine and Nueces rivers.

In 1826 the Fredonian Rebellion occurred; a band of Americans, led by Hayden Edwards, proclaimed the eastern part of the territory the independent Republic of Fredonia. A skirmish in which one man was killed and one wounded ended the uprising. In 1830 the Mexican government passed a decree severely limiting American immigration to Texas. Other decrees, many of which were designed to curtail the expansion of the American settlers, were passed by the government, and in 1835 war broke out between the American settlers and the Mexican government. The first battle of the Texas Revolution, fought at Gonzales on Oct. 2, 1835, was won by the Texans. San Antonio was captured by the Texans in the same year, a provisional government was set up, and Sam Houston (q.v.) was named commander in chief of the Texan armies. Many Americans from the States hastened to the assistance of the Texans. In February-March of 1836 occurred the heroic defense of the

Alamo (q.v.) by about 180 Americans commanded by Col. William B. Travis and Col. David Crockett. The massacre of Goliad, in which all the Texans captured in a previous battle by the Mexicans were ordered slain by Antonio López de Santa Anna (q.v.), president and commander of the Mexicans, also occurred in March. On March 2, 1836, the Texans issued a declaration of independence. On April 21, at San Jacinto (see SAN JACINTO, BATTLE OF), the Texan army under Houston inflicted a disastrous defeat upon the numerically superior Mexican army, and captured its commander, Santa Anna. The victory insured the independence of Texas. In September, 1836, Sam Houston was elected president of the Republic of Texas.

Indian wars, raids by Mexican forces, and financial difficulties beset the young republic, which had been quickly recognized by the United States, France, Great Britain, Holland, and Belgium. The question of the annexation of Texas to the Union became a national issue and James Knox Polk (q.v.) was elected President of the U.S. on a platform favoring the admission of Texas, but before he took office Congress passed a joint resolution offering Statehood to the republic. This offer was quickly accepted and on Dec. 29, 1845,

Texas was admitted to the Union. The Mexican War (q.v.), originating in a dispute over the boundaries of Texas, followed, and the first fighting took place near the Rio Grande at Palo Alto on May 8, 1846. In 1848, by the Treaty of Guadalupe Hidalgo, ending the war, the Rio Grande was recognized by Mexico as the southern boundary of Texas. At this time, Texas included, in addition to its present area, present-day Colorado, the eastern half of New Mexico, s.w. Kansas, and portions of Wyoming and Oklahoma. Texas and the U.S. agreed to the Compromise of 1850, in which for the payment to Texas of $10,000,000 the U.S. received all the territory claimed by Texas except that area which now comprises the State (see COMPROMISE MEASURES OF 1850).

Texas grew rapidly after its entrance into the Union. As a Southern, slave-holding State, it seceded from the Union on Feb. 1, 1861. Little fighting occurred in Texas during the Civil War. Galveston was occupied by Federal forces for a short time, and the last battle of the war, which took place one month after General Robert E. Lee's surrender at Appomattox on April 9, 1865, was fought on the lower Rio Grande on Texas soil. The Reconstruction (q.v.) period proved difficult for Texas, but the State recovered rapidly as it expanded its agricultural and manufacturing industries. The discovery of the first great oil field in the State at the beginning of the 20th century greatly spurred the industrialization process.

The events attending the Civil War and the Reconstruction period engendered powerful anti-Republican traditions in Texas, and the voters of the State have almost invariably voted for Democratic Party candidates in State and national elections since its readmission to the Union. Between 1876 and 1952 Texans have cast a majority or plurality of their ballots for the Democratic candidate in every Presidential election year except 1928 and 1952. In the election of 1928 Herbert Hoover, the Republican candidate, carried the State over Alfred E. Smith, the Democratic candidate by 367,036 votes to 341,032 votes. In 1952 the Republican candidate Dwight D. Eisenhower received 1,102,878 votes; the Democratic candidate Adlai E. Stevenson received 970,128 votes.

TEXAS AGRICULTURAL AND MECHANICAL COLLEGE, a State-controlled land-grant college for men, located at College Station, Brazos Co., Tex., and founded in 1871. Courses in agriculture, engineering, and architecture are offered leading to bachelors' and doctors' degrees. A four-year course in veterinary medicine leads to the degree of D.V.M. The United States Department of Agriculture operates a number of experiment stations and an extensive branch of its forestry service in connection with the curricula of the college. Since 1947–48 the department of agriculture has included a five-year course in food technology. The department of aeronautical engineering trains pilots for examinations granting private or commercial licenses and flight instructor ratings. In 1953 the enrollment at the College was 5495, including 5277 full-time students, and the faculty numbered 552.

TEXAS CHRISTIAN UNIVERSITY, a coeducational institution of higher education, controlled by the Disciples of Christ Church in Texas, and located at Fort Worth, Tex. It was chartered as a private school in 1873 under the name of the Add Ran Christian University, and became the property of the Christian Church of Texas in 1890; the present name was adopted in 1902. Courses are offered in the liberal and fine arts, education, business, music, oratory, and law, leading to bachelors' and masters' degrees. A School of the Bible confers the degree of bachelor of divinity. Special programs of study in engineering, home economics, journalism, and nursing are included in the curricula. In 1953 the enrollment was 5870, including 3565 full-time students, and the faculty numbered 237.

TEXAS CITY, a city of Galveston Co., Tex., situated on Galveston Bay, opposite the city of Galveston and about 40 miles s.s.e. of Houston. Transportation facilities include two railroads. Texas City is a leading seaport, ranking 11th in the U.S. in tonnage of cargo handled. It has a fine, deep-water harbor, and is an important shipping point for cotton, oil, and sulfur. In a recent year, over 8,000,000 tons of cargo passed through the port. Among the industrial establishments in the city are oil refineries, chemical plants, the largest tin smelter and processing plant in the world, and factories manufacturing cotton bagging. On April 16, 1947, an explosion occurred in the harbor aboard a French cargo ship carrying explosive chemicals; the explosion caused fires in adjacent chemical plants and oil refineries in the city. Next day occurred a similar explosion on an American freighter carrying similar cargo. As the result of both disasters, considered the worst in U.S. shipping, 592 persons were killed and missing in Texas City and 800 injured. Extensive areas of the city were destroyed by fire, the property damage being estimated at $50 million, but rebuilding commenced almost immediately. Pop. (1950) 16,620.

TEXAS FEVER, also known as BOVINE PIROPLASMOSIS, BABESIASIS, SPLENETIC FEVER, TICK FEVER, SOUTHERN CATTLE FEVER, HEMOGLOBINURIA, REDWATER, DRY MURRAIN, BLACKWATER, or SPANISH FEVER, a febrile infectious disease of cattle, usually observed in epizootic extension in the course of which hemoglobin appears in the urine as a result of the breaking down of red blood corpuscles. It is caused by (*Piroplasma*) *Babesia bigemina* in the red blood corpuscles. This protozoan is transmitted to uninfected cattle by the progeny of ticks, particularly cattle ticks of the genus *Margaropus* or *Boöphilus*, that have developed on infected animals. The disease is characterized by fever, greatly enlarged spleen, destruction of the red blood corpuscles, escape of the coloring matter of the blood through the kidneys, giving the urine a deep-red color, yellowness of the mucous membranes and fat, rapid loss of strength, and fatal results in a large proportion of cases.

TEXAS TECHNOLOGICAL COLLEGE, a coeducational, State-controlled institution of higher education, located at Lubbock, Tex., and opened in 1925. Courses are offered in agriculture, home economics, and engineering (including petroleum and textile engineering) leading to bachelors' and masters' degrees. In 1953 the enrollment was 4550, including 3902 full-time students, and the faculty numbered 318.

TEXAS, UNIVERSITY OF, a coeducational, State-controlled institution of higher education, with its main campus at Austin, Tex., and schools of medicine, pharmacy, and nursing at Galveston, of dentistry at Houston, and the College of Mines and Metallurgy at El Paso, Tex. The University was organized in 1881 with a grant of over 2,000,000 acres of land from the State. This land subsequently proved to be enormously rich in oil, gas, and minerals; accumulated revenue from its holdings provided the University with the unusually large endowment of nearly $181 million in 1953. The University departments of arts and sciences, law, engineering, education, and a bureau of economic geology and technology are located at Austin. Courses are offered in all schools leading to undergraduate and graduate degrees. The department of education, as a part of its teacher-training program, conducts extensive experimental work in the study of child development, speech, psychology, counseling, and guidance. In 1953 the enrollment was 12,144, including both full-time and part-time students; the faculty numbered 656; and the library contained 973,259 volumes.

TEXEL, an island belonging to the province of North Holland, at the entrance to the Zuider Zee. It is separated from the mainland by a narrow strait, called the Marsdiep, and it contains about 35,000 acres of arable and pasture lands. The Marsdiep channel or part of it is often called the Texel, and in it many important naval battles have been fought: Blake defeated Van Tromp and De Ruyter in 1653; Prince Rupert fought De Ruyter in 1673; and Duncan blockaded the Texel in 1797.

TEXTILE PRINTING. Block printing of textiles in one form or another can be traced back among the Egyptians, Assyrians, and Chinese to remote ages, and it was closely associated with other similar processes that produce similar results, such as painting, stenciling, and dyeing. In printing fabrics the color is stamped on from an engraved block or roller. Pliny says that the Egyptians figured fabrics by applying several mordants with different powers of resistance, presumably by stamping or stenciling, in such a way that one dipping in the dye pot produced a pattern in several colors. During the twelfth, thirteenth, and fourteenth centuries, in Germany, the place of the rich Saracenic, Byzantine, and Italian damasks and brocades was largely taken by inexpensive block-printed imitations. There survive examples of Rhenish thin-printed silks with simplified patterns in gold and silver; and coarse linens outlined in dark browns and blacks. In the seventeenth century the industry revived and Augsburg was famous for its printed linens, supplying Alsace and Switzerland with many trained workmen. In 1676 textile printing was introduced into England by a French refugee who opened an establishment on the Thames near Richmond. In the last half of the eighteenth century the art was brought to a high point of perfection in France, especially at Jouy, near Versailles, where Oberkampf produced printed linens.

At the end of the eighteenth century metal rollers took the place of wooden blocks for the production of simple repeat patterns inexpensively, and the modern machine pe-

Metropolitan Museum of Art

TEXTILE PRINTING. *Top, left: Print on French linen of the 18th century. Top, right: Design on German linen of the 19th century. Bottom: English printed cotton, about 1800.*

riod had begun. The invention of rollers is attributed in France to Oberkampf and in Great Britain to Bell. In the last quarter of the nineteenth century William Morris raised the standard of design greatly by his introduction of ingenious and richly colored flower and bird patterns, going back for his inspiration to Persian and Indian flat ornament.

Stenciling is nearer painting than printing, the colors being applied with a brush through sheets of thick paper or thin metal from which the pattern has been completely cut out with a sharp knife, the uncut portions covering the parts of the surface that are to be left uncolored. A peculiarity of stenciled patterns is the ties that have to be left to keep detached or nearly detached portions of the background connected with the rest of the stencil. These ties spoil the design when badly placed, but when skillfully used add distinctive charm. The Japanese are especially skillful in the use of stencils, often employing them in connection with painting and with block printing.

The printing of woolen and silk cloths is similar to that of cotton, except that the woolen cloth requires more preparation before printing and the silk cloth less; and that silks are particularly adapted to discharge and reserve effects. See DYEING.

TEXTUAL CRITICISM, the criticism of existing texts of literary works with a view to the detection of variations from the original manuscript. Such criticism may be concerned with any literary production which is no longer under the control of the author, but is most usually applied to the manuscripts of the Old and New Testaments and of the works of ancient Greek and Latin authors, which were changed by the inaccurate work of those who copied them by hand before the invention of printing; and to the texts of such later writers as William Shakespeare, whose works were often changed by the printers who set them in type. Textual criticism involves two distinct processes: *recension*, or the collection and examination of the most trustworthy documentary evidence as a basis for the establishment of the correct text; and *emendation*, or the attempt to eliminate the errors which even the most accurate manuscripts contain, by the deliberate overruling of the documentary evidence and the substitution, by conjecture, of material which is in accord with both transcriptional and intrinsic probability. The results of the latter process are not considered thoroughly reliable unless they are confirmed, as sometimes happens, by the subsequent discovery of new evidence.

The criticism, for example, of the texts of Greek and Latin authors is based primarily upon a careful study and comparison of all existing manuscripts. The secondary consideration is subsidiary evidence, known as *testimonia*, which may be in the form of ancient or medieval references to, or quotations and reminiscences of, the passage under consideration; scholia (see SCHOLIASTS); or translations into another language, such as the Latin and Arabic renderings of certain works of Aristotle. Most classical manuscripts, excluding documents on papyri discovered during the past hundred years (see PAPYRI, DISCOVERIES OF), date from the 9th to the 15th century; a few are as early as the 4th century, and some, generally of little value, as late as the 15th and 16th centuries. No existing manuscript is free from errors. The scribes often did their work mechanically and ignorantly, and the blunders thus made were perpetuated by each succeeding copyist. Such errors may be corrected by comparison with a manuscript which does not contain the identical blunders, but if all existing manuscripts are descended from the same incorrect original, or archetype, the same errors probably appear in all. In such an event, the only resort is to conjectural emendation. If a number of manuscripts have for the same passage different readings, all of which are intelligible, recension is used to determine which of the several readings is the one intended by the author.

The textual critic must establish the interrelationship of the various texts by systematized comparisons. Generally, identity of reading implies identity of source. Although an early text is presumed to be more valuable, having been less exposed to repeated corruptions, it may be filled with errors, whereas a later manuscript may be a fairly accurate copy of a more reliable text, now lost. A majority of manuscripts need not give the more correct reading; three extant copies of a corrupt text, now lost, have less value in textual criticism than a single good manuscript. In the critical examination of the evidence, all copies of a manuscript still extant may be disregarded, provided that none has drawn material from another source which is no longer in existence.

Certain types of errors were commonly made by scribes in the copying of manuscripts, and may be divided into the following classes: (1) errors of *omission,* known as haplography, involving the leaving out of one of two identical letters, syllables, or words, or the omission of entire clauses or sentences in prose or lines in poetry, such as often occurred when two sentences or lines ended with the same word; (2) errors of *insertion,* known as dittography, involving the repeating of a letter, syllable, or word, or the addition to the text of an explanatory word, gloss, or marginal note; (3) errors of *substitution,* such as the substitution of an explanatory gloss for the word it defined, or of a classical form for an archaic form which the scribe failed to understand; (4) errors of *transposition,* such as the misplacing of letters, syllables, words, or lines, usually ascribed to the inaccurate insertion of material previously omitted by a copyist; (5) errors of *emendation,* occurring chiefly in manuscripts dating from the 9th century or later and especially common in manuscripts written by Renaissance scholars, arising from the wrong division of words, or from attempts to correct mistakes already made of obscure words and phrases which were deemed corrupt; and (6) errors due to the *confusion of letters and contractions,* occurring seldom in capital and uncial writing (see PALEOGRAPHY), but often in minuscule manuscripts, especially with the increasing use of contractions and arbitrary signs.

Frequently the textual critic, in following the process of emendation, finds manuscripts which contain meaningless or metrically impossible passages, or phraseology in violent contradiction to or deviation from an author's normal usage. In all such instances the passage is pronounced corrupt, in spite of the external evidence in its favor, and emendation is resorted to as a means of restoring the original reading of the text. All such conjectural emendation must be based on expert knowledge of paleography and the principles of textual criticism, and of the style and subject matter of the author and the age in which he lived. Conjectural emendation has been termed "at once the highest and the most difficult part of the textual critic's task".

TEYTE, MAGGIE (1890–   ), English lyric soprano, born in Wolverhampton. She made her debut at Monte Carlo in 1908 as Zerlina in Mozart's *Don Giovanni.* For the next two years she was a member of the Opéra Comique, where Beecham heard her and engaged her for his first operatic season in London (1910). On coming to the United States, she became a member of the Chicago Opera Company (1910–15) and made extensive concert tours of the States. Her favorite roles were Mimi in *La Bohème* and Mélisande in *Pelléas et Mélisande.*

THACKERAY, WILLIAM MAKEPEACE (1811–63), one of the greatest of English novelists, born in Calcutta, India. In 1829 Thackeray was entered at Trinity College, Cambridge. He left the university after two years without taking his degree.

On leaving Cambridge Thackeray traveled for two years. From the first he had a passion for drawing and literary composition, his fancy in both running to caricature. Early in 1833 he became a contributor to the *National Standard and Weekly Journal of Literature, Science, Music, Theatricals, and the Fine Arts,* a weekly journal. With the nineteenth number Thackeray took the editorship, and subsequently became the proprietor. The paper came to an end after a year's existence. However, art, not literature, was Thackeray's ambition and he went to Paris to study painting. After his return to London he made the famous application to illustrate *Pickwick.* By 1837 financial reverses made him become a literary hack. He contributed regularly in the *Times,* and also the *New Monthly, Fraser's Magazine,* and in Cruikshank's *Comic Almanacks.* In 1840 his wife, after the birth of the third daughter, became affected in mind, and never recovered, though she lived till 1894. This misfortune broke up the home, and for a time caused much misery to Thackeray. But his genius was by this time asserting itself.

In 1840 appeared his first book, *The Paris Sketchbook,* a series of reprints, followed in 1841 by the *Comic Tales and Sketches,* which contained the *Yellowplush Papers* from *Fraser, Major Gahagan* from the *New Monthly,* and the *Bedford Row Conspiracy.* In the same year the *Hoggarty Diamond* and the *Shabby Genteel Story* appeared in *Fraser,* followed by *Barry Lyndon* and *Men's Wives* in the same magazine. In 1843 and 1846 appeared respectively the *Irish Sketchbook* and *Cornhill to Cairo,* and in 1842 he joined the staff of *Punch.* The publication of *Vanity Fair* began, in monthly numbers, early in 1847 and by the time it was finished it had made the author's reputation.

The last number of *Vanity Fair* appeared in July, 1848. It was followed in November of the same year by the first installment of *Pendennis. Pendennis* was followed by *Henry Esmond*, published in three volumes in 1852. Thackeray then sailed for America with his lectures on the humorists. On his return in 1853 *The Newcomes* began to appear; and on its conclusion in 1855, after the publication of *The Rose and the Ring*, which was begun in Rome, Thackeray again made a journey to America with his lectures on the "Four Georges". In 1857 the *Virginians* came out.

On January 1, 1860, the *Cornhill Magazine* made its appearance, with Thackeray as editor. To the *Cornhill* he contributed *Lover the Widower* and *Philip*. But if the *Cornhill* did not bring out Thackeray's best work as a novelist, it furnished the occasion for the *Roundabout Papers*. In 1862 he gave up the editorship of the *Cornhill*, not being equal to the task of refusing manuscripts, but he continued to work for the magazine. He now began to write *Denis Duval*. But his health failed. No immediate danger was feared, but he was found dead in his bed on the day before Christmas, 1863.

THADDÆUS, one of the twelve Apostles in the list given in Mark 3:16–19 and Matthew 10:2–4. In the corresponding lists in Luke 6:14–16 and Acts 1:14 he is named Judas [son] of James, doubtless to distinguish him from Judas Iscariot. As so named he may be the Judas referred to in John 14:22. Some inferior manuscripts in the lists of Mark and Matthew substitute Lebbæus for Thaddæus, a reading possibly due to some scribe who, ignorant of the identity of Levi with Matthew, introduced the former into the apostolic list under this name. The ecclesiastical historian Eusebius of Cæsarea makes Thaddæus one of the Seventy, and refers to him as sent by Thomas the apostle to Abgar, King of Edessa, in fulfillment of a promise of Christ to him to heal him of an incurable disease and to evangelize his household. Eusebius claims to have taken this story direct from Syrian sources. In the Greek *Acts of Thaddæus* the apostle is identified with Lebbæus, and referred to as evangelizing Syrians and Armenians. The Syrian tradition embodied in the *Doctrine of Addai* makes Addai, one of the Seventy, the apostle of the Syrian church.

THAI or **TAI,** a group of peoples of Farther India, including the Thos and Muongs in the northeast (Tongking and China), the Shans in the northwest (Burma, Siam, China), the Laotians in the south (the Laos

William Makepeace Thackeray

States, French Siam), and the Siamese in the southwest (Siam). The term "Thai" is applied by certain writers to the Siamese in particular, but their proper appellation is rather Little Thai, their ancestors, the Shans, being called the Great Thai. The Thai peoples speak languages belonging to the same linguistic stock. The Siamese present the Thai type, much changed by intermixture with Khmers, Hindus, Kuis, Malays, and other stocks. They are of medium stature and brachycephalic, while the Laotians are shorter and less broadheaded. The primitive Thai type is best seen in some Shan tribes.

THAILAND or **SIAM,** kingdom of s. Asia, situated in Indochina (q.v.) and officially known (1939–45, 1949–   ) as Thailand. Except for its s. extremity, a long narrow portion of the Malay Penninsula (q.v.), Thailand lies entirely within Indochina proper, being bounded by Burma on the N. and w. and by the Associated States of Indochina on the N. and E. The Indochinese region is bounded on the s. by the Gulf of Siam, an arm of the South China Sea, which also adjoins the E. coast of the peninsular region. On the s. the peninsular region is bounded by the Federation of Malaya. The w. coast of peninsular region adjoins the Bay of Bengal, an arm of the Indian Ocean. Including about 45,000 sq.m. on the Malay Peninsula, the area of Thailand is 200,148 sq.m. The capital, largest city, and chief seaport of the kingdom is Bangkok (q.v.). Other important cities are Ayuthia, Chiengmai (qq.v.), Khonkaen, and Chieng Rai. For administrative purposes, the kingdom is divided into seventy provinces, locally known as *changwads*. The population (1956 est.) is 20,686,000.

The physiography of Thailand is highly diversified, but the mountain systems are the predominant feature of the terrain. A series of parallel ranges, with a N. and S. trend, occupy the N. and W. portions of the country. Extreme elevations occur in the westernmost ranges, which extend along the Burmese frontier and project into the Malay Peninsula. Among the outstanding summits of these uplifts are Doi Intanon (8454 ft.), Kao Prawa (5862 ft.), and Mogodok (5495 ft.). Outstanding peaks in the peninsular area are Kao Luang (5813 ft.) and Kao Prong (4478 ft.). Another mountain system projects, in a N. and S. direction, through central Thailand. At its S. extremity, the system assumes an eastward trend and extends to the E. frontier. Doi Pia Fai (4199 ft.) is the highest peak. The region to the N. and E. of this system consists largely of a low, barren plateau. Between the central and western uplifts is a vast alluvial plain. This plain, which is traversed by the Menam R. (q.v.), the chief stream of Thailand, is the richest agrarian and most densely populated section of the kingdom.

Thailand has a tropical climate, characterized by sharply defined local and seasonal variations. From May to October the country is under the influence of the S.W. monsoon, a steady wind from the Bay of Bengal. Precipitation is excessive during this period, attaining a maximum of about 240 inches in the western uplifts and about 50 inches in the vicinity of Bangkok. Daytime temperatures average around 85°F. in the wet season, and humid conditions are prevalent throughout the country. In the dry season, the N.E. monsoon period extending from November to April, generally lower temperatures prevail, falling to as low as 40°F. in the N. uplands after sunset. However, temperatures over 100°F. are common in the interior during the period of the N.E. monsoon.

The flora and fauna of Thailand are typical of those of S.E. Asia. Jungles and swamps are scattered through the coastal areas. In these areas are extensive stands of tropical

Erwin Berghaus, from Black Star

Shops on a street in Bangkok, capital of Thailand

P. E. Robinson, Black Star

SCENES IN BANGKOK, THAILAND

Above: A baby toddling about near a fruit vendor's stall. Right: Thai temples bordering Temple Walk.

trees, including such species as the mangrove, rattan, ironwood, sapanwood, ebony, and rosewood. The upland areas are also heavily wooded, the most valuable species being teak, agalloch, oak, and conifers. In addition, a wide variety of tropical fruit trees and plants are indigenous to Thailand. Many species of animals inhabit the jungles and forests. Elephants, widely used as beasts of burden, are abundant. Other large quadrupeds include the rhinoceros, tiger, leopard, gaur, water buffalo, and gibbon. There are more than fifty species of snakes, including several poisonous varie-ties. Crocodiles are numerous, as are various species of fish and bird life.

Thailand has extensive natural resources. Besides the forests, which yield a large annual volume of timber, notably teak, varied mineral deposits and extensive tracts of arable lands are situated in the country. The national economy is predominantly agrarian. The chief crops, which are produced mainly in the alluvial plain, are rice and raw rubber. In a recent year the respective output of these crops was 4,500,000 tons and about 53,000 tons. Other staple crops are soy beans.

coconuts, sugar cane, tobacco, pepper, raw silk, and cotton. Livestock raising is also important, the chief herds being, according to a recent census, buffaloes, 3,900,000; bullocks, 3,100,000; horses, 65,000; and elephants, 3600. Annual teak production recently totaled about 62,000 tons. The fisheries, especially those in the Gulf of Siam, are another important source of national wealth. Rice milling and the production of lumber are the only manufacturing industries of consequence.

Thailand ranks among the foremost tin-producing countries in the world. In a recent year the output of tin ore, which was mined almost exclusively in the peninsular region, totaled 1410 tons. The country also contains valuable deposits of rubies, sapphires, wolfram, gold, silver, mercury, lead, zinc, copper, iron, coal, manganese, antimony, scheelite, molybdenum, and cement.

The Thai railway system, which totals about 2000 m. of trackage, is owned and operated by the state. Consisting of a network of lines radiating from Bangkok, the system extends as far N. as Chiengmai, southward to the frontier of the Malayan Federation, and eastward to Ubol Rajadhani. Another line extends northwestward to the Burmese frontier. The Menam R., navigable for about 50 m. from its mouth, is an important inland waterway. Highways suitable for automotive traffic total about 2700 m. Fourteen international air lines maintain regular service to and from Bangkok.

Thai, a people of the Indochinese linguistic family, comprise the overwhelming majority of the population. The chief minority groups are Chinese, who total about 3.5% of the population, Malayans, and Indians. Siamese and Chinese are the principal languages. Approximately 95% of the people of Thailand are Buddhists, and the country has more than 18,000 Buddhist temples and nearly 141,000 Buddhist priests. The most important religious minorities are Moslem and Christian.

Free elementary schools are maintained, and attendance of children is compulsory. In a recent year the local and municipal schools in the country numbered more than 11,000 and enrollment was more than 1,387,000. Many of these schools are situated in Buddhist monasteries. The foremost institution of higher learning is Chulalongkorn University, at Bangkok.

The government of Thailand, a constitutional monarchy, is based on the constitution of 1947. By the terms of this document, executive power is nominally vested in the king, who exercises his prerogatives through a state council. The latter body consists of no more than twenty-four members, fifteen of whom, including the prime minister, are selected from the parliament. The parliament is a bicameral, popularly elected organization. All men and women over twenty years of age are eligible to vote in Thailand.

History. Various tribes of the Indochinese linguistic stock began to migrate into the region now called Thailand about the middle of the 6th century A.D. The Thai, as the invaders became known, subjugated the native peoples in the course of the following centuries, penetrating to the tip of the Malay Peninsula before 1160 and as far E. as Cambodia (q.v.) before 1284. In 1350 a unified Thai kingdom was established by a ruler known posthumously as Phra Rama Thiboda. This king founded Ayuthia and made it his capital. Despite intermittent warfare with the Cambodians and Burmese, the Thai kingdom flourished during the next four centuries, conquering Cambodia and the surviving states in the N. Meanwhile, the Thais had established close commercial relations with various European and Asiatic nations, including Portugal, the Netherlands, Great Britain, and China.

The Burmese launched a full-scale attack on Thailand in 1764. In 1767, following a two-year siege, Ayuthia was captured and destroyed. Burmese overlordship in Thailand was shortly terminated through an uprising led by General Phaya Takh Sin, who proclaimed himself king. On the death (1782) of the latter the crown passed to General Phaya Chakkri, founder of the present dynasty of Thai kings. The British and Thai governments concluded a commercial treaty in 1826. In consequence of the rights and privileges obtained by this agreement, British influence was in the ascendancy in Thailand for the remainder of the 19th century.

In 1893 Thailand became embroiled in a boundary dispute with France, then the dominant power in Cochin China, Annam, and Tongking. The French dispatched warships to Bangkok and forced the Thais to yield Cambodia and all territory E. of the Mekong R. Additional Thai territory, situated W. of the Mekong R., was acquired by France in 1904 and 1907. Thailand ceded four states in the Malay Peninsula to Great Britain in 1909. In exchange, the British relinquished most of their extraterritorial rights in the rest of the kingdom. The Thai government entered World War I on the side of the Allied Powers in July, 1917. Thailand subsequently became a founding member of the League of Nations.

In June, 1932, during the reign of King Prajadhipok, a small group of Thai military and political leaders organized a successful revolt against the government, until then an absolute monarchy. The insurgents proclaimed a constitutional monarchy on June 27. Royalist opposition was finally overcome in October, 1933. In March, 1935, King Pra-

jadhipok abdicated in favor of his nephew Prince Ananda Mahidol. Thailand denounced all of its treaties with foreign nations in November, 1936. Under the provisions of new treaties negotiated in the following year, the government obtained complete autonomy over its internal and external affairs.

With Japanese encouragement and support, the Thai government made demands on France, beginning in 1940, for the return of the territory ceded in and after 1893. The dispute was settled, through Japanese mediation, in May, 1941. By the terms of the settle-

SCENES IN BANGKOK, THAILAND

Right: Thai dancers performing one of their typical, exotic dances. Below: A row of Buddhas lining a wall in Watpoh Temple.

Metcalf and Black Star

ment, Thailand received about 21,000 sq.m. of territory, including part of N. Cambodia and all of Laos W. of the Mekong R. The relations between Japan and Thailand became increasingly friendly thereafter. On December 8, 1941, a few hours after the Japanese attack on Pearl Harbor, the Thai government granted Japan the right to move troops across the country to the Malayan frontier. Thailand declared war on the United States and the United Kingdom on January 25, 1942. Although the pro-Japanese government of the country was overthrown in July, 1944, and considerable sympathy for the Allied cause developed among the Thai people, Japanese occupation of the kingdom continued for the duration of World War II.

Thailand concluded a treaty with the United Kingdom and India in January, 1946, renouncing, among other things, its claims to Malayan territory obtained during the war. Diplomatic relations with the United States were resumed in the same month. In November, 1946, Thailand reached an agreement with France providing for the return to France of the territory obtained in 1941. Thailand was admitted to the United Nations on December 15, 1946, becoming the 55th member. Meanwhile, on June 9, King Ananda Mahidol had died under mysterious circumstances. A regency was appointed to rule during the minority of his brother and successor King Rama IX (q.v.).

On November 9, 1947, a military junta led by Luang Pibul Songgram, a prime minister during the Japanese occupation, seized control of the government. A provisional constitution, largely based on the constitution of 1946, was immediately proclaimed by the junta. Except for a brief interlude early in 1948, when a group headed by Khuang Abhaiwong, leader of the Democratic Party, held power, Songgram thereafter retained control of the government. The Songgram regime, essentially a dictatorship, based its foreign policy on the maintenance of close relations with the United States and the United Kingdom. Notable domestic developments during 1949 included steadily improving economic conditions, the institution of stringent measures against the Chinese Communist Party, and the readoption of "Thailand" as the country's official name. King Rama IX assumed the throne on May 5, 1950. After the outbreak (June, 1950) of the Korean War, Thailand assigned a contingent of 4000 men to the United Nations fighting forces.

On Nov. 29, 1951, a group of army officers seized control of the government in a bloodless *coup d'état* and re-established the authoritarian constitution of 1932, with some changes. Pibul Songgram was retained as premier. In March, 1952, the king signed the revised constitution. Meanwhile a "Free Thai" movement, supported by the Chinese Communists and headed by a former premier of Thailand, had been formed in China. On Aug. 30, 1953, the Thai government reported that it had frustrated a Red plot to assassinate the Thai cabinet members and overthrow the government.

Thai representatives took part in the Geneva Conference (April, 1954) which ended the war in Indochina. In September 1954, Thailand was one of the eight nations attending the Manila conference on the defense of Southeast Asia; the country was the first to ratify the resulting Southeast Asia Collective Defense Treaty. Thailand also participated in the Asian-African Conference, a meeting of 29 Asian and African States held (April, 1955) in Bandoeng, Indonesia.

THALAMUS, in neuroanatomy, a term applied to each of two ovoid nuclei of the brain, situated on either side of the third ventricle, and serving as the principal lower centers of sensation. The function of the thalamus is co-ordination of sensations of gross perception of pain or other tactile stimuli and the reflexes triggered or conditioned by optic stimulation; it is the primary relay nucleus also for the transmission of optic stimuli to the cerebral cortex. The thalamus is considered by comparative anatomists to be the highest center of the "primitive brain", that is, the center in control of bodily actions and reactions in animals lacking distinct cerebral hemispheres. The thalamus, in addition to being the principal substation for sensation between the spinal tracts and the cerebral cortex and the center of optic reflexes, is also regarded by anatomists as the center controlling emotion; lesions in this region have been demonstrated in cases of uncontrollable emotional states, such as laughing and weeping. Endocrinologists have recently discovered that the thalamus secretes a hormone which probably effects emotional development.

THALES (about 640–546 B.C.), Greek philosopher, born in Miletus, Asia Minor. He was the founder of the Ionian school (q.v.) of philosophy, and was considered one of the Seven Wise Men (q.v.) of Greece. Thales was famed for his knowledge of astronomy, and predicted an eclipse of the sun which occurred on May 28, 585 B.C. He also, by founding the geometry of lines, established the science of abstract geometry. Thales is regarded as the first Greek to have speculated on the nature of the universe, seeking a first principle. According to him the original principle of all things is water, from which everything proceeds and into which everything is again resolved. Although Thales left no writings, and even among the ancient Greeks considerable doubt prevailed as to his exact teachings, he is given the title of father of Greek science and philosophy.

THALIA, one of the nine Muses (q.v.) of the ancient Greeks. In the assignment of specific functions to the Muses, Thalia became the muse of comedy and pastoral poetry, and was represented as holding the comic mask.

THALICTRUM, a genus of hardy, perennial herbs belonging to the Crowfoot family, Ranunculaceae, and commonly called meadow rue. The genus, which contains approximately 90 species, is native to temperate and tropical regions throughout the world, and is cultivated extensively in gardens of the U.S. The small, petalless, greenish-white, purple, or yellow flowers, arranged in corymbs and loose panicles, have four or five petallike sepals, numerous stamens, and a solitary pistil. The fruit is a single-seeded achene. Feathered columbine, *T. aquilegifolium*, is a white-sepaled, purple-stamened species native to Europe and N. Asia, and attaining a height of 3 feet. *T. dipterocarpum*, native to Yunnan Province in China, has large, rose-colored flowers and is slightly smaller than the feathered columbine. Common American thalictrums include *T. confine*, a small species, growing 20 in. high, native to the mountainous regions of South Dakota. The early meadow rue, *T. dioicum*, bears numerous greenish-white or purple flowers, and is found in E. North America from Labrador to Alabama. It attains a height of 2 feet.

THALLIUM (Gr. *thallos*, "a young shoot"), a metallic element of atomic number 81, atomic weight 204.4, and symbol Tl, insoluble in water and soluble in nitric and sulfuric acids. The element was discovered spectroscopically in 1861 by the English chemist Sir William Crookes, who named it from the green line it produces on the color spectrum. It was first isolated by the French chemist Claude August Lamy in 1862. Thallium ranks 61st in abundance among the elements in the earth's crust, and is a mem-

ber of the aluminum family of metals. It occurs in combination with pyrites, zinc blende, and hematite, and is often recovered from the flue dust produced by pyrites ovens in which sulfur and iron are separated. Occasionally it is extracted from the mud produced in the lead chambers used in manufacturing sulfuric acid. A few deposits of thallium-rich pyrites occur in Sweden and Macedonia. Thallium has a bluish-gray color which turns to dark gray upon exposure to the atmosphere. It has a specific gravity of 11.9, melts at 303.5°C. (578.3°F.), and is very soft and malleable. It forms two series of salts, such as thallous chloride, $TlCl$, and thallic chloride, $TlCl_3$, which are univalent and trivalent respectively. Thallous oxide, Tl_2O, a black solid which, when molten, attacks glass and porcelain, is made by heating thallium in air at very high temperatures. Thallium salts, which are very poisonous, are used in insecticides and rodenticides. Thallium has a high index of refraction, and is therefore important in the manufacture of several types of optical glass.

THALLOPHYTA. See BOTANY: *Classification.*

THAMES, the most important river in Great Britain, flowing with a southeastern trend through the southern portion of the kingdom and passing through London.

Its headwaters, rising on the southeast slope of the Cotswold Hills, in Gloucester, five miles S. of Cheltenham, converge on Oxford and flow thence in a southeasterly direction to Reading, through a gap in the Chiltern escarpment. The Thames thereafter follows a generally eastward trend. A few miles below Gravesend it expands into a wide estuary and enters the North Sea. Its length is about 215 miles. The upper part of the river is sometimes called the Isis. At London Bridge the width of the river is about 290 yards; at Woolwich, 490 yards; at Gravesend pier, 800 yards; 3 miles below Gravesend, 1290 yards; at Nore Light, 6 miles; and at its mouth, between Whitstable and Foulness Point, about 8 miles below the Nore, the estuary is 18 miles across.

The London docks embrace more than 35 miles of the river from the Tower Bridge to Tilbury Dock, and the largest steamships are moored at these docks. While the upriver docks are tidal, the lower admit any vessel at any stage of the tide.

The Thames is also the main source of the water supply of London, the daily supply delivered exceeding 225,000,000 gallons. The

Art Institute of Chicago

Preparing the Thanksgiving Day feast (painting by the American artist Doris Lee)

part of the river immediately below London Bridge is called the Pool, and the part between the bridge and Blackwall is called the Port. Two embankments have been formed, one on the north shore from Blackfriars Bridge to Westminster, and one on the south shore from Westminster Bridge to Vauxhall. Among the historic and otherwise noteworthy places on the Thames are Putney, Mortlake, Hampton Court, Twickenham, Richmond Staines, Eton, Windsor, and Henley.

THAMUGAS. See TIMGAD.

THAMYRIS, in Greek mythology, a Thracian bard who challenged the Muses (q.v.) to a singing contest. He was defeated by them and as a punishment was blinded and deprived of his gift of song.

THANATOS, in Greek mythology, the god of death, a son of Erebus and Nyx and the twin brother of Hypnos (see SOMNUS), god of sleep, with whom he is usually represented. When Thanatos carried off Alcestis (q.v.), the hero Hercules compelled him to restore her to her husband Admetus (q.v.).

THANET, ISLE OF, the N.E. extremity of Kent County, England, bounded on the N. and E. by the North Sea and separated from

the remainder of the county by two branches of the Stour R. The Isle of Thanet is approximately rectangular in shape and extends about 8 m. in an E. and W. direction and about 5 m. in a N. and S. direction. The chief feature of the terrain is a succession of steep cliffs fronting the North Sea. North Foreland, one of the highest of these headlands, is the site of a famous lighthouse. Thanet is also the site of a number of popular beach resorts, including Margate, Westgate, Broadstairs, Ramsgate, and Minster. During the Roman occupation of Britain, the invaders maintained two forts on the isle. Pop., about 95,000.

THANKSGIVING DAY, in America, the name of a national holiday, which originated in New England. After the first harvest of the New England colonists in 1621 Governor Bradford made provisions for a day of thanksgiving and prayer. In 1623 a day of fasting and prayer in the midst of drought was changed into thanksgiving by the coming of rain during the prayers; gradually the custom prevailed of appointing thanksgiving annually after harvest. These appointments were by proclamation of the governors of the several New England colonies. During the Revolution a day of national thanksgiving was annually recommended by Congress.

In 1817 New York adopted it as an annual custom, and it spread through many of the States by the middle of the 19th century. In 1864 President Lincoln appointed a day of thanksgiving, and since then the Presidents have issued a Thanksgiving proclamation generally designating the last Thursday of November.

THAR DESERT or **INDIAN DESERT,** extensive region of arid sand dunes, situated in the N.W. section of the Union of India and in w. Pakistan, and enclosed by the Sutlej R. on the N., the Aravalli Range on the E., the Rann of Cutch and the Arabian Sea on the s., and the Indus R. on the w. Extending in a N.E. and s.w. direction, it is approximately 500 m. in length and 300 m. in width, and has a total area of about 100,000 sq.m. The terrain consists largely of rolling sand hills, and there are intermittent outcroppings of thin scrub on which the flocks of nomadic herdsmen feed. The altitude ranges between 250 ft. and 750 ft. Rainfall is scanty, averaging from 3 to 10 inches annually, and temperatures are high throughout the year. Part of the N. and w. border areas are made suitable for agriculture through irrigation. The political divisions covered by the Thar Desert include large sections of Rajasthan Union and Punjab State, in the Union of India, and parts of Bahawalpur, Khairpur, and Sind provinces, in Pakistan.

THASOS, the most northerly island in the Ægean Sea, near the coast of Macedonia. Exports include oil, honey, and timber. The surface is covered with wooded hills, the summit of Hypsaria being 3428 feet high. Area, 167 sq.m.; pop., about 12,000.

THAYER, ABBOTT HENDERSON (1849–1921), American artist, born in Boston. He studied painting under Gerome at the École des Beaux Arts, Paris. From 1879 to 1891 he painted portraits and landscapes, but after that devoted himself chiefly to figure subjects, a branch of art in which he was conspicuously successful.

His favorite subject was a young female figure, alone or in company with one or two accessory figures. They were treated with much ideality, and great dignity and charm of expression. Fine examples of his work are "Young Woman" (Metropolitan Museum of Art, New York City), "Caritas" (Boston Museum), "Winged Figure" (Albright Art Gallery, Buffalo), "A Virgin" (Freer collection, National Gallery, Washington, which also possesses several other works), and "Virgin Enthroned". He was elected a member of the National Academy of Design in 1901, and was one of the original members of the Society of American Artists, of which he was president for two years.

THAYER, SYLVANUS (1785–1872), American soldier, born in Braintree, Mass., and educated at the U.S. Military Academy at West Point. He was instructor in mathematics at West Point (1808–12). He served in the War of 1812 at Niagara, Lake Champlain, and Norfolk, and was promoted captain (1813). After visiting Europe to witness the operations of the Allies around Paris (1815), he was appointed superintendent of West Point. During his term of office he so reorganized it that he won the title of "Father of the United States Military Academy". He held the post till 1833 and won the brevet of lieutenant colonel.

He was subsequently engaged on the defenses of Boston harbor, and retired from the service in 1863 with the brevet of brigadier general. He is buried at West Point, where a statue to his memory was unveiled in 1883.

THEATER. The classical theater arose among the Greeks and was a place devoted to dramatic and musical performances. The central circle was the *orchestra,* in which the chorus sang and danced. Round the orchestra, the stone seats for the audience rose tier above tier like a large flight of steps. The theater of Dionysus at Athens held nearly 30,000 persons, and that at Megalopolis, 44,000.

The stage was a long, narrow platform, standing about 12 feet higher than the orchestra, and was used by the actors, as distinguished from the chorus. The stage and back wall were called the *proskēnion;* the side walls, or wings, in each of which was an entrance door, being named *paraskēnia.* A flight of steps connected the stage with the orchestra, and these steps, continued out of sight, were the means by which apparitions from the lower world ascended. The wall of the dressing rooms, which formed the back wall of the stage, was ornamented with columns, and represented the front of a temple or other building, before which the action of the play was supposed to take place.

When the action of the play required a different scene, the back of the stage was covered with painted curtains or boards. For machinery there was a platform on

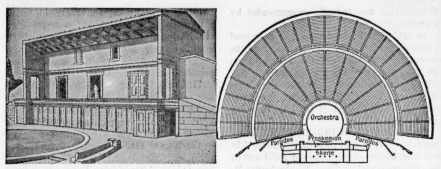

THE ANCIENT GREEK THEATER. *Left: Drawing of the stage and back wall (proskēnion) of the theater at Epidaurus. Right: A ground plan of the theater at Epidaurus.*

which a tableau, depicting an incident which could not be shown on the stage, was rolled forward from one of the doors, exhibited to the audience, and rolled back again. There was also the *mēchane* (*machina*), by which a god could be lowered from heaven to earth, which was probably some sort of crane. From it we derive the phrase *Deus ex machinâ.* In dealing with the early Greek theater it must always be remembered that the stage was only of secondary importance, the orchestra being deemed the chief point of interest.

The Romans, whose theaters were founded in most respects on Greek models, differed in this point. They transferred all the singing and dancing to the stage, and gave up the orchestra to the most important section of the audience. The most perfect existing specimens of the early Greek theater are at Epidaurus, at Aspendus in Pamphylia, and at Athens. At Orange, in the south of France, there is a splendid specimen of an ancient Roman theater.

During the Middle Ages, when the drama existed only in the form of mysteries and miracle plays, and was under the management of the Church, theaters were not required. Plays were represented generally in cathedrals or monasteries, and the most elaborate scenery ever used was a three-story scaffold to represent heaven, earth, and the nether world. In Max Reinhardt's production of *The Miracle*, performed in London (1912), the idea of transforming the Olympia Music-Hall into a vast cathedral came from this medieval practice. With the revival of learning in the 16th century came also a revival of the drama, and theaters began to be built. The earliest was probably a playhouse of some sort in the Hôtel de Bourgogne, Paris,

built about 1548; the first regular theater was that which Bramante constructed at Rome (1580), while the earliest theater built on modern lines was constructed by Aleotti at Parma in 1618.

In all the early Continental theaters the construction was founded on Greek models, but in England a simpler idea served. There the earliest dramatic performances took place in booths, on tennis courts, or in the open courtyards of inns; and it was not till the end of the 16th century that the first permanent building was erected for theatrical purposes. This was "The Theater", built by Burbage in Shoreditch in 1576, which was founded, not on any classical model, but on the inn yards in which the actors had been accustomed to play.

The stage was literally a stage, a platform erected against one side of the building, and on three sides of this platform the spectators stood or sat in the pit (then called the *yard*), while all round it ran the galleries or boxes (then called *rooms*) exactly like the galleries of an inn yard. There was no provision for scenery. The locality in which the scene was laid was indicated only by a ticket stuck up bearing such an inscription as "A Garden", "Thebes", or "Rhodes". *Properties* were, however, largely used to give verisimilitude to the action.

After the Restoration, under the supervision of Charles II, who was familiar with the French stage, the English theater came more into line with the Continental. The stage was gradually withdrawn closer and closer to the proscenium opening, until, by the middle of the 18th century, the appearance of the interior of Drury Lane was not seriously different from that which it presents at this day. In the years immediately following the Restoration elaborate scenery and the playing of female parts by women were introduced. The first American theater is said to have been at Williamsburg, Va., where an English actor named Hallam played in 1752. Hallam also opened a theater in New York (1753), and at the beginning of the 19th century we find theaters in Charleston, Boston, Albany, Baltimore, and Richmond.

Modern Theater. Since the last decade of the 19th century the theater has developed so enormously on all sides that it cannot easily be described in terms of anything previously existing. This change has been due, first, to the literary genius which was thrown into dramatic writing in the second half of the 19th century, an amount of genius greater than the theater has had at any time since the age of Elizabeth; and second, to the rapid progress of the physical sciences, especially in electricity. These two influences have raised the theater from the position of a third-rate institution, scarcely related to literature or the arts, to one of unsurpassed power as a cultural force and an artistic instrument. Dramatic literature, which had for two centuries been held in rigid conventional grooves, has been freed to take all knowledge as its province. All types of social questions can now be discussed in dramatic form; nearly all genres of literary production have their dramatic parallels; and all types of pictorial and plastic art can be reproduced in the scenic setting. The theater is now the only one of the arts which makes use of all the others. In the last quarter of the 19th century it was absorbing artistic and literary forces from the outside; in the first quarter of the 20th it was established as a creative force and was reflecting back new influences to the other arts.

The modern theater is divided into two or three parts, kept distinct in the structural scheme. First, there is the stage, with all necessary dressing rooms and mechanical equipment for the production of the play, together with space at each side and above for the storing of scenery. Next there is the auditorium with its corridors and lounging rooms. Finally, there is the outer lobby with its approaches. This is often made a part of the auditorium structure. There are several modern types of theater differing

J. Arthur Rank Organization

Actors on stage of an Elizabethan theater (scene from the motion picture "Henry V")

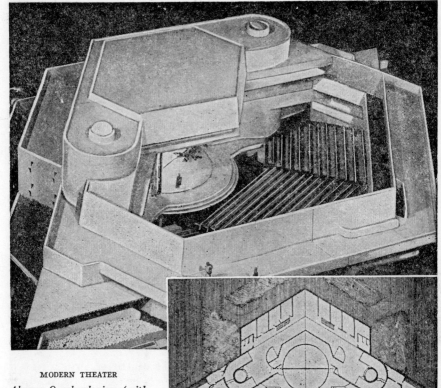

MODERN THEATER

Above: Overhead view (with roof removed) of "The New Theatre," designed by Frank Lloyd Wright. It introduces many new features in theater architecture. Right: Ground plan of the hexagonal structure, showing the seating arrangement and the revolving stage. Below: Vertical section shows large space for backstage operations.

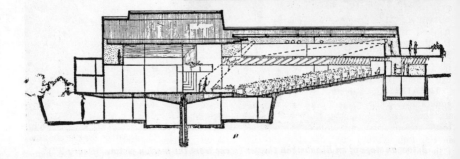

from the traditional type based on the Italian opera house, which has its balconies in horseshoe shape and its seats generally in curved rows.

Modern practice in theater-building tends to make both the balconies and the rows on the ground floor straight. The larger opera houses, which seat upward of 3000, may have as many as five distinct balconies, including those composed of boxes. But the normal theater for the spoken drama usually has a capacity between 1100 and 1500. A distinct type of playhouse, however, is the little theater, which may have a capacity as small as 99, and rarely goes above 400. This is a direct result of the intimate and lifelike character of many modern plays which demand the most accurate attention. Recently, too, the large outdoor theater, modeled on the Greek, has come into fashion.

In the auditorium, the modern theater has been strongly influenced by German methods. In addition to making straight rows, modern theater architects incline to a steeply pitched floor, sometimes so much as to give the spectators of each row a clear view over the heads of those sitting in front. This type of auditorium is known as the amphitheater, without implying a semicircular plan. Modern custom also tends to the elimination of boxes and loges, or to placing them at the rear. The galleries must of course be more steeply pitched than the ground floor. In the matter of decoration, too, modern taste follows the German. The ornate quality which is to be found in the Italian opera house is giving place to straight and bare walls, with a simple and harmonious color scheme.

Lighting methods, in recent times, have undergone much change and experimentation, especially in Germany. The "Fortuny system" and related methods throw upon the stage an indirect light reflected from bands of silk or plaster surfaces. Subtle gradations of color can be obtained by the mixing of the primary hues under this method. In some theaters it is the practice to illuminate the stage by means of arc lamps placed in the first balcony, thus eliminating the unreal lighting from beneath that exists under the footlight system.

THEATINES, a Roman Catholic religious community, which played, next to the Jesuits, the most important part in the movement for reform from within the Church in the 16th century. Its founders were St. Cajetan (Gaetano da Tiene) and Giovanni

Pietro Caraffa, at that time bishop of Chieti, from the Latin title of whose see, Theate, the order took its name. With two other friends, they obtained a charter from Pope Clement VII, dated June 24, 1524, formally constituting the new brotherhood, with the three usual vows, and with the privilege of electing their superior, who was to hold office for three years. They were all to be priests. Their first convent was opened in Rome, and Caraffa was chosen as superior. He was succeeded in 1527 by Cajetan, and the congregation began to extend to the provinces. After a time, however, it was thought advisable to unite it with the somewhat analagous Order of the Somaschians; but Caraffa, who was elected pope, under the name of Paul IV, restored the original constitution in 1555. The Theatines extended themselves over Italy, and into Spain, Poland, and Germany, especially Bavaria. The first French house was founded in Paris under Cardinal Jules Mazarina in 1644. To their activity and zeal many historians ascribe much of the success of the Counter Reformation in the south of Europe. In 1909 Pope Pius X united the order with the Spanish congregation of the holy family at Barcelona.

THÉÂTRE FRANÇAIS. See COMÉDIE FRANÇAISE.

THEATRE GUILD, INC., THE, an organization devoted primarily to the artistic development of the theater. The plan was first started in New York City by the Washington Square Players in 1916, but World War I put an end to the activity of producing one-act plays. In 1919 the little band of theatrical pioneers reorganized and the Theatre Guild came into existence. The Guild has subscription audiences in about twenty-one cities, and produces an average of six new plays a year and occasional revivals. It presented a weekly radio program entitled *Theatre Guild on the Air* from 1945 to 1953.

THEBAN CYCLE, the name given to a series of ancient Greek epics, no longer extant, treating the legends of Thebes. It included the *Thebaïd*, the story of the Seven Against Thebes (q.v.); the *Epigoni*, a poem of about 7000 lines, telling of the capture of the city by the descendants of the heroes of the *Thebaïd*; and the *Œdipodeia*, attributed to Cinæthon, a Lacedæmonian, and presenting, in about 6000 lines, the tragic story of Œdipus (q.v.), King of Thebes.

THEBES (Egypt. *Weset* or *Newt*), a celebrated ancient city and, for many centuries, the capital of ancient Egypt. It was named

Thebes by the Greeks, who knew it also as *Diospolis* ("city of Zeus"); it is the city identified in the Old Testament as *No* ("city") or *No-Amon* ("city of Amon"). Its site, on both banks of the Nile R. about 480 miles s. of present-day Cairo, is partly occupied by the modern towns of Karnak and Luxor (qq.v.). Scattered over the site, which reputedly had a maximum circumference of 16 m., are the remnants of numerous temples, tombs, and other ancient monuments. Of prehistoric origin, Thebes began to figure in the recorded history of Egypt during the Old Kingdom (3400?–2445 B.C.). Tombs dating from the VIth dynasty (2625–2475 B.C.) of Egyptian pharaohs have been discovered in the original necropolis, which is situated on the w. side of the Nile. As the Biblical name of Thebes indicates, the local deity of the city was Amon (q.v.), originally the Egyptian god of the reproductive forces and, later as Amen-Ra, the "father of the gods". The ruined temple of Amon, which ranks among the best preserved and most magnificent structures of Egyptian antiquity, is situated at Karnak.

Under the pharaohs of the IXth and Xth dynasties (2445–2160 B.C.), Thebes emerged as the administrative center of a powerful line of nomarchs. The Theban nomarchs successfully challenged the Heracleopolitan pharaohs, winning complete control of Egypt about 2160 B.C. With this event and the establishment of the Theban dynasty of pharaohs, Thebes became the capital of Egypt. The city retained this status until the reign (1375–58 B.C.) of Amenhotep IV. Many of the great temples, the avenue of sphinxes, a number of beautiful tombs, and numerous other lasting monuments were erected in and around Thebes during the period. Thebes was re-established as the seat of the Egyptian government shortly after the death of Amenhotep IV. Subsequently, in particular during the XIXth and XXth dynasties, the pharaohs made additional contributions to the architectural splendor of the city. The Assyrians sacked Thebes in the 7th century B.C. Although it was later partly restored, the city declined steadily after the collapse (332 B.C.) of the New Kingdom. Thebes was destroyed by the Romans late in the 1st century B.C.

Several of the chief ruins of Thebes are described in the articles dealing with Karnak and Luxor. (For additional information on these and other Theban ruins, see EGYPTIAN

ARCHITECTURE.) Among the ruined Theban edifices of great archeological importance are the tombs of the pharaohs. These structures, situated in the so-called Valley of the Kings on the w. side of the Nile, were erected between the 16th and 11th centuries B.C. The tomb of Tutankhamen, who reigned about the middle of the 14th century B.C., was discovered in this region in 1922. Other celebrated Theban ruins are the Ramesseum, a temple built during the reign (1292–25 B.C.) of Ramses II, the temple of Ramses III, the temple of Queen Hatshepsut, and the Colossi of Memnon.

THEBES, the principal city of Bœotia in ancient Greece, situated N. of Mount Cithæron, about 44 miles N.W. of Athens. Its acropolis was called Cadmeia, from the legend that it was founded by a colony of Phenicians under Cadmus (q.v.). No city of ancient Greece was more celebrated in myth and legend. The cycles of myths include stories of the twin brothers Amphion and Zethus; the tragic fate of its king Œdipus (q.v.) and the rivalry of his two sons, Eteocles and Polynices, which culminated in the expedition of the Seven Against Thebes (q.v.) and the later capture and destruction of the city by the Epigoni (q.v.); the return of the god Dionysus (q.v.) and the introduction of his worship at Thebes; and the birth and exploits of the famous Theban hero Hercules (q.v.).

Thebes in historical times was long an enemy of Athens, and in 479 B.C., during the Persian invasion under Xerxes I (q.v.), the Thebans sided with the invaders and fought against the confederated Greeks at Platæa. When the Peloponnesian War broke out in 431 B.C., Thebes joined the side of Sparta, and at the close of the war was eager for the destruction of Athens; it soon, however, began to dread the heightened power of its ally, and sheltered the Athenian exiles from the rule of the Thirty Tyrants. Hence arose a bitter antagonism between Thebes and Sparta, and a struggle ensued which resulted in a short period of Theban supremacy over all Greece, won by the victory of Epaminondas (q.v.) at Leuctra in 371 B.C., and brought to an end by the hero's death at Mantinea in 362 B.C.

The eloquence of the Athenian orator Demosthenes (q.v.) induced the Thebans to unite with the Athenians in opposition to the encroachments of Philip of Macedon (q.v.), but their combined forces were of no avail and in 338 B.C., by the battle of

Chæronea, the power of Greece was crushed. After the death of Philip the Thebans made a fierce but unsuccessful attempt to regain their freedom; their city was taken by Alexander the Great (see ALEXANDER III) in 335 B.C. and leveled to the ground, the entire surviving population being sold into slavery. Alexander is said to have spared only the temples and the house of the poet Pindar (q.v.). Although the city was rebuilt by Cassander in 315 B.C. and prospered for a time, it had dwindled to a wretched village by the 1st century B.C. At present the site of the acropolis named after Cadmus is occupied by the town of Thebai (pop., about 8000).

THECLA, a virgin saint, a member of a noble family of Iconium in Lycaonia, where she was converted by the preaching of St. Paul, and, having devoted herself to a life of virginity, suffered persecutions from her intended bridegroom, and from her parents. She is said to have died at the age of ninety in Seleucia.

THEILER, MAX (1899–   ), South African physician, born in Pretoria, and educated at London University. From 1922 to 1930 he was lecturer and assistant in tropical medicine at Harvard University, and in the latter year joined the staff of the Public Health Division of the Rockefeller Foundation, New York City. He was appointed director of the laboratories of the Division of Medicine and Public Health of the foundation in 1951. Known for his contributions to tropical medicine, Theiler was awarded the 1951 Nobel Prize in medicine. Theiler's works include a monograph contributed to the symposium *Yellow Fever,* published by the Rockefeller Foundation. See YELLOW FEVER.

THEINE. See CAFFEINE.

THEISM, belief in God, and as such opposed to atheism. Theism is now usually understood to mean the doctrine of the One, supreme, personal God, "in whom we live, and move, and have our being", as distinguished from polytheism, which recognizes more gods than one; from pantheism, which denies the divine personality; from agnosticism, which denies that we can know anything of God; and from deism, which, etymologically equivalent to theism, is generally defined as recognizing the personality of God, but denying His providence and active presence in the life of the world.

The four great arguments for theism or a belief in God are: (1) the *ontological* argument first formulated by St. Anselm,

which proceeds from the notion of a most perfect being to infer his existence; without actual existence the idea would fall short of perfection. The argument was restated in a different way by Descartes, and is still an element of the claim that without a God the world is a chaos; (2) the *cosmological* argument, employed by Aristotle, Aquinas, and many others, and which is an application of the principle of causality. We cannot conceive an infinite regression of finite causes; therefore beyond the last or first of the finite causes is the Infinite. From motion the argument is to a mover; (3) the *teleological* argument, or argument from design; this argument proceeds from the order and arrangement of the universe, the reign of law and beauty and adaptation, to the intelligent and supreme fountain of order; and (4) the *moral* argument which was relied on by Kant when he destructively criticized the other three; it forms a part of most modern theistic arguments. God is a postulate of our moral nature; and the moral law in us implies a lawgiver without us. See CAUSALITY; GOD.

THEISS, an important affluent of the Danube, and the chief river of Hungary. It rises by two streams, the Black Theiss and the White Theiss, in the Carpathian Mts. It winds 850 miles N.E., S.W., and finally southward, joining the Danube after running parallel to it for 300 m. The river is famous for its fish.

THEME, in music, a subject or motive (q.v.). Every composition is built up from themes which constitute the basic material. In a specific sense, the theme of a fugue is the subject (dux). In variations the theme is a complete musical idea, generally of periodic structure. It is usually played in its entirety before the variations begin. See SONATA.

THEMIS, in Greek mythology, the personification of justice, who presided over the assemblies of gods and men, and hence the goddess and the guardian of the law and harmony of nature established by the gods. She was considered a Titaness (see TITANS), the daughter of Uranus, god of heaven, and of Gæa, goddess of the earth. By her husband Zeus, ruler of the Olympian deities, her children were the Horæ and the Mœræ, or Fates (q.v.); by another husband, a Titan, she was the mother of the hero Prometheus (q.v.). Originally Themis may have been identical with Gæa, for popular conceptions of the two goddesses seem not

Themistocles (from a bas-relief)

to have been sharply differentiated. In art Themis is represented as holding a cornucopia and a pair of scales.

THEMISTOCLES (527?–460? B.C.), Athenian general and statesman. Upon the defeat of the Persians at Marathon (q.v.) in 490 B.C., Themistocles had the keen insight to realize that only by having a strong navy might the Greeks remain free of Persian domination. After the expulsion of his rival Aristides (q.v.) in 483 B.C., Themistocles controlled Athenian politics, and convinced his fellow citizens that a powerful fleet was necessary for their welfare. When it was learned that King Xerxes I of Persia was preparing for another invasion of Greece, and the Athenians had been told by the oracle at Delphi to defend themselves with "wooden walls", Themistocles interpreted this answer as referring to the Athenian ships. The Athenians, terrified, abandoned the city and sent the women and children to the neighboring states; on the eve of the battle of Salamis (q.v.), in 480 B.C., the Greek forces were about to disperse, despite the exhortations of Themistocles to await the attack of the enemy. He is said to have precipitated the contest by a secret message to Xerxes to attack before the Greek fleet had an opportunity to flee. He himself commanded the Athenian fleet, which comprised more than half of the total Greek forces, the entire fleet being under the command of

the Spartan admiral Eurybiades. The battle of Salamis resulted in a crushing defeat for the Persians, and Themistocles was acclaimed the foremost man of his time.

Eventually, however, his popularity began to wane, because his arrogance provoked the anger and resentment of the citizens. He was ostracized (see OSTRACISM) about 470 B.C. and retired to Argos, subsequently gaining favor at the court of Artaxerxes I, King of Persia. The town of Magnesia was appointed to supply him with bread, Lampsacus with wine, and Myus with other provisions. He lived at Magnesia until his death. In spite of the discreditable conclusion to his career, Themistocles was a statesman of outstanding ability, and his strong naval policy laid the foundations of the Athenian empire. He also was one of the first Athenians to plan colonization in the west, and he opened Athens to foreign merchants, encouraging trade.

THEOBALD, LEWIS (about 1688–1744), early Shakespearian editor and critic, born in Sittingbourne, Kent, England. He wrote and adapted plays, and made translations from Sophocles, Aristophanes, and other Greek authors. In 1725 Pope published an edition of Shakespeare, which Theobald sharply reviewed in a volume entitled *Shakespeare Restored* (1726). Pope retaliated by making Theobald the first hero of the *Dunciad* (1728). Early in 1734 Theobald brought out his own edition of Shakespeare in seven volumes.

THEOBROMINE or **THEOBROMIN,** a white, bitter, crystalline alkaloid, $C_7H_8N_4O_2$, obtained in large amounts from chocolate, cacao, cola nuts, and tea (qq.v.), and closely related to the drug caffeine (q.v.). Salts and other derivatives of theobromine are employed extensively in medicine as diuretics.

THEOCRITUS (fl. 3rd century B.C.), Greek bucolic poet, born probably in Syracuse, Sicily. Few details are known of his life, except that he spent considerable time on the island of Cos, and lived also at the court of the Egyptian king Ptolemy II Philadelphus, in Alexandria, where he composed several of his poems about 275–270 B.C. and was a member of the *Pleiad* (q.v.) of Alexandrian poets. Thirty-one poems, mostly in dactylic hexameter, and a number of short epigrams have been preserved under his name. His language is for the most part a modified Doric (see GREEK LANGUAGE), but three lyric poems are composed in the literary Æolic, the traditional meter of lyric poetry. Of the longer poems of Theocritus ten are bucolic or pastoral in form, and three are mimes (q.v.), similar to the recently discovered mimes of Herodas (q.v.). Theocritus raised pastoral poetry to a new and highly perfected form of literature. The poems, each of which represented a single scene of country life, came to be called idyls (q.v., "little pictures"), a name probably not used by Theocritus himself. He introduced into pastoral poetry the themes and conventions adopted by later poets, such as the responsive singing matches of shepherds, the use of invocations and melodious refrains, songs of unrequited love, and dirges sung to commemorate the death of some pastoral hero. Among the Greeks, Theocritus was imitated by Bion (q.v.) and Maschus; his most successful follower was Vergil (q.v.), who in his *Bucolics*, or *Eclogues*, introduced the pastoral form into Latin poetry.

THEODORA (about 508–48 A.D.), Byzantine Empress, the wife of Justinian I (q.v.), and said to have been the daughter of Acacius, a keeper of wild beasts at the circus of Constantinople. She was successively an actress, dancer, and courtesan, before becoming the mistress of Justinian, whom she married in 523 A.D. Four years later she was crowned empress and became Justinian's trusted counselor. She bore a chief share in the work of government, and saved the throne by her high courage at the crisis of the Nika riots in 532 A.D., when she prevented Justinian from fleeing and brought about the suppression of the insurrection. Most information concerning Theodora is derived from the *Anecdota,* or *Secret History,* of Procopius, who gives lurid details about her early life and describes her as a cruel and tyrannical empress whose numerous spies ferreted out all who were opposed to the government. These details are not supported by other writers, but all authorities agree upon her beauty and intellectual gifts.

THEODORIC or (Ger.) **DIETRICH,** surnamed THE GREAT (454?–526 A.D.), the founder of the Ostrogothic kingdom in Italy, born in Pannonia. From the age of seven to seventeen he was a hostage at the court of the Eastern Roman emperor at Constantinople. In 474 A.D. Theodoric succeeded his father Theodemir as head of the Ostrogothic naton, and fifteen years later invaded Italy with the permission of the Eastern emperor Zeno (see GOTHS: *Ostrogoths*). Odoacer, the first Germanic king of Italy, was defeated in three decisive battles and blockaded in Ravenna; the whole of Italy having been subdued by Theodoric, Odoacer surrendered in 493 A.D. and was treacherously slain by the Ostrogothic king. Theodoric then assumed the title of king of Italy and made Ravenna his capital, occasionally moving his court to Verona when his northern frontier was threatened.

Theodoric's reign of thirty-three years was devoted primarily to the consolidation and development of his new kingdom, and was a period of unexampled peace in Italy. He showed no desire for further conquest, and zealously promoted agriculture and commerce. He ruled all classes of his subjects with irresistible authority, but with justice and moderation, and, although himself an Arian (see ARIUS), exhibited an unusual tolerance of all other sects. The government was administered by Romans on Roman lines; separate codes of law were used for Romans and Goths. Among the Romans who held high office under Theodoric were Anicius Manlius Severinus Boethius (q.v.) and Flavius Magnus Aurelius Cassiodorus (q.v.); the former incurred the suspicion of the monarch toward the end of his reign and was unjustly put to death. Theodoric left no son, but was succeeded in 526 A.D. by his daughter Amalasuntha as regent for her son Athalaric. To the Germans Theodoric is known as Dietrich von Bern (Bern being the German name for Verona), and is one of the great heroes of Germanic legend.

THEODOSIUS I, called THE GREAT (346?–95 A.D.), Roman Emperor, son of Theodosius the Elder, born in Spain, probably in Cauca. He accompanied his father on his British campaigns, but upon the latter's death in 376 he retired to the family estate in Spain. Upon the death of the emperor Valens, the co-emperor, Gratianus, realizing his inability to govern the empire alone, invited Theodosius in 379 A.D. to become emperor in the East. In 380 A.D. Theodosius was baptized as a Trinitarian, or orthodox Christian, and, as a consequence, the restoration of the religious unity of the empire was restored and various edicts against Arianism (see ARIUS) and other heresies were promulgated. Upon the murder of Gratianus at Lyons, his rule was threatened by the advance toward Italy of the upstart Maximus, proclaimed emperor in Britain, and the arrival of Valentinian II; Theodosius defeated Maximus at Aquileia in 388 A.D. and made Valentinian emperor in the West.

Saint Ambrose barring Theodosius the Great from the church

For some years thereafter Theodosius lived at Milan, enjoying the friendship and respect of its bishop, St. Ambrose (q.v.). In 390 A.D., when the governor of Thessalonica was lynched by a circus mob for his punishment of a brutal but favorite charioteer, Theodosius ordered the people of the city to be invited into the circus and there massacred. At least 7000 were thus put to death. The subsequent humiliation of Theodosius and his submission to the penance demanded by St. Ambrose for the massacre was regarded by the Church as one of its greatest victories over the temporal power. In 392 A.D. Valentinian II was murdered, and in 394 A.D. Theodosius, then in Constantinople, again marched westward, this time against the Frankish general Arbogast and his puppet emperor Eugenius. After a stubborn fight at the river Frigidus, Theodosius gained a complete victory, and for four months ruled as sole Roman emperor. Upon his death the empire was divided between his two sons, Honorius and Arcadius.

THEOGNIS (fl. late 6th cent. B.C.), Greek elegiac poet, born in Megara. During the conflict in his native city between the aristocratic and democratic parties, in which he took the side of the aristocrats, he lost his estate and was driven into exile. He appears to have visited Sicily, Bœotia, Eubœa, and Sparta, but later, apparently under changed conditions, he returned to Megara. Theognis is the only elegiac poet of the early period whose works are extant in almost complete condition. A collection of his short poems totaling 1389 verses exists, but is believed to have suffered from interpolations. The elegies to his friend Cyrnus, which are undoubtedly genuine, are filled with ethical and political precepts and give valuable evidence as to the state of Greek political parties and social conditions of his time. The poetry of Theognis provides the best extant example of that form of verse, usually embodying moral precepts and general maxims of conduct, known as gnomic poetry.

THEOGONY. See HESIOD.

THEOLOGY, literally, a speaking concerning God. It is that branch of theological science which treats of God, including (1) the being of God, (2) the attributes of God, (3) the doctrine of the Trinity, and (4) creation and providence. The word first occurs in Plato and Aristotle. Scholasticism understood by theology the whole of Christian doctrine, to which in England the name divinity is given. In its widest sense, the term "theology" now includes all the various theological disciplines, the sacred languages, and the interpretation of the Bible; the history of the church, and the history of religions in general; the contributions of our own age to the knowledge of the objects of theological study from other sciences, such as biology; systematic theology, or the system of doctrines and duties; and, finally, practical theology, or the application of theology to life, in the pulpit, in church administration, and in the various forms of contact with the world. But more strictly and correctly, the term "theology" is employed at present of systematic theology, which may be defined as the science of Christianity, of the scientific explanation of the Christian life, the development of its characteristic principles, conditions, and general relations. Viewed thus it yields a system of doctrines and a system of duties, or dogmatics and ethics.

Dogmatic theology is the exposition of the dogmas in which the church has found its historical expression. To the end of the 17th century it was for the most part associated with ethics, and the two were combined as *sacra doctrina* or *Theology*, but from that time the separation became general, and the name *dogmatica theologia*, first used by the Lutheran Buddæus in 1724, was applied to the theoretical part of Christian doctrine. It combines the results of exegetical and historical inquiry. It is not a product of the consciousness of the individual, but is drawn from historical sources.

In what is known as the *New Theology*, the results of historical criticism are applied to a restatement of exegetical theology. It accepts evolution both in the spiritual and material spheres, employs the methods of the higher criticism, rejects verbal inspiration and emphasizes revelation, takes a subjective view of the atonement, minimizes the supernatural, and has a strong tendency to universalism.

THEOPHRASTUS (372?–287? B.C.), Greek philosopher, scientist, and author, born on the island of Lesbos. He studied philosophy at Athens, first under Plato and subsequently under Aristotle, whose devoted pupil he became. He is believed to have accompanied the latter to Stagira and to have returned with him to Athens when Aristotle in 334 B.C. opened his school of philosophy in the Lyceum. Aristotle retired to Chalcis in 323 B.C., and Theophrastus succeeded him as head of the Peripatetic School (see PERIPATETIC PHILOSOPHY); upon his master's death Theo-

phrastus inherited Aristotle's entire library, the largest then known, including the philosopher's original manuscripts and unpublished writings. Theophrastus lectured at the Lyceum for thirty-five years, during which period he is said to have had 2000 pupils.

As a writer Theophrastus displayed an amazing versatility and was the reputed author of 227 works. For many years his authority remained paramount in logic, psychology, ethics, politics, rhetoric, physics, and metaphysics. His scientific writings are for the most part lost, but his *History of Plants* and *On the Causes of Plants* are extant; these two works present the first thorough treatment of the science of botany. Also extant are portions of his treatises *On Stones, On Fire, On the Senses,* and *Metaphysics*; and his book of thirty ethical sketches, called *Characters*, each one depicting a certain type of person, such as the disreputable man, the loquacious man, the tactless man, the surly man, and the superstitious man. The collection *Characters* became famous in world literature, and its form and style were imitated by many French and English writers of the 17th and 18th centuries, notably by Joseph Hall in *Characters of Vertues and Vices* (1608), Sir Thomas Overbury in *A Wife . . . Wherevnto Are Added Many Witty Characters* (1614), John Stephens in *Satyricall Essayes Characters and Others* (1615), John Earle in *Microcosmographie, or a Peece of the World Discovered* (1628), Jean de La Bruyère in his *Caractères* (1688), and Samuel Butler (q.v.) in *The Genuine Remains in Verse and Prose of Mr. Samuel Butler, Author of Hudibras* (1759).

THEORELL, (AXEL) HUGO (1903–), Swedish biochemist, born in Linköping, and educated at Stockholm University and at the Royal Caroline Medico-Surgical Institute in Stockholm. He obtained an M.D. degree, but was forced to abandon his career as a practitioner because of a crippling attack of poliomyelitis. From 1930 to 1936 he served as assistant professor of chemistry at Uppsala University, and during that period he conducted important biochemical research. In 1937 he became head of the biochemistry department of the newly organized Nobel Institute, in Stockholm.

Theorell is recognized as an outstanding researcher in enzyme (q.v.) chemistry. In 1934, using an apparatus of his own invention, he isolated the so-called yellow enzyme, or yellow ferment, and split it into its component parts. His subsequent studies led to an understanding of the structure and action of other enzymes, notably the oxidation enzymes involved in respiration. Theorell was awarded the 1955 Nobel Prize in medicine.

THEOREM, in mathematics, a proposition to be demonstrated. A theorem consists of two parts: the hypothesis, or the given; and the conclusion, or what is to be proved. One theorem is the converse of another when the conclusion and the hypothesis are interchanged in the two theorems. The converse of a theorem is, however, not necessarily true. A corollary of a theorem is a truth easily deduced from it and not requiring a separate demonstration. A lemma is generally a theorem used to prepare the way for another theorem.

THEORY OF AVERAGES. See PROBABILITY.

THEORY OF EQUATIONS, the branch of mathematics concerned with finding the solutions of algebraic equations, or proving that such solutions cannot be found. Although many types of equations other than algebraic equations are important in modern mathematics (for example, differential equations; see CALCULUS), the theory of equations is restricted to algebraic equations, and in general to a particular type of algebraic equation. This type of equation contains but one unknown, usually called x; the equation states that zero is equal to some *function* of this unknown, the function consisting of the sum of a number of *terms,* each term consisting of some known number multiplied by x raised to some integral power (for example, x, x^2, x^7, or in general x^n where n is any positive whole number). The number by which x^n is multiplied in each term is called the *coefficient* of that term, and is often represented by a letter such as a, b, or c, indicating a known number. The general equation of this type may thus be expressed in the following form:

$$a + bx + cx^2 + dx^3 - \ldots ex^n = 0$$

In this equation any of the known numbers other than e and n may be any number, positive or negative or zero, real or imaginary, or complex; the number e cannot be zero, and, as stated above, the number n must be a positive whole number. The magnitude of n is called the *degree* of the equation.

When n equals one, the equation is of the first degree, and is called a *linear equation.* Every such equation can be expressed in the form $ax + b = 0$, and the solution is easily obtained: $x = -\dfrac{b}{a}$. When n equals two, the equation is of the second degree, and is called a quadratic equation. Every such equation can be expressed in the form $ax^2 + bx + c = 0$, and the solution is as follows:

$$x = \frac{-b \pm \sqrt{b^2 - 4ac}}{2a}.$$

Equations of the third degree are called *cubics,* and equations of the fourth degree are called *biquadratics* or *quartics*. These equations are exceedingly difficult to solve. However, the solution of the cubic equation was discovered in the 16th century by the Italian mathematicians Jerome Cardan and Niccolò Tartaglia and the solution of the quartic equation was discovered by Cardan's pupil Ludovici Ferrari later in the same century. The general solution of equations or higher degree proved extremely difficult, and the *quintic* equation, as an equation of the fifth degree is called, resisted the attempts at solution by the ablest mathematicians of the 17th and 18th centuries. At the beginning of the 19th century the German mathematician Karl Gauss showed that every algebraic equation has at least one root; his proof, however, did not imply that such a solution can be found. In the 19th century the Norwegian mathematician Niels Hendrik Abel, the Irish mathematician Sir William Hamilton, and the French mathematicians Évariste Galois, Charles Hermite, and Jules Henri Poincaré proved that in many cases equations of the fifth and higher degrees cannot be solved, even though such equations have roots. Mathematicians have also shown that every equation of degree n has exactly n roots. For example, the equation $x^2 = 9$ has two roots, $x = 3$ and $x = -3$. The equation $x^3 = 1$ has three roots: $x = 1$, $x = \dfrac{\sqrt{-3} - 1}{2}$, $x = \dfrac{-\sqrt{-3} - 1}{2}$. Sometimes two or more of the roots have the same value; for example, the equations $x^2 - 2x + 1 = 0$ has two roots, both $x = 1$.

Extracting the roots of an equation is called solving the equation. Formulas can be found for solving cubic and quartic equations, but these formulas are extremely cumbersome. Such equations are normally solved by *transformations*; the equation is transformed into a different equation, usually of lesser degree, which can be solved, and the roots of this new equation bear a simple known relationship to the roots of the original equation. Equations of the fifth and higher degree can always be simplified by such transformations; for example, any equation of the fifth degree can be transformed into an equation of the form $x^5 + ax + b = 0$. However, the latter cannot be solved by means of a finite number of simple arithmetical operations, and in this sense is insolvable. The value of each of the roots can, however, be computed to within any desired degree of accuracy by simple methods. Moreover, the roots can be expressed in terms of the coefficients by various complex mathematical functions. But the roots cannot in general be expressed in such a way that they can be computed from the coefficients by a finite number of additions, subtractions, multiplications, divisions, or extractions of square roots. Only when the roots can be so expressed, can the equation be considered "solved".

THEORY OF NUMBERS, the branch of mathematics which deals with the properties and relationships of numbers (q.v.). According to this broad definition, the theory of numbers includes most of mathematics, and particularly of mathematical analysis. Generally, however, the theory of numbers is confined to the study of integers, or occasionally to some other set of numbers which has properties similar to the set of all integers (an integer is a whole number, as opposed to a fraction). Elementary arithmetic, for example, is part of the theory of numbers, and some of the unsolved problems in this branch of mathematics are no more complicated than ordinary arithmetic.

One of the simple concepts in the theory of numbers is the concept of prime and composite numbers. A composite number may be factored; that is, it is equal to the product of two or more other numbers. A prime number may not be factored; that is, it cannot be divided by any number (other than itself or one) without leaving a remainder which is a fraction. For example, the numbers 1, 2, 3, 5, 7, and 11 are prime; the numbers 4, 6, 8, 9, and 10 are composite.

With increasingly larger numbers, the probability that a number chosen at random will be prime becomes smaller, because there are so many smaller prime numbers which may be factors of it. For example, between 1 and 10 there are five prime numbers; be-

tween 1000 and 1010 there is only one prime number: 1009. 1001 is not prime because it is equal to $7 \times 11 \times 13$; 1003 is not prime because it is equal to 17×59; and 1007 is not prime because it is equal to 19×53. The ancient Greek mathematicians speculated on the possibility of the existence of a number so large that no number larger than it is prime. This problem was solved by Euclid (q.v.) about 2000 years ago. The proof that there is no largest prime number is a typical example of some of the techniques employed in the theory of numbers.

Euclid's proof proceeds by assuming the existence of a largest prime number and then proving the assumption absurd, because there must be larger prime numbers. The proof follows. The largest prime number is defined as p. The number q is designated as equal to the product $1 \times 2 \times 3 \times 4 \times 5 \times \ldots \times p$, where the dots represent all of the numbers between 5 and p. The number r is set equal to $q + 1$. The number q must be an even number (i.e., it must be divisible by 2) because 2 is one of the numbers which was multiplied in obtaining it; hence r must be an odd number, and so not divisible by 2. Similarly q is divisible by 3, and hence r cannot be divisible by 3. Similarly, r cannot be divisible by any number up to and including p. Hence r is either a prime number, or else it is a composite number the factors of which are prime numbers larger than p. In either case, p is not the largest prime number. But whatever the largest prime number might be assumed to be, one can always, by this method, find a larger prime number. Hence, no largest prime number exists.

The above proof indicates the essentially simple nature of some of the theorems in the theory of numbers. Others of the theorems are extremely complex. For example, mathematicians long wondered exactly how many primes there are in the first million numbers, or in the first billion numbers, or in the first trillion numbers. It is impossibly difficult to make this calculation by simple methods. To find out whether such a number as 13,692,487 is a prime number is an extremely arduous task, because a mathematician must attempt to divide it by each smaller prime number, and discover whether there is a remainder. Formulas have been worked out for predicting the number of primes in the first n numbers (where n in any number), but the methods of deriving these formulas involve mathematics which would be far beyond the average college graduate. (The number of primes in the first n numbers, if n is extremely large, is approximately n divided by the natural logarithm of n.)

For an example of a famous unsolved problem in the theory of numbers, see FERMAT'S LAST THEOREM. See also INDETERMINATE EQUATION.

THEOSOPHICAL SOCIETY, a religio-philosophical organization founded in New York City in 1875 by Elena Petrovna Blavatsky (q.v.), with the assistance of Henry Steel Olcott and William Quan Judge. In 1879 the international headquarters were transferred to Adyar, near Madras, in India, where the Society maintains numerous buildings, including a library, printing plant, auditorium, business offices, and residences. The objects of the Society are to promote the universal brotherhood of mankind; to investigate the ancient religions, philosophies, and sciences of the world; and to make systematic inquiries respecting the occult powers of man. Since it was instituted in 1875, the Society has established over sixty national organizations on five continents. The American organization is known as *The Theosophical Society in America.* Each national organization is autonomous and carries on its work of study and teaching in small groups, known as lodges or branches, which are also autonomous.

The first president of the Theosophical Society at Adyar was Olcott. He was succeeded in 1907 by Annie Besant (q.v.), who visited the United States in 1926, bringing with her the young Hindu Krishnamurti, whom she claimed to be the chosen vehicle through which the "Messiah" or World Teacher would speak when he should come again. Dr. George Arundale succeeded Annie Besant as president in 1934, and C. Jinarajadasa became head of the Society in 1946. The American organization has its headquarters at Wheaton, Illinois, where it maintains a spacious executive and student building constructed in 1927 on a forty-acre estate. The world membership of the Theosophical Society in a recent year was about 40,000.

See also THEOSOPHY.

THEOSOPHY (fr. Gr. *theos,* "god"; *sophos,* "wise"), the designation for any religio-philosophical system purporting to furnish authoritative knowledge of God, and of the universe in relation to God, by means of direct mystical intuition, philosophical inquiry, or both. The earliest examples of theosophic thought are found in the Sanskrit metaphysical treatises known as the Upanishads (q.v.). All Hindu philosophy subsequent to the introduction of the Upanishads (about the 8th century B.C.) has been predominantly theosophic in tone. From India this form of speculative philosophy was transmitted to Persia, where it was adopted by the Arabs after their conquest of Persia in the first half of the 7th century A.D. In China, the *I Ching* ("Book of Changes"), one of the so-called Five Classics (see CHINESE LANGUAGE AND LITERATURE) of the Confucian (see CONFUCIUS) religion, and the *Tao Tê Ching* ("Book of the Virtuous Way"), the chief treatise of the religio-philosophical system known as Taoism (q.v.), both contain theosophic elements. A distinctive theosophy was expounded in the Cabala (q.v.), a mystical interpretation of the Scriptures current among the Jews of Europe between the 12th and 16th centuries. The doctrines of the Cabala were profoundly influenced by two Western theosophic systems, namely, Neoplatonism (q.v.), as represented in the writings of Ammonius Saccas, Plotinus, Proclus (qq.v.), and Porphyrius; and Gnosticism (q.v.), as exemplified chiefly in the works of Basilides and Valentinus (qq.v.). In the Middle Ages theosophic teachings were expounded by Johannes Eckhart (1260?–1327?), Johannes Tauler (1300?–61), and Theophrastus Bombastus von Hohenheim, known as Philippus Aureolus Paracelsus (q.v.), and in later periods, by Robert Fludd, Jakob Böhme, and Jan Baptista van Helmont (q.v.).

In modern times, the term "theosophy" has been employed with particular reference to a system of occult philosophy set forth by Madame Elena Petrovna Blavatsky (q.v.), who maintained that she had received her doctrines from various Oriental religious teachers who were supposed to have reached a higher plane of existence than that of other mortals. The concepts and terminology of Blavatsky's system are derived for the most part from Buddhism and Hinduism (qq.v.; see also THEOSOPHICAL SOCIETY). According to her teaching, God is infinite, absolute, and unknowable. No attempt is made, therefore, to qualify or describe the Great Unknown, which is held to be the source of both spirit and matter. Spirit and matter are regarded as the two indissociable aspects of one root nature. By the operation of an immutable law, spirit is said to descend into matter, and matter to ascend into spirit. Thus a cyclical action is posited, from spirit downward to matter, and from matter upward to spirit.

In the cosmological application of this theory, all worlds are represented as passing through seven great periods of manifestation, called rounds. Spiritual at first, these worlds become denser and darker in their descent toward materiality, until they reach the fourth and densest round (corresponding to the present condition of our own material world). Thence begins their upward movement toward spirituality through the three ascending rounds. In its psychological application, the theosophic doctrine represents all souls as being the same in essence, although differing in degrees of development. The more advanced souls are supposed to be the natural guardians of the less developed.

Man, according to the theosophists, is composed of seven principles, which are divided into a lower (mortal) and higher (immortal) nature. The lower nature, constituting man's personality, is fourfold. Of this fourfold nature, one fourth, constituting the physical body, is visible; the remaining three fourths are invisible. These three invisible principles are, respectively, the astral body, a subtle counterpart of the physical body, on which is molded the physical atoms; the life principle; and the principle of desire. The physical body is matter without form; it receives its form, or "entelechy", from the astral body, and is animated by the principle of desire. This fourfold nature, common to all animal beings, is mortal and subject to dissolution at death. The higher nature of man is threefold, and comprises the mind, soul, and spirit. This higher nature, when freed by death from the trammels of the lower nature, ascends to heaven, in which it enjoys a period of happiness and tranquillity proportionate to its virtuous thoughts and high ideals while on earth. With the exhaustion of its accumulated good, however, the higher nature descends once more to earth.

One mundane life is not sufficient to effect the total redemption of the soul from the corruption of its lower nature, hence the cycle of birth-death-rebirth through which the soul must pass until it has altogether purged away the moral consequences of its earthly deeds, both good and evil (see TRANSMIGRATION). By purification and training of the body, the theosophists maintain, the divine powers latent in man are acti-

vated. The bonds of personality then no longer bind him to the attractions of the senses. Having consciously related himself to the source of his being, he becomes one with the divine. See also METAPHYSICS; MYSTICISM; OCCULTISM; VEDANTA.

THEOTOKOPOULOS, KYRIAKOS. See GRECO, EL.

THERAPEUTÆ, an ascetic sect, mentioned in the *De Vita Contemplativa*, doubtfully ascribed to Philo, as living chiefly on Lake Mareotis, near Alexandria, Egypt. Their discipline resembled that of the Essenes (q.v.). Throughout the week each lived in his lonely dwelling, but on the Sabbath they assembled for worship.

THERAPEUTICS, the science of healing; that division of medicine which treats of the actions of remedies on the diseased animal system, or the means by which nature can be aided in return to health. The conception of disease which is found among primitive races is associated with the idea of demon possession. The earliest therapeutic measures were devoted to driving out these demons from the bodies of their victims. Two methods were employed: one consisted in the recital of charms or magic over the ailing part, or over the sick person; and the other consisted in internal administration or external application of certain aromatic or bitter herbs. In the early history of both Eastern and Western nations there was a blending of the office of priest and physician.

Among the ancient Egyptians the treatment of disease had acquired a character by no means unscientific. They used remedies of vegetable, mineral, and animal nature, many of acknowledged value. Careful directions as to administration of drugs and indications for their use have been found. Egyptian physicians' knowledge of hydrotherapy, dietetics, and hygiene was far advanced. Among the Hebrews the infliction and cure of diseases is on various occasions in Scripture ascribed to the direct interposition of God. Their methods of treatment consisted principally of strict hygienic means, attention to diet, ablution, separation, and combustion of infected garments. A large list of remedies is mentioned in the Bible.

The Chinese assert that with them the study of medicine was coeval with the foundation of their empire. They possess works on treatment of great antiquity. Ginseng they regarded as a panacea, and also employed opium, mercury, and many other drugs of value. The Greeks may have borrowed something from the Eastern nations of their knowledge of medicine and treatment; but researches have shown that under the scientific spirit of Hippocrates they had evolved a fairly good system. Hippocrates ascribed disease to alterations of the humors of the body (the blood, phlegm, and yellow and black bile). He employed baths, diet, exercise, blood-letting, the actual cautery, and an extensive series of medicines. Galen represented the highest development of Greek medicine. He explained the operation of drugs by reference to their elementary qualities, heat, cold, dryness, and moisture.

In the early periods of Roman history medicine was practiced by the slaves and freedmen and its highest development was reached under the influence of the Greek school. In the Dark Ages medicine was practiced by the monks. Magic and astrology were potent influences. Toward the middle of the eighteenth century the practice of therapeutics had reached a most complicated stage. There were theories and countertheories, and physicians were prescribing huge doses of unpleasant mixtures in the hope of securing good from all the remedies recommended. A natural reaction set in which resulted in the establishment of homeopathy.

Modern therapeutics may be said to have begun with the discovery of morphine, an alkaloid of opium, in 1817. The present method of treatment is embodied in rational therapeutics, which implies the use of remedies based on a knowledge of the diseased condition present in the patient, a knowledge of the nature of disease itself, and of the physiological action of the agent employed, as determined by experimental investigation on animals, from which may be deduced the action on men. The knowledge of the action of drugs must include the manner in which they effect nerve centers, respiration, circulation, and especially their influence on blood pressure and on body temperature. The range of medicinal doses, as well as the minimum and maximum fatal doses, must also be determined.

In treating disease it is the aim of the physician to seek the cause of the condition present and to endeavor from a true appreciation of the knowledge of drug action to administer curative remedies. A remedy which will usually cure a certain disease is called a specific. Such is the action of mercury and salvarsan in syphilis, and quinine in malaria. Empirical therapeutics was based on the cumulative evidence that cer-

tain drugs were of service in certain conditions, and experiment was the sure guide. Symptomatic treatment aims to relieve the symptoms of disease irrespective of their cause. Rational or scientific therapeutics recognizes that both these previous methods may have to be followed at times, but it aims especially at the removal of the cause of disease by appropriate treatment of whatever sort. It has been developed by the increased knowledge of disease which we have acquired through the growth of the sciences of pathology and bacteriology. *Materia medica* comprises a knowledge of the remedies employed in medicine; while the methods by which drugs are prepared and combined for administration, as well as the separation of the active principles of drugs, belongs to the department of therapeutics known as pharmacy. It is essential that there should be a uniform standard of strength and purity of medicinal products, as well as uniformity in their preparation, and to attain this object the various countries have standards established by law or by professional authority, to which the drugs prepared by the pharmacists must conform. These standards are published by each nation in works known as *Pharmacopœias*. The first United States *Pharmacopœia* was published in 1820, previous to which time European works were used. This work is revised every ten years by a committee of physicians and pharmacists. Those preparations which follow its direction and are named in the work are called official. Unofficial preparations, including many newer drugs, are in use. Some of these, provided they are of sufficient value, are included in the *Pharmacopœia*.

The term "therapeutics" is usually restricted to the administration of medicinal drugs, but in its broadest sense, general therapeutics, it includes every form of treatment. Natural therapeutics is the healing power of nature to cure disease through the operation of the so-called *vis medicatrix naturæ*. In what is known as expectant treatment the physician depends solely on this force and sustains the patient's strength by food and nursing. Treatment by surgical means is regarded as a special and separate department of medicine. A large number of other means than treatment by drugs are in use and each is designated by an appropriate prefix. Electrotherapeutics, the use of electricity as a healing agent, is especially valuable in certain cases of disease of the nervous system or local injury to a nerve. Radio-therapy or X-ray therapy is the use of the Röntgen rays. Suggestive therapeutics is the name given to treatment in the form of suggestion made to the patient while in an induced hypnotic state, with the object of the patient's following the suggestion when out of the hypnotic state. Thermotherapeutics is the treatment of disease by the application of heat. Therapeutics fully recognizes the value of diet in disease in the department known as dietetics or dietotherapeutics.

THEREMIN, LEO (1896–), Russian musician and engineer, born in St. Petersburg (now Leningrad), and educated at the University of St. Petersburg and at the St. Petersburg Musical Institute. In 1919 Theremin was made director of the Laboratory of Electrical Oscillations at the Leningrad Physico-Technical Institute; soon afterward, he invented an electronic musical instrument which bears his name. The initial public demonstration of the theremin was given by its inventor in August, 1920, at the Eighth All-Soviet Union Electrical Congress. Seven years later Theremin visited the United States, giving a series of recitals on his instrument in New York and other principal cities. He returned to the Soviet Union in 1938.

The theremin consists of a compact cabinet, from the right rear corner of which a vertical, antennalike rod projects; from the left side a loop of metal extends in an almost horizontal direction. Musical sounds are generated by two vacuum-tube oscillator circuits. One of these circuits functions at a fixed frequency; the frequency of the other circuit is controlled by the motions of the instrumentalist's hand in the air close to the vertical rod. The pitch of the sound emitted by the instrument is raised or lowered as the hand of the performer is moved toward or away from the rod; a range of approximately six octaves may be achieved by moving the hand within a radius of about three feet from the rod. Volume is controlled by a switch, which is located on the front panel of the cabinet and fixes the volume level, and by the motion of the instrumentalist's left hand above the horizontal loop of metal on the left side of the cabinet. When the hand is raised upward from the loop the volume of the tone is amplified; conversely, when the hand is lowered the tone diminishes until it finally becomes inaudible. Few compositions have been written especially for the theremin as either a solo or ensemble instrument; among the most notable is the *First Airphonic Suite* (1929), by the Russian-American composer Joseph Schillinger.

THERESA, SAINT. See TERESA.

THEREZINA, the capital of Piauhy State, Brazil, on the Parnahyba River, with cotton mills and soap works. Pop., about 58,000.

THERIODONTIA, an animal classification, proposed by Owen, to include the mammallike reptiles with mammallike teeth, from the South African Karrov formation. The group has since been subdivided, the Lower Permian types forming the Therocephalia, and the Upper Triassic, the Cynodontia.

THERMOCHEMISTRY, the division of the science of chemistry treating of the energy phenomena involved in chemical reactions. Nearly all chemical reactions are accompanied by energy changes which are usually in the form of heat transfers. Most of these reactions result in heat energy being liberated, and are said to be *exothermic*. Thus the burning of coke, in which solid carbon and gaseous oxygen from the air unite to produce carbon dioxide, is an exothermic reaction which results in the release of heat. Thermochemistry also includes those changes in which energy is liberated in forms other than heat, such as light and electrical energy. Other reactions may occur in which heat is absorbed rather than released, i.e., heat, or energy in some other form, disappears during the reaction. Reactions of this type, which absorb heat or other types of energy, are called *endothermic*. Melting of ice is an endothermic reaction in which heat is absorbed from the surrounding air, thereby lowering the air temperature. Similarly, hydrated sodium thiosulfate, dissolved in water at room temperature, produces a solution which is cooler than the original water; the heat lost by the water is necessary to dissolution of the solid.

Energy produced by a chemical change, either in the form of liberated or absorbed heat, may be accurately measured by performing the reaction in an instrument called a calorimeter; see CALORIMETRY. A specific name is applied to the energy absorbed or emitted, according to the type of reaction with which it is associated. Thus, the heat absorbed or given off when a unit of solute is dissolved in a unit of solvent is called the *heat of solution*. Other terms include: *heat of combustion*, which is produced by the burning of a substance in air; *heat of formation*, utilized or emitted in the process of a chemical combination by which a distinct compound is formed; *heat of solidification*, produced by the transformation of a liquid or gas into the solid state; *heat of condensation*, released by the return of a gas to the liquid state; and *heat of hydration*, given off or absorbed when a substance combines with water. Except in atomic reactions (see ATOMIC ENERGY AND ATOMIC BOMB), the energy produced by chemical reactions in the form of heat loss or gain can neither disappear nor be destroyed, but may be converted into other forms. For example, a steam engine may convert heat energy to mechanical energy, and the mechanical energy may be converted by a generator into electrical energy. Similarly, in reversible chemical reactions (see REACTION, CHEMICAL), the amount of heat liberated by the exothermic process in one direction will be equal to the amount absorbed by the endothermic reaction in the reverse direction.

In order to express the energy change which has been observed and calculated experimentally, various forms of chemical equations have been utilized. These equations, in addition to indicating the substances involved, must also take into account the physical state of the reaction substance. For example, a reaction in which 68,400 calories of heat are liberated when one gram molecule of hydrogen gas reacts with one-half gram molecule of oxygen gas to produce one gram molecule of liquid water is expressed by the formula:

$$H_2(gas) + \frac{1}{2}O_2(gas) \rightarrow H_2O(liquid) + 68,400 \text{ cal.}$$

Some chemical reactions take place in several steps, each step absorbing or freeing varying amounts of energy. However, the total quantity of energy involved in a reaction depends only on the initial and final substances and conditions, and is not affected by any intermediate phenomena. This general principle, commonly referred to as the law of constant heat summation, was originated in 1840 by the French chemist Germain Henri Hess. It may be illustrated by the two different methods of chemical reaction which result in the preparation of barium oxide, BaO.

(1) *Direct method*:

$$Ba(solid) + \frac{1}{2}O_2(gas) \rightarrow BaO(solid) + 124,400 \text{ cal.}$$

(2) *Indirect method*:

$$Ba(solid) + O_2(gas) \rightarrow BaO_2(solid) + 141,600 \text{ cal.}$$

$$BaO_2(solid) \rightarrow BaO(Solid) + \frac{1}{2}O_2(gas) - 17,200 \text{ cal.}$$

The amount of heat energy liberated by the solid barium is therefore the same in the direct method (124,400 cal.) as in the indirect (141,600 + 17,200 = 124,400). With a knowledge of the various intermediate steps involved in chemical reactions, it is possible, through the law of constant heat summation, to predict accurately the heat of reaction of any process not measurable by physical means; see THERMODYNAMICS.

THERMODYNAMICS, the branch of physical science which deals with the relation between heat and work (qq.v.). It forms the basis of the modern doctrine of energy (q.v.), and the science of applying mechanics to heat phenomena. With the development of the theory, the names of Colding, Hirn, Davy, Rumford, Joule, and Mayer are closely associated. In 1843 Joule obtained a measurement of the mechanical or dynamical equivalent of heat, commonly called Joule's Equivalent. By demonstrating that wherever energy in the dynamical form is lost an exact equivalent of heat is always obtained, Joule established what is known as the First Law of Thermodynamics. Briefly, this law is the statement that heat is energy, and can be measured in the same units.

Others who developed the science, which embraces the functions of steam engines, gas engines, and all machines which do work by combustion of fuel, were Carnot, Rankin, Clausius, and Thomson (Lord Kelvin). Sadi Carnot, in his *Réflexions sur la Puissance du Feu* (1824), laid down the lines along which the complete theory must be developed. His own argument was vitiated by the assumption of the then accepted caloric theory of heat. But we know from his posthumous papers, published in 1878, that Carnot, before 1832, recognized that heat was energy, and had fully enunciated the First Law of Thermodynamics.

The novel feature of Carnot's method was the invention of the cycle of operations, and especially the reversible cycle. An engine or working substance will have passed through a cycle of operations when all its parts have recovered exactly those physical conditions (volume, pressure, temperature, and the like) which they had at the beginning. It is only when such a cycle has been completed that we have any right to reason about the equivalence of the transformations of energy which have taken place during the progress of the operations which constitute the cycle.

The perfect or reversible engine, as imagined by Carnot, is capable of going through a cycle of operations in either direction. During the direct process, the heat engine does work at the expense of an equivalent amount of heat which disappears; during the reverse process the heat is restored at the expense of an equivalent amount of work done on the engine. On account of the tendency of heat to diffuse in the direction of diminishing temperature, this condition of things cannot be practically realized; but as the temperature differences become smaller and smaller, the conditions for true reversibility become more and more closely approximated. If there were available an absolute nonconductor of heat, we should be able to study transformations without gain or loss of heat to the working substance. Under such *adiabatic* conditions, as they are called, reversibility would be realizable.

A valuable deduction from Carnot's principle was made by Thomson (Lord Kelvin), who defined temperature in a manner quite independent of the properties of any particular substance. So defined, it is known as the absolute temperature (q.v.). The greatest possible efficiency of a heat engine is measured by the ratio of the difference of temperatures of the source and refrigerator to the temperature of the source. This absolute scale is found to be in close accordance with the scale of the air thermometer; and its zero, as determined by Lord Kelvin and Joule, lies 274° C. below the freezing point of water. Thus a perfect engine working between temperatures 0° to 100°C. would have an efficiency of a little more than one fourth. Practically, it will hardly exceed half that value.

When a substance takes in or gives out heat it is said to change its *entropy*, an index of the relative amount of unavailable energy in a physiochemical system: the length on a diagram in which area is energy, in heat units, and height is absolute temperature.

THERMOELECTRICITY, electricity generated by difference of temperature, as by two different metals in double contact and at different temperatures; also, that part of the science of electricity embracing phenomena related to the resistance caused by passage of current in a conductor, developing heat or light. See ELECTRICITY: *Current Electricity.*

THERMOMETER, an instrument for measuring temperature. The ordinary thermometer consists of a glass tube of narrow bore, which opens into a bulb at one end. The bulb and part of the capillary tube are filled with a substance, generally mercury. sometimes alcohol or other liquid. Mercury is pre-

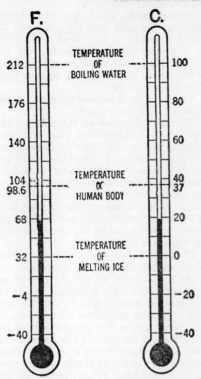

Fahrenheit (left) and centigrade thermometers

eminently suitable for thermometric purposes. It remains liquid through a long range of temperature; expands regularly as heat is applied to it; it is opaque, and therefore easily read; and does not wet the surface of the glass with which it is in contact. For low temperatures alcohol and ether thermometers are valuable, these substances having a low freezing point and a high expansibility.

The two standard temperatures universally used in graduating a thermometer are the freezing and boiling points of water. In the modern centigrade, or Celsius, scale, the freezing point of water is taken at zero, and the boiling point under a pressure of 760 millimeters (29.92 in.) of mercury as 100°. In the Fahrenheit thermometer, the freezing point of water is 32° and its boiling point 212°.

Réaumur divided the interval between the freezing and boiling points into eighty divisions, and his scale is still largely used.

The centigrade scale is used almost exclusively for scientific purposes. British and American meteorologists, however, prefer the

Fahrenheit scale, which has two distinct merits as compared with the centigrade. Its degree is smaller, so that, reading to tenths, it is a more delicate instrument; and the freezing point being at 32°, it is only under severe wintry conditions that negative temperatures are found.

Various modified forms of thermometers are used for particular purposes.

Maximum and *minimum* thermometers belong to the self-registering class of instrument. In one form of maximum thermometer the mercury pushes a small index, which remains to show the highest point reached. In the minimum thermometer, the index is set in the alcohol used as the thermometric substance. As the alcohol contracts, it drags with it the index, and its upper end indicates the lowest point reached by the curved capillary surface of the liquid.

Clinical thermometers are small instruments specially designed for determining the body temperatures of animals (mouth or rectum). They are self-registering, usually by a trap in the capillary tube between the bulb and the lowest graduation on the scale, of the correct size, so that the mercury can expand through the trap in fine globules, but cannot flow back. From one-half to three minutes are required to obtain the final temperature indication when placed in the mouth, and before the thermometer is used again the mercury column must be shaken down into the bulb. To avoid the objection that the graduations may retain disease germs not readily removable by antiseptic liquids, clinical thermometers are sometimes made with the scale inclosed in a glass tube, or the thermometer completely covered by a thin glass envelope.

For continuous registration of temperature, or for self-registration of temperatures at short intervals, intermittent photography is used.

Historically older than and scientifically superior to the mercurial thermometer is the *air* thermometer. It is indispensable for measuring the very low temperatures that must be reached before the ordinary gases can be liquefied under great pressure.

Thermoelectricity has provided delicate methods of measuring the most minute changes of temperature.

The invention of the thermometer must be attributed to Galileo, who about the year 1593 made an open-air thermoscope, consisting of a bulb with a long tube attached, which was provided with a scale and dipped below the surface of a liquid, water or wine. Some of the air was expelled from the bulb, and so the liquid rose in the tube. This thermometer was later used (1611) by Sanctorius in the diagnosis of fevers. The word thermoscope was used by Bianconi in 1617 and thermometer in 1624 by Leurechon. The first scaled thermometers were those of Ferdinand II, Grand Duke of Tuscany (1641). They contained alcohol. In 1661 Fabri made a scale, using as the fixed temperatures those of snow and of midsummer heat. Robert Hooke in 1664 proposed the freezing point of water as one of the fixed temperatures; and in 1694 Renaldini proposed this as one, and the boiling point of water as the other. In 1709 Fahrenheit introduced his alcohol thermometers, and in 1714 his mercury ones. About 1731 Réaumur devised his scale, which until recently was in extensive use on the continent of Europe. In 1742 Celsius proposed a centigrade scale, with the temperatures of melting ice 100° and boiling water 0°. Christin, working independently of Celsius, proposed a centigrade scale in 1743 which is the Celsius scale inverted, and is the one used now.

THERMOPYLÆ (Gr., "Hot Gates"), a pass famous in ancient Greek history, lying between Mount Œta and the Maliac Gulf and leading from Thessaly into Locris. The pass, which received its name from the existence of several hot sulphur springs in the vicinity, was the main route by which an invading army could penetrate from northern into southern Greece. In ancient times it was a narrow track about fifty ft. wide passing under a cliff, but alluvial deposits have so altered the coast line that it is now a broad swampy plain from one and a half to three miles broad. Thermopylæ won eternal fame as the scene of the heroic death of Leonidas I (q.v.) and his 300 Spartans in their attempt to stem the tide of Persian invasion in 480 B.C. The Spartans were betrayed by Ephialtes, a Thessalian, into the hands of the Persians, who, by following a path over the mountain, attacked the Greeks from the rear. In 279 B.C. Brennus, at the head of a Gallic force, traveled the same path and forced the united Greeks to withdraw from the pass. Again, in 191 B.C., Antiochus III (q.v.), King of Syria, endeavored to check the Romans at this point, but Marcus Porcius Cato stormed the fortress which commanded the path, and, aided by a frontal attack of the main Roman force under Manius Acilius Glabrio, routed and almost annihilated the Syrian army.

THERMOSTAT, an automatic device employed to maintain or regulate the temperature of an enclosed area by controlling the operation of a heat-producing apparatus. Nearly all thermostats are operated by the expansion of liquids or solids subjected to varying degrees of heat. Thus, in a typical metallic-element thermostat, two metals, such as steel and bronze, having different coefficients of expansion, are fastened together and arranged in a spiral or as a straight rod. The metal spiral or rod is then securely attached at one end to a fixed point, the other end being fastened to a pointer or indicator. When the temperature of the surrounding atmosphere rises above a predetermined point, the unequal expansions of the two metals force the coiled or rod-shaped strip to bend the pointer toward one of the contacts, automatically causing the heating unit to cease functioning temporarily. Similarly, a drop in temperature below that desired will force the strip and the indicator in the reverse direction and against the opposite contact, thereby causing the heating unit to function until the pointer returns to its neutral position.

The wafer-type thermostat, constructed of numerous flat, circular shells called sylphons, operates on the principle of the expansion of liquids when heated. The pressure resulting from water heated within this form of thermostat is exerted upon the walls of the very flexible sylphons, causing an undulating motion which is in turn transmitted to the valves regulating the operation of a heating system. Other types of thermostats, used in more specialized cases, may be operated by the action of electric currents, or may depend upon the varying resistances of metallic conductors. The principle of the thermostat is also used to put out fires in houses and factories by setting automatic sprinkler systems into operation.

THERSITES, in Greek legend, a Greek warrior, son of Agrius, who fought in the Trojan War. Homer in his *Iliad* describes him as the ugliest and the most impudent of the Greeks massed before Troy. After the withdrawal of the hero Achilles (q.v.) from the fighting, Thersites reviled Agamemnon (q.v.), the commander in chief of the Greek forces, and was beaten by the hero Ulysses, to the amusement of the assembled Greeks. According to later writers, he mocked Achilles for mourning the death of Penthesilea, the Queen of the Amazons, and was slain by Achilles.

Theseus slaying a Centaur (Greek painting)

THESEUS, the great national hero of the ancient Athenians, and, next to Hercules, the most famous character of Greek legend. He was said to be the son of Ægeus (q.v.), King of Athens, and Æthra, daughter of King Pittheus of Troezen, but early legend also recognized the paternity of Poseidon, god of the sea; modern writers suggest that Ægeus was originally a local name of the sea god.

Theseus, having grown to maturity in Troezen, set out for Athens with the sword and sandals left behind by Ægeus. On this journey he killed many dangerous men and beasts, his adventures recalling the more illustrious exploits of Hercules; Theseus slew, among others, the brigands Procrustes (q.v.), Sinis, and Sciron. Arriving at Athens, Theseus narrowly escaped poisoning at the hands of the sorceress Medea (q.v.), who, after her crimes at Corinth, had sought refuge with Ægeus in Athens. Ægeus, recognizing the sword and sandals as his own, acknowledged the youth as his son. Theseus next captured the fire-breathing bull of Marathon, which had been brought from Crete by Hercules. Then came the famous expedition to Crete to deliver Athens from the necessity of paying human tribute to the monstrous Minotaur (q.v.); this creature Theseus killed with the assistance of Ariadne (q.v.), the daughter of King Minos, whom he took from Crete but later deserted on the island of Naxos. On his way home from Crete he founded a festival at Delos in honor of the god Apollo, and to this shrine the Athenians thereafter sent an annual embassy. Theseus, on setting out from Athens with black sails, as was customary for the ships which bore the Athenian youths and maidens to the Cretan sacrifice, had promised to change the sails from black to white if he returned in safety; Theseus forgot the promise, however, and Ægeus, seeing the black-sailed ship returning and believing that his son had perished, hurled himself from a rock into the sea.

Theseus now became king of Athens. He took part in several legendary expeditions, including that of the Argonauts (q.v.), the Calydonian hunt (see CALYDONIAN BOAR; MELEAGER), and that against the Amazons (q.v.). As a result of this last trip, the Amazons invaded Attica, but were finally repulsed by Theseus, who secured as wife their queen, Antiope or Hippolyta (q.v.), by whom he had a son, Hippolytus (q.v.). After the death of his wife, Theseus married Phædra (q.v.), the daughter of Minos and sister of Ariadne. Having formed a firm friendship with Pirithoüs (q.v.), King of the Lapithæ, he aided the latter in his fight against the Centaurs; with the assistance of Pirithoüs, he later carried off Helen (see HELEN OF TROY) from Sparta, but she was subsequently rescued by her brothers Castor and Pollux. Theseus also accompanied Pirithoüs to the lower world when the latter desired to carry off Persephone (q.v.) as his bride, but both heroes were imprisoned in the underworld; Pirithoüs never returned, and Theseus remained in captivity until Hercules, on his quest for Cerberus, prevailed upon Hades to release him. During Theseus' absence from Athens, his wife Phædra fell in love with Hippolytus, her stepson, and, being repulsed by the youth, committed suicide, leaving a false accusation against Hippolytus. Theseus returned from the underworld and, believing the charge, cursed his son, who was later dragged to his death, the curse being fulfilled by the god Poseidon. Theseus was unable to re-establish his authority after his return to Athens and went to the island of Scyros, where he was murdered by King Lycomedes.

Although most of the tales concerning Theseus seem pure myth, the ancient Athenians themselves looked upon him as a historical figure, one of their early kings, to whom was attributed the consolidation into one state of the twelve independent communities of Attica.

THESPIS (fl. 6th century B.C.), Athenian poet, known as the father of Greek tragedy. His first victory in a dramatic contest is said to have been about 534 B.C. To him was attributed the introduction of an actor to converse with the leader of the chorus, who previously had recited the adventures of the god Dionysus (q.v.) to the chorus and had been answered by the chorus. Originally only the chorus and its leader were on stage. Thespis' introduction of an actor to respond to and interrupt the leader's exposition represents the beginning of dialogue in Greek drama. Thespis is also said to have introduced the use of a linen mask, which made possible more dramatic action, because the actor, by disguising himself, could represent various characters in the same play.

THESSALONIANS, FIRST AND SECOND EPISTLES TO THE. The first epistle, which is the earliest extant epistle of Paul, was written at Corinth, about 53 A.D. or 54 A.D. Of its two parts the first is mainly personal and explanatory (1–3), and the second ethical and doctrinal (4, 5). Baur, who was the first to deny the genuineness of this epistle, has not been followed in this by the more recent representatives of the Tübingen school.

The second epistle consists of three parts. The first is introductory (1:1-12). The second (2:1-12) is eschatological, and warns readers against supposing "that the day of the Lord is now present". The concluding part of the epistle (2:13-3:18) substantially repeats the exhortations of 1 Thessalonians. The genuineness of this epistle was first doubted by J.E.C. Schmidt (1801), which doubt has steadily increased since that time. Assuming the hypothesis of its genuineness, 2 Thessalonians must have been written shortly after 1 Thessalonians and before the apostle's sojourn of eighteen months in Corinth had come to an end. Apart indeed from 2:1-12, 2 Thessalonians may conceivably have been written before 1 Thessalonians.

THESSALONICA. See SALONIKA.

THESSALY, the largest division of ancient Greece, a vast plain, separated on the N. from Macedonia by the Cambunian Mountains, on the W. from Epirus by the Pindus range, and on the S. from Locris and Phocis by the Maliac Gulf. The Ægean Sea is on the E. The plain is drained chiefly by the Salambria (anc. Peneus) River and its tributaries, and is the most fertile in all Greece; the river flows into the sea through the famous mountain gorge of Tempe, between mounts Olympus and Ossa. In ancient times the plain produced an abundance of grain and cattle, and a breed of horses considered the finest in Greece. In Greek mythology, Thessaly was the home of the Centaurs (q.v.) and the Lapithæ, and from Thessaly Jason and the Argonauts (q.v.) set out in quest of the golden fleece.

The government of Thessaly in the early historical period appears to have been oligarchical in the separate cities, of which Pharsalus, Larissa, Heracleum, and Pheræ were the most important; during the 6th and 5th centuries B.C. the principal power was in the hands of the two families of the Aleuadæ of Larissa and the Scopadæ of Crannon and Pharsalus. About 374 B.C. Jason, tyrant of Pheræ, was elected *tagus*, or chief magistrate, of all Thessaly. The rule of Jason's successors became so unbearable that aid was sought from Philip of Macedon, who in 344 B.C. subjugated the country. Thessaly remained subject to the Macedonian kings until the victory of Titus Quinctius Flamininus at Cynoscephalæ in 197 B.C. brought it under the protection of Rome. Under the Roman emperors Thessaly was united with Macedonia, but after the reign of the emperor Constantine (306–37 A.D.) it became a separate province. In 1204 A.D., along with other portions of the eastern empire, Thessaly came under the dominion of the Venetians, and in 1335 was taken by the Turks. Turkey ceded Thessaly to Greece in 1881, as a result of the Congress of Berlin (1878) which followed the Russo-Turkish War. In 1897 Thessaly was the principal battleground of the Greco-Turkish War.

Today the plain of ancient Thessaly, over 5000 sq.m. in area, comprises the Greek departments of Larissa and Trikkala, with a population of nearly 500,000. The region is essentially agricultural and pastoral.

THETFORD MINES, town of Wolfe Co., Quebec, 80 miles s.w. of Quebec. It has extensive asbestos mines. Pop., about 10,000.

THETIS, in Greek mythology, the daughter of the sea divinities Nereus (q.v.) and Doris, and the most famous of the Nereids (q.v.). She was wooed both by Zeus, father of the gods, and by Poseidon, god of the sea, until they learned the prophecy that she would bear a son who would be mightier than his father; thereupon she was forced against her will to marry a mortal, Peleus (q.v.), the ruler of the Myrmidons. At the marriage of Peleus and Thetis, Eris, the goddess of discord, threw a golden apple, inscribed "To the Most Beautiful", among the assembled guests; the resultant strife among the three goddesses Hera, wife of Zeus, Athena, goddess of wisdom, and Aphrodite, goddess of love, led ultimately to the Trojan War (see PARIS). By Peleus, Thetis became the mother of the hero Achilles (q.v.). She lived in the depths of the sea with her father, and had, like Proteus (q.v.), the power of changing her shape.

THIBAULT, JACQUES ANATOLE. See FRANCE, ANATOLE.

THICKHEAD FLY, common name for any of the flies of the family Conopidae, a group comprising species with large heads broader than the thorax. They are rather large insects, but are generally slender and with a stalked abdomen. They frequent flowers, and their larvae are parasitic, chiefly upon bumblebees and wasps, and, more rarely, upon grasshoppers. About 30 species are found in the United States.

THIERRY, JACQUES NICOLAS AUGUSTIN (1795–1856), French historian, born in Blois. In 1814 he joined the ranks of the Parisian Liberals. Soon after appeared his first book, entitled *De la Réorganisation de la Société Européenne.* In 1820 he contributed *Lettres sur l'Histoire de France* to the *Courrier Français.* In 1825 he published his masterpiece, *L'Histoire de la Conquête d'Angleterre par les Normands.*

THIERS, LOUIS ADOLPHE (1797–1877), French historian and politician, born in Marseilles. His articles in *Constitutionnel* on political and literary subjects gained influence for him. In 1830, he, with Carrel, Mignet, and others, started the *National,* and in it combated the Polignac administration. The ministry met the opposition by the Ordonnances of July. The result was the revolution which drove Charles X into exile.

Thiers was elected a deputy; appointed secretary general to the minister of finance; and passed through several cabinet offices on his way to the premiership, which he attained in 1836. In August of the same year he resigned and became the leader of the opposition. In 1840 he was again summoned to office as president of the Council and foreign minister. In a few months he was a terror to the peace of Europe. He talked menacingly of setting aside the treaties of 1815 and of extending the French frontier to the Rhine. On his application to the British government, Napoleon's remains were removed from St. Helena to the Invalides (1840). After the *coup d'état* of 1851 he was arrested, and banished for several months.

The collapse of the Second Empire enabled Thiers to play the greatest of his parts, that of "liberator of the territory". He made an abortive diplomatic mission, after Sedan, to procure the intervention of the Great Powers, but was instrumental in securing for his country an armistice which permitted the holding of a national assembly with a view to the negotiation of peace. He was placed at the head of the provisional government, and was elected (1871) president of the French Republic. He held office till 1873, and was instrumental in securing the withdrawal of the Germans from France, and the payment of the war indemnity. His histories are eulogies of revolutionary and Napoleonic ideals.

THIRD (COMMUNIST) INTERNATIONAL, known as the COMINTERN, a world-wide union of communist parties, founded in Moscow in 1919 by the Bolshevik leader Nikolai Lenin (q.v.) and his associates for the purpose of overthrowing all "bourgeois" governments and establishing an international federation of Soviet republics. The First International (see INTERNATIONAL WORKINGMEN'S ASSOCIATION), founded in London in 1864 under the leadership of Karl Marx, was dissolved in 1876. The Second International (q.v.) was founded in Paris in 1889. The formation of the Third International marked the complete break of the communist revolutionary movement from the socialist world organization, the Second International. Of the fifty-one delegates representing eight countries who attended the first congress of the new organization, the majority were members of the Russian Communist Party, which had issued the invitation to the meeting. Most of the other delegates represented various groups which had previously constituted a dissident left wing in the Second International, opposing the patriotic support given by right-wing leaders to their governments during World War I. The congress elected the Russian Bolshevik leader Grigori Zinoviev (q.v.) first president of the Comintern, proclaimed its dedication to the cause of establishing in all countries a proletarian dictatorship modeled on the Soviet regime, and announced its uncompromising hostility to those who placed patriotism and pacifism before the cause of the revolution.

By 1921 the Third International had grown both numerically and in the consolidation of its policy. Over two hundred delegates attended the second congress held in Moscow in 1920. A twenty-one-point program, the endorsement of which was required for membership, placed paramount emphasis on the revolutionary purpose and disciplinary methods of communism. The second congress issued a formal statement declaring that the world was in a state of "acute civil war", and outlined an attack, not only against capitalism and capitalist governments, but also against all socialists who believed in reformist methods and in political democracy. In order to carry out this attack, the congress demanded that all groups affiliated with the Third International accept the Bolshevik organizational system and the disciplinary leadership of the Russian Bolshevik Party. Provision was made for the creation in each country of an "illegal" (or underground) party, in control of the work of the "legal" (open) party. The illegal parties were charged particularly with the task of carrying on secret propaganda and agitation in the ranks of the army, navy, and police. All national communist parties were commanded to seek control of the labor unions of their respective countries and to convert them into "powerful weapons of the revolution". A Red International of Labor Unions (Profintern) was set up to oppose the socialist Amsterdam International Federation of Trade Unions and to win the adherence of organized workers to the Comintern and its revolutionary aims (see TRADE UNION). The specific means whereby the aims of the Comintern were to be achieved by the communist parties of all nations were described in detail in the program drafted by the congress. Under this program, the world communist movement was pledged to support and aid the "Soviet Republics" (i.e., the U.S.S.R.) in the event of war with other nations.

At the fifth congress of the Comintern, held in Moscow in 1924, a constitution was drawn up setting forth the organizational structure in detail. Nominally, the highest governing body of the Comintern was the world congress of representatives of the member parties. The congress was to meet biannually; after 1928, however, only one congress convened, namely the seventh congress which met in Moscow in 1935. Between sessions of the congresses, supreme authority was vested in the Executive Committee, which was to meet twice a year. A Presidium composed of about thirty members drawn from the Executive Committee was to meet every two weeks, and to conduct the business of the Executive Committee during the intervals between the latter body's meetings. The Presidium was empowered to elect from among its members a Political Secretariat composed of twelve individuals; the Political

Secretariat actually functioned as the highest executive organ of the Comintern, formulating its fundamental strategy and tactics, laying down the "Party line", and exercising effective control over both the Presidium and the Executive Committee. Under the constitution the revolutionary tasks before the Comintern were assigned to various departments, the most important of which were the departments of organizations (Orgburo), of information and statistics, and of propaganda and agitation. The communist parties throughout the world were grouped into a number of geographical sections, such as the Scandinavian and Balkan sections, each directed by a Central Committee controlled by the Executive Committee.

During the 1920's, as the postwar political situation in Europe moved toward stabilization, the prospect of a world-wide civil war receded. Communist uprising in several countries of Europe, notably Germany and Hungary (see GERMANY: *History*; HUNGARY: *History*), were brief and unsuccessful. The newly formed communist parties throughout the world were thrown into confusion by this apparent refutation of the most basic tenets of Marxist theory, and the leaders of the Third International made frequent adjustments and alterations of program and policy. In 1928 a sixth congress held in Moscow emphasized the authoritarian character of the organization and objectives of the Comintern. The new program, drawn up primarily by Joseph Stalin (q.v.), head of the Russian Communist Party and of the Soviet state, reaffirmed the absolute and unqualified dedication of the Third International to world revolution. The disciplinary organization of the national communist parties, which had been established in almost fifty countries, was tightened, and instructions for immediate action and revolutionary propaganda were more explicitly defined. Considerable emphasis was placed on the duty of all communists throughout the world to defend the U.S.S.R. against military attack by the capitalist powers. After the sixth congress of 1928, the Comintern changed little in organization or policy. From its inception it was a strongly centralized body, denying any autonomy whatever to the separate communist parties of the various nations. Strict party discipline was demanded of all individual members, who were expected to execute promptly the decisions of the Communist International and its various organs, and the active membership had no opportunity to partici-

pate in the formulation of party policy.

The Communist International had no formal connection with the Soviet government. The existence, however, of a close bond between the two was evident. The headquarters of the Comintern were located in Moscow, and its financial support came chiefly, although secretly, from the Soviet government. The Soviet Communist Party was always dominant in the International, both in numbers (almost three fourths of the total membership were Soviet communists in 1928) and in the positions of power held by its members. The guiding force of the Comintern was from the beginning the head of the Soviet state, i.e., from 1919 to 1924, Nikolai Lenin, and after 1924, Joseph Stalin.

The program adopted by the sixth congress in 1928 made more stringent the conditions for membership laid down by the second congress in 1920 and extended them to require the subordination of all local interests to the interests which the leading bodies of the Comintern decided should take precedence. That these decisions often reflected internal factional disputes in the Soviet state and the exigencies of Russian foreign policy is indicated by the frequent changes in the policy of the Comintern. Its policy alternated between extreme revolutionism (leftism) and a "united front" with reformist social democrats (rightism), depending on which policy best served the requirements of the U.S.S.R.

After several quick shifts from leftism to rightism in the 1920's, the Comintern made a sharp turn to the left in 1929, and followed this course until 1934. The conditions existing when the turn was made in 1929 were as follows: in the Soviet Union, Joseph Stalin had overcome all factional opposition to his personal power and established himself as undisputed master of the Soviet state and the Soviet Communist Party; the democratic countries were undergoing a severe depression, with unparalleled unemployment and almost chaotic social dislocation; and in Germany, the National Socialist Party, led by Adolf Hitler (q.v.), was plotting the overthrow of the republican government (see NATIONAL SOCIALISM). Among the leaders of the Comintern these conditions were interpreted as the precursors of a new era of revolution. They welcomed Hitler's coming to power in 1933 as a step forward in the destruction of the old order, paving the way for a workers' revolution. Throughout this period, from 1929 to 1934, the Communist International prohibited any co-operation between its members on one hand and democratic socialists and reformist organizations on the other.

The victory of Hitler proved far more substantial than the communist leaders had expected, removing temporarily all hopes of a revolution led by the communists in Germany and also presenting a military threat to the Soviet Union. Alarmed by the growing danger to Soviet security, the Comintern suddenly proclaimed, in February, 1934, a "Popular Front" policy of unity between communists and all who believed in any form of democracy. The basic doctrine of revolution was apparently put aside. For the next five years this policy was maintained, and communists openly entered the governmental and educational services of the democratic states. In August, 1939, the policy of the Comintern turned leftward again when the Soviet Union signed a nonaggression pact with the government of Hitler, presumably for reasons of military strategy, and a few weeks later, upon the outbreak of World War II, joined the Nazis in the invasion and conquest of Poland. The communist parties of all countries were unsparing in their condemnation of the war as an imperialist struggle. When, in June, 1941, Germany invaded the Soviet Union, the Comintern made another extreme rightward swing to a Popular Front with the democracies. In this new stage the continued existence of the Communist International, and its avowed aim of overthrowing the "bourgeois" (i.e., democratic) states, became a strong obstacle to the collaboration of the U.S.S.R. with the democratic powers in their war effort against a common enemy. On May 22, 1943, without any apparent consultation with its member parties, the Executive Committee announced the dissolution of the Communist International, declaring "that the forms, methods, and regulations of the Comintern had become obsolete".

Four years later, in September, 1947, representatives of the communist parties of nine European countries (Russia, Yugoslavia, France, Italy, Poland, Bulgaria, Czechoslovakia, Hungary, and Romania) met in Poland and announced that a Communist Information Bureau would be established in Belgrade, Yugoslavia, to act as a co-ordinating agency for communist parties. The manifesto issued by the nine parties called for all communist parties to "place themselves in the vanguard of the opposition" to the "expansion and aggression" of the United States

"in all spheres (military, strategic, economic, ideological)". The newly formed organization, generally called the Cominform, was regarded by the foreign offices of the Western democracies as a continuation of the Comintern, though Stalin and the other leaders of the Cominform declared the new organization to be fundamentally different in organization and methods from its predecessor. The first internationally important action of the Cominform was its denunciation in June, 1948, of Marshal Tito (q.v.), who had acquired considerable personal power as head of the communist government of Yugoslavia. Tito was accused of not conforming to communist doctrine and slandering the Soviet Union. The conflict ended in a complete break between the Soviet Union and Yugoslavia, the expulsion of Tito from the Cominform, and the removal of the headquarters of the Cominform from Belgrade to Bucharest, Romania. The rupture was accepted by most Western governments as convincing proof that the Cominform was an international organization identical in purpose with the Comintern, and was, as the Comintern had been, an instrument of the Soviet Union, dedicated to the revolutionary overthrow of capitalism and the establishment of a proletarian dictatorship throughout the world.

THIRTY-NINE ARTICLES. See ARTICLES, THE THIRTY-NINE.

THIRTY YEARS' WAR, a series of European conflicts, extending from 1618 to 1648, involving most of the countries of western Europe, and fought chiefly in Germany. At its inception, the struggle was primarily a product of the profound religious antagonisms engendered among Germans by the events of the Protestant Reformation (see REFORMATION). Religious animosity, especially as manifested by non-German coreligionists of the contending Protestant and Roman Catholic factions, broadened the war and ranked as a substantial factor in its later stages. As the struggle gained momentum, however, its direction and character were decisively influenced by various other issues, including the dynastic rivalries of ambitious German princes and the determination of certain European powers, notably Sweden and France, to curb the power of the Holy Roman Empire (q.v.), then the chief political instrument of Austria and the Hapsburgs (q.v.). The religious hatreds that flared into the Thirty Years' War had smoldered for more than half a century prior to 1618. In large measure, this situation had resulted

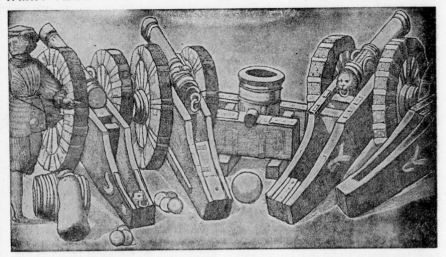

Cannon of the type used in the Thirty Years' War (from an early drawing)

from the weaknesses of the Peace of Augsburg (see AUGSBURG), an agreement concluded in 1555 between the Holy Roman emperor and the Lutheran princes of Germany. The treaty, while effecting a truce between the German Catholics and Protestants, failed to reconcile their basic differences. By several of its provisions, the treaty sharpened these differences. (For further information regarding the political and religious complications flowing from the Peace of Augsburg, see GERMANY: *History*.) The Thirty Years' War, probably the most calamitous and destructive conflict, to that time, in the history of Europe, may be divided into four phases, usually styled and dated as follows: the Palatine-Bohemian (1618–25); Danish (1625–29); Swedish (1630–35); and French (1635–48).

Palatine-Bohemian. With respect to the immediate background of the first phase of the war, it should be noted that religious tensions were seriously aggravated in Germany during the reign (1576–1612) of the Holy Roman emperor Rudolf II. Protestant churches in many parts of Germany were destroyed, restrictions were placed on the rights of Protestants to worship freely, and the Treaty of Augsburg became, in the hands of the emperor's officials, the basis for a general resurgence of Catholic power. With the establishment (1608) of the Evangelical Union, a Protestant defensive alliance of princes and cities, and of the Catholic League, a similar organization of Catholics, in the

next year, a violent solution of the crisis became inevitable. The Bohemian section of the Evangelical Union struck the first blow. Outraged by the aggressive policies of the Roman Catholic hierarchy in Bohemia, the Bohemian Protestants, a majority of the population, demanded that King Ferdinand intervene. The king, an ardent Catholic and the Hapsburg heir presumptive, ignored the Protestant appeal. On May 23, 1618, the enraged Protestants of Prague invaded the royal palace, seized two of the king's ministers, and heaved them out of a window. This act, known in history as the Defenestration of Prague, inaugurated a national Protestant uprising.

Under the leadership of Count Heinrich von Thurn, the Protestant forces achieved numerous initial successes, and the rebellion swiftly spread to other parts of the Hapsburg dominions. For a brief period early in 1619 even Vienna, the Hapsburg capital, was threatened by Union armies. Later in 1619 the Bohemians bestowed the crown of the deposed Ferdinand on Frederick V, Elector of the Palatinate. Several sections of the Evangelical Union, which consisted chiefly of Lutherans, thereupon withdrew from the struggle, because Frederick was a Calvinist. Taking advantage of Protestant dissensions, particularly a declaration of war against Bohemia by Lutheran Saxony, and of a Spanish invasion of the Palatinate, Ferdinand, who had become Holy Roman emperor in August, 1619, quickly assumed the offensive. On November 8, 1620, a Catholic League army, commanded by Count Tilly (q.v.), routed the Bohemians at White Mountain, near Prague. Sanguinary reprisals were inflicted on the Protestants of Bohemia on the heels of this victory, and Protestantism was outlawed. Although the Evangelical Union disintegrated, Frederick and a few allies continued the struggle in the Palatinate. The Protestants defeated Tilly's army at Wiesloch in April, 1622, but thereafter met with successive disasters. By the end of 1624 the Palatinate, which was awarded to Maximilian, Duke of Bavaria, had been forcibly returned to the Catholic fold.

Danish. In its second phase the war, essentially, a German civil conflict up to that point, began to assume an international character. On the one hand, the rulers of various German Protestant states, fearful of resurgent Catholicism and indignant over the harsh treatment accorded their coreligionists, found it expedient to seek foreign assistance; on the other hand, the rulers of the United Kingdom, France, and certain other w. European powers were profoundly alarmed at the growing might of the Hapsburgs. Both France and the United Kingdom, then allies against Spain, were obliged to forego immediate intervention in the war because of domestic difficulties. At this juncture Christian IV (q.v.), King of Denmark and Norway, came to the aid of the beleaguered German Protestants. Christian's intervention was substantially motivated by nonreligious considerations, mainly territorial ambitions in N.W. Europe and a determination to end Hapsburg control of the Danish duchy of Holstein.

Supported by Lutheran and Calvinist German princes, Christian mobilized a large army in the spring of 1625 and invaded Saxony. The Protestant expedition encountered little effective resistance until the spring of 1626. In the meantime Albrecht von Wallenstein (q.v.), Duke of Friedland, had created a powerful army of mercenaries and entered the service of Ferdinand II, whose only other available force was that of the Catholic League under Tilly. Wallenstein's mercenaries won their initial victory at Dessau in April, 1626. On August 27, 1626, Tilly completely defeated the main body of Christian's army at Lutter am Barenberge. The combined imperial armies subsequently overran all of N. Germany, leaving innumerable pillaged towns and villages in their wake. With Wallenstein in pursuit, Christian retreated (1627) into the Jutland peninsula.

Total victory for the imperial cause was signalized when, on March 6, 1629, Ferdinand issued the Edict of Restitution. By the provisions of this document, Protestant titles to all Catholic property acquired through the Peace of Augsburg were nullified. On May 12, 1629, King Christian accepted the Peace of Lübeck. Its terms deprived him of numerous small holdings in Germany.

Swedish. Ferdinand's successes in the second phase of the war sharpened the anti-Hapsburg orientation of Cardinal Richelieu (q.v.), chief minister of the French monarch Louis XIII. Unable because of recurring internal crises to intervene directly in Germany, Richelieu made overtures to the Swedish ruler Gustavus II (q.v.), better known as Gustavus Adolphus. A zealous Lutheran, Gustavus had already received appeals from the hard-pressed N. German Protestants. This circumstance, the promise of French support, and Swedish ambitions for hegemony in the Baltic region brought him into the conflict. In the summer of 1630 Gustavus landed a well-trained army on the coast of Pomerania. The rulers of Pomerania, Brandenburg, and Saxony shortly adopted a vacillatory policy on the question of participation in the Swedish venture, seriously delaying the start of the campaign. While Gustavus marked time, Tilly, who had been given command of Wallenstein's army, laid seige to Magdeburg, then in a state of insurrection against the Holy Roman Empire. The imperial armies captured the city on May 20, 1631, sacked and burned it, and massacred the Protestant inhabitants.

Tilly was repulsed by the Swedes on three occasions in the following summer. In the last of these battles, fought at Breitenfeld in September, Gustavus, with the help of the Saxons, routed Tilly's troops, about 6000 of whom were killed. Following Breitenfeld the Swedish army moved into s. Germany, where it spent the winter. The spring campaign brought numerous victories, notably the defeat (April 14, 1632) of Tilly, who was killed on the banks of the Lech R., and the capture of Munich. Faced with complete disaster, Ferdinand had meanwhile recalled Wallenstein to command the imperial war effort. Wallenstein, who hurriedly recruited a new army of mercenaries, invaded Saxony in the fall of 1632. The Swedish army followed and on November 16 attacked the imperial force, then intrenched at Lützen. At the conclusion of the ensuing battle, which cost Gustavus his life, Wallenstein's army was forced to withdraw. Bernhard, Duke of Saxe-Weimar, who succeeded to Gustavus' command at Lützen, overran Bavaria after this victory, but during 1633 Wallenstein struck repeated blows against the Swedish strongholds in Silesia. Toward the close of 1633 Wallenstein initiated a peace movement among leading circles of the imperial armies. Removed from his command by Ferdinand on suspicion of treason, Wallenstein then entered into peace negotiations with the Protestant leaders. His attempts to end the war aroused the enmity of his own officers, and on February 25 he was assassinated. The imperial armies inflicted a devastating defeat on Duke Bernhard at Nördlingen on September 6, 1634. Dismayed by this catastrophe, the leaders of the Protestant coalition swiftly abandoned the struggle. The Peace of Prague (1635), which formally ended the third phase of the war, provided for certain concessions to the Saxon Lutherans, particularly basic modifications of the Edict of Restitution.

French. In its final phase, the war became an imperialist conflict between the Hapsburgs and France, which was still under the leadership of Richelieu, for hegemony in w. Europe. Religious issues figured insignificantly in the final phase, which opened, in May, 1635, with a French declaration of war against Spain, the chief Hapsburg dominion aside from Austria. In alliance with Sweden and various German Protestant leaders, including Duke Bernhard, France quickly overcame serious difficulties that developed during the first stage of the fighting. The Swedish general Johan Banér defeated a combined force of Saxons and Austrians at Wittstock on October 4, 1636, materially damaging the Hapsburg position in Germany. In 1636, Spanish invasions of French territory were repelled. The Hapsburg position in Germany was further damaged by a defeat inflicted by Duke Bernhard at Rheinfelden on March 3, 1638. Following these setbacks the imperial armies were forced to surrender one after another of their European strongholds. Between 1642 and 1645 the Swedish general Lennart Torstenson scored numerous triumphs, overrunning Denmark, which had become allied with the Empire, and ravaging large sections of w. Germany and Austria. In the w., the French, under generals Vicomte Turenne and Louis II, Prince de Condé (qq.v.), were also generally successful. Condé routed a Spanish army at Rocroi in May, 1643. In the following November the French suffered a severe defeat at Tuttlingen, but

thereafter the Hapsburg war effort produced very few successes, and those largely of a minor character.

The combined armies of Condé and Turenne badly mauled a Bavarian army at Freiburg im Breisgau in August, 1644. On August 3 of the next year the French commanders defeated an Austro-Bavarian army at Allersheim, near Nördlingen. Representatives of the Empire and the anti-Hapsburg coalition began peace discussions at Westphalia and Osnabrück in 1645, but the negotiations, primarily a concession to the war-weary peoples of w. Europe, were destined to remain fruitless for a protracted period. However, an invasion of central Bavaria forced Maximilian I to conclude a separate peace early in 1647.

Despite these and other reverses, Ferdinand III, the son and successor (1637) of Ferdinand II as Holy Roman emperor, refused to capitulate. Desultory fighting continued in Germany, Luxembourg, the Low Countries, Italy, and Spain throughout the remainder of 1647. In the fall of 1647 Maximilian I re-entered the war on the side of the Empire. Another army of Bavarians and Austrians was defeated in May, 1648. This defeat, Swedish investment of Prague, French and Swedish investment of Munich, and an important French victory (August 5) at Lens compelled Ferdinand, who was also confronted with the threat of an assault on Vienna, to agree to the victors' peace conditions.

Incorporated in the document known in history as the Peace of Westphalia (see WESTPHALIA, PEACE OF) and signed at Münster on October 24, 1648, the peace conditions fundamentally influenced the subsequent history of Europe. In addition to establishing Switzerland and Holland (the Netherlands) as independent states, the treaty, among other things, permanently and gravely weakened the Holy Roman Empire and the Hapsburgs, insured the emergence of France as the chief power on the Continent, and disastrously retarded the political unification of Germany. The economic, social, and cultural consequences of the war were incalculable, with Germany, previously one of the most prosperous regions of Europe, the principal victim. According to conservative estimates, no less than half of the German people perished during the war. Countless German cities, towns, villages, and farms were totally destroyed. Approximately two thirds of the industrial, agricultural, and commercial facilities of Germany were in ruins. Religion no

New York State Museum
Swamp thistle (Cirsium muticum)

longer figured as a potent factor in German life, and education and other forms of intellectual activity had come to a virtual standstill.

THISTLE, common name applied to a family of plants, the Carduaceae. The Thistle family, also sometimes called the Aster family, is the largest family of flowering plants, containing about 800 genera and over 10,000 species. The plants are world-wide in distribution; many of them are cultivated ornamentals. The Thistle family and the Chicory family (see CICHORIACEAE) were formerly included in the family Compositae (q.v.). For further information on well-known members of the Thistle family, see ARNICA; ASTER; CHRYSANTHEMUM; COREOPSIS; EUPATORIUM; GOLDENROD; IRONWEED; RUDBECKIA; SENECIO; SUNFLOWER.

The name "thistle" is applied in a restricted sense to plants in several genera of the Thistle family, including *Cirsium, Carduus, Echinops, Onopordum, Silybum, Centaurea,* and *Cnicus*. The common characteristic of plants in these genera is the possession of spiny leaves and branches, and of sharp, spiny bracts surrounding the flowers. The common, plumed, or bull thistle is *Cirsium lanceolatum* which bears purple flowers; the Canada thistle, *C. arvense*, bears small

lilac or white flowers. *Carduus* includes the plumeless thistles; *C. nutans*, the musk thistle, is common in fields in northeastern United States and bears purple flowers. The globe thistle, *Echinops sphaerocephalus*, which bears whitish or blue flowers, is frequently cultivated in the United States, as is the milk thistle or lady's thistle, *Silybum marianum*, which bears purple flowers. The cotton or Scotch thistle, *Onopordum acanthium*, has large heads of purple flowers. *Centaurea* contains the star thistle, *C. calcitrapa*, with purplish flowers; the blessed thistle, *Cnicus benedictus*, bears large heads of yellow flowers.

The name "thistle" is often erroneously applied to spiny plants which resemble true thistles but do not belong to the Thistle family. The sow thistles, for example, constitute the genus *Sonchus* of the Chicory family, and the Russian thistle, *Salsola pestifer*, belongs to the Saltwort family.

THISTLE, ORDER OF THE, called also the ORDER OF ST. ANDREW. The earliest known mention of the thistle as the national badge of Scotland is in the inventory of the effects of James III. The Order of the Thistle was revived by James VII (II of England) in 1687. After falling into abeyance during the reign of William and Mary, the order was revived by Queen Anne in 1703. The statute of 1827 limits the number of knights to sixteen members of the Scottish nobility, in addition to the sovereign and princes of the blood. The motto is *Nemo me impune lacessit*.

THOMA, HANS (1839–1924), German painter, born in Bernau (Black Forest), noted for his versatility. His works include "At Lake Garda" (Metropolitan Museum of Art, New York City). He was also known as a lithographer and etcher.

THOMAS, SAINT (fr. Aramaic, *Te'ōma*, "twin"), in the New Testament, one of the Twelve Apostles (see APOSTLE) of Jesus Christ. He is mentioned by the name "Thomas" in the Synoptic Gospels (see GOSPEL) and in the Acts of the Apostles (q.v.). In 11:16 and 20:24 of the Gospel According to John (see JOHN, GOSPEL ACCORDING TO), however, it is made clear that "Thomas" is only an appellative, since the Apostle in question is alternately referred to as Didymus, the Greek word for "twin". An early identification of Thomas with Judas, the son of James, is implied in John 14:22 of the Sinaitic Syriac manuscript of the New Testament, in which "Thomas" is substituted for "Judas". This identification appears also in the apocryphal *Acta Thomæ* ("Acts of Thomas"), and in the Syriac source from which the theologian Eusebius (q.v.) of Cæsarea translated the story of Abgar, the ailing King of Edessa, who was healed by the Apostle Thaddæus (Judas). The Gospel According to John is the only one of the Gospel narratives which furnishes any information about Thomas. It represents him as one inclined to overestimate difficulties (14:5) and to be troubled with doubts (20:24,25), but, at the same time, as one whose loyalty to the Master made him willing to face the greatest difficulties (11:16), and whose response to the Master's assurances instantly changed his doubts into faith (20:26-28).

Though nothing more is said of Thomas in the New Testament, he figures prominently in the traditions concerning the propagation of Christianity in the Far East. An account older than that of Eusebius designates the ancient country of Parthia in Asia Minor as the sphere of Thomas's missionary activity. According to the *Acta Thomæ*, however, he is the Apostle of India. To him the "Thomas Christians" of southern India assign their origin. Mount St. Thomas, near Madras, is the site of his reputed martyrdom. As the Thomas Christians were in close communication with the Christians of eastern Syria, it is not unlikely that the basis of the whole fabric of tradition is some actual missionary work of Thomas in eastern Syria.

THOMAS, AUGUSTUS (1857–1934), American playwright, born in St. Louis, Mo. He became a member of the American Academy of Arts and Letters, received in 1913 the gold medal of the National Institute of Arts and Letters, of which he was chairman, 1914–16, and was executive chairman (1922–25) of the Producing Managers' Association. His plays include *Arizona, The Witching Hour, As a Man Thinks,* and *The Copperhead.*

THOMAS, BRANDON (1856–1914), English actor and playwright, born in Liverpool. He is the author of the farce *Charley's Aunt* (1892). He wrote a number of other plays, including *Fourchette and Co.* (1904) and *A Judge's Memory* (1906).

THOMAS, (CHARLES LOUIS) AMBROISE (1811–96), French composer, born in Metz. He won the Grand Prix de Rome in 1832 and became director of the Paris Conservatory in 1871. His compositions include the operas *Le Songe d'une Nuit d'Été* (1850), *Psyché* (1857), *Mignon* (1866), *Hamlet* (1868), and *Françoise de Rimini* (1882).

THOMAS, (CHRISTIAN FRIEDRICH) THEODORE (1831–1905), American orchestral conductor, born in Esens, East Friesland, Germany. He came with his parents to America in 1845 and was a member of the orchestra of the Italian opera in New York. In 1861 he began the formation of an orchestra and in 1864 gave his first symphony concerts in New York. In 1866 he instituted summernight festivals. For nine years from 1869 he made an annual round of the principal American cities. In 1878 he became director of the College of Music at Cincinnati, but in 1880 returned to New York, where he was conductor of the Philharmonic Society until 1890. The orchestra he built up in Chicago, where he lived thereafter, came to be recognized as one of the great orchestras of the world.

THOMAS, DYLAN MARLAIS (1914–53), Welsh poet and short story writer, born in Swansea, and educated at Swansea Grammar School. He was a reporter for the newspaper *South Wales Evening Post* for a brief period after completing his formal education. In his first volume of verse *Eighteen Poems* (1934), a book that won instant critical acclaim in Great Britain, he revealed unusual power in the use of diction and imagery. Thematically, these poems and much of his later work are surrealistic and often obscure. The Freudian influence and introspective tendency is less apparent, however, in *Deaths and Entrances* (1946) and *In Country Sleep* (1951), which are generally regarded as his finest writings. Thomas' other works include *Twenty-Five Poems* (1936); *The Map of Love* (1939), consisting of poems and short stories; *A Portrait of the Artist as a Young Dog* (1940), autobiographical sketches; documentary motion-picture scripts (during World War II); *Under Milk Wood* (posthumously published, 1954), a prose radio play; and *Adventures in the Skin Trade* (posthumously published, 1955), an unfinished novel and prose pieces. After World War II he was a literary commentator for the British Broadcasting Company.

THOMAS, GEORGE HENRY (1816–70), American soldier, born in Southampton County, Va., and educated at the U.S. Military Academy at West Point. He served in the Mexican War, and, following the outbreak of the Civil War, commanded a brigade in the first Shenandoah campaign and, early in 1862, won the battle of Mill Springs, Ky. He commanded the right wing of the Army of the Tennessee during the siege of Corinth, and was in full command during a great part of June, 1862. Thomas held command of the

Wide World Photo

Norman Thomas

center of the Army of the Cumberland, and, though appointed to supersede Buell as commander of the whole army, asked to remain in a subordinate position. He rendered conspicuous service at Perryville and Stone River, and led the Fourteenth Army Corps in the campaign of middle Tennessee in the summer of 1863. At Chickamauga, Sept. 19-20, 1863, Thomas resisted the concentrated attack of a victorious enemy, gaining the title of "the Rock of Chickamauga". Soon after he reluctantly succeeded to the post held by Rosecrans, and commanded the Army of the Cumberland at Missionary Ridge, and in the campaign of 1864 up to the capture of Atlanta. When Sherman marched thence to the sea, Thomas was sent into Tennessee, where, in the battle of Nashville, Dec. 15-16, 1864, he crushed Hood's army. He was at once appointed a major general in the regular army. From 1865 to 1867 he held commands in Tennessee, and was subsequently in command of the Military Division of the Pacific.

THOMAS, JOHN CHARLES (1891–   ), American baritone, born in Meyersdale, Pa. First starred in New York musical plays, including *Apple Blossoms, Maytime,* and *The Highwayman,* he made his concert recital debut in 1921 and appeared in *Aïda,* in Wash-

ington, D.C. in 1925. He was a member of the Metropolitan Opera Company, New York City, in 1933–34, and filled various radio and motion-picture engagements.

THOMAS, LOWELL (1892–   ), American author and lecturer, born in Woodington, Darke County, Ohio. He began public life as a journalist and was instructor in oratory at the Chicago Kent College of Law (1912–14) and in English at Princeton (1914–16). Thomas was chief of the civilian mission sent to Europe by President Wilson to prepare a historical record of World War I, acted as historian of the Palestine campaign and Arabian revolution, and was observer with the Hedjaz forces.

Thomas was with the Prince of Wales on his tour of India (1922), historian of the first world flight (1924), and conducted a 25,000-mile flight in Europe, Asia, and North Africa in the study of international aviation (1926–27). An editor of *Asia* (1919–23), he became a radio news commentator in 1930, and commentator for Twentieth Century Fox Movietone in 1935. In 1949, at the invitation of the Dalai Lama, Thomas made an expedition to Tibet. He recorded his Tibet experiences in the travelogue *Out of This World* (1954).

Notable among Thomas' earlier works are *With Lawrence in Arabia* (1924), *Beyond the Khyber Pass* (1925), *The Boy's Life of Col. Lawrence* (1927), *The Sea Devil* (1927), *Raiders of the Deep* (1928), *Adventures in Afghanistan for Boys* (1928), *Woodfill of the Regulars* (1929), *The Sea Devil's Fo'c's'le* (1929), *The Hero of Vincennes* (1929), *Lauterback of the China Sea* (1930), *The Wreck of the Dumaru* (1930), *Tall Stories* (1931), *Kabluk of the Eskimo* (1932), and *Old Gimlet-Eye: The Adventures of Smedley D. Butler* (1933). His later works include *The Untold Story of Exploration* (1935), *Magic Dials* (1939), *Pageant of Adventure* (1940), *These Men Shall Never Die* (1943), *Back to Mandalay* (1951), and *Seven Wonders of the World* (1956).

THOMAS, NORMAN MATTOON (1884–   ), American socialist leader, born in Marion, Ohio, and educated at Princeton University and the Union Theological Seminary. While preparing for the ministry he was assistant pastor of the Brick Presbyterian Church, New York City, and in 1911 he became pastor of the East Harlem Church, New York City. In 1917 Thomas became an active Socialist; he opposed the entrance of the United States into World War I and participated in the New York City mayoralty campaign in behalf of Morris Hillquit (q.v.), the Socialist candidate. Thomas resigned his pastorate in 1918; in the same year he became secretary of the Fellowship of Reconciliation, a Christian pacifist organization, and editor of the magazine *The World Tomorrow*, a pacifist publication. In 1921–22 he was an associate editor of the liberal periodical *The Nation*. From 1922 to 1935 he was a codirector of the League for Industrial Democracy, a Socialist Party auxiliary organization. In the election of 1928 he was the Socialist Party candidate for U.S. President.

Thomas resigned from the ministry entirely in 1931. In the struggle in the Socialist Party in the 1930's, he was the leader of the younger members, who called themselves "militants" and demanded of the older leaders in control of the party that they adopt a more radical declaration of principles and a militant policy in the day-to-day work of the party in the trade unions and the organizations of the unemployed; see SOCIALIST PARTY. In the national election campaigns of 1932, '36, '40, '44, and '48, Thomas was the Socialist Party candidate for President. The largest vote he polled was close to 900,000, in 1932. He wrote *The Conscientious Objector in America* (1923, revised and published as *Is Conscience a Crime?*, 1927), *America's Way Out—A Program for Democracy* (1930), *Socialism on the Defensive* (1938), *What Is Our Destiny?* (1944), *Appeal to the Nations* (1947), *A Socialist's Faith* (1951), *Test of Freedom* (1954), and *Mr. Chairman, Ladies and Gentlemen* (1955).

THOMAS, SETH (1786–1859), American merchant, born in Wolcott, Conn. He settled in Plymouth Hollow (now Thomaston), Conn., and with two partners began the manufacture of clocks, finally becoming sole proprietor of an establishment which developed into one of the largest clock factories in the world.

THOMAS, SIDNEY GILCHRIST (1850–85), British metallurgist and inventor, born in London. In 1875, by using a basic lining of magnesian limestone in the Bessemer converter, he solved the problem of the dephosphorization of pig iron, and produced a new substance, basic slag or Thomas slag. He patented his process in 1877. In 1881 and 1883 he visited the United States.

THOMAS A BECKET. See BECKET.

THOMAS A KEMPIS, the traditional name of THOMAS HAMERKEN VON KEMPEN (1380–1471), German Catholic ecclesiastic and writer, born in Kempen, Prussia, and edu-

cated at Deventer, the Netherlands. In 1407 he entered the Augustinian monastery at Mount St. Agnes, near Zwolle, in the Netherlands; he was ordained a priest in 1413. He was made subprior of the monastery in 1425. The greater part of his outwardly uneventful life was passed in the seclusion of the cloister. Thomas a Kempis is celebrated principally as the author of the religious treatise *De Imitatione Christi* ("Concerning the Imitation of Christ"). His other writings include sermons, religious biographies, and devotional books for the young.

THOMAS AQUINAS. See AQUINAS.

THOMAS THE RHYMER (1220?–97?), name given to the earliest poet of Scotland, Thomas Rymour of Ercildowne. The history of his life and writings is involved in obscurity. For centuries all sorts of prophecies were connected with his name. A collection of them was published in Edinburgh in 1603 under the title *The Whole Prophesie of Scotland*. The other poems attributed to him are chiefly descriptive of his interviews with the Fairy Queen and his adventures in Fairyland.

THOMASVILLE, county seat of Thomas Co., Ga., situated 12 miles N. of the Florida boundary and 230 miles S. of Atlanta. It is served by two railroads. The city has long

Thomas a Kempis

Dorothy Thompson

been famous as a winter resort, and is the trading center of an agricultural area in which cotton, sugar cane, pecans, peanuts, garden truck, and melons are the principal crops. Thomasville is a market for horses and mules, and contains meat-packing plants, fruit and vegetable canneries, sawmills, and factories manufacturing cheese and wood products. The city is situated in a region noted for pine forests, and is celebrated for its beauty; in and around the city are many picturesque estates and plantations. Thomasville is renowned for its rose gardens, and a rose show in which 150,000 blooms of many varieties are exhibited is held there annually. Another attraction at Thomasville is a huge oak, 250 years old, which has a spread of 210 ft., a height of 50 ft., and a trunk circumference of $21\frac{1}{3}$ ft. In the vicinity of the city are abundant facilities for fishing and hunting. Thomasville was settled about 1825, incorporated as a town in 1831, and chartered as a city in 1889. Pop. (1950) 14,424.

THOMPSON, BENJAMIN, COUNT RUMFORD (1753–1814), Anglo-American physicist, statesman, and philanthropist, born in Woburn, Massachusetts Bay Colony. At the age of fourteen, while serving as an apprentice to a storekeeper in Salem, he predicted the appearance of a solar eclipse within four seconds of its actual occurrence. Thereafter until the outbreak of the American Revolutionary War

he conducted various chemical and mechanical experiments, and practiced engraving. As a British sympathizer during the war, he emigrated to England, was appointed to a clerkship in the Office of Foreign Affairs, and shortly thereafter became British undersecretary of state. During this period, however, he continued his scientific studies, devoting himself to investigations of the explosive force of various gunpowders, the improvement of firearms, and the development of a signal system practicable for communication between ships at sea. In 1783, after the official cessation of hostilities between the British and the American colonies he served briefly with the Austrian army against Turkey, and thereafter for eleven years in several administrative offices of the Bavarian civil and military service. In recognition of his service to the Bavarian state he was created a count of the Holy Roman Empire in 1791 and assumed the title of Count Rumford. After the defeat of the Bavarian elector Maximilian in 1795 he visited England, and in 1798 settled in London. Six years later he moved to France, where he died.

Rumford is particularly known for his investigations of the nature of heat. In his "Enquiry Concerning the Source of Heat Which is Excited by Friction", presented to the Royal Society in 1798, he became one of the first to declare that heat is a form of motion rather than, as was popularly believed until the mid-19th century, a material substance. Rumford also devised methods for eliminating smoky chimneys and developed the principles according to which fireplaces and chimneys are still constructed (see HEATING, VENTILATION, AND AIR CONDITIONING). Among his other numerous scientific contributions are the development of a calorimeter and a photometer.

In 1799 Rumford suggested the establishment of the Royal Institution, which was chartered by King George III the following year. He established and was the first recipient of the Rumford medal of the Royal Society and originated a similar award bearing his name for the American Academy of Arts and Sciences. He also endowed the Rumford chair of physics at Harvard University. In 1779 he was elected a Fellow of the Royal Society.

THOMPSON, DOROTHY (1894–   ), American journalist, born in Lancaster, N.Y., and educated at Lewis Institute, Chicago, at Syracuse University, and at the University of Vienna. After her graduation from Syracuse, she campaigned in New York State for woman suffrage from 1915 to 1917, engaged in social-service work from 1917 to 1920, and subsequently went to Europe and became a free-lance journalist. She was correspondent for the Philadelphia *Public Ledger* and New York *Evening Post*, first in Vienna (1920–24) and later, as chief of the Central European services of these newspapers, in Berlin (1924–28). After her return to the United States, she spent her time in writing and study until 1936, when she began writing a column of political comment and analysis, *On the Record*. The column, noted for its vigor and sincerity, and written from the point of view of a conservative liberal, was syndicated by the N.Y. Herald Tribune Syndicate from 1936 to 1941 and thereafter by the Bell Syndicate and then the New York Post Syndicate. She conducted a radio program of political comment in 1938–39, and became well known as a public speaker. She frequently contributed articles to American and British periodicals. From 1928 to 1942 Dorothy Thompson was married to the novelist Sinclair Lewis. Among her books are *New Russia* (1928), *Political Guide* (1939), and *Listen, Hans* (1942).

THOMPSON, FRANCIS (1860–1907), English poet, born in Preston. His first volume of poems (published 1893) ran through several editions and won the admiration of Browning. This volume was followed by *Sister Songs* (1895) and *New Poems* (1897). Thompson's early privations broke down his health, and he died of tuberculosis. Essentially a mystic, he takes high rank among the poets of his time. In prose, he wrote literary criticism for the *Academy* and the *Athenæum; Health and Holiness* (1905), and the following books posthumously published: *Life of St. Ignatius Loyola* (1909); *Shelley* (2nd ed., 1909); *A Renegade Poet, and Other Essays* (1910); and *Life of John Baptist de la Galle* (1911). A three-volume edition of his *Works* appeared in New York in 1913.

THOMPSON, LAUNT (1833–94), American sculptor, born in Abbeyleix, Ireland. When fourteen years of age he came to Albany, N.Y. In 1857 he opened a studio in New York, and in 1862 became a National Academician. He visited Rome in 1868–69, and from 1875 to 1887 was again in Italy, living for most of the time at Florence. Among his important works are "Napoleon the First" (Metropolitan Museum of Art, New York); "Abraham Pierson", **first** president of Yale University (New **Haven,** Conn.); "Admiral

S.F. Du Pont" (Washington, D.C.) ; "General John Sedgwick" (West Point, N.Y.) ; and a bust of "William Cullen Bryant" (Metropolitan Museum of Art, New York).

THOMPSON, SETON. See SETON, ERNEST THOMPSON.

THOMSON, ELIHU (1853–1937), Anglo-American electrical engineer and inventor, born in Manchester, England. He was educated at the Philadelphia Central High School, at which he served as professor of chemistry and mechanics from 1870 to 1880. Three years later, with the American electrical engineer Edwin James Houston, he organized the Thomson-Houston Electric Company, which in 1892 was merged with the Thomas Edison Company to form the General Electric Company. Among the more than seven-hundred inventions for which Thomson received patents are a process of electric welding, the three-phase alternating-current generator, the centrifugal cream separator, the common watt meter, and the now obsolescent street arc lamp.

THOMSON, JAMES (1700–48), Scottish poet, born in Ednam, Roxburghshire. In 1726 in London he began the publication of his poem on the *Seasons*. The first, *Winter*, was immediately successful. *Summer* and *Spring* followed in the next two years. In 1730 *Autumn* completed the *Seasons*. In 1729 his tragedy of *Sophonisba* was produced. His other tragedies were *Agamemnon* (1738), *Edward and Eleonora* (1739), *Tancred and Sigismunda* (1745, in which Garrick and Mrs. Cibber played the principal parts), and *Coriolanus*, produced after his death. In 1740 the *Masque of Alfred* was produced. It contains the song "Rule, Britannia". Thomson's last and finest work is *The Castle of Indolence* (1748).

THOMSON, JAMES (1834–82), English poet, born in Port-Glasgow, Scotland. From 1860 he was a contributor to the *National Reformer*, in which many of his poems first appeared. In 1862 he became a lawyer's clerk; he went to America as a mining agent (1872) ; was war correspondent with the Carlists (1873) ; and from 1875 depended for livelihood largely on contributions to *Cope's Tobacco Plant. The City of Dreadful Night and Other Poems* was published as a book in 1880, and was followed by *Vane's Story, Essays and Phantasies, A Voice from the Nile* (1884, with *Memoir* by Bertram Dobell), and *Shelley, a Poem* (1885). He wrote under the pseudonym "Bysshe Vanolis".

Brown Brothers
Henry David Thoreau

THOMSON, SIR JOSEPH JOHN (1856–1940), English physicist, born near Manchester, and educated at Manchester and Cambridge universities. He was Cavendish professor of experimental physics at Cambridge University from 1884 until his death, and from 1905 to 1918 served also as professor of physics at the Royal Institution in London. Thomson developed the famous Cavendish Research Laboratory at Cambridge University, at which he conducted investigations of the electrical conductivity of gases, the charge and mass of the electron, and the nature of radioactivity. He was particularly influential in developing and advancing the modern ionic theory of electricity. In 1884 he was elected a Fellow of the Royal Society, serving as the Society's president in 1915. He was awarded the 1906 Nobel Prize for physics and was knighted two years later. Among his works are *Elements of the Mathematical Theory of Electricity and Magnetism* (1895), *Rays of Positive Electricity and Their Application to Chemical Analyses* (1913), and *The Electron in Chemistry* (1923).

THOMSON, WILLIAM. See KELVIN, 1st BARON, WILLIAM THOMSON.

THOR, in Scandinavian mythology, the god of thunder, war, and agriculture, son of Odin and Jord, and the champion of the Aesir. He was the implacable foe of the

giants whom he destroyed with his magic hammer. The thunder was supposed to be the sound of the rolling of his chariot.

THOREAU, HENRY DAVID (1817–62), American naturalist and author, born in Concord, Massachusetts, and educated at Harvard University. For some years after graduation, he engaged in schoolteaching and tutoring in Concord, and on Staten Island, N.Y. From 1841 to 1843 he lived in the home of the essayist and philosopher Ralph Waldo Emerson (q.v.), at which he met the transcendentalists (see TRANSCENDENTALISM) Amos Bronson Alcott, Margaret Fuller (qq.v.), and George Ripley. Two years later, he took up his abode in a crude hut on the shores of Walden Pond, a small body of water on the outskirts of Concord. There he lived until 1847, resided again with Emerson during 1847–48, and spent the years from 1849 with his parents and sister at Concord. During his sojourn at Walden Pond and elsewhere in Concord, Thoreau supported himself by doing odd jobs, such as gardening, carpentering, and land surveying. The major portion of his time he devoted to the study of nature, to meditating on philosophical problems, to reading Greek, Latin, French, and English literature, and to long conversations with his neighbors.

Of the numerous volumes which comprise the collected works of Thoreau, only two were published during his lifetime, *A Week on the Concord and Merrimack Rivers* (1849) and *Walden, or Life in the Woods* (1854). The material for the other volumes was edited posthumously by the author's friends from his journals, manuscripts, and letters. *A Week on the Concord and Merrimack Rivers* is the narrative of a boating trip taken in August, 1839; it is a delightful combination of nature study and metaphysical speculation, and bears the distinctive impress of the author's engaging personality. *Walden,* Thoreau's most popular work, is generally acknowledged to be one of the most original and sincere productions in the entire range of American letters. It gives a plain and straightforward statement of the author's reasons for adopting the contemplative life, and a graphic account of the principal details of that life. The literary quality of Thoreau's writing is high; he had a pronounced gift for style, and wrote with great care and unfailing freshness.

THOREZ, MAURICE (1900–), French communist leader, born in Noyelles Godault, in the coal-mining region of Pas-de-Calais. At the age of twelve he joined his father and grandfather as a mineworker. During World War I, when his native region was invaded and its inhabitants had to flee, he went to central France, and there was employed as a farm hand. Upon his return to Pas-de-Calais after the armistice, Thorez became a communist. During the next three years, while earning his living as a house painter and bricklayer, he participated actively in communist union work and helped organize a number of strikes. In 1923 he gave up all other employment and went to work as the paid secretary of the Communist Party of Pas-de-Calais. A year later he was named to the party's Central Committee. In 1925 he visited Russia; upon his return he established his headquarters in Paris, first as a communist leader and later as secretary general of the French Communist Party. Between 1929 and 1931 he served two prison sentences for incitement to violence among the armed forces. He was a member of the Executive Committee of the Comintern (see THIRD [COMMUNIST] INTERNATIONAL) from 1928 to 1943, when the organization was dissolved. From 1929 to 1939 he was a member of the French Chamber of Deputies.

At the outbreak of World War II Thorez was mobilized into the French Army, but deserted and fled to Moscow. He was sentenced to death *in absentia*, but in 1944 General Charles de Gaulle, who was eager to establish unity among all political factions of the French people, granted him a pardon and restored his full rights of citizenship, and he returned to Paris. Thorez was minister of state without portfolio in the De Gaulle cabinet from November, 1945, to January, 1946, and vice-premier in the three following coalition cabinets. In November, 1946, he was elected a member of the National Assembly. He went to the U.S.S.R. for medical treatment in November, 1950. In June, 1951, Thorez was elected a member of the National Assembly, *in absentia*, and in April, 1953, he returned to France.

THORITE, a rare, radioactive mineral consisting of thorium silicate, $ThSiO_4$, and crystallizing in the tetragonal system. It has a specific gravity of 4.5 to 5.4, exhibits prismatic cleavage, and shines with a vitreous luster. The color usually ranges from brown to black, but is orange yellow in the variety *orangite*. In luster, density, and transparency, thorite closely resembles the mineral zircon (q.v.). Scattered deposits of thorite are found throughout Sweden and Norway. In combination with uranium oxide, known as

uranothrite, it occurs in parts of Madagascar and Ontario, Canada.

THORIUM, radioactive metallic element of atomic number 90, atomic weight 232.1, and symbol Th, insoluble in water, soluble in hydrochloric and sulfuric acids, and slightly soluble in nitric acid. It was discovered in 1819 by the Swedish chemist Jöns Jakob Berzelius, and ranks 35th in abundance among the elements in the earth's crust. It has a melting point of 1845°C. (3353°F.), a specific gravity of 11.5, and is dark gray in color. Small quantities are found in combination with such minerals as thorite, orangite, and thorianite, the larger deposits occurring mainly as thorium oxide, ThO_2, in the monazite sands of Brazil and India.

There are several natural and artificially produced isotopes of thorium. The isotope Th-232 is the first member of the radioactive-decay series ending with the stable lead isotope Pb-208; see RADIOACTIVITY.

Thorium is currently important as an atomic-fuel source, as neutron bombardment of Th-232 yields the fissionable uranium isotope U-232. The process is accomplished in breeder reactors, which produce 15 percent more fissionable uranium than the amount of fuel consumed. Chemical techniques are employed for the recovery of the new fuel from the reactor debris. See ATOMIC ENERGY AND ATOMIC BOMB.

THORN APPLE. See DATURA; JIMSON WEED.

THORNDIKE, EDWARD LEE (1874–1949), American psychologist and educator, born in Williamsburg, Mass., and educated at Wesleyan, Harvard, and Columbia universities. He joined the psychology faculty of Teachers College of Columbia University in 1899, serving as adjunct professor of educational psychology from 1901 to 1904 and as professor of psychology from 1904 until his retirement in 1940. From 1922 to 1940 he also was director of the psychology division of the Institute of Educational Research at Teachers College. Thorndike is particularly known for his construction of various intelligence tests. He contributed to the development of the Army Alpha and Army Beta intelligence tests used by the U.S. Army during World War I (see PSYCHOLOGICAL TESTING: *Intelligence Testing*) and was responsible for the preparation of numerous other tests measuring individual achievement and skills. In the field of educational theory, Thorndike is best known for his repudiation, on the basis of experiment, of the belief that

Ossip Garber Studios
Edward Lee Thorndike

such primarily intellectual subjects as languages and mathematics discipline the mind; as a result he greatly encouraged the inclusion of various informational subjects such as the physical and social sciences in elementary and secondary-school curricula. In 1934 he served as president of the American Association for the Advancement of Science. Among his works are *Educational Psychology* (1903), *Mental and Social Measurements* (1904), *Animal Intelligence* (1911), and *Human Nature and the Social Order* (1940).

THORNDIKE, DAME SYBIL (1882–   ), British actress, born in London. Her first appearance in the United States was in 1903–07 in a Shakespearean repertoire with Ben Greet; three years later she toured America with John Drew. In 1928, she produced *Judith of Israel* in London, playing the title role; in 1929, after a tour of South Africa, she revived *Jane Clegg* and the *Medea*. She played in 1938 in *Time and the Conways* (in New York), in 1940 in *Macbeth,* in 1941 in *Candida,* in 1953 in *A Day by the Sea,* and in 1957 in *The Potting Shed* (in New York).

THORNTON, WILLIAM (1762–1828), American architect, born in Tortola Island in the West Indies. In 1793 he submitted plans

for the proposed Capitol in Washington to the commissioners of the District of Columbia. These plans were approved by President Washington. Thornton's design, though later modified in detail, survives in the central block of the Capitol, in spite of the fire of 1814. He also designed the "Octagon" mansion in Washington. From 1802 until the time of his death Thornton held the office of commissioner of pensions.

THORODDSEN, JÓN THÓRDARSON (1819–68), Icelandic poet and novelist, born in Reykhólar, and educated at the University of Copenhagen. He took part in the war against the Schleswig-Holstein insurgents and in 1850 returned to Iceland. He died at Borgarfjartharsysla. In point of both time and excellence, Thóroddsen is the first Icelandic novelist. His best-known works are his first novel, *Piltur og Stúlka* ("Lad and Lass", 1850) and *Mathur og Kona* ("Man and Wife"; published posthumously, 1876). These books are characterized by a faithful delineation of Icelandic life and by a quaint and pleasing humor. Thóroddsen also wrote a number of witty and satirical poems, published in 1871.

THORPE, JAMES FRANCIS, popularly JIM; original name WA-THO-HUCK (Ind., "Bright Path") (1888–1953), American athlete, born near Prague, Indian Territory (now in Oklahoma), and educated at Haskell Institute, in Lawrence, Kans., and at Carlisle Indian School. His parents were Sac and Fox Indians of partly Caucasoid ancestry. In his first year (1907) at Carlisle he displayed remarkable athletic prowess, particularly in football and track, and won the special attention of Glenn Scobey ("Pop") Warner, then Carlisle's coach of these sports. He performed brilliantly on the varsity football team the following year, but in 1909 he withdrew from the school and went to North Carolina. There he worked as a farmhand and played semiprofessional baseball. Returning to Carlisle in 1911, Thorpe won a position as halfback on the varsity eleven. He played sensationally that year and the next, contributing largely to Carlisle victories over some of the most powerful teams in the country. Both in 1911 and 1912, when he established a new scoring record (198 points), he made the All-American Team, the honorary college eleven chosen by the American sports authority Walter Camp. Thorpe excelled during this period in many other sports, including track and field, baseball, lacrosse, basketball, hockey, swimming, boxing, tennis, and archery.

A member of the U.S. track and field team

at the Olympic Games of 1912, he acheved universal recognition as the world's greatest all-around athlete by winning both the pentathlon and the decathlon. In the latter event he scored 8412 points, a record that has been surpassed only once. However, early in 1913 the Amateur Athletic Union, having learned that he had played semiprofessional baseball, voided his amateur status, disallowed his Olympiad victories, and forced him to relinquish his recently won medals.

Thorpe played professional baseball, notably with the New York "Giants" and the Boston "Braves", from 1913 to 1919, when his weakness as a hitter forced him to retire. He had meanwhile organized (1915) the "Bulldogs", a professional football club of Canton, Ohio. After a series of outstanding seasons with that and other teams he retired from the sport in 1929. His subsequent career included periods as the recreation supervisor of the Chicago Park System, a small-part actor in motion pictures, a lecturer on Indian culture, and during World War II a seaman in the U.S. Merchant Marine. In 1950 nearly 400 American sports writers and broadcasters, voting in a nationwide poll, selected Thorpe as the greatest all-around athlete and football player of the first half of the 20th century. He is the coauthor, with T. F. Collison, of *Jim Thorpe's History of the Olympics* (1932).

THORVALDSEN or **THORWALDSEN,** BERTEL (1770–1844), Danish sculptor, born in Copenhagen. The collection of his works is one of the chief glories of that city. He was at his best in classical and mythological subjects. Of his works those best known are the reliefs "Night" and "Morning". Of his portrait busts, those of Byron, now in Cambridge, and Oehlenschläger are the most notable. His "Memorial Lion" in Lucerne, Switzerland, is familiar to travelers.

THOTH, Egyptian name for the god Hermes or Mercury, mythical inventor of the arts and sciences, music, and astronomy, and especially of speech and hieroglyphs or letters, over which he was supposed to preside.

THOUGHT, the act, process, or power of thinking. Thought, as a mental achievement, is a complex process involving all the elementary forms of intellectual activity. Of these the most important and distinctive are *comparison, identification,* and *generalization.* But they are themselves based upon the yet more elementary processes of the ideating or representative faculty so called. Naming and thought are also closely correlated. The essential thing about the more elaborate forms

of thought is the act of judgment; for conception, reasoning, and the construction of scientific system have their essential character expressed as the formation of series of connected judgments. See IDEA; LOGIC; PHILOSOPHY; PSYCHOLOGY; RATIONALISM.

THOUSAND ISLANDS, a group of small islands, numbering about 1700, situated in an expansion of the St. Lawrence River, about 40 m. long and from 4 to 7 m. wide, between Ontario, Canada, and Jefferson and St. Lawrence counties, New York. They are favorite resorts for summer tourists on account of their picturesque beauty.

THRACE (Lat. *Thracia,* fr. Gr. *Thrakē*), an area, predominantly agricultural, forming part of present-day Greece, Bulgaria, and European Turkey. The name was first applied by the ancient Greeks to the little-known land N.E. of Macedonia. In later Greek history, the name was used for the greater part of the E. Balkan Peninsula, bounded on the N. by the Danube R., on the E. by the Euxine (Black Sea), on the s. by the Propontis (Sea of Marmara), the Bosporus, the Hellespont (Dardanelles), the Ægean Sea, and Macedonia, and on the w. by Illyria and Macedonia.

Ancient Thrace was largely uncultivated and covered with forests; large mineral deposits, particularly of gold, made the region a coveted possession. The Thracians were a barbaric, warlike people who established their own kingdom in the 5th century B.C. In later history, Thrace became successively a Macedonian, Roman, and Byzantine province. After the fall of Constantinople in 1453, Thrace came under the control of the Ottoman Turkish Empire. As a result of the Russo-Turkish War (1878) and the Congress of Berlin which followed it, the N. part of Thrace was constituted an autonomous district, under the Turkish government, and was called Eastern Rumelia; the s. portion of Thrace became the Turkish vilayet of Adrianople (see EDIRNE). The Conference of London in 1913, ending the Balkan Wars (q.v.), gave Eastern Rumelia to Bulgaria, and by the Treaty of Bucharest, later in 1913, Bulgaria also acquired the region between the Mesta and Maritsa rivers, known as Western Thrace. Turkey retained Eastern Thrace, E. of the Maritsa R. Following World War I, Bulgaria was compelled by the Treaty of Neuilly (Nov. 27, 1919) to cede Western Thrace to Greece. In 1919 Greek troops also occupied Eastern Thrace, resulting in war with Turkey. By the Treaty of Lausanne

California thrasher

(July 24, 1923) Eastern Thrace was returned to Turkey. Greek (Western) Thrace is composed of three prefectures, Evros, Xanthi, and Rhodope. Area of Greek Thrace, 3315 sq.m.; pop. (1951) 336,736.

THRACIAN SAMOS. See SAMOTHRACE.

THRALE, MRS. See PIOZZI, HESTER LYNCH.

THRASHER, common name applied to any of the American oscine birds constituting the genera *Toxostoma* and *Oreoscoptes*, and belonging to the family Mimidae, which also contains the mockingbirds and catbirds. Thrashers are slender, long-billed, long-tailed birds, over 8 inches in length, and tinted with drab grays, browns, blacks, and white. They are excellent singers and are surpassed only by the mockingbird in powers of mimicry. The birds, which subsist on insects, nest in thick bushes or tangles of vines. Their nests are large, composed of twigs and weeds lined with small rootlets and grasses. The females lay two to six bluish-green eggs, marked with lavender and brown, in a clutch.

The common thrasher of eastern United States is the ground thrush, brown thrush, or brown thrasher, *Toxostoma rufum*, which is about 11½ inches long. The bird is chestnut above and is white, marked with wedge-shaped black spots, below. It habitually perches on the edge of a limb and sings for hours at a time. The bird is extremely timid, and darts for cover at the approach of man. The sage thrasher, *Oreoscoptes montanus*, inhabits the sagebrush regions of the Western States. It is about 8½ inches long and is brownish gray above and grayish white below, marked on the chest and sides with heavy brown spots. One of the most unusual of the thrashers is Leconte's thrasher, *T. lecontei*, a buff-colored bird inhabiting the deserts of western United States. This bird is usually found in the hottest portions of the desert, living where the temperature often reaches 130°F. (73°C.); despite the heat of its environment, the bird is capable of running extremely rapidly along the ground. The

California thrasher, *T. redivivum*, which is about 12 inches long, is chiefly brown in color and has a downward-curving bill. This bird characteristically raises its tail as it runs along the ground.

THREAD HERRING, or MACHUELO, small fish, *Opisthonema oglinum*, closely related to sardines and menhaden, common along the southern coast of the U.S. It is 12 in. long, bluish above and silvery below, with an indistinct bluish shoulder spot, and has a long dorsal-fin filament, from which the fish receives its name.

THREADNEEDLE STREET, a London thoroughfare that got its name from the Merchant Taylors' Company, whose present hall is built on an estate acquired by them as early as 1331. It leads from Bishopsgate Street to the Bank of England, which hence is often called the "Old Lady in Threadneedle Street".

THREADWORM, common name applied to any of the worms constituting the phylum Nemathelminthes, some of which are free-living and many of which are important internal parasites of man and lower animals. Threadworms have cylindrical, nonsegmented bodies, tapering at both ends, and covered by an elastic cuticle. Their digestive tract is a narrow tube which is partially absent in some species and completely lacking in others. The nervous system consists of a ganglionic ring about the esophagus and of several cords running from this ring longitudinally through the body; the largest of these cords are the dorsal and ventral nerve tracts. Most of the threadworms are contained within the class Nematoda (see NEMATODES) which contains such parasites as the filaria (q.v.) and the hookworm (q.v.). The other classes of threadworms are Nematomorpha, which contains many of the hairworms (q.v.), and Acanthocephala. See PARASITE.

THREE-COLOR PROCESS, a photomechanical process of reproducing in color applicable either to stone or metal. It consists in first making three photograph negatives of the same subject through three different color screens representing the three primary colors, red, yellow, and blue. From these three negatives printing blocks are made and the result is obtained by making three printings, one from each block, with three different pigments, each pigment representing as nearly as possible the color originally used in the color screen. In much of the best modern color work a fourth plate printing in black or gray is employed to give greater depth to the shadows.

THREE RIVERS (*Trois Rivières*), chief town of St. Maurice County, Quebec, at the confluence of the St. Maurice and St. Lawrence rivers, 95 m. by rail N.E. of Montreal. It has a large trade in lumber, and manufactures boots and shoes. Water power is afforded by the falls at Shawanegan, Grande Mère, and other places on the St. Maurice. Three Rivers was founded by Champlain in 1634. Pop. (1951) 46,074.

THRESHER SHARK, THRASHER SHARK, FOX SHARK, or SWINGLETAIL, common name applied to *Alopias vulpinus*, belonging to the family Alopiidae. This elasmobranch, which inhabits the warmer parts of the Atlantic Ocean and Mediterranean Sea, has the upper lobe of its tail elongated to more than the length of the body proper. It uses its long tail to flail the water about it, stunning the smaller fish on which it feeds. The thresher shark attains a total length of about 13 feet.

THRIFT (*Armeria*), genus of plants of the family Plumbagineae, having the flowers collected into a rounded head, a funnel-shaped, dry, and membranous calyx, five petals united at the base, and narrow, often grasslike leaves. The sea pink, *A. maritima*, grows in turflike tufts, with linear leaves, scapes a few inches high, and beautiful rose-colored, purple, or white flowers, which form an ornament of the sea coasts of Britain and of Europe generally; it is also frequently found on high mountains.

THRIPS, genus of minute insects of the order Thysanoptera. They are found on the leaves of plants, and damage the essential organs of flowers. Some species attack corn. Over thirty are found in the United States.

THROAT, DISEASES OF THE. See LARYNX; TONSIL.

THROMBOSIS, CORONARY. See HEART, DISEASES OF.

THRONDHJEM. See NIDAROS.

THRUSH, common name applied to any of the numerous, widely distributed, oscine birds constituting the family Turdidae. The family contains such well-known song birds as the nightingale, robin, bluebird, solitaire, hermit thrush, and veery (q.v.). Members of the Thrush family feed chiefly on fruits, especially berries, but also destroy large numbers of insects. They live in varied habitats, including wooded areas, plains, and rocky regions, and build nests in locations suitable to their environment. The typical nests of the thrushes of northeastern United States are large, cup-shaped structures made of grass, twigs, bark, and leaves, often cemented with mud, and lined with rootlets, mosses, and pine needles. The female thrush lays three to five bluish or greenish eggs in a clutch.

Among the best-known European thrushes are the merle (q.v.) and the song thrush, *Turdus musicus*, which is also known as the "redwing", "mavis", and "throstle". This latter bird, which is about 10 inches long, is popular as a singing cage bird. It is greenish brown above and is white, tinted with tan and heavily spotted with black, below.

Among the American thrushes, the wood thrush or American song thrush, *Hylocichla mustelina*, is most common in eastern United States. This bird, which is slightly over 8 inches in length, is reddish brown above and is white, spotted with black, below. It inhabits woods and thickets and has a clear, powerful song.

The name "thrush" is often applied to birds of different families resembling the true thrushes in coloration or song. Among such birds are the shrike thrushes and babbling thrushes constituting the family Timaliidae, the ground thrushes or ant thrushes constituting the family Pittidae, the water thrushes constituting the genus *Seiurus* of American warblers, and the brown thrush, which is one of the thrashers.

THUCYDIDES (471?–400? B.C.), Greek historian, considered the first and greatest critical historian of antiquity, born in the Attic deme Halimus, the son of Olorus, a rich and aristocratic Athenian. Thucydides was well educated; tradition relates that he was the pupil of Antiphon in rhetoric and of Anaxagoras in philosophy. When the Peloponnesian War broke out in 431 B.C., Thucydides discerned the importance of the conflict and formulated plans for recording its course and outcome. In 424 B.C. he was appointed one of the generals to command the Athenian

Wood thrush

Portrait head of Thucydides

fleet off the Thracian coast, but failed to arrive in time to relieve Amphipolis, which was besieged by the Spartan general Brasidas (q.v.). For this failure Thucydides was exiled from Athens and spent the next twenty years abroad, living part of the time at his estate in Thrace and also devoting considerable time to travel. In 403 B.C. he was recalled from exile, after the restoration of the democracy at Athens, in which he spent the last years of his life.

Thucydides' great work, the *History of the Peloponnesian War*, covers three phases of the war: the conflict between Athens and Sparta from 431 to 421 B.C., ended by the peace of Nicias; the Sicilian expedition of the Athenians from 415 to its disastrous failure in 413 B.C. (see ALCIBIADES; SYRACUSE); and lastly the renewed war between Sparta and Athens from 413 to 404 B.C. The history is incomplete, however, breaking off in the middle of the year 411 B.C., and the division of the work into eight books was probably made by later scholars. Thucydides brought to his undertaking a practical acquaintance with politics and military science, enabling him to pass impartial judgment on the events which he narrated. His material was obtained in the main by personal observation or by questioning those who had participated directly in the fighting. He was most successful in his characterization of the leaders of the conflict, ascribing to them lengthy speeches which sometimes represent the author's idealized conception of events. In form, Thucydides' history is strictly annalistic, the account being given by summers and by winters, and his work suffers from his failure to group events effectively. His style, although occasionally obscure and difficult to understand, because he molded the then immature Greek language into new forms to suit the complexity of his thought, was greatly admired in antiquity, and became the model for many historians in later centuries (see SALLUST; TACITUS, CORNELIUS). Thucydides is noted for his style of writing, his scientific method, and especially his conception of the causes of historical events.

THUGS (from the Hindustani *thaga*, "deceive"), a religious fraternity in India, which, in honor of the goddess Kali, was addicted to murders and the plundering of its victims. They considered their murders pious rites. The confraternity appears to have come into existence under the early Mohammedan rulers of India.

THULE, the name generally given by the ancients to the most northerly part of Europe known to them. Pytheas (q.v.) of Massilia, a Greek navigator of the 4th century B.C., discovered Thule, reaching it after a six days' sail from Britain; he related in his account of the discovery that the midsummer sun never set there. In antiquity Thule was considered to be Mainland, the largest of the Shetland Islands, but modern scholars believe that Pytheas reached either Iceland or Norway. The Romans sometimes used the phrase *Ultima Thule* to denote the most distant unknown land.

THULIUM, a rare, metallic element of atomic number 69, atomic weight 169.4, and symbol Tm, belonging to the group of elements known as rare earths (q.v.). It was discovered in 1879 by the Swedish chemist Per Teodor Cleve. Thulium ranks 60th in abundance among the elements in the earth's crust, and is found in small quantities in such rare-earth minerals as euxinite, gadolinite, and blomstrandine. Its principal compounds are in the form of pale-green salts. Until recently thulium had little practical application. In 1954 the Argonne National Laboratory developed a small portable X-ray machine which uses artificially radioactive thulium as its X-ray source.

THUMB, TOM. See STRATTON, CHARLES SHERWOOD.

THUNDERCLOUD (about 1856–1916), American Blackfoot Indian chief, born in Canada. He served as a scout for the United States Army in 1872–76, and participated in the capture of Red Cloud. He was one of the Indian guides of the Prince of Wales, later King Edward VII, when he hunted in the Northwest. Later Thundercloud became famous as an artist's model, posing for Remington, Abbey, and Sargent. He is found in many of the historical paintings in the capitol in St. Paul, Minn.

THURBER, JAMES GROVER (1894–), American cartoonist and author, born in Columbus, Ohio, and educated at the University of Ohio. He was a code clerk in the U.S. State Department from 1918 to 1920, a reporter with the Columbus, Ohio, newspaper *Dispatch* from 1920 to 1924, and on the Paris staff of the *Chicago Tribune* in 1924–25. Beginning in 1926, he contributed regularly to the weekly humorous magazine *The New Yorker*. In most of his drawings Thurber depicts sad-faced animals and humans contending persistently with diabolically frustrating circumstance; his writings, replete with fantastic characters and zany situations, include highly effective satires of various types of contemporary literature, notably pseudoscientific books dealing with sex and psychoanalysis. Among his works, some of them collections of his contributions to *The New Yorker,* are *Is Sex Necessary?* (with Elwyn Brooks White, 1929), *The Owl in the Attic and Other Perplexities* (1931), *The Seal in the Bedroom and Other Predicaments* (1932), *My Life and Hard Times* (1933), *The Middle Aged Man on the Flying Trapeze* (1935), *Let Your Mind Alone* (1937), *The Last Flower* (1939), *Fables for Our Time, and Famous Poems Illustrated* (1940), *My World —and Welcome To It* (1942), *Men, Women, and Dogs* (1943), *The Beast in Me, and Other Animals* (1948), *The 13 Clocks* (1950), *The Thurber Album* (1952), *Thurber Country* (1953), *Thurber's Dogs* (1955), and *Further Fables for Our Time* (1956). He is co-author, with the American playwright and actor Elliott Nugent (1900–47), of *The Male Animal* (1940), a play, and he also wrote several fantasies for children including *Many Moons* (1943) and *The White Deer* (1945).

THURGAU, a canton of N.E. Switzerland, separated from Germany by Lake Constance. The capital is Frauenfeld (pop. in 1950, 11,-114). The surface of the canton is elevated but not mountainous. The valley of the principal river, the Thur, traverses the canton from E. to S.W. The chief industries are agriculture, notably grape growing, and cotton spinning, dyeing, and weaving. The district was controlled by the Swiss Confederation after 1460, and became a canton in 1803. Area, 388 sq.m.; pop. (1950) 149,738.

THURINGIA, region of E. Germany, including the former State of Thuringia and the government district of Erfurt (formerly in Saxony), bounded on the N. by Saxony-Anhalt and Lower Saxony, on the E. by Saxony, on the S. by Bavaria, and on the W. by Hesse. Thuringia was constituted as a State of the federal German republic on Dec. 24, 1919, by the union of the following former States of the German Empire: Saxe-Weimar-Eisenach, Saxe-Meiningen, Saxe-Altenburg, Schwarzburg-Rodolstadt, Schwarzburg-Sonderhausen, Saxe-Gotha (Coburg having merged with Bavaria), and Reuss. The chief city of Thuringia is Weimar. A great part of the area is occupied by mountain ranges, notably the Thuringian Forest (q.v.). Over 40% of the land is arable. The greatest of the considerable mineral resources are lignite and potash. The industries include the manufacture of glass, textiles, earthenware, and machinery.

The region acquired its name from the Thuringians, a Germanic tribe which established a kingdom there in the 5th century. The landgraviate of Thuringia was founded in 1130 and was an important principality during the 12th and 13th centuries. The seat of the landgraves was the famous castle of Wartburg, near Eisenach (q.v.), noted as the site of contests of minnesingers (q.v.). The old line of landgraves became extinct in 1247. The landgraviate then passed to the house of Wettin, which ruled in the margraviate of Meissen, and which in the 15th century also acquired the electoral duchy of Saxony (q.v.). When the Saxon dominions were partitioned in 1485, most of Thuringia passed to the Ernestine branch of the Wettin house. During the Reformation, the Saxon duchies and principalities were separated, becoming again merged, into the state of Thuringia, following World War I. Following World War II Thuringia was included within the Soviet Zone of Occupation.

THURINGIAN FOREST or **THURINGER WALD,** mountain range of central Germany, extending from the banks of the Werra near Eisenach in a S.E. direction to the N. boundary of Bavaria, where it joins the Frankenwald, a ramification of the Fichtelgebirge. It forms the s.w. boundary of the trough of Thuringia, which in outward features resembles a plateau extending to the Harz Mountains. Its length is about 70 m.; its highest summit is Gross-Beerberg, 3238 ft. The range falls steeply toward the N.E. and is covered to the summits with pine forests. The Triassic deposits which once clothed its surfaces have been worn away, exposing older granites, porphyries, and schists. It is rich in minerals, among which iron ore, copper, manganese, and gypsum are the most important.

THURMOND, JAMES STROM (1902–), American political leader, born in Edgefield, S.C., and educated at Clemson Agricultural College, S.C. He taught in the public schools of his native State from 1923 to 1929, and during the following years, until 1933, was superintendent of education of Edgefield Co. He was a State senator from 1933 to 1938, and a State circuit judge from 1938 to 1946. During World War II he served in the U.S. Army in both the European and Asiatic theaters of operations. In 1947 he was elected governor of South Carolina. Thurmond, who had been a delegate to the national conventions of the Democratic Party in 1932 and 1936, achieved national prominence in 1948 as the Presidential candidate of the States' Rights Democrats, a group of dissident Southern Democrats, popularly called Dixiecrats, who rejected the nominee of the Democratic Party, Harry S. Truman; see STATES' RIGHTS; POLITICAL PARTIES IN THE UNITED STATES. In the election, Thurmond received about one million votes, or 2 percent of the total cast. He was elected to the U.S. Senate in 1954 and resigned in March, 1956, but was returned to the U.S. Senate in the election of November, 1956.

THUTMOSE or **THOTMES,** the royal name of four kings of the XVIIIth (Diospolite) dynasty of Egypt.

1. THUTMOSE I, successor to Amenhotep I, king from about 1540 to 1501 B.C. and again from 1496 to 1493 B.C. The first recorded military expedition of Thutmose I was against the Nubians, whom he conquered. Not long thereafter, Thutmose I invaded Asia, and advanced as far as the Euphrates River, where he erected a stele, or pillarlike monument, commemorating his achievement. The remainder of his reign was peaceful, and was largely devoted to various building projects. At Karnak (q.v.) he built two pylons and two hypostyle halls, and raised two obelisks (q.v.) one of which is still standing.

2. THUTMOSE II, son of the foregoing, king jointly with his father from 1496 to 1493 B.C., following the deposition of his sister and wife, Queen Hatshepsut (q.v.), and of Thutmose III (see below). According to an inscription discovered at Aswan, Upper Egypt, Thutmose II sent an expedition against Nubian tribes who had made incursions into his realm. He is also said to have warred against the Bedouins (q.v.), a nomadic people of the Arabian and Syrian deserts. Thutmose II made additions to the great temple of Amen at Karnak, and his name is inscribed on ancient buildings in many parts of Egypt. The mummy of the king was found in 1881 at Der el-Behri.

3. THUTMOSE III, son of Thutmose I by the concubine Isis, and half brother and husband of Queen Hatshepsut, king jointly with Hatshepsut from about 1501 to 1496 B.C. and again from 1493 to 1481, and sole king from 1481 to 1447. Soon after deposing his father in 1501 B.C., Thutmose III was forced into the background by Hatshepsut, who became the supreme ruler until Thutmose I and Thutmose II drove her from the throne and regained their power by means of a revolution. After the death of Thutmose I in 1493 B.C., Thutmose III and Hatshepsut again assumed the throne, but the queen once more exercised the supreme authority, assigning to her husband merely a nominal role in the government. With the death of Hatshepsut twelve years later, however, Thutmose III at last became the sole ruler of Egypt. He then entered upon a career of conquest unrivaled in the annals of Egyptian history. Invading Syria through the passes of Mount Carmel, he vanquished the Syrian forces on the Plain of Jezreel (now Esdraelon) and forced them to take refuge in the city of Megiddo, which he captured in 1479 B.C. after a brief siege. The conquered Syrian chiefs were made vassals of Egypt, and Thutmose III returned home in triumph.

His victory proved incomplete, however, for a number of Syrian and Phenician cities offered stubborn resistance to Egyptian rule, aided by the powerful state of Mitanni, which at that time occupied the territory now included in northern Syria and northern Iraq. Thutmose III then waged war against Mitanni, ravishing its territory and capturing a number of its cities, notably Carchemish on the Euphrates River. Although this conflict netted the Egyptian sovereign no permanent territorial possessions, it served to neutralize Mitannian power while he extended his dominion over northern Palestine and Phenicia. At the city of Ni, near the lower course of the Orontes River, he erected a stele to mark the limit of the Egyptian Empire in that region. During his reign Thutmose III conducted seventeen successful campaigns into Asia, lavishing the booty and tribute thus obtained upon the Egyptian temples. As a builder Thutmose III was hardly less energetic than as a warrior, and his monuments occur in many places throughout Egypt and northeastern Africa. He made important additions to the great temple of Amen at Karnak and caused his annals to be inscribed upon its walls. He also fostered building projects in the Egyptian cities of Heliopolis, Memphis, Abydos, and Isna. The mummy of Thutmose III was excavated at Der el-Behri.

4. THUTMOSE IV, son of Amenhotep II and grandson of Thutmose III, king from about 1420 to 1411 B.C. He conducted military expeditions to Nubia and to Phenicia, collecting booty and tribute in both countries. He completed the last obelisk erected by Thutmose III and cleared away the sand from the Great Sphinx (q.v.). Thutmose IV maintained friendly relations with Babylonia and with Mitanni, and married the daughter of Antatama, King of Mitanni. See EGYPT: *History.*

THYESTES, in Greek legend, the son of Pelops (q.v.) and Hippodamia, and the brother of Atreus (q.v.). Having seduced the wife of Atreus, he was banished from Mycenæ, and in revenge sent Plisthenes, Atreus' son, whom he had reared as his own son, to slay his real father. Atreus, not recognizing Plisthenes as his son, killed him, and then exacted a horrible vengeance on Thyestes by summoning him to Mycenæ and placing before him at a feast the flesh of Thyestes' two sons. Upon discovering the truth Thyestes fled, invoking a curse upon his brother. Another son of Thyestes, Ægisthus, carried on the feud; he killed Atreus and later seduced Clytemnestra, with whom he conspired to kill her husband, the famous hero Agamemnon (q.v.), son of Atreus.

THYLACINE, *Thylacynus cynocephalus,* largest of the extant predaceous marsupials, now restricted to Tasmania. The thylacine is somewhat smaller than a wolf, has a doglike muzzle, a long, tapering, tail, and is grayish brown in color, with black cross bands on the hind part of the back and loins. It is called also "Tasmanian wolf" and "hyena".

THYME (*Thymus*), a genus of half-shrubby plants, of the mint (q.v.) family, Labiatae. Garden thyme, *T. vulgaris,* is 6 to 10 in. high, with narrow, almost linear leaves, and whitish or reddish flowers, which grow in

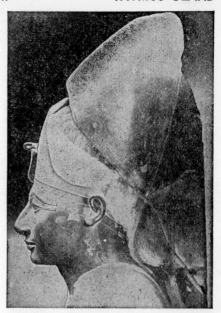

Detail of a sculpture of Thutmose III

separate whorls, six in a whorl. Wild thyme, *T. serpyllum,* has a precumbent stem with many branches, forming tufts, low and dense, a few inches to a foot wide, oval leaves and purplish flowers, arranged in whorls, which are united in a head. It is less fragrant than garden thyme, but both species contain an aromatic essential oil.

THYMUS GLAND, name applied to a structure located just behind the top of the sternum in almost all vertebrates. The thymus gland consists chiefly of lymphatic tissue and contains a few small areas of epithelial tissue which are known as *Hassall's corpuscles.* The human thymus gland increases in weight until the age of one year, and from then until puberty it maintains a constant weight of about 1½ ounces. After puberty, the lymphatic tissue of the thymus gland is replaced by fat, and in the adult human the organ is chiefly composed of fatty tissue. A great deal of contradictory experimental evidence is available concerning the functions of the thymus gland. Many scientists believe that the organ has no glandular secretory functions whatsoever, and is merely an evolutional remnant of some organ which was formerly functional in the ancestors of the vertebrates. Other scientists claim that the organ is an endocrine gland producing hormones which control calcium metabolism and

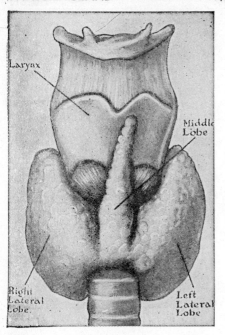

Drawing of the three-lobed thyroid gland of man, located in the neck below the larynx

the growth of the skeleton. Scientists generally accept the thymus gland as the seat of some formation of white blood cells. Abnormal enlargement of the thymus gland occurs in such conditions as exophthalmic goiter, myasthenia gravis, and suprarenal insufficiency, but the reason for such enlargement has not yet been explained.

THYROID GLAND, or THYROID BODY, name applied to an endocrine gland found in almost all vertebrate animals and so called because it is located directly in front of the thyroid cartilage of the larynx. The thyroid gland in its early evolutional stages was a digestive organ; the gland is homologous with the endostyle of ascidians. In vertebrates, the gland has lost its digestive function and serves to secrete a hormone (q.v.) which controls metabolism in adult and young animals and which is an important factor in the growth and development of young animals.

The gland in human beings is a brownish-red organ which normally weighs about one ounce. It consists of cuboidal epithelial cells arranged to form small sacs known as *vesicles*, *acini*, or *alveoli*. The vesicles are supported by connective tissue which forms a framework for the entire gland. In the normal thyroid gland, these vesicles are usually filled with *colloid substance* or *thyroglobulin*, the secretion of the thyroid gland. The amount of secretion elaborated by the thyroid is controlled by the thyrotropic hormone of the pituitary body (q.v.). Thyroglobulin is especially rich in iodine (q.v.); although the thyroid gland constitutes about one two-hundredth percent of the total human body weight, it holds about one fifth of the total iodine in the human body. Thyroglobulin contains also several amino acids, the most active of which is the thyroid hormone, thyroxine (q.v.). Thyroxine is released from the gland directly into the blood stream through the walls of numerous capillaries which traverse the thyroid gland. The thyroid hormone acts directly on the cells of the vertebrate body, serving as a catalyst to accelerate biological oxidations.

Deficiency of secretion of the thyroid gland results in a number of abnormal body conditions characterized by lowering of the basal metabolic rate (see METABOLISM), lethargy, and decreased activity; among such abnormal conditions are cretinism (q.v.), myxedema (q.v.), and simple goiter (see GOITER). Overactivity of the thyroid gland results in increased metabolism and activity, and in the condition known as exophthalmic goiter. The thyroid hormone is also believed to influence other endocrine glands, especially the pituitary and suprarenal glands, and disturbance of the thyroid often precedes or accompanies disturbances of these glands.

THYROXINE, TETRAIODOTHYRONINE, or THYROXIN, a complex organic compound, $C_{15}H_{11}I_4NO_4$, which is one of the most active ingredients of thyroglobulin, the hormone of the thyroid gland (q.v.). Thyroxine, which was isolated in 1919 by the American biochemist Edward Calvin Kendall (1886–   ) and which was synthesized in 1927 by the British physiologist Charles Robert Harington (1897–   ), is a white or yellowish substance which is one of the most active substance which is obtained in crystalline needles. It melts at 235° to 237°C. (457° to 460°F.), and is slightly soluble in water and insoluble in alcohol and ether. Thyroxine is closely related to the amino acid tyrosine, from which many scientists believe thyroxine is synthesized in the body. In the normal adult human being, about .0005 oz. of thyroxine circulates throughout the entire body; the thyroid gland manufactures about .0001 oz. of thyroxine each day. Synthetic thyroxine is used in medicine in the treatment of various conditions resulting from deficient functioning of the thyroid gland; a person completely lacking the thyroid gland can be maintained in good health by the administration of slightly more than .0001 oz. of thyroxine a day. The compound is also sometimes used for relief in cases of obesity.

THYSANURA, an order of wingless insects of small size (see INSECTS). The abdomen usually bears peculiar structures, which seem to be abortive limbs, and the name Thysanura or bristletails refers to terminal appendages which are sometimes long and hairy.

THYSSEN, AUGUST (1842–1926), German industrial leader. He founded, in Mülheim-Ruhr, the firm of Thyssen and Company, parent house of his many industrial interests. He became the chief owner of a mining company employing about 18,000 men, of 641 coke ovens, and of 7 blast furnaces. He built the first 500-ton blast furnace in Germany, the first 100-ton Martin furnace, and the first large tube works.

TI (Polynesian name), *Cordyline terminalis,* a treelike plant of the family Liliaceae, found in southeastern Asia, the eastern archipelago, and the Hawaiian and other Pacific islands. It sometimes exceeds 12 feet in height. The reddish, lanceolate leaves are used as cattle food, as thatch for houses, and as food wrappers. Their fibers are sometimes made into cloth. The large, hard, fibrous, and almost insipid root becomes soft and sweet when baked. It is very nutritious, and is much used as an article of food. The juice is used for making sugar, a fermented beverage, and a distilled liquor. Fully 25 varieties of Cordyline are grown under glass for their ornamental, often variegated, foliage.

TIAHUANACO, an ancient, ruined city in Bolivia, situated on an arid plain, about 12,000 ft. above sea level, between lakes Titicaca and Aullagas, about 40 miles w. of La Paz. The ruins of the city are remarkable for the remains of stone buildings, presumed by archeologists to have been the work of the Aymaras, a pre-Incan people (see PERUVIAN ARCHEOLOGY). The present-day village of the same name stands near the ruins and is built for the most part of stones from the ancient buildings. Five enormous structures within the old city are known as the Fortress, the Temple, the Palace, the Hall of Justice, and the Sanctuary. The Temple, believed to be the oldest of the Tiahuanaco buildings, is a rectangle 388 ft. by 455 ft., defined by erect stones between 8 and 10 ft. high, 2 to 4 ft. wide, and 20 to 30 in. thick. Many of the building stones are of andesite, a hard volcanic rock, transported from far-distant areas. The masonry is laid without mortar, the stones being tongued and grooved at their ends; bronze pins and T-clamps were used to hold the courses together.

The ruined city is one of the great archeological enigmas. Its history is lost in remote antiquity, but it is thought to predate the Christian era. The carvings and building style are similar to those of later structures on the Isla del Sol, in Lake Titicaca. A widely-held theory considers Tiahuanaco to have been a port city, when the lakes covered the present dry plain. According to this theory, a prehistoric flood forced the emigration of the inhabitants to the lake island.

TIAN-SHAN, or THIAN SHAN ("Celestial Mountains"), a great mountain system, consisting of several ridges, mostly parallel, in central Asia, extending from the Pamir to the N. of the Tarim depression in Turkestan. It forms the boundary of the great Tarim Basin, which it separates from the watersheds of Lake Balkash and the Syr-Darya. It is connected by broken ranges with the Altai Mountains to the north, and, through the Sarikal, with the Kuen-lun, Hindu-Kush, and Himalaya systems. In the central portion there is a main ridge forming an unbroken wall covered with perpetual snow throughout its length, and culminating in the west in the Khan-Tengri, a peak bearing enormous glaciers and reaching an altitude of 24,000 feet. East of this ridge the mountains descend in a broad plateau with scattered peaks and ridges from 6000 to 10,000 ft. high. In the west portion there are several important passes affording routes between Western and Eastern Turkestan. The system incloses numerous large longitudinal valleys whose bottoms form wide steppe regions. Above, the slopes are covered with spruce forests succeeded by an alpine flora to the snow line. The loftiest group in the eastern portion, the Bogdoola, is held sacred by the Mongolians.

TIARA, the triple crown of the pope, which is symbolical of his temporal authority. It is composed of a cap of gold cloth, encircled by three coronets, with a mound and cross of gold on the top. The original papal crown consisted of the cap alone, and was first used by Nicholas I (858–67); Alexander II added the second coronet (1065). Urban V (1362–70) added the third.

TIBBETT, LAWRENCE MERVIL (1896–   ), American baritone, born in Bakersfield, Calif. He made his debut on the concert stage in

Lawrence Tibbett

1917, and on the operatic stage in 1923. In the same year, he appeared at the Metropolitan Opera House, New York, as Valentine in Gounod's *Faust*. He visited Europe several times, and appeared in moving pictures after 1929.

TIBBUS, TIBUS, or **TUBUS** ("rock people"), a people inhabiting Tibesti, in the eastern Sahara, and extending southward into the Sudan. Possibly related to the central Sudanese Negroes, they vary greatly in hair and features. There are only 70,000 of them spread over an area of 300,000 square miles, under the names Tedas, Dasas, Bedeyat, Zoghawa, and Bulzeda. In religion they are Mohammedan.

TIBER (anc. *Tiberis*; It. *Tevere*), the principal river of central Italy, rising in the Apennine Mountains of Tuscany, in the province of Arezzo, about 30 miles E. of the source of the Arno R., and flowing S. in a winding course across the province of Perugia (ancient Umbria). In antiquity the river formed the boundary between Etruria on the W. and Umbria and Latium on the E. and S. About 3 m. above Rome it is swelled by the Teverone (ancient Anio); passing through the city, it forms an island, the ancient Insula Tiberina, now Isola di San Bartolomeo, and enters the Tyrrhenian Sea about 21 m. below Rome.

The total length of the Tiber is 244 m.; its breadth at Rome is about 250 ft. The sediment deposited at the mouth of the Tiber extends the land at the rate of more than 10 ft. a year, so that the ruins of Ostia (q.v.), the ancient harbor of Rome, are now more than 4 m. inland. The delta is formed of two mouths, enclosing the Isola Sacra: the fiumicino, originally a channel dug by the emperor Trajan for his harbor, the Portus Trajani, and now the larger and navigable branch; and the fiumara, now almost choked by sand banks. Although the depth of the river between its mouths and Rome is normally only 9 to 20 ft. and, in places, at low water, not more than 4 ft., the Tiber is navigable by small steamers in that part of its course; smaller craft can ply 60 m. beyond Rome. The river is subject to frequent and often disastrous flooding. Among the more famous floods are that mentioned by the Roman poet Horace; that of 1598, when the water at Rome rose 51½ ft.; and that of 1900, when the river reached a flood height of almost 54 ft. above the river bed. To remedy this evil, the government, beginning in 1876, constructed massive embankments at Rome at an expense of more than $25,000,000, but the carefully planned work proved defective. In the flood of 1900 fully a quarter of a mile of the south embankment was carried away by the water.

TIBERIAS. See GALILEE.

TIBERIUS, in full TIBERIUS CLAUDIUS NERO CÆSAR (42 B.C.–37 A.D.), the second emperor of Rome, ruling from 14 to 37 A.D., elder son of Tiberius Claudius Nero and Livia Drusilla. Four years following his birth his mother divorced his father and married the triumvir Octavian, later the emperor Augustus, who had Tiberius carefully educated. The boy early manifested intellectual power and military skill. In 20 B.C. he commanded an expedition to Armenia, restored to the Armenian throne Tigranes, grandson of Tigranes the Great, and brought back the standards lost at the defeat of Marcus Licinius Crassus in 53 B.C. In 15 B.C. Tiberius cooperated with his younger brother, Nero Claudius Drusus, in subduing the Rhætians (see RHÆTIA) and the Vindelicians; he fought against the Pannonians (see PANNONIA) from 12 to 9 B.C., and in the campaign that followed the death of Drusus in 9 B.C. traversed Germany between the Rhine and the Elbe rivers.

Marcus Claudius Marcellus, the youthful nephew of the emperor Augustus, had died in 23 B.C., and Marcus Vipsanius Agrippa, the son-in-law of Augustus, died suddenly in 12 B.C., leaving only two boys of eight and five between Tiberius, the stepson, and the succession. In 11 B.C. Tiberius was compelled by Augustus to divorce Vipsania Agrippina, daughter of Agrippa by a former wife, Pomponia, in order to marry Augustus' daughter Julia, the widow of Agrippa. Shortly after this marriage Tiberius was sent to crush a revolt in Dalmatia and Pannonia. In 6 B.C. he retired to the island of Rhodes, where he devoted himself to study for seven years. When he returned to Rome in 2 A.D., Julia had been banished to Pandataria, and within the next two years the deaths of both the young princes Lucius and Gaius (in 2 and 4 A.D., respectively) paved the way for the adoption of Tiberius as heir to the imperial dignity. He was formally adopted by Augustus in 4 A.D. Tiberius spent the next seven years in active service in northern Germany against Marbo, King of the Marcomanni, in quelling formidable insurrections in Pannonia and Dalmatia, and finally in securing the frontier and taking vengeance upon the enemy, who had annihilated the army of Publius Quintilius Varus in the Teutoburger Wald in 9 A.D. Accompanied by Germanicus (q.v.) Cæsar, his nephew and adopted son, Tiberius made two more marches into the heart of Germany in 9 and 10 A.D., returning to enjoy a triumph in 12 A.D.

Upon the death of Augustus at Nola in 14 A.D. Tiberius succeeded to the throne without opposition. The first years of his reign were marked by revolts of the troops in Pannonia and Germany, but these were soon suppressed; then followed the campaigns of Germanicus in Germany in 15 and 16 A.D. Other military events were the revolt of the Numidians (17–24 A.D.), the rebellion in Gaul (21 A.D.), the suppression of a revolt in Thrace (25 A.D.), and an expedition against Parthia (35 A.D.). In domestic affairs the reign of Tiberius was at first beneficent. He improved the civil service, kept the army in strict discipline, and managed the finances with great ability and generosity; the provinces were better governed during his reign than ever before. Gradually, however, a change took place, and the latter part of his reign is notable for a series of conspiracies and consequent executions. In 26 A.D. Tiberius left Rome and withdrew to Campania, and the following year went to the island of Capreæ (modern Capri), leaving Rome under the power of Lucius Ælius Sejanus, the prefect of the Prætorian Guard. Finally, realizing that Sejanus was trying to seize the imperial power, Tiberius had him and his supporters put to death in 31 A.D. Tiberius continued to live at Capreæ until 37 A.D., and then returned to Italy; shortly thereafter he died at Misenum, being said by some ancient historians to have been smothered by Nævius Sertorius Macro, Sejanus' successor as prefect of the Prætorian Guard. He was succeeded by Germanicus' son Gaius, usually known as Caligula (q.v.).

Estimates of the character of Tiberius differ widely; most modern scholars, however, reject the tales of his cruelty, hypocrisy, and debauchery which are related by the ancient historians Publius Cornelius Tacitus (q.v.) and Gaius Suetonius Tranquillus (see SUETONIUS). Tiberius seems to have been an able soldier and administrator, who endeavored to govern with justice and humanity, retaining the republican forms of government as much as possible and giving to the Roman senate, in the early part of his reign, a large amount of authority. His coldness and reserve, and his desire for economy in government, however, rendered him unpopular with the people.

TIBET or (Chin.) **SITSANG,** semiautonomous province of the People's Republic of China, formerly constituting (1914–51) an independent state. It is bounded on the N. and E. by China, on the S. by the Union of India, Bhutan, and Nepal, and on the W. by Kashmir and the Union of India. Tibet is enclosed on three sides by vast mountain systems, namely the Himalaya (q.v.) on the S., the Kuen-Lun Mountains (q.v.) on the N., and the Karakorum chain on the W. Largely because of the impassable character of these natural barriers, Tibet is one of the most isolated regions in the world. It is also the most elevated region in the world, having an average elevation of more than 16,000 ft. The capital and only important city of Tibet is Lhasa (q.v.). The estimated area of the province is 470,000 sq.m.; the population (1953) is 1,273,969.

As indicated in the foregoing, S. Tibet falls wholly within the Himalaya mountains. Many of the highest summits known to man are situated in the main Himalayan chain extending along the entire S. frontier. Among these summits are Everest (q.v., 29,141 ft.), the highest peak ever discovered; Gosainthan (26,291 ft.); Gurla Mandhata

(25,355 ft.) ; and Kula Kangri (24,784 ft.). Another Himalayan chain, commonly known as Trans-Himalaya, lies parallel to the main chain on the N. Between this chain, which is dominated by peaks up to 24,000 ft., and the main chain are the valleys of the Brahmaputra (q.v.), known in Tibet as the Tsangpo, Sutlej (q.v.), and Indus (q.v.) rivers. The Trans-Himalayan chain slopes northward to the Tibetan Plateau, a vast tableland extending to the Karakorum and Kuen-lun systems on the w. and N. respectively. The Tibetan Plateau, which is broken by mountainous outcroppings and lakes,

slopes gradually eastward and southward. Elevations in the plateau region average between 14,000 and 17,000 ft.

Tibet is a region of great aridity, precipitation being negligible virtually everywhere except in the S.E. Excluding the S.E., the average annual precipitation is about 8 inches. The most equable climatic conditions are confined to the river valleys. Because of the rarefied atmosphere, the climate in the mountainous and plateau regions is marked by sharp variations. Precipitate drops of temperature after sunset are a common phenomenon.

Vegetation is extremely sparse in the plateau region, consisting for the most part of grasses and shrubs. Scattered wooded areas occur in the extreme w. and E. In the main, however, the flora of Tibet is concentrated in the valleys of the Tsangpo, Indus, and Sutlej. These areas support several species of trees, including conifers, oak, cypress, poplar, and maple. Apple, peach, and apricot trees are cultivated in the river valleys, practically the only arable sections of the province

Left: Tibetan woman wearing hat with cone-shaped crown. Her hair is worn in numerous finely braided strands. Below: Tibetan warriors and their horses in a forest camp.

Pix

Pix

Lamas gathering for a solemn mass at a temple in Tibet

The fauna of the province is quite diversified. Musk deer, wild sheep, wild goat, wild ass, yak, and Tibetan antelope are common in the mountainous areas. Other large quadrupeds are the leopard, bear, sloth bear, wolf, fox, wild dog, and monkey. Bird life includes the bar-headed goose, teal, and other species of waterfowl, the pheasant, and sand grouse.

Extensive portions of Tibet have never been explored, but the province is known to contain valuable mineral deposits. Gold occurs in many areas, and gold panning is an occasional occupation. There are deposits of coal, iron ore, silver, salt, potash, borax, granite, quartz, slate, and clay. Jade, lapis lazuli, and other precious and semiprecious stones are found. However, mining occupies an insignificant place in Tibet's economy.

The chief sources of livelihood and national wealth in Tibet are livestock raising, farming, and foreign commerce. Livestock raising is the primary occupation of nomadic inhabitants of the plateau region. Besides sheep, cattle, and goats, the herds include camels, yaks, mules, and other beasts of burden. The principal crops, produced almost exclusively in the river valleys, are barley, wheat, buckwheat, potatoes, turnips, cabbages, and fruits. Textiles and religious objects, the only manufactures of consequence, are produced by home and other small-scale enterprises.

Tibet possesses no railroads and few modern highways, but considerable trade is carried on with neighboring nations, particularly India and Pakistan, by means of camel, mule, and yak caravans. Caravan routes radiate in all directions from Lhasa, the chief commercial center. Exports consist mainly of musk, wool, hides, furs, yak tails, livestock, herbs, salt, and borax. The principal imports are manufactured articles, tea, rice and other foodstuffs, and silk.

The people of Tibet belong predominantly to the Mongolian race. Modified racial types, the product of intermarriage with the Indian and Chinese people, are common in the frontier regions and larger communities. Tibetan, a branch of the Indo-Chinese linguistic family, is the language of the country. The religion of the overwhelming majority of the population is Lamaism (q.v.), a modified version of Buddhism. Large numbers of Tibetans are Lamaist monks, known as lamas. According to some estimates the lamas, most of whom are celibates, number nearly 500,000. Among noteworthy features of the Tibetan social structure are polyandry, which is practiced among the peasants, and polygamy, which is common among the wealthy classes.

History. Prior to the 7th century A.D., when Buddhism was introduced into Tibet, the history of the region is legendary and obscure. Buddhist missionaries developed an alphabet for the Tibetan language, initiated translations of the Buddhist sacred books, and conducted a relentless struggle against Shamanism (q.v.), the indigenous religion. In the period of Buddhist penetration, which led to the development of Lamaism and a powerful Lamaist hierarchy, Tibet was a strong kingdom. Toward the close of the 10th century the kingdom began to disintegrate, eventually splitting into a number of petty principalities. The Mongol conqueror Genghis Khan incorporated the area into his empire in 1206. In 1270 political power was bestowed on the head of the Lamaist hierarchy.

The Chinese Empire acquired sovereignty over Tibet in the 17th century, but in the course of the following two centuries Chinese authority steadily diminished. Meanwhile, British colonial officials in India, initially Warren Hastings (q.v.), attempted to secure a foothold in the region. These efforts were fruitless, mainly because of Tibetan resentment over a Nepalese invasion (1790), which had British support. In 1904 Tibet, then virtually independent of Chinese authority, was invaded by the British, who were alarmed over Russian influence in the country. The expedition laid the foundations for an Anglo-Chinese convention (1906). By the terms of this agreement, the Chinese Empire acquired recognition as the sovereign power in Tibet. The agreement also provided for the payment of a large indemnity to the British, who subsequently withdrew their troops. In 1907 the British and Russian governments concluded an agreement which pledged noninterference in Tibetan affairs.

Tibet attained nominal independence from China following the revolutionary overthrow (1912) of the Manchu dynasty. All Chinese officials and troops were expelled from the country by 1913. In 1914, at a conference, held at Simla, of representatives of the British, Chinese, and Tibetan governments, tentative agreement was reached on a convention regulating mutual relations. Among other things the convention provided for an autonomous Tibet and for Chinese sovereignty in the region, called Inner Tibet, contiguous to China proper. The Chinese government subsequently repudiated the convention, which was signed by the United Kingdom in July, 1914. In 1918 the strained relations between Tibet and China culminated in armed conflict. A truce was arranged, with British help, in September of that year. Subsequent efforts to conciliate the dispute were unsuccessful. In October, 1950, little more than a year after the Communist victory in the Chinese civil war, Tibet was invaded by Red troops. To rally the nation, presumably, against the advancing Reds, the regency invested the Dalai Lama with full authority in November, 1950, three years before he attained his majority. However, the Tibetan government capitulated in May, 1951, signing a treaty that provides for the maintenance of the Dalai Lama's power in domestic affairs; for Chinese control of Tibetan foreign and military affairs; and for the return from China of the Lamaist spiritual leader, the Teshu, or Panchen, Lama, reputedly a partisan of the Communist regime. Communist military units reached Lhasa in October. The Panchen Lama arrived there in April, 1952.

During 1952 the Chinese, accelerating a communications-improvement program launched the previous year, completed airfields in various parts of Tibet and continued with the construction of military highways, notably a road linking Lhasa and Kangking, China (730 m.). According to press reports a purge of anti-Communists was in progress in Tibet early in 1953.

TIBULLUS, ALBIUS (54?–18 B.C.), Roman elegiac poet. Few details of his life are known, except that he was the chief poet in the literary circle of Marcus Valerius Messala Corvinus, whom he is believed to have accompanied on a military mission to Gaul about 30 B.C. and later on a mission to the East. He was obliged by illness to return from the latter expedition, and thenceforth lived at Rome, devoting himself to poetry. The collection of elegiac poems under his name is preserved in three books, but is usually published in four, the third book having been divided into two by Italian scholars in the Renaissance. The first book, concerned chiefly with his love for his mistress Delia, and the second book, devoted to his love for the courtesan Nemesis, are undoubtedly the work of Tibullus; the remainder of the collection seems to have been written largely by other members of the circle of Messala, including Lygdamus, an inferior poet, and Sulpicia, Messala's niece. The poetry of Tibullus reflects his unselfish, amiable, and winning personality, its two chief themes being love and a desire for an idyllic country life. His death, which followed immediately after that of Vergil, was the subject of a magnificent elegy by the poet Ovid.

TIBUR. See TIVOLI.

TICINO (anc. *Ticinus*), a tributary of the Po R., situated in S. Switzerland and N. Italy. From its sources in the Saint Gotthard range of the Alps, the river flows generally southward across Ticino Canton, Switzerland, to Lake Maggiore, reappears at the S. extremity of the lake, and courses southward and eastward to its confluence, S.E. of Pavia, with the Po. Part of the boundary between Piedmont and Lombardy is formed by the Ticino. The river, which is navigable S. of Lake Maggiore, is about 155 m. in length.

TICINO (Ger. *Tessin*), the most southerly of the cantons of Switzerland (q.v.), bounded on the N. by the cantons of Uri and Grisons, on the E. by Grisons and Italy, on the S. by Italy, and on the W. by Italy and the canton of Valais. The capital is Bellinzona; other important cities are Locarno (q.v.) and Lugano. The region is very mountainous, with the Lepontine Alps on the N. and the Adula Alps on the E., and is traversed by the river valleys. The N. part of Lake Maggiore and almost all of Lake Lugano are within the canton. The S. is comparatively low and is the most fertile portion. About two thirds of the canton is under cultivation, the principal crops being cereal grains and fruits, particularly grapes. The inhabitants are, for the most part, Italian-speaking, and Roman Catholic in religion. During the late Middle Ages the area was part of the duchy of Milan, from which it was wrested during the 15th and 16th centuries by the Swiss Confederation. In 1803 the separate districts were united into the canton of Ticino, which received a constitution in 1830. Area, 1086 sq.m.; pop. (1950) 175,055.

TICINUM. See PAVIA.

TICKELL, THOMAS (1686–1740), English poet, born in Bridekirk, Cumberland. He held the office of secretary to the lords justices of Ireland (1725–40). The most memorable incident in his life was his translation of the first book of the *Iliad* about the same time

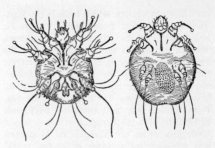

Ticks. Left, male; right, female.

as the first part of Pope's *Homer*. His longest poem is "Kensington Gardens"; his most popular, the ballad of "Colin and Lucy"; his finest, the exquisite elegy to Addison prefixed to his edition of Addison's *Works* (1721).

TICKNOR, GEORGE (1791–1871), historian of Spanish literature, born in Boston, Mass. He went to Europe in 1815, and for four years resided successively in London, Göttingen, Paris, Geneva, Rome, Venice, Madrid, and Lisbon. His journal is full of the best sort of interviewing of all the literary personages of the day. Returning to America, he became professor of French and Spanish and of the belles-lettres at Harvard University. In 1835 he went to Europe, where he remained three years, collecting materials for his great *History of Spanish Literature* (1849), an exhaustive and admirable work which has been translated into Spanish and German. Other works by him were *Lives* of Lafayette (1824) and Prescott (1864).

TICKS, common name applied to mites of the order Acarida, the members of which attack man, cattle, dogs, birds, reptiles, and some other animals. They live in woods or among thick vegetation, and it is likely that their primary food supply is derived from vegetable juices. The mitelike body has a tough skin; there are four pairs of clawed legs; the mouthparts consist (1) of a paired anchoring organ or "rostrum", covered with recurved hooks, and equivalent to a "maxillary lip" or to the pedipalps of other Arachnids, and (2) of a pair of sharp mandibles which play backward and forward in two longitudinal channels on the rostrum. Fastening themselves to the skin of an animal, they cut a hole and suck the blood.

TICONDEROGA, a village of Essex Co., N.Y., situated on the La Chute R., which connects Lake George with Lake Champlain, 100 m. by rail N.N.E. of Albany. The falls in the river supply ample water power for the village industries, which include the manufacture of paper, paper pulp, machinery, and pencils. In the vicinity of Ticonderoga are rich deposits of graphite. The site of the present village was of considerable strategic importance during the French and Indian War as a portage point on the water route between Canada and the English settlements. Fort Carillon was built there by the French in 1755. In 1758 the French garrison of about 4000 men under the Marquis de Montcalm was besieged by a force of about 16,000 troops under the British general James Abercrombie, but the attack was repelled by the French, with severe losses suffered by the British forces. However, in 1759, when the French garrison had been reduced to 400 men, British forces numbering about 11,000 men under Lord Jeffrey Amherst captured Fort Carillon and renamed it Ticonderoga. During the Revolutionary War Ethan Allen and Benedict Arnold, with a small force of Americans, captured the fort by a surprise attack on May 10, 1775. The Americans held the fort until July, 1777, when it was evacuated in the face of the advance of a large army, led by General John Burgoyne, from Canada. British troops occupied the fort until after the surrender of Burgoyne at Saratoga in October, 1777. After the American Revolution the fort was abandoned but it has now been restored and is maintained as a historic monument. The village of Ticonderoga was incorporated in 1889. Pop. (1950) 3517.

TICUNAS, or JAMANAS, a tribe of South American Indians inhabiting the Paramayo and Upper Amazon basins. Tall and graceful in person, they wear nothing but feather ornaments. Themselves a peaceable people, they trade in poison with their more warlike neighbors. They live mainly by hunting and fishing, and, though partially civilized, preserve many curious pagan customs, notably that of burying their dead in jars with their faces toward the rising sun.

TIDAL WATERS, in the law of real property in England and the United States, navigable waters or streams which may be used by the public for navigation and commerce. In the old common law of England navigable waters included only those waters subject to the ebb and flow of the tide; however, with the modern development of waterways and commerce many other waters, such as canals, lakes, and rivers, came to be used for navigation and to be legally included under the term "tidal waters". In modern law any stream which is of such size and character

that it can be used regularly for the purpose of transportation and commerce, is considered a navigable stream or a tidal water.

The legal questions involving tidal waters concern the water itself, the shore adjacent to it, and the land under water. In England the waters, the shore, and the land under the waters belong to the crown. In the United States, title to streams that have been declared to be public waters, and to the land thereunder, is in the separate States, although the Federal government, under its power to regulate foreign and interstate commerce, exercises jurisdiction over interstate waterways. The ownership and use of the banks of a stream and of the shore involve questions of riparian rights. The owner of land adjoining tidal waters has the right of access to the point of navigation, i.e., he may build a pier or wharf to the navigable part of the water, but he must not in any way interfere with the public right to use such streams for the purposes of navigation.

TIDELANDS OIL CONTROVERSY, a dispute between the Federal government of the United States and a number of States over ownership of tidelands in the Pacific Ocean and the Gulf of Mexico. As employed in this controversy, the term "tidelands" has a larger signification than its customary dictionary definition of coastal lands which are alternately uncovered and covered by the ebb and flow of the tide, or that part of the shore lying between the low-water and high-water marks; instead, the term includes all the land beneath the marginal sea, that is, the land underlying the territorial waters for a distance of three nautical miles from the average low-water mark.

The controversy was initiated in 1937 in the second administration of President Franklin Delano Roosevelt, who was seriously concerned with the need of conserving the decreasing petroleum resources of the country, and with the vital importance of oil for the armed forces and the national security of the United States. Important economic interests and profound legal problems were involved in the ownership of the tidelands. Included in the economic aspects of the controversy were the ownership of the tideland oil resources of the United States, discovered about 1900; some estimates of the amount of this reserve are as high as one hundred billion barrels, though most conservative estimates are set at five to ten billion barrels. Less important, but by no means inconsequential, was the determination of the proper recipient of the royalties paid by the private companies engaged since 1921 in exploiting the tideland oil resources. The principal legal problems involved in the dispute related to the ownership of the tidelands themselves; ever since the establishment of the United States, the lands were presumed in State and Federal legislative enactments and judicial decisions to comprise part of the territory of the States, but ownership was never specifically determined by the U.S. Supreme Court.

The origin of the controversy may be traced to August 14, 1937, when Senator Gerald P. Nye (1892–   ) of North Dakota introduced a resolution in the Senate, establishing all tidelands as part of the U.S. public domain. Congress did not act on that resolution, nor on similar measures offered in 1938 and 1939, but the issue had been joined between proponents of Federal and of State ownership. During World War II, the Federal government did not press the issue. After the war, however, the dispute was waged vigorously by the administration of President Harry S. Truman, which supported Federal ownership, and by Congress, which, by a large majority, supported the rights of the States. In the fall of 1945, the U.S. Supreme Court took original jurisdiction of a suit instituted by the Federal government against the State of California, in which the United States sought ownership of the California tidelands. On September 28, President Truman issued a proclamation declaring that the tidelands and all their resources were under the "jurisdiction and control" of the U.S. government. By executive order, he placed control of the tidelands in the Department of the Interior, pending Congressional action or judicial determination of the controversy. On July 22, 1946, Congress passed a joint resolution quitclaiming Federal interests in the tidelands and affirming State ownership of them. Truman vetoed the measure on August 1.

In June, 1947, the Supreme Court handed down its decision in *U.S. vs. California*. The court decided that California did not hold title to the land beneath the marginal sea, and that the United States had always had "paramount rights in and full dominion and power" over the tidelands and all their resources. This decision was not based by the court on an ascertainable chain of title to the tidelands on the part of the United States. It was predicated in large part on the principle of "national external sovereignty", that is, on the paramount and overriding right of the Federal government to control the tidelands as an aspect of its dominion over areas and functions involved in relations with other nations.

While the court's decision definitely eliminated ownership of the tidelands by California, it did not as positively establish the ownership of the United States. In his dissent from the court's opinion, Associate Justice Felix Frankfurter pointed to this ambiguity in the verdict, which, he held, established the tidelands as "unclaimed land". The Truman administration contended that the terms "paramount rights" and "full dominion", employed by the court, included ownership. This view appeared to be borne out in a decision made by the Supreme Court in June, 1948, in another case in which it employed language implying its intention in its 1947 decision of investing ownership of the tidelands in the Federal government. However, the ambiguity persisted and, led by the administration, proponents of Federal ownership introduced legislation in Congress designed to establish U.S. proprietorship definitively.

On the other hand, opponents of Federal ownership, supported by officials of all the States except Washington and Arizona, and by numerous private interests, including especially oil companies, introduced measures in Congress vesting ownership of the tidelands in the States. Among important considerations motivating the States and private interests other than the oil companies was concern over the legal status in coastal cities, including those on the shores of the Great Lakes, of docks, other shipping facilities, and numerous municipally and privately owned enterprises, situated on land reclaimed from the marginal sea. They also contended that a legal precedent had been established for effecting Federal ownership of land beneath navigable inland waterways, which, according to various Supreme Court decisions, are the property of the States. In urging these considerations, the proponents of State ownership discounted stipulations by the Federal government that it had no intention of contesting the titles of ownership of reclaimed lands, and Federal disclaimers of interest in ownership of land underneath inland waterways; the advocates of State ownership contended that such reassurances were not permanent and might not be observed by later administrations.

Congress did not act on the tidelands oil controversy in 1948 and 1949. The Federal government, however, moved to dispose of the controversy in the courts. In May, 1949, it received permission from the U.S. Supreme Court to institute suit against Louisiana and Texas in order to determine ownership of the tidelands of those States. By means of that suit it hoped to remove all ambiguity inherent in the 1947 decision. The court's ruling (June, 1950) amounted essentially to a reaffirmation oi its opinion in the California case.

On May 15, 1950, Congress gave final approval to a bill granting the States clear title to offshore deposits of petroleum and other minerals. President Truman vetoed this bill two weeks later, declaring that "it would turn over to certain States, as a free gift, very valuable lands and mineral resources" belonging "to all the people of the country".

The controversy began to figure in the 1952 election campaign as early as June 18, when Gen. Dwight D. Eisenhower, a leading contender for the Republican Presidential nomination, went on record in favor of the States' claims to the oil-rich lands. The States' claims were unequivocally endorsed in the platform adopted by the Republican National Convention.

President Truman, on Jan. 16, 1953, only four days before he relinquished his office to President-elect Eisenhower, issued an executive order establishing the offshore lands as "a naval petroleum reserve". Republican Congressional leaders shortly thereafter introduced legislation granting the States title to submerged resources within their "historic boundaries". The measure was approved, despite stubborn opposition in the Senate. Under the terms of the legislation, signed by President Eisenhower on May 22, Texas and Florida gained ownership of submerged oil lands extending 10½ miles into the Gulf of Mexico; California won title to submerged oil lands within 3 miles of its coast. In a dispute over the historic offshore boundary of Louisiana, the State claimed title to the submerged oil lands within 10½ miles of its coast; the Federal government contended that the State boundary was 3 miles offshore. The U.S. Supreme Court refused (October, 1955) a Justice Department request to strike down Louisiana's claim.

TIDES, the periodic rise and fall of all ocean waters, including those of open sea, gulfs, and bays, resulting from the gravitational attraction of the moon and the sun upon the water, and upon the earth itself. The moon, being much nearer to the earth than the sun, is the principal cause of tides.

When directly over a given point on the surface of the earth it exerts a powerful pull on the water, which therefore rises above its normal level. It simultaneously exerts its pull throughout the entire earth, the force decreasing rapidly in proportion to the distance of a particular portion of the earth from the moon. Thus, the portion of the earth furthest from the moon is also subject to this pull, but to a lesser extent than the water covering it; another distinct dome of water on the farther side of the earth, providing the basis for a second wave, is thereby formed. The lunar wave crest directly beneath the moon is called *direct tide*, and the crest on the side of the earth diametrically opposite is called *opposite tide*. At both crests the condition known as *high water* prevails, while along the circumference of the earth perpendicular to the sublunar point there are phases of *low water*.

Low and high waters alternate in a continuous cycle. The variations which naturally occur in the level between successive high water and low water are referred to as the *range* of tide. At most shores throughout the world there occur two high waters and two low waters every lunar day, the average length of a lunar day being 24 hours, 50 minutes, and 28 seconds. One of these high waters is caused by the direct-tide crest, and the other by the opposite-tide crest. Two successive high waters or low waters are generally of about the same height. However, at various places outside of the Atlantic Ocean these heights vary considerably; this phenomenon, known as *diurnal inequality*, is not completely understood.

Accompanying the vertical rise and fall of water are various horizontal or lateral movements commonly known as *tidal currents* or *tidal streams*, which are very different from the common ocean currents; see OCEAN AND OCEANOGRAPHY. In confined areas a tidal current flows for about 6 hours, 12 minutes in an upstream or shoreward direction, corresponding to high water; it then reverses and flows for approximately the same time in the opposite direction, corresponding to low water. During the period of reversal, the water is characterized by a state of rest or calm known as *slack water*. A current flowing toward the shore or upstream is called *flood current*; that flowing in a direction away from land or downstream is known as *ebb current*. At various times there occur on the open sea gigantic waves, called *tidal waves*, which strike the surrounding shore

Ewing Galloway

Bales of cotton on barges in the harbor of Tientsin, China

with tremendous force and cause considerable damage to life and property. These waves are not caused by natural tidal phenomena, but by earthquakes, midocean volcanic eruptions, and serious atmospheric disturbances.

The sun, likewise, gives rise to two oppositely situated wave crests, but because the sun is far from the earth, its tide-raising force is only about four ninths, or 46 percent of the moon's. The sum of the forces exerted by the moon and sun result in a wave consisting of two crests, the positions of which depend upon the relative positions of the sun and moon at different times. During the periods of new and full moon, when the sun, moon, and earth are directly in line with each other, the solar and lunar waves coincide. This results in the condition known as *spring tides* in which the high water is higher and the low water lower than usual. However, when the moon is at first or at third quarter, it is in a position perpendicular to the sun relative to the earth and the heights of the waves are subject to the resultant force produced by the attraction of both the sun and moon. Under these conditions, *neap tides* are produced in which the high water is lower, and the low water higher, than normal height. Spring and neap tides occur very soon after the corresponding phases of the moon, the intervening period of time being known as the *age of the tide* or *age of the phase inequality*, and lasting

about 60 hours. The interval of time which elapses between the crossing of a meridian by the moon at one point and the next high water at that point is called the *lunitidal interval*, or the *high-water interval* for that point. The *low-water interval* is the period between the moon's crossing of the meridian and the next low water. Average values for the high-water lunitidal intervals during periods of new and full moon are known as the *establishment of the port*. Values for the intervals during other periods of the month are often referred to as the *corrected establishment*. See also BORE.

TIECK, JOHANN LUDWIG (1773–1853), German author, born in Berlin. He dramatized versions of the old fairy tales, which he made the vehicle for satire on contemporary literature. Besides superintending the completion of Schlegel's translation of Shakespeare's plays, he edited the doubtful plays and wrote a series of essays (*Shakespeare's Vorschule,* 1823–29). He also translated *Don Quixote* (1799–1804). He holds an honorable place in the ranks of Germany's dramatic and literary critics, by virtue of his *Dramaturgische Blätter* (2nd ed., 1852) and *Kritische Schriften* (1848). Some of his fairy tales and novels were translated into English by Carlyle and Thirlwall. See WACKENRODER, WILHELM HEINRICH.

TIENTSIN, a municipality and former treaty port in the province of Hopeh, China, situated on the s. bank of the Pei R., at its confluence with the Hun R. and the Grand Canal, 30 m. by rail w. of the Yellow Sea and about 70 miles s.s.e. of Peiping. The former Italian concession in Tientsin, consisting of about half a square kilometer on the N. bank of the Pei, was ceded to China in 1947 by the terms of the Italian peace treaty of that year. Tientsin is the port of Peiping, and is connected by rail with that center, and with Manchuria, Hankow, and other industrial centers. The city itself is comparatively small, with houses generally made of pressed mud or brick and one story high. The foreign quarter, N. of the city, which was until recent years enclosed by high walls, was designed as a European city, with broad streets and many public buildings. The Tientsin suburbs are extensive, and contain most of the trading establishments of the city. Tientsin is a great center for domestic Chinese commerce, with a vast trade in salt and tea. The city has few factories; the principal manufactures are straw braid, cured skins, tobacco products, and rugs.

Tientsin was made an open port in 1858 (see CHINA: *History*). The city figured prominently in the Boxer rebellion (q.v.) against foreign interests in China in 1900. It was captured by the foreign powers and made the base of operations against the Boxers. In 1937, during the undeclared Sino-Japanese War, Japanese troops took the city on Aug. 2. On Oct. 6, 1945, some five weeks after the surrender of Japan in World War II, Japanese troops in Tientsin formally surrendered to a token force of U.S. marines, who accepted and took the city in the name of Generalissimo Chiang Kai-shek. On Jan. 15, 1949, during the civil war between the Chinese nationalists and communists, Tientsin was taken by the Chinese communist army. Pop. (1950 est.) 1,795,000.

TIEPOLO, GIOVANNI BATTISTA (1696–1770), the last great master of the Venetian school of painting and trained in Venice. It is impossible to fix the dates for his pictures before 1737. He was famous long before that date, however, and was patronized by Doge Giovanni II Cornaro and noble Venetian families and by many cities and churches in northern Italy. The first of his principal works that can with certainty be dated are the beautiful decorations of the Villa Valmerana at Vincenza, executed in 1737. The subjects are taken from the works of the classic Roman poet Vergil and of the Italian poets Ariosto and Torquato Tasso. In fresh-

ness and charm, in conception and technique, they bear favorable comparison with the Italian painter Paolo Veronese's masterpieces in the Villa Maser. In 1739 followed the three ceiling decorations in Santa Maria del Rosario (Venice), including the "Institution of the Rosary", and in 1743–44 those of the church of the Scalzi, the chief of which represents "Angels Bearing the Casa Santa from Nazareth to Loreto" (these were ruined by an Austrian bomb in 1915, during World War I). To the same period belong the ceiling paintings of the Palazzo Rezzonico, and about 1745 Tiepolo decorated the grand hall of the Palazzo Labia. The ceiling is highly fantastic, and the illusive architectural decorations of the walls form an admirable framing for two of his best frescoes, "Cleopatra's Banquet" and the "Embarkment of Cleopatra and Antony". The date of his decorations in the archiepiscopal palace at Udine, which are among his best works, is not known.

Under the patronage of Karl Philipp of Greifenklau, Bishop of Würzburg, Tiepolo passed the years 1750–53 in that city, engaged in decorating the episcopal (later the royal) palace. On the lofty ceiling over the grand staircase he painted frescoes of "Olympus" and of the "Four Quarters of the Earth"; in the Kaisersaal, three scenes from the life of Frederick Barbarossa; in the chapel, two large altarpieces, the "Ascension of the Virgin" and the "Fall of the Angels". Returning to Venice in 1754, he became director of the Venetian Academy. Between this time and his departure for Spain he painted another grand ceiling decoration, the "Triumph of Faith", in the Chiesa della Pietà, and perhaps most of his easel pictures. In 1763 he was summoned by King Charles III to Spain to decorate the royal palace. In the guard room he painted the "Smithy of Vulcan", in the anteroom an "Apotheosis of Spain", and in the throne room magnificent ceiling frescoes of "Spain and Her Provinces". At Madrid he executed most of his etchings, about fifty plates, the most important, showing the influence of the Spanish painter Francisco José de Goya y Lucientes, being the series *Scherzi di Fantasia*.

In the classical reaction immediately following Tiepolo's death, scant justice was done him, and not until comparatively recent times has he been accorded his place. His art is essentially decorative, and harmonizes perfectly with the rococo architecture of the day. The color is light and flaky,

"Victory," painting by Giovanni Battista Tiepolo in the Palazzo Labia, Venice, Italy

and exquisitely delicate, and the treatment of light is above reproach. To a wonderfully rich fantasy and invention he joined an equal facility of execution. Sometimes he degenerates into extravagances, and what prevents him from ranking with the greatest artists of all time is the frivolity of his conceptions and the artificiality consequent upon the lack of a more direct contact with nature.

Tiepolo's easel pictures show the same grace of form and charm of color as his frescoes, and are more carefully composed and executed. Among the best known are "Christ in the Garden of Olives" and "Calchas and Iphigenia", in the Lichtenstein Gallery in Vienna; "St. Catharine of Siena" and an "Adoration of the Kings", in the Imperial Gallery, also in Vienna; "Martyrdom of St. Agatha" and "After the Bath", in the Kaiser Friedrich Museum in Berlin; the "Immaculate Conception" at Vicenza and Madrid; and a "Holy Family with St. Gaetano", in the Venetian Academy. In the Venetian churches are several altarpieces, including "Madonna in Glory" in the church of the Jesuits and "Christ Bearing the Cross" in Sant' Aluise. He is represented in the Metropolitan Museum of Art,

New York City, by five canvases, including two sketches for ceiling decoration.

TIERRA DEL FUEGO (Sp., "Land of Fire"), an archipelago at the s. extremity of South America, from which it is separated on the N.W. by the Strait of Magellan, and belonging partly to Argentina and partly to Chile. The islands are bordered by the Atlantic Ocean on the E., the Antarctic Ocean on the s., and the Pacific Ocean on the w.; their s. extremity is Cape Horn. The archipelago consists of a large main island, sometimes called King Charles South Land and including more than four fifths of the total area, and many smaller islands. The Argentine portion, lying E. of a line connecting the E. entrance of the Strait of Magellan with the middle of Beagle Channel, includes the main island and Staten Island at the S.E. extremity; it has an area of 8344 sq.m. and a population (1951 est.) of 6888. The remainder, and greater portion, of the archipelago is included politically in the Chilean Territory of Magellanes; see CHILE. Area of the entire archipelago, 27,600 sq.m. Pop., about 10,000.

The E. portion of the main island is a continuation of the Patagonian plateau; see PATAGONIA. All the islands are mountainous, the highest peaks being Mt. Sarmiento (7200 ft.) and Mt. Darwin (about 7500 ft.). The mean annual temperature is about 43°F., and annual precipitation is about 25 in. On the mountain slopes facing the wind, rain is almost continuous. Gold deposits are found, and seams of lignite, but minerals are little exploited. The most important industry is the raising of livestock, particularly of sheep. The aboriginal Indians, the Onas in the w. and the Yahgans (qq.v) in the s., are thought to be related to the Indians of Patagonia; they are few in number, and are rapidly disappearing. The archipelago was discovered in 1520 by the Portuguese navigator Ferdinand Magellan, who named it. No systematic exploration took place until several British expeditions were undertaken in the 19th century. The most famous of these expeditions was the survey (1831–36) described by the British naturalist Charles Darwin in his *Zoology of the Voyage of the Beagle* (1840).

TIFFANY, CHARLES LOUIS (1812–1902), American merchant, born in Killingly, Conn. In 1848 when the political unrest in Europe caused great depreciation in the price of precious stones, Tiffany invested heavily in diamonds, which were sold at a great profit a few years later. The firm became Tiffany, Young & Ellis in 1841. At the beginning of the Civil War, foreseeing that the jewelry business would suffer, he turned to the manufacture of medals and similar productions. In 1868 the company was incorporated, and branches were established in London and Geneva. Tiffany was the originator of many ideas and methods in the jewelry trade since generally adopted. The sterling silver standard 0.925 fine, adopted by him in 1851, became the recognized standard throughout the country. He was also a patron of art.

TIFFIN, county seat of Seneca Co., Ohio, situated on the Sandusky R., 47 miles S.S.E. of Toledo. It is served by three railroads and maintains a municipal airport. Tiffin is the trading center of a fertile agricultural area which also contains deposits of sand and clay. In addition, it is an important manufacturing center, with factories producing electric motors, heavy machinery, sheet-metal products, abrasive grinding wheels, glass, pottery and other clay products, copper wire, brass and bronze castings, metal ceilings and stampings, automatic doors, insulating material, woodwork, church furniture, stage curtains and scenery, cigars, and dairy products.

Tiffin is the site of Heidelberg College (Reformed Church), established in 1850, of a State hospital of St. Francis Convent and Home for the Aged (Roman Catholic), and of the National Home of the Daughters of America. The site of the present city was settled in 1817 and named in honor of Edward Tiffin, first governor of the State. It was incorporated as a town in 1835 and as a city in 1850. Pop. (1950) 18,952.

TIFLIS. See TBILISI.

TIGER (*Felis tigris*), feline Carnivore, belonging to the same genus as lion and leopard, lynx and cat, puma and jaguar. It most resembles the lion, from which it differs only in superficial characters, such as the color-striping, the absence of a mane, and in trivial skeletal features, especially of teeth and skull.

In distribution the tiger is exclusively Asiatic. The tiger may exceed the lion in length. Adult males measure 5½ to 6½ ft. from the nose to the root of the tail, and the tail measures about 3 ft. The predominant color is rufous fawn or tawny yellow, and is barred by dark or black cross stripes; the under parts are whitish. The favorite haunts of the tiger are grassy plains and jungle swamps. In attacking a large animal, such as a bullock, the tiger seizes the nape of the neck with its teeth, holds the victim firm with its sharp claws, and with a powerful wrench dislocates the vertebrae. From two to six cubs are born at once. Occasional cannibalism is recorded.

TIGER BEETLE, predaceous cicindelid beetle, generally metallic golden-green, with spots or stripes on the wing covers, frequenting sandy districts. They are voracious and savage. Some 1500 species are known, the majority inhabiting the tropics. Some species are wingless, others active; some are found only on the mounds of termites; some frequent the trunks of trees, which they ascend in a spiral manner. Less than 100 species are known in the United States, but tiger beetles are abundant and are seen everywhere. The largest American form is *Amblychila cylindriformis*, found in sandy regions in the mid-Western States. *Tetracha carolina* and *Tetracha virginica* are large greenish species occurring in the Atlantic and Southern States. The genus *Cicindela* contains more than half of the species in the entire family, and a very large number of the forms found in North America.

TIGER CAT, any wild cat of medium size that resembles the tiger in form or markings. The ocelot, serval, margay, and especially the

N.Y. Zoological Society

The tiger, a powerful animal of the Asiatic jungles

chati of South America, and clouded tiger or clouded leopard of India, are frequently so called.

TIGER LILY. See LILY.

TIGER MOTH, a name applied, because of their coloration, to certain moths of the family Arctiidae, as, for example, to *Arctia nais,* and especially to the Isabella tiger moth, *Isia isabella,* an American species, grayish yellow with black markings. The caterpillar is known as the woolly bear, and is densely clothed with reddish brown and black hairs. It feeds upon a great variety of low-growing herbage.

TIGRIS, a river, about 1030 m. long, in Asiatic Turkey and Iraq. The Tigris rises in S.E. Turkey in two branches, one s. of Lake Geuljik and the other s.w. of Lake Van. The branches join at Til, and the river flows in a winding S.E. direction, forming the extreme N.W. boundary between Lebanon and Turkey, and passing Diyarbekir, Mosul, Samarra, Tikrut, and Baghdad. It unites with the Euphrates R. (q.v.) at Korna to form the Shatt-al-Arab, which flows 120 m. to the Persian Gulf. The Tigris receives many smaller rivers from both E. and w. in its upper course. Its chief tributaries, all in Iraq, come from the E. and include the Diyala, the Great and Little Zab, and the Adhem. The Tigris is shallow in many parts and contains numerous obstructions, but is navigable by some form of craft for most of its course; small river steamers can ascend the river as far as Baghdad. The main portion of the region in Iraq between the Tigris and Euphrates, now in part known as Al Jazira, was ancient Mesopotamia (q.v.). On the Tigris

Ewing Galloway

Tigris River at Baghdad. Floating in river is a gufa, a round boat made of wickerwork.

banks are the ruins of ancient Nineveh (opposite Mosul), Seleucia, and Ctesiphon.

TIKI-TIKI. See AKKA.

TILBURG, town of North Brabant Province, Netherlands, 14 m. from Breda. It has manufactories of calico, cloth, leather, soap and tobacco. Pop. (1950) 120,491.

TILDEN, SAMUEL JONES (1814–86), American statesman, born in New Lebanon, N.Y. In 1868 he had become the leader of the Democrats in the State, and he strengthened his position by the energy and determination with which he attacked Tweed and his supporters (see TAMMANY). In 1874 he was elected governor of New York, owing largely to his efforts in overthrowing the Tweed Ring. As governor he fought the "Canal Ring", and introduced many economies into the management of the State canals. In 1876 he was the Democratic candidate for the Presidency (for the disputed election, see HAYES, R.B.). Twice afterward his party would have nominated him had he been willing. He left a great part of his fortune to found and endow a free library in New York City. See NEW YORK PUBLIC LIBRARY.

TILDEN, WILLIAM TATEM, JR. (1893–1953), American tennis player, born in Philadelphia, Pa. He won the national singles championship of the United States from William M. Johnston in 1920 and retained the title five years. He was a member of the American Davis Cup team (since 1920). Tilden won the British amateur singles championship in 1920, 1921, and 1930. He regained the United States championship in 1929 and the championship of Switzerland and the Netherlands in 1929. He entered motion pictures in 1924. In 1930 he became a professional and in 1931 became American professional tennis champion. His works include *The Phantom Drive, and Other Tennis Stories* (1924); a play, *They All Want Something,* produced in 1926; and *How to Play Better Tennis* (1950).

TILDY, ZOLTAN (1889–   ), Hungarian statesman, born in Losoncz, and educated in Hungary and at Assembly College, Belfast, North Ireland. Upon returning to Hungary, Tildy was ordained a Protestant minister and became a teacher. In 1930, after participating in the movement to improve the conditions of the peasants, he collaborated with Ferenc Nagy, later the premier of Hungary, in founding the Independent Small Landholders Party. As a leader of this party, Tildy was elected in 1936 to the lower house of the Hungarian parliament, in which he became a prominent advocate of measures in behalf of the peasants. During World War II he attracted international attention when, in 1944, he warned parliament that German occupation of Hungary was imminent and declared that only a truly democratic regime could save his native land from complete ruin. Immediately afterward he went into hiding, successfully eluding the Nazi Gestapo which raided his home and arrested his son.

Thereafter, while Hungary was under German domination, Tildy was active in the anti-Nazi underground movement. After Budapest was liberated by Soviet forces in 1945, the Small Landholders Party won a majority in the parliamentary elections held in November of that year, and Tildy became head of the coalition government which took office. In January, 1946, he was unanimously elected president of Hungary by the National Assembly. He became in effect an "independent" figurehead of a government controlled by the Hungarian communist puppets of the Soviet government; see UNION OF SOVIET SOCIALIST REPUBLICS: *History*. Tildy resigned the presidency on July 30, 1948, after his son-in-law, Victor Csornoky, former Hungarian minister to Egypt, had been arrested in Budapest on charges of espionage and treason. Tildy declared that his resignation was not motivated by political disagreements with the government but was prompted by a feeling that he could not "expect the confidence of the Hungarian people" in view of the "great crime" committed by one of his "close entourage". Tildy served as state minister without portfolio in the short-lived government of Premier Imre Nagy in October-November, 1956.

TILES, plates of baked clay, of various shapes and patterns, according to their use, some being for roofs, some for facing walls, and others for pavements. Marble and stone slabs used for covering roofs are also sometimes called tiles.

Encaustic tiles are ornamental tiles made of earthenware, and extensively used for floors, walls, and other purposes. The name applies to decorative tiles with a pattern produced by layers of different colored clays.

Fireproofing, structural, or hollow tiles are rapidly growing in use (see FIREPROOF CONSTRUCTION), particularly for fitting around steel columns and girders forming partitions, floor arches, and ceilings. Their lightness is greatly in their favor. They are divided into three classes: dense, porous or terra-cotta lumber, and semiporous.

Roofing tiles, when of clay, are something like terra cotta in their composition and manufacture.

Wall tiles of a highly decorative character were made at least as early as the 12th century in Persia, and it is very probable for a long time before that. The manufacture was continued into the 17th century before the artistic merit of the designs declined. Beautiful wall tiles were made at Damascus, Rhodes, and various other places in the 16th century.

TILIACEAE. See LINDEN.

TILL. See GEOLOGY: *Glaciers.*

TILLY, JOHAN TSERCLAES, COUNT OF (1559–1632), German soldier, born in the castle of Tilly in Brabant. He was given the command of the Catholic army at the outbreak of the Thirty Years' War, and in conjunction with Duke Maximilian gained (1620) the battle of Prague. During the course of this war he defeated the margrave of Baden at Wimpfen (1622), and expelled Christian of Brunswick from the Palatinate, defeating him at Höchst (1622) and at the desperate struggle at Stadtlohn (1623). Created a count of the empire, he next defeated the king of Denmark at Lutter (1626), and in conjunction

Samuel Jones Tilden

Dutch tiles dating from the first half of the 17th century

with Wallenstein compelled him to sign the Treaty of Lübeck (1629). Next year he succeeded Wallenstein as commander in chief of the imperial forces, and took by storm the town of Magdeburg. From this time fortune deserted him, for his next opponent was Gustavus Adolphus, who completely routed him at Breitenfeld (1631); in 1632 the king forced him to retreat behind the Lech in Bavaria, and forced the passage of the river right in his front, after a desperate conflict, in which Tilly received his death wound.

TILSIT, a former city of Germany in East Prussia (q.v.); following World War II it was included in the Kaliningrad Region of Soviet Russia. Tilsit lies on the Niemen R., 72 miles N.E. of the city of Kaliningrad (formerly Königsberg). It is an industrial center, with paper and sugar mills, oil refineries, iron foundries, breweries, distilleries, and chemical factories. Tilsit was founded in 1288 by the Teutonic Knights, and was chartered as a city in 1552. The Treaty of Tilsit (see TILSIT, TREATY OF) was signed there in 1807. Pop., about 51,000.

TILSIT, TREATY OF, either of two treaties signed in July, 1807, between France and Russia (July 7) and between France and Prussia (July 9), ending the War of the Third Coalition. Preliminary discussions were held by Napoleon I of France and Alexander I of Russia during a famous meeting on a raft in the Niemen R., on June 25, 1807, following the defeat of Russia by France in the battle of Friedland (June 14, 1807). By the terms of the treaties, Prussia was reduced, until the conclusion of the Napoleonic Wars in 1815, to the status of a second-rate European power and its territory was diminished by 43,088 sq.m. Prussia was forced to cede all its territory w. of the Elbe R. to Napoleon, who used it to create the Kingdom of Westphalia. Prussia also relinquished to France the Polish territory it acquired in the 1793–95 partitions, out of which Napoleon created the duchy of Warsaw; and Danzig was made a free city. Prussia joined the Continental System (q.v.), for the blockade of England, and closed its ports to British vessels. The Prussian army was reduced to 42,000 men. Prussian forts and provinces taken by the French were occupied until a war indemnity fixed at 120,000,000 francs was paid in substantial part. The sovereignty of Napoleon's three brothers (the kings of Naples, Holland, and Westphalia) was recognized. Russia obtained only a small portion of East Prussia, Alexander I having signed the treaty with France mainly to be in the victor's camp. In effect, by the agreements, France and Russia divided the political control of Europe between them. See RUSSIA: *History*.

TIMBRE, CLANG, TINT, or TONE COLOR, in acoustics, the special quality of a continuous sound or musical note, as of the human voice, a stringed instrument, or a wind instrument. The term applies to *quality* of tone as distinguished from *intensity* and *pitch*. Helmholtz demonstrated that the difference of timbre or quality in a fixed note is caused by the harmonics, or overtones, which accompany the foundation sound. By its timbre, therefore, we are enabled to distinguish between the sound of a piano, an oboe, a violin, and a trumpet, although all may be pitched to the same note.

TIMBREL, a small musical instrument, in use in ancient times. It was carried in the hand, and was apparently similar to the modern tambourine.

TIMBUKTU, or TIMBUCTOO, a town in the French Sudan, on the southern edge of the Sahara Desert. It stands on a trade route between the interior and the west and south, and its importance has increased through the gradual extension of French influence. Timbuktu is notable for its commerce, and is the focus of the caravan trade in west-central Africa. Gums and rubber are the leading articles. Gold, ivory, wax, salt, hardware, beads, and cheap cloth are also prominent items. The trade is chiefly by barter. The few local manufactures include cottons, leather articles, and pottery. French goods and money are replacing those of other countries. Timbuktu is a center of Mohammedan learning and has a large Moslem library. It was apparently founded in the 11th century, and first became known to Europeans in the 14th century. Pop., about 6000.

TIME, in music, the division of a measure into the fractional parts of a whole note. The sign which indicates the character of the subdivision is called the time signature. This is generally a fraction (2/4, 3/4, 6/8, etc.) placed after the clef at the beginning of a movement. In the fraction the lower figures represent the kind of notes to be used as time standards, while the upper figure shows how many of them are to be given in a bar. There are two general classes of time, duple and triple; in the former, the number of beats in a bar is divisible by two; in the latter, by three. Common time, so called, is 4/4 and is represented by the sign C. Compound duple time and compound triple time differ only from their originals in that each beat (containing a dotted note or its equivalent) is divisible by three. See RHYTHM.

TIME, STANDARD, the time in common use for regulating the ordinary affairs of life. It is derived from the sun. When that celestial body is on the meridian of any place we call the time at that place noon, or 12 o'clock. It follows that when it is noon at any given place it is similarly noon at all other places having the same meridian, and at places having different meridians, it is either forenoon or afternoon. In other words, when it is noon in a given place it is already afternoon in places to the eastward, and still forenoon in places to the westward. The farther east one travels, the later is the local time.

In 1882 the United States Congress passed a joint resolution authorizing the President to call an international conference to fix and recommend for universal adoption a common prime meridian to be used in reckoning longitude, and in the regulation of time throughout the world. The conference assembled in Washington, Oct. 1, 1884. Delegates representing twenty-six countries were present, but they were not able to agree unanimously upon a prime meridian. However, most of them favored the adoption of Greenwich, England, as the origin of longitudes. When the Prime Meridian Conference met, the United States and Canada had already selected a series of standard meridians, differing in longitude from

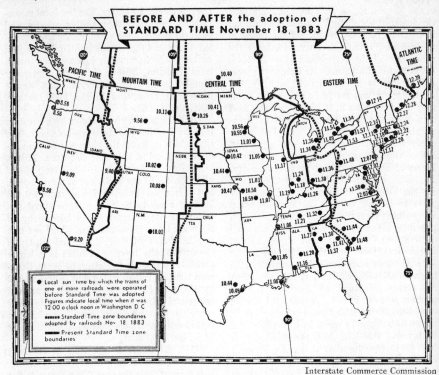

Interstate Commerce Commission

Map of U.S. showing early and revised standard time-zone boundaries used by railroads

that of Greenwich, by exact multiples of 15°. Now 15° of longitude corresponds exactly to one hour of time difference, and therefore the local times of the several standard meridians differ from Greenwich by an even number of hours without fractional minutes and seconds. In the United States the standard time meridians are those whose longitudes are west of Greenwich 60°, 75°, 90°, 105°, and 120°. The times of these meridians are respectively 4 hours, 5 hours, 6 hours, 7 hours, and 8 hours slow on Greenwich time. The time of the 60th meridian is called Colonial, that of the 75th meridian Eastern, that of the 90th Central, that of the 105th Mountain, and that of the 120th Pacific time. The limiting lines of the time zones have been so drawn arbitrarily that they never divide any town. Where such a division is theoretically unavoidable, the dividing line for actual use is drawn on the map with a crook in it, so as to put the whole town on one side of the line.

Most of the countries throughout the world now use standard time based on one of the even hour meridians as reckoned from Green-wich. See DAY; DAYLIGHT SAVING; INTERNATIONAL DATE LINE.

TIME STUDY. See SCIENTIFIC MANAGEMENT.

TIMGAD or THAMUGAS, an ancient city situated on the northern slopes of the Aurès Mountains in Algeria, about 22 miles S.E. of Batna, in the department of Constantine. It was founded by the Roman emperor Trajan in 100 A.D. and named, in honor of his sister, Colonia Marciana Trajana Thamugas. The ruins of the city are extensive, and it is hence known as the "Numidian Pompeii". The ruins, all of which except a 7th-century basilica date from the 2nd century, include the remains of an arch, known as the arch of Trajan, a forum, a library, and a theater having a seating capacity of nearly 4000. Baths with paved and mosaic floors have been found in a perfect state of preservation; numerous large private dwellings have been uncovered, one house sometimes occupying a whole block. The existence of several churches indicates that the city was a center of Christianity in the 3rd century. With the decline of the Roman Empire, Thamugas ceased to flourish, and suffered from the invasions of the Vandals, the Byzantines, and the Arabs. After 647 A.D., when the Arabs defeated Gregorius, the last Byzantine governor of Africa, Thamugas declined rapidly to its present deserted state.

TIMIŞOARA (Hung. *Temesvár*), a city of western Romania, situated on the Bega River and Canal, 75 miles N.E. of Belgrade. The city consists of an inner town, which formerly was fortified, and four suburbs which are separated from the inner town by parks. Timişoara is a commercial center, and the fourth-largest city in population in Romania. The principal industries include oil refining and the manufacture of paper, tobacco products, woolen goods, alcoholic beverages, flour, and leather. The city is the site of a university, founded in 1945. Buildings of interest include an 18th-century Roman Catholic cathedral, a 15th-century castle, and a museum, town hall, county hall, and a Greek Orthodox cathedral. A Gothic column in the city's main square was erected by the Austro-Hungarian emperor, Francis Joseph, in 1851 to commemorate the resistance of Timişoara during a 107-day siege by the Hungarian revolutionary army in 1849.

The city is of ancient origin. It was destroyed by Tatars in 1242, but was again a populous community in the following century. During the Middle Ages the city was, for a time, the residence of the king of Anjou, Charles Robert. During the 16th century it was captured by the Turks and in 1716 it was recaptured by Prince Eugene of Savoy. Following World War I, Timişoara became a part of Romania. Pop., about 110,000.

TIMMINS, a town of Cochrane County, Ontario, Canada, situated on the Mattagami R., about 175 miles N.E. of Sault Ste. Marie. The town, which is served by a railway, lies in the Porcupine Gold Field, one of the richest gold-producing regions in Canada. Industries in Timmins include meat packing, sawmilling, and the manufacture of wood pulp and paper, mining machinery, tools, and wood products. A considerable trade in agricultural products is also carried on in the town. Pop. (1951) 27,743.

TIMOR, the largest and most southeasterly island of the Lesser Sunda Islands of the Malay Archipelago, situated about 700 miles E. of Java and belonging partly to Portugal and partly to the Republic of Indonesia. Portuguese Timor consists of the E. part of the island of Timor together with the territory of Ambeno (an enclave within Indonesian Timor) and the adjacent islands of Pulo Cambing and Pulo Jako. Its capital is Dili (pop., about 3000), on the N.E. coast of Timor. Area, 7330 sq.m.; pop., about 463,800. Indonesian Timor consists of the w. part of the island of Timor together with the nearby islands of Sumbawa, Sumba, Flores, and the Solor and Alor islands, and its capital is Kupang (pop., about 7000), on the s.w. coast of Timor. Area, 24,449.5 sq.m.; pop., about 1,657,000.

Timor Island (area, 13,700 sq.m.) extends from s.w. to N.E., with a length of about 280 m. and an average width of 55 m. Its coasts are, for the most part, steep and lined with coral reefs. The island is traversed from E. to w. by parallel mountain ranges, the highest peak being Mt. Rameau (9600 ft.), in the Portuguese portion. Mineral resources of gold, copper, gypsum, and petroleum are little exploited. The climate is hot and unhealthful in the coastal regions, and rainfall is slight, especially in the s. The flora and fauna are transitional between the Malaysian and Australian varieties. The aboriginal inhabitants of Timor are a people of mixed Malay, Polynesian, and Papuan descent. Head-hunting was formerly prevalent. Agriculture is carried on by primitive methods, and native industry consists mainly of weaving, making weapons and ornaments, and, along the coast, fishing and the production of copra. Exports include coffee, sandalroot, copra, and wax.

The first Portuguese colonies were founded in the early 16th century, and the Dutch made their first landings in 1613. Strife between the two countries for possession of the island lasted until 1859, when a treaty settled the main boundaries. During World War II, the island was occupied by Japanese troops from 1942 to 1945. See REPUBLIC OF INDONESIA.

TIMOSHENKO, SEMËN KONSTANTINOVICH (1895–), Soviet army commander, born in Furmanka, Bessarabia. He had little formal education and was working as a farm laborer when he was conscripted into the imperial Russian army in 1915. In 1917 he was court-martialed and jailed for striking an officer, but was set free by the revolution of that year. Timoshenko joined the Red army, and became commander of the 4th and 6th cavalry divisions, and a military hero during the Civil War. He became a close friend of Joseph Stalin. Following the war he rose rapidly in the Red army and was commander of the Kiev military district when World War II began in Sept., 1939. During the Russo-Finnish War

Republic of the United States of Indonesia
Natives of Indonesian Timor

(1939–40) Timoshenko commanded the final victorious Soviet offensive which broke the Mannerheim Line. He also directed the Soviet occupation of E. Poland in 1939. On May 8, 1940, he was appointed people's defense commissar and raised to the rank of marshal. After the German invasion of the Soviet Union, in June, 1941, Stalin replaced Timoshenko as commissar, and the marshal was put in command of the Soviet armies in the w. In Oct. he was transferred to the s. front, where he recaptured Rostov (Nov. 29, 1941). He commanded the Soviet retreat in summer, 1942, when the German army advanced toward Stalingrad, and later in the year commanded on the N.W. front, around Leningrad. In summer of 1943 he resumed command of the s. front and conducted the victorious Russian counteroffensive in the Taman peninsula and Bessarabia. After the war he became a member of the Ministry of Defense. In 1949 he was reported to be commander of all Soviet western army groups. He was elected to the Bureau of the Communist Party's Central Committee in Byelorussia in 1954.

TIMOTE, a group of small tribes apparently constituting a distinct linguistic stock, whose modern representatives still occupy the mountainous district of Mérida, southward from Lake Maracaibo, in western Venezuela. In former times they usually went naked, with their bodies painted red, and were agricultural, cultivating corn, chile, and edible roots. They buried their dead, with sacred clay figurines, in caves or in underground vaults.

TIMOTHY (Gr. *Timotheos,* "honoring God"), one of the assistants of the apostle Paul, born in Lystra, Lycaonia, the son of a Gentile father and a Jewish mother. The circumstances of his conversion to Christianity are unknown. To avoid unnecessary offense to the Jews, he was circumcised. Until the close of Paul's life Timothy was one of his most faithful, trusted, and intimate disciples. He was intrusted several times with important missions to the churches founded by the Apostle. At Berea (Acts 17:14), Athens, and Thessalonica (1 Thess. 3:1–6), at Corinth and later at Ephesus (1 Cor. 4:17, 16:10), and again in Macedonia (Acts 19:21–22) he rendered important services, and is joined by Paul in the addresses of several of his epistles. His important and delicate mission to Corinth, however, seems to have had unfavorable results (see CORINTHIANS, EPISTLES TO THE). Though Timothy went to Jerusalem with Paul (Acts 20:4), he was probably engaged in labors elsewhere when the apostle embarked on his voyage to Rome. He visited his master in Rome (see the opening words of Philippians, Colossians, and Philemon), and was probably sent by Paul, shortly before his release, with a message to Philippi (Phil. 2:19). According to the usual interpretation of 1 and 2 Timothy, after the apostle's release he joined Timothy in the East, and later left him in charge of Ephesus in a position full of great responsibility. In his anxiety Paul wrote him the letter of advice and warning known as 1 Timothy. When Paul was imprisoned the second time, and probably not long before his death, he wrote 2 Timothy, summoning his beloved disciple to come to him as quickly as possible. At some later date Timothy himself was arrested, but afterward released (Heb. 13:23). According to tradition he passed the remainder of his days as bishop of Ephesus.

TIMOTHY AND TITUS, EPISTLES TO. The first and second Epistles to Timothy, with the Epistle to Titus, make up the three "Pastoral Epistles" whose claim to have been written by Paul has been recognized by Catholic tradition since the 2nd century. They owe the name to the fact that they are addressed to Timothy and Titus, with reference mainly to the discharge of the pastoral office. The general purpose of the Pastorals may be said to have been to furnish the church with a convenient set of instructions regarding the administration of church affairs and the necessity of combating the insidious and corrupting forms of error that threatened to work the moral undoing of the church.

External and internal evidence go to show that all three epistles belong to nearly the same date; and it is now agreed that this cannot have been earlier than the Neronian persecution (64 A.D.). The stay of Timothy in Ephesus postulated by 1 Tim., the captivity of the apostle after having been recently at Troas, Corinth, and Miletus, which is presupposed in 2 Tim., and his visit to Crete and proposed sojourn in Nicopolis (Epirus) which are mentioned in Titus, all require us to assume a continued activity of the apostle after his first Roman imprisonment, an activity,

however, of which (apart from the pastoral epistles themselves) tradition knows nothing. Assuming the genuineness of all three, the order in which they were written must have been 1 Tim., Titus, 2 Tim. To sum up the present state of criticism, the pastoral epistles are admittedly late; but how late is impossible to say with our imperfect knowledge of the state of the church during the decades immediately following 64 A.D. But all that the apologists can say is that their Pauline authorship is not inconceivable.

TIMOTHY GRASS (so called from Timothy Hanson, who introduced its cultivation into the Carolinas about 1720), *Phleum pratense,* the most valuable species of the genus for hay and pasturage. It is the herd's grass of New England and New York, and along with the other species of the genus, is in England often called cat's-tail grass. In the United States timothy hay is considered one of the most valuable hays made wholly from grass and is commonly used as the standard with which to compare other hays.

U.S.D.A., Bur. Plant Ind., Soils, & Ag. Eng.
Timothy grass

TIMPANOGOS CAVE NATIONAL MONUMENT, a national monument in N. central Utah, established in 1922. The monument covers an area of 250 acres on the S. slopes of American Fork Canyon, about 15 miles N. of the city of Provo. It contains a limestone cavern cut into the canyon walls at an elevation of 6776 ft. and stretching for a length of about 1200 ft.

TIMUCUA, a group of tribes, constituting a distinct linguistic stock, formerly occupying central and northern Florida from about Tampa Bay and Cape Canaveral northward to St. Mary's River. When first known to the Spaniards they had about forty settlements, principally along the lower St. John's River. French Huguenots landed on the east coast in 1564, and were received with friendship, which continued during the brief existence of the French colony. At this time there seem to have been at least five cognate tribes, with differing dialects. On the expulsion of the French the Timucua came under the dominion of the Spaniards, by whom they were compelled to work upon the fortifications of St. Augustine. In 1687, greatly diminished, they made an unsuccessful attempt to revolt. In 1702–06 inroads of the English of the colony of Carolina, with their hundreds of Indian allies, wiped out the mission villages of the Timucua who fled to the upper waters of St. John's River, where Tomoco River in the present Volusia County preserves their name. The Seminole Indians took their abandoned territory.

TIN, an important metallic element, of atomic number 50, atomic weight 118.7, and symbol Sn, insoluble in water and soluble in hydrochloric, sulfuric, and dilute nitric acids. The metal has been known since very early times, and ranks 27th in abundance among the elements in the earth's crust. It has been found in the tombs of ancient Egyptians, and was exported to the European continent in large quantities from Cornwall, England, during the Roman period. The ancient Egyptians considered tin and lead to be different forms of the same metal.

Tin is a silvery-white metal with a specific gravity of 7.3, and is very ductile and malleable at 100° C. (212° F.). At temperatures below 18°C. (64°F.) it often decomposes into an allotropic form known as gray tin, which is an amorphous, grayish powder with a specific gravity of 5.75. Because of the mottled appearance of tin objects undergoing this decomposition, the action is commonly referred to as *tin disease* or *tin pest*. Ordinary bar tin,

when bent, issues a crackling sound called "tin cry", caused by the friction of the tin crystals.

The principal ore of tin is the mineral cassiterite, or tinstone, SnO_2, found abundantly in Cornwall, England, and in Czechoslovakia, Germany, the Malay Peninsula, Bolivia, and Australia. No workable deposits of tin occur in the United States. In extraction of tin the ore is first ground and washed to remove all impurities, and is then roasted to oxidize the sulfides of iron and copper. After a second washing, the ore is reduced by carbon in a reverberatory furnace, the molten tin that collects on the bottom being drawn off and molded into blocks known as "block tin". In this form, the tin is resmelted at low temperatures, with the impurities forming an insoluble mass. Tin may also be purified by electrolysis, using pure tin anodes and cathodes immersed in a bath of sulfuric acid and fluosilicic acid, H_2SiF_6.

Tin forms stannic acid, H_2SnO_4, when heated in air or oxygen at high temperatures. It dissolves in hydrochloric acid and in aqua regia to form stannous chloride, $SnCl_2$, and stannic chloride, $SnCl_4$, respectively, and reacts with sodium hydroxide solution to form sodium stannite and hydrogen gas. In cold and very dilute nitric acid, tin dissolves to form stannous nitrate and ammonium nitrate; in concentrated nitric acid, it produces metastannic acid, H_2SnO_3. Stannous sulfide, SnS, is yielded as a dark-brown precipitate by the action of hydrogen sulfide on a solution of stannous chloride. Stannic sulfide, SnS_2, is produced by passing hydrogen sulfide through a solution of stannic salt, and forms a thiostannate when dissolved in ammonium. The two hydroxides of tin, $Sn(OH)_2$ and $Sn(OH)_4$, are produced by adding a soluble hydroxide to solutions of stannous and stannic salts. Stannous oxide, SnO, a black, insoluble powder, is obtained by heating stannous oxalate in the absence of air. In the presence of air stannous oxide burns to form the dioxide, or stannic oxide, SnO_2, a white, insoluble solid. The dioxide may also be prepared by heating stannic acid, or by heating tin metal in air at very high temperatures.

Tin is a widely sought metal today and is employed in hundreds of industrial processes throughout the world. In the form of tin plate, it is used as a protective coating for various metals employed in the manufacture of tin cans, copper vessels, and similar articles. Tin is important in the production of the common alloys such as bronze (copper and tin), solder (tin and lead), and type metal (tin, lead, and antimony); see PEWTER. Stannic sulfide, under the name of *mosaic gold,* is used in the powdered form for bronzing articles made of plaster of Paris and wood. The United States uses considerably more tin than the rest of the world combined, and the metal has always been among the leading imports of the country. In a recent year, more than $200,000,000 worth of the pure metal and its ore was imported and used in numerous industries throughout the United States. These imports, amounting to more than 108,000 long tons, were supplied mostly by the Federation of Malaya, Bolivia, the Republic of Indonesia, Nigeria, and Thailand.

TINAMOU (*Tinamus*), a South American genus of birds sometimes called partridges. Their flight is strong and swift, but of short duration and very direct, yet they haunt the undergrowth of dense forests or bushy and grassy flats, run with amazing rapidity, and conceal themselves with great skill, rather than take to flight. Their food is miscellaneous, and their flesh is edible.

TINGUIAN, or ITNEG, a pagan mountain people of northwestern Luzon, Philippine Islands.

TINIAN, one of the Marianas (q.v.), in the S. Pacific Ocean, administered since 1947 by the United States under a trusteeship of the United Nations, and formerly (1919–44) administered by Japan under a mandate of the League of Nations. Tinian is a coral island about 10 m. long and a little over 4 m. wide. It is notable for its herds of wild cattle and its prehistoric ruins, consisting of two rows of truncated pyramids built of masonry. Following World War I the island, formerly a German possession, became one of the most heavily fortified Japanese bases in the Pacific. During World War II, U.S. forces invaded Tinian on July 23, 1944, and brought the island under American control within a week. Tinian then became a powerful base for air operations against the Japanese home islands. See SAIPAN.

TINKER, JOSEPH BERT (1880–1948), American professional baseball player, born in Muscotah, Kans. His first important professional engagement was as shortstop for the Chicago club (Cubs) of the National League, with which he played from 1902 to 1912, as a member of one of the best defensive infield combinations in the history of baseball, noted particularly for its skill in making double plays. In addition to Tinker, the combination included John Joseph Evers as second baseman,

and Frank Leroy Chance (qq.v.) as first baseman; the three became famous through the popular phrase, descriptive of their throwing procedure, "Tinker to Evers to Chance". The Chicago teams on which the trio played won four National League championships and two world championships. In 1912 Tinker became manager of the Chicago team, and later was manager of the Cincinnati club of the National League, the Chicago club of the Federal League, and also a number of minor-league teams. During his career he played in 1799 games and had a batting average of .263. He was appointed to the Baseball Hall of Fame in 1946.

TINKER'S ROOT. See FEVERWORT.

TINNÉ, a collective term sometimes used as synonymous with Athapascan stock, but more usually employed to designate the tribes of that stock residing in the Canadian northwest. See ATHAPASCAN STOCK.

TINNEVELLI, or TINAVELLY, the capital of a district of Madras, India, on the Tambraparni River. The most striking edifice is the Siva Temple. Cotton goods are extensively manufactured. Pop., about 60,000.

TINTERN ABBEY, a beautiful monastic ruin in England, on the river Wye, 9 miles below Monmouth. Theodoric, British King of Glamorgan, was said to have fallen in battle against the Saxons here, 600 A.D. The abbey was founded in 1131 for Cistercian monks by Walter de Clare; the church was begun a century later through the munificence of Roger de Bigod, Earl Marshal, and dedicated in 1268. The tower and roof are gone, but the church remains a fine example of the Decorated style —the English High Gothic—beautiful in composition and delicate in execution. The nave is 228 feet long, the transept 150 ft., and the width of nave and choir 37 feet. Tintern Abbey is well known through Wordsworth's poem.

TINTORETTO, IL, real name JACOPO ROBUSTI (1518–94), Italian painter, one of the chief masters of the High Renaissance in Venice, born in Venice, the son of a dyer (*tintore*), whence his name. At an early age he began to study with Titian. Following his great aim to unite Michelangelo's design with Titian's color, he drew constantly from casts of the former's sculptures. He dissected bodies to learn anatomy, studied foreshortening and movement from suspended figures, worked by day and lamplight for chiaroscuro, and even learned from house painters the secrets of their craft. One of Ruskin's "five supreme

Tintern Abbey, a monastic ruin near Monmouth, England

painters", he was unquestionably a great master of composition, drawing, and color; his conceptions are often grand and his chiaroscuro startlingly effective. But he was strangely unequal; some of his earlier pictures are very carefully finished, but his later ones are dashed off with a fatal haste that justifies the epithet *Il Furioso*. Many of his pictures are of prodigious size. Venice contains many undoubted specimens of his art; there are a number in England, including "St. George and the Dragon" in the National Gallery in London. The Metropolitan Museum of Art, New York City, possesses "Doge in Prayer before the Redeemer" and the large "Miracle of the Loaves and Fishes". Other famous pictures from his hand are "Belshazzar's Feast" and the "Writing upon the Wall" (fresco for the Arsenal in Venice), "The Tiburtine Sibyl", "The Last Supper and the Washing of the Disciples' Feet", "The Crucifixion", "The Worship of the Golden Calf", "The Last Judgment", "St. Agnes Restoring to Life the Son of a Prefect", "The Miracle of St. Mark", "The Resurrection", "The Slaughter of the Innocents", and the largest picture on canvas by any great master, the "Paradise" (1558) of the Ducal Palace in Venice. It is 34 ft. high by 74 long, and contains over 100 figures.

TIPPECANOE, BATTLE OF, an engagement fought on Nov. 7, 1811, near the site of the present village of Battle Ground, on the Tippecanoe River, in Tippecanoe Co., Ind., between an American force of about 800, including 500 Indiana and Kentucky militiamen, under William Henry Harrison, then governor of Indiana Territory, and an Indian force, estimated by Harrison at about 6000, but probably much smaller, under the actual command of White Loon, Stone Eater, and Winnemac. While Harrison was building a stockade on the side of Terre Haute, one of his sentinels was killed from ambush, and Harrison, considering this the beginning of hostilities, soon afterward marched against the town on the Tippecanoe, where Tenskwatawa, called the Prophet, a brother of Tecumseh, was supposed to be inciting the Indians to attack the whites because of the alienation of Indian lands. The Indians attacked the camp with great ferocity and bravery, but after more than two hours of stubborn fighting were driven from the field. On the following day Harrison advanced to the town, found it deserted, and almost completely destroyed it. The loss of the whites in the battle in killed and wounded was about 190; that of the Indians, though undoubtedly large, is not definitely known. The battle rendered virtually impossible the realization of Tecumseh's plans, weakened and almost destroyed the prestige of the Prophet, hastened the general outbreak of hostilities by the Indians against the Americans in the Northwest, and greatly enhanced the reputation of General Harrison, who later became President of the United States.

TIPPERARY, inland county of Munster, Republic of Ireland, touching Galway on the N. and King's Co., Queen's Co., and Kilkenny on the E. The county of Tipperary for the most part lies in the basin of the Suir R. The surface is generally level, but is diversified by several mountain ridges or groups. These mountains are the Galtees, rising to 3008 ft., Knockmeledown (2609 ft. high), and Slievenaman on the s.; Keeper Mt. on the w.; and the Slievardagh Hills on the E. The soil of the plain is productive, especially the district called the Golden Vale, in which stands the town of Tipperary (pop., about 7000). Anthracite coal is worked; copper, lead, and zinc occur in smaller quantities; and slates and pipeclay are available. The principal occupation in the county is agriculture, especially dairy farming. Area, 1659 sq.m.; pop. (1951 est.) 133,347.

TIPTON, a town and municipal borough of Staffordshire, England, situated 4 miles s.s.E. of Wolverhampton and 8 miles w.N.w. of Birmingham. Tipton contains coal mines and blast furnaces, and is a center of the iron industry in England. Pop. (1951 prelim.) 39,382.

TIRANË or **TIRANA,** the capital of Albania, situated in the central part of the country, about 25 miles E. of Durrës. Tiranë is a picturesque town, in which are many mosques, olive groves, and gardens. Moslems comprise nearly 75 percent of the population. Tiranë was founded in the 17th century, during the Turkish domination of Albania. Pop. (1949 est.) 40,000.

TIREE. See HEBRIDES.

TIRESIAS, in Greek mythology, a Theban seer. He was said to have been struck blind by the goddess Athena, because he had seen her bathing, but to have been recompensed by her with the gift of prophecy. According to another version, he was for a time transformed into a woman, and later, having become a man again, he was asked by Zeus and Hera, king and queen of the gods, to tell which sex had more pleasure in love; when he replied

"Minerva Expelling Mars," painting by Il Tintoretto

Austrian State Tourist Dept.
TIROL, AUSTRIA
Left: Mountain view from a rocky crag. Right: An old church in the town of Solbad Hall.

that woman had nine times as much pleasure as man, Hera in anger blinded him, but Zeus granted him long life and the gift of prophecy. Tiresias played a prominent part in Theban legends, delivering prophecies to Œdipus (q.v.), King of Thebes, and to his sons in the war of the Seven Against Thebes (q.v.). Even after death he uttered prophecies; according to Homer, the hero Ulysses, visiting the shades of the dead, consulted Tiresias before returning to Ithaca.

TIROL or **TYROL,** province in Austria, bounded on the N. by Bavaria, on the S. by Italy, and lying between the Austrian provinces of Salzburg and Vorarlberg. Formerly it extended S. to Lake Garda, but as a result of World War I the Trentino was ceded to Italy. The province is situated in the Alps and is traversed by a number of rivers, including the Inn, Otz, Ziller, Lech, and Issar. Railway communication in the western section is confined principally to the Arlberg pass and railway tunnel. The capital of the province is Innsbruck. The chief occupations of the inhabitants are lumbering, cattle-grazing, dairy farming, and mining for lead and salt.

At one time Tirol was a part of the Roman Empire. It passed into the hands of Austria in 1363, was ceded to Bavaria in 1805, but was restored to Austria in 1814. Following World War II it was included in the French Zone of Occupation. Area, 4882 sq.m.; pop. (1951 prelim.) 426,499.

TIRPITZ, ALFRED VON (1849–1930), German naval officer, born in Küstrin. He became a naval cadet in 1865, and rose to the position of lord high admiral by 1911. He served as secretary of state of the imperial navy from 1897 to 1916 and to his efforts was due the creation of a navy capable of meeting that of Great Britain. In World War I, Tirpitz was a vigorous advocate of unrestricted submarine warfare, and this insistence caused a breach with Von Bethman-Hollweg, the imperial chancellor, and the resignation of his office in March, 1916. As the outcome of this policy, many belligerent and neutral vessels were destroyed by German submarines, one of the most spectacular catastrophes being the sinking of the *Lusitania.* The loss of American lives on such vessels severely strained the relations between Germany and the United States, and eventually led to the participation of the United States in World War I against Germany. The following year Tirpitz associated himself with Kapp in the upbuilding of the Fatherland Party, and he sat in the Reichstag from 1924 to 1928. He published

My Memories in 1920, and a work on the rise of German world power in 1924.

TIRYNS, an ancient city of Argolis, Greece, in the Peloponnesus, situated a short distance S.E. of Argos, about 3 miles inland from the head of the Argolic Gulf. According to tradition it was founded by Proetus, the brother of Acrisius, King of Argos. Proetus was succeeded on the throne of Tiryns by Perseus (q.v.), grandson of Acrisius. A later mythological king of Tiryns was Eurystheus, to whom the hero Hercules (q.v.) was in servitude and for whom he performed his famous labors; hence Hercules was sometimes called *Tirynthius.* In the historical period Tiryns was often subject to Argos, although during the Persian Wars it was independent and in 479 B.C. sent troops to Platæa. Some time later, probably about 468 B.C., the city was taken by the Argives; after this period Tiryns remained uninhabited, and only the massive walls of its citadel were left standing, the wonder and admiration of later ages. These walls, about twenty-five ft. thick and constructed of huge stones 6 to 10 ft. long and about 3 ft. wide, were believed by the ancient Greeks to be the work of the Cyclopes.

The greatness of Tiryns dates from the prehistoric period. The city seems to have been inhabited from the third millennium B.C. and to have attained its greatest splendor in the late Mycenæan period, about 1400–1200 B.C. (see ÆGEAN CIVILIZATION; MYCENÆAN ART AND ARCHITECTURE). The palace on the summit of the citadel was excavated in 1884–1885 by Heinrich Schliemann (q.v.), and, until the later discoveries in Crete, was considered the most complete example of the home of a prehistoric king in the Ægean area. It includes entrance gates, paved courts, large halls, vestibules, smaller rooms, and a bath, and was apparently built by stages, the complex of buildings representing both an earlier and a later palace.

TISCHENDORF, LOBEGOTT FRIEDRICH KONSTANTIN VON (1815–74), German Biblical scholar, born in Lengenfeld, Saxony. His labors in search of manuscript of the New Testament, in which he was assisted by the Saxon and Russian governments, were exceedingly valuable, especially those in 1844, 1853, and 1859, which resulted in the discovery of the Sinaitic Codex at the monastery on Mt. Sinai. It was bought by the British Museum in 1933.

TISELIUS, ARNE VILHELM KAURIN (1902–), Swedish biochemist, born in Stockholm, and educated at Uppsala University. In 1925 he joined the faculty of Uppsala as a research assistant in physical chemistry, becoming assistant professor of chemistry in 1930 and professor of biochemistry in 1938; in 1948 he was appointed to the university's newly created Tiselius chair in biochemistry and to the directorship of the newly established Institute of Biochemistry, affiliated with the university.

Tiselius' principal work was on the development of new techniques for the study of various physiologically important substances. He is best known for his development of two new methods for the analytical study of biological substances, especially proteins. The first of these methods involves the adaptation of the principles of cataphoresis to the molecular separation of biochemical materials and has been effectively used in the study of living tissue and the determination of the purity of various protein complexes. His second method utilizes the techniques of adsorption analysis to distinguish proteins from such compounds as salts, sugars, and acids; Tiselius improved older methods of adsorption analysis by devising an apparatus which automatically registers the distinguishing properties of the substances under analysis; on the basis of readings made from this apparatus the density of the solution is computed, thereby making separation of the various substances possible. In recognition of this work Tiselius was awarded the 1948 Nobel Prize for chemistry. From 1944 to 1947 he served on several Swedish government research committees, including the atomic energy and natural science research committees. He was chairman of the Swedish Natural Science Research Council from 1946 to 1950. In 1947 he became vice-president of the Nobel Foundation, and from 1951 to 1955 he served as president of the International Union of Pure and Applied Chemistry. Among his scientific writings on chemistry and biochemistry are papers which have appeared in such international scientific journals as *Nature, Research,* and *Chemical and Engineering News.*

TISSUES. See HISTOLOGY.

TISZA, ISTVÁN (1861–1918), Hungarian statesman, born in Budapest. He entered the Hungarian Ministry of the Interior in 1882 and in 1886 became a member of the Hungarian Parliament. As the leader of the Liberal Party Tisza became premier and minister of the interior in 1903, but was dismissed in 1906. He returned to power as premier on June 9, 1913, holding office until

June, 1917. On Oct. 31, 1918, he was assassinated.

TIT. See TITMOUSE.

TITANIA. 1. In Roman mythology, a female descendant of a Titan (see TITANS). The epithet was applied by the Roman poet Ovid to Latona and Diana, as daughter and granddaughter respectively of the Titan Cœus; to Pyrrha, as granddaughter of Iapetus; and to Circe, daughter of the sun god Helios and granddaughter of Hyperion. **2.** The name of the fairy queen, the wife of Oberon (q.v.), in *A Midsummer Night's Dream,* by William Shakespeare.

TITANIC DISASTER. The Royal Mail steamship *Titanic* of the White Star Line, sailing on her maiden voyage from Southampton to New York with 2223 passengers and crew, was sunk at sea by collision with a submerged iceberg at night on Sunday, April 14, 1912, and 832 passengers and 685 of the crew perished. Among those lost were John Jacob Astor, Archibald W. Butt, Benjamin Guggenheim, F.D. Millet, William T. Stead, and Isidor Straus. The *Titanic* was the largest ship in the world at the time, with a length of 852.5 feet and a gross tonnage of 46,328.

TITANITE. See SPHENE.

TITANIUM, a metallic element, of atomic number 22, atomic weight 48.1, and symbol Ti, belonging to the tin (q.v.) group of metals. It was discovered in 1789 in the mineral menachanite by the English clergyman William Gregor, who named the new element menachite. Three years later, the German chemist Martin Heinrich Klaproth rediscovered Gregor's element in the mineral rutile, and named it titanium in allusion to the strength of the mythological Greek Titans. The metal was isolated in 1910. It ranks ninth in abundance among the elements in the earth's crust. Titanium is never found in the pure state, but occurs as an oxide in the minerals ilmenite, $FeTiO_3$; rutile, TiO_2; and sphene, $CaO \cdot TiO_2 \cdot SiO_2$; see articles on each mineral. To separate titanium oxide from its ore, the mineral is ground and mixed with potassium carbonate and aqueous hydrofluoric acid to yield potassium fluotitanate, K_2TiF_6. The fluotitanate is extracted with hot water and decomposed with ammonia. The resulting ammoniacal hydrated oxide, when ignited in a platinum vessel, yields titanium dioxide, TiO_2. Titanium is obtained in the pure form by first treating the oxide with chlorine to form titanium tetrachloride, a volatile liquid, and then reducing the liquid with magnesium in a closed iron chamber to yield metallic titanium. The metal is then melted and cast into ingots.

Pure titanium is silver white in color, soluble in hot water and in sulfuric and hydrofluoric acids, and insoluble in cold water, it has m.p. 1800°C. (3272°F.), b.p. 3000°C. (5452°F.), and specific gravity of 4.50. The metal is extremely brittle when cold, but is readily malleable and ductile at a low red heat. It burns in oxygen at 610°C. (1130°F.) to form titanium dioxide, and burns in nitrogen at 800°C. (1472°F.) to form titanium nitride, TiN. Titanium exhibits valences of 4, 3, and 2, and forms the salts titanium tetrachloride, $TiCl_4$; titanium trichloride, $TiCl_3$; and titanium dichloride, $TiCl_2$.

Because of its strength and light weight, titanium is used primarily in metallic alloys and as a substitute for aluminum. Common alloys in use today include: ferrocarbon titanium, made by reduction of ilmenite with coke in an electric furnace; cuprotitanium, formed by reduction of rutile to which amounts of copper have been added; and manganotitanium, produced by reduction of rutile to which manganese or oxides of manganese have been added. The relative inertness of titanium makes it available as a replacement for bone and cartilage in surgery, and as a pipe and tank lining in the processing of foods. In metallurgy, titanium alloys are employed as deoxidizers and denitrogenizers to remove oxygen and nitrogen, respectively, from molten metals. Titanium dioxide, commonly known as titanium white, is a brilliant white pigment used widely in ceramics and in the rubber industry.

With the recent development of supersonic aircraft, titanium has become a structural metal of primary importance. Current research is concerned with the attempt to improve its qualities by various means, such as the development of protective coatings, and to discover new methods of processing which might reduce the present high cost of the metal.

TITANOSAURUS, or ATLANTOSAURUS, genus of extinct, sauropodous, herbivorous dinosaurs found fossil in the Jurassic rocks of the Rocky Mountain region and Dakota, whose species were among the most gigantic land animals that ever existed, one specimen, exhumed in Colorado by O.C. Marsh, measuring about 60 feet long and standing about 30 feet high.

TITANS, in Greek mythology, the six sons and six daughters of Uranus (q.v.), god of heaven, and Gæa (q.v.), goddess of earth. The sons were Oceanus, Cœus, Crius, Hyperion, Iapetus, and Cronus; and the daughters Theia, Rhea, Themis, Mnemosyne, Phœbe, and Tethys. Of these the most important were Iapetus, father of Atlas, Prometheus, and Epimetheus; Hyperion and Theia, parents of the sun god Helios, the moon goddess Selene, and the dawn goddess Eos; Oceanus and Tethys, parents of the ocean nymphs and the river gods; and Cronus and Rhea, parents of six Olympian deities Hestia, Demeter, Hera, Pluto, Poseidon, and Zeus (qq.v.; see also OLYMPUS). Uranus and Gæa were also the parents of the Cyclops (q.v.) and the Hekatonchires, or hundred-handed giants, whom Uranus imprisoned in Tartarus (q.v.). Instigated by their mother, the Titans, under the leadership of Cronus, rose against their father, emasculated and deposed him, and liberated their brothers from Tartarus. In the later war with the Olympian deities, the Titans were defeated and, with the exception of Oceanus, were consigned to Tartarus.

The Titans belong to a very remote past, several of their names appearing to be non-Greek. Mnemosyne hardly belongs with the other Titans as she is little more than an abstraction, the personification of memory. As a group the Titans are taken as types of lawlessness, great strength, and gigantic size, possibly representing the wild, disorderly forces of Nature, eventually overcome by the Olympian deities who represent peace and order. The name of Titans was given also to the descendants of the original Titans, such as Atlas, Helios, and Prometheus.

TITCHENER, EDWARD BRADFORD (1867–1927), Anglo-American psychologist, born in Chichester, England, and educated at Oxford and Leipzig universities. In 1892 he was appointed assistant professor of psychology at Cornell University; from 1895 to 1909 he served the University as Sage professor of experimental psychology, and thereafter until his death as research professor of experimental psychology in the graduate school. Titchener was the leading proponent of the theories of the German psychologist Wilhelm Wundt. Like Wundt, he emphasized introspective analysis of consciousness as experimentally validated techniques as opposed to the mechanistic concepts of behaviorism (q.v.). Among his works are *Experimental Psychology* (1901–05), *Lectures on the Experimental Psychology of the Thought-Processes* (1909), and *A Textbook of Psychology* (1909–10).

TITHE (AS. *tēotha,* "tenth"), originally a tenth of such things as annually increase or render an annual crop. For many centuries it constituted the usual tax or assessment. The term is applied to predial tithes, e.g., grain and fruit; mixed tithes, e.g., the young of animals, milk, etc.; and personal tithes, or gain arising from labor.

Tithes figured extensively in the Old Testament and are described in detail in Leviticus 27 and Deuteronomy 14. The system was adopted into the Christian Church, and has survived in a modified form in Great Britain.

TITHONUS, in Greek legend, a son of King Laomedon of Troy, and the brother of Priam. He was carried off by the dawn goddess Eos, who bore him a son, the hero Memnon (q.v.). Eos obtained from the gods the gift of immortality for Tithonus, but because she forgot to ask that he remain eternally young, Tithonus in his old age withered away to a decrepit and shriveled old man. A later account related his final transformation into a grasshopper.

TITIAN, or (It.) TIZIANO VECELLI or VECELLIO (1477–1576), one of the most celebrated Venetian painters of the High Renaissance, born in Pieve di Cadore. When he was about ten years old his parents sent him to Venice, where he became a pupil first of Gentile Bellini and then of Giovanni Bellini, both of whom were among the most noted painters of the time. He was also influenced by the work of Il Giorgione, with whom he is believed to have formed a partnership. Until about 1512 Titian painted in a style similar to that of Giorgione, but bolder and more clearly defined in line and color. His reputation was established through a number of early works, dating from about 1505, which include "Christ Carrying the Cross" (Chapel of San Rocco, Venice) and "Man of Sorrows" (Scuola di San Rocco, Venice). In 1507 and 1508 he was associated with Giorgione in the execution of frescoes in the Fondaco de' Tedeschi, but these works are no longer extant. Subsequently he painted "The Tribute Money" (Dresden Picture Gallery), "Tobias and the Angel" (Church of San Marziale, Venice), "Pope Alexander VII Presenting Jacopo Pesaro to Saint Peter" (Antwerp Museum), and "Saint Mark Enthroned" (Church of the Salute, Venice). Some time between 1510 and 1512 he executed one of the best known of his early works, the allegorical "Sacred and Profane Love" (Villa Borghese, Rome), in which a nude and a clothed figure are represented in a sunny landscape.

"Flora," painting by Titian

During the same years he visited Padua, and painted in the Scuola di San Antonio there a series of frescoes depicting scenes from the life of Saint Anthony. He returned to Venice in 1512 and about that time executed the paintings entitled "Three Ages" (Bridgewater House, London), "Noli Me Tangere" (National Gallery, London), and "Salome with the Head of the Baptist" (Doria Gallery, Rome). In 1513 he was appointed superintendent of the government works of Venice; three years later he succeeded Giovanni Bellini as official painter to the state, and was given an annual pension. In 1518 he completed one of his masterpieces, the "Assumption of the Virgin" (San Nicolò dei Frari, Venice), a vast oil painting in which a number of the figures are almost nine feet tall. This work created a sensation and marked the beginning of Titian's international reputation. Subsequently he received numerous commissions from patrons outside Venice. For Alfonso d'Este, Duke of Ferrara, he painted three pictures with mythological themes: "Worship of

Venus", "Bacchanal" (both in the Prado, Madrid), and "Bacchus and Ariadne" (National Gallery, London). In 1552 he painted "Resurrection of Christ" (Church of San Nazaro e Celso, Brescia), and about the same time "Flora" (Uffizi Gallery, Florence) and "Venus Anadyomene" (Bridgewater House, London). Also of this period is the portrait of "Alfonso d'Este" (Metropolitan Museum of Art, New York City) and the fresco of "St. Christopher Carrying the Infant Christ" (1523), in the doge's palace at Venice. Another of his masterpieces, the dramatic "Entombment of Christ" (Louvre, Paris) was completed in 1523.

In 1527 Titian became a friend of the writer Pietro Aretino, and according to many art historians painted several portraits of him. In 1530 his most distinguished patron, Holy Roman Emperor Charles V, summoned Titian to Bologna, where he executed a portrait of the emperor, who became his friend and in 1533 made him count palatine and knight of the Golden Spur. He also executed numerous commissions for Federigo II Gonzago, Duke of Mantua, including the "Madonna del Coniglio" (Louvre). Other famous patrons for whom he worked included members of the Medici family and Guidubaldo della Rovere, Duke of Urbino (1514–72). As an international celebrity, Titian maintained in Venice a luxurious home, which became the center of a famous literary and artistic circle. Occupied with important private commissions, he neglected his official duties as state painter, and in 1538 was dismissed from his post; he was reinstated a year later, however, after completing an elaborate painting, "Barbarossa's Victory at Spoleto", which was later destroyed by fire. Another great work completed in 1538 is the "Presentation of the Virgin in the Temple" (Academy, Venice). His "Adonis with His Dog" (Metropolitan Museum of Art) was also painted about 1538. A number of paintings executed about 1540 show the influence of Michelangelo in their emphasis on muscular form; these include "Cain Killing Abel", "Sacrifice of Abraham", and "David and Goliath" (Church of the Salute, Venice), and "Ecce Homo" (Vienna Gallery).

In 1545 Titian was invited by Pope Paul III to visit Rome, where he was received with high honors, and executed several portraits of his patron. Titian's paintings subsequent to his stay in Rome were executed in a free, somewhat impressionistic style; they are best seen at a distance, rather than close up. At this time he also changed the predominant colors of his works, and adopted deep yellow and blue in place of the earlier red and green. He was called to Augsburg, Germany, in 1548 and again in 1550 to paint portraits of Emperor Charles V and other notables. The most celebrated of these works is the equestrian portrait, "Charles V at the Battle of Mühlberg" (Prado, Madrid). Titian also executed many commissions for Philip II, son of Charles V. These include works painted about 1558, such as "Diana and Actæon" (Bridgewater House, London), "Europa on the Bull" (Gardner Museum, Boston), and "Actæon Torn to Pieces by His Dogs" (Louvre). In 1564 he completed his "Last Supper" (Escorial, Madrid), a very large canvas, which was sent to Philip II. At about the same time he executed "Adoration of the Magi" (Prado), "Saint Jerome" (Escorial), "Religion Aided by Spain" (Prado), and "Venus and the Lute Player" (Metropolitan Museum of Art). The principal works of Titian's last years, also executed for Philip II, include "Philip Presenting His Son to Victory" (Prado). His last painting, "Pietà" (Academy, Venice), left incomplete at his death, was finished by Jacopo Palma the Younger.

Although Titian was not a many-faceted genius of the type of Michelangelo and Leonardo da Vinci, he attained supremacy in the field of painting and carried the use of glowing and vivid color, characteristic of the Venetian school, to its highest development. Working until the very end of his extraordinary life span of ninety-nine years, he painted a tremendous number of works, the majority of which are outstanding. In his rapid and sweeping brushwork, he revolutionized painting, departing from the former meticulously detailed style and establishing a new free treatment of form, light and shade, and atmospheric perspective, subsequently further developed by Rembrandt and Velasquez. The landscape backgrounds of his works, usually idealized scenes of Venetian lagoons or of the Alps in the vicinity of his native village, set a standard which was subsequently surpassed only by the 17th-century French landscape painter Nicolas Poussin. He was unequalled as a portraitist and his realistic and striking characterizations of kings and nobles rank among the best of his work.

TITICACA, LAKE, the largest lake in South America, on the boundary of Peru and Bolivia, about 12,500 feet above the sea. The lake has a length of 130 miles with an average breadth of 30 miles. The region around Lake Titicaca was one of the seats of early Indian civilization; it contains many architectural remains, some of which antedate the Incan periods.

TITLARK. See PIPIT.

TITLE, REGISTRATION OF. See TORRENS SYSTEM.

TITMOUSE, name given to several genera of Passerine birds in the family Paridae. They are more numerous in cold and temperate than in tropical regions, those which are found within the tropics being mostly inhabitants of elevated mountainous districts. The bill is small, short, somewhat conical, the tip entire, the base beset with hairs, and the nostrils generally concealed by feathers. The plumage is soft, lax, and fluffy, often gay. The chickadee or blackcap tit, *P. atricapillus,* is very common in North America.

TITO, assumed name of JOSIP BROZ (1892–   ), Yugoslav communist statesman, born in Zagorye, near Zagreb, Croatia, then in Austria-Hungary. On the outbreak of World War I he was conscripted into the Austrian army. In 1915 he deserted to the Russians and was held as a military prisoner; he was liberated following the Russian Revolution of 1917. He remained in Soviet Russia, became a communist, and fought in the Red Army during the civil war of 1919–21. He went to Yugoslavia in 1923; became a leader of the metal workers' union, and was active in the underground communist movement. From 1923 to 1928 he was imprisoned in Yugoslavia for his revolutionary activities. After his release he became a leader of the underground labor and revolutionary movements; subsequently he became general secretary of the communist party of Yugoslavia.

During the civil war in Spain in 1936–39, Tito organized and led the Yugoslav contingent of the International Brigade which fought against the fascist forces of Francisco Franco. In World War II, after the occupation of Yugoslavia by the Germans and Italians in 1941, Tito organized and led the underground resistance forces, called the Yugoslav Army of National Liberation, and referred to as the Yugoslav Partisans. He conducted guerrilla warfare against the fascist invaders and civil war against the Croatian partisan forces led by General Draža Mihajlović (1893?–1946), called the Chetniks, which collaborated with Italians and Germans. By 1943 Tito, who was supported by the Soviet Union, commanded an army of approximately 200,000 and was dominant in the Anti-Fascist Council for National Liberation, which controlled about one-third of Yugoslavia. In 1944, he was recog-

nized by the allied powers as their principal ally in Yugoslavia; in the fall of the year his forces established contact with Soviet armies moving eastward. In imitation of Joseph Stalin, Soviet dictator, he assumed the rank of marshal.

Tito was prime minister and minister of war in the provisional government of Yugoslavia, established in the spring of 1945. Following the abolition of the monarchy and the establishment of the Federal People's Republic of Yugoslavia as a satellite of the Soviet Union in November, 1945, Tito became dictator of Yugoslavia; through the institution of a five-year plan and other measures, he began the economic, political, and social transformation of the country in the image of the Soviet Union. In 1947 he became a leader of the Information Bureau of Communist and Workers' Parties, or Cominform, created in that year to replace in part the Third (Communist) International (q.v.) which had been formally dissolved in 1943. Economic difficulties caused Tito, at the beginning of 1948, to modify the rate of implementation of the five-year plan and to appeal for assistance first to the Soviet Union, and, when it was not forthcoming, to western capitalist powers. He was subsequently denounced by the Cominform and the Soviet government and its satellites as a traitor to socialism and a fascist ally of warmongering imperialist powers bent on the destruction of the Soviet Union. Tito became president of Yugoslavia in 1953, when the governmental structure was altered. Diplomatic relations with the U.S.S.R. were reestablished the same year, and in June, 1955, Tito and Soviet Premier Nikolai Bulganin formally proclaimed the resumption of cordial relations between the two countries.

TITOGRAD, formerly CETINJE, capital of the Republic of Montenegro, Yugoslavia, located in the s.w. portion of the country, 2068 ft. above sea level, 19 miles E. of Cattaro and about 12 miles from the Adriatic Sea. Its principal industry is the bottling of mineral water. The town consists of two main thoroughfares connected by smaller streets and the houses are chiefly whitewashed cottages. The principal buildings are a 15th-century church, an old and a modern palace, a seminary, library, museum, theater, and hospital. The town was founded in 1484 by Ivo the Black, Prince of Montenegro, who made it his capital. During World War II, in 1941, the town and all of Montenegro came under Italian control with the dismemberment of Yugoslavia (see YUGOSLAVIA: *History*). Following the close of the war and the return of Montenegro to Yugoslavia, the town was renamed in honor of Tito, the premier of Yugoslavia. Pop. (1948) 12,206.

TITUS, in full TITUS FLAVIUS SABINUS VESPASIANUS (about 40–81 A.D.), Roman Emperor from 79 to 81 A.D., the second of the Flavian emperors and elder son of Titus Flavius Vespasianus (later the emperor Vespasian, q.v.), born in Rome and educated at the court of the emperor Claudius. As a young man, Titus served as a military tribune in Germany and Britain, and fought under his father in Palestine. Upon Vespasian's elevation to the throne in 69 A.D., Titus was left to carry on the Jewish War, which he brought to a close by the capture of Jerusalem in 70 A.D. after a long siege. Upon his return to Rome, he was given a joint triumph with Vespasian in 71 A.D., the victory being later commemorated by the Arch of Titus, erected by the emperor Domitian, the brother of Titus. Titus was associated with his father in the government of the empire, but gave himself over to the pursuit of pleasure in many forms, outraging public opinion by his affair with Berenice, the sister of the Judean king Herod Agrippa II.

Upon the death of his father in 79 A.D. Titus was proclaimed emperor, and by his generous gifts and lavish entertainments soon made himself popular with the Roman people. The first act of his reign was to discontinue all prosecutions for *læsa majestas,* and to decree heavy punishments against informers. He assumed the title of pontifex maximus; completed and dedicated in 80 A.D. the great Flavian amphitheater (q.v.), later called the Colosseum, gratifying the populace by lavish games lasting 100 days; and built N.E. of the Colosseum the extensive baths which bear his name. During his reign occurred the famous eruption of the volcano Vesuvius in 79 A.D., which overwhelmed Herculaneum, Pompeii (qq.v.), and Stabiæ; and the great fire at Rome in 80 A.D. which raged for three days, destroying the temple of Jupiter Capitolinus and numerous public edifices, and was followed by a dreadful pestilence. For his beneficence to the sufferers of these disasters he became the idol of the populace. At his death, like his father, he was deified.

TITUSVILLE, a city of Crawford Co., Pa., situated on Oil Creek, 42 miles S.E. of Erie. It is served by two railroads. The city lies in the midst of the oil and gas fields of N.W. Pennsylvania. The surrounding region is also an agricultural area, yielding buckwheat and dairy products. The principal industries in the

city are oil refining, and the manufacture of oil-well machinery and supplies, iron and steel forgings, machine and tool steel, cutlery, building supplies, explosives, small boats, patent medicines, and silk ribbon. The history of Titusville is closely allied with that of the development of the oil and gas industries of the State. The first artesian oil well in the U.S. was drilled at Titusville on Aug. 27, 1859, by Col. Edwin L. Drake (1819–80). The site of the original well is now contained in Drake Well Memorial Park, which houses a museum with exhibits of the oil industry. A monument to Col. Drake in Woodlawn Cemetery was erected in 1902. The city was the center of opposition of independent oil-well operators to the Standard Oil Company until 1875, in which year John D. Archbold of Titusville, leader of the opposition, became a director of the Standard Oil Company. The first commercial development of the natural-gas fields of Pennsylvania took place at Titusville about 1872. In 1892 a disastrous flood occurred, during which oil tanks wrecked by the flood caught fire, destroying one third of the city and taking sixty lives. Titusville was settled in 1796 by Jonathan Titus, incorporated as a borough in 1847, and chartered as a city in 1866. Pop. (1950) 8923.

TIVOLI (anc. *Tibur*), a town of the province of Roma, central Italy, situated 18 miles N.E. of Rome on the slope of the Sabine hills. At Tivoli the river Teverone (anc. Anio) issues from the mountains over lofty, picturesque waterfalls, and the town affords an excellent view of the Roman Campagna and of the city of Rome. In antiquity Tibur became an ally of Rome in the 4th century B.C., and its inhabitants acquired Roman citizenship about 90 B.C.; it long remained a favorite summer residence of wealthy Romans, and was praised by many Roman poets, especially by Horace. In and around Tivoli are many remains of temples, villas, bridges, and tombs. In a commanding position near the waterfalls rises the so-called Temple of the Sibyl, a circular edifice in good preservation. About two and a half miles from Tivoli are the imposing remains of the magnificent villa constructed for the emperor Hadrian. On the western slope of the town lies the famous Villa d'Este, dating from about 1550, with a beautiful garden containing numerous terraces, fountains, and cypress trees, said to be the finest Renaissance garden in Italy. Tivoli has long been famous for grapes grown in the surrounding area, and for its travertine quarries. Pop. of commune, about 19,000; of town, about 15,000.

The common toad

TLAXCALA, the smallest and most densely populated State of Mexico, situated in the central portion of the country, bounded on the N., E., and S. by Puebla, and on the W. by Mexico State. Tlaxcala lies in the central Mexican plateau. Several mountain peaks rise on the W. and S. frontiers. The chief industry is agriculture and the principal products are corn and other grains. The natives are of Nahua descent. The Nahuas founded an Indian republic there in the 13th century. The republic kept its independence, despite Aztec incursions, until 1519, when it was taken by the Spanish under Hernando Cortes. Area, 1555 sq.m.; pop. (1950) 282,495.

TLEMCEN, town of Algeria, 80 miles S.W. of Oran. It is surrounded by olive plantations and vineyards. Pop. (1948) 69,668.

TLINGIT, name of a group of sixteen Indian tribes, inhabiting the Pacific coast in the southern extension of Alaska. They form a homogeneous people, speak the same tongue, and are maritime in habit, their canoes being made from the trunks of large cedar trees. They show no knowledge of pottery, but are experts in carving, many of their domestic utensils being made of wood. They are fine basketmakers.

TNT. See TRINITROTOLUENES.

TOAD (*Bufo*), a genus of amphibians (see AMPHIBIA), typical of the family Bufonidae. Toads are distinguished from frogs by the absence of teeth, by the roughness of the skin, by peculiarities in the breastbone, and by the shorter hind legs.

The common toad is a shy, nocturnal animal, hiding during the day in dark, damp places, crawling about at night in search of insects, grubs, slugs, worms, and the like. Its appearance is familiar, a brownish-gray color, a warty skin, a flat head, swollen parotid glands above the ears, bright, jewellike eyes

with a transverse pupil, and slightly webbed toes. They are heavier and clumsier than frogs, and cannot leap as far. During winter they hibernate in the mud or in holes. In spring they pair, and the females lay in the water pools their numerous ova in gelatinous strings about 3 or 4 ft. in length. The tadpoles are smaller and darker than those of frogs, and do not accomplish their transformation into terrestrial toads until autumn.

The natterjack or rush toad is of a light yellowish-brown color, clouded with a dull olive, with a bright yellow line running down the back. It is found in dry locations. It is less timid than the common toad, and its eyes are more prominent, its warts larger, its tadpoles smaller, their metamorphoses much shorter.

The genus *Bufo* includes over seventy different species. These are widely distributed over most parts of the continent, but are most abundant in tropical regions. The common toad of North America is *Bufo americanus,* ranging everywhere E. of the Rocky Mountains. In the southern States another very similar species, *B. lentinosus,* is numerous, and other species are found in the West. The largest, *B. marinus* of tropical America, measures 8 in. in length. The *bombinator,* a small European frog (*bombinatoridae*) is sometimes mistaken for a toad.

TOADFLAX, common name applied to herbs of the genus *Linaria,* belonging to the Figwort family, very closely allied to snapdragon, from which genus it is distinguished chiefly by the spur at the base of the corolla, and the capsule opening by valves or teeth.

TOADSTOOL. See FUNGI.

TOBACCO, common name applied to *Nicotiana tabacum,* an herb belonging to the Nightshade family, and cultivated for its leaves, which when cured are used for smoking, chewing, and as snuff. It has broad leaves, terminal panicles of flowers, and two-celled, five-valved fruits (many-seeded capsules). It is a native of the Western Hemisphere, where the aborigines cultivated and used it from remote times. Its generic name is in honor of Jean Nicot, who introduced it into France in 1559 from Spain, where it had been introduced from Santo Domingo in the same year. In 1585 it was taken to England by Sir Francis Drake, and the practice of pipe smoking was introduced among the Elizabethan courtiers by Sir Walter Raleigh. Its use rapidly extended throughout Europe, and soon became extensively prevalent among Oriental nations. Tobacco was at first recommended

Liggett & Myers; Standard Oil

GROWING TOBACCO. *Above: Seedling nursery covered with cloth as protection from wind and cold. Right: Transplanting seedlings. One man drops them on ground; others set them. Below: Tractor drawing planting machine on which four men sit. Each two plant one line.*

Liggett & Myers; Ga. Agric. & Ind. Devel. Bd.

GROWING TOBACCO. *Above: Tractor pulling cultivator through a field of plants. Left: Shade-grown tobacco under cheesecloth covering (barely visible in picture) stretched across the tops of poles. Below: Harvesting the full-grown leaves.*

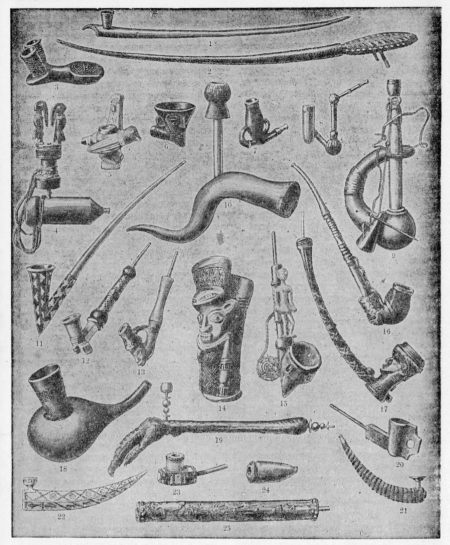

TOBACCO PIPES. *1 to 18, native African pipes; 19, native Australian; 20, native Brazilian; 21 and 22, Eskimo; 23, Patagonian; 24, Brazilian; 25, Paraguayan.*

for medicinal virtues, but soon became an article of luxury.

In America the culture of tobacco began in Virginia with the earliest settlement of the colony. It is recorded that in 1615 the gardens, fields, and even the streets of Jamestown were planted with tobacco, which immediately became, not only the staple crop, but the principal currency of the colony.

India is the second-largest producer of to-bacco in the world and likewise the second-largest consumer, consuming most of its own tobacco. Indonesia produces great quantities of leaf for export, and Japan nearly supplies its own needs. Turkey, France, Canada, Italy, Greece, and Romania produce considerable quantities, as do also Cuba, Puerto Rico, Santo Domingo, the Philippines, and Mexico. Brazil leads among the South American countries.

The principal manufactured products are cigars and cheroots, cigarettes, smoking tobacco (for pipes and cigarettes), snuff, and chewing tobacco—plug, twist, and fine cut. Both the cigar and cigarette manufacture have been revolutionized by machinery. See NICOTINE.

TOBACCO PIPE, an implement for the smoking of tobacco. Aside from the specimens discovered in ancient sites in Europe, the greatest prehistoric distribution of the pipe is in America. Most of the inventions have grown out of the desire to cool the smoke and relieve it of acrid principles, giving rise to the great class of water pipes widespread in Asia and Africa, as the hookah or narghile, and the ornate Chinese water pipe, and in other countries resulting in absorbing bowls, as the meerschaum, calabash, clay, brier root, or other substances, as well as devices for condensing the nicotine in a receptacle below the bowl, as in the German *lange Pfeife*. The opium pipe of China is a special development with a large bowl for the inhalation of a small quantity of fumes from a pellet of burning opium. The hemp pipe of India is a form of water pipe in which tobacco or a mixture of tobacco and hemp may be smoked. The majority of the high class pipes used in United States and Europe are made from Algerian and Italian brier.

TOBAGO. See TRINIDAD AND TOBAGO.

TOBIT, THE BOOK OF, in the Old Testament apocrypha, the book telling of Tobit, and Tobias his son. Tobit was a pious Israelite of the tribe of Naphtali, carried captive to Nineveh by "Enemassar" (Shalmaneser). Among his good works was the practice of defying the prohibition of the Assyrian kings by secretly burying the bodies of his slain fellow countrymen. He was discovered, and his goods confiscated. To add to his misfortune he became blind. In his poverty he resolved to send his son Tobias to Rhagæ (Rai) in Media to recover a debt from a friend. Tobias finds a companion in an unknown youth (really the archangel Raphael) who gives him much advice. Acting on this, he catches a great "fish" in the Tigris, and secures its heart, liver, and gall. By means of the first two he is able to deliver from the power of the evil spirit Asmodeus his cousin Sara, daughter of Raguel, at Ecbatana, whom he marries and, after recovering the debt, leads back to his father's house. At home he is able with the gall of the fish to cure his father's blindness. The book closes with Tobit's psalm of thanksgiving, and relates how he enjoyed a hundred years' happiness after these events, Tobias also living to the age of 127.

TOBRUK, a seaport of the district of Cyrenaica, in the independent kingdom of Libya, situated on the N. coast of Africa, about 275 miles E. of Bengasi and about 390 miles W.N.W. of Alexandria, Egypt. It has an excellent natural harbor, deep and well sheltered, with a maximum depth of 40 ft. Harbor facilities were considerably improved by the Italian government prior to the entrance of Italy into World War II. Tobruk is also served by a fine motor road to Tripoli, and is connected by rail via the Egyptian coastal railway with Istanbul, Turkey. The city is the trading center and port for the rich oases in the interior, where date palms abound.

Tobruk was an important supply port during World War II and the site of intense desert fighting between Italo-German and Allied forces. In the first phase of the North African campaign the heavily fortified city was captured by Australian troops within 24 hours on January 22, 1941, following a combined assault by British ground, air, and naval forces. About 25,000 Italian defenders of Tobruk were taken prisoner by the British, who then swept westward along the coast, leaving a small garrison to hold the city. During the Axis offensive launched late in March, 1941, by General (later Field Marshal) Erwin Rommel, commanding the specially trained task forces comprising the *Afrika Korps,* Tobruk was threatened, and by April 13, completely encircled. The beleaguered garrison at Tobruk, although isolated from other British ground troops, was supplied by British naval forces, and consequently was able to withstand a prolonged siege of about eight months. In November, 1941, the British commenced a counteroffensive from Egypt, striking into Libya and pushing westward toward Tobruk, while at the same time the garrison of that city attacked the encircling Axis troops. The final relief of the city remained in doubt until Dec. 10, when the Axis forces withdrew from the Tobruk region and retreated westward. However, a second major Axis offensive, begun by General Rommel on May 26, 1942, once again drove British forces back across Libya, and Tobruk, with its garrison of 25,000 troops, fell on June 21. The gain to the Axis by the capture of the city was considerable, both from the point of view of morale and of war equipment, the British having left large quantities of matériel in Tobruk, including about 100 tanks. Not until Nov. 13, 1942, when Rommel's forces were in full retreat before the final and victorious British offensive launched from El Alamein on Oct. 22, was Tobruk at last recaptured. Pop., about 2500.

TOCANTINS, an important river of Brazil, rising in the State of Goyaz. It flows N. through the State of Pará, and finally, after a course of 1500 m., widens into the Pará, 138 m. from the Atlantic. Its principal affluent is the Araguaia (q.v.), which joins it at the northern extremity of Goyaz.

TOCCATA, in music, a term originally applied to compositions written for keyed instruments, thus having a somewhat more restricted meaning than sonata, a composition for any instrument. The oldest toccatas preserved are some written for the organ by the Italian composer Claudio Merulo (published 1598). They generally begin with full chords which gradually give way to passage work among which small fugato sections are interspersed. The modern toccata does not differ materially from that of Merulo.

TOCQUEVILLE, ALEXIS CHARLES HENRI CHÉREL DE (1805–59), French writer and statesman, born in Verneuil, Seine-et-Oise. In 1831 he accepted a government mission to America, to report on the working of the penitentiary system, but the chief fruit of which was his great work, *De la Démocratie en Amérique* (1835). He became successively a member of the Academy of Moral Sciences and of the French Academy. In 1839 he was returned to the Chamber of Deputies by his neighbors, the Norman farmers, by an overwhelming majority, and in 1849 became vice-president of the Assembly, and from June to October in the same year was minister of foreign affairs. His other works include *L'Ancien Régime et la Révolution* (1856) and *Œuvres et Correspondance Inédites* (1860). A collected edition of his works appeared in Paris (1860–65).

TODAS, a people of the Nilgiri Hills in southern Hindustan, considered to be of Dravidian stock (see DRAVIDIAN). They are tall, well built, and dolichocephalic, with prominent nose, features approaching the Caucasian, full beard, black hair, and rather light-brown skin. They live a simple pastoral life and are concerned almost solely with the care of the dairy. The Todas form a typical polyandrous community in which when a woman marries it is understood that she becomes the wife of her husband's brothers.

TOGA. See COSTUME: *Roman.*

TOGO, COUNT HEIHACHIRO (1847–1934), Japanese admiral, born in Kagoshima, Japan. He studied naval science and navigation in

England (1871–78), and first attained prominence, as captain of the cruiser *Naniwa*, by sinking the Chinese troopship *Kowshing* (1894), thus precipitating the Sino-Japanese War. In the subsequent Russo-Japanese War (1904) he was appointed commander in chief of the Japanese fleet, and under his direction various brilliant operations took place, culminating in the battle of the Sea of Japan when the Russian fleet was annihilated. He received the title of count (1907) and was made the admiral of the fleet (1912).

TOGOLAND or **TOGO**, a region of West Africa lying between the Gold Coast and Dahomey, and bounded on the S. by the Bight of Benin in the Gulf of Guinea, and on the N. by French West Africa. Formerly a German protectorate, and, after World War I, mandated by the League of Nations in part to France and in part to Great Britain, Togoland is now divided into Togoland, a United Nations Trusteeship territory which is administered by Great Britain as a part of the Gold Coast (q.v.), and Togo, a U.N. Trusteeship territory administered by France.

The low, sandy coast of the region rises toward the interior, which has an undulating surface. The coast contains a number of lagoons, and is about 32 m. long. In the interior are the Aposso Mts. The principal rivers are the Oti, Sio, Haho, and Mono. The climate is moist and unhealthful. Rubber trees, coconut and oil palms, and dyewood trees grow in the region. The S. portion is inhabited by various Negro tribes, of which the most important are the Ewe-speaking peoples (see EWE), related to the Bantus. In the N. are found natives descended largely from Hamitic tribes. Most of the natives are pagan, although Mohammedanism is well represented in the N., and many in the S. are Christian.

Togoland (British). The British portion consists of approximately one third of the original area of Togoland and is located in the western interior of the region. The administrative center is Ho, with a population of about 3000. Kete-Krachi, in the N. of British Togoland, has a population of about 9000. The chief industry is agriculture and the principal crops include cacao and cotton. Coffee, kola nuts, and palm kernels and oil are also produced, and cattle are raised. Area, 13,041 sq.m.; pop. (1956 est.) 436,000.

Togoland (French). The French portion of Togoland is commonly called Togo and includes the entire coastline of the region. The capital and chief port is Lomé (pop., about 31,700, including about 1100 Whites). The prin-

British Info.; French Embassy

IN TOGOLAND. *Above: Native chiefs (in white) in British Togoland. Left: Drying cacao in British Togoland. Below: Open-air school, French Togoland.*

cipal industries are farming and the raising of cattle, sheep, and pigs. Crops include yams, cotton, millet, palm kernels, cacao, palm oil, rubber, coconuts, groundnuts, plantains, corn, and manioc. Native industries include lumbering, weaving, and the making of pottery and fiber products. The natives also mine and smelt iron. Togo is governed by a commissioner, aided by a privy council and 11 elected district councils; it is represented in the French National Assembly by one deputy, in the Council of the Republic by two councillors, and in the Assembly of the French Union by one delegate. Area, 21,893 sq.m.; pop. (1955 est.) 1,080,000.

History. The German colony of Togoland or Togo was founded in 1884 when the native ruler of the region signed a treaty granting suzerainty to the Germans. In 1899 Germany, Great Britain, and France fixed the territorial limits of the German colony after a long period of negotiation. The Germans created the port of Lomé and developed the resources of the region to the point at which Togo was self-supporting. In August, 1914, during the first month of World War I, the Germans surrendered the region to French and British forces. The two nations divided the region in 1919, but the French were dissatisfied because the port of Lomé went to the British. In 1920, a new division took place and Lomé and the entire coastline was assigned to French Togo in exchange for enlarging the British territory in the interior. In 1922 the League of Nations granted France and Great Britain mandates over their respective territories. During World War II French Togo remained loyal to the government at Vichy (see FRANCE: *History*) following the French defeat in June, 1940. With the invasion of Africa by Allied forces in Nov., 1942, the colony joined the Free French. On Dec. 13, 1946, the United Nations granted France and Great Britain trusteeships over Togo and Togoland, respectively, to supersede the mandates established by the League of Nations.

TOJO, EIKI or HIDEKI (1884–1948), Japanese soldier-statesman. He entered the army in 1915, was resident officer in Germany, 1919, became chief of staff of Japanese army in China, 1937, war minister, 1940, premier, 1941, and army staff chief, 1944. In July he resigned but remained in the cabinet. Tojo was tried as a war criminal by the Allied powers; he was convicted and executed.

TOKAY (Hung. *Tokaj*), a town of Zemplén County, Hungary, situated at the confluence of the Tisza and Bodrog rivers, about 130 miles N.E. of Budapest. The town is the commercial center of a region especially noted for its vineyards and containing productive mineral deposits, chiefly of salt, sapphire, and carnelian. More than thirty wines are produced in the vineyard region, a hilly plateau almost 150 sq.m. in area, and all are designated by the name of the town. Among the most celebrated Tokay wines, which are usually topaz in color and moderately strong, are *Tokaji Essencia* and *Tokaji Austruch.* Pop., about 5800.

TOKUGAWA, the name of the great family which ruled Japan between 1600 and 1868. Its founder was Ieyasu, who, with four other generals, ended centuries of feudal strife and anarchy. The fifteenth shogun resigned his powers to the emperor in 1868.

TOKYO, or TOKIO, the capital and largest city of Japan, and one of the largest cities in population in the world, situated on the S.E. coast of the main island of Honshu, at the head of the Bay of Tokyo and on both sides of the Sumida R., 18 m. by rail N.E. of Yokohama. The Sumida is too shallow for vessels of large draft, and Yokohama serves as the port of Tokyo; the rail route between the two cities is bordered by industrial plants. Tokyo, with its many suburbs, covers about 225 sq.m., and is more a collection of towns and villages than an integrated metropolis. It is a financial and commercial center, with varied industries. The western portion of the city is built on hills from 50 to 130 ft. in altitude, and the eastern portion extends along the flat, low section on the river banks. The lower section, intersected by canals, stretches between the two largest Tokyo parks, the Ueno on the N. and the Shiba on the S., both of which contain the tombs of the Tokugawa shoguns. Ueno park is also the site of the imperial library, the imperial museum, and zoological gardens. Of the many city divisions, Hongo and Kanda, in the N., contain most of the educational institutions, notably the Tokyo Imperial University (1877), the oldest and foremost center of education in Japan. In Kojimachi-ku, in the S.W., are the imperial palace, government buildings, and foreign embassies and legations. Nearest the sea are the districts of Nihonbashi, Kyobashi, and Asakusa, which are industrial and commercial. Situated in the Asakusa district is the celebrated temple of Kwannon, the goddess of mercy, and a popular recreation center.

The city was originally an obscure village

Daniel L. Burkett, from Black Star

A busy street corner in Tokyo, Japan

called Yedo ("Gate of the Inlet"), first mentioned in the 12th century, when the waters
of the bay and lagoons covered the commercial districts of the modern city. A castle
was built there about 1457 by a provincial
general, but Yedo had little importance until,
in 1590, Tokugawa Iyeyasu, first of the shoguns of that family, took possession of it
(see JAPAN: *History*). In 1603 Iyeyasu made
Yedo his capital, as opposed to the imperial
capital at Kyoto. In 1868, with the fall of
the shogunate, the imperial court was transferred to Yedo and the name of the city was
changed to Tokyo ("Eastern Capital").

The city site is often subject to earthquakes,
and Tokyo has frequently suffered disastrous
fires. Of these natural catastrophes, the most
serious in modern history was the earthquake
and fire of 1923 (see EARTHQUAKES, MEM-
ORABLE), which destroyed the greater part of
the city. In the subsequent reconstruction completed in 1930, over 200,000 new buildings,
including many on the Western model, and
seven reinforced concrete bridges spanning
the Sumida were erected. A number of new

parks were also laid out, and in one was constructed a Hall of the Nameless Dead as a
memorial to the approximately 30,000 people killed in Tokyo in the disaster.

During World War II Tokyo was severely
bombed. Its first and most famous raid occurred on April 18, 1942, when a squadron of
U.S. Air Force planes under the direction of
Lt. Col. (later Lt. Gen.) James H. Doolittle
(q.v.) bombed the city. Tokyo was occupied
by American troops from September, 1945 to
April, 1952. Pop. (1950) 6,277,500.

TOKYO, UNIVERSITY OF, a Japanese university founded in 1868 by the union of two
older schools, as one of the results of the
great political and social revolution of that
year. It has grown with the growth of modern Japan. At first officered largely by foreigners, these have been gradually superseded by
Japanese, for the most part trained in Europe
and the United States. The university is a
government institution. Its administration is
vested in a president and a board of councilors, two from each college, named by the
minister of education, for a term of five years.

The colleges comprise law, medicine, engineering, literature, science, and agriculture.

TOLEDO, port of entry and county seat of Lucas Co., Ohio, situated on Maumee Bay at the s.w. end of Lake Erie, and at the mouth of the Maumee R., 95 miles w. of Cleveland. Transportation facilities include sixteen major railroads, eight branch-line railroads, lake steamers, and a municipal airport of over 500 acres, with service by two transcontinental air lines. The city lies on both banks of the river, with seven bridges connecting the two sections. It is the largest coal-shipping port in the world, the second-ranking Great Lakes port in tonnage, an important market for grain, hay, winter vegetables, coffee, spices, iron ore, and petroleum products, and a leading manufacturing and distributing center. The harbor, with a depth of 25 ft., has a shore line of 35 miles; facilities include extensive railroad docks, coal docks, and warehouses. In a recent year the total cargo handled by the port amounted to more than 30,000,000 tons, comprising chiefly exports of coal and imports of grain, wood pulp, sand, and gravel. Among the industrial establishments in the city are shipbuilding yards, oil refineries, flour and feed mills, and large factories producing glass, automobiles, automobile parts and accessories, machine tools, dies, machinery, steel products, oil-well supplies, gas furnaces and heating equipment, weighing devices, giant presses, institutional and industrial food-conveying equipment, children's vehicles, playground equipment, wheelchairs, tinware and cans, vacuum cleaners, rubber products, spray-painting equipment, atomizers, plastics, and porcelain-enameled products.

Toledo is the site of the University of Toledo, established in 1872 and made a municipal institution in 1884; of De Sales College (Roman Catholic), established in 1936; Mary Manse College (Roman Catholic) for women, founded in 1922; and a State hospital for the insane. Cultural and recreational facilities include the Toledo Museum of Art, sixth-largest museum in the U.S.; a museum of natural science; a symphonic society; a choral society; one of the largest municipal zoos in the U.S.; and a park system covering more than 2200 acres. Toledo is also noted for its opera season.

Fort Industry was built on the site of the present city in 1794 by General Anthony Wayne as an outpost against the hostile Indian tribes of the region. Two towns, Port Lawrence and Vistula, were founded on the site in 1817 and 1832 respectively, and in 1833 they were united as Toledo. The area around Toledo was a part of the disputed territory in what was known as the "Toledo War" between Ohio and Michigan in 1835–36. Both Michigan and Ohio claimed the territory, and when the Ohio legislature prepared the way for the organization of new townships in the area, Michigan sent a division of Territorial militia which occupied Toledo in March, 1835. The territory was awarded to Ohio by Congress in June, 1836, and Toledo was incorporated as a city in 1837. Pop. (1950) 303,616.

TOLEDO, a province in the Castille region of Spain, bounded on the N. by Madrid and Ávila provinces, on the E. by Cuenca, on the s. by Cuidad Real, and on the w. by Cáceres. The capital is Toledo (q.v.). The region is largely mountainous. Gold, silver, iron, lead, mercury, copper, and tin are mined. Lumbering and farming are also carried on. Manufactured products of the province are textiles, soap, confections, wine, arms, and earthenware. Area, 5925 sq.m.; pop. (1950) 532,-278.

TOLEDO, capital of the Spanish province of the same name, situated on the Tagus R., about 45 miles s.s.w. of Madrid. The city is built on a promontory, 2400 ft. above sea level, bordered on three sides by a bend in the Tagus, with the land side protected by an inner and outer wall. Its many towers, old gates, narrow, winding streets, massive houses, and predominantly Moorish architecture give the city a medieval aspect. In the center of Toledo rises the principal edifice, the Gothic cathedral, built between 1227 and 1493, with forty chapels. Other noteworthy architectural features are the Gothic church of San Juan de los Reyes and its adjoining convent, a gift of Ferdinand and Isabella in 1476; El Tránsito, a medieval synagogue dating from 1366 and made a church after the expulsion of the Jews in 1492; and the church of Santo Tomé, originally a mosque and rebuilt as a church in Gothic style in the 14th century. The churches and religious treasures of Toledo contain some of the greatest works of art in Spain, notably those by El Greco. On the highest ground stands the Alcázar, a vast, square edifice with four towers, now a military academy, around which the houses of Toledo are grouped in a semicircle. The great square, or Zocodover, Moorish in architecture, is a fashionable promenade, and was long the site on which victims of the Inquisition were burned and bull fights took place. The most famous industry is the manufacture of swords, both by private companies and the government factory. Other industries are the manufacture of beer, confectionery, church ornaments, textiles, bricks, and fans. The origin of the city is lost in prehistory. It was in turn occupied by the Carpetani, probably by the Carthaginians, and by the Romans, who named it *Toletum*. From about 534 to 712 Toledo was the capital of the Visigothic kingdom in Spain (see GOTHS), and became a great ecclesiastical center. After its conquest by the Arabs, in 712, the city became an important Moorish center and in the 11th century the capital of a short-lived Moorish kingdom (1035–85). In 1085, after a memorable siege, the city was captured by the forces of Castile and annexed to the Castilian realms, of which it was made the capital (1087–1560). During the Spanish Civil War (1936–39) rebel forces in the Alcázar were besieged for seventy days by Loyalist forces (July–Sept., 1936). Area of province, 5923 sq.m.; pop. (1950 prelim.) 524,935. Pop. of city, about 31,000.

TOLIMA, a quiescent volcano in Colombia rising from the Central Cordillera of the Andes, 75 miles w. of Bogotá. It is the highest peak in the country, having an altitude of 18,325 feet.

TOLLER, ERNST (1893–1939), German dramatist. He was second chairman of the council of working men, soldiers, and peasants during the revolution in Munich (1919) and after a successful counterrevolution was imprisoned. He left Germany for London when Hitler came to power (1933). He came to New York (1936), where he lived until his death. His plays include *Wandlung* (1919), *Masse Mensch* (1921), *Die Ludditen* (1921), *Hinkemann* (1922), *No More Peace* (1937), *Learn from My Youth* (autobiography, 1934), and *Look through the Bars* (1937).

TOLSTOI, COUNT LEV NIKOLAEVICH (1828–1910), Russian novelist, moral philosopher, and social reformer, born in Yasnaya Polyana, in the province of Tula, and educated at the University of Kazan. In 1851 he joined an artillery regiment in the Caucasus; he was transferred to the staff of Prince Mikhail Dmitrievich Gorchakov on the Danube River during the initial phase of the Crimean War (q.v.), and commanded an artillery unit in 1855 at the unsuccessful Russian defense of Sevastopol. During the period of his military service Tolstoi wrote the idyllic and semi-autobiographic sketches *The Story of Yesterday* (1851), *Childhood* (1852), and *Boyhood* (1854), the philosophical tale *The Cossacks*

(1854), and the war sketches *Sebastopol in December of 1854, Sebastopol in May of 1855,* and *Sebastopol in August of 1855.* The last-named compositions, with their uncompromisingly realistic delineation of the horrors of war, immediately placed Tolstoi among the important writers of his day.

After his resignation from the army in 1857, he made a trip abroad, but was profoundly disillusioned by the materialism and predatory commercialism of Western civilization. Another European tour, made three years later, confirmed him in his pessimistic outlook on modern society. Upon his return to Russia, Tolstoi settled on his estates at Yasnaya Polyana, manumitted his serfs in conformity with the provisions of the Emancipation Act of 1861, and established a school for peasant children in his neighborhood. In 1862 he married Sofya Andreevna Behrs, a girl sixteen years younger than himself. About this time he began work on *The Decembrists,* a long novel, of which only the first three chapters were published. Historical research in connection with this project, however, led Tolstoi to study the reign of the Russian emperor Alexander I. His interest gradually centered on Napoleon's abortive invasion of Russia in 1812, which became the basic theme of his novel *War and Peace* (1866), a colossal prose epic depicting the whole range of Russian society at the beginning of the 19th century. Thereafter Tolstoi once more resumed his pedagogical activities. From 1875 to 1877 his novel *Anna Karenina* appeared periodically in the *Russian Herald.* This somber work details with consummate realism the history of an ill-fated marriage, in which the inability of the beautiful and romantic wife of a prosaic government official to assume her domestic obligations leads her to infidelity and at length to suicide.

Sometime after 1876, Tolstoi, who had developed profound spiritual misgivings about the prosperous and self-satisfied life he was leading, turned for solace to the Russian Orthodox Church. Its ritualism and pageantry proved unacceptable to him, however, and he devoted himself instead to an intensive independent study of the Gospels, as a result of which he formulated a new type of Christianity. This new religion is epitomized in the words from *Matthew* 5:39 "that ye resist not evil", which Tolstoi interpreted as containing the whole message of Christ. The doctrine of nonresistance to evil, analogous in many respects to the creed of nonviolence expounded by the Indian religious and political leader

Sovfoto

Above: The birthplace of Count Lev Nikolaevich Tolstoi, in Yasnaya Polyana, U.S.S.R.
Right: Count Lev Nikolaevich Tolstoi.

Mohandas Gandhi (q.v.), asserts that evil, in whatever form, should not be resisted by violent means (see PACIFISM). *Tolstovstvo* ("Tolstoyism"), as this religion was known, became an established sect about 1884, and soon acquired a large number of converts.

Meanwhile, Tolstoi set forth his new faith and the circumstances of his conversion in a series of memorable works, including *A Confession* (1879), *Commentary on the Gospel* (1883), *The Memoirs of a Madman* (1884), *The Death of Ivan Ilyich* (1886), *The Power of Darkness* (1889), *What Is Art?* (1896), and *Resurrection* (1899–1900). In the enthusiasm attendant upon his conversion, Tolstoi wished to dispossess himself altogether of his property and live in the humble fashion of a peasant; his wife, however, unwilling to see her children thus disinherited, prevailed upon him to sign over his estates to her. In 1910, in pursuance of a long-held plan to end his days in solitude, Tolstoi suddenly fled his home, but contracted pneumonia during his journey and died in a small railway station at Astapovo.

TOLTECS. See MEXICO: *History.*

TOLUCA, the capital of the State of Mexico, Mexico, situated on the s.w. border of the Anahuac plateau, 34 miles s.w. of the city of Mexico. Toluca lies at an altitude of 8650 ft. above sea level and possesses a cool and healthful climate. Industrial establishments include breweries, cotton mills, and flour mills. The Mexican government maintains a college and a meteorological station at Toluca. The Nevada de Toluca, an extinct volcano (15,155 ft.) is nearby. According to Mexican historical tradition, the city was founded by the Toltecs. It was an Aztec pueblo called Tollán at the time of the Spanish conquest in the 16th century. Pop. (1950) 115,422.

TOLUENE, TOLUOL, or METHYL BENZENE ($C_6H_5CH_3$), one of the group of hydrocarbons known as alkyl benzenes. It is formed by destructive distillation of many organic products, such as tolu balsam (hence the name), but is always obtained, together with benzene, from the first distillates of coal tar, and purified by fractional distillation. See BENZENE; TRINITROTOLUENE.

TOMAHAWK, a light war-hatchet of the North American Indians. The early ones were made of stone or of deer horn put through a handle of wood, or fastened to the handle by sinews or cords of skin. European traders supplied the Indians with hatchets of steel.

TOMATO, common name for *Lycopersicon esculentum*, a vinelike annual herb belonging to the Nightshade family, and native to the Andean regions of South America. It was formerly much cultivated for the decorative effect of its bright red fruit, which was generally thought to be poisonous; it is now known to be not only edible, but a valuable source of food minerals and vitamins. The numerous varieties vary greatly in plant form and fruit type, ranging from the small "currant" size through cherry, plum, and pear forms to the varieties, now most used in cultivation, which bear large, oblate fruits, 4 inches and more in diameter. All forms include both red- and yellow-fruited varieties.

The tomato is propagated principally from seed which, in temperate regions, is started in greenhouses, hotbeds, or coldframes, the plant being set out in the field when danger of frost is past. The plants thrive best in well-fertilized, sandy loams, but grow well on almost any type of fertile, well-drained soil. Tomatoes are cultivated in most temperate regions throughout the world. In the United States, large markets are supplied with tomatoes throughout the year, the winter crop being field grown in Florida, Texas, and California, and greenhouse grown in the North Central and New England States. In a recent year the production of tomatoes in the United States totaled about 5,470,000 tons.

TOMB, a monument erected over a grave. Some of the most remarkable rock tombs are those of Egypt. The rock tombs of Iran and Lycia have imposing architectural façades. See CATACOMBS.

The pyramids were the sepulchers of the Egyptian monarchs from the 4th to the 12th dynasty. The tombs of Greece, and of the Greek colonies in Asia Minor were sometimes pillars, or upright stone tablets, and sometimes small buildings in the form of temples; the most celebrated was the Mausoleum.

The first step which led to the burial of the dead in churches was the custom of erecting churches over the graves of martyrs. In the 13th century a species of tomb was introduced, consisting of a sarcophagus, on which rests a recumbent figure of the deceased, the whole being surmounted by a canopy. The tombs of the Scaligers at Verona with their beautiful wrought-iron railing are famous. In the Renaissance period of art the tombs became more and more complex. The most beautiful of all mausoleums is the Taj Mahal (q.v.) at Agra. See BURIAL.

TOMBAUGH, CLYDE WILLIAM (1906–), American astronomer, born in Streator, Ill., and educated at the University of Kansas. He joined the staff of the Lowell Observatory in Flagstaff, Ariz., in 1929, becoming assistant astronomer in 1938. In 1946 he was appointed astronomer of the Aberdeen Ballistics Laboratories Annex at White Sands Proving Grounds, Las Cruces, N.M. Tombaugh is best known for his discovery in 1930 of the trans-Neptunian planet Pluto, the existence of which had been predicted by Percival Lowell (q.v.). Among his other contributions to astronomy are his discovery of a new globular star cluster, six new galactic star clusters, extensive investigations of asteroids and variable stars, and studies of the surface features of the moon. In 1931 he was awarded the Jackson-Guilt Medal and Gift of the Royal Astronomical Society of England.

TOMBIGBEE RIVER, one of the chief rivers of Alabama. It rises in the northeast part of Mississippi and runs generally S.S.E., uniting with the Alabama to form the Mobile R. The length of the Tombigbee is about 450 m. and it is navigable to Aberdeen, Miss., 410 m. from Mobile Bay. Its chief tributary is the Black Warrior.

TOMBSTONE, a city of Cochise Co., Ariz., situated about 65 miles S.E. of Tucson. Transportation facilities include a railroad and a municipal airport. Tombstone is a popular health and pleasure resort, with a colorful

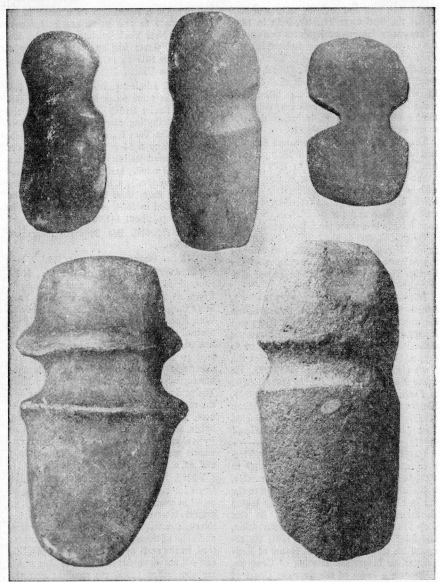

American Museum of Natural History

TOMAHAWK HEADS. *Top, left and middle: From Manhattan Island, New York. Top, right: Double-bit, from Tennessee. Bottom, left: From Tennessee. Bottom, right: From Delaware.*

history as an old mining camp. The city lies between the Dragoon and Huachuca mountains at an altitude of 4500 ft. above sea level. The climate is especially beneficial to persons suffering from respiratory diseases, and the city contains a general hospital and the Father

Aull Clinic. The principal industries in the surrounding region are cattle raising and the mining of lead and zinc; industries in the city are the manufacture of leather novelties and cement blocks. Points of interest include what is said to be the largest rose bush in the world, 9 ft. high and covering an area of 3000 sq.ft.; the Bird Cage Theater, built in 1881, where many famous entertainers performed; the old county courthouse, completed in 1882, scene of many dramatic trials in Tombstone's violent early days; the O.K. Corral, where feuding pioneers fought a gun duel in 1882 in which several men were killed and wounded; and Boot Hill Graveyard, containing about 300 graves, including those of many outlaws and lynching victims.

The site of the present town was first settled in 1877 by Edward Schieffelin, a prospector. The town was laid out in 1879 and by about 1895 was a flourishing mining center, with a population of approximately 15,000. Rising underground waters forced most of the mines to close and the population decreased considerably in a short time. Pop. (1950) 910.

TOMCOD, one of the small codfish of the genus *Microgadus,* including *M. tomcodus* of the Atlantic coast and *M. proximus* of the Pacific. They are very abundant and of considerable importance as food.

TOMLINSON, HENRY MAJOR (1873–), British journalist, essayist, and travel writer. He was a war correspondent in Belgium and France (1914–15), official correspondent at the general headquarters of the British armies in France (1915–17), and literary editor of the *Nation* and the *Athenæum* (1917–23). He wrote *The Sea and the Jungle* (1912), *Gifts of Fortune* (1926), *Essay on Hardy* (1928), *Illusion: 1915* (1928), *The Snows of Helicon* (1933), *The Day Before* (1940), *A Mingled Yarn* (1953), and *The Trumpet Shall Sound* (1957).

TOMPKINS, DANIEL D. (1774–1825), Vice-President of the United States from 1817 to 1824, born in Fox Meadows (now Scarsdale), Westchester Co., N.Y. He was admitted to the bar in New York City in 1797. Early taking an interest in political questions, he was elected to the State Constitutional Convention, and later to the Assembly of 1801. He resigned his seat in the Federal House of Representatives before the meeting of Congress, to become a judge of the Supreme Court of New York (1804), and three years later was elected Democratic governor of the State (1807), being re-elected in 1809 and in 1811. His action in preventing the establishment of the Bank of North America in succession to the United States Bank of Philadelphia caused his defeat in 1813. During the War of 1812 Governor Tompkins recruited and equipped 40,000 militia in New York State, providing funds for this raised partly on his personal

security. On a recommendation made in his last message to the legislature in January, 1817, the New York legislature passed a law setting all slaves free on and after July 4, 1827. From 1817 to 1825 he was Vice-President of the United States.

TOMSK, administrative center of the Region of the same name in the Siberian territory of Soviet Russia. The city, one of the major distributing centers of Siberia, is situated on the Tom R., a tributary of the Ob, and linked by a 54-m. branch line with the Trans-Siberian Railway. Tomsk is a Siberian educational center, and has a university (established in 1888), a museum, and a library containing more than 225,000 volumes. The city, founded in 1604, is one of the oldest in Siberia. Pop., about 141,000.

TOM THUMB. See STRATTON, CHARLES SHERWOOD.

TON. See WEIGHTS AND MEASURES.

TONAWANDA, a city of Erie Co., N.Y., situated on the Niagara R. and Tonawanda Creek, at the w. terminus of the New York State Barge Canal, and 8 miles N. of Buffalo. With North Tonawanda it forms a single industrial community. The two cities share a fine harbor and the traffic of the port ranks next to that of Buffalo in volume. Hydroelectric power is furnished the numerous manufacturing establishments by Niagara Falls. The principal industries are boatbuilding and the manufacture of beaverboard, paper products, plastics, office supplies, steel, roofing, hoists, and chains. The name of the city is an Indian word meaning "swift water". Tonawanda was incorporated as a village in 1854 and as a city in 1903. Pop. (1950) 14,617.

TONE, in music, the name given to the larger intervals (q.v.) in the diatonic scale, so called in contradistinction to the semitones, or smaller intervals. Theoretically some of the intervals called tones are larger than others, and none of them are equal to two semitones; thus, in the scale of C, the intervals CD, FG, and AB are all equal; but DE and GA, which are also called tones, are smaller; and the semitones, EF and BC, are larger than half even of the larger tones. In instruments, however, which are tuned according to the equal temperament, all the tones are made equal, and each equivalent to two semitones.

TONGA, or FRIENDLY, ISLANDS, an independent Polynesian kingdom, and protectorate of Great Britain, in the Pacific Ocean, situated about 180 miles S.E. of Fiji. It consists of some 150 islands and islets forming three main groups called respectively Tonga-tabu, Haaibai, and Vavau, and, in addition, several outlying islands. The capital is Nuku-alofa, a small seaport on the northern coast of Tongatabu Island. The islands lie generally in a long north and south chain; the Tongatabu and Haapai groups contain low-lying islands of coral formation; the Vavau group is volcanic and mountainous. Tongatabu Island, which is 20 m. long, is the largest and most fertile of the Tonga Islands and possesses about half the total population of the group. The total area of the Tonga Islands is about 250 sq.m.; pop. (1955 est.) 54,000.

The main islands are covered with luxuriant vegetation, notably palm trees. The fauna is comparatively insignificant, and includes a large, fruit-eating bat. The climate is healthful and mild. More than 75 inches of rain falls a year. Serious earthquakes occasionally occur, and small islands rise suddenly at times as a result of earthquakes and volcanic action, and as suddenly disappear. Falcon Island, which is located in the southwestern part of the group, has risen from the sea three times, the last time in October, 1927. Commercial produce consists almost entirely of copra and bananas. Citrus fruits, taro, breadfruits, and yams are grown, and fishing is carried on. Regular steamship trips are made between the islands and New Zealand. The inhabitants are almost entirely native Polynesians (q.v.), and all are Christians. Free education and medical and dental care are provided by the British.

The kingdom is governed by a native ruler and a legislative assembly, which consists of seven ministers of the Crown, seven elected representatives of the people, seven nobles elected by their own peers, and a speaker. The kingdom is under the jurisdiction of the British High Commissioner for the Western Pacific, but Tongan courts exercise complete jurisdiction over all offenses and crimes committed in the kingdom by natives and by British or foreign nationals, except crimes which are punishable by death or by imprisonment for more than two years. Crimes of the latter categories are under the jurisdiction of the High Commissioner's court.

A portion of the Tonga Islands was discovered in 1616 by two Dutch navigators; the main part of the group was first seen in 1643 by the Dutch mariner Abel Janszoon Tasman. Other explorers visited the group during the next two centuries. In 1845, the natives of the Tonga Islands were united into a kingdom by the chief George Tubou I. The islands and kingdom became a protectorate of Great Brit-ain on November 14, 1899, according to the terms of the Anglo-German Agreement of November 14, 1899 (see SAMOA: *History*).

TONGUE, a symmetrical, muscular organ in the mouth, extending from the hyoid bone upward and forward to the lips in front, and occupying the buccal cavity. The superior surface, borders, and anterior third of the inferior surface are free; elsewhere it is attached to adjacent parts by the investing mucous membrane and subjacent structures. At certain points this membrane forms distinct folds, containing fibrous or muscular tissue, which act to a certain extent as ligaments to the tongue. The most considerable of these folds is termed the *fraenum* (or bridle) of the tongue, and connects its anterior free extremity with the lower jaw. Other folds of mucous membrane pass from the base of the tongue to the epiglottis; while from the sides of the base, passing to the soft palate, are seen two folds on either side, the "pillars of the fauces". The superior surface of the tongue is divided into two symmetrical lateral parts by a median longitudinal furrow, commencing at the tip, and extending back about two thirds of the tongue's length. The muscles of the tongue are usually divided into two groups: the extrinsic muscles, which attach the tongue to certain fixed points external to it, and move it on them; and the intrinsic muscles, which pass from one part of the tongue to another, constitute its chief bulk, and move it on itself. These intrinsic muscular fibers run vertically, transversely, and longitudinally, and are so interlaced as mutually to support one another, and to act with the greatest advantage. See TASTE.

TONIKAS, or TUNICAS, a North American Indian tribe, forming a distinct linguistic stock. They are now practically extinct. Their original home was in the Louisiana-Mississippi region. They became close allies with the French, and in 1802 were found, reduced to 120, opposite Pointe Coupée, below Red River. Their language has some remarkable peculiarities, which distinguish it from that of the surrounding tribes.

TONKA BEAN, the seed of *Dipteryx odorata,* which is a large tree, of the order Leguminosae, having pinnated leaves and axillary racemes of purplish flowers. The fruit is an oblong, dry, fibrous pod, containing a single seed, which has a strong, agreeable odor, owing to the coumarin which it contains.

TONKAWA, a tribe of North American Indians constituting a distinct linguistic stock. Their original home was in s. or w. Texas.

Woman in Tonkin carrying a baby and hollow bamboo canes containing water

They were a roving tribe who built thatched houses, lived by hunting and on wild fruit, and were believed by the other tribes to be cannibals. The few survivors are located in a reservation in northern Oklahoma.

TONKIN, or TONGKING, a component part of the republic of Viet-Nam (q.v.) in the Associated States of Indochina (see INDOCHINA, ASSOCIATED STATES OF), bounded on the N. by China, on the E. by the Gulf of Tonkin, on the s. by Annam, and on the s. and w. by Laos. The capital and largest city of Tonkin is Hanoi, and its industrial center and chief port is Haiphong (qq.v.). Tonkin contains the deltas of the Thai-Binh and Red rivers, the most densely populated regions of Indochina. A heavily forested plateau in the N. and w. descends to a rolling plain, with exceedingly fertile soil. Rice is the most important crop; corn, arrowroot, tobacco, tea, and coffee are also grown, and raw silk is an important agricultural product. Mineral resources of coal, iron, zinc, tungsten, bauxite, and manganese are little exploited. Tonkin has a hot, tropical climate with heavy rainfall. The great bulk of the population is Annamese, with primitive Muongs and Thôs inhabiting some N. districts.

Tonkin was an independent state until 1802, when it came under the control of Annam. In 1882 the French government, long covetous of the delta of the Red R. for French colonial commerce, sent an expedition against the Black Flags, predatory bands of Chinese rebels living in the delta, and occupied Hanoi. A year later France compelled Annam to accept a French protectorate. As a result, France became involved in a war with China

(1884–85), which claimed suzerainty over Annam. After much severe fighting French domination was established in 1885. Area, 40,530 sq.m.; pop., about 9,930,000.

TONSIL, name applied to any of a number of masses of lymphoid tissue embedded in and forming a ring around the walls of the pharynx or throat. These masses consist of cells, similar to the lymphocytes of the blood stream, embedded in fibrous connective tissue and covered by a single layer of epithelium. The lymphoid cells are phagocytic (see PHAGOCYTE) and serve to protect the pharynx from invasion by disease-producing bacteria. When tonsils have insufficient resistance to subdue infectious organisms, they become inflamed and serve as a source of infection for the rest of the body. Such a condition, called tonsillitis, is usually caused by streptococcus infection. The tonsils most often affected are the palatine tonsils, situated on each side of the throat. Tissues surrounding the tonsils frequently form pus during or following acute attacks of tonsillitis; this condition is called quinsy. Pharyngeal tonsils, located at the back of the throat, become abnormally large when inflamed, and are then called adenoids. Acute cases of tonsillitis are often treated by injections of such antibiotics as penicillin. Chronic tonsillitis is treated by surgical removal of the palatine and often of the pharyngeal tonsils, followed by administration of antibiotics.

TONTO NATIONAL MONUMENT, a national monument in Arizona, established in 1907 to preserve the ruins of two prehistoric habitations of cliff dwellers. It is situated in the Tonto National Forest, about 3 miles S.E. of Roosevelt, and covers an area of 1120 acres. The ruins, which were inhabited about the 14th century, are constructed with adobe walls, two stories in height, and are in a good state of preservation.

TOOTHACHE TREE. See HERCULES'-CLUB.

TOOWOOMBA, a city of Queensland, Australia, situated about 100 m. by rail w. of Brisbane. The city, lying in a hilly region more than 1900 ft. above sea level, is a popular summer resort, often described as the "Garden City of Queensland". It is also a railway junction and commercial center, with an extensive trade in dairy products, wheat, fruits, timber, and coal. Among the chief manufactures are butter, cheese, beer, flour, and lumber. Pop. (1950 est.) 37,500.

TOPAZ, a mineral aluminum fluosilicate, crystallized in the orthorhombic system. It has a vitreous luster and may be colorless, yellow, green, blue, or red. Topaz occurs in gneiss or granite associated with beryl, mica, tourmaline, etc., and occasionally with apatite, cassiterite, and fluorite, and also in certain talcose rocks, mica slate, rhyolite, and in alluvial deposits and drift. The crystallized varieties, owing to their hardness, are valued as gems, and the best of these come from Ceylon and other parts of India, the Urals, Minas Gerais, Brazil, and in the United States from various localities in Maine, Colorado, and Utah. The most popular color for topaz gem stones is a rich orange yellow somewhat resembling the color of sherry wine. Rose topaz is a delicate rose pink in color. It is the birthstone for November. The true Oriental topaz is the yellow sapphire, and the Saxon, Scottish, Spanish, smoky, and false topaz are yellow varieties of quartz. See GEM.

TOPE, common name applied to a small shark, *Galeus canis,* found chiefly around the southern coasts of Great Britain. The fish attains a length of about 6 ft.; its coloring is dark gray above, white below. A score or more young are born viviparously at a birth. In France and Italy the tope is eaten fresh or after drying; the liver is used for oil.

TOPE, a Buddhist tumulus for the preservation of relics, of more or less sold masonry, in which the relics were deposited. The chief one of a great group at Sanchi, near Bhilsa, in central India, is 42 ft. high and 106 ft. in diameter. In Ceylon they are called dagobas. Some topes are rock-cut.

TOPEKA, capital of Kansas and county seat of Shawnee Co., situated on both banks of the Kansas R., 70 miles w. of Kansas City. It is served by four railroads, and maintains a municipal airport. Among the industrial establishments in the city are large railroad repair shops; extensive printing and publishing plants; foundries; meat-packing, food-processing, poultry, and egg-packing plants; creameries; flour mills; and factories producing tires, rubber products, iron, steel office equipment, and other steel products. Topeka is an insurance center; it is the site of the home offices of five large insurance companies.

Educational and cultural facilities of Topeka include Washburn Municipal University, founded in 1865 and made a municipal university in 1941; Kansas Vocation School for Negroes; the Mulvane Art Museum, on the University campus, which contains collections of American painting and sculpture; the collection of the Topeka Art Guild; and the museum of the Kansas State Historical Society. The principal public build-

British Information Services

A tope in Sarnath, near Benares, India

ings are the State capitol, constructed between 1866 and 1903 and modeled on the Federal capitol in Washington, D.C.; and the Kansas Memorial Building, which contains the collections of several patriotic and historical societies. Topeka is the site of the State Industrial School for Boys, the State Printing Plant, the State hospital for the mentally ill, a U.S. veterans hospital, and the annual Kansas Free Fair. The municipal park system totals more than twenty parks, including Gage Park, containing the Reinisch Memorial Rose and Rock Gardens, which are among the most beautiful gardens in the U.S. Recreational facilities in the parks include tennis courts and swimming pools.

The site of the present city was settled between 1852 and 1854, near the dividing point of the old Santa Fe and Oregon trails. For several years Topeka was a center of conflict in Kansas between the proslavery and antislavery factions. It was chartered as a city in 1857, became the temporary Territorial capital in 1859, and was made the permanent State capital in 1861, following the admission of Kansas into the Union. Pop. (1950) 78,791.

TORAH, or THORAH, Hebrew term technically applied to the Pentateuch (q.v.). Be-

sides the term Torah there is also used *Tōrath Mōshe,* i.e., Law of Moses, on the basis of the tradition which ascribes the whole Pentateuch (the historical as well as the legal portions) to Moses. Traces of the original sense of Torah as oracle are to be found in various passages of the Old Testament.

TORNADO (Lat. *tonare,* "to turn"), in meteorology, a violent, whirling wind, characteristically accompanied by a funnel-shaped cloud, which moves frequently for many miles in a narrow path over land. The rapidity of the wind's motion in a tornado is too great to be measured and its impact is often sufficiently strong to destroy and lift otherwise permanent, heavy structures. Tornados occur throughout the land areas of the world but are particularly common in the central Mississippi Valley of the United States. The term is sometimes restricted to squalls off the west coast of Africa in which a swiftly revolving wind moves beneath an arch of dark clouds similar to those usually preceding a thunderstorm.

TORONTO, capital of the province of Ontario and second-largest city in population in Canada, situated on the N. shore of Lake Ontario, 313 miles W.S.W. of Montreal and 60 miles N.W. of Buffalo, N.Y. Toronto is built on a plateau rising from the N. shore of an inlet, Toronto Bay, and has a water frontage of about 10 m. The port, considered one of the finest on the Great Lakes, accommodates the largest vessels that pass through the Welland Canal. The Humber R. forms the w. limit of the city and the Don R. flows through the E. portion. Of the many notable buildings of Toronto, the best known are in Queen's Park near the center of the city, and include the provincial parliament buildings, of red sandstone and blue dolomite, and the buildings of the University of Toronto (see TORONTO, UNIVERSITY OF). Other buildings include the City Hall, with a 300-ft. clock tower; the Canadian Bank of Commerce, one of the highest buildings in the British Commonwealth; Casa Loma, an ornate mansion on the crest of a hill; and Government House, in Rosedale, residence of the provincial lieutenant governor. Toronto, a notable music center, contains the Hambourg Conservatory and the Toronto Conservatory of Music, and is the home of the Mendelssohn Choir and the Toronto Symphony Orchestra. Its museums and collections include the John Ross Robertson Historical Collection, the Art Museum of Toledo, and the Royal Ontario Museum, con-

taining historical and geological relics. The medical facilities of the city include ten public hospitals, the largest being the $2,000,000 General Hospital. The city has sixty-nine parks and playgrounds with a total area of 2065 acres. The largest are High Park (354 acres), Island Park (371 acres), Exhibition Park (216 acres), Humber Boulevard (129 acres), and Riverdale (109 acres). Exhibition Park is the site of the Canadian National Exhibition, which has been held annually since 1878, except for the war years 1942–46 inclusive, when the buildings were used to house army troops and installations.

Toronto is a leading distribution, commercial, financial, and industrial center of the Dominion. The port receives freighters with grain from w. Canada, and supplies them with manufactures for N.W. regions. The two Canadian transcontinental railroads, the Canadian Pacific and Canadian National, originate in Toronto yards. The city contains a large mining exchange and possesses five of the ten chartered banks of Canada. Electric power is supplied by Niagara Falls dynamos, and the city is close to sources of raw materials. Industrial establishments in Toronto include iron and steel foundries, and factories producing electrical apparatus and supplies, packed

Nat. Film Bd.

Casa Loma, a mansion in Toronto, Canada

meats and meat products, biscuits, confectionery, machinery, lumber, wallpaper, stationery, clothing, pianos, bicycles, carpets, brewery and distillery products, stoves, iron rails, and drugs. The city also contains large shipyards, is the principal Canadian center for the rubber, publishing, lithographing, and farm-implement industries, and is the leading Canadian wholesale center for dry goods, leather, shoes, hardware, groceries, and fruits.

The site of the city was long a meeting place for Indians, who called it *Toronto,* meaning "a place of meeting". In 1749 a French fort, Fort Rouillé, was built there for the Indian trade. In 1759, during the French and Indian War, the fort was destroyed by the French garrison in order to prevent its occupation by the British. The present city was founded in 1794 as York, the capital of Upper Canada (see CANADA: *History*). It was occupied and burned by American troops in 1813 during the War of 1812. In 1834 the provincial legislature granted a charter of incorporation, creating a city which took the Indian name of Toronto. Pop. (1951) 1,117,470.

TORONTO, UNIVERSITY OF, an institution of higher education in Toronto, Canada, established in 1827. It has an annual average enrollment, apart from that in affiliated colleges and extension courses, of 12,000 students. There are nine faculties: arts (including sciences and commerce), medicine, applied science and engineering, household science, education (Ontario College of Education), forestry, music, school of graduate studies, and dentistry. There are four arts colleges: University College, Victoria College, Trinity College, and St. Michael's College. In addition, there are several schools: School of Hygiene, School of Nursing, School of Physical and Health Education, School of Social Work, Library School, and School of Law. There are three federated theological colleges: Knox College, Wycliffe College and Emmanuel College. Affiliated with the University of Toronto are the Ontario Agricultural College, Ontario Veterinary College, Ontario College of Pharmacy, and Ontario College of Art. In conjunction with the government of Ontario, the university controls the Royal Ontario Museum.

TORP, OSCAR (1893–), Norwegian political leader, born in Skjeberg, Östfold, and educated as an electrician. He joined the trade-union movement in his youth, and in 1918 he was elected to the executive committee of the Norwegian Labor Party. In 1923 he became the party's chairman, a post he held until 1940. When, in 1934, the Labor Party assumed power, he was appointed deputy minister of defense. Torp remained in the government until November, 1947, serving successively as minister of social affairs, finance, defense, and supply and reconstruction. After leaving the last-named post he headed the Labor Party caucus in the parliament until November, 1951, when he succeeded Einar Gerhardsen (1897–) as prime minister. Torp resigned in January, 1955, and Gerhardsen again became prime minister.

TORPEDO, self-propelled underwater weapon carrying a high-explosive charge and launched from a surface vessel or submarine (q.v.) or from a low-flying aircraft. Formerly the term "torpedo" was applied to any underwater weapon designed to destroy a ship by blowing a hole in the hull below the water line. In current usage the term is restricted to the self-propelled device; weapons set adrift or moored at a particular site undersea presently are called submarine mines; see MINES, SUBMARINE.

At the beginning of the 19th century the American inventor Robert Fulton demonstrated for the first time that a ship could be sunk by exploding a large gunpowder charge underwater against the hull. Crude devices called spar torpedoes were used effectively during the American Civil War against ships at anchor. The spar torpedo consisted of a charge of gun-cotton attached to the end of a long pole projecting from the bow of a small boat. The charge was submerged to a depth of about 10 ft., driven against the hull of the enemy ship, and exploded by electricity.

The first practical, self-propelled torpedo was invented in 1866 by the English engineer Robert Whitehead (1823–1905). It had a cylindrical steel casing and was driven by a reciprocating compressed-air engine providing a speed of 7 knots. The depth of operation was regulated by rudders controlled by hydrostatic pressure, but there was no mechanism for keeping the torpedo on a straight course toward its target. In 1896 the gyroscope (q.v.) was added to the Whitehead torpedo for horizontal steering, and with other, later improvements this type of torpedo became a highly accurate and deadly weapon.

A variation of the Whitehead type, called the Bliss-Leavitt torpedo, was adopted by the U.S. Navy about 1908. Though similar to the Whitehead in many respects, the Bliss-Leavitt type contained two important innovations, namely a method of preheating the compressed air with burning alcohol and a turbine (q.v.) in place of the reciprocating engine.

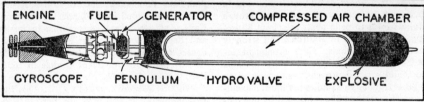

ENGINE FUEL GENERATOR COMPRESSED AIR CHAMBER

GYROSCOPE PENDULUM HYDRO VALVE EXPLOSIVE

Acme; Mechanix Illustrated

Top: A torpedo seen at the moment of launching from the deck of a destroyer. Bottom: a cut-away drawing showing parts of a torpedo.

These innovations greatly increased the speed and the range of the torpedo.

The typical Bliss-Leavitt torpedo consists of a cylindrical steel casing divided into several chambers which house the operating and storage units. In the nose of the torpedo is the warhead, containing several hundred pounds of high explosives (q.v.). The central section contains the air flask, charged with compressed air at pressures up to 3000 lbs. per square inch. In the third section, known as the afterbody, are the fuel tank, combustion chamber, turbines, and steering controls. The tail section carries two contrarotating propellers, horizontal vanes, and vertical rudders. The

torpedo has an average effective range of more than 4000 yards at a speed of 45 knots. At lower speeds its effective range is longer. The main disadvantage of the Bliss-Leavitt type of torpedo is that it leaves a trail of bubbles on the surface of the sea, and this wake serves to warn target ships of its approach and indicates the position of the submarine that launched the torpedo.

During World War II the Germans developed the electric torpedo, which leaves no visible trace of its path through the water. In this type storage batteries are carried in the central section to provide power for electric motors in the afterbody. Because of the comparatively heavy weight of the batteries, the electric torpedo has a shorter effective range than the Bliss-Leavitt torpedo traveling at the same speed.

Another innovation developed by the Germans in World War II was a guiding mechanism which steers the torpedo automatically to its target. Torpedoes equipped with such a mechanism are called acoustic torpedoes, as the device operates in response to the sound of the target ship's propellers.

A torpedo may be fired from the tubes of submarines, patrol torpedo craft (see TORPEDO BOATS, MOTOR), and destroyers, or dropped horizontally by aircraft flying at low altitudes.

TORPEDO, or ELECTRIC RAY, a ray of the family Narcobatidae, which inhabits warm seas and often is of large size. These rays have a broad, flat body with a comparatively slender tail and are of interest because of the electrical powers which they possess. (See ELECTRIC FISH.) There are about fifteen species, of which the best known is *Torpedo marmoratus* of southern Europe. A similar species, the crampfish or numbfish, *T. occidentalis,* occurs on the Atlantic coast of the United States and is said to attain a weight of 200 pounds. See RAY.

TORPEDO BOATS, MOTOR (abbr. MTB), also known as PATROL TORPEDO CRAFT (PT) or MOSQUITO BOATS, small vessels whose main offensive armament is a torpedo shot through a tube. Motor torpedo boats are about 80 feet long, displacing up to 300 tons, and strongly resembling speedboats. Their armament includes four torpedoes, two 50-caliber machine guns, and often depth charges. Speed of an MTB is from 50 to 85 miles per hour, depending on the weather. She is manned by one officer and eight men.

For defense and protection, MTB's rely upon their speed and great maneuverability. Although built sturdily to stand the poundings of high waves at terrific speeds, they have no protective armor.

MTB's are used for routine patrol, piloting, daring duels with regular ships of the line, rescue, and even strafing. Under attack by planes, they can zigzag and run, and have proven their ability to down aircraft. They carry depth charges and are an indispensable part of antisubmarine patrol.

The first known boat of torpedo design was built for the British Navy in 1875, especially for torpedo attack. Long before 1900 the torpedo boat had become an important part of the navies of the world, together with coun-

terweapons, such as the quick-fire gun and the torpedo-boat destroyer. The latter soon drove the old type T-boat out of existence, but remained itself to evolve into the modern destroyer. It was the invention and development of the internal-combustion engine which revived interest in torpedo boats. The Italians developed the forerunner of the modern torpedo boats, calling it the MAS, which scored successes against the Austrians in World War I. The British developed their own ML's and the German counterpart were the PMB's. It was not until war had actually broken out in Europe in 1939 that the first American motor torpedo boats made trial runs after General Douglas MacArthur had advocated a new type of motor torpedo boat to bolster the defenses of the Philippines in 1937. By 1939, both England and Italy were already using small caliber boats.

Torpedo Planes, known as VT's and also used as horizontal bombers, are armed with torpedoes very much like those employed by surface craft. The big planes must gain favorable positions to release their torpedoes and depend upon their speed and smoke screens not to disclose their whereabouts until within striking distance of their intended victims.

TORQUAY, a fashionable health resort of South Devon, on the N. side of Tor Bay, 23 miles s. of Exeter and 220 miles s.w. of London. Some remains exist of Tor Abbey. Kent's Cavern, discovered in 1824, and the Brixham Cave, discovered in 1858, are rich in fossils and have supplied the earliest English evidences of prehistoric man. Torquay was the landing place of William of Orange in 1688. Pop. (1951 prelim.) 53,216.

TORQUEMADA, TOMÁS DE (1420–98), the first inquisitor general of Spain, born in Valladolid. When prior of a Dominican monastery at Segovia, he persuaded Ferdinand and Isabella to crave from the pope the appointment of the "Holy Office" of the Inquisition. Torquemada in 1483 was named grand inquisitor for Castile and Aragon. He has been accused of wanton cruelty on the evidence of his own code of procedure and on the evidence of the historians Juan de Mariana and Juan Antonio Llorente. Llorente was general secretary of the Inquisition (q.v.) and made a careful study of its archives.

TORRANCE, a city of Los Angeles Co., Calif., situated about 15 miles s. of the center of Los Angeles and about 4 miles E. of Redondo Beach. The city is served by two railways and is an industrial center, with railway repair shops, oil wells, and plants engaged in the manufacture of petroleum products, steel, oil-well equipment, brick and tile, and rubber products. Founded in 1911 by Jared Sydney Torrance, a financier and native of Pasadena, the city was developed in accordance with modern principles of municipal planning, notably the separation of industrial and residential districts. Pop. (1950) 22,241.

TORRENCE, (FREDERIC) RIDGELY (1875–1950), American poet, born in Xenia, Ohio. He held editorial positions with *Cosmopolitan* (1905–07) and *The New Republic* (1920–34). He was a member of the faculty at Miami University in 1920–21 and joined the university again in 1941. His work includes *The House of a Hundred Lights* (1900); *El Dorado: A Tragedy* (1903); *Abelard and Eloise* (1907), a poetic drama; *Rituals for the Events of Life* (1910); *Plays for a Negro Theater* (1925); *Poems* (1941); and *Story of John Hope* (1948).

TORRENS SYSTEM, in the law of real property in England and the United States, a system of registration of title to real property. The system was first introduced in Australia by Sir Robert Richard Torrens in 1857 and subsequently adopted in England, New Zealand, parts of Canada, and in several States of the United States, including Massachusetts, Illinois, California, and Minnesota. The purpose of the Torrens System is to avoid the need for and the expense of an examination of the title of the seller of property every time a conveyance is made; it is a substitute for the system of registering deeds or the instruments of title required under recording acts.

The principal characteristics of the system are as follows. (1) Registration of title must be made by the owner of property in the office of the registrar. Before title can be registered an investigation of the owner's documents of title is made by the registrar; a certificate of ownership is given the registrant and his documents of title are filed in the registrar's office. (2) Provision is made for special proceedings to establish the validity of title, if such should be necessary, before a certificate of ownership is issued. (3) Transfer of title to registered land is made by entry on the register, and the certificate of title is given to the new owner. (4) The holder of a land title certificate is guaranteed a perfect title. An indemnity fund is provided to compensate for any loss suffered by a purchaser of land as a result of an error in the title certificate issued by the registrar.

TORREÓN, a city of Coahuila State, Mexico, situated about 250 miles S.E. of Chihuahua. The city, which is served by a railway, lies in a rich agrarian region especially noted for the production of cotton, and ranks among the chief industrial cities of northern Mexico. Among the manufacturing establishments in Torreón are flour mills, textile plants, iron foundries, a brewery, and a rubber factory. The city was founded in 1893. Pop. (1950) 132,101.

TORRES STRAIT, a channel that lies between the northernmost part of Australia and the south of New Guinea. The channel is from 80 to 90 m. in width, and its navigation, though practicable, is dangerous. It was discovered in 1606 by Luis Vaez de Torres, a Spanish navigator.

TORREY, JOHN (1796–1873), American botanist and chemist, born in New York City, and educated at the New York College of Physicians and Surgeons. He practiced medicine in New York City from 1818 to 1824, when he became professor of chemistry and mineralogy at the U.S. Military Academy at West Point. From 1827 to 1855 he served as professor of chemistry at the New York College of Physicians and Surgeons, and from 1830 to 1854 was also professor of chemistry and natural history at Princeton University. From 1854 until his death he was chief assayer in the New York Assay Office, New York City. In 1843, while serving as botanist of the New York Geological Survey, he made extensive investigations of the flora of New York State. Torrey is best known for his studies of the vegetation of North America. He collaborated with Asa Gray (q.v.) in the preparation of *Flora of North America,* published from 1838 to 1843. He served as president of the American Association for the Advancement of Science in 1855, and eight years later was designated by the U.S. Congress as a charter member of the National Academy of Sciences. His writings include *Flora of the Northern and Middle States* (1824) and *Flora of the State of New York* (1843).

TORREYA, a genus of conifers belonging to the Taxineae, or yew tribe, and comprising four species of remarkable distribution. All of the species are local, but occur in restricted localities in Florida and California in the United States, Japan, and China. The California species known as California nutmeg is the largest, reaching a height of 70 feet and occasionally 100 feet.

TORRICELLI, EVANGELISTA (1608–47), Italian mathematician and physicist, born in Faenza, and educated at the Collegio di Sapienza. He served as secretary to the Italian astronomer and physicist Galileo from 1641 until the latter's death in 1642; he was then appointed to the chair of philosophy and mathematics at Florentine Academy and became mathematician in the court of the grand duke of Tuscany. Torricelli is best known for his discovery of the physical principles upon which the barometer (q.v.) is based, and in 1643 devised the earliest known form of the instrument. Since that time the space between the top of the mercury column in a barometer and the top of the barometric tube has been known as a *Torricellian vacuum*; for many years the instrument itself was known only as the *Torricellian tube*. He was also one of the first to construct a simple microscope and made numerous improvements in the construction of the telescope. In pure mathematics, he is best known for his work on the properties of the cycloid. He was the author of *Trattato del Moto* (1641).

TORRINGTON, a city of Litchfield Co., Conn., situated on the Naugatuck R., 25 miles w. of Hartford. Torrington is a manufacturing center, surrounded by a fertile agricultural area and lying in the foothills of the scenic Berkshire Hills. In the vicinity are five lakes. The city has been noted for the manufacture of brass since 1834, when the first brass kettles made by machinery in the U.S. were manufactured there. In addition to brass goods, the principal industries are the manufacture of steel knitting needles, machine tools, gaskets, heavy industrial machinery, sporting goods, and uniform cloth. Places of interest include the Turner Museum, containing collections of manuscripts, rugs, firearms, glass, china, jewelry, and lace. Torrington was the birthplace of John Brown, the famous Abolitionist. It was founded and incorporated as a town in 1740, incorporated as a borough in 1887, and chartered as a city in 1923. Pop. (1950) 27,820.

TORSION, the strain produced in a bar or wire when one end is kept fixed and the other rotated about the axis. The torsion is measured by the inclination of the diameter of any section to the diameter originally parallel to it of the section at unit distance. The moment of the forces which produce the torsion is called the torsional stress or *torque,* and the coefficient of torsion is the ratio of the stress to the strain. For wires and bars of circular section the coefficient of torsion varies as the fourth power of the radius.

TORSION BALANCE, an instrument for measuring very minute forces by measuring the angle through which an arm turns before the resisting force of torsion brings it to rest. It was originally designed by the Reverend John Mitchell and, after his death, improved by Henry Cavendish, who used it in performing the well-known Cavendish experiment of determining the mass of the earth. The apparatus was reinvented by Coulomb and is often known by his name, having been used by him to study electrical and magnetic attractions. It consists of a horizontal rod suspended by a fine wire or, in more recent experiments, a fiber of quartz, and carrying at each end two small spheres having a mass equivalent to one gram. Adjacent to, but on opposite sides of, these small masses are two large spheres of lead, which attract the two smaller masses and cause the horizontal rod to deflect, the movement being observed by a mirror and telescope and scale, as in the case of the reflecting galvanometer. The force of attraction between two different masses can thus be ascertained and, as the attraction of the earth for a unit mass, as well as its radius, is known, we can thus determine the mass of the earth. In electricity, charged conductors were substituted for the masses, and to study the strength and action of magnetic poles a long, thin magnet was suspended and a similar magnet placed in a vertical position near one of its poles. The amount of force exerted was ascertained by finding the angle through which it was necessary to turn the head carrying the wire in order to keep the suspended bar at its original position. The Cavendish experiment enables the physicist to compute the mass of the earth and to determine also its mean density, which according to Boys is 5.5268.

TORT, in law in England and the United States, a wrongful act involving a breach of a legal duty imposed by the state and which results in injuries to another for which the injured party may institute a civil action for damages. A tort differs from a crime in that a tort is an offense against an individual, whereas a crime is an offense against the state, for which the state inflicts punishment. A tort differs from a breach of contract in that the legal duty breached by the tort is one imposed by the state, whereas in the case of breach of contract, the obligation breached is one which the contracting parties have voluntarily assumed. The same act may be both a tort and a crime, as assault (q.v.) and nuisance; each is a tort because it is an offense against an individual, and a crime because it is an offense against society. Torts may also arise out of

Australian News & Information Bureau

TORTOISES AND TURTLES. *Left: Australian aborigines pulling a large turtle, captured near Darwin, Australia, aboard their canoe. Right, top: Young Brazilian painted tortoises. Right, bottom: Young spiny tortoise of Borneo.*

contractual relations, as the inducing of an individual by fraudulent representations (see FRAUD) to purchase merchandise. An act may be simultaneously a breach of contract, a tort, and a crime; for example, the misappropriation of funds by a trustee is a breach of the contract of trust, the tort of conversion, and the crime of embezzlement.

TORTOISES AND TURTLES, a well-defined order of reptiles (q.v.), distinguished especially by the dorsal and ventral shields which protect the body. Although terrestrial Chelonians are often called tortoises, and aquatic Chelonians turtles, the distinction cannot be sustained. The dorsal shield or carapace, within shelter of which the head, limbs, and tail can be more or less completely sheltered, is formed (a) along the middle line by the vertebrae whose neural spines are flattened, (b) by expansions of the parts which in other animals form well-defined ribs, and (c) along the edge by marginal plates ossified in the

under skin or dermis. The dorsal vertebrae and ribs are thus rigidly involved in the carapace; the neck and the tail are the only flexible parts. The ventral shield or plastron consists of nine bony pieces, one anterior and four on each side. They arise as membrane bones in the dermis. Overlapping, but not corresponding to, the bones of the shields are horny epidermic plates of "tortoise shell", which, although hard, are not without sensitiveness, numerous nerves ending upon them.

The bones of the skull are immovably united together; there are no teeth, although in an embryonic turtle (Trionyx) traces of them have been detected. There is no breastbone, and, according to most authorities, there are no clavicles. The heart, as in other reptiles except crocodiles, is anatomically three-chambered, but the presence of an incomplete partition in the ventricle makes it work almost as if it had four chambers.

The Chelonians can be subdivided into

two groups: (a) Athecata, where the carapace is flexible and represented by only one species, the leather turtle, common in tropical seas; and (b) the Testudiana, in which the carapace is rigid. The Greek tortoise, *Testudo graeca,* is a land tortoise. To this group belong all the ordinary turtles, including the green turtle and the hawksbill turtle. The hawksbill turtle, *Caretta* or *Eretmochelys imbricata,* is a ferocious carnivorous form occurring along the coasts of the United States. In fresh water in the United States occur the snapping turtle, *Chelydra serpentina,* and its southern ally, the alligator turtle, *Macroclemmys temmincki,* both powerful and vicious forms.

TORTOISE-SHELL BUTTERFLY, any one of the butterflies of four or five common American genera. They are usually of medium size and have the wings on the upper side of some shade of black or brown marked with red, yellow, or orange. The commonest species in the eastern United States are the following. *Aglais (Euvanessa) antiopa* is called the mourning cloak and in England is known as the Camberwell beauty. *Aglais milberti* is common in the northern United States and Canada. Its caterpillars feed upon the nettle plants of the genus *Urtica. Eugonia californica* is confined to California and in the larval stage feeds upon *Ceanothus. Aglais j-album,* the Compton tortoise, is a northern species whose larvae feed upon willows.

TORTOLA, an island of the West Indian group. See VIRGIN ISLANDS, BRITISH.

TORTUGA or **TORTUE,** an uninhabited island off the north coast of Haiti, West Indies. Its surface is broken. It was formerly occupied by buccaneers and produced sugar and tobacco. Area, about 80 sq.m.

TORTUGAS, a group of islands off the coast of Florida. See DRY TORTUGAS.

TORTURE (Lat. *tortura,* "a twisting", "torture"), in law, the infliction of severe bodily pain either as punishment or for the purpose of compelling the person tortured to give evidence in judicial proceedings or to confess a crime. Among primitive and savage peoples torture has been used as a means of ordeal (q.v.) and as a means of punishing captured enemies. Examination by torture, often called "the question", has been used in many countries as a judicial instrument. Such examination involved the use of instruments of torture to extort evidence from unwilling witnesses. In ancient Athens slaves were always examined by torture, and their evidence seems on this account to have been deemed more valuable than that of freemen. No free Athen-

ian could be examined by torture, but torture seems occasionally to have been used in executing criminals. Under the Roman Republic only slaves could be legally tortured, and as a general rule, they could not be tortured to establish their master's guilt. Under the Empire, however, torture, besides being much used in examining slaves, was by order of the Emperor frequently inflicted even on freemen, to extract evidence of the crime of *læsa majestas.* Cicero and other enlightened Romans condemned its use. Until the 13th century torture seems to have been unknown to the canon law; about that period the Roman treason law began to be adapted to heresy as *crimen læsæ majestatis Divinæ.* A decree of Pope Innocent IV issued in 1282, calling on civil magistrates to put persons accused of heresy to the torture to elicit confessions against themselves and others, was probably the earliest instance of ecclesiastical sanction being extended to this mode of examination. Gradually the ecclesiastical courts developed from the Roman law and applied a system of torture which reached its culmination in the atrocities of the Inquisition (q.v.).

The influence of the Church during the Middle Ages undoubtedly contributed to the adoption of torture by the civil tribunals. It was early adopted by the Italian municipalities, but its introduction into western Europe as an instrument of judicial inquisition as distinguished from the ordeal or compurgation was slow. It first appeared in France in the latter part of the 13th century and in Germany in the 15th century and ultimately became part of the legal system of every European nation except Sweden and England. The use of torture never became a part of the common law of England, although its use by exercise of the royal prerogative was lawful both in state trials and in the case of ordinary crimes. The first instance we have of its use is in 1310, in aid of the ecclesiastical law, during the struggle between Pope Clement V and the Templars. Edward II, when asked to sanction the infliction of torture by the Inquisitors in the case of certain Templars accused of heresy and apostasy, at first refused; but on a remonstrance by Clement he referred the matter to the Council. On the recommendation of the Council the Inquisitors were authorized to put the accused to the torture, but without mutilation or serious injury to the person, or effusion of the blood. During the Tudor period the Council frequently assumed the power of directing torture warrants to the lieutenant of the Tower and other officers both against state prisoners and those accused of other serious crimes; and similar warrants were at times issued under the royal signature. Under James I and Charles I torture was less resorted to and only in state trials. The last recorded instance of the use of torture in England was in the reign of Charles I (1640) to compel a confession of treason. The use of torture was never legal in the English colonies and the few instances of torture in the American colonies were properly forms of execution, or the infliction of *peine forte et dure* as a means of compelling the defendant to plead guilty or not guilty to an indictment.

Even during the period when the use of torture was most prevalent its cruelty was recognized and its employment deplored as an evil necessary to the due administration of justice. In all ages there have been leading writers and thinkers who denounced the use of torture, not only because of its cruelty and its debasing effect upon public morals, but because of its unreliability as a means of discovering the truth, since it often led the innocent from weakness and exhaustion to plead guilty or accuse others of crimes which had not been committed. The horrors of the Inquisition and the excessive use of judicial torture from the fourteenth to the sixteenth century led to a gradual but nevertheless progressive change of public sentiment, which ultimately caused its disuse in all the countries of Europe. Legal torture was abolished in Prussia, Saxony, Austria, and Switzerland by the middle of the eighteenth century. Its use in Russia was limited by command of Catherine II in 1762 and finally abolished in 1801. In France it was abolished in 1789 (although temporarily restored by the Bourbons in 1814), in Württemberg in 1806, in Bavaria in 1807, in Hanover in 1822, and in Baden in 1831.

TORY (Ir. *toiridhe,* "a pursuer"), a name first given to certain bands of outlaws, half robber, half insurgent, who professed the Roman Catholic faith, and harassed the English in Ireland. About 1679, the time of the Popish Plot, it began to be applied as a term of reproach to the Cavalier or Court Party, as supposed abettors of that trumped-up conspiracy. The nickname was soon adopted by one of the two great political parties in Great Britain. During the Revolutionary War the British loyalists were called Tories.

TOSCANINI, ARTURO (1867-1957), Italian orchestral conductor, born in Parma. He received his education at the Conservatory of Parma, studying piano, cello, and composition. Having made his debut as operatic conductor in Turin, he was engaged for the Dal Verme in Milan. There his brilliant work attracted such general attention that Gatti-Casazza, who assumed the directorship of La Scala in 1895, secured his services.

From 1908 to 1915 he was principal conductor at the Metropolitan Opera House in New York City.

During World War I he conducted innumerable concerts throughout Italy for the benefit of various war activities. In 1918 he gave in Milan a series of twelve symphony concerts, the entire proceeds of which he distributed among Italian musicians who had been reduced to want by the war. After La Scala, in Milan, had been rebuilt and enlarged, he was made sole artistic director in 1921.

Among the world premières given there, two stand forth as musical events of international importance, the production of Boito's *Nerone* (May 1, 1924) and Puccini's *Turandot* (April 25, 1926). During the spring of 1929, he took the entire La Scala company on a tour to Vienna and Berlin, arousing unbounded enthusiasm in both cities. He announced unexpectedly after the final Berlin performance (*Aïda,* May 29) that on that occasion he had made his farewell appearance as an operatic conductor, as he had severed his connection with La Scala in order to devote his entire time to concerts. At the same time, however, he accepted the invitation of Siegfried Wagner to conduct the performances of *Tristan und Isolde* in Bayreuth during the festival of 1930. It was the first time that this honor was conferred upon a foreign conductor.

Supreme as Toscanini stood as an operatic conductor, he was equally great as a symphonic conductor. He directed without score a repertory of almost 100 operas of all nationalities and schools and, in addition, an extensive concert repertory. Even during rehearsals he conducted by memory. His first appearance in concert in the United States occurred during his engagement at the Metropolitan Opera House on April 13, 1913, when he produced Beethoven's *Ninth Symphony.* In 1921 he made a concert tour of the U.S. with his entire La Scala Orchestra.

Toscanini was conductor of the New York Philharmonic Symphony Orchestra from 1926 to 1933, and general music director from 1933 to 1936. In 1937 he became organizer and conductor of the National Broadcasting Com-

NBC Photo

Arturo Toscanini

pany Symphony Orchestra. The world-famous conductor resigned from this post on April 4, 1954.

TOTALITARIANISM, a modern form of dictatorship. It differs from all other forms of tyrannical government in three essential respects which constitute the negation and antithesis of democracy (q.v.). The control exercised by totalitarian governments is absolute and total, that is, it extends to all phases of societal existence; that control is exercised in behalf of an elite ruling group through a mass political party which is identified in law with the state and which is invested with a monopoly of political organization and activity; and the individual, in law and in fact, is completely subordinated to the state. Because the totalitarian, or, as it is frequently called, the state party, is a mass party, totalitarian dictatorships sedulously cultivate the appearance of popular sanction of their actions and policies. Among other distinguishing features of totalitarianism are the regulation by the state of all economic processes; abolition of civil rights and individual liberty, and, with the exception of the elite ruling group, the regimentation and terrorization of the entire population in the interest of the state; and, in a number of states, the institution of systematic slave labor as an integral part of the economy.

Historically, totalitarianism is a relatively new phenomenon, which made its first appearance in Europe between World Wars I and II. Its principal embodiments before World War II were of two types: the fascist governments of Italy, Germany, and Spain; and the government of the Soviet Union. The fascist dictatorships of Germany and Italy were destroyed at the end of the war. That of Spain survived, and the totalitarian state of the Soviet type was extended after the war to the Soviet satellite states in eastern and central Europe. The communist conquest of China in 1948–50 resulted in the creation of the first totalitarian dictatorship in Asia.

Because totalitarianism is a relatively new historical phenomenon, is still in process of development, and is, moreover, one of the most controversial of contemporary subjects, sufficient time has not elapsed for historians and social scientists to acquire the necessary knowledge and historical perspective to formulate a definitive theory of its origin, structure, and functions. An important problem in this connection is the determination of the economic and social origins of totalitarianism. The problem arises principally from the existence of the two types of totalitarian state described above; under the short-lived fascist dictatorship of Nazi Germany, the national economy continued to be based on capitalist private property but was closely integrated with, and strictly regulated by, the state; under the continuing dictatorship in the Soviet Union, the means of production and distribution of wealth are national property. During the existence of the Nazi regime, some scholars posited a simultaneous development of German and Russian society in the direction of a new authoritarian form of state. Others professed to see in totalitarianism in Germany and the Soviet Union different forms of state socialism. A number of political analysts hold that socialism, because it is based on collective ownership of the means of production and distribution, must lead inevitably to totalitarianism. Others believe that totalitarianism and socialism, which postulates a society free of the economic exploitation and coercion of man by man, are mutually exclusive and irreconcilably antagonistic. In the most widespread view, the fascist and Soviet types of totalitarian state are held to be basically identical and the differences between them are regarded as of minor importance. For a detailed description of the totalitarian state under fascism, see FASCISM; NATIONAL So-

Canadian National Railways; Museum of the American Indian

Top, left: Figure of a beaver on a totem pole of a British Columbian tribe, symbolizing a totemic relationship between beavers and people of the tribe. Top, right: Dog totem in British Columbia. Bottom: Tlingit chief's house and totem pole in Alaska.

CIALISM; SPAIN: *Government*. For a detailed description of the totalitarian state of the Soviet type, see UNION OF SOVIET SOCIALIST REPUBLICS. See also GOVERNMENT; STATE; LIBERTY; RIGHTS, CIVIL.

TOTEM, a natural object, not an individual, but one of a class, taken by a tribe, a family, or a single person, and treated with superstitious respect as an outward symbol of an existing intimate unseen relation.

TOTEMISM. The wide distribution of totemism among the nations of the Old World, civilized as well as savage, and its significance as at once a religious and a social system, was first pointed out by J.F. M'Lennan about 1868. In North America totemic complexes are represented, roughly speaking, in five areas: the Pacific Northwest, the Southwest, the Southeast, the Northeast, and the Eastern Plains area inhabited by tribes speaking Siouan languages and divided into totemic gentes.

Totemism forms the foundation of a vast social system of alternate obligation and restriction. It governs marriage and all sexual relations, for a man may not touch a woman of the same totem as himself. Sometimes the prohibition extends only to a man's own totem clan, but more frequently it includes several clans, in none of which is it permissible to marry. Such an exogamous group of clans within the tribe is a *phratry*, which was no doubt originally itself a totem clan that had since undergone subdivision. Search for the origin of exogamy (q.v.) reveals that it was based on an antecedent system of totemism, evidence of which was generally found in all rude societies acknowledging kinship through women only, the same association being found almost as generally in those rude societies which know kinship through males, while the worship of plants and animals (see ANIMAL WORSHIP; NATURE WORSHIP) in more advanced societies acknowledging kinship through males was lineally descended from totemism.

TOTONAC, ancient nation whose territory embraced the northern portion of the present State of Veracruz, with the adjacent portion of Puebla, Mexico. Their language has numerous Mayan and Nahuatlan affinities, but appears to be of distinct stock. They claim to have come from the northwest about 800 years before the Spanish conquest and to have been the builders of the remarkable ruins of Teotihuacán, about 10 miles N.W. of Mexico City. For several centuries they had maintained their independence, but had been conquered by the Aztec emperors some time before the coming of the Spaniards. The Spanish conqueror of Mexico, Hernando Cortes, made his first landing in their territory. They were fully as advanced as the Aztecs. Their capital, Cempoalla, was about 5 miles from the seacoast, with houses built of brick and mortar, each house in the center of a small garden watered by a constantly flowing stream; the city itself was surrounded by fruit trees and fields of grain. Their religion was a ceremonial sun worship, and they practiced circumcision and head flattening. They still constitute an important part of the population of their former territory, retaining many of their ancient rites interwoven with those of the conquering religion.

The superbly carved stones of peculiar shapes that are commonly ascribed to the Totonac are second in quality only to Maya sculpture. The most interesting stones are shaped like a capital U and are called sacrificial yokes, although their original use is unknown. Human and reptile motives are combined in the elaboration of these yokes. Other stones of peculiar shapes bear remarkable sculptures of birds, etc. In pottery the most beautiful objects are the so-called "laughing faces", which are infectious in their realism. All of these faces wear broad smiles. It is in the Totonac area that the art of the Archaic Mexican type seems to have first come under the influence of the Maya. The most famous ruin is that of Papantla.

TOTTENHAM, a town in Middlesex, England, a connecting suburb of London, 6 miles N.E. of St. Paul's on the river Lea. The town is mainly residential, and among its public parks is the Bruce Castle Park, the site of the old Bruce estate and castle in which King Robert's father died in 1303. Alexandra Palace, a pleasure resort, is partly within the urban limits. Pop. (1951 prelim.) 126,921.

TOTTORI, the capital of the prefecture of Tottori, in west Honshu, Japan, 70 miles N.W. of Kobe. It has manufactures of cotton and silk goods. Pop., about 52,000.

TOUCAN, a family of birds, Ramphastidae, numbering more than fifty species, and inhabiting tropical America. There are five genera. The legs of the toucan are strong, rather short, and with large scales; the toes are arranged in pairs, the first and fourth being turned backward. The form of the body is short and thick; the tail is rounded, varying in length in the different species from half the length to almost the whole length of the body. The neck is short and thick; the enormous bill is at the base of the full width and depth of the head, and is in some species more than half the length of the body. It is arched toward the tip, irregularly toothed along the margins of the mandibles, and extremely cellular and light, yet strong in structure. The tongue is long, narrow, and singularly feathered on each side, the processes which give it this feathered appearance possibly adding to its sensibility as an organ of taste.

A species of toucan

Toucans eat fruits with avidity; but they also seize and devour small birds and lizards. They make a clattering noise with their great mandibles and emit a harsh cry. They live chiefly in the depths of the South American forests, in small flocks. Almost nothing is known of their life histories, but they are supposed to lay white, glossy eggs in hollows of trees, making little if any nest for them. Toucans are easily tamed and in captivity readily eat rice, bread, potatoes, eggs, meat, and other kinds of food and make amusing pets. The colors of the bill are in most species brilliant during life, but disappear from stuffed specimens.

TOUCH, the tactile sense, the least specialized of the senses. The sense organs of the various groups of animals are discussed in the articles on the various groups. In the nervous system of man the organs of touch or feeling are central end organs; conducting nerve fibers; and peripheral end organs. Nerves end in the skin in two ways. In the simplest mode of termination they form a plexus in the dermis, pass outward from this, lose their medulla, divide into fibrils, and are lost to view in or between the cells of the epidermis.

Nerves end in this way in all parts of the skin, but the relative number of such terminations in different parts of the skin cannot be determined by present methods of research; they may be easily seen in the cornea. In the more complex form the nerves terminate in little swellings or end bulbs of greater or less complexity. In every case we have a nervous portion, composed of the termination of the axon of the nerve and an enclosing fibrous sheath. Very characteristic forms, the Pacinian corpuscles, are found in the sensitive pad of the fingers. In measuring the acuteness of the sense of touch, an instrument called the aesthesiometer is often used. It consists essentially of two needle points, and the nearer these can be separately felt, the greater is the delicacy of touch.

The point of greatest delicacy of touch is the tip of the tongue, and the seat of the least developed tactile sense is the skin over the spinal column. The sense of touch, like all other perceptions, can be sharpened by use. This improvement is not to be explained by an increased development of the terminal organs, nor by a growth of new nerve fibers in the skin, but by a more exact limitation of the sensation areas in the brain. Many artisans acquire a highly specialized sense of touch. The delicacy of the tactile sense in the blind is well known; they are able to read fine raised letters and to make articles of delicate structure in a manner impossible to individuals who can see.

TOUCH IN ANIMALS, a general term for the cutaneous senses of pressure, pain, and temperature, as evidenced by the selective reactions of animals to contact, warmth, and cold. Mammals behave as if sensitive to contact, and it is probable that the hairs which are found upon the skin of all mammals are organs of pressure. The vibrissae of rats have been shown to be highly developed forms of such pressure organs.

Most mammals, moreover, appear to possess a sense of support; thus, they will not, when blinded, walk off the edge of a table. The ability of bats to avoid small wires stretched in the path of their flight depends to a great extent upon the excitability of the ears, as is shown by the result of stopping the auditory meatus. It has been suggested that the drumskin of the ear acts in this case as an organ of touch, excited by the condensations of the air which occur when the bat approaches a wire. Fish and amphibia show many responses to contact. Some fish are unequally sensitive to pressure in different regions; and some, it is thought, swim against the current of a stream in response to pressure cues from the flowing water.

French National Tourist Office
Church in the city of Toulouse, France

In general, mammals are sensitive to thermal stimuli. Rats and squirrels have been trained to discriminate between two temperatures separated by as little as 10° C. A study of the dependence upon temperature of the breathing rhythm of the decerebrized frog makes it appear that the frog, at least in a reflex manner, is as sensitive as the human being to thermal changes.

TOUCH-ME-NOT. See BALSAM.

TOUCHSTONE, a hard, black stone, occasionally used in assaying. The original kind was a peculiar bituminous quartz or flinty slate obtained from Lydia in Asia Minor, and hence known as Lydian stone; but black basalt may be employed. Its test of the fineness of gold is the color of the streak made by the metal on the stone.

TOULON, a seaport and naval station of France, capital of the arrondissement of Toulon in the department of Var, situated on a bay of the Mediterranean Sea, 42 miles E.S.E. of Marseille. The site is partly surrounded by hills, on which are situated forts. Toulon consists of an old town, with narrow, crooked streets, and a new town on the N., with handsome avenues and public buildings. The principal squares are the Place D'Armes, the Place de la Liberté, and the Jardin de la Ville, an attractive promenade; the last-named two are connected by the Boulevard Strasbourg, the main avenue of Toulon. Among the notable structures are the 11th-century Romanesque Church of Ste. Marie Majeure, the vast naval and military hospital, and the marine arsenal, which covers 650 acres. The harbor has five principal basins. The E. portion of the port is used for merchant shipping, and that on the w. for the French navy. Toulon, second only to Brest as a naval station, is the headquarters of the French Mediterranean fleet, and the leading French naval dockyard. Its industries include ship building, lace making, wine making, and fishing. Its port is a center for exports of salt, fruit, nuts, bauxite, and cloth, and its principal imports include wood, coal, hemp, and corn.

The ancient Roman city of Telo Martius, noted for its dye works, once stood on the site. It was destroyed by the Saracens in 889, rebuilt, and in 1259 taken by Charles of Anjou. Toulon was strongly fortified by kings Henry IV and Louis XIV. In 1707, during the War of the Spanish Succession, Toulon withstood the allied fleets of England and the Netherlands. In 1793, during the French Revolutionary period, royalists within the city delivered Toulon into British hands. Later in the year the French republican army besieged and recaptured the city; in this battle Napoleon Bonaparte won military distinction as an artillery commander. During World War II, when, in Nov., 1942, German troops were ordered into unoccupied France, the bulk of the French war fleet (about 200,000 tons), which was anchored at Toulon, was scuttled by French crews to prevent its acquisition by Germany. Pop. (1947) 125,742.

TOULOUSE, capital of Haute-Garonne Department, s.w. France, situated on the E. bank of the Garonne R., 443 miles s.w. of Paris and 159 miles s.e. of Bordeaux, by rail. Three bridges, one a 16th-century stone structure of seven arches, connect Toulouse with the suburb of Saint-Cyprien on the w. bank of the river. The principal structures are the Church of Saint-Sernin, a Romanesque edifice begun in the 11th century and restored by the architect Eugène Viollet-le-Duc in the 19th century; the Church of Notre-Dame de la

Dalbade, with a square tower and a Renaissance portal; and the Cathedral of Saint-Étienne, in a combination of architectural styles. In the center of Toulouse is its 16th-century town hall, called the Capitole. The museum of fine arts occupies, in part, an ancient convent. The city is famous for its many mansions in the French Renaissance style, particularly the Hôtel Bernuy, the Hôtel Lasbourde, and the Hôtel d'Assézat. The latter mansion became in 1895 the home of the Académie des Jeux Floraux, an organization which since 1323 has annually held a poetry contest, the prizes being flowers of gold and silver. The University of Toulouse, founded in 1230, is attended annually by about 7700 students. Other educational institutions include an agricultural institute, a Catholic institute of theology and letters, and art and music schools. The city is the industrial and commercial center of the region and former province called Languedoc (q.v.). It is the site of the national tobacco factory and also contains factories producing textiles, steam engines, leather, stained glass, agricultural machinery, and airplanes.

Toulouse, as the ancient Gallic city of Tolosa, was important long before the Roman conquest of Gaul. It became the capital of the Visigothic kingdom of Toulouse (see GOTHS) in 419, and in 507 was taken by the Franks. Later it became the capital of the rulers of Aquitaine, under the Merovingian kings. For several centuries the city was the capital of the county of Toulouse (see TOULOUSE, COUNTY OF), which in the 11th century became the greatest principality in s. France. In the early part of the 13th century Toulouse suffered greatly because of the Albigensian religious conflict (see ALBIGENSES). During the wars of religion which devastated France during the 16th century, 4000 Huguenots of the city were killed in 1562, and the Toulouse Huguenots later attempted to deliver the city to the Protestant leader, Louis de Bourbon, Prince de Condé. On April 10, 1814, Marshal Nicholas Soult, one of Napoleon's generals, made an unsuccessful stand at Toulouse against the Allied armies commanded by the Duke of Wellington. Pop. (1947) 264,411.

TOULOUSE, COUNTY OF, a feudatory state in s. France which became one of the greatest principalities of w. Europe. It was established by Charlemagne when that king, about 780, created the kingdom of Aquitaine for his son Louis. The city of Toulouse became its capital and gradually, with surrounding territory, acquired the status of a

feudal domain. About 852 Raymond, Count of Quercy, became Count of Rouergue and Toulouse, beginning the famous line of Toulouse rulers. Gradually the county emerged from its position of dependence upon the French crown, and by the 11th century became a large and powerful principality, its dominions including Languedoc, Rouergue, and parts of Guienne and Provence. Count Raymond IV (d. 1105), who was in addition, the marquis of Provence and duke of Narbonne, played a distinguished part in the First Crusade (1096–99). His son, Bertrand, established the principality of Tripoli on the coast of Syria during the Crusade. Raymond VI (1156–1222) was famous as a patron of Provençal poets and partisan of the Albigenses (q.v.). When he refused to take severe measures against the Albigenses, he incurred the wrath of the pope. Raymond's possessions were given by the Fourth Lateran Council to Simon de Montfort, and the latter was sent against the Count. Montfort, however, was killed at the siege of Toulouse in 1218, and Raymond shortly afterward succeeded in recovering most of his domains. In 1229 Raymond VII was forced to cede a large part of his holdings to Louis IX of France and to acknowledge the king as his feudal lord. Jeanne, daughter and heiress of Raymond VII, was married to Alphonse of Poitou, brother of the French king. On the death of Alphonse, in 1271, the County of Toulouse was united with the French crown.

TOULOUSE-LAUTREC, in full, HENRI MARIE RAYMOND DE TOULOUSE-LAUTREC MONFA (1864–1901), French postimpressionist (see POSTIMPRESSIONISM) painter, lithographer, and illustrator, born in Albi in the department of Tarn. Toulouse-Lautrec's interest in art was first aroused by the painter René Princeteau; he subsequently studied painting under Léon Bonnat and Fernand Cormon. Toulouse-Lautrec frequented the colorful cafés in the Montmartre district of Paris, where his scintillating wit attracted a large group of artists and intellectuals, including the Irish author Oscar Wilde, the Dutch painter Vincent van Gogh, and the French singer Yvette Guilbert. He preserved his impressions of these and other celebrities in portraits and sketches of striking originality and power. His frequent periods of dissipation at length brought on a paralytic stroke, to which he succumbed on his family estate at Malarmé. Toulouse-Lautrec was a prolific creator, producing great numbers of paintings, drawings, etchings, lithographs, and posters, as well as illustrations for various contemporary newspapers.

TOURACO, TURACOU, TURACO, or TURA-KOO, common name applied to any of the African cuculiform birds constituting the family Musophagidae. These birds usually range in length from 1 to 2 feet, are brightly colored, and have loose, fluffy plumage. They have long tails and short, thick bills with saw-toothed cutting edges; their heads bear erectile crests of feathers. The birds feed on bananas and plantains, and occasionally on insects. The giant touraco, *Corythaeola cristata,* which is found in western and central Africa, is the largest of these birds, attaining a length of almost 3 feet. It is bluish green with a red and yellow bill. Touracos are also known as "helmet birds", "plantain eaters", and "plantain cutters".

TOURAINE, one of the former provinces of France, corresponding to the present department of Indre-et-Loire. The capital was Tours. After having been under the rule of its own counts Touraine was united about the middle of the 11th century with Anjou.

Wildenstein & Co.
"Jane Avril," painting by Toulouse-Lautrec

With Anjou it passed in 1154 to England. It was reacquired by France half a century later, was made a duchy in 1356, and was definitively united with the crown in 1584.

TOURCOING, capital of an arrondissement in the department of Nord, France, situated less than a mile from the Franco-Belgian border, 8 miles N.E. of Lille. The town is part of the industrial center of Roubaix (q.v.), with which it is joined by a canal and a tramway. Tourcoing has a fine modern Gothic church and schools of painting, drawing, music, and architecture. It is one of the most important French textile centers, and its greatest industries are the manufacture of carpets, cotton goods, linens, silks, and such related products as dyes and textile machinery. Its woolen goods have been famous since the Middle Ages. In 1477 the town was heavily fortified by its Flemish inhabitants, but in a dispute between France and Burgundy for possession of Tourcoing it was captured by French troops. In 1794 the allied British and Austrian armies were defeated there by the French Republican army; a monument erected in 1866 commemorates the event. During World War I the city was severely damaged. Pop. (1947) 76,080.

TOURMALINE, a mineral which has a very complex and somewhat variable chemical composition. The chief constituents are silica and alumina in nearly equal proportions, and forming about three fourths of the whole. The remainder consists of boracic acid, ferrous oxide, manganous oxide, magnesia, lime, soda, potash, and lithia, which are not all present, however, in any specimen. Tourmaline is harder than quartz, but not as hard as topaz.

The mineral has a vitreous luster. The most common colors are black, brownish black, and bluish black; blue, green, and red varieties also occur; but white or colorless kinds are rare. Red tourmaline is known as *rubellite*; pale blue or bluish black as *indicollite*; Berlin-blue and transparent as *Brazilian sapphire* (in jewelry); green and transparent as *Brazilian emerald, chrysolite,* or *peridot of Brazil*; honey-yellow as *peridot of Ceylon*; colorless as *achroite*; and black as *schorl.*

TOURNAI, or TOURNAY, capital of an arrondissement in the province of Hainaut, Belgium, situated on the Schelde R., 48 miles s.w. of Ghent. Its most famous edifice is the five-towered Romanesque cathedral of Notre Dame, begun in 1030, with a nave dating from 1146 and a pointed Gothic choir built in 1242. Other architectural features include a belfry, the oldest in Belgium, built in 1187 and restored in the 19th century; the church of

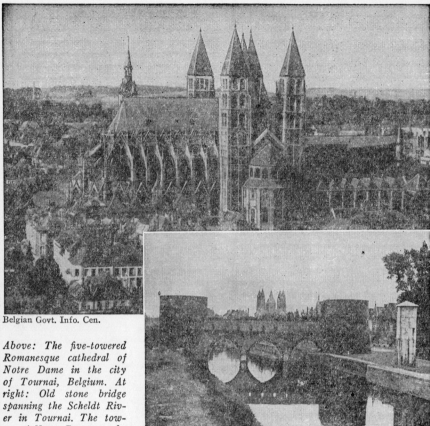

Belgian Govt. Info. Cen.

Above: The five-towered Romanesque cathedral of Notre Dame in the city of Tournai, Belgium. At right: Old stone bridge spanning the Scheldt River in Tournai. The towers of Notre Dame can be seen in the distance.

Saint-Quentin in the Transitional Gothic style; and the church of Saint-Brice, containing the tomb of Childeric, 5th-century king of the Franks, in which were discovered 300 golden bees. Over the Scheldt is the 13th-century Pont des Trous. The town hall occupies an ancient former monastery. Tournai contains an art gallery, a natural history museum, and a library containing 60,000 volumes. The city is noted for the manufacture of carpets, porcelains, hosiery, and textiles.

Tournai was the capital of the Belgic tribe of the Nervii, and after the Roman conquest was named *Civitas Nerviorum* or *Turnacum*. In the 5th century the Merovingian kings made their royal residence there until the death of Clovis in 511. The town was at various times in the possession of England, Spain, and France, the last-named country relinquishing its control in 1748. In the course of

the German invasion of Belgium in 1940, during World War II, Tournai was in part destroyed. Pop. (1950 est.) 32,451.

TOURNAMENT or **JOUST,** a military sport of the Middle Ages in Europe, in which combatants engaged one another with the object of exhibiting their courage and skill in the use of arms. A tournament was usually held on the invitation of a prince, who sent a herald through his own dominions and to foreign courts. The intending combatants hung up their armorial shields on the trees, tents, and pavilions round the arena for inspection, to show that they were worthy candidates for the honor of contending in the lists in respect of noble birth, military prowess, and unspotted character. The combat took place on horseback, although the combatants who had been dismounted frequently continued it on foot.

Mounted knights with lances in combat at a medieval tournament

The usual arms were blunted lances or swords. The period when tournaments were most in vogue comprised the 12th, 13th, and 14th centuries, and the place where the most celebrated English tournaments were held was the tiltyard near St. James's, Smithfield, London. But by 1500 the alteration in the social life and warfare of Europe had changed their character, and they are rather to be regarded as state pageants than as real combats. The development of firearms helped to put them out of fashion.

TOURNAY. See TOURNAI.

TOURNEUR, CYRIL (1575?–1626), English dramatist. He found employment in the Low Countries and served as secretary to Sir Edward Cecil in the expedition to Cadiz (1625). He wrote two plays, *The Atheist's Tragedie* (written probably about 1603, published 1611) and *The Revenger's Tragedie* (published 1607). The latter is a powerful though lurid tragedy, in praise of which the 19th-century English poet Algernon Charles Swinburne wrote several essays. Tourneur also wrote elegies and other nondramatic pieces.

TOURS, capital of the department of Indre-et-Loire, France, situated on the left bank of the Loire R., 145 m. by rail s.w. of Paris. The city is built on a plain between the Loire and Cher rivers, above their confluence. Near the Loire, in the N.E. section of Tours, is the famous Gothic cathedral of St. Gatien, begun in 1170 and completed about 1550, with a richly ornamented façade, magnificent stained-glass windows, a rose window, and two towers. Near the center of Tours are the detached towers of St. Martin and Charlemagne, the only remains of the abbey-church of St. Martin, demolished in 1802. In the principal square, site of the Palais de Justice, stands a famous statue of Honoré de Balzac, a native of Tours. In the immediate vicinity of the city is the ruined chateau of Plessis-lez-Tours, favorite residence of Louis XI of France. Other famous structures include the 13th-century (restored 19th century) Notre-Dame-la-Riche, the 15th-century St. Saturnin, and the 13th-century St. Julien churches. Industrial establishments in the modern city include steel plants, foundries, printing plants, and factories producing automobiles, porcelain, and shoes. Tours is the commercial center for the wine, brandy, confectionery, and dried fruits of the Touraine region.

The city derives its name from the Gallic tribe of Turones. After its conquest by Rome, it was named *Altinos,* and later *Cæsarodunum.* It was Christianized about 250, and in early times became the seat of an important bishopric, later an archbishopric. In the 5th century the name of the city became *Civitas Turonorum* ("City of the Turones"), later corrupted to Tours. Tours was captured by the Visigoths in 473 and by Clovis, King of the Franks, in 507. In 732, between Tours and nearby Poitiers, Charles Martel (q.v.) repulsed the invading Saracens and thus arrested their advance northward. Later, the city became the capital of Touraine (q.v.). Under the Valois kings of France, particularly Louis XI, who established a silk industry there, Tours became an important commercial center. In October, 1870, after the fall of Paris in the Franco-German War, the Government of National Defense was organized at Tours, remaining there until the city was occupied by German troops on Jan. 10, 1871. Pop. (1947) 80,044.

TOUSSAINT L'OUVERTURE, PIERRE DOMINIQUE (1743–1803), West Indian revolutionist, born a slave, who joined the Negro insurgents (1791), and for his services against the Spaniards was made by the French Convention general of brigade (1795), general of division (1797), and a little later chief of the army of San Domingo. Bonaparte having later proclaimed the reestablishment of slavery in San Domingo, Toussaint declined to obey, whereupon General Le Clerc was sent with a strong fleet to compel him. The liberator submitted, but was arrested, sent to France, and flung into a dungeon at Fort de Joux, near Besançon, where he died.

TOWER. See BELL TOWER.

TOWER OF LONDON, structure near and without the eastern wall of the city of London and on the northern bank of the Thames, begun by Bishop Gundulf at the direction of William the Conqueror in 1078, and not completed for more than thirty years. The tower liberty consists of 26 acres, of which 12 are enclosed within the ditch. The principal towers of this structure are: the White Tower (erected for William the Conqueror by Gundulf, Bishop of Rochester, 1079–80); the Middle Tower (forming the main entrance); the Byward Tower (the chief entrance to the external line of fortifications); Traitor's Gate, or St. Thomas's Tower (the entrance for prisoners taken to the Tower by water); Bloody Tower (so called from the tradition that young Prince Edward V and the Duke of York were murdered there), Record or Wakefield Tower (where the Records were formerly kept and the regalia is now guarded); Beauchamp Tower (named after Beau-

Toussaint L'Ouverture (contemporary portrait)

British Information Services

Visitors being led on a tour of the Tower of London in England

champ, Earl of Warwick); Devereux Tower (where the Duke of Clarence is said to have been drowned in a butt of malmsey); and Jewel Tower (where the regalia was formerly kept). The Chapel of St. John is a pure and fine example of Norman architecture. Henry III used the tower for a residence, it was long a prison for political offenders, and it has now a collection of armor and is the repository of the regalia of the kingdom.

Early writers have alleged that Julius Cæsar built the tower of London as a Roman fortress. The spot was in fact occupied by some structure before the time of William the Conqueror, as is shown by the massive foundations discovered in the course of later erections; but of the nature of these earlier buildings we know little. The White Tower, already mentioned, is the beginning of the historical Tower of London. During the reigns of the first two Norman kings the tower seems to have been used as a fortress merely. In Henry I's time it was already a state prison. That monarch and his successors gradually increased the size and strength of the ramparts and towers, until the whole became a great feudal stronghold. The kings frequently lived there, holding their courts, and often sustaining sieges and blockades at the hands of their rebellious subjects. On the accession of Queen Elizabeth I, however, the tower ceased to be a palace. Of the long list of executions for political offenses which it witnessed, those occurring during World War I (1914–18) were the first after those of the rebellion of 1745.

The Tower of London is in charge of the War Department and contains arms and accouterments for the complete equipment of a large army. The government of the tower is vested in a constable, who is usually a military officer of long service and distinguished rank, whose position is honorary; the deputy constable, also an officer of repute, is the actual governor. He has under him a small staff and the corps of Yeomen of the Guard, popularly known as "beefeaters".

TOWN, the name applied generally throughout the United States to small municipalities, larger than the village and smaller than the city. In New England it more often denotes a quasi-corporate area, either urban or rural, constituting a subdivision of the county, which elsewhere is usually called the township. The New England town is the most important local administrative unit in the governmental system. The center of political activity is the town meeting, which meets usually once a year and may be attended by all the legal voters of the town. It discusses measures of general interest to the town, elects the town officers, and votes the taxes for the ensuing year. The government of the New England town is therefore a pure democracy and the only real example of the kind in the American political system. The town meeting governs through a body of officers, varying according to the needs of the community. These are usually the selectmen, varying in number from three to nine, who are the executive magistrates of the town, the town clerk, treasurer, constables, tax assessors, overseers of the poor, and school trustees. In some towns there are such officers as field drivers, pound keepers, fence viewers, measurers, and sealers. In England the word "town" applies to the small municipalities as in the United States, although the word "borough" is used to designate certain of the old towns. See TOWNSHIP.

TOWN, ITHIEL (1784–1844), American architect, born in Thompson, Conn. Town built several government buildings at Washington and a number of bridges, including one over the James River near Richmond, Va. He was one of the original members of the National Academy of Design, New York. A large part of his extensive library on art went to Yale College. He published many architectural works.

TOWNSHEND, CHARLES, 2nd VISCOUNT (1674–1738), English statesman, born in Raynham, Norfolk. He entered public life as a Tory, but soon afterward co-operated with the Whigs. In 1709 he visited The Hague as ambassador, and negotiated with the states-general the Barrier Treaty, which pledged the states-general to the Hanoverian succession. He took part in arranging for the accession of George I, who, while still at The Hague, on his way to his new kingdom, made him secretary of state. He held the office till 1730, except for the years 1716 to 1720. With Stanhope he formed a ministry entirely Whig, in which Sir Robert Walpole, his brother-in-law, became chancellor of the exchequer.

TOWNSHEND, CHARLES (1725–67), English statesman, grandson of the 2nd Viscount Townshend. He entered the House of Commons (1747) as a supporter of the Pelham (Whig) administration. His first great speech was against the Marriage Bill (1753). Upon the dissolution of the Whig government the Earl of Bute gained him by the offer of the post of secretary at war; but on Bute's resignation (1763) he was appointed first lord of trade and the plantations. In the Chatham ministry (1766) he became chancellor of the exchequer and leader of the House of Commons. When Lord Chatham abdicated the post of first minister Townshend proposed and carried those measures of taxation of commodities in America that led to the loss of the American colonies. See TOWNSHEND ACTS.

TOWNSHEND, GEORGE, 1st MARQUIS (1724–1807), British soldier. He served in the Netherlands and at Culloden and Laufeld. In 1759, as brigadier general, he joined Wolfe's expedition against Quebec, commanded the left wing on the Heights of Abraham, and at Wolfe's death succeeded to the chief command. In 1764 he took the family title. Viscount Townshend. He was lord lieutenant of Ireland in 1767–72, and was made marquis in 1786 and field marshal in 1796.

TOWNSHEND ACTS. The Stamp Act was repealed in March, 1766, but three measures were introduced by Charles Townshend on

May 13, 1767. These included suspension of the functions of the legislature of New York; the establishment of commissioners of the customs to superintend laws relating to trade; and an impost duty upon glass, red and white lead, painters' colors, paper, and tea. This reawakened the agitation created by the Stamp Act, and brought the quarrel between England and the colonies nearer the final rupture.

TOWNSHIP, territorial subdivision of a county with certain corporate powers of municipal government for local purposes; also, the corporation or government thereof. The designation applies also to one of the tracts of the United States, formerly public lands, 6 miles square, as surveyed and designated of record under the provisions of the acts of Congress of 1785 and 1796. Upon the settlement of the country these townships are usually continued as civil townships in States adopting that form of local government.

TOWNSVILLE, chief city and port of North Queensland, on Cleveland Bay on the east coast of Australia, 870 miles N.W. of Brisbane. It has a fine harbor, and is the see of an Anglican bishop. Pop. (1950 est.) 35,880.

TOXEMIA, a poisoned condition of the blood due to the circulating in it of toxic materials, either chemical or bacterial in their nature. These toxins (q.v.) may be derived from putrefactive or other fermentative changes in the intestinal tract or from the products of bacterial activity in the tissues circulating the blood. When bacteria themselves find entrance into the blood stream, the condition is known as bacteremia.

TOXICOLOGY, the science of poisons, embracing the physical and chemical history of all the known poisonous substances, as well as the methods of testing for them, their action on the living body, and the post-mortem results they occasion. See POISON.

TOXINS, specific poisonous substances elaborated by the metabolic activities of certain microorganisms. A few varieties of bacteria secrete their toxins in the tissues or culture media in which they grow and are known as soluble, exogenous, extracellular, or true toxins. Other bacteria retain most of the poisonous material within themselves and hence are known as intracellular or endotoxins, these being liberated only when the bacteria become disintegrated by chemical, physical, or mechanical means. In addition to bacterial toxins there are characteristic poisons produced by various plants and animals and termed respectively phytotoxins and zootoxins. The more important true toxins causing infection in man are those of diphtheria, tetanus, botulism, dysentery, and staphylolysin. Owing to their extreme susceptibility to various chemical and physical influences, such as light, heat, and age, toxins are difficult to isolate in their pure state. Oxidizing agents destroy them, and our knowledge of them has been gained chiefly through the lesions and symptoms which they produce when injected into susceptible animals. They are all poisonous, but in order to become effective must enter into chemical combination with the animal cells. They are, with the exception of botulin, destroyed by the gastrointestinal juices. While their exact chemical nature is unknown, it is the general belief that they are toxalbumins and closely allied to proteins. It has also been abundantly demonstrated that they are colloid in nature and bear a close resemblance to enzymes. They differ from ptomaines (q.v.) in that they are absolutely specific synthetic products, whereas ptomaines are cleavage products from the medium upon which the bacteria grow. Toxins, moreover, can give rise to antibodies, whereas ptomaines cannot produce them. See ANTITOXIN.

TOXODONTIA, an extinct suborder of ungulate mammals found fossil in the Tertiary deposits of Argentina and Patagonia, South America. The best-known genus, *Toxodon,* comprised heavily built animals as large as a rhinoceros, with a large heavy head placed on a short neck which sloped down from the shoulders, so that the head was much lower than the back. The teeth were large, compressed laterally, and either triangular or prismatic in section, and they grew from persistent pulps. The bones of the skeleton are all massive, the legs short and thick, and the feet are three-toed. *Nesodon,* an earlier genus than *Toxodon,* was of smaller size and slighter build.

TOYAMA, town in Japan, 160 m. from Tokyo. It is the capital of Toyama prefecture, and a center of trade and manufactures. Pop., about 100,000.

TOYNBEE, ARNOLD JOSEPH (1889–   ), British historian, born in London, and educated at Winchester College, a public school, and Balliol College, Oxford University. From 1912 to 1915 Toynbee was a fellow and tutor in ancient history at Balliol; during that period he began his career as an interpreter of modern history and politics. In 1915 he entered the British government service, working until 1919 in the Political Intelligence Department of the Foreign Office; he then became a member of the Middle Eastern Section of the

British delegation to the Paris Peace Conference. After World War I, in 1919, he was appointed Koraes Professor of Byzantine and modern Greek languages, literature, and history at the University of London. The University appointed him research director of international history in 1925, and in the same year he became director of studies in the Royal Institute of International Affairs in London. He retired in 1955. During World War II he served as director of foreign research and press service of the Royal Institute (1939–43), and director of the research department of the Foreign Office (1943–46). In 1946 Toynbee was a member of the British delegation to the Paris Peace Conference.

Toynbee's most significant contribution to historiography is considered to be the theory embodied in A Study of History (vols. 1-6, 1934–39; vols. 7-10, 1954), which he began writing in 1922. His primary thesis regards history as the progress of civilizations rather than of nations. He discusses the twenty-six civilizations which, in his opinion, have so far existed, and analyzes their genesis and growth to meet the challenges of their environments, and also their declines, seen as their inability to respond to challenges other than those of physical environment. An abridgement of A Study of History has been published (vols. 1-6, 1946; vols. 7-10, 1954). Other writings include The Western Question in Greece and Turkey (1922), Greek Civilization and Character (1924), A Journey to China (1931), Civilization on Trial (1948), The World and the West (1953), and An Historian's Approach to Religion (1956). Toynbee prepared a series of international yearbooks, A Survey of International Affairs, issued between 1924 and 1938 by the Royal Institute of International Affairs, and edited A Survey of International Affairs, 1939–1946, issued by the Institute beginning in 1952.

TOYOHASHI, maritime town of Japan, on Honshu Island, 95 m. from Kioto. Pop., about 106,000.

TRABZON or **TREBIZOND** (anc. Trapezus), city, seaport, and capital of the il of the same name, Turkey, in Asia, situated on the s.e. coast of the Black Sea, about 110 miles n.w. of Erzurum. The city lies on a small tableland extending between two precipitous, parallel valleys to the coast and terminating in a low promontory. Medieval walls surround the city, and its highest point is surmounted by an ancient citadel. Astride the historic trade route between Persia (Iran) and the European continent, Trabzon is a shipping and commer-

British Information Services
Arnold Joseph Toynbee, British historian

cial center with an export trade in textiles, carpets, tobacco, flour, corn, nuts, and raisins. The industries include wool, silk, and linen weaving, tanning, dyeing, and the manufacture of filigree. Trabzon is famed for many architectural landmarks dating from Byzantine times. Noteworthy are the church of the Virgin of the Golden Head, the church of St. Eugenius, both of which are now mosques, and the church of Hagia Sophia. Near Trabzon is the 14th-century monastery of Sumelas.

Greek colonists from Sinope founded Trapezus on the site of present-day Trabzon early in the 8th century b.c. Seized by the Romans in the 1st century a.d., it was subsequently incorporated into the Byzantine Empire. The city attained wide renown as an artistic, cultural, and commercial center during the Middle Ages, when it was the capital of the Trebizond Empire, established in 1204 by Alexius I (1180?–1222), a member of the Comnenus family of Byzantine rulers. It flourished until 1461, when the empire was conquered by the Turkish sultan Mohammed II and made part of the Ottoman Empire. In succeeding centuries the city declined in importance. Turkey ceded Trabzon to the short-lived autonomous republic of Armenia in 1920, but regained it the next year. In 1923 the Turks deported the city's sizeable Greek population. The port facilities of the city were enlarged and improved between 1945 and 1949. Area of il, 1787 sq.m., pop. (1950) 419,148. Pop. of city (1950) 33,969.

TRACE ELEMENTS, name applied to natural elements required in minute amounts, or "traces", for normal growth and development of most living organisms, and known also as micronutrients. The importance of trace elements in plant and animal physiology was overlooked by 19th-century biologists because the minute amounts in which they were utilized by organisms made their detection impossible by the analytical methods then known. The so-called "major" elements, such as calcium, potassium, magnesium, phosphorus, sulfur, carbon, oxygen, sodium, nitrogen, and hydrogen, which constitute the bulk of all living matter, were thought to be responsible for maintaining most biological processes; diseases which could not be attributed directly to a deficiency of one or more of the dominant elements were ascribed to supernatural powers, or to "soil sickness". As late as the 18th century, when the existence of many "minor" elements was recognized, the presence of these elements was presumed by biologists to exist in plant and animal tissue only because of inability of the organisms to differentiate sufficiently between various nutrients. In 1897, the French biochemist Gabriel Émile Bertrand grew plants in dilute aqueous solutions of various salts, and discovered that manganese was essential for normal growth. Experiments which followed Bertrand's discovery eventually proved the importance to plants of copper, cobalt, boron, molybdenum, zinc, iodine, and other elements. Results of early plant-nutrition experiments were inaccurate because sufficient amounts of trace elements were present in the containers used or available as impurities in the salt solutions employed. Most present-day knowledge of the biochemical functions of trace elements has been derived from analytical chemical determinations and from the use of radioactive isotopes, or "tracers" (q.v.).

In analytical determinations, mineral nutrients are extracted from various parts of plants and animals, which are analyzed to determine the concentration of a particular trace element in a specific organ or tissue; see MICROCHEMISTRY. For the purpose of detecting and measuring such minute quantities as trace elements, ordinary microchemical techniques are of little use, and it is necessary to employ special instruments such as the absorptiometer, which can measure quantities of one milligram or less. The absorptiometer, which is an adaptation of the colorimeter, measures,

with the aid of an electric cell, the depth of color of a solution of unknown concentration by matching it against a standard solution of the same material. Such analysis of trace elements is often made from the ash of animal or plant organisms. To prepare the ash for analytical purposes, the tissues to be analyzed are extracted and dried in an oven, powdered by grinding, and then incinerated in a furnace at a temperature of 450-600° C. (842-1112°F.). The ash is then dissolved in a mineral acid and the solution evaporated to dryness, the resulting residue being dissolved in a definite volume of water or dilute acid. Tissue extracts are also analyzed by a flame-spectrum method, which consists either of placing the unknown extracts on a piece of filter paper and placing the paper in a flame, or of spraying a solution of the extracts directly onto the flame. The density of the resulting spectral line is then measured by such instruments as a microphotometer to determine the composition of the extract.

In horticulture, a method known as visual diagnosis is often used to analyze soils for deficiencies or excesses of one or more of the trace elements, and to observe the effects of these deficiencies or excesses upon plant life. This method employs various plants called indicators, which are extremely sensitive to excesses or deficiencies of specific elements, and which indicate this sensitivity by marked changes in color and structure when grown in certain soils. The vegetables most commonly used as indicators are cauliflower and broccoli, which are especially sensitive to iron and boron; potato, which is sensitive to manganese; globe beet, used to indicate deficiency or excess of boron and manganese; rutabaga, sensitive to boron; and pea, sensitive to manganese. The fruits commonly used as indicators include plum and pear, which are sensitive to iron; apple, which is sensitive to boron, iron, and manganese; sweet cherry, sensitive to manganese; raspberry, sensitive to iron and manganese; and strawberry, sensitive to iron. Plants which do not respond readily as indicators when grown in soil are often grown in solutions containing varying amounts of mineral concentrations; see HYDROPONICS.

After a deficiency of one or more specific trace elements has been recognized in a plant or animal, the element or elements can usually be supplied to the organism by several well-established methods. In animals, deficiencies are corrected mainly by dietary supplements or by direct injection into the tissues. In plants, deficient trace elements are applied as sprays on the leaves; in the form of fertilizer (see SOILS AND SOIL MANAGEMENT) ; or in the form of solid salts which are injected into various portions of the plant body. Usually, injections are applied either through the veins of the leaf, the tip of the leaf, the leaf stalk, the stem tip, the branch tip, the individual branches or roots, or to many parts of the tree at the same time. Injections often supply sufficient quantities of needed elements for a period of three or four years, and then the procedure must be repeated.

With the aid of experimental procedures such as those described above, trace elements have been shown to function biologically as important components of specifically acting chemical catalyzers, called enzymes (q.v.), which are responsible for the high-velocity reactions between organic and inorganic substances in all organisms. When conditions become unfavorable for activity of enzymes, the vital life processes are retarded or entirely inhibited. Although all trace elements are involved in biochemical reactions in living tissues, only the most important trace elements and their major specific functions can be discussed here. The element *zinc* is necessary for the elaboration of a zinc-protein enzyme, carbonic anhydrase, which occurs in the gastric mucosa and erythrocytes of mammals. The enzyme catalyzes the chemical breakdown of carbonic acid into carbon dioxide and water, and furthers the escape of carbon dioxide from the blood into the alveolar spaces. In plants, zinc serves as a catalyst to sulfhydryl compounds such as cysteine in the regulation of the oxidation-reduction potential in the cells. Zinc is also important in maintaining a normal auxin supply in plant cells, thereby regulating plant growth. The element *copper* enters into the composition of the copper-protein oxidizing enzymes known as catechol oxidases, or polyphenol oxidases, which are widely distributed throughout all plant cells. Catechol oxidase catalyzes the oxidation of catechol, pyrogallol, and other compounds of the orthodihydroxyphenol group. Copper also forms the copper-protein compound haemocuprin, present in minute amounts in the blood of mammals; hepatocuprin, found in the liver of mammals; and hemocyanin, the pigment concerned with the respiration of most crustaceans and many other lower animals. Copper is present in many protein and enzyme complexes such as ascorbic acid oxidase and phenol oxidase, and is involved in the formation of such enzymes as catalase, which decomposes hydrogen peroxide into water and gaseous oxygen.

Boron serves mainly to influence the absorption of calcium, regulate the water concentration of protoplasm, help in the absorption of cations, and retard the absorption of anions. It is also partly responsible for carbohydrate and nitrogen metabolism, and assists in the formation of pectic substances in the cell wall. The element *manganese,* in plants, has a direct effect upon oxidation, and also catalyzes nitrate assimilation. In animals, it aids lactation; prevents degeneration or atrophy of the testes, and serves as a component of such enzymes as arginase, which splits the amino acid arginine into ornithine and urea; peptidase, which accelerates the hydrolysis of peptides; and phosphoglucomutase, which accelerates the breakdown of sugar-phosphorus compounds. *Iron,* although present in the soil and the mammalian body in comparatively large quantities, is usually considered as a trace element because of its close connection with the elements mentioned above. It is present in nearly all human tissue, and serves as the central atom in ferriheme, the hemoglobin complex found in mammalian erythrocytes and muscle tissue and concerned with oxidation; see BLOOD. Iron is stored in vertebrates as ferritin, a protein containing ferric hydroxide, and found in the liver, spleen, and bone marrow. *Iodine,* which in the animal body is located entirely in the thyroid gland, is the active principle in the thyroid-regulating chemical thyroxine, or tetraiodothyronine. *Aluminum* is a constituent of the succino-oxidase enzyme system important in sugar metabolism, and is usually interchangeable in this system with the element *chromium. Arsenic* and *cobalt* are also found in most animals and plants but their biochemical functions are not yet understood by biologists. *Fluorine* is a constituent of tooth enamel and minute traces of this substance in the diet have been found to reduce the incidence of dental caries.

Deficiency Diseases in Plants. Diseases produced in plants by deficiency of one or more trace elements are numerous, and are usually characteristic of specific soils and localities. Manganese deficiencies are common to reclaimed, heavily limed soils, in which certain soil bacteria render manganese salts insoluble and thereby reduce the resistance of plants to disease. Typical manganese-deficiency diseases are characterized by development of small chlorotic patches localized in intravenal areas of the leaves. In grasses, the patches take the form of stripes or streaks which correspond to the parallel venation; in reticulate-veined dicotyledonous leaves, the patches are spotted, speckled, or mottled. The discoloration is usually followed by reduction or cessation of growth throughout the entire plant, and necrosis of the leaves and seeds. Gray speck of oats, commonly called gray stripe, gray spot, or dry spot, is a typical manganese-deficiency disease common to grasses in Europe, North America, and Australia. It is so called because it produces grayish discoloration on the leaves of affected plants. In the pabola blight of sugar cane, the chlorotic areas of the leaves take the form of long, white strands, which are eventually replaced by irregular, red spots. Other manganese-deficiency diseases include the speckled yellow of sugar beet and spinach, marked by a yellow chlorosis of the leaves; marsh spot of peas, in which cavities or brown or black spots appear on the cotyledon tissue of the seedlings; and frenching of tung trees, in which a premature abscission of the leaves occurs. Most manganese-deficiency diseases are combatted successfully by the application of manganese sulfate, $MnSO_4$, in the form of a top dressing or spray.

Zinc deficiences are injurious chiefly to orchard trees, in which they cause an intrevenal leaf chlorosis and produce a variety of diseases. Injuries to the leaf include a longer and spongier palisade layer, a deeply stained nuclear cytoplasm, and injury to the plastids. Pecan rosette, a disease injurious to the pecan tree *Carya olivaeformis,* causes crinkling and yellow mottling of the terminal leaves, and decreases production of fruit. The mottleleaf or little-leaf disease, which attacks great numbers of citrus trees, affects the roots and causes a yellow mottling of the leaves. Other zinc-deficiency diseases include: rosette of deciduous fruit trees, in which the normal elongated shoots are replaced by rosettes of small, stiff leaves; bronzing of tung trees, in which the leaves become deformed and assume a bronze coloration; and white bud of maize, which attacks the maize plant, *Zea mays,* and produces light-yellow streaks between the veins of the older leaves. Zinc-deficiency diseases are corrected or prevented by application of zinc sulfate, $ZnSO_4$.

Copper deficiencies, especially common to reclaimed acid peats in Holland, Denmark, and N. Germany, produce several diseases in oats, wheat, barley, beets, and legumes. Typical diseases are exanthema, or dieback, of fruit trees, in which the young shoots develop small, blisterlike swellings and the fruit becomes smaller and brown-spotted; and reclamation disease of grasses, in which the leaf tips lose their color and the seed production is markedly decreased. Most copper-deficiency diseases are controlled by applying a dressing of 50 pounds of copper sulfate per acre of deficient soil. Deficiencies of the element boron are widespread in alkaline and dry soils and result in such diseases as heart rot, crown rot, or dry rot of sugar beet; brown heart of rutabagas and turnips; browning of cauliflower; internal cork and corky core of apples; cracked stem in celery; yellowing in lucerne; and "top sickness" in tobacco plants. The diseases are controlled by the application of small amounts of borax to the soil. Iron deficiencies, common mostly to alkaline soils, produce diseases in fruit trees and bushes, conifers, rice, and certain legumes; the iron-deficiency diseases are marked by a chlorosis of the leaves, and are due to the destruction of the chloroplasts. Most iron-deficiency diseases are corrected by injecting solid ferrous sulfate into the trunks of the affected trees. Molybdenum deficiencies, which rarely occur in nature, cause chlorosis and eventual necrosis in the leaves of most grasses and various other plants.

Deficiency Diseases in Animals. Animals, like plants, require an adequate amount of trace elements to grow normally. Failure to receive the required amounts of one or more of these elements results in serious, often fatal diseases peculiar to the particular deficiency. Deficiencies of iodine produce in human beings the condition known as goiter (q.v.). This condition, which is essentially an enlargement of the thyroid gland, is also common to livestock, especially in parts of California and the Middle West, where the soil is deficient in iodine. Manganese deficiencies, also common in the animal kingdom, produce in poultry the disease known as perosis, slipped tendon, or hock disease, in which deformity of the leg and wing bones occurs. Usually accompanying the deformities in female birds are loss of maternal instinct and progressive loss of fertility. The disease is usually arrested by supplementing the diet with ten parts of manganese for every million parts of food. Boron deficiencies, especially common in Scotland, New Zealand, and Australia, produce in sheep and cattle the often-fatal disease called pining, enzootic marasmus, or bush sickness. Early symptoms of the disease are usually a progressive debility, accompanied by anemia and emaciation. The coats of the affected animals become rough, the eyeballs become deeply sunken, and the visible mucous membranes, especially the conjunctivas, become pale.

A deficiency of copper often causes in cattle the diseases known as licking sickness, and salt sickness, which are both marked by anemia, loss of appetite, and general bodily degeneration. Cattle thus affected are usually treated with regulated doses of copper sulfate solutions. A copper-deficiency disease of lambs, commonly known as sway-back, swing back, swingle back, or enzootic ataxia, is usually noticeable at birth, and is marked by paralysis, anemia, and cavitation of the brain tissue. The disease is checked by supplementing the daily diet of the ewes with 10 mg. of copper salts during the gestation period.

Excess Diseases in Animals. An overabundance of one or more trace elements in the animal body is often as dangerous as a deficiency of the same element or elements, and produces various common diseases. A typical excess disease in the human body is iodism, caused by too great a concentration of iodine in the thyroid gland, and resulting in headaches, emaciation, skin eruptions, and eventual atrophy of the thyroid gland. Among horses, cattle, pigs, and poultry, a common excess disease is selenium poisoning, or alkali disease, which results from poisoning by grain or forage containing comparatively large amounts of selenium; see LOCOWEED. The disease is marked by a loss of hair from various parts of the body, a sloughing off of the hoof, emaciation, lesions in the heart, liver, spleen, and kidneys, and a failure of poultry eggs to hatch properly. It is usually controlled by adding varying amounts of sulfur to the soil, and thereby reducing the amount of selenium capable of being absorbed by plants. An excess of molybdenum, especially in herbage such as clover, produces a disease in cattle called scouring, or tart lands. Cattle afflicted with the disease excrete watery, foul-smelling, yellowish-green dung and suffer a marked decrease in the yield of milk. The diseased cattle are usually transferred to safer pastures, and are fed one or two grams of copper sulfate daily. See individual articles on all of the elements mentioned above. See also METABOLISM; NUTRITION; PHYSIOLOGY; VITAMIN.

TRACERS, in biology, term applied to the radioactive or stable isotopes (q.v.) of various elements, which are suitable for use in studying the biochemical and physiological role of each element and its compounds. These isotopes, although used to some extent to determine the concentration of specific elements in various organisms, are employed mainly to measure the assimilation, distribution, conversion, and elimination of one or more elements in certain plant and animal tissues; see METABOLISM.

Until the early part of the 20th century, the only method available for studying the physiology of most elements within organisms was the direct chemical approach, in which the techniques of either quantitative and qualitative chemical analysis, or the visual diagnosis of induced chemical disturbances, were utilized. With these techniques, it was not possible to differentiate in any way between the atoms or molecules of elements administered experimentally and atoms or molecules of the same elements naturally absorbed and already present in living tissue. In 1923, the Hungarian chemist Georg von Hevesy conducted a unique investigation by using radium D, the naturally radioactive isotope of lead, to trace the metabolism of lead in plants. Hevesy's experiment, which consisted of introducing quantities of radium D into the vascular system of several plants, made possible the quantitative measurements of the circulation and absorption of lead by determining the radioactivity of different portions of the plant body. Tracer methodology received its most important impetus, however, in 1934, when the French physicists Irène and Frédéric Joliot-Curie (qq.v.) discovered the principles of induced radioactivity, and succeeded in synthesizing radioactive elements from ordinarily stable elements. Several years following the Joliots' discovery, Hevesy became the first to use artifically produced radioisotopes in biological research by performing experiments on the metabolism of phosphorus in rats.

Natural radioactivity, as exhibited by such elements as uranium, radon, and radium, occurs in all elements higher than bismuth in the periodic table; these elements are too heavy for the electromagnetic forces which bind their individual components together, and are therefore continuously undergoing transmutations; see RADIOACTIVITY. Induced radioactivity, in which normally stable elements are made unstable, and thereby radioactive, depends upon producing certain significant changes in the atomic nuclei of certain elements. In order to produce these nuclear changes, it is necessary to increase in some manner the nuclear mass or electrical charge of a particular atom, and thus decrease the stability of the atom. Most nuclear transformations are produced today either by bombarding the nuclei of various target atoms with helium atoms, or by bombarding the target nuclei with deuterium atoms. The latter, which are stable isotopes of hydrogen (q.v.) and are commonly known as deuterons or "heavy" hydrogen, consist essentially of one proton, or positively charged particle, and one neutron, or neutrally charged particle, both of which are held together within the nucleus of the deuterium atom; see ATOM AND ATOMIC THEORY.

A typical application of deuterium atoms is in the production of radioactive phosphorus. All natural phosphorus is stable, containing 15 protons and 16 neutrons in its nucleus, and being represented by the symbol $_{15}P^{31}$, in which 31 signifies the total nuclear mass and 15 the positive nuclear charge. When a highly accelerated deuterium nucleus comes in contact with the phosphorus nucleus, the positive charge of the latter repels the positively charged deuterium proton. If this repulsion attains an energy of 2.2 million electron volts (mev), the deuterium proton is pulled away from its neutron, and the neutron, being neutrally charged, enters the target nucleus. This phenomenon is commonly known as the Oppenheimer-Phillips process after the American scientists J. Robert Oppenheimer and Henry Bayard Phillips, and is the most effective known method of adding a neutron to the nucleus of an atom. As a result of the deuterium bombardment described above, the nuclear charge on the phosphorus atom remains the same, but the nuclear mass is increased by one, thereby producing a phosphorus atom having an atomic weight of 32 and indicated as $_{15}P^{32}$. The electronic formula symbolizing this reaction may be represented as follows:

$$_1H^2 + {}_{15}P^{31} = {}_{15}P^{32} + {}_1H^1.$$

Phosphorus produced by this method is unstable and radioactive, but still maintains its 15 orbital electrons, and therefore exhibits chemical properties identical with those of stable phosphorus. Eventually, the unstable form of phosphorus will emit an electron and thereby be converted to the stable form of $_{16}S^{32}$.

Most biologically useful radioisotopes are produced by the Oppenheimer-Phillips process, in each case the deuteron being shot at a target nucleus for the purpose of adding a neutron to the target nucleus. Typical radioisotopes produced by neutron capture are radioactive sodium 24, derived from sodium 23; and radioactive iron 56, derived from iron 55. Occasionally, bombardment of an atom with deuterons may result in the capture of a proton, rather than a neutron, by the bombarded nucleus, resulting in the formation of an element with one more unit of charge and mass than the target element. For example, beryllium, when bombarded with a deuteron nucleus, accepts a proton and rejects the neutron, thereby increasing its nuclear charge by one and effecting its transmutation to the element boron, which is the next highest element in the periodic table. The radioactive boron atom thus formed emits a gamma ray and is converted immediately to stable beryllium, as indicated in the following formula:

$$_1H^2 + {}_4Be^9 \rightarrow {}_5B^{11} \longrightarrow \diagdown\!\!\!\!\!\diagup \; {}_5^{\Gamma}B^{10}.$$

Although no appreciably permanent radioactivity is produced in this case, the same process of proton capture is used in the bombardment of tellurium nuclei by deuterium to produce radioactive iodine, which has an appreciable half-life (q.v.). The deuterium neutrons which are expelled during proton capture have a velocity of approximately 21 mev and are sometimes harnessed when a large supply of neutrons is required for specific purposes.

Helium nuclei, which are composed of two protons in combination with two neutrons, are commonly called *alpha particles* because of their resemblance to some of the particles emitted by naturally radioactive elements. Because of their double positive charge, they require tremendous velocities to overcome the repulsion of the target nuclei, and are rarely used to bombard the heavier, and therefore more highly charged, elements. A target nucleus, when bombarded by an alpha particle, usually either accepts one or both protons and rejects the neutrons, or captures the neutrons and rejects one or both protons, depending on the method of bombardment. An example of element transmutation by alpha bombardment is the use of nitrogen 14 to form radioactive flourine with an atomic mass of 18. The flourine immediately decays by emitting a proton, and is converted to stable oxygen with a mass of 17.

Many radioisotopes are also produced today by a method known as pile irradiation, which utilizes the energy produced by a radioactive pile of uranium 235; see URANIUM. When uranium is subjected to fission by high-speed neutrons, it in turn liberates many more neutrons traveling at ultrahigh speeds. Stable elements or their compounds can be placed in such radioactive uranium piles and subjected to the intense neutron irradiation, thereby being converted to a radioactive form. In all methods of radioisotope production by proton or neutron capture, the incidence of helium or deuterium nuclei hitting its target nucleus is small, and depends almost entirely on the direction of the bombardment and the cross section of the particular target nucleus. In general, bombardment by high-speed helium or deuterium nuclei achieves one direct hit upon a target nucleus for each million nuclei used.

Other, less common methods of inducing radioactivity include the photodisintegration of target nuclei by high-energy gamma rays, and the bombardment of nuclei by high-frequency X rays, and in that case the bombarded nuclei release one neutron to yield an isotope reduced in mass by one unit. The high velocities required by particles to bombard various target nuclei effectively are supplied by such machines as the cyclotron and betatron (qq.v.), in which enormous energies are imparted to particles by accelerating them progressively.

Stable isotopes, as well as radioisotopes, are often used as tracers in biological investigations. To be useful as tracers, the normal concentrations of stable isotopes should not exceed a few percent. The isotopes can then be highly concentrated by electromagnetic separation, and their metabolism measured with the aid of a mass spectrometer. The most important stable isotopes used as tracers are hydrogen 2, carbon 13, nitrogen 15, and oxygen 18 among the lighter elements; and sulfur 35, 36, potassium 40, 41, calcium 44, iron 57, 58, zinc 70, krypton 78, strontium 84, mercury 196, 204, and lead 204 among the heavier elements. Radioactive and stable isotopes are available for almost all elements which are essential to normal plant and animal growth.

Detection and Application of Radioisotopes. Most radioactive substances are detected by their emission of beta particles, or high-speed electrons; by their emission of gamma or alpha rays; or by their emission of beta, alpha, and gamma rays. Beta particles, by shooting through the air and knocking electrons off the outer rings of the atoms

they encounter, leave a wake of positively and negatively charged atoms which can be collected and measured as a current of electricity. Gamma rays, although possessing no charge, can be absorbed by a gas and detected by the secondary electrons which they cause to be ejected from the atoms of the gas. Various sensitive instruments are employed to detect and record the volume of charged atoms, or ions, which are produced as a result of radioactivity. The most common of these instruments, the Geiger-Mueller counter, is a modification of the ionization chamber (q.v.). It operates on the principle that the formation of one or more paired ions produces a large number of secondary ions which collect along a wire in the counter, and produce a momentary electrical impulse. Another instrument, called the scintillation counter (q.v.) is rapidly replacing the Geiger-Müller counter, as it not only counts the number of particles involved in the ionizing radiations but also can determine their energy distributions. Permanent photographs of radio-activity may be obtained by use of a technique known as autoradiography. This technique employs a photographic-emulsion plate to intercept the alpha, beta, and gamma rays resulting from radioactive decomposition. The rays, when striking the plate, lose their energy by collision with the emulsion atoms, and produce in the emulsion many thousands of charged ions which cause a darkening of the film plate. The differences in color on the photographic plate are then interpreted, and information regarding the radioactive element and its compounds established. To measure the concentration of beta rays, a device known as the cloud chamber (q.v.) is often used. This device utilizes the principle of fog condensing on the ions produced by beta radiation to produce a series of fog droplets all along the path traced by the ions.

By the methods of radiation detection described above, radioactive elements and their compounds administered to plants and animals may be traced in their course through various tissues. At present, the two principal methods used for gathering physiological data with the aid of radioisotopes are: the direct measurement of radioactive samples of tissue after their removal from the body; and the measurement of the radioactivity of bodily structures *in situ*. In the first method, which is used mainly to determine the total volume of a specific element in various tissues, radioelements are administered as simple inorganic compounds; for example, radiosodium is given as sodium chloride, radiophosphorus as disodium phosphate, and radioiodine as sodium iodide. A sufficient time after the compound has been administered, the tissues or groups of tissues to be analyzed are removed from the body. The element in question is isolated, and its radioactivity compared with the total radioactivity of the isotope administered. Very often, the removed tissue is sectioned and the techniques of autoradiography applied to determine the tissue regions of greatest mineral deposition. In the second method of gathering data, that of detecting radiation from tissues *in situ,* radioactive minerals are administered in a manner similar to that of the first method. Their radiations, however, are measured by such instruments as the Geiger counter, which can be operated from outside the body. This method avoids the removal of tissue, and makes it possible to trace an element throughout its entire course in the plant or animal body.

Results of Tracer Methodology. The application of tracer methodology to biological research has resulted in the formation of many new concepts regarding plant and animal physiology. In agriculture, the incorporation of tracers in various fertilizers has enabled scientists to study the rate and efficiency of absorption by numerous plant crops of the essential elements, and has thereby resulted in the production of more efficient fertilizers. Tracers have also made it possible to compare the utility of a given element which already exists in the soil with that of the same element added to the soil as fertilizer. In the form of radiophosphorus, tracers are used to study the effects of sulfur sprays and other insecticides, and are used extensively in the investigation of photosynthesis (q.v.). In animal physiology, dozens of stable and radioactive isotopes have been used successfully to trace and analyze practically every process involved in animal metabolism. Sodium, one of the most abundant elements, has been used in radioactive forms to determine salt and water metabolism, and to assist in calculating the volume of extracellular fluids in the body, thereby aiding investigation of such diseases as dehydration and edema in farm animals. Radioactive isotopes of phosphorus, calcium, and strontium, by their manner of deposition in various tissues, have provided valuable information on calcification and the formation of bone. Radioactive iodine, when injected into the blood, enables hematologists to measure quickly and accurately the volume of blood in the body,

and thereby aids in the study of such diseases as anemia and chlorosis. Chlorine isotopes are being employed in the investigation of electrolyte metabolism, and those of argon in the investigation of breathing and rate of gas exchange. For information regarding the physiology of such elements as zinc, boron, and cobalt, which are present in minute amounts in most animal and plant tissues and are essential for normal growth, see TRACE ELEMENT.

Radioisotope Therapy. The discoveries resulting from tracer methodology have led to the use of radioisotopes as therapeutic agents in the treatment of various diseases. From the time it was first observed that the nuclei of fast-growing tumors absorbed radiophosphorus tracer material more rapidly than did normal-tissue nuclei, radioisotopes have been used to penetrate and destroy radiation-sensitive diseases such as leukemia, lymphoma, myeloma, polycythemia vera, and numerous cancers of the skin; see NEOPLASM. Common therapeutic radioisotopes include radiostrontium, which deposits itself in bone tissue and is used in the treatment of primary and metastatic bone tumors; and radioiodine, which is deposited in the thyroid gland and is used in the treatment of goiter (q.v.). Artificially induced radioisotopes, because of their comparatively short half-lives, are more valuable as therapeutic agents than naturally radioactive substances such as radium (q.v.), which were formerly used a great deal in the treatment of abnormal cell development.

In the use of radioactive tracers and therapeutic agents, there is always the danger of excess radiation disturbing chemical equilibrium and interfering with the normal metabolism of plant and animal cells. Before administering radioisotopes, either orally or intravenously, it is therefore necessary to determine the tolerance values, or maximum permissible dosages, for each of the radioelements employed. All tolerances of radioactive substances are measured in *roentgens,* or r's, a tolerance of one roentgen being equal to the quantity of gamma radiation which produces one esu (electrostatic unit) when falling on dry air under standard conditions of temperature and pressure. Because the effects of radiation by gamma, beta, alpha, neutron, and other forms of radioactive emission are different, the term *roentgen equivalent physical* (rep) is used to represent the equivalent strengths of radiations produced by rays other than gamma rays. The term *roentgen equivalent for man* (rem) is used to represent the amount of radiation which will produce the same damage to man as will one roentgen of gamma radiation. Today, the maximum exposure value for most radioisotopes administered as tracers or as therapeutic agents has been set as .1 rem for every 24-hour day.

Precautions against excessive exposure to radiation are taken by persons employed in the production, utilization, and administration of radioisotopes, as well as by those persons subjected to radioisotope analysis and therapy. Typical precautionary measures include: proper shielding from radiation; maintenance of adequate radiation-detection instruments; and the "monitoring" of persons and materials located in the vicinity of radioactive materials, in order to disclose any radioactivity above the maximum, or safe, exposure values; see ATOMIC ENERGY AND ATOMIC BOMB.

TRACERY, beautiful forms in stone with which the arches of Gothic windows are filled or traced for the support of the glass. These forms vary with every variety of Gothic architecture, from the simple early forms to the Decorated and Flamboyant.

Tracery was developed during the Gothic period chiefly in France and England from its germ in two openings grouped under an arch with a decorative opening pierced in the spandrel above them. This early phase, called *plate tracery,* is seen in the early rose windows of Chartres (1170) and in English churches of the 12th century. The openings were multiplied and in later examples replaced by slender mullions, arches, circles, cusps, and foils of stone (*bar tracery*). The general frame of each window inclosed several separate lights, and above and between their arched summits were minor foiled openings. The rose or wheel windows, such as those of Notre Dame in Paris, and the clerestory and chapel windows of the cathedrals of Reims and Amiens, illustrate the various stages of this development. This tracery spread gradually from the windows until it overran almost every part of the church with its delicate lace patterns, solid ground (*wall tracery*) or pierced.

The period of a Gothic structure can generally be judged with tolerable accuracy by the style of its tracery. This is particularly the case in England, where two of the three main divisions of the Gothic movement, the Decorated and the Perpendicular, are so called on account of their distinctive styles of tracery. During the Decorated period the tracery, at first composed of simple arches, circles,

and cusps (*geometric*), later assumed freer curved lines (*curvilinear* or *flowing*). About 1375 there is an almost abrupt transition to the *Perpendicular* tracery, in which vertical mullions dominate the design. The English tracery is richer and more varied than the French. The finest French examples are the great rose windows of the west fronts and especially the transepts of the great cathedrals (whence the term *Rayonnant*). The *Flamboyant* style in France, contemporary with the English Perpendicular, had tracery composed of swaying and flowing lines. German tracery followed in the main, but with variations, the French types (e.g., Strasbourg, Freiburg). With a few exceptions Italian tracery is negligible, as large windows were not in favor.

TRACHEA or **WINDPIPE,** term applied to the section of the mammalian respiratory tract located between the larynx and the bronchi. The trachea is made up of numerous cartilaginous half-rings, the open ends of which are directed backward. These rings, located one above the other, are connected by muscular and fibrous tissue. The trachea, in man, is about 4 inches long and 1 inch in diameter, and is lined internally with a ciliated mucous membrane. See RESPIRATION.

TRACHOMA, disease of the eye characterized by hard pustules or granular excrescences on the inner surface of the eyelids, and inflammation of the membrane. Kentucky has a bureau for trachoma and blindness, the disease being common there. Twenty-five percent of the Navajo and Pueblo Indians in Oklahoma have also been found to be affected, and special measures have been adopted there to combat it. It is a major cause of blindness among populations living under unhygienic conditions. According to some authorities the disease is caused by a virus which has not been isolated. In its early stages trachoma responds readily to the administration of sulfonamides or broad-spectrum antibiotics.

TRACK AND FIELD, term denoting a group of athletic events contested at both indoor and outdoor meets. The basic categories of track and field events are the runs, walks, jumps, throws, and decathlon. Running events, which comprise the largest group of track and field sports, range from the 40-yard dash to the 26-mile Marathon race. In the United States and Great Britain the distances covered are expressed usually in yards. In Europe and in the Olympic Games (q.v.) the distances are expressed in meters.

Dashes. The shortest and swiftest running events are the dashes, or sprints. Indoor dashes are run over distances of 40, 50, or 60 yards. Outdoors, the most popular distances are 100 and 220 yards. In running the dashes the athlete crouches at the starting line, leaps into full stride at the crack of the starter's pistol, and races to the finish line at top speed. The chief characteristics of efficient sprinting style are high knee lift, free-swinging arm movements, and a forward lean of about 25 degrees. Sprinters of championship caliber usually run the 100-yard dash in 9.5 seconds or less, and 220 yards in under 21 seconds.

Hurdling. Hurdling events are essentially long dashes in which competitors must clear a series of wooden barriers called hurdles. The most popular outdoor hurdling events are the 120-yard high hurdles, the 220-yard low hurdles, and the 440-yard intermediate hurdles. Indoor races are run over high hurdles at distances varying from 60 to 75 yards. High hurdles stand 3 feet, 6 inches from the ground, low hurdles are 2 feet, 6 inches high, and intermediate hurdles are 3 feet in height. Good hurdling form consists in leaning well forward and clearing each barrier smoothly without breaking the rhythm of the running stride. The first leg to clear the hurdle is brought down to the track sharply. The trailing leg meanwhile clears the hurdle at almost a right angle to the body. Running speed, gymnastic ability, and superior co-ordination are prerequisites of success in hurdling.

Middle-Distance Runs. Races ranging from 440 yards to 2 miles are known as middle-distance events. The most popular indoor distances are 600 yards, 1000 yards, 1 mile, and 2 miles. The outdoor races are the 440-yard, 880-yard, 1-mile, and 2-mile runs. The 440-yard event closely resembles a sprint race, for it is run at almost full speed. During a typical 440-yard contest a runner achieves his top speed in the first 200 yards, "coasts" or "floats" for another 150 yards, then finishes the race in a final burst of speed. Some runners prefer to sprint at top speed for the first 200 or 300 yards, then coast through the remaining distance. In coasting or floating, the runner conserves his energy by relaxing, lengthening his stride, and allowing his momentum to carry him along close to top speed. Champions run the 440-yard distance in 46 seconds or less.

Competitors in the longer middle-distance runs must maintain a pace far below their top running speed in order to avoid exhaustion. By regulating his speed carefully, a mediocre runner often can defeat good runners who squander their energy through bad pacing. Some middle-distance runners change their speed several times during a race, while others strive to maintain an even pace throughout. The great Finnish runner Paavo Nurmi (1897–   ) carried a stopwatch during races as a means of checking on his pace. The running form best suited to middle-distance events differs considerably from that employed in the sprints. Knee action is much less pronounced, the stride is shorter, and the lean forward is less extreme than that used by sprinters.

Distance Runs. Runs longer than 2 miles are considered distance events. Distance running is especially popular in Europe, where races of 5000 to 10,000 meters are commonplace. In the running style employed by champion distance runners all waste motion is avoided. The knee action is slight, arm movements are reduced to a comfortable minimum, and the strides are much shorter than those used in sprinting or middle-distance running. When in full stride, the distance runner lands on the ball of his foot, lowers his heel to the ground briefly, then drives forward off his toes.

Among the most grueling distance runs are the cross-country and marathon races. Unlike other distance races, which are contested on flat cinder tracks, cross-country races are run over rough, rolling terrain and the marathon usually is run on paved roads. Runners in these events must learn to ascend hills with short, efficient strides and to descend hills rapidly without jarring themselves. On level surfaces, cross-country running style requires an erect carriage and the ball-heel-ball foot action used in other distance runs. A steady, even pace is essential to good cross-country performance. Cross-country races seldom exceed 7 miles.

The marathon is an exacting race over a course of 26 miles, 385 yards. In the United States marathon runs are sponsored annually by the Boston (Mass.) Athletic Association and the Amateur Athletic Union. The event is contested also at the Olympic Games.

Relays. Relay races are team events in which an athlete runs a given distance, called a "leg", then passes a wooden baton to his successor. The pass must be accomplished within a zone extending 20 yards. In the 440- and 880-yard relays the passer places the baton in the hand of the receiver, who is thus free to get underway while facing forward. In longer relays the receiver looks back and takes the baton, for the passer is likely to be badly fatigued. Ideally, receiver and passer should be in full stride and about 2 yards apart when the baton is handed over. If the legs of a relay race vary in length, e.g., 880, 220, 220, and 440 yards, the contest is called a medley relay. In so-called shuttle relays, the members of the competing teams shuttle back and forth along a single stretch of track. Upon completion of each leg the runner touches his successor instead of passing a baton.

Steeplechase. The steeplechase is an obstacle race, run usually over a 3000-meter course containing hurdles, water jumps, and other hazards. An extremely exhausting event, it is run at the Olympics, but is rarely contested in U.S. meets.

Walks. The walking events are foot races contested at distances ranging from 220 yards to 30 miles. The cardinal rule of such races is that the heel of the forward foot must touch the track before the toe of the trailing foot leaves the ground. The rule is designed to prevent running by the contestants. Walking events are contested at the Olympics, but seldom are scheduled at American meets.

The jumping events, among the most color-

MEN'S WORLD RECORDS

RUNNING

Event	Record	Holder	Country	Place	Date
100 yd. dash	9.3s.	Melvin Patton	U.S.A.	U.S.A.	May 15, 1948
		H. D. Hogan	Australia	Australia	March 13, 1954
		James Goliday	U.S.A.	U.S.A.	May 14, 1955
		Leamon King	U.S.A.	U.S.A.	May 12, 1956
		David Sime	U.S.A.	U.S.A.	June 9, 1956
220 yd. dash	20.0s.	David Sime	U.S.A.	U.S.A.	June 9, 1956
440 yd. run	45.8s.	Jim Lea	U.S.A.	U.S.A.	May 26, 1956
880 yd. run	1m.47.5s.	Lon Spurrier	U.S.A.	U.S.A.	March 26, 1955
1 mile run	3m.58.0s.	John Landy	Australia	Finland	June 21, 1954
2 mile run	8m.33.4s.	Sandor Iharos	Hungary	Gt. Britain	May 30, 1955
3 mile run	13m.14.2s.	Sandor Iharos	Hungary	Hungary	Oct. 23, 1955
6 mile run	27m.43.8s.	Sandor Iharos	Hungary	Hungary	July 15, 1956
10 mile run	48m.12.0s.	Emil Zatopek	Czechoslovakia	Czechoslovakia	Sept. 29, 1951
15 mile run	1hr.14m.01.0s.	Emil Zatopek	Czechoslovakia	Czechoslovakia	Oct. 29, 1956
1 hour run	12mi.809yds.	Emil Zatopek	Czechoslovakia	Czechoslovakia	Sept. 29, 1951
100 meter dash	10.1s.	Willie Williams	U.S.A.	Germany	Aug. 3, 1956
		Ira Murchison	U.S.A.	Germany	Aug. 4, 1956
200 meter dash	20.0s.	David Sime	U.S.A.	U.S.A.	June 9, 1956
400 meter dash	45.2s.	Lou Jones	U.S.A.	U.S.A.	June 30, 1956
800 meter run	1m.45.7s.	Roger Moens	Belgium	Norway	Aug. 3, 1955
1000 meter run	2m.19.0s.	Audun Boysen	Norway	Sweden	Aug. 30, 1955
		Istvan Rozsavolgyi	Hungary	Hungary	Sept. 21, 1955
1500 meter run	3m.40.6s.	Istvan Rozsavolgyi	Hungary	Hungary	Aug. 3, 1956
2000 meter run	5m.02.2s.	Istvan Rozsavolgyi	Hungary	Hungary	Oct. 2, 1955
3000 meter run	7m.52.8s.	Gordon Pirie	Gt. Britain	Sweden	Sept. 4, 1956
5000 meter run	13m.36.8s.	Gordon Pirie	Gt. Britain	Norway	June 19, 1956
10,000 meter run	28m.30.4s.	Vladimir Kuts	U.S.S.R.	U.S.S.R.	Sept. 11, 1956
20,000 meter run	59m.51.8s.	Emil Zatopek	Czechoslovakia	Czechoslovakia	Sept. 29, 1951
25,000 meter run	1hr.16m.36.4s.	Emil Zatopek	Czechoslovakia	Czechoslovakia	Oct. 29, 1956
30,000 meter run	1hr.35m.03.6s.	Antti Viskari	Finland	Finland	Oct. 21, 1956
3000 meter steeplechase	8m.35.6s.	Sandor Rozsnyoi	Hungary	Hungary	Sept. 16, 1956
1 hour run	20,052 meters	Emil Zatopek	Czechoslovakia	Czechoslovakia	Sept. 29, 1951

WALKING

Event	Record	Holder	Country	Place	Date
2 mile walk	12m.45.0s.	Verner Hardmo	Sweden	Sweden	Sept. 1, 1945
5 mile walk	34m.32.8s.	J. Dolezal	Czechoslovakia	Gt. Britain	Oct. 15, 1955
7 mile walk	48m.15.2s.	Verner Hardmo	Sweden	Sweden	Sept. 9, 1945
10 mile walk	1hr.10m.45.8s.	J. Dolezal	Czechoslovakia	Czechoslovakia	April 30, 1954
20 mile walk	2hr.33m.09.4s.	J. Dolezal	Czechoslovakia	Czechoslovakia	May 14, 1954
30 mile walk	4hr.12m.03.4s.	L. Moc	U.S.S.R.	Czechoslovakia	June 21, 1956
1 hour walk	8mi.1025yds.	John Mikaelsson	Sweden	Sweden	Sept. 1, 1945
2 hour walk	16mi.126yds.	A. Vedjakov	U.S.S.R.	U.S.S.R.	Oct. 7, 1955
3000 meters	11m.51.8s.	Verner Hardmo	Sweden	Sweden	Sept. 1, 1945
5000 meters	20m.26.8s.	Verner Hardmo	Sweden	Sweden	Sept. 1, 1945
10,000 meters	42m.39.6s.	Verner Hardmo	Sweden	Sweden	Sept. 9, 1945
15,000 meters	1hr.05m.59.6s.	J. Dolezal	Czechoslovakia	Czechoslovakia	April 30, 1954
20,000 meters	1hr.27m.58.2s.	M. Lavrov	U.S.S.R.	U.S.S.R.	Aug. 13, 1956
30,000 meters	2hr.20m.40.2s.	A. Vedjakov	U.S.S.R.	U.S.S.R.	Oct. 7, 1955
50,000 meters	4hr.21m.07.0s.	L. Moc	U.S.S.R.	Czechoslovakia	June 21, 1956

HURDLES

Event	Record	Holder	Country	Place	Date
120 yard	13.4s.	Jack Davis	U.S.A.	U.S.A.	June 22, 1956
220 yard	22.2s.	David Sime	U.S.A.	U.S.A.	May 5, 1956
440 yard	51.3s.	Yuri Lituyev	U.S.S.R.	Gt. Britain	Oct. 13, 1954
110 meter	13.4s.	Jack Davis	U.S.A.	U.S.A.	June 22, 1956
200 meter	22.2s.	David Sime	U.S.A.	U.S.A.	May 5, 1956
400 meter	49.5s.	Glenn Davis	U.S.A.	U.S.A.	June 29, 1956

FIELD EVENTS

Event	Record	Holder	Country	Place	Date
High jump	7ft.½in.	Charles Dumas	U.S.A.	U.S.A.	June 29, 1956
Running broad jump	26ft.8¼in.	Jesse Owens	U.S.A.	U.S.A.	May 25, 1935
Running hop, step, and jump	54ft.3¾in.	Adhemar F. da Silva	Brazil	Mexico	March 16, 1955
Pole vault	15ft.7¾in.	C. Warmerdam	U.S.A.	U.S.A.	May 23, 1942
16-lb. shot-put	63ft.1¾in.	Parry O'Brien	U.S.A.	U.S.A.	Nov. 1, 1956
16-lb. hammer throw	220ft.10in.	M. P. Krivonosov	U.S.S.R.	U.S.S.R.	Oct. 22, 1956
Discus throw	194ft.6in.	Fortune Gordien	U.S.A.	U.S.A.	Aug. 22, 1953
Javelin throw	281ft.2in.	Egil Danielson	Norway	Australia	Nov. 26, 1956

WOMEN'S WORLD RECORDS

Event	Record	Holder	Country	Place	Date
100 yd. dash	10.4s.	Marjorie Jackson	Australia	Australia	March 8, 1952
220 yd. dash	23.6s.	Maria Itkina	U.S.S.R.	U.S.S.R.	July 22, 1956
880 yd. run	2m.06.6s.	N. Otkalenko	U.S.S.R.	U.S.S.R.	June 10, 1956
60 meter dash	7.3s.	Stella Walasiewicz	Poland	Poland	Sept. 24, 1933
100 meter dash	11.3s.	Shirley S. De La Hunty	Australia	Poland	Aug. 4, 1955
200 meter dash	23.4s.	Marjorie Jackson	Australia	Finland	July 25, 1952
		Betty Cuthbert	Australia	Australia	Nov. 30, 1956
		Maria Itkina	U.S.S.R.	U.S.S.R.	Oct. 14, 1956
800 meter run	2m.05.0s.	N. Otkalenko	U.S.S.R.	Yugoslavia	Sept. 24, 1956
80 meter hurdle	10.6s.	Z. Gastl	Germany	Germany	July 29, 1956
Running high jump	5ft.9¼in.	Mildred McDaniel	U.S.A.	Australia	Dec. 1, 1956
Running broad jump	20ft.9¾in.	Elzbieta Dunska-Kreskinska	Poland	Hungary	Aug. 20, 1956
Shot-put	54ft.11¾in.	Galina Zybina	U.S.S.R.	U.S.S.R.	Oct. 13, 1956
Discus throw	187ft.1½in.	N. Dumbadze	U.S.S.R.	U.S.S.R.	Oct. 18, 1952
Javelin throw	182ft.0in.	N. Konjaeva	U.S.S.R.	U.S.S.R.	Aug. 6, 1954

ful of track and field contests, include the high jump, pole vault, broad jump, and the hop, step, and jump.

High Jump. The aim in high jumping is to leap over, or "clear", a crossbar resting between two upright standards. Though there are many jumping styles, champion jumpers mainly employ the "Western Roll" and the "Straddle". In preparing to use either style, the athlete runs toward the bar at a 45 degree angle and springs upward, combining a powerful kick of his outside leg with a leaping takeoff from his inside foot. To execute the Western style, the jumper then snaps his takeoff leg up sharply, and rolls across the bar on his takeoff side. To execute the Straddle, known also as the "Belly Roll", he clears the bar face down in a prone position. The Straddle is preferred generally by top performers. Champion jumpers consistently clear heights within a few inches of 7 feet.

Pole Vault. In pole vaulting the athlete attempts to clear a high crossbar with the aid of a steel, aluminum, or bamboo pole from 12 to 16 feet long. Grasping the pole several feet from its top, the vaulter races down a short runway, digs the tip of the pole into a box or slot in the ground, and swings upward toward the bar. The abrupt conversion of his forward speed into upward momentum enables the vaulter to project himself to heights often greater than that of his pole. As his feet near the bar the vaulter does a virtual handstand on the pole, thrusting his body across the bar face down. He then descends into a soft pit in the track below. Vaulters usually possess above-average running speed, powerful shoulder muscles, and all-round gymnastic ability. A number of American vaulters have cleared 15 feet.

Broad Jumps. In broad jumping, the contestant dashes along a cinder path and springs into the air from a take-off board, with the aim of covering the greatest possible distance. The jump is nullified if he falls backward after landing. While still in the air the jumper throws both feet far forward of his body. Though adding distance to the jump, this maneuver will cause him to topple backward unless he succeeds in flinging his body forward upon landing. Broad jumping requires strong leg and abdominal muscles, running speed, and leg spring. Several jumpers have surpassed the 26-foot mark.

Hop, Step, and Jump. The aim in the hop, step, and jump is to cover the greatest distance possible in a series of three quick leaps. In the first phase of the sequence the jumper sprints along a running path, "hops" into the air from a take-off board, and comes down on his take-off foot. He then springs or "steps" forward off the take-off foot and lands on the opposite foot. In the same motion he "jumps" into the air once more and lands on both feet, like a broad jumper. A number of athletes have exceeded 50 feet in the hop, step, and jump. The event is contested at the Olympic Games but only rarely at U.S. meets.

The throwing events include the shot put and the discus, hammer, and javelin throws.

Shot Put. The aim in shot putting is to propel a 12- or 16-pound ball through the air for a maximum distance. The lighter ball is used in high-school competition. The action in shot putting is confined to a circle 7 feet in diameter. In the first phase of the event, the athlete holds the shot in the fingers of his throwing hand and rests the hand against his shoulder. He then bounds or hops across the circle in a half-crouch, building up speed as he goes. When he reaches the opposite side of the circle he straightens suddenly and puts the shot with an explosive uncoiling of his arm and body. The shot is pushed into the air, not thrown. If the contestant steps outside the circle, the throw is disallowed. Champion shot putters often approach and, in some cases, exceed the 60-foot mark.

Discus Throw. The discus, a steel-rimmed hardwood platter measuring 8⅝ inches across and 1¾ inches in thickness and weighing 4 pounds, 6.4 ounces, is thrown from a circle 8 feet, 2½ inches in diameter. The athlete holds the discus flat against the palm and forearm of his throwing arm. He then whirls around rapidly and propels the discus outward with a whipping motion of his arm. The longest throw, measured from the outside of the circle to the point of first contact with the ground, wins the competition. Some throws exceed 190 feet. The discus throw is a traditional event in U.S. track meets and at the Olympic Games.

Hammer Throw. Hammer throwers compete by hurling a heavy ball attached to a length of wire which has a metal handle. The ball, wire, and handle weigh 16 pounds and form a unit no longer than 4 feet. The action takes place in a circle 7 feet in diameter. The athlete grips the handle with both hands and, without moving his feet, whirls the ball around in a circle passing above and behind his head and just below his kneecaps. As the hammer gains momentum, the athlete suddenly whirls his body around three times to impart even greater velocity to the ball. The hammer is then released upward and outward at a 45-degree angle. If it falls outside a prescribed 90-degree arc, the throw is invalid. Hammer throwers are usually tall and muscular, but success in the event is dependent also upon timing and co-ordination. Several athletes have thrown the hammer more than 200 feet.

Javelin Throw. The javelin is a steel-tipped wooden spear with a minimum length of 8 feet and a minimum weight of 1¾ pounds. The contestant grasps the javelin near its center of gravity and sprints toward a check line. As he nears the line he twists to one side, draws back the javelin, and prepares to throw. Meanwhile, in order to maintain his running speed while leaning back for the throw, he executes a hop or fast cross step. At the check line he pivots forward abruptly and hurls the javelin into the air. The throw is disallowed if he steps across the line or if the javelin does not fall to earth point first. Top competitors throw the javelin more than 250 feet.

Decathlon. The decathlon is a 2-day, 10-event contest which places a premium on stamina and versatility. The events are, in order, the 100-meter dash, broad jump, shot put, high jump, 400-meter run, 110-meter high hurdles, discus throw, pole vault, javelin throw, and 1500-meter run. The athlete's performance in the various events is rated against an ideal score of 10,000 points. The highest point total determines the winner.

History. Track and field events have been contested for thousands of years. The first organized meets known to history were the Olympian Games (q.v.), which the Greeks initiated in 776 B.C. For many years the chief Olympian competition was the pentathlon, which comprised discus and javelin throwing, foot racing, broad jumping, and wrestling.

Other contests, including foot races for men clad in full armor, were later added to the program. The Romans continued to hold the Olympian contests after they conquered Greece in 146 B.C. In 394 A.D. the games were abolished by the Roman emperor Theodosius. For eight centuries thereafter no organized track and field competitions were held, although informal running, jumping, and throwing contests often took place among soldiers in training. Revived in England about the middle of the 12th century, track and field gradually became a favorite English sport. The first modern athletic club was founded in Necton, Suffolk, England, in 1871, and in 1834 a group of English enthusiasts agreed on the minimum standards of performance expected of athletes competing in certain track and field events, notably the 440-yard run (60 seconds), one-mile run (5 minutes), 2-mile run (10 minutes), broad jump (20 feet), and high jump (5 feet, 6 inches). Other 19th-century landmarks in track and field included the first college meet (1864), between Oxford and Cambridge, the first national meet, in London in 1866, and the first U.S. amateur meet, held indoors in 1868.

Track and field subsequently gained a large following in the United States, and in 1876 a number of eastern colleges formed the Intercollegiate Association of Amateur Athletes of America (I.C.A.A.A.A.). The Amateur Athletic Union of the United States (A.A.U.), an organization serving the needs of collegians and noncollegians alike, was founded in 1888. In 1896 the Olympic Games, a modified revival of the Olympian Games, were initiated in Athens, Greece. Thereafter the games were held in various countries at intervals of four years, except in time of war. During the 20th century many track and field records long regarded as ultimate accomplishments were either equaled or surpassed, notably 4 minutes for the mile, 7 feet for the high jump, 60 feet for the shot put, and 46 seconds for the 440-yard run.

TRACTARIANISM, popular name for the Oxford Movement referring to the ninety *Tracts for the Times,* published at Oxford in 1833–41. The principal writers were Pusey, Newman, Keble, Hurrell Froude, and Isaac Williams. See OXFORD MOVEMENT.

TRADE. See COMMERCE.

TRADE, BOARD OF, a department of the British executive which exercises important functions in all commercial matters falling within the purview of the government. Crom-well in 1655 was the first to establish a permanent committee for matters of trade. Charles II continued the policy and in 1660 created two separate councils for trade and for foreign plantations, which in 1672 were consolidated into one. In 1786 the present department was established as a permanent committee of the Privy Council. The board as now constituted consists of the president, who is a member of the cabinet, together with the first lord of the treasury, the chancellor of the Exchequer, and numerous other ex-officio members; but, like the Treasury Board, the Board of Trade does not meet and consists in practice of the president and his staff. The board consists of two main departments, Home Trade Matters and Foreign and Commercial Relations. The latter includes branches for Trade treaties and Export Licensing.

TRADE ASSOCIATIONS, associations of manufacturers, tradesmen, or businessmen engaged in the furtherance or protection of their mutual interests. In England these associations antedate the 19th century. In the United States some were founded before 1850; by 1890 they had been formed in most well-established industries; while by 1900 they had spread to almost every subdivision of the industrial world. Trade association may include one or more of three classes of functions—the commercial, the industrial, and the protective. Associations to do the work of business agencies display most clearly the commercial function. The London Association of Guardians for the Protection of Trade was established as far back as the year 1776.

The operation of the earlier societies was confined chiefly to compilations of registers of bankruptcies, insolvencies, and private settlements with creditors. Societies may undertake investigations into the circumstances connected with a bankruptcy and perform the general agency business of their members. Many establishments maintain separate credit departments in the charge of special credit men who have formed a national association, with branches in many chief U.S. cities.

The general industrial functions include the surveillance of important influences, such as legislation, railway rates, the tariff, laws affecting labor, the quality, the method of sale, or the inspection of goods. In the second place, associations may seek to keep their members informed of new inventions or processes, of market conditions, etc. Provision may be made for exhibits at fairs, trade schools may be encouraged, selling agencies established, bureaus of employment maintained, or local improvements furthered, or, a system of mutual insurance may be attempted.

At present the typical forms of protection are: (1) against introduction of so-called unfair methods within the trade; (2) against railroad discrimination in rates; and (3) against labor organizations.

In recent years there has been a rapid growth of trade associations of employers in the United States formed to deal with labor unions and to conclude agreements on wage scales and on conditions of labor.

TRADE CYCLE. See BUSINESS CYCLE.

TRADE FAIRS. See EXHIBITIONS AND EXPOSITIONS.

TRADE-MARK, in law in the United States, as defined under the Trade-Mark Act of 1946, any word, name, symbol, or device, or any combination thereof, adopted and used by a manufacturer or merchant to identify his goods and distinguish them from those made or sold by others. Examples of trade-marks are "Kodak", "Duz", and "Nu-Enamel". Under common law, ownership of a trade-mark depends on proof of the earliest use. Federal statutes govern trade-mark registration; registration gives prima-facie evidence of the registrant's ownership of the trade-mark; it is evidence of the registrant's exclusive right to use the trade-mark and gives the registrant the right to sue others for using it. Applications for trade-mark registration must be filed in the patent office; the trade-mark must be used in interstate or foreign commerce before it can be registered. Trade-marks are not protected by the copyright laws.

A trade-mark cannot be registered if it is identical with that used by another party on the same class of goods, or if it so nearly resembles another trade-mark as to be likely to cause confusion in trade. No one can register a trade-mark containing immoral or scandalous matter, or one which includes the flag or coat of arms or other insignia of the United States, of any State or municipality, or of any foreign nation, or the emblem of any fraternal society. No portrait of a living individual may be registered as a trade-mark except by the written consent of the individual; the portrait of a deceased President of the U.S. cannot be registered during the life of his widow except by her written consent.

The law of trade-marks is of recent development. The first trade-mark statute in the United States was passed in 1881. Important changes in legislation governing trade-mark registration were made in the acts of February 20, 1905; March 19, 1920; June 10, 1938; and July 5, 1946. The 1946 act became effective on July 5, 1947, and repealed all previously existing trade-mark statutes. Under the 1946 statute, also known as the Lanham Act, two registers were established, designated a principal register and a supplemental register. Registration on the principal register corresponds to registry under the 1905 act and is merely evidence of the registrant's exclusive right to the use of the trade-mark; the registrant may, however, under the present law, acquire "incontestability" of his registration, after five years of undisputed use, by filing an affidavit stating its continuous use and that there has been no decision adverse to registrant's claim of ownership and that no proceeding is pending in the courts involving such rights. Under the act of 1905 a petition to cancel a registrant's trade-mark could be brought at any time, inasmuch as registration under the 1905 act gave only prima-facie evidence of ownership, which could be contested at any time by a party claiming prior use of the trade-mark. The effect of the present statute is to compel disputants to assert their claims against the registrant's use of the trade-mark in the first five years after it has been registered.

Registration on the supplemental register corresponds to that provided for in the 1920 act, which permitted registration of certain marks not previously registerable. Under the 1905 act trade-marks with a geographic or descriptive meaning could not be registered. Under the 1920 act a geographical name, or words descriptive of the goods, could be registered provided that such mark had been in use in interstate or foreign commerce for at least a year; such registration, however, did not give prima-facie evidence of ownership to the registrant. Trade-marks registered in accordance with the 1905 act may be re-registered on the principal register; trade-marks registered under the 1920 act expire within twenty years of registration and are not renewable; they may be re-registered on the principal register only if the mark has acquired a distinctive meaning. Thus trade-marks previously unregistrable, consisting, for example, of a descriptive term, a surname, or a geographical term, are now registrable on the principal register, if such names have become distinctive of the owners' goods in commerce. A trade-mark registered under the 1920 act that is not suitable for the principal register may be re-registered on the supplementary system only if the registrant would otherwise lose a foreign registration. Under the new law the term of a trade-mark registration is twenty years, renewable at twenty-year intervals.

A complete application for registration of a trade-mark comprises a drawing of the mark, made by a competent draftsman, and five facsimiles of the drawing; a petition which contains the name, residence, and citizenship status of the applicant; and a statement as to the date of applicant's first use of the mark, the goods to which the mark is to be applied, and the manner in which the mark is used on such goods. The filing fee must accompany the application; the fee for a new registration is $25, and $10 for reregistration, or publication of a previously registered trade-mark. After the applicant for registration of a trade-mark files his application, an examination is made in the patent office to determine whether the applicant is entitled to have his trade-mark registered; if he is so entitled the trade-mark is then published in the official gazette of the patent office.

Any person who believes he would be damaged by the registration of another's trade-mark may oppose registration by filing notice of opposition, with the ground of such opposition, in the patent office within thirty days after the publication of the mark; if no notice of opposition is filed within that time, a certificate of resignation is issued to the applicant. If there is opposition to registration or if the patent office rejects the registrant's application because it interferes with a trade-mark registered by another party, a hearing is held by an examiner in charge of interferences to determine the question of the right of registration to the trade-mark. An appeal from the decision of the examiner in charge of interferences may be made to the commissioner of patents; an appeal from the decision of the commissioner of patents may be made to the U.S. Court of Customs and Patent Appeals.

In suits for trade-mark infringement the plaintiff must prove that the defendant knows, or had notice of, his registration of the trade-mark. The Lanham Act provides that notice of the registrant's exclusive use to the trade-mark registered on the principal register or registered under the acts of 1881 and 1905 is given when the mark is displayed on trade-marked goods by the words "Registered in U.S. Patent Office", "Reg. U.S. Pat. Off.", or the letter "R" enclosed within a circle.

In every other action for trade-mark infringement, recovery of damages is predicated on the infringer having received notice of the registration. The act forbids the importation of goods bearing infringing trade-marks.

A registered trade-mark, or a trade-mark for which application for registration has been made, is assignable in connection with the good will of the business, or that part of the good will of the business in which the trade-mark is used.

See also PATENT.

TRADE NAME, in law in the United States, the name or title lawfully adopted and used by any manufacturing, industrial, commercial, agricultural, or other organization engaged in trade or commerce. A trade name used by a manufacturer or merchant to identify his goods and distinguish them from those manufactured or sold by others may be registered as a trade-mark (q.v.). The statutes of the several States specify the formalities required for an individual or partnership desiring to do business under a trade name; the name adopted by a corporation is its trade name and may not be adopted by any other. A firm which uses the established trade name of another may be enjoined by a court of equity from such use and is liable for damages to the injured party resulting from such use. According to the courts, such wrongful use constitutes both a form of unfair competition with the injured party, involving fraud and deceit against the public, and an unlawful appropriation of the property of another. A trade name constitutes a significant part of a firm's good will.

TRADE SCHOOLS. See TECHNICAL EDUCATION.

TRADE UNION, an association of workingmen, organized primarily for the protection and improvement of the economic status of its members through the conduct of collective bargaining and such other joint actions as the boycott and the strike (qq.v.). Specifically, trade unions seek to improve, and to prevent adverse changes in, the wages, hours, and other conditions of employment of the workers; they may also provide the workers with health and welfare benefits, and cultural and recreational facilities. Trade unions are of two principal types: craft unions, composed of all workers performing a specific type of work, such as dressmakers, locomotive engineers, and teamsters; and industrial unions, comprising all workers in a given industry, such as steel workers, automobile workers, and maritime workers. In most industrial countries the unions are organized into national federations, which usually consist principally of either craft or industrial unions, but may include both types. In the United States, for example, the American Federation of Labor (q.v.) is composed chiefly of craft unions, while the Congress of Industrial Organizations (q.v.) consists chiefly of industrial unions.

Trade unions frequently engage in political activities; they may endorse candidates for political office who are deemed friendly to the unions, conduct political campaigns in opposition to hostile candidates, and publicly support legislation favoring the interests of the workers. This form of activity, however, generally serves as an auxiliary means of carrying out the fundamentally economic functions of trade unionism. On some occasions, trade unions have been used as primary instruments of revolutionary movements, particularly movements espousing the doctrines of syndicalism (q.v.).

Historically, the trade-union movement stemmed from and was a concomitant feature of the development of capitalist society. Like capitalism, trade unionism received great impetus from the Industrial Revolution (q.v.) of the 18th century, which made possible the establishment of large factories employing masses of workers; see also FACTORIES AND THE FACTORY SYSTEM. The earliest trade unions were formed during the 18th and early 19th centuries in countries having the highest relative degree of industrial development, such as England, Germany, France, and the United States. These early unions frequently took the form of local associations of skilled craftsmen and artisans, and in many respects resembled the guilds (see GUILD) formed by skilled workers in the later Middle Ages. In many cases, the organization of unions had to be carried on secretly in order to circumvent repressive legislation enacted in several countries declaring the trade unions to be illegal combinations and conspiracies in restraint of trade. Notable among these restrictive laws were the Combination Acts passed in England in 1799–1800 and the Le Chapelier Law enacted in France in 1791. In the United States, repression of the early trade unions often occurred in the form of judicial action; for example, in 1806 the leaders of the Federal Society of Journeymen Cordwainers, a union of shoemakers organized in Philadelphia in 1792, were tried and convicted of the charge of "conspiracy to raise wages". For a detailed account of the

history of the U.S. trade-union movement, see TRADE UNIONS IN THE UNITED STATES.

The development of trade unions in Europe during the 19th century was characterized by the gradual abolition of the most flagrant forms of legal repression, and by a steady growth in union membership. The leading country in industrial development and consequently in trade-union organization was Great Britain, which by 1900 had more than 2,000,000 workers organized into trade unions. About 1,250,000 of the unionized British workers were members of unions affiliated with the Trades Union Congress, the leading national labor federation. The number of union members in Germany in 1900 exceeded 850,000; in France, however, the trade unions developed more slowly than elsewhere, principally because the proportion of industrial workers in the entire population was still comparatively low at the beginning of the 20th century. The membership of the principal French trade-union federation, the Confédération Générale du Travail, only slightly exceeded 100,000 in 1900.

During the closing years of the 19th century a movement developed in Europe for the formation of an international trade-union federation. This goal was realized in 1903 with the establishment of the International Secretariat of National Trade Union Centers, an organization set up with the active support of the Second, or Labor and Socialist, International (q.v.). In 1904, the year following its foundation, the International Secretariat had a total membership of more than 2,500,-000 workers belonging to trade unions in fourteen European countries. Five years later its membership was considerably raised by the affiliation of the American Federation of Labor, which gave the organization intercontinental coverage and led to the changing of its name to the International Federation of Trade Unions. The membership of the IFTU mounted rapidly; by 1912 it had almost 7,400,000 members in nineteen countries. The outbreak of World War I in 1914 was followed by a lapse in the activities of the IFTU. In July, 1919, after the conclusion of hostilities, a reorganizing conference was held in Amsterdam, Holland, and the organization resumed its prominent role in the world labor movement. Of an estimated total trade-union membership of 42,000,000 in thirty countries in December, 1919, the IFTU accounted for 23,000,000 members in twenty-one countries.

The sharpening of the conflict between the

world socialist and communist movements which occurred after the Bolshevik Revolution of 1917 was reflected in a split within the IFTU. In 1921 the Third (Communist) International (q.v.) set up the Red International of Labor Unions as a communist rival to the socialist-led IFTU. The question of relations with the Red International caused a division among the IFTU leaders, weakening the influence and prestige of the organization. Further damage was done to the position of the IFTU by the establishment in Berlin in 1923 of a syndicalist federation, the International Workingmen's Association, which attracted large numbers of workers in Spain, Portugal, Germany, and Latin America. For these and other reasons, the IFTU membership declined considerably during the 1920's.

The severe depression which followed the world-wide economic crisis of 1929, however, was marked by a notable rise in IFTU membership, which in 1937 approximated 18,000,-000 persons. The year 1935 was notable for the dissolution of the Red International of Labor Unions by the Communist International, which urged those of its members not living in the Soviet Union to affiliate with the noncommunist unions in the interest of forming a "united front" against the aggressive forces of fascism (q.v.; see also NATIONAL SOCIALISM). In 1938 a proposal was submitted to the General Council of the IFTU to admit the trade unions of the U.S.S.R. to membership. As a precondition for their affiliation, the Soviet trade unions, which had a membership of about 20,000,000, demanded that the IFTU alter its structure to provide for the election of two presidents and two general secretaries enjoying equal powers, with one of each to be elected solely by the Soviet trade unions. This condition was found unacceptable by the IFTU leadership, and the proposal was rejected.

During World War II, the IFTU affiliates in the various countries warring against the Axis Powers actively supported the war efforts of their respective countries. In conformity with its policy of accepting only one representative trade-union organization from each country, the IFTU continued to recognize the American Federation of Labor and to bar the Congress of Industrial Organizations from membership. Moreover, in accordance with its traditional hostility to the Soviet Union, the IFTU continued its policy of non-co-operation with the trade unions of the USSR. The British Trades Union Congress, one of the leading affiliates of the IFTU and the representative of virtually all organized labor in the United Kingdom, became increasingly dissatisfied with these policies of the IFTU, and in 1944 convoked a world labor conference, primarily for the purpose of forming a new international trade-union federation. Among those invitied, in addition to the IFTU affiliates, were the Soviet trade unions, the CIO, and a number of independent U.S. unions. The AFL refused the invitation, charging that the conference was aimed at splitting the world labor movement, and that the Soviet trade unions were not free and democratic organizations. The conference met in London in February, 1945, and organized the World Federation of Trade Unions, comprising unions from fifty-six countries with a combined membership of about 66,000,000. In December of the same year the IFTU, its membership greatly diminished by the defection of such large affiliates as the British Trades Union Congress and the Dutch Federation of Labor, and of many lesser trade-union bodies, was formally dissolved.

In the years following the conclusion of World War II in 1945, the unity of the WFTU was subject to increasing tension owing to the developing antagonisms between the communist-led unions of the U.S.S.R. and other nations of Eastern Europe, on the one hand, and the unions of the Western nations, particularly Great Britain and the United States, on the other. The growing dissension culminated in January, 1949, in the withdrawal from the WFTU of the American CIO, the British Trades Unions Congress, and the Dutch Federation of Labor, which charged that the federation had come under the domination of the Soviet communists, and that the latter had converted it into an organ for propaganda and revolutionary activities. Soon after their resignation, the dissident unions launched preparations for the organization of a new trade-union federation. Late in 1949 delegates representing over 47,000,000 workers convened in London and founded the International Confederation of Free Trade Unions. Both the AFL and the independent United Mine Workers Union (U.S.) joined the new organization. In 1951 the trade unions of the newly established Chinese People's Republic affiliated with the WFTU. The latter organization intensified its activities in Asia, Africa, and Latin America during 1950 and 1951; by the middle of 1951 its claimed membership totaled 78,000,000 in 56 countries. Substantial advances were registered in 1951 by the

ICFTU, which reported (July) a membership of 52,000,000 in 66 countries. In 1952 its membership increased by 1,000,000. The ICFTU held its first World Congress in Stockholm, Sweden, in July, 1953.

TRADE UNIONS IN THE UNITED STATES.
The early development of the trade-union movement in the United States was basically parallel to the development of unions in other countries (see TRADE UNION). The first to organize were the skilled workers; during the 1790's organizations resembling the craft unions of the present day were formed by the carpenters and shoemakers of Philadelphia, the tailors of Baltimore, and the printers of New York City. Many other types of skilled workers began to form similar associations during the early decades of the 19th century, and in several cities these associations were organized into local federations known as "Trades' Unions". In addition to carrying on activities aimed at the improvement of the members' wages and working conditions, the federations actively espoused various social reforms, such as the establishment of free public education, the abolition of imprisonment for debt, and the adoption of universal manhood suffrage.

Attempts were made during the 1830's to organize the city-wide federations and various independent local unions into a national federation, but the economic crisis of 1837 and the ensuing depression led to a sharp decline in union membership, temporarily halting the movement toward federation. Union organization again began to progress after the revival of business in the 1840's and early 1850's, and many local unions of workers employed in the same crafts banded together to form the first national craft unions. Included among the categories of skilled workers who formed these national unions were the typographers (organized in 1852), the journeymen stonecutters (1853), the hat finishers (1854), the blacksmiths and machinists (1857), and the iron molders (1859). The economic crisis of 1857 resulted in another drastic curtailment of trade-union membership, however, and caused even the dissolution of several national unions.

During and after the Civil War the industrialization of the United States proceeded at an accelerated pace, and was accompanied by a corresponding development of unionization among the workers. More than thirty national craft unions were established during the 1860's and early 1870's. The year 1866 was especially notable for the formation of

the National Labor Union, the first federation of national and local unions and city-wide trade-union organizations. The NLU was short-lived, however; its concentration on political action alienated many of its constituent unions, whose membership regarded purely economic struggles as the sole proper function of trade unions. The withdrawal of several national unions led to the dissolution of the NLU in 1872.

Despite the militant opposition of many employers to the growing trade-union movement, the decade of the 1870's was a period of widespread labor agitation and unrest, owing largely to the difficult economic conditions which prevailed among the workers after the disastrous crisis of 1873. Strikes against wage reductions and the displacement of workers by labor-saving machinery were conducted by unions in many industries. On some occasions, as in the railroad workers' strike of 1877, the strikes culminated in outbreaks of such violence that Federal troops were used to restore order. The 1870's were also marked by the steady growth of the Knights of Labor (q.v.), a trade union originally formed in 1869 as a secret fraternal order by a group of garment workers in Philadelphia. This organization subsequently developed into an "inclusive union"; i.e., a union embracing workers of all trades. Its secret and fraternal character was eliminated in 1881; thereafter it functioned exclusively as a trade union, organizing and participating in many of the militant struggles conducted by the workers. By 1886 its membership exceeded 700,000.

In December, 1886, a number of craft unions which had for some years been affiliated with the Knights of Labor seceded from the organization because of a disagreement with its leaders, and established the American Federation of Labor. The organizational structure of the AFL was based on the principle of autonomy for the individual craft-union affiliates, each of which enjoyed the right to deal with the employers independently. Only workers already employed in the crafts represented by the individual unions were admitted to active membership. Moreover, the AFL concerned itself almost exclusively with the organization of skilled workers, carrying on little or no organizational activity among the semiskilled and the unskilled. During the 1890's, the unions of the AFL conducted several successful campaigns; the affiliated unions of the building-trades workers, the printers, and the coal miners, for example, finally achieved the long-sought goal of the eight-hour workday. These victories, coupled with the expansion of industrial activity after the Spanish-American War of 1898–99, resulted in a notable growth in the membership of the trade unions of the United States. By 1904 more than 2,000,000 workers had been organized into unions; of this number, almost 1,700,000 belonged to the AFL.

The year 1905 witnessed the formation in Chicago, Ill., of a type of trade union new to the United States, the Industrial Workers of the World (q.v.), which publicly espoused the revolutionary trade-union principles of syndicalism (q.v.). Led by such prominent figures as Eugene V. Debs, William D. Haywood (qq.v.), and Daniel De Leon, the IWW rejected the practice of collective bargaining in favor of "direct action", principally in the form of strikes, as the only effective means of improving the economic status of the workers and of ultimately securing the overthrow of capitalism and the establishment of a workers' society. The IWW also repudiated the craft-union principles of the AFL, proclaiming as its objective the inclusion of all workers, skilled, semiskilled, and unskilled, in "one big union". At the peak of its strength in 1912 the IWW membership probably did not exceed 100,000; nevertheless, it constituted a significant and unique component of the U.S. trade-union movement. During the period from 1906 to 1917, the IWW conducted numerous strikes notable for the violence practiced by both the strikers and the employers. Its militancy and its active opposition to the participation of the United States in World War I led in 1917 to the arrest and conviction of most of its leaders and hundreds of its members on various charges including sedition and criminal syndicalism; thereafter the IWW was never able to re-establish itself as a major factor in the American labor movement.

In the years immediately preceding the entry of the United States into World War I in 1917, organized labor won several major gains from the Federal government. In 1913 the Congress created the Department of Labor (see LABOR, DEPARTMENT OF), thereby according to labor the privilege of representation in the Cabinet, the highest agency of the executive branch of the Federal Government. Of equal importance to the development of the trade-union movement was the passage in 1914 of the Clayton Act (q.v.), restricting the use of injunctions (q.v.) by employers seeking to curb union activities during labor disputes. In 1916 the independent railroad unions, comprising one of the most powerful sections of organized labor, won a signal victory through the enactment by Congress of the Adamson Eight-Hour Act; although this law limited the working hours of railroad workers only, its passage considerably strengthened the struggle of all unions for shorter hours. All of the foregoing achievements contributed to a sharp rise in trade-union membership, which by 1920 totaled more than 5,100,000 persons, more than 80 percent of whom were members of the AFL.

These gains were not unaccompanied by serious defeats for organized labor, however. One of the worst setbacks for the trade-union movement was the total defeat of the strike of the iron and steel workers in 1919. Despite the fundamental importance of the iron and steel industry in the national economy, no significant attempts to organize these workers occurred until 1918, when the AFL set up a National Committee for the Organization of the Iron and Steel Industry. The ensuing organizational campaign was notably successful; the workers, many of whom were then working twelve hours daily and seven days weekly, welcomed the advent of unionization. The iron and steel companies refused to bargain collectively with the union, and discharged large numbers of union members. An industry-wide strike was called in September, 1919; it involved almost 370,000 workers, and hence was one of the greatest strikes in U.S. history. Both the intransigeance of the employers and the lack of unity among the strikers, whose ranks were divided by splits between the native-born and foreign-born and between the skilled and unskilled workers, were the causes of the eventual termination of the strike without any gains by the workers. Iron and steel manufacturing remained an "open-shop" (q.v.) industry for more than a decade thereafter.

Several factors contributed to a general decline in trade-union membership during the 1920's. A major cause was the severe postwar depression of 1921–22, during which unemployment rose sharply and the unions were unable to prevent wage reductions in many industries. Employment in certain industries continued to decline even after the return of business prosperity, leading to drastic losses of membership in such unions as those of the coal and metal miners and of the garment workers. Many employers sought to prevent the unionization of their employees; for example, they removed their establishments to areas not yet entered by the unions, abrogated existing collective-bargaining agreements and refused to conclude new agreements, engaged in paternalistic practices such as the establishment of company health-and-welfare plans, and required their employees to join only those unions actually formed under the sponsorship of the companies. An equally important obstacle to trade-union progress was the failure of the AFL to organize the semiskilled and unskilled workers of the mass-production industries, which underwent a notable expansion during the 1920's; it should be noted, however, that these industries were not suited to the craft-union type of organization, and that their unionization would have required a fundamental revision of principles by the craft-unionist AFL leadership. For these and other reasons, union membership dropped from the peak of 5,100,000 in 1920 to less than 3,500,000 in 1929.

The cataclysmic economic crisis of 1929 and the ensuing depression were accompanied by a precipitous increase in unemployment and a corresponding further decrease in union membership. The unions, attempting to offset the adverse effects of the depression upon wages and working conditions, launched numerous strikes, many of which were defeated by the widespread use of injunctions by employers. In 1932 the Congress came to the aid of the unions, enacting the Norris-La Guardia Act, which curtailed the use of injunctions far more drastically than had the Clayton Act of 1914. This law proved to be the forerunner of the large body of labor legislation enacted after the election of Franklin D. Roosevelt to the Presidency in November, 1932.

The first of the many laws passed by Congress, under the direct sponsorship of Roosevelt, for the specific purpose of mitigating the effects of the depression and protecting and stimulating the growth of the trade-union movement, was the National Industrial Recovery Act (q.v.) of June, 1933. One of the most controversial sections of this law stipulated that "employees shall have the right to organize and to bargain collectively through representatives of their own choosing, and shall be free from the interference, restraint, or coercion of employers . . . in the designation of such representatives". The unions were quick to take advantage of this legislative encouragement, and during the ensuing twenty-two months carried out successful organizing campaigns in many industries. The membership of the AFL, which had dropped to about 2,500,000 in 1932, rapidly

mounted to more than 3,000,000 workers. In May, 1935, the United States Supreme Court declared certain sections of the NIRA unconstitutional, but two months later Congress enacted a law providing even stronger governmental support to organized labor, the National Labor Relations Act (q.v.). The NLRA not only reaffirmed labor's right to organize freely and to bargain collectively, but also designated as "unfair labor practices" and fixed penalties for certain acts carried out by employers in resisting unionization. One of its most significant provisions illegalized the domination of or contribution of financial support to unions by employers, thereby eliminating the company-dominated unions which had been organized in many industrial establishments.

The year 1935 was also notable for the rise to prominence within the AFL of a group of union leaders who demanded the revision of AFL craft-union principles to facilitate the organization of the workers in the mass-production industries into industrial rather than craft unions. In November, 1935, the leaders of eight AFL unions, led by John L. Lewis (q.v.) of the United Mine Workers, formed the Committee for Industrial Organization to carry out an organizing campaign in the mass-production industries. By August, 1936, the number of AFL unions participating in the Committee for Industrial Organization had risen to ten; in that month the Executive Council of the AFL suspended the dissident unions, charging them with precipitating a split in the ranks of labor. The recalcitrants persisted in their industrial organizing activities, however, and in May, 1938, they were officially expelled from the AFL. Six months later they formed the Congress of Industrial Organizations, then comprising thirty-two international unions and nine organizing committees. Among the basic industries unionized by the CIO were steel and iron production, automobile manufacturing, rubber production, electrical and radio manufacturing, and shipping. These organizational campaigns were accompanied by the greatest wave of strikes in U.S. history, a large proportion of which were called primarily for the purpose of winning union recognition from employers in previously unorganized industries.

The combination of favorable legislation and revitalized organizing drives inevitably resulted in an unprecedented growth of union membership. By 1940 the total number of workers organized into all unions in the United States had risen to about 8,500,000, and was still rapidly mounting. In that year, with many of the countries of the world already engaged in World War II, the Federal government called upon organized labor for assistance in furthering a broad national-defense program. Labor representatives were appointed to many key Federal agencies and in January, 1942, one month after the entry of the United States into World War II, Congress established the National War Labor Board to adjudicate wartime labor disputes, with equal representation on the Board afforded to both labor and management. Thereafter, all of the trade unions of the nation pledged themselves, in the interest of the war effort, to a minimum of strikes and work stoppages; although several strikes did occur during the war, their frequency and duration were comparatively negligible. The unions did, however, take advantage of the high rate of employment, the scarcity of labor, and the tremendous industrial expansion during the war years (1941–45), to increase their membership, which by 1945 exceeded 14,-000,000.

The first postwar year, 1946, was marked by a resurgence of trade-union struggles for higher wages and improved working conditions. More strikes than ever before occurred during 1946, and unprecedented numbers of workers were involved. The general success of these strikes led many conservative legislators to denounce the waxing power of the unions as dangerous to the nation, and in the following year the conservative Republican majority in Congress secured the enactment of the Labor Management Relations Act, commonly termed the "Taft-Hartley Act" (see NATIONAL LABOR RELATIONS ACT), embodying a number of provisions generally designed to curb the power of organized labor. The unions vigorously opposed this law, and in the election campaign of 1948 they supported the Democratic Party and its Presidential candidate Harry S. Truman (q.v.), who had vetoed the law only to see it enacted, with the support of several Democratic members of Congress, over this veto.

For some years prior to 1948, a struggle had been developing between the right-wing affiliates of the CIO, comprising about 5,000,-000 members, and the left-wing affiliates, numbering about 1,000,000 members. At the national CIO convention held in 1948, the right-wing majority voted to support not only the domestic policies of President Truman, but also such components of his foreign policy as the European Recovery Program, the North Atlantic Treaty (qq.v.), and the Truman Doctrine. These measures were regarded by the right wing, whose leaders were strongly opposed to communism, as essential to the containment of the dynamic world-communist movement. The left-wing affiliates of the CIO, on the other hand, denounced the Truman foreign policy as a manifestation of U.S. imperialism, and announced its support of the Presidential candidate of the Progressive Party, Henry A. Wallace (q.v.). Philip Murray (q.v.), president of the CIO, and other right-wing leaders accused the leftists of accepting the domination of the Communist Party, and threatened them with expulsion from the CIO unless they acceded to the policies favored by the majority. During the ensuing year the left-wing unions persisted in their opposition to Truman and to certain policies of Murray. At the 1949 CIO convention the largest of the left-wing affiliates, the United Electrical, Radio, and Machine Workers, with about 450,000 members, was officially expelled, and in succeeding months ten other unions were expelled by order of the CIO executive board. In some cases the CIO chartered new international organizations, most notably the International Union of Electrical Workers, to absorb workers who resigned from the left-wing unions; in others, organizing committees were established to operate in the fields covered by the ousted affiliates.

A new wave of strikes broke out in steel production, coal mining, and railroading during 1949 and 1950, but increasing efforts were made to prevent strikes from crippling the American economy. Thus, in December, 1950, a nationwide strike of railroad switchmen was dropped when President Truman, speaking as commander in chief, called upon the strikers to end their threat to national security. After December 16, when the President proclaimed a state of national emergency, American trade unions pledged themselves to co-operate fully in plans for national economic mobilization. In February, 1951, a new crisis arose when the major unions withdrew their representatives from all mobilization agencies, charging that labor's interests were being ignored in defense planning. Labor's boycott of the agencies was dropped in April of the same year, following establishment by President Truman of the National Advisory Board on Mobilization Policy. This body, representative of labor, industry, and the public, secured various reforms favorable to labor, including formation of a new Wage Stabilization Board, which was authorized, unlike its predecessor, to settle strikes. Other significant trade-union developments during 1951 were Congressional legislation easing restrictions on union-shop contracts and the growth of harmonious relations between the CIO and AFL. In the view of some observers the latter development might eventually lead to merger of the two federations.

During 1952 man-days lost as a result of work stoppages exceeded the total of every previous postwar year except 1946. The most serious stoppage, a 53-day strike by the United Steelworkers, CIO, was preceded by a series of dramatic developments, notably seizure of the steel industry by President Truman and a Supreme Court ruling that his action was unconstitutional.

The platform adopted by the Democratic National Convention of 1952 strongly advocated repeal of the Taft-Hartley Act. Retention of the act, with the adoption of such amendments as "further protect the rights of labor, management, and the public", was advocated by the Republican National Convention. Both the CIO Executive Board and the AFL Convention endorsed the Democratic Presidential nominee Adlai Ewing Stevenson. No Presidential candidate had ever before been endorsed by an AFL convention.

President Dwight David Eisenhower, following his inauguration, appointed the AFL leader Martin P. Durkin secretary of labor. Durkin resigned his post in September, 1953, charging that the President had "reneged" on promises to initiate proposed amendments to the Taft-Hartley Act. This accusation was denied by White House spokesmen and, implicitly, by the President himself. Meanwhile (May) the AFL and CIO had moved further toward organic unity by reaching tentative agreement on a pact to prohibit membership raids by rival affiliates.

Agreement to merge the two organizations was reached by AFL and CIO committees on Feb. 9, 1955. The committee completed a draft constitution for the projected body on May 2. The merger was effected during the week of Dec. 5.

See also LABOR RELATIONS.

TRAFALGAR, CAPE, a low promontory on the south coast of Spain, about 29 miles s.w. of Tarifa, at the western entrance to the Strait of Gibraltar. It is memorable for the great naval victory obtained off its shores by the British fleet under Nelson over the combined fleets of France and Spain under Villeneuve, on Oct. 21, 1805. On this occasion 27 ships of the line, with 2138 guns, outfought 33 ships, mounting 2640 guns, but Nelson was mortally wounded by a musket ball. See NELSON, HORATIO.

TRAFFIC REGULATION, a system of rules and regulations, aided by mechanical apparatus, traffic engineering bureaus, and special policemen, to avoid congestion in the largest cities of the world. In the smaller cities, where congestion does not warrant elaborate electrical equipment to facilitate traffic movement, stop and go signs are operated by policemen, direction arrows, traffic buttons, and automatic red and green lights are used, many ot the devices eliminating the need of the traffic patrolman altogether. The designation of one-way streets is another method adopted by many American cities and towns.

New York City, with a traffic problem of first magnitude, has the most elaborate, costly, and varied system in the world. Special policemen are stationed at all important and congested sections of the city. The traffic control light system is general throughout the city, extending to even lesser populated areas. The synchronized block system of traffic lights is employed in most sections of the city. In this system signals simultaneously show green on a series of parallel streets, permitting traffic to move, and at the same instant signals on the intersecting arteries show red, bringing traffic to a halt. After a brief period, usually two minutes, the operation is automatically reversed. As the result of a recently adopted improvement of the system, both the red and the green lights show for a short interval before the expiration of each period, warning drivers and pedestrians of the impending change in the direction of traffic. Because congestion and delay are unavoidable in the synchronized block system, in recent years New York City authorities have installed the progressive system of traffic lights on a number of the major arteries. In this system signals at successive intersections along the artery are timed to change from red to green at staggered intervals, permitting a vehicle which maintains a constant speed (usually 20 to 25 m.p.h.) to proceed from one end of the artery to the other without a stop.

In New York, as in most large urban areas of the U.S., the efficiency of a traffic-control system is determined by a variety of factors, among them the degree of enforcement of regulations against such violations as parking in restricted areas and double-parking. Where enforcement is lax the resultant congestion

Photos by Charles Simmons

TRAFFIC REGULATION IN NEW YORK CITY. *Top, from left to right: One-way sign above traffic light; pedestrian-crossing marker; pedestrian safety zone. Bottom: Parking-regulation markers. Left, sign reserving space for taxicabs; right, sign in restricted area.*

renders the system ineffective and causes grave economic loss. At the root of most of the traffic problems in New York and other large U.S. cities is the failure of municipal government and private enterprise to provide sufficient, reasonably priced off-street parking facilities. Establishment of such facilities is prerequisite to an effective system of traffic control, in the view of many authorities.

TRAGEDY. See DRAMA.

TRAIL, a Canadian mining community situated in the southeastern portion of British Columbia, on the Columbia R., a few miles N. of the State of Washington and about 2 miles E. of Rossland. The mines in the vicinity yield gold, silver, lead, zinc, bismuth, and cadmium. Manufacturing industries in the town include ore refineries and a factory producing sulfuric acid. Pop. (1951) 11,430.

TRAJAN, or (Lat.) MARCUS ULPIUS TRAJANUS (52 or 53–117 A.D.), Emperor of Rome from 98 to 117 A.D., born in Italica, near Seville, Spain, of a family probably Roman in origin. He was trained as a youth in Roman arms, and took an active part in the Parthian and German campaigns during the reigns of the emperors Titus and Domitian (79-96 A.D.), achieving the reputation of being a general of outstanding ability. He was prætor in 85 A.D. and consul in 91 A.D., and was adopted by the emperor Nerva (q.v.) in 97 A.D. as his colleague and successor. Upon the death of Nerva the following year, Trajan, who was at that time inspecting the Roman frontier in Germany, became the sole ruler of the empire. He did not return to Rome until several years later, however. He celebrated his accession by largesses to the soldiers and to Roman citizens and their children, and also made provision for the maintenance of the children of poor freemen in Rome and other Italian cities, thus continuing the system of governmental benevolence initiated by Nerva. In 101 A.D. Trajan set out on his first campaign against the Dacians (see DACIA). The struggle was long and fierce, but the Romans at last gained a decisive superiority, and in 107 A.D. completely subdued the country, which became the Roman province of Dacia. This conquest, the first since the death of the emperor Augustus, was celebrated by a triumph and by games which lasted four months. The famous column of Trajan was erected later (about 114 A.D.) to commemorate this victory (see COLUMN OF TRAJAN).

In 113 A.D. the emperor left Italy for his great expedition in the East, directed mainly against the Parthians. Landing in Syria he

Sculpture of the Roman emperor Trajan

made Armenia and Mesopotamia Roman provinces, and advanced to Ctesiphon on the Tigris, meeting, however, with defeat at Hatra. Meanwhile the Jews rose in Cyprus and Cyrene, and other enemies, taking advantage of the emperor's absence in the far east, revolted. Trajan, in failing health, set sail for Italy, but died en route at Selinus in Cilicia. Although the greater part of Trajan's reign was spent in the field, the internal administration of Rome was carefully and excellently guided. The improvement and beautifying of Rome was carried on; better roads, canals, and bridges were constructed; new towns were built; the Via Appia was restored; the Pontine Marshes were partially drained; the magnificent Forum Trajani was erected at Rome; the harbor of Centum Cellæ, modern Civitavecchia, was constructed; and new cities\were founded in Numidia (see TIMGAD).

TRAJAN, COLUMN OF. See COLUMN OF TRAJAN.

TRANQUILIZING DRUGS. See CHLOR-PROMAZINE; RESERPINE.

TRANSCAUCASIA. See CAUCASIA.

TRANSCENDENTALISM. The two words transcendental and transcendent were employed by Duns Scotus to describe conceptions that, by their universality, transcend the ten Aristotelian categories. The primary conception was declared transcendent because it pertained to "being" before *descent* into existence took place.

Between transcendental and transcendent Immanuel Kant (q.v.) drew a distinction. By "transcendental" he designates the nonexperiential, a priori elements of thought especially the forms and categories (space and time, causality, etc.) which, though not products of experience, are manifested only in experience, and contribute to all experimental knowledge. "Transcendent" Kant reserves for those among the transcendental or a priori elements that transcend and lie beyond all experience, and are so far illegitimate as cognitions. Such are the "ideas of the pure reason", God, an immaterial soul, etc.

For post-Kantian systems which affirmed the identity of subject and object the distinction of transcendental and transcendent ceased to exist, and absolute knowledge was practicable; such systems are said to be or contain *transcendentalism*. "Transcendental philosophy" was the name given by the German philosopher Friedrich Wilhelm Joseph Schelling (q.v.) to part of his system. Transcendental has often been used by "commonsense" philosophers and the association school for the a priori generally. The epithet of Transcendental School has come, however, to be specially associated with a group of American authors and thinkers who early in the 19th century led a reaction against Puritan prejudices. The movement was identified with idealism, vague pantheism, mysticism, and eclectic orientalism. Among the main exciting causes were the influence of Carlyle and the discovery of German literature. Brook Farm (q.v.) was one outcome of the school. The first meeting of the Transcendental Club took place in 1836 in the house of George Ripley; other members were Margaret Fuller and Theodore Parker. The thinker who gave the movement the most important expression was Ralph Waldo Emerson (q.v.).

TRANSEPT. See CHURCH: *Architecture*.

TRANSFORMER, a device consisting of one coil of wire placed in proximity with one or more coils, used to couple two or more circuits together by employing the inductance (q.v.) between the two coils. It is also used to raise or lower ("step up" or "down") alternating voltages and currents. When the voltage of a line is increased by a transformer the current is decreased in like proportion and vice versa. In this case one coil is wound directly upon the other. The coil connected to the source of power is called the *primary* and the other coil the *secondary*. A transformer in which the secondary voltage is higher than the primary voltage, and the secondary current lower than the primary current is a *step-up transformer*; a transformer in which the relations of primary and secondary voltages and currents are reversed is a *step-down transformer*. The ratio of the primary to the secondary voltage of a transformer is called the *ratio of transformation*. In the case of an iron-core transformer this ratio is approximately the same as the ratio of the turns in the two windings. The transformer is of great importance in radio apparatus, in which it may be found under any of the following aspects.

Air-cooled transformer, a transformer which is not cooled by oil or other liquid.

Air-core transformer, a transformer in which the core consists of the air inside of the coils, since with high-frequency currents it is the general practice not to use iron cores as these tend to choke off the oscillations.

Audio- or low-frequency transformer, a transformer which is used in an audio-frequency amplifier. It may be an input transformer (as from a telephone line), an *interstage* (or *intervalve*) *transformer*, or an output transformer (as to a loud speaker). It should be capable of dealing with all frequencies between 30 and 10,000 cycles per second so that none is favored more than another, if it is used in a broadcasting receiver. It consists essentially of two separate windings on an iron core.

Auto-transformer, a transformer either for radio-, audio- or power-frequency in which the *primary* and *secondary* windings are formed by one and the same coil having three connections to it.

Closed-core transformer, a transformer in which the iron core forms a continuous magnetic circuit, i.e., it has no air gap. Compare *open-core transformer*.

High-frequency transformer. See *Radio- or high-frequency transformer,* below.

Intervalve transformer, a transformer used in *intervalve coupling* which is inductive. *Intervalve coupling* is the term applied to the components used to transfer oscillations from the anode circuit of one valve or tube to the grid circuit of the following valve or tube in a multi-stage cascade amplifier. See VACUUM TUBES, THERMIONIC. It may be designed for radio- or audio-frequencies.

Low-frequency transformer. See *Audio-* or *Low-frequency transformer.*

Microphone transformer, a small transformer for coupling a microphone to a line or amplifier.

Oil-cooled transformer, a transformer in which the coils are placed in oil.

Open-core transformer, a transformer in which the magnetic circuit consists partly of iron and partly of air. Owing to its bad characteristic curve an open-core transformer is never used in a low-frequency amplifier. Compare *closed-core transformer.*

Oscillation transformer, a transformer used in conjunction with a condenser and a tube to produce oscillation at a given frequency.

Power transformer, a transformer for commercial alternating current for lighting, heating, and power. In radio it is the transformer used to deliver the high voltages for the plate circuits and low voltages for the filament circuits of tubes.

Radio- or *high-frequency transformer,* a transformer for coupling together high-frequency circuits, e.g., an *interstage transformer* in a high-frequency amplifier.

TRANSFUSION OF BLOOD, the surgical procedure by which the blood of one individual is introduced into the blood stream of another. The techniques of blood transfusion are technically classed as types of plastic surgery because transfusion involves the transfer of living tissue (blood). Blood transfusion is an extremely important method of therapy; it has saved hundreds of thousands of lives of persons suffering from severe bleeding, shock (q.v.), and blood-destroying diseases. Blood transfusion is employed routinely in cases of surgery and childbirth involving great loss of blood. See BLOOD; BLEEDING.

The earliest successful attempt to transfer blood into a human being was made in France during the 17th century by Jean Baptiste Denis (d. 1704). The source of the blood used in this attempt was a sheep; most later attempts to transfuse whole sheep's blood into a human were unsuccessful. Later physicians, therefore, restricted the source of their blood supply to human beings; despite this restric-

tion, more patients into whom blood was transfused died than survived. Blood from unhealthy donors often transmits such diseases as syphilis and malaria to the patient. Of even greater danger are the dissimilar antibodies (see IMMUNITY) which the blood of the donor may carry and the possibility of anaphylactic shock when the foreign protein of the donor's blood is injected into the recipient. Almost all of the dangers of blood transfusion have been eliminated during the 20th century.

Blood Types. During the early part of the 20th century physicians discovered that four chief types of human blood existed. These blood types were classified in 1901 by the Austrian pathologist Karl Landsteiner (q.v.), who discovered that blood types are transmitted by Mendelian heredity; see HEREDITY: *Human Heredity.* The four types are known as A, B, AB, and O. Blood of type O may usually be given to persons with any of the four blood types, and consequently persons with this type blood are often called "universal donors"; patients with blood of type AB may usually be transfused with blood of any type, and consequently such persons are often "universal recipients". However, persons transfused with blood of type O occasionally suffer illness caused by blood incompatibility; physicians attempt wherever possible to transfuse blood identical in type with that of the recipient. The serum of blood incompatible with the blood of the recipient causes the red blood corpuscles of the recipient to agglutinate, often resulting in death.

Besides the primary blood types, several other hereditary blood groupings have been discovered recently. The types M and N have no importance in transfusions but are important in legal cases involving proof of paternity of a child. Much more important is the Rh factor (q.v.), discovered during the second quarter of the 20th century.

Transfusion of Whole Blood. Prior to World War II, most blood transfusions were performed directly from donor to recipient. This practice was inefficient because it often involved difficulty in locating a donor of the proper blood type at the necessary time. When repeated transfusions were necessary, impositions on the time of a suitable donor were impossible to avoid. During World War II surgeons developed techniques of removing whole blood from a donor, treating the blood with an anticoagulant, and storing it in sterile containers under refrigeration. By means of this method blood could be preserved for

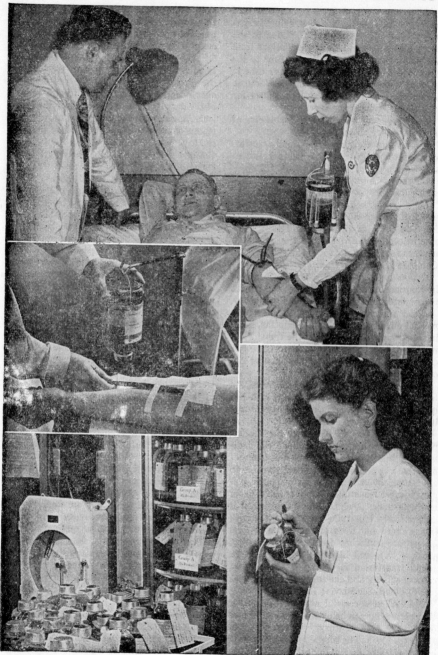

American Red Cross

TRANSFUSION OF BLOOD. *Top: Red Cross attendants taking blood from the arm of a donor. Middle: Needle punctures the vein and blood passes through tube to a collection bottle. Bottom: Blood from mobile Red Cross collection units is classified for hospital use.*

about a week. Improved methods of blood processing, particularly the elimination of coagulants by the ion-exchange technique (see ION EXCHANGE), subsequently extended the storage time to three weeks. Processed blood is available at blood banks, set up by hospitals, charitable agencies such as the Red Cross, and private pharmaceutical companies throughout the United States, and serve to route blood of the desired types in needed quantities to hospitals or private physicians having patients needing transfusions.

An outstanding advance in blood transfusion has been made in recent years in the treatment of infants with blood-destroying conditions caused by incompatibility of the mother's blood with the blood of the child she carries. When an Rh-positive baby is born to an Rh-negative mother, the mother's blood develops antibodies to combat the presence of the Rh factor. Such antibodies may enter the infant's blood, causing an acute anemia called *erythroblastosis fetalis*. After birth, almost the entire blood supply of the erythroblastotic infant is slowly drained from its body while, at the same time, a supply of non-sensitized Rh-negative blood is injected into the infant.

Transfusion of Plasma. In cases of severe edema or of shock the number of red blood corpuscles in the circulating blood remains constant, while the amount of circulating fluid decreases. The purpose of transfusion in such cases is to increase the amount of circulating fluid, and to reverse the osmotic pressure within the blood vessels to prevent further loss of circulating fluid. For such transfusions, plasma or the plasma component, called serum albumin, is used; see BLOOD: *Plasma; Plasma Proteins.* Unlike whole blood, dried plasma may be stored indefinitely, requires no refrigeration, and does not need to be typed; like whole blood, it transmits such virus diseases as hepatitis if the virus happens to be present in the donor's blood. Such virus contamination cannot be determined by any definitive test available to blood banks and the virus cannot be destroyed by processing techniques. Solutions of serum albumin may be sterilized, however, and this technique eliminates the risk of virus infection. Serum albumin transfusions are often performed in cases of severe kidney disease. In addition, such transfusions inhibit nerve damage in cases of infantile paralysis.

Various synthetic plasma substitutes, such as the carbohydrate compound dextran, have been developed in recent years. Also known as plasma volume expanders, these substances are available in unlimited amounts and are reported (1953) to be more effective than whole blood in cases of sudden shock. Present-day research indicates that the plasma volume expanders may be useful also in various other conditions requiring transfusions.

TRANSISTOR, electronic device designed to amplify or oscillate electric current and employed in various fields of technology, notably in communications. The device was developed in 1948 in the course of research on semiconductive materials, such as germanium (q.v.) crystals. In its original form the transistor is a tiny triode, the size of a pea, consisting of thin layers of specially treated germanium. As an amplifier (q.v.) it operates over a wide range of frequencies and is superior to thermionic vacuum tubes in several respects; it is hardier, lighter, and smaller, and, requiring no heater current, is more economical to operate. However, because germanium loses its amplifying properties if subjected to temperatures over 100° C., transistors, as originally designed, could not be used in many types of electronic equipment. Recent reports indicate (1954) that transistors made of an alloy containing germanium and silicon (q.v.) will operate reliably at temperatures as high as 177° C., and that those made of layers of silicon, coated with indium, are impervious to even higher temperatures. Other recent advances include tetrode and pentrode transistors, providing 2 and 3 times the power output of the triode without an increase in size.

As a substitute for various types of vacuum tubes the transistor has many uses. It was first employed commercially in hearing aids (q.v.). In a later application, the device made possible the development of a radio set about the size of a wrist watch and capable of receiving broadcasts over a distance of 40 miles. This wrist radio is now standard equipment in the U.S. Signal Corps. Heat-resistant transistors are eminently suitable for use in aircraft equipment, such as radar, in guided missiles, and in electronic computers.

TRANSIT, the passage of one heavenly body over the disk of another, as of Mercury or Venus over the disk of the sun, or of a satellite over its primary. A transit of Mercury or Venus can take place only when the planet passes the sun at the time it is near one of its nodes. The first recorded transit of Venus was that of 1639. In 1679 Halley pointed out that these transits could be utilized for determining the distance of the sun. There are usually two transits of Venus within 8 years

Keuffel & Esser Co.

A transit instrument

of one another, and then a lapse of 105 or 122 years, when another couple of transits occur with 8 years between them.

TRANSIT INSTRUMENT, one of the most important of astronomical instruments, consisting of a telescope fixed to a horizontal axis, so as to revolve in the plane of the meridian. It is employed in the observation of the meridian transits of the heavenly bodies, i.e., the apparent passage of the heavenly bodies across the observer's meridian. The axis consists of a hollow sphere or cube, to opposite sides of which are tightly fastened the bases of two cones in whose apices the pivots are screwed; the sphere or cube is pierced for the admission of the telescope, which is firmly soldered at right angles to the axis. One of the pivots is hollowed so that a stream of light can be directed from a lantern, through an aperture in the side, and half way along the interior of the axis, into the telescope tube, where, being received by an annular mirror set at a 45° angle to the axis and telescope tube, it is directed to the eyepiece, and brilliantly illumines the field of view, while the annular form of the mirror prevents any interference with the passage of rays from the object under observation to the eye. One extremity of the axis carries one and sometimes two small

graduated circles, each supplied with index, clamping screws, and vernier. There are three adjustments necessary before a transit can be observed: the axis must be horizontal; the line of collimation must be at right angles to the axis of motion; and the latter must be placed so as to point accurately E. and W. To note accurately the instant of time by the astronomical clock at which the object (e.g., a star) is seen to pass the center of the field of view is the essential part of a transit observation. This is effected by the agency of electricity. At a certain point of its swing a seconds pendulum makes a dot on a uniformly moving slip of paper. The instant of transit is similarly noted by the observer's tapping an electrical contact key; and the distance of this dot from the previous seconds one, compared with the distance between two seconds dots, gives the time accurately almost to 1/100 of a second.

The *transit circle* differs mainly from the older transit instrument in the addition, on the axis of rotation, of two large graduated circles which are read off by microscopes fixed on an independent coaxial wheel called an alidade, any variation in the position of which may be detected by a large spirit level attached to it.

TRANSJORDAN. See JORDAN, HASHEMITE KINGDOM OF.

TRANSMIGRATION, or METEMPSYCHOSIS, the transition of the soul after death into another substance or body from what it occupied before. It is to be distinguished from the metamorphosis of living men, which we find in witchcraft; it is wider in its range than the doctrine of the resurrection of the body; and it presupposes a belief in the immortality of the soul. The simplest form of this belief is found in several tribes of Africa and America who think the soul at death must look out for a new host to inhabit, and if need be will enter the body of an animal. This reincarnation is most often considered as taking place through the soul of a dead man animating the body of an infant of his own kindred, thus accounting for the likeness between parents and children and for the phenomena of atavism. Both Brahmins and Buddhists admit human descent into beasts, plants, and trees, and the Buddha himself, before his last birth as Sakyamuni, underwent as many as 550 births through such stages as a hermit, a king, a slave, an ape, elephant, snipe, fish, frog, and the genius of a tree. When he attained the perfect knowledge of the Buddha he was able to recall all these existences, and these accounts form the *Jatakas*. The doctrine of transmigration (Samsâra) does not seem to have belonged to the early Aryan faith, but it lies at the heart of the accepted Indian philosophy.

The ancient Egyptians believed in the transmigration of souls; among the Greeks it was a doctrine especially associated with Pythagoras. Pythagoras recognized in the temple of Hera the shield he had borne as Euphorbus at the siege of Troy. The general lot is to live anew according to the degree of guilt to be atoned for. This same doctrine of purificatory wandering is found again in Plato's speculations on the future life. Among the Jews the Cabalists accepted the doctrine, and it formed an essential part of the Manichæan philosophy. Into Christianity it has never made way. See ANIMAL WORSHIP; ANIMISM; BUDDHISM; HINDUISM; IMMORTALITY; NATURE WORSHIP; THEOSOPHY; VEDANTA; YOGA.

TRANSPADANE REPUBLIC, a republic formed by Napoleon in 1796 on the south side of the Po and in 1797 united with the Cispadane Republic, on the N., to form the Cisalpine Republic (q.v.).

TRANSPIRATION, the evaporation of water from the aerial surfaces of plants. In most land plants transpiration takes place by the passage of evaporated water from cells bordering the interior air chambers through the stomata (q.v.). The rate of transpiration is determined by the relative humidity of the outer air, temperature, wind, light, etc. Transpiration is necessary for cooling and advantageous for the movement of dissolved salts.

TRANSPOSING, in music, changing a piece of music in performance from the key in which it is written to another key. To play at sight an accompaniment for such an instrument as the pianoforte or organ, transposed from one key to another, requires considerable artistic skill.

TRANSUBSTANTIATION. The meaning of the theological term is apparent in the following canon of the Council of Trent: "If any one shall say that, in the most holy sacrament of the Eucharist, there remains the substance of bread and wine together with the body and blood of our Lord Jesus Christ; and shall deny that wonderful and singular conversion of the whole substance of the bread into the body, and of the whole substance of the wine into the blood, the species of bread and wine alone remaining—*which conversion the Catholic Church most fittingly calls Transubstan-*

tiation—let him be anathema" (*Conc. Trid. Sess.* 13 Can. 2).

The doctrine of transubstantiation was not adopted into the phraseology of the church before 1215, when it was employed by the fourth Lateran Council. The Council of Trent (1551) formally reaffirmed the dogma, and it was inserted as an article of faith in the creed of Pope Pius IV.

Transubstantiation is a doctrine not only of the Roman, but also of the Greek, Church. At the Synod of Jerusalem (1672) the doctrine was confirmed as essential to the faith of the entire Eastern Church. In transubstantiation the external manifestations, as shape, color, flavor, and odor, and the other forces and characteristics of bread and wine, continue. The dogma was repudiated by the Anglican Church in the 28th Article. The term *consubstantiation* denotes the Lutheran doctrine of the actual, real, substantial presence of the body and blood of Christ, coexisting in and with the bread and wine used at the Lord's Supper. See MASS.

TRANSVAAL, formerly THE SOUTH AFRICAN REPUBLIC, a province of the Union of South Africa (q.v.), bounded on the N. by Southern Rhodesia and Bechuanaland, on the E. by Portuguese East Africa and Swaziland, on the S. by Natal and the Orange Free State, and on the W. by the province of the Cape of Good Hope and Bechuanaland. The capital of the province is Pretoria and its largest city is Johannesburg (qq.v.). Most of the Transvaal territory is a plateau containing grasslands (*velds*) and studded with small hills (*kopjes*); about a third of the E. portion is occupied by the Drakensberg mountain range, culminating in the Mauchberg (8725 ft.). The Lebombo Mts. form the E. boundary with Portuguese East Africa. Across the W. veld stretches the Witwatersrand ("White Water Ridge") range, between the basins of the two principal river systems, the Limpopo and the Vaal. This range contains some of the richest gold fields in the world.

The great wealth of the Transvaal is its mineral resources, of which the most important are gold, diamonds (found chiefly in the Pretoria district), coal (in the districts of Barberton, Middelburg, and Pietersburg), copper, and tin. The total value of production of these five minerals up to 1949 was about £3,050,-000,000. Stock raising is the second most important occupation, and in a recent year Transvaal herds included about 3,880,000 cattle and 3,830,000 sheep. The cultivated area is comparatively small, and the principal crops

South African Railways & Harbours

IN TRANSVAAL, UNION OF SOUTH AFRICA. *Top: Natives harvesting cotton on a plantation. Bottom, left: Public building, Pretoria. Bottom, right: A statue of Stephanus Johannes Paulus Kruger, South African statesman who helped found the Transvaal state, Pretoria.*

are cereal grains. Manufacturing establishments include iron and steel foundries, notably in Pretoria and Vereeniging, breweries, grain mills, brick and pottery works, and wagon factories. The great majority of the population consists of native Africans, living chiefly in N. Transvaal and including the Bechuana, Basuto, Zulu, and Amaswazi people. The provincial government is headed by an administrator, appointed for five years by the Union ministry, an elected provincial council of 64 members, and an executive committee of 4 members elected by the council on the basis of proportional representation. The council deals with local matters and other matters delegated it by the Union parliament, and its ordinances are subject to veto by the Union ministry. Area of province, 110,450 sq.m.; pop. (1951 prelim.) 4,802,405, including 1,205,458 whites.

History. In 1848 the Boers (q.v.), descendants of the Dutch colonists of South Africa, who had migrated from Cape Colony because of their opposition to British rule, founded the South African Republic (see ORANGE FREE STATE). The region also became known as the Transvaal, its territory being beyond the Vaal R. Great Britain recognized the Boer republic in 1852. During the succeeding two decades constant warfare between the Boers and the hostile African tribes, and friction between Boer factions, almost bankrupted the republic and severely weakened its political strength. In 1877 it was annexed by Great Britain. The Boers revolted against British rule in 1880, and after the British forces were completely defeated in the battle of Majuba Hill (Feb. 27, 1881), the Transvaal was recognized as autonomous, under British suzerainty.

The discovery of gold in the Witwatersrand area in 1884 brought a sudden influx of immigrants, coming in such numbers that the Boers were soon outnumbered. To maintain Boer supremacy, the foreigners, or *Uitlanders,* were not permitted to share in the Transvaal government. Constant agitation resulted on the part of the Uitlanders, and in 1895 they helped bring about the abortive Jameson raid (see JAMESON, SIR LEANDER STARR). In 1899 the Uitlanders of the Boer state petitioned Queen Victoria for aid, and Great Britain actively intervened in their behalf. Negotiations led to the repudiation of British suzerainty by the Boers, mobilization of Boer troops, and the South African War (q.v.). The British were victorious and in 1902 the Transvaal, together with the Boer Orange Free State, was governed as a British crown colony until 1906,

when it was granted self-government. In 1910 it was united with the Orange Free State, Natal, and the Cape Colony into the Union of South Africa.

TRANSYLVANIA, province of Romania, and before 1918 a part of Hungary. The region is an elevated plateau entirely surrounded by the Transylvanian Alps (see CARPATHIAN MOUNTAINS), which curve around it like a wall and in various places spread over the land. Transylvania is rich in minerals, including gold, silver, salt, and coal. During the 11th century the region became part of the kingdom of Hungary. In 1526, after the defeat of Hungary by the Turks, Transylvania became a separate principality under the protection of the Turkish sultan. In 1699, by the Treaty of Karlowitz which concluded war between Austria and Turkey, Austria, which had previously claimed Transylvania, obtained possession of the region. In 1765 the region was made a grand principality of Austria, and in 1849 an Austrian crownland, but was reunited to the Hungarian kingdom in 1867 upon the formation of the dual monarchy of Austria-Hungary. Transylvania became a part of Romania in Dec., 1918, following World War I. Hungary persisted in claiming the area because of its large Magyar population. In 1940, during World War II, by the Italo-German award of Aug. 30, the N. part of Transylvania, including 17,000 sq.m. with a population of 2,370,000, was given to Hungary. Following the war the ceded area was returned to Romania. Area, 22,312 sq.m.; pop., about 3,218,000. See HUNGARY: *History;* ROMANIA: *History.*

TRAP, general term used to designate dense and generally fine-grained igneous rocks of black or dark-green color. The term is almost synonymous with basalt or diabase but might include gabbro, peridotite, and pyroxenite. When altered such rocks assume a green color from the secondary minerals developed in them and are then known as greenstone. Both greenstone and trap include a wide range of rock families.

TRAPA. See WATER CALTROP.

TRAPANI, seaport of Sicily, Italy, and capital of a province of the same name in the N.W. of the island, standing on a tongue of land 40 miles w. of Palermo, but 141 m. by railroad. It has a trade in wheat, wine, olives, sumach, salt, tunny fish, sponges, and coral. It was founded by the Carthaginians, who here defeated the Romans in a naval battle in 249 B.C. Area of province, 968 sq.m.; pop., about 375,000. Pop. of city, about 63,000.

TRAPDOOR SPIDER, common name for any one of the large hairy tropical spiders of the family Theraphosidae, which make long tubes in the earth, lining them with silk and fashioning at the entrance a bevel-edged, hinged, accurately fitting trapdoor made of alternate layers of earth and silk. The upper surface is covered with earth or gravel so as to disguise the entrance. The spider hides in the nest when not seeking prey, and with some species a branch to the tunnel is built with a separate door.

The digging of the burrow (always on high, sloping ground) is a laborious task. The earth is loosened with the mandibles and is carried away piece by piece supported by the mandibles and maxillae. A species common in the southwestern United States, *Cteniza californica,* digs holes nearly an inch in diameter and sometimes a foot in length. When the spider is on guard, holding the door down from the inside by means of its mandibles and feet, it is impossible to raise the trapdoor without tearing it. Experimenters at San Diego, Calif., removed the trapdoors of 60 nests, unhinging them at night. Without exception the spider had by morning completed a new door. Continued removal resulted in a falling off in the quality of the doors, owing to the failure of the spider's supply of silk. The fifth door made, by a single spider, was almost entirely of mud with hardly enough web to coat and hinge it. When the trapdoors were fastened down, a side branch with a new door was always made overnight with an opening near the original mouth.

The nests are generally in pairs, but it is not known whether they are occupied by different sexes. The young hatch in the mother's burrow and live there for a few weeks; then they leave the nest and begin small tubes of their own. The food of these spiders consists largely of ants and other crawling wingless insects. They have been known to eat earthworms and large caterpillars. The trapdoor spiders of southern Europe make thin covers which rest loosely on the top of the hole, but they are covered with leaves or other material in order to disguise them.

TRAPPING, the snaring or capture of wild animals and birds by various devices. In some cases a pitfall or enclosure (usually of splints, wire, or netting, with a funnel-shaped entrance) is used into which an animal is lured, but whence it cannot readily escape. Lobster pots, pounds, fish traps, fish slides, and fish wheels are examples of this kind of trap. In other devices bait is used, and so arranged that its disturbance by game causes the trap to close or fall, thereby capturing or killing the game.

The trapping industry of North Africa has lost its former importance with the disappearance of animals valuable for their fur or their flesh. The animals trapped in America include bears, wolverines, coyotes, foxes of all sorts, lynxes, raccoons, skunks, otters, beavers, fishers, martens, minxes, and weasels.

India is noted for its trappers, who in many cases form a "caste" of their own. The largest of all traps is the elephant *keddah,* a palisaded enclosure in which a whole herd of elephants can be captured. Panthers are taken in a contrivance resembling the ordinary mousetrap. In trapping wolves a kid is hung in a basket over a deep staked pit, and just beyond the spring of a wolf. The wolves leap at the kid, and fall into the pit. In Africa antelopes, zebras, and other animals are trapped primitively by driving them into pits.

TRAPPISTS, a religious order, celebrated for its austerities, named from a Cistercian abbey, founded in the middle of the 12th century, in the valley of La Trappe, near Mortagne, in the Norman department of Orne, by Armand-Jean le Bonthillier de Rancé. The monks are forbidden the use of meat, fish, wine, and eggs, and all intercourse with externs is cut off. Perpetual silence is enjoined.

TRAPSHOOTING, the sport of shooting at clay pigeons, saucers made of river silt and pitch, or other artificial targets such as glass balls; the targets are propelled into the air by machines, known as traps, worked by springs. The sport originated in England in the early part of the 19th century as a substitute for the hunting of live birds, and was introduced into the United States in the late 1870's. After 1900 the sport in the United States was governed by the American Trapshooting Association, which in 1924 became known as the Amateur Trapshooting Association. This organization today has associate members in each of the States and also in Canada. State tournaments take place annually, and the winners meet in an annual tournament at the Association's headquarters at Vandalia, Ohio, to determine the national champion. Several events are contested at Vandalia annually, including the Grand American Handicap, for men; the Grand American Handicap, for women; the North American Clay Targets, for men and women; and the North American Doubles and the Governor's Cup Contest, both for men.

Pix; Dept. of M. & R., N.W.T. & Yukon; Mo. Cons. Comm.; Mo. Devel. Comm.

TRAPPING. *Top: Antelope driven into a net trap in New Mexico. Above: Canada lynx in a jaw trap. Right: Trapper in Missouri removing muskrat from a jaw trap. Below: A fisherman with a lobster trap in his boat.*

TRASIMENO, or PERUGIA, LAKE, a shallow lake lying between the towns of Cortona and Perugia, in Umbria, Italy. The lake is surrounded by hills, and is about 10 m. long and 8 m. wide. Called Lake Trasimenus by the ancient Romans, it was the scene of a great victory of the Carthaginian general Hannibal in 217 B.C. (see PUNIC WARS). Hannibal concealed most of his forces in the mountains N. and E. of the lake. The Roman consul Gaius Flaminius (q.v.), unable to see the troops of the enemy because of the morning mists, led his army along the N. shore of the lake. His troops were surrounded by the Carthaginians and about 15,000 were killed; only the vanguard broke through and escaped to the east.

TRAVANCORE-COCHIN, THE UNITED STATE OF, southernmost State of the Union of India, situated at the s.w. extremity of the Indian Peninsula. Prominent topographic features of the State include a low, sandy coast; numerous lagoons, which are linked by canals, forming an inland waterway; a central plains region; and the Western Ghats, which extend from a point near the s. extremity of the State along the entire eastern boundary. The maximum elevation of the Western Ghats in Travancore-Cochin is about 8000 ft. Heavy stands of timber, including teak, cover the w. slopes of the range. Numerous rivers traverse the State.

The principal industries are the processing of cashew nuts and the manufacture of coir and coir products. Among other industries are tea processing, salt making, and the manufacture of textiles, ceramics, refined sugar, matches, glass, chemicals, and cement; monazite, an important source of thorium, is mined. Agricultural products include coconuts, sugar cane, rice, rubber, pepper, tea, and coffee. Cashew nuts, spices, tea, and coir and coir products are the leading exports. Trivandum (q.v.) is the capital; other important communities are Ernakulum, Alleppey, Quilon, and Nagercoil.

Prior to the termination (1947) of British paramountcy in India the region contained in the present-day State was occupied by the separate princely states of Travancore and Cochin. The princely regimes adhered to the Indian Union in 1947; the United State was formed in 1949. Area, 46,710 sq.m.; pop., about 8,000,000.

TRAVELER'S TREE (*Ravenala madagascariensis* or *Urania speciosa*), plant of the order Scitamineae, a native of Madagascar. A tree often has twenty or twenty-four leaves, the stalk of each leaf being 6 or 8 ft. long, and the blade 4 or 6 ft. more. Forty or fifty fruits grow in a bunch, and three or four bunches may be seen at once on the tree. It recevied its popular name, *Arbre des voyageurs,* first from the French on account of the stores of pure water found in the large, cuplike sheaths of its leafstalks, readily obtained by tapping the sheaths at the base.

TRAVERSE CITY, county seat of Grand Traverse Co., Mich., situated on Grand Traverse Bay, an arm of Lake Michigan, and at the mouth of the Boardman R., 140 miles N. of Grand Rapids. It is served by three railroads and by lake steamers. The city is a famous cherry-packing center and market, and the hub of an extensive resort area. The principal industries are the manufacture of automobile parts, machine tools, and foundry products. Traverse City is the site of the U.S. Coast Guard Air Station for the Great Lakes, and of Northern Michigan State Hospital. Parks include Clinch Park, containing an aquarium, a zoo, a bathing beach, and a museum. Interlochen State Park, an area of pine forests and sandy beaches, is 15 miles s.w. of the city. Grand Traverse Bay is noted for deep-water trout trolling. Traverse City was settled in 1847, incorporated as a village in 1881, and chartered as a city in 1895. Pop. (1950) 16,974.

TRAVESTY, term applied in literature to denote a burlesque representation of something previously executed in a serious and lofty manner. It differs from parody in this respect: that while the latter changes the subject matter and the dramatis personae, but mockingly imitates the style of the original, the former leaves the subject matter partially, and the dramatis personae wholly, unaltered; producing a purely comic effect by the substitution of the mean and grotesque in action or speech, for the serious, noble, or heroic.

TRAVIS, WILLIAM BARRETT (1811–36), American soldier, born in Edgefield Co., S.C. After studying law he began practice in Claiborne, Ala., but removed to Texas in 1832 and took part in its successful struggle for independence. Becoming a colonel in the revolutionary army, he was captured by the Mexicans but subsequently released. With about 180 men he defended the Alamo (q.v.) from Feb. 23 to March 6, 1836, against General Santa Anna (q.v.) and about 4000 Mexicans. Desperate fighting continued until only Travis and five others were left, but after a short and determined resistance they were all killed.

TRAWL. See FISHERIES.

TREASON, in criminal law in England and the United States, an overt act of treachery or a breach of allegiance to the government. The crime is neither a felony or misdemeanor, but a grade of crime in itself. Anyone aiding or abetting in the commission of treason is liable as a principal. The United States Constitution (Art. III, Sec. 3) provides that treason against the United States shall consist "only in levying war against them, or in adhering to their enemies, giving them aid and comfort". Levying war under this provision has been construed to mean a defiance of the government by armed force; it must amount to more than a riot (q.v.) or an interference with the execution of the laws for some private purpose. Adhering to or giving aid and comfort to the enemies of the United States means the voluntary giving of material assistance to countries with which the United States is at war. The Constitution provides that "no person shall be convicted of treason unless on the testimony of two witnesses to the same overt act, or on confession in open court". The penalty for treason is death or imprisonment and fine at the discretion of the court; the minimum penalty is five years' imprisonment and a fine of $10,000. The act constituting treason may be committed by an alien temporarily residing in the United States, inasmuch as he owes the duty of allegiance to the country while residing under the protection of its laws.

In England under the old common law, there were two distinct classes of crime, respectively designated high treason and petit, or petty, treason. High treason, although not clearly defined, involved disloyalty to the sovereign or a violation of allegiance due him; petit treason was a violation of the allegiance owed by an inferior to a superior, as a wife to her husband or a servant to his master, such violation consisting of the killing of the superior by the inferior. In 1828 the crime of petty treason was abolished, and the acts formerly constituting petty treason were made felonies. The terms "high treason" and "treason" are now used synonymously. The crime of high treason was first specifically defined by statute in 1351, in the reign of Edward III, to include (1) "compassing and imagining the death of a king", or any act directed at a sovereign's life; (2) violating the king's wife, his oldest unmarried daughter, or the wife of the king's oldest son and heir; (3) levying war against the king by taking arms to dethrone him or under pretense to reform religion or the laws; (4) giving aid and comfort to the king's enemies, as by sending intelligence or provisions or selling arms; and (5) slaying the chancellor, treasurer, or the king's justices while they were administering justice. Subsequent statutes enacted during the reigns of Anne and George III extended the crime of treason to include an attempt to hinder the next in succession under the act of settlement from succeeding to the crown, and a plot to inflict bodily harm or death on the king or his heirs whether evidenced by an overt act or by publication of any writings. By a statute enacted in the reign of William III, and still in effect, a copy of an indictment for treason and a list of the witnesses and jurors, together with the addresses of the latter, must be delivered to the prisoner ten days before the trial; the prisoner may also have counsel assigned to defend him.

The punishment for treason was the most severe of the harsh punishments imposed by the common law. The traitor was drawn on a hurdle to the place of execution, hanged by the neck, his head then severed from his body, the body divided into four quarters, and the head and quarters placed at the disposal of the crown. In 1870 this practice was abolished and the penalty was changed to execution by hanging. Among the famous treason trials in English history were those of Sir Walter Raleigh, Mary, Queen of Scots, Lord George Gordon, and Sir Roger David Casement (qq.v.). Among the most famous treason trials in American history were those of Aaron Burr, John Brown, and Jefferson Davis (qq.v.). No treason trials in America developed as a result of World War I, but after World War II several prosecutions for treason took place in the U.S.; the most notable of these were against the radio propagandists popularly known as Axis Sally and Tokyo Rose. The treason trials in the Soviet satellite states which took place in the period following World War II were similar to the famous Soviet treason trials of 1936–38 (see UNION OF SOVIET SOCIALIST REPUBLICS: *History*). See LESE MAJESTY; MISPRISION.

TREASURY DEPARTMENT, an executive department of the government of the United States controlling the national finances. Established by Act of Congress in September, 1789, it was the successor of the Treasury Department created by the Congress of the Confederation in 1781. The most extensive and complex of the departments, it stands next in rank to the Department of State. At its head is the secretary of the treasury (appointed by the President), second among

Giles, Black Star; Acme

U.S. TREASURY
DEPARTMENT

Above: The entrance to the Treasury Building, Washington, D.C. Right: Aerial view of the U.S. gold repository at Fort Knox, Kentucky.

cabinet officers in line of succession to the presidency. The only qualification for the office is the negative one that the secretary shall not be interested in foreign commerce. He is aided by an undersecretary, a deputy to the secretary, two assistant secretaries, a fiscal assistant secretary, and an administrative secretary. The business of the department is distributed among many offices, bureaus, and divisions, the most important of which are the Office of the Secretary, the Office of the Comptroller of the Currency, the Bureau of Customs, the Bureau of Engraving and Printing, the Bureau of Internal Revenue, the Bureau of the Mint, the Bureau of Narcotics, the Fiscal Service, the U.S. Savings Bonds Division, the U.S. Secret Service,

and the U.S. Coast Guard. The department maintains many field offices throughout the country.

TREATIES, INDIAN. The first step of the United States government in determining its policy in regard to the Indians, whether expressed or implied, was to decide as to the nature of their territorial rights, this being the chief and altogether the most important factor in their relations with the whites. The decision reached on this point is distinctly stated by the United States Supreme Court in the case of Johnson and Graham's Lessee vs. McIntosh, as follows: "It has never been contended that the Indian title amounted to nothing. Their right of possession has never been questioned. The claim of the government extends to the complete, ultimate title, charged with the right of possession, and to the exclusive power of acquiring this right." The next step was to determine the branch of the government to carry out this policy. When the Constitution was framed this authority was conferred upon the legislative department in the following brief statement: "To *regulate commerce* with foreign nations and among the several States, and with the *Indian Tribes*". It is apparent, from the use of the term "tribes", that the framers of the Constitution had in contemplation the method of dealing with the Indians as tribes through treaties. This is clearly shown by the Act of March 1, 1793, in which it is stated that no purchase or grant of lands from the Indians shall be of any validity "unless the same be made by a treaty or convention entered into pursuant to the Constitution". From the formation of the government until March 3, 1871, 653 treaties were made with 97 different tribes or recognized tribal organizations. During all this time Indian titles to lands were extinguished only under the treaty-making clause of the Constitution.

It was ordered by the act of March 3, 1871, that "No Indian nation or tribe within the territory of the United States shall be acknowledged or recognized as an independent nation, tribe, or power with whom the United States may contract by treaty." As the title to reservations is derived in most cases from the United States, and title by purchase is derived directly or indirectly from the same source, it may be stated that the Indian title to all the public domain, except in Alaska, had practically been extinguished by the year 1890. See INDIAN RESERVATIONS.

Other respects in which the power of Congress intervenes in reference to Indian lands, or is necessary to enable the Indians to carry out their desires in regard thereto, are the following. (1) Allotments of land in severalty previous to the Act of Feb. 8, 1887, could be made only by treaty or by virtue of an act of Congress, but by this act general authority is given to the President for this purpose. (2) Leases of land, sale of standing timber, granting of mining privileges, and right of way to railroads are all prohibited to the Indians without some enabling act of Congress. On the other hand, it is obligatory on the government to prevent any intrusion, trespass, or settlement on the lands of any tribe of Indians except where their consent has been given by agreement. See INDIAN AFFAIRS. BUREAU OF; AMERICAN INDIANS.

TREATY, in international law, an agreement entered into between the governments or sovereigns of two or more states. The right to enter into treaty relations is one of the essential attributes of sovereignty. The usual conditions essential to the validity of a treaty are that the contracting parties shall have the requisite capacity to enter into treaty engagements, the plenipotentiaries who negotiate the treaty must be properly authorized, and freedom of consent on the part of the signatory powers must exist. In the case of a treaty of peace, following a war, however, the element of duress is frequently present in the negotiations, and freedom of consent is not a requisite to the validity of the treaty. The extent of the treaty-making power is practically unlimited. It includes the acquisition of foreign territory, the disposal of domestic territory, the recognition of new states, the formation of alliances, the granting of special privileges with respect to commerce, the delimitation and rectification of boundaries, and the guarantee of territorial integrity.

Among the more important types of treaties are treaties of alliance, treaties of guarantee, and reciprocity treaties. A treaty of alliance is an agreement between two or more states with a view to concerted action in war. The alliance is defensive when it is formed with a view to preventing armed aggression against either of the signatory powers; it is offensive when it is formed for the purpose of waging war against another state or states. Treaties of guarantee are entered into for the reaffirmations of the terms of previous treaties made by the signatories; for the purpose of securing the observance of existing treaties made by other signatories; or for the maintenance of certain existing conditions, such as the independence or neutrality of certain states. Reciprocity treaties provide for reciprocal commercial advantages, such as reduced customs tariffs on the products of each signatory state when imported into the other signatory states; in recent times, such treaties usually contain a clause stipulating that each signatory will extend to the other signatory or signatories treatment equally favorable to that accorded any nation with which it has, or may have in the future, a commercial treaty (q.v.; see MOST-FAVORED-NATION CLAUSE). Other types of treaties are those conferring extraterritorial jurisdiction to the signatory powers (see EXTRATERRITORIALITY), those providing for the submission of international disputes to arbitration (see ARBITRATION, INTERNATIONAL) and those regulating commercial matters as copyrights. Treaties may be terminated in various ways. The treaty itself may provide for its termination at a specified time or may provide that either one of the signatories may "denounce", i.e., give notice to terminate, the treaty. A treaty may be terminated by the refusal of one of the signatories to perform mutual stipulations, thus releasing the other party from its obligations; such a unilateral termination of a treaty may result in retaliatory measures by the other signatory. A treaty is also considered to be terminated when the state of affairs assumed by the signatory parties, and therefore the real basis of the treaty, no longer exists, as when a state is destroyed or loses its national character.

With regard to the form of a treaty, no fixed rule prevails, except that the stipulations of the treaty are usually preceded by a recital of the names and titles of the negotiators, with a statement of the purpose which the treaty is intended to accomplish. A copy of the treaty is prepared for each contracting party and signed by its representatives. The treaty must then be ratified by each of the contractual parties; after formal ratification, the treaty becomes operative.

In the United States the treaty-making power is vested in the President and the Senate by Art. II, Sec. 2 of the Constitution, which provides that the President "shall have power by and with the advice and consent of the Senate to make treaties, provided two-thirds of the Senators present concur". Under Art. I, Sec. 10 of the Constitution the power to "enter into any treaty, alliance or confederation" is expressly denied to the States. It is also provided that no State shall, without the consent of Congress, "enter into any agreement or compact with another State or with a foreign power, or engage in war, unless actually invaded, or in such imminent danger as will not admit of delay." The President exercises the treaty-making power through negotiations carried on by the State Department or through special plenipotentiaries appointed for the purpose. The treaty drafted by the negotiating authorities must be ratified by the Senate. The Senate may approve a treaty, it may refuse to ratify, or it may make its ratification conditional upon the adoption of amendments.

Among important treaties entered into by the United States following World Wars I and II were the Treaty of Versailles (1919), under which the all' imposed terms on which German's national status was to be established, and reparations were to be paid; the Treaty of Locarno (1925), under which provision was made for the demilitarization of the Rhineland; the Pact of Paris or "Kellogg Pact" (1928), under which war was renounced as "an instrument of policy"; the Treaty of London (1930), under which a program for limiting naval armaments was arranged; the Teheran Agreement (1943), affirming the determination of the United States, the United Kingdom, and the Union of Soviet Socialist Republics to co-operate in defeating the Axis Powers in World War II, and to continue their co-operation in the postwar period; the Bretton Woods Agreement (1944), whereby the United States, acting in concert with forty-three other nations, created the International Monetary Fund and the International Bank for Reconstruction and Development (qq.v.); the Yalta Declaration (1945), containing numerous decisions relating to the postwar treatment of Germany and to various related questions, concluded by President Franklin D. Roosevelt, Prime Minister Winston Churchill, and Premier Joseph Stalin; the Potsdam Agreement (1945), whereby the United States, the United Kingdom, and the U.S.S.R. established the Council of Foreign Ministers to carry out the preparatory work on the World War II peace treaties, and agreed on a wide variety of subjects affecting postwar international relations; the Treaty of Rio de Janeiro (1947), a mutual-defense and assistance treaty concluded by the United States and eighteen Latin-American nations; the treaties of peace after World War II with Italy, Romania, Bulgaria, and Hungary (1947); the North Atlantic Treaty (1949), a defensive alliance, with Canada and ten West European democracies, against the threat of Soviet aggression; the Japanese Peace Treaty (1951), formally ending World War II in the Far East and restoring sovereignty to Japan; the Japanese Defense Alliance (1951), providing for the maintenance of U.S. land, sea, and air forces in Japan; the "Anzus" treaty (1951), a security pact with Australia and New Zealand; and the Southeast Asian Treaty (1954), a defensive alliance with Great Britain, France, and five nations of s.e. Asia and the s.w. Pacific.

TREBIZOND EMPIRE. See TRABZON.

TREE, a perennial plant having an upright woody main stem, which is usually the tallest of plants at maturity. Trees differ from shrubs (q.v.) in that they usually produce a single

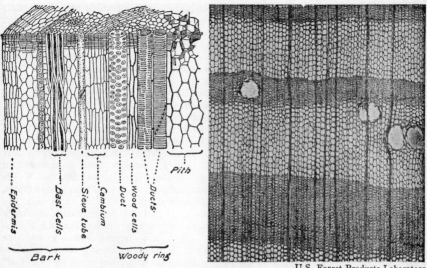

Epidermis . . . . .

Bast Cells

Sieve tube

Cambium

Duct

Wood cells

Ducts

Pith

Bark

Woody ring

Left: Cross and longitudinal section through the woody stem of a tree. Right: Cross section of a trunk of a pine tree, seen under a microscope, showing the annual rings.

main stem, or trunk, and from herbs (q.v.) in that the stem is composed almost entirely of woody tissue. Trees of some smaller species sometimes develop with more than one stem, like a shrub, but most species of larger size grow only in tree form. Some species at maturity are only 10 feet high, with trunks as slender as 6 inches in circumference; the largest species reach as high as 350 feet, with a trunk circumference of 100 feet.

Trees are usually divided into two broad categories: evergreen and deciduous trees. Evergreens are those which bear foliage throughout each year, constantly shedding a small proportion of the older leaves and replacing them with new leaves. Evergreens include two major subdivisions: (1) conifers, native primarily to temperate and cold regions, and bearing needlelike or scalelike leaves which contain large amounts of tough, durable tissue called mechanical tissue; and (2) broad-leaved evergreens, native to warm-temperate and hot regions, and having soft, flat, bladelike leaves. Deciduous trees are broad-leaved and lose their foliage each year, usually at the approach of the coldest season.

Classification and Distribution. All trees are seed-bearing plants belonging to both divisions of the phylum Spermatophyta: Gymnospermae, cone-bearing plants commonly called "softwoods"; and Angiospermae, flowering plants, the trees of which are commonly called

"hardwoods". All seven orders of gymnosperms (q.v.), the most important of which is Coniferales (the conifers), consist primarily of tree species. Among the angiosperms (q.v.), few tree species belong to the class Monocotyledoneae; the only monocotyledonous family containing a preponderance of tree species is the Palm family, the genera of which are native to tropical and subtropical regions throughout the world. The angiospermous class Dicotyledoneae contains most of the broad-leaved trees, which are distributed throughout the world. Of the sixty to seventy thousand species of trees identified by botanists, all are dicotyledonous except a few hundred monocotyledonous species and less than a thousand gymnospermous species. In the United States, native trees belong to about 850 species which are classified in 222 genera of 16 families; the most notable of the latter are the Pine, Yew, Palm, Maple, Cashew, Walnut, Beech, Birch, Magnolia, Rose, Laurel, and Willow families; see separate articles on each of these families. Of the tree species native to the United States, about 150 are hawthorns (see CRATAEGUS), and about 110 are tropical and subtropical trees which grow in s. Florida. About 60 species of trees from Europe and Asia are naturalized in the United States after centuries of cultivation, and more than 200 species of foreign trees are commonly grown in the United States as ornamental,

Amer. For. Prod. Ind.; Fresno, Cal., C. of C.;
Canadian Nat. Railways

TREES. *Above, left: Walnut trees, a flower-bearing deciduous type. Above, right: Pine trees, coniferous evergreens. Left: Fan palm, a flower-bearing evergreen.*

shade, and fruit trees. Tree species comprise about 3½ percent of the plant species found in the United States.

Trees have been in existence since the Devonian period of the Paleozoic era. The oldest trees known to paleobotanists are those of the genus *Cordaites,* which originated in the early Devonian period and became extinct during the Jurassic period of the Mesozoic era. The oldest known surviving order of trees, the broad-leaved, gymnospermous Ginkgoales, is now represented by a single species, the maidenhair tree, *Ginkgo biloba* (see GINKGO). Coniferous trees have existed since the middle of the Carboniferous period. Angiospermous trees first appeared in the Jurassic period of the Mesozoic era, and by the beginning of the Pliocene epoch of the Cenozoic era virtually all tree genera now in existence were growing profusely. The majority of fossil tree leaves found in Pliocene rocks are indistinguishable from leaves of present-day trees.

Trees grow in all regions of the world having adequate ground water available for the major portion of the year. Trees do not grow profusely in desert areas or in areas in which the ground-water table is sufficient only for grassland vegetation; in such areas trees grow successfully only under careful cultivation, in desert oases, or along the banks of rivers and streams. In areas bordering a grassland or desert, trees are frequently stunted and gnarly in growth. In high mountains or at the edge of the northern coniferous forests, for example, trees grow as scattered, twisted dwarfs called *Krumhölz*, or elfinwood. Under normal conditions, however, trees grow in large aggregations called forests (q.v.).

The climatic and soil requirements of trees are somewhat different for each species. Most tree species grow over large areas of which only a small proportion permits optimum growth of the plant. When a tree species is the most prolific of any tree species in a given area, it is called the *dominant* species of the

area. In the eastern half of the United States, for example, spruce and fir dominate in Maine and northern New York; beech and maple dominate in the southern portions of New York, Michigan, and Wisconsin; oak, chestnut, and poplar dominate throughout the mountainous areas; longleaf, loblolly, and slash pines dominate in the Gulf States; and oak and hickory dominate in Ohio, Indiana, Illinois, Missouri, and the southern portions of Michigan and Wisconsin. Some of the States have chosen the blossoms of characteristic native trees as State flowers; apple, *Pyrus malus,* is the State flower of Michigan and Arkansas; hawthorn, *Crataegus mollis,* of Missouri; southern magnolia, *Magnolia grandiflora,* of Louisiana and Mississippi; peach, *Amygdalus persica,* of Delaware; flowering dogwood, *Cornus florida,* of Virginia; and the cone and tassel of white pine, *Pinus strobus,* of Maine. For further information on the ap-

TREES. *Below: Blossom of a magnolia tree. Below, right: Cones on branch of Nordmann's silver fir, a coniferous evergreen. Right: Fruit and leaves of the maindenhair tree, the last remaining representative of the oldest order of trees known, Ginkgoales.*

Cal. Mission Trails; Ohio Dept. Hwys.

TREES. *Above: Giant redwood trees in California. Left: Trees warped by prevailing winds on the coast of California. Below: Isolated Logan elm in Ohio, with crown widely spread.*

pearance, distribution, uses, diseases, and pests of most of these and many other common trees, see separate articles listed under common names of the trees.

Life Processes. Most of the physiological processes undergone by trees are common to all higher plants, but, because the structure of all trees is basically similar, many processes are carried on in uniform ways by most trees. Growth of trees, like that of shrubs, requires the successive addition of many layers of woody tissue to the stem of the original young seedling. The axis (root and stem) of a tree seedling is divided into three main layers. The outermost layer, called the epidermis, is composed of thin-walled cells, and protects the inner layers of the axis. The middle layer, called the cortex, is composed of larger, thin-walled cells, which function temporarily as storage cells. The innermost layer, or stele, is composed of a layer of tough pericyclic cells, a multicellular layer of phloem cells, a multicellular layer of xylem (wood) cells, and an inner core of thin-walled cells which is called pith.

Early in the development of the plant, an embryonic layer of cells, called the cambium, is differentiated between the phloem and xylem layers. The cambium layer alternately produces additional phloem and xylem cells by constant division; when a cambium cell divides to form xylem cells, the inner of the two resulting cells develops into a xylem cell and the outer continues to function as cambium in the next division, in which the outer cell develops into a phloem cell and the inner cell continues to function as cambium. The constant divisions of the cambium gradually increase the circumference of the axis. The cambium continually increases in circumference as the area of wood enlarges from the increase in xylem cells, but the tissues outside the cambium, namely, phloem, pericycle, cortex, and epidermis, soon rupture, form deep fissures, and eventually split off. A new cambium, called the cork cambium or phellogen, develops outside the phloem, and produces successive layers of cork cells which protect the axis. As the axis continues its expansion, the layers of cork develop characteristic fissures at the surface, and as each cork cambium is split by the expansion of wood, a new cork cambium develops to replace it. At maturity, the tree axis normally consists of several layers of cork cells, the outer portion of which is fissured, the cork cambium, a few layers of crushed phloem, a few layers of functioning phloem, the cambium, and many layers of

xylem. The xylem layers usually comprise more than ninety-five percent of the diameter of the axis. The xylem layers are collectively called wood, and the layers outside the cambium are collectively called bark. The cork cambium divides the bark into outer bark and inner bark.

Because the xylem cells produced in the spring of the year are large, and those produced later in the year are smaller, and because an interruption of growth occurs during the winter, each year's growth of wood appears as a distinct ring, called an annual ring. Older annual rings are usually darkened and nonfunctional, and are collectively called heartwood; younger layers are lighter in color, and function in transporting sap, and are therefore called sapwood; see Wood.

The sapwood of the axis functions to carry water and dissolved mineral nutrients upward from the soil to the leaves. In the leaves the water is used, in combination with carbon dioxide taken in through the leaves, in a process of food manufacture called photosynthesis (q.v.). The sapwood also transports the gaseous products of respiration (q.v.), which occurs in all living cells of the plant, to the leaves, from which the gases are released into the atmosphere. Food, manufactured by photosynthesis, and oxygen, absorbed from the air and used in respiration, are transported downward to the roots by the phloem.

Reproduction in trees is usually carried on by asexual processes; that is, the reproductive organs of both sexes are usually borne on the same flower (q.v.) or the same inflorescence (q.v.) of a single tree. In holly, ash, many maples, yew, juniper, and ginkgo (qq.v.), however, the trees are either male or female. Trees are usually wind- or insect-pollinated (see Pollination), but several species of birch produce fertile seeds without pollination.

The normal age span of trees is different for each species. Some birches, for example, normally die after about 40 years of life. The sugar maple, on the other hand, frequently lives as long as 500 years, some oaks as long as 1500 years, some junipers as long as 2000 years, and some giant sequoias as long as 4000 years.

Uses. Trees and tree products are among the most important commodities used by man. For information on the growth of trees for timber and their subsequent use as wood, see Forestry; Lumber Industry; Wood; and separate articles on timber trees. For information on the use of trees as food sources,

Pan Amer. World Air.; U.S. Forest Service; Australian News & Information Bureau

TREES. *Top: Bananas growing on a tree in Brazil. Bottom, left: Leaves and fruit of the butternut tree. Bottom, right: Baobab tree, Australia. Bark is used for cordage fiber.*

see FRUIT; HORTICULTURE: *Fruitgrowing*; ORCHARD; and separate articles on common fruit trees. For use of trees in erosion control, see CONSERVATION; EROSION. Many trees are used as ornamental plants in parks, along avenues and boulevards, and in gardens; see LANDSCAPE ARCHITECTURE. The accompanying table lists the trees most commonly used as ornamental and shade trees in the United States; similar trees of the same genera are used under corresponding climatic conditions in other parts of the world.

COMMON SHADE TREES OF THE UNITED STATES

SCIENTIFIC NAME	COMMON NAME
Acer platanoides	Norway maple
A. rubrum	Red maple
A. saccharum	Sugar maple
Betula lutea	Yellow birch
Carya illinoensis	Pecan
Castanea dentata	American chestnut
Catalpa speciosa	Northern catalpa
Celtis occidentalis	Hackberry
Cercis canadensis	Redbud
Chionanthus virginica	Fringe tree
Fagus grandifolia	Beech
Fraxinus americana	White ash
Ginkgo biloba	Maidenhair tree
Gleditsia tricanthos	Honey locust
Gymnocladus dioica	Kentucky coffee tree
Ilex opaca	American holly
Juglans cinerea	Butternut
J. nigra	Black walnut
Juniperus virginiana	Eastern red cedar
Libocedrus decurrens	Incense cedar
Liquidambar styraciflua	Sweet gum
Liriodendron tulipifera	Tulip tree
Magnolia grandiflora	Southern magnolia
M. soulangea	Saucer magnolia
Mimosa ferruginea	Mimosa
Picea glauca	White spruce
P. pungens	Colorado blue spruce
P. rubens	Red spruce
Pinus nigra	Austrian pine
P. resinosa	Red pine
P. sylvestris	Scotch pine
Platanus occidentalis	American sycamore
Pseudotsuga taxifolia	Douglas fir
Quercus bicolor	Swamp white oak
Q. borealis	Northern red oak
Q. macrocarpa	Bur oak
Q. palustris	Pin oak
Q. stellata	Post oak
Robinia pseudoacacia	Black locust
Salix nigra	Black willow
Sorbus americana	Mountain ash
Thuja occidentalis	Eastern arborvitae
Tilia americana	American linden
T. vulgaris	European linden
Tsuga canadensis	Eastern hemlock
Ulmus americana	American elm
U. procera	English elm

TREE, SIR HERBERT BEERBOHM (1853–1917), English actor-manager, born in London. He became widely known for his elaborate productions of Shakespearean plays, in most of which he took leading parts. In 1905 he in-augurated a Shakespeare Festival, which was repeatedly successful. With his company he visited Germany in 1907, at the invitation of Emperor William, and in 1916 played in the United States, presenting *Henry VIII* and *The Merchant of Venice.* He was the author of *Thoughts and Afterthoughts* (1913).

TREE COBRA. See MAMBA.

TREE CYPRESS. See PHLOX.

TREE DUCK, common name applied to any of several tree-dwelling wild geese belonging to the genus *Dendrocygna* and noted for their extremely long legs and neck. The chestnut-colored feathers are often specked in many places with white and black. The black-bellied tree duck, *D. autumnalis,* and the fulvous tree duck, *D. bicolor,* are native to tropical America, and are common in the southern portions of the United States during summer; see GOOSE.

TREE FERN, common name applied to any of several true ferns belonging to the Fern family, Polypodiaceae, and to the Cup-Fern family, Cyatheaceae. The tree ferns differ from other true ferns in possessing fronds borne on thick erect, columnar trunks. The thick trunks, formed by the consolidation of the bases of the fronds, are enlarged stems which contain a central area of soft, parenchyma tissue. Most species of tree ferns belong to the Cup-Fern family, and are native to tropical and subtropical regions throughout the world. The hardiest and most beautiful of these, be-

N.Y. Zoological Society
White-faced tree ducks (Dendrocygna viduata)

longing to the genus *Dicksonia*, grow abundantly in many regions of the South Pacific Ocean. The principal species, *D. antarctica*, native to Australia and Tasmania, often attains a height of 35 feet. *Alsophila australia*, an elaborately pinnate-leaved tree fern found in most tropical regions of the Eastern and Western hemispheres, grows about 40 feet high. A less common species, *A. excelsa*, reaches a height of 80 feet. Other genera include *Cyathea*, common in Colombia and the West Indies, and *Cibotium*, native to Mexico and Polynesia. The most common tree ferns of the family Polypodiaceae belong to the genus Blechnum, native to Brazil and the West Indies. Plants of the genus rarely exceed 15 feet in height. Most tree ferns are cultivated as ornamental plants in greenhouses or outdoors in porous soils throughout many warm areas.

The name "tree fern" is also commonly but erroneously applied to the gray polypody, *Polypodium polypodioides*, found growing on rocks and the trunks of trees throughout North America, and to the royal fern, *Osmunda regalis*, a flowering fern which bears numerous fruit clusters. Compare FERN; PTERIDOPHYTA.

TREE FROG or **TREE TOAD**, common name applied to any of several small, brightly colored frogs of the family Hylidae, found living among the branches of trees and shrubs in many temperate and tropical areas throughout the world. Unlike most other frogs they possess disklike suction cups at the tips of the fingers and toes; these cups enable them to cling tightly to branches, tree trunks, and rocks. Their diet consists mainly of insects, which they catch while jumping across bushes or the branches of trees. In general, the skin of the tree frog is smooth above but extremely warty on the abdomen and the inside of the legs. The general body color ranges from brown and gray to green, changing, chameleonlike, to blend with the surrounding area. During the spring, the female lays one to several eggs in a pond; the eggs become attached to pond plants and hatch in several days.

The common North American tree frog, *Hyla versicolor*, is found near decaying trees or old fences throughout the eastern part of the United States. It ranges in color from dark brown to mottled gray, has a short, rounded head, and attains a length of 2 inches. *H. regilla*, the Pacific tree toad, occurs widely in North America, and is similar to *H. versicolor* in habit and structure. The largest-known tree toad, *H. vasta*, is native to Dominica, where it attains a length of 5 inches.

The only species common to Europe, *H. arborea*, is similar to the North American species, except that it is usually colored greenish above and yellowish or white below. *Acris gryllus*, a less common species native to s.w. United States, is colored gray above, greenish below and averages 1½ inches in length. It is characterized by a red dorsal line and by three large, black, white-margined spots which run along the sides. The common South American tree toad, *Hylodes faber*, usually known as *ferreiro*, attains a length of 2 inches. Tree toads have a melodious, chirping song; because the song is most intense in damp weather or before a rain, the toads are regarded as weather prophets in various parts of the world. During the winter, they bury themselves in the decayed stumps of trees or within the earth and wait for the coming of spring. Compare FROG; SPRING PEEPER.

TREE HOPPER, any insect of the homopterous family. Membracidae, a very strange group comprising a variety of grotesque forms. The species are very numerous, and the group is one of wide distribution. The most bizarre forms occur in tropical regions, but many curious species are found in the temperate zone. A common form in the United States is the little humpbacked *Telemona monticola*, which sometimes swarms on the branches of the Virginia creeper in June. Another interesting form, *Entilla sinuata*, is found upon the leaves of the sunflower and other annual plants. The buffalo tree hopper, *Ceresa bubalus*, so called from its horned prothorax, is a species of considerable economic importance; it damages the small twigs of fruit trees in the act of laying its eggs.

TREE KANGAROO, common name for kangaroos of the genus *Dendrolagus*, which inhabit trees in the forests of northern Australia and New Guinea. They embrace several species, of which the black tree kangaroo, *Dendrolagus ursinus*, of New Guinea is the best known. Unlike ordinary kangaroos, tree kangaroos have the hind limbs only slightly longer than the fore limbs.

TREE LIZARD. See DRAGON, OR FLYING DRAGON.

TREE OF HEAVEN. See AILANTHUS.

TREE SHREW or **SQUIRREL SHREW,** common name applied to any of several small, insectivorous animals belonging to the family Tupaiidae, and found living in trees throughout the East Indies and southern Asia. They greatly resemble the common shrew (q.v.) in external appearance, but differ in having five clawed toes on each foot. Because of their

N.Y. Zoological Society

Tree shrew (Tupaia ferruginea)

soft, gray, gleaming fur and long, bushy tail they are often mistaken for squirrels. Approximately fifteen species of tree shrews are known, the most common being the Malayan banxring, *Tupaia glis,* found in abundance throughout the Malay Peninsula, and the Madras tree shrew, *Anathana ellioti,* native to India. Both animals are very similar in appearance, and feed on insects and fruits. The Bornean tree shrew, *Ptilocercus lowii,* also known as *pentail,* is native to Borneo and feeds on insects and fruit; its tail is naked at the base.

TREE TOAD. See TREE FROG.

TREE WORSHIP, in primitive times, or among primitive races, reverence paid to trees because of the belief that they were inhabited by a supernatural being or were beloved by some god whose favor should be propitiated. This veneration survives in the Chersonese, and among native races of America, Asia, Africa, and Oceania. It was much developed among the Canaanites, Buddhists, Druids, and Greeks, and gave rise to a large class of fables and folklore. The sacred bo tree of India, destroyed in 1887, the oak of the Druids and of Dodona, the laurel of Apollo, the fig of the Acropolis, and the legends of dryads, fauns, and satyrs are products of tree worship. See DRUIDISM.

TREITSCHKE, HEINRICH VON (1834–96), German historian and political writer, born in Dresden. After first considering a journalistic career he became in 1858 a lecturer in history at the University of Leipzig, and he spoke before large audiences on the constitutional history of Germany. In 1864 he published an essay *Bundesstaat und Einheitsstaat,* one of his most important writings and by many

considered his best work, in which he attacked the German confederacy and advocated a German union. In 1866 he became editor of the *Preussische Jahrbücher* in Berlin. But in the same year he was called to the University of Kiel, in 1867–73 he was a professor at Heidelberg, and in 1873 he accepted a chair at Berlin. After the foundation of the German Empire he was elected to the Reichstag, at first as a member of the National Liberal party, later becoming a conservative. He attracted attention as a parliamentary orator and was noted for his speeches against the Ultramontanes and the Socialists. One of the most brilliant works of the kind in the German language is Treitschke's *Deutsche Geschichte im Neunzehnten Jahrhundert* (5 vols., 1874–94; Eng. trans., "History of Germany in the Nineteenth Century", 7 vols., New York, 1915 et seq.). Treitschke was the last and greatest of the Prussian school and his book is written throughout from a Prussian standpoint.

After the outbreak of World War I Treitschke was attacked as one of its spiritual instigators.

TRELAWNY, EDWARD JOHN (1792–1881), English author and adventurer, whose name is linked with the names of Shelley and Byron. He was born in London and entered the Royal Navy at the age of thirteen, serving in the fleet blockading Cadiz (1805). Subsequently he deserted and passed through exciting adventures in the East Indies. He made the acquaintance of Shelley at Pisa in 1822, and he took part in the burning of the poet's body on the shore near Viareggio. Next year he accompanied Byron to Greece, and joined in the war of independence. After living in Italy and traveling in the United States (1833–35), he settled in London where he was much sought after on account of his rich fund of anecdote. He was the old arctic voyager in Millais' *Northwest Passage.* Trelawny published two books, *The Adventures of a Younger Son* (1831) and *Recollections of the Last Days of Shelley and Byron* (1858), the latter republished, with changes, as *Records of Shelley, Byron, and the Author* (1878).

TREMATODA. See FLUKE.

TREMOLITE, a compact, granular, transparent to translucent mineral usually composed of hydrated calcium magnesium silicate, $Ca_2Mg_5Si_8O_{22}(OH)_2$. The mineral crystallizes in the monoclinic system in fibrous or columnar form. It has a hardness of 5 to 6, a specific gravity of 3.0 to 3.3, and exhibits perfect prismatic cleavage. The color ranges from light green to white; excess amounts of iron sometimes replace the magnesium in part, causing a slightly darker color. Tremolite is a member of the group of minerals called amphiboles. A hard, compact variety of tremolite, known as *nephrite,* yields the mineral jade (q.v.); a variety having more than two percent of iron is called actinolite. All varieties shine with a vitreous luster.

The mineral occurs in various talc (q.v.) schists, and is often found in impure, crystalline varieties of dolomitic limestones; see DOLOMITE. Less frequently, it is discovered in the pyroxene (q.v.) deposits of igneous rocks. In the United States, tremolite is mined extensively in several areas of upper New York State. Other deposits occur in the Italian, Swiss, and Austrian Alps and throughout the mountain areas of s. Turkestan. Fibrous tremolites are a minor source of asbestos (q.v.).

TREMOLO, a term in vocal music used to designate the wavering tone produced when the voice is caused or allowed to become unsteady. The *involuntary vibrato* is generally caused by imperfect control of the breath, but tremolo may be intentionally and legitimately employed in certain dramatic situations. In instrumental music the word signifies that the notes are to be rapidly reiterated during their time values, instead of being played as sustained sounds.

TRENCH. See FORTIFICATION AND SIEGECRAFT.

TRENCH FOOT, a morbid condition of the foot, common during World War I, caused by repeated exposure to wet, low temperatures, tight or ill-fitting shoes, and neglect of personal hygiene. The chief symptoms are burning, numbness, and tingling; the feet being red or livid and insensitive. Tetanus and gangrene were frequent complications. Curative measures in simple cases were rest and cleanliness; gangrenous conditions sometimes required surgical treatment.

TRENCH MOUTH or **VINCENT'S ANGINA,** an acute inflammation of the mucous membranes of the mouth and throat, characterized by painful ulcerations. The disease was prevalent among soldiers of World War I and is still common among people suffering from pyorrhea, Vitamin-B deficiency, and tooth decay. *Fusiformis dentium,* a bacillus, and *Borrelia vincenti,* a spirillum, are often found in trench mouth lesions; most physicians believe that the organisms do not cause the disease, but are instead secondary invaders of tissue which has been injured or irritated. Trench mouth is treated by local applications and intramuscular injections of penicillin, which reduce the intensity and duration of the disease.

TRENGGANU, a British protected Malay State. See MALAYA, FEDERATION OF.

TRENT, a river of central England, rising on the northwest border of Staffordshire, and flowing through the counties of Derby, Nottingham, and Lincoln, till it unites with the Ouse to form the Humber, about 15 miles w. of Hull. Length, 170 m.

TRENT. See TRENTO.

TRENT, COUNCIL OF, the eighteenth ecumenical council of the Roman Catholic Church, assembled at Trent, and held with intermissions from 1545 until 1563 under the pontificates of Paul III, Julius III, and Pius IV.

The council opened at Trent on December 13, 1545. In the fourth session (1546) sacred tradition was put on a par with Scripture, all the books contained in the Vulgate, including the so-called Apocrypha, were declared to be canonical, and the Vulgate version was pronounced "authentic". The doctrine of Justification was after much discussion laid down (1547) in terms which involved the emphatic condemnation of the Lutheran teaching. One of the most prolonged struggles arose out of a discussion on the laws regarding episcopal residence. In 1547 the council was moved to Bologna and in 1551 the council was reassembled at Trent, but after the sixteenth session the sittings were suspended for two years.

To Pius IV (1560–66) belongs the credit of renewing the council, and bringing it to a successful conclusion. Disciplinary decrees were passed regarding episcopal duties, the

Cathedral and Great Tower in the town of Trento, Italy

religious orders, the education of the priest-hood, and the censorship of books. Clandestine marriages were by a new law made invalid. Doctrinal decrees were issued on the Mass, purgatory, the veneration due to saints, and the doctrine of indulgences.

The decrees of the entire council were confirmed, January 25, 1564, by Pius IV, who in the same year published the profession of the Tridentine Faith, a brief summary of doctrines, generally known as the *Creed of Pope*

Pius. The council set the standard of Roman Catholic faith and practice to the present day. The only things added have been the two definitions of the Immaculate Conception and the Infallibility of the Pope. The tercentenary of the council was celebrated in June, 1863.

TRENTE ET QUARANTE. See Rouge et Noir.

TRENTO or **TRENT** (Ger. *Trient;* anc. *Tridentum*), city and capital of the province of the same name, Italy, situated on the Adige R., about 45 miles N. of Verona. The city lies on the historic route, via Brenner Pass, between Austria and Italy and is an important railroad junction and commercial center. Industrial establishments include foundries, alcohol distilleries, wineries, and glassworks, and plants engaged in the manufacture of chemicals, cement, foodstuffs, and electric motors. Among noteworthy points of interest are the Cathedral of San Vigilio, begun in the 11th century and completed in the 15th century; the 13th-century Castello del Buon Consiglio, once the residence of the prince-bishops of Trento and now containing a museum of antiquities and fine arts; and the 16th-century church of Santa Maria Maggiore, in which the celebrated Council of Trent took place.

Little of an authentic nature is known concerning the origins of ancient *Tridentum*. It was seized from the Celts late in the 3rd century B.C. by the Romans, and under their rule it became a powerful defense bastion. The Ostrogoths captured *Tridentum* in the 5th century A.D. and lost it to the Lombards in the 6th century. In 774 the latter were subdued by the Franks, under whom the city became the seat of a duchy. Trento subsequently became a German possession, and in 1027 the Holy Roman emperor Conrad II made it an episcopal principality. The prince-bishops, under Hapsburg sovereignty after 1363, governed Trento (except for periods of French occupation in 1797 and 1801) until 1803, when the principality was secularized and merged with Austrian Tirol. Seized again by the French in 1809, Trento remained under their rule until it was returned to Austria in 1814. After the formation (1861) of the Kingdom of Italy the city was a center of Italian Irredentism. Trento was transferred to Italy in 1919 under the provisions of the Treaty of Saint-Germain, the peace settlement imposed on Austria following World War I. Area of province, 2516 sq.m.; pop., about 391,000. Pop. of city, about 37,000.

TRENTON, capital of New Jersey and county seat of Mercer Co., situated on the E. bank of the Delaware R. at the head of navigation, 30 miles N.E. of Philadelphia, Pa. Transportation facilities include two railroads, an airport, and barges and small steamers on the Delaware R. Harbor facilities include wharves, warehouses, and municipal terminals. Trenton is a manufacturing center, noted for the production of pottery and other clay products, and wire rope and cable, and as the site of the John A. Roebling's Sons Corporation (see ROEBLING, JOHN A.), builders of the Brooklyn and George Washington bridges, New York City, and the Golden Gate Bridge, San Francisco. Other important products are rubber goods, electrical goods, hardware, asbestos fabrics, airplane equipment, parachutes, silk and woolen yarns, foundry products, and cigars. Among the educational institutions are the New Jersey State Teachers College, established in 1855, and Rider College, founded in 1865. The city also contains the New Jersey School for the Deaf, the State Home for Girls, the State Hospital for the Insane, the State prison, and the State arsenal. Trenton is an episcopal see of both the Roman Catholic and Protestant Episcopal churches. The State capitol, or State House, dating in part from 1792, and the State Capitol Annex, completed in 1931 and containing the State museum and library, are the principal public buildings. Of historical interest are the old "Hessian" barracks, built in 1758, occupied in turn during the Revolution by British, Hessian, and American troops; the Trenton Battle Monument, commemorating the Battle of Trenton; Trent House, dating from 1719, the oldest house in Trenton; the Friends Meeting House (1739); and Bow Hill, a red brick house in which Joseph Bonaparte, brother of Napoleon, lived for a time prior to 1822. The municipal park area covers more than 260 acres and includes Cadwalader Park, containing zoological gardens.

The site of the present city was first permanently settled in 1680 and in 1714 the settlement became known as Trent-Town or Trenton, after William Trent, a wealthy landowner who later became chief justice of New Jersey. During the American Revolution Trenton was the site of the decisive Battle of Trenton following George Washington's famous crossing of the Delaware. The U.S. Congress met at Trenton for a short period in Nov., 1784. In 1790 Trenton became the capital of New Jersey. It was chartered as a city in 1792. Pop. (1950) 128,009.

TRENTON, BATTLE OF. See PRINCETON, BATTLE OF.

TREPANG, the dried body of a holothurian, esteemed in China as a food. It passes also under the name of *bêche de mer,* or sea slug. The ordinary kind resembles a prickly cucumber. The average size is about 8 in. long, but some are 2 ft. in length. They are often found in the coral sand, the tentacles only appearing above it. Large ones are sometimes speared in shallow water, but most are taken by divers. Macassar is the center of the trade. Trepang is also gathered and prepared in California. It is gelatinous and nutritious, and is used as an ingredient in soups.

TREPANNING or **TREPHINING,** the surgical removal of a disk of bone from the skull to provide entrance to the brain or to relieve cerebral pressure or irritation. The operation is accomplished by cutting the cranial bones with a small cylindrical saw, called a trepan or trephine, equipped with a center pin. The center pin extends a short distance beyond the blade of the saw and is inserted first to prevent slipping. In modern surgery the disk is replaced by a metal plate after the completion of an operation. Trepanning is the most ancient form of surgery for which objective evidence exists. The operation is established as having existed in a well-developed form in the Neolithic Age. In ancient times trepanning was performed on live patients suffering from fractured skulls, convulsions, and insanity. Disks of bone from the skulls of cadavers were often carved and used as religious amulets in ancient Egypt and Sumeria.

TRESPASS, in law in England and the United States, a tort (q.v.) consisting of unlawful entry on real property in the possession of another. An entry need not be by an individual; it may be made by animals, such as cattle, which are allowed to stray on another's land, or by propelling stones upon another's property, as by blasting. The entry may originally have been lawful and authorized, but the person entering may later become a trespasser; thus, the purchaser of a theater ticket who creates a disturbance and refuses to leave when requested is a trespasser. The party in possession of property may use force if necessary to prevent a trespass or eject a trespasser. A trespasser on another's property who sustains injuries because of the defective condition of the property cannot recover damages against the owner of the property for such injuries. A trespasser is liable to the aggrieved party for damages resulting from his wrongful act.

TREVANDRUM. See TRIVANDRUM.

TREVELYAN, GEORGE MACAULAY (1876–   ), British historian, born in London. He was regius professor of modern history at Trinity College, Cambridge, from 1927 to 1940, and master of Trinity College, Cambridge, from 1940 to 1951. In 1949 he became chancellor of Durham University. He served in a British ambulance unit in Italy during World War I, and was twice decorated by that country. His later works include *The Two-Party System in English Political History* (1926), *History of England* (1926), *The Present Position of History* (1927), *Sir George Otto Trevelyan: A Memoir* (1932), *Grey of Fallodon* (1937), *Illustrated English Social History* (4 vols., 1950–52), and *A Layman's Love of Letters* (lectures, 1954).

TREVELYAN, SIR GEORGE OTTO (1838–1928), English statesman and historian, the only son of Sir Charles Edward Trevelyan, born in Rothley Temple, in Leicestershire. He was a member of the House of Commons from 1865 until 1897, and successively held the appointments of civil lord of the admiralty (1868), secretary of the admiralty (1880–82), chief secretary for Ireland (1882–84), chancellor of the duchy of Lancaster, with a seat in the cabinet (1884–85), and secretary for Scotland from February to April, 1886, and from 1892 to 1895. He was mainly instrumental in securing the abolition of purchase in the army and the extension of household suffrage to the counties. He wrote several biographies and histories and published, among other works, *The Life and Letters of Lord Macaulay* (new ed., 1923), *The Early History of Charles James Fox* (1880), and *The American Revolution* (4 vols., 1912–14).

TREVES. See TRIER.

TREVISO (Rom. *Tarvisium*), capital of an Italian province of the same name, on the Sile, 18 miles N. of Venice with which it is connected by a canal. It has a Duomo dating from the 15th century, with pictures by Titian and Pordenone. Treviso figured among the cities of the Lombard League. It came under the rule of Venice in the 14th century. Pop., about 30,000.

TREVITHICK, RICHARD (1771–1833), English mechanical engineer and inventor, one of the pioneers of railroad locomotion, born in Cornwall. In 1796 he exhibited models of high-pressure steam engines. One which he designed in 1800 was soon in wide use in the mines of Cornwall and Wales. In 1801 he completed and operated a full-sized vehicle for which he received a patent in the following year. In 1804, with the assistance of Andrew Vivian, he made the first application of steam to the hauling of loads on a railway, and this led to the construction of further steam locomotives operating on rails. He is considered by many entitled to the credit of being the real inventor of the locomotive steam engine. His discoveries were of the greatest use to other engineers when practically applied. See LOCOMOTIVE.

TRIAD, in music, a chord of three tones built upon any tone with its third and fifth above. It varies materially according to the character of the intervals (major, minor, augmented, or diminished).

TRIAL, in law, in a general sense, the investigation and decision of a matter in issue between parties before a competent tribunal, including all steps taken in the case from its submission to the trial court or jury to the rendition of judgment. A trial may be defined broadly and comprehensively as a judicial examination of the issues between the parties.

Trials are usually held before a judge sitting alone, a referee (see below), or a judge and jury. In most States of the United States the details of trials in the various courts are regulated by the State codes of civil and criminal procedure and the State constitutions. Civil cases are divided into two classes: equity cases, which are usually tried by a judge sitting without a jury; and actions at law, which are usually tried before a jury. In civil cases the right to a trial by jury may, in most jurisdictions, be waived. In some States the defendant may waive his right to be tried by a jury even in criminal cases, although in most jurisdictions the rule obtains that in all cases involving the commission of felonies the defendant must be tried by a jury.

The procedure usually followed in the trial of either a civil or criminal action is as follows. A panel of jurors (see JURY) is convened in the court in which the case is to be tried; the names of prospective jurors are drawn by lot by the clerk of the court, and as the names are called the prospective jurymen take their seats in the jury box. The attorneys for the respective parties are then permitted to examine the jurors at length for the purpose of determining their qualifications to sit as jurors. Each side has the right, depending upon the type of case and the jurisdictions involved, to challenge a certain number of jurors peremptorily. Prospective jurors who exhibit bias or prejudice can be challenged for cause. The first twelve persons who are accepted as satisfactory by both sides usually constitute the jury.

The opening remarks to the jury, in most jurisdictions, can be waived in both civil and criminal cases. If not waived, it is customary for the attorney for the plaintiff in a civil case and the prosecuting officer in a criminal case to make the first opening address to the jury, which consists of a statement of what the plaintiff or the prosecution intends to prove. The defendant's attorney then makes his opening address to the jury, which consists of a similar statement as to what proof will be adduced on behalf of the defendant. In criminal cases, in a number of jurisdictions, the opening address on behalf of the defendant is not made until the prosecution has completed its part of the case.

After the opening addresses, it is incumbent upon the plaintiff in a civil case and the prosecution in a criminal case to substantiate the allegations set forth in the plaintiff's complaint or the various charges made by the indictment in a criminal case by the introduction of such proof as may be available to them (see EVIDENCE). The examination of the witnesses called by either of the parties is called direct examination; examination by opposing counsel is called cross-examination. In a civil case, the plaintiff must at the outset sufficiently prove the allegations of his complaint to require the defendant to adduce controverting testimony. In the event that the plaintiff fails to make out such a "prima facie" case, the court may, upon motion of the attorney for the defendant, dismiss the case for failure of proof. If a prima facie case has been made out by the plaintiff, the defendant has the choice of either resting his case without offering any testimony in his behalf or producing his proof before the jury. In a criminal prosecution, the burden is upon the State or other prosecuting agency first to establish by its proof that the defendant is guilty of the crime or crimes charged in the indictment beyond a reasonable doubt. In the event that no proper proof is produced, defendant's counsel, at the end of the State's case, may make a motion to dismiss the indictment, and if the requirement with regard to the degree of proof has not been satisfied by the prosecution, the court must dismiss the indictment; upon such dismissal, the prosecution is terminated completely.

At the conclusion of the case, it is customary for both sides to make their summations, which consist of comments by counsel with regard to the testimony of the various witnesses who have testified at the trial, and the inferences to be drawn therefrom. In both civil and criminal cases, in most jurisdictions, counsel for the defendant sums up first, and the attorney for the plaintiff or the prosecuting officer makes the concluding summation. After the summations, the court charges the jury. The charge of the court consists of a statement and an exposition of the rules of law applicable to the issues in the case, for the guidance of the jury. After the charge is made, counsel for either party can except to those portions of the charge which they consider objectionable and make requests that additional charges be given by the court. After the conclusion of the charge, the jury retires from the courtroom to decide on its verdict. The verdict (q.v.) of a jury terminates the trial. In a case tried before a judge sitting alone, the decision of the judge constitutes a termination of the trial.

In law in the United States, a referee is an attorney authorized by a civil court to act as an officer of the court in the determination of a proceeding or suit referred to him. Reference of an issue to a referee may be either voluntary or compulsory; it is most frequently resorted to in actions involving long and complicated accounts, such as bankruptcy actions, and in actions in which privacy and secrecy are considered desirable in the public interest, such as divorce actions. The findings and decision of a referee are submitted in a report which is filed with the court ordering the reference; a trial before a referee is terminated when the referee's decision is confirmed by that court.

A trial conducted before a referee or a judge sitting alone is identical with a jury trial, except that the opening remarks and summations described above are omitted.

TRIAL BY COMBAT. See BATTLE, WAGER OF.

TRIANGLE, a musical instrument formed of a steel rod bent in triangle form, open at one angle. It is suspended from the performer's left hand, his desk, or his drums by means of a string attached to the upper angle, and struck with a steel beater. Modern composers frequently use it in marches, dances, and fantasias.

TRIANON, TREATY OF, the treaty of peace concluded between Hungary and the Allied Powers following World War I, and signed at the Grand Trianon, Versailles, France, on June 4, 1920. Its terms were similar to those of the Treaty of Saint Germain (see SAINT GERMAIN, TREATY OF) between the Allies and Austria, except for specific territorial adjustments. In accordance with the treaty Hungary lost about three fourths of its territory through the cession of Slovakia and Carpathian Ruthenia to Czechoslovakia, of Transylvania and a part of the Banat province to Romania, of Croatia-Slavonia and the remainder of the Banat province to Yugoslavia, and of the Burgenland region to Austria. In addition, the port of Fiume on the Adriatic Sea was re-established as a free city. The population of Hungary was reduced by two thirds because of these territorial losses. The Hungarian army was limited to 35,000 men. The treaty also provided that livestock was to be furnished by Hungary for devastated countries, and that Yugoslavia was to receive without cost annual allotments of coal from Hungary for five years. Reparations were to be paid in part by May 1, 1921, and the balance in sixty-six semiannual installments; the total amount was to be fixed subsequently by the Reparations Commission. See HUNGARY: *History*; REPARATIONS; WORLD WAR I: *The Peace Treaties.*

TRIASSIC PERIOD, the first geological period of the Mesozoic era. The Triassic followed the Permian period of the Paleozoic era and preceded the Jurassic period. The Triassic began approximately 200,000,000 years ago and lasted for about 50,000,000 years. Its beginning was marked by the Appalachian revolution, a vast folding of the earth's crust, in what is now the northeastern U.S., which produced the Appalachian mountains. The last geological event of the period was the Palisade disturbance, an upheaval in the same area. This disturbance thrust up once again the same chain of mountains, which had been greatly eroded during the period.

Triassic North America. At the beginning of Triassic times the Atlantic shoreline of the continent was probably located far east of the present coasts; none of the deposits of the period found in the eastern U.S. are marine in character. The newly-formed Appalachian chain, stretching from the present area of New Brunswick to Alabama, was high and rugged at the beginning of the period and joined with another chain of mountains, the Ouachita Mountains, which ran from the Texas panhandle through southern Arkansas, northern Louisiana, and Mississippi. In the western portion of the continent a long arm of the Pacific Ocean extended from southern California, through Nevada and a portion of Arizona, northward to Utah, Wyoming, Montana, and British Columbia. This arm of the sea represented the troughs of three geosynclines, or sag troughs in the earth's crust extending inland and parallel with the coast. These troughs included one in California, one in British Columbia, and a third following the axis of the modern Rocky Mountains. Throughout the Triassic period these troughs continued to subside and by the end of the period the sea had invaded the continent from the north. On the shores of this shallow inland sea were great stretches of low plains.

In the eastern portion of the continent, the Appalachians were eroded to a low, rough plain, or *peneplain,* by the middle of the period, when faulting or slippage of great blocks of the earth's crust occurred. The troughs formed by these faults, which occurred in Connecticut, north New Jersey, Pennsylvania, Maryland, Virginia, and North Carolina, gradually became filled with coarse sediments from the uplifted portions of the faults. These sediment beds, which are the most prominent Triassic strata of the eastern U.S., reach thicknesses between 10,000 and 13,000 feet. The beds are interspersed with three separate sheets or flows of igneous rock, and in some places are cut by vertical igneous dikes, indicating that much volcanic activity occurred during the last half of the Triassic period.

Outside of the North American continent notable Triassic deposits occur in the British Isles and Europe (particularly in the region of the Alps, where the deposits reach a thickness of 25,000 feet), Asia, South Africa, and South America.

Climate. From the fossilized remains of animals and plants found in Triassic strata, geologists infer that the general climate of the North American continent was warm and that subtropical conditions existed as far north as Wyoming and New England. In the eastern part of what is now the United States rainfall was extensive but probably occurred during only one part of the year. In the plains to the east of the inland sea in the western U.S. there was little rainfall.

Fauna. The most important animals to make their appearance in the Triassic period comprised the dinosaurs. The earliest members of this group did not attain the huge dimensions of the dinosaurs of later Mesozoic times and were for the most part comparatively slim animals no more than 10 to 15 feet in length. Another important reptilian group of the Triassic were the ichthyosaurs, which were marine reptiles with long snouts and bodies shaped like those of modern dolphins. Other marine reptiles of the period were the turtles and the pleisiosaurs, which had broad, turtlelike bodies, long necks and tails, and large flippers. The Triassic period is considered by many geologists to mark the emergence of the first mammals, but little is known of their structure. The only fossil remains so far discovered consist of a few teeth and part of a single skull. From this evidence, some geologists believe that they were small animals, probably no larger than rabbits; others consider them to be reptilian, rather than warm-blooded. Among the invertebrates, insects were represented in the Triassic by the first species to undergo complete metamorphosis from larva through pupa to adult. Other invertebrates of the period were the squidlike belemnites, the ammonites, and the first lobsters.

Flora. The landscapes of Triassic times were dominated by evergreen trees. Most of these were conifers, not unlike modern pines, and ginkgos. The cycad palms and scale trees which were the most prominent flora of the preceding Coal Measure period still survived but were not as numerous or varied as the evergreens.

See GEOLOGY, SYSTEMATIC; MESOZOIC ERA; and articles on many of the animals and plants named.

TRIBE, a social, often territorially defined, group of varying size, composed of a number of families possessing a common language and culture, and united in a single political organization. Originally, the families of a tribe were supposed to descend from a common ancestor; the twelve tribes of Israel, for example, were said to be descended from the twelve sons of Jacob. In its primitive form, the tribe usually consists of members loosely organized under a central authority, such as a headman or chief. Among African tribes the monarchical principle generally prevails. Ancient Rome had its beginnings in the union of three tribes, the Latin, Sabine, and Etruscan, and the word "tribe" derives from *tribus* (Lat., "one of the three"). In western civilization the tribal system persists among the Scotch Highlanders (see CLAN) and the American Indians.

TRIBOLUMINESCENCE. See FLUORESCENCE AND PHOSPHORESCENCE.

TRIBUNE, in ancient Rome, the official title of several kinds of public official, the most important of whom were the following.

1. MILITARY TRIBUNES. In the traditional organization of Roman citizens by Romulus, first legendary king of Rome, the leader of the quota of warriors furnished by each of the three tribes was called *tribunus militum.* From 444 to 367 B.C. military tribunes with consular power were frequently elected in place of the regular consuls, the normal number of the college of consular tribunes being six. The college was abolished by the Licinian-Sextian laws of 367 B.C., which provided that one consul should be a member of the plebs (q.v.; see also ROME: *History*). In the time of the republic each Roman legion was under the

Smithsonian Institution, U.S. National Museum

Museum model of Triceratops elatus, a horned dinosaur

command of six military tribunes, at first appointed by the consuls, who were the commanders in chief, but from 362 B.C. on elected by the people in the *comitia tributa,* or assembly of tribes (see Comitia). The number was gradually increased to twenty-four, sufficient for four legions; when more tribunes were needed, they were nominated by the consuls. The importance of the military tribune was greatly diminished at the end of the period of the republic, when the actual command of the legion in the field was entrusted to a skilled officer, called *legatus legionis,* and the tribunes were retained as an honorary staff of the general. In the *cursus honorum,* or sequence of offices for men of senatorial rank, the military tribuneship was the stepping stone to the higher offices.

2. People's Tribunes. In the early period all the perquisites and prerogatives of government in Rome were in the hands of the patricians (q.v.), while the plebs (q.v.), the bulk of the people, had only the burdens of taxation and military service. This condition was partly remedied by the secession of the plebs in 494 B.C., when they secured the right to have annual magistrates, called *tribuni plebis,* chosen from their number to look after their especial interests and needs. The number was perhaps originally two, but was soon raised to five, and by 450 B.C. had been increased to ten. The tribunes of the plebs were invested with three important privileges: the right to defend a member of the plebs on any charge; the right to veto any measure proposed by the Roman senate; and personal inviolability during their term of office. To the activity of the

plebeian tribunes was due the gradual extension of political rights to all the people. The emperor Augustus took to himself the power and rights of the tribunes (*tribunicia potestas*), thus acquiring sacrosanctity for his person and becoming the champion of popular rights. As the tribunician power was held by all later emperors, the office itself lost its importance, becoming merely a function for senators of plebeian rank, held between the quæstorship and the prætorship.

TRICERATOPS, a fossil reptile, a horned dinosaur of formidable aspect, of which skeletons are found in the Upper Cretaceous rocks of Colorado, Dakota, Wyoming, and Montana. The animal was about 25 feet long, with heavily built legs and powerful tail. The most peculiar feature is the strong armature of the massive head. The skull is larger than that of any other known land animal, with a length of 6 feet and a width across the crest of about 5 feet. It is wedge-shaped and narrow in front of the small orbits and expanded behind into a broad solid bony crest which projects far backward over the neck and shoulders, with edges armed with a row of sharp projections that were covered by horn. On the facial region are three horns: a long, outward-spreading pair over the orbits and a small horn on the nose. The jaws have strong, turtlelike beaks on their tips and series of two-rooted teeth placed in sockets in their posterior portions. The feet were three-toed, and the beast walked on all fours and fed on plants. The brain of this creature was relatively smaller than that of any other known vertebrate, with a ratio of bulk to body of 2 pounds to 10 tons.

TRICHINA. See Trichinosis.

TRICHINOPOLY, officially **TIRUCHIRA-PALLI,** capital of the district of the same name, Madras, India, on the right bank of the Cauvery R., 56 m. from the sea. It is dominated by a hill (273 ft.), upon which there are two temples. Cheroots are manufactured in large quantity from tobacco grown in the vicinity. Weaving and the manufacture of hardware, cutlery, jewelry, gold chains, harness, and saddlery are extensively carried on. Trichinopoly was governed by a line of rajahs that died out in 1732 when it came under the rule of the nawab of Arcot. It came under British control in 1801. Area of district, 5514 sq.m.; pop. (1951) 2,943,882. Pop. of city (1951) 218,921.

TRICHINOSIS, Trichiniasis, or Trichinelliasis, common name applied to a disease of rats, swine, bears, cats, dogs, and humans caused by infection with the larvae of a parasitic nematode worm (see Nematodes), the trichina worm, *Trichinella spiralis.* The minute trichina worm is almost world-wide in distribution. The adult female is about ⅛ inch long; the adult male is about 1/16 inch long.

Animals are infected with trichinosis by eating flesh in which the larvae of the trichina worm are encysted. The encysted larvae are freed from their cysts by the digestive juices of their host's intestine; two days after entering the intestinal tract they become adults and mate. The adult male trichina worm dies shortly after mating; the ovoviparous females burrow into the lining of the intestine and, after six days, begin to bear numerous larvae. The female lives for about thirty to thirty-seven days, and bears an average of about fifteen hundred young. Seven days after the trichina worms have been ingested by the host, the newly born larvae migrate into the lymph channels of the intestine, from which they enter the blood stream. From the blood stream, the larvae travel through any of a number of organs, including the heart and sometimes the lungs, and finally penetrate the striated (voluntary) muscles about fourteen days after birth. The muscles most frequently affected are the diaphragm, the calf, the biceps, the muscles of the cheek, the muscles between the ribs, and the muscles of the larynx, tongue, and eyes. Within these muscles the larvae mature until they are sixteen days old; they then cease developing and form a capsule about themselves from the sheath (sarcolemma) of the host's skeletal muscle. The host then secretes lime salts which are deposited in the capsule, eventually transforming the capsule

into a completely calcified cyst; the process of encystment usually takes about six months. The larvae are incapable of developing further until ingested by a new host, in the intestine of which the cyst is digested. The dormant larvae are usually viable for about twelve years and sometimes for as long as thirty years.

Man most often acquires trichinosis by eating infected pork, and infrequently from infected bear meat. Despite rigid standards of meat inspection in the United States, infected pork often passes inspection because the disease is extremely difficult to recognize. The trichina cysts of pork may be completely destroyed by heating the meat to 55°C. (123°F.) and maintaining it at this temperature for 30 minutes for each pound of meat; ordinary curing and smoking processes do not render pork safe for consumption. Refrigeration of pork for six days at −17.7°C. (0°F.) will also destroy the trichina larvae.

Trichinosis in man takes numerous forms, depending on the organs injured during the migrations of the trichina larvae. The symptoms are classified in three stages, infection, migration, and maturation, linked to the life cycle of the trichina worm.

During the state of infection, after liberation of the immature trichina worms from their cysts, the maturing larvae cause severe irritation of the intestinal tract. Burrowing of the fertilized female into the intestinal walls increases this irritation. The symptoms marking the stage of infection include abdominal pain, nausea, vomiting, and watery stools. Also frequent are prostration, high fever, accelerated pulse, edema of the eyelids, and urticaria.

With the release of the newly formed larvae into the blood stream, the symptoms of infection become intensified. During the stage of migration embryo trichina worms may be found in the blood and in the feces of the patient. The face very often becomes puffy and swollen, especially surrounding the eyes, and headache and even delirium occur. During the migration of the larvae, the heart muscles are often traversed and damaged. The eyes are damaged in about one third of all cases.

The migration of the larvae into the skeletal muscles lasts for seven to fourteen days, and many larvae are still migrating while others are invading muscle tissue; the division between the stage of migration and the stage of invasion, therefore, is not very marked. A characteristic feature of the stage of invasion is a change in the nature of the white blood cells; an unusual type of granulocyte (see BLOOD), characterized by the presence of red-staining granules and known as an *eosinophil,* becomes predominant in the blood stream, sometimes constituting fifty percent of all the white blood cells of the host. Muscle spasm and pain in the muscles and joints are pronounced during the stage of invasion. The stage of invasion usually terminates in recovery by encystment of the larvae in about six months; in one to thirty percent of all cases in a single outbreak, the stage of invasion terminates in death in from two to six weeks, the causes of death being exhaustion, heart failure, or secondary infection of the lesions produced by the migrating larvae. Persons recovering from trichinosis often suffer permanent heart and eye damage.

The diagnosis of trichinosis is extremely difficult because of the number of abnormal conditions this disease superficially resembles.

Effective treatment of trichinosis can be performed only before the stage of migration; at this time the immature larvae and the adult females can be purged from the body by intestinal washings. Because of the difficulty of diagnosis, the disease is rarely arrested during the stage of infection; present methods of treatment of later stages relieve the patient's discomfort but are incapable of destroying the trichina worms.

TRICHOMANES. See HYMENOPHYLLACEAE.

TRICHOMONIASIS. See PARASITE.

TRIENT. See TRENTO.

TRIER, or TRÈVES, city of Rhineland-Palatinate, West Germany, on the Moselle R., 69 miles S.W. of Coblenz. There are tanneries, iron foundries, dye works, furniture factories, and glass-painting works. The trade is extensive in wine, fruit, and wood. There are many mines in the vicinity.

Trier is considered the most ancient town of Germany. It was the capital of the Celtic Treviri, from whom it took its name (anciently *Augusta Trevirorum*). The Romans made it a colony. It was an imperial residence in the later period of the Roman Empire. It fell into the hands of the Franks about the middle of the 5th century.

In the 14th century it was created an electorate. The archbishopric is reputed the oldest in Germany, its foundation being said to date before the 7th century. A "Holy Coat" in the cathedral caused much excitement in 1844 by miracles associated with it. The city was the capital of the French department of Sarre from 1794 till 1814, when it passed to Prussia. Pop. (1950 prelim.) 74,709.

TRIESTE (Ger. *Triest;* Yugoslav *Trst;* anc. *Artemidorus*), city and free port of Italy, situated on the Gulf of Trieste, at the N.E. extremity of the Adriatic Sea, and about 70 miles E.N.E. of Venice. The city has many picturesque features, notably a 15th-century castle atop a high hill, an old section lying on the lower slopes of the hill, and a modern section fronting the harbor. Among other landmarks are an amphitheater dating from ancient Roman times, a medieval cathedral, a number of museums, and the University of Trieste (1924). Trieste has an excellent harbor with three basins, extensive freight-handling facilities, and rail connections with major European points. Shipbuilding is a major industry; other industries include petroleum refining and the manufacture of iron and steel products, textiles and clothing, foodstuffs, soap, paint, and alcoholic beverages.

Trieste was built as a Roman port and after the dissolution of the Roman Empire in the 5th century came under the rule of the patriarchs of the city of Aquileia, 22 m. inland, and later became a free commune. Strife with the city-state of Venice induced Trieste, in 1382, to place itself under the protection of Austria. From that time until 1919 the port was under Austrian control, except for two periods (1797–1805 and 1809–13) in which it was incorporated into French-dominated Italy. In 1719 Charles VI of Austria made it a free port. With surrounding territory, it was constituted a separate crownland in 1867. The Austrian government revoked the city's free-port privileges in 1891, but authorized a free-trade zone. As the only Austrian seaport and a natural outlet for the countries of central Europe, Trieste prospered throughout the 19th century; its growth was especially marked in the decades preceding the outbreak of World War I. The armed forces of Italy captured the city, long an Italian irredentist center, on Nov. 3, 1918. In 1919, by the terms of the Allied Treaty of St. Germain with Austria, the city and adjoining area were assigned to Italy. Though the free-trade zone was maintained, Trieste declined as a shipping center under Italian rule. Its port facilities were badly damaged during World War II. Yugoslav troops captured the city in May, 1945. By the terms of the peace treaty imposed on Italy after the war, Trieste was made part of the Free Territory of Trieste. See TRIESTE, FREE TERRITORY OF for subsequent developments. The city was returned to Italian control under the provisions of an agreement (Oct. 5, 1954) among Yugoslavia

Lee Thody, from Black Star

Street scene in the city of Trieste, in the Free Territory of Trieste

Italy, the United States, and the United Kingdom. Pop. (1951) 271,452.

TRIESTE, FREE TERRITORY OF, formerly and nominally, a United Nations protectorate provided for under the terms of the Allied peace treaty (1947) with Italy after World War II. The U.N. Security Council was unable to implement the terms of the treaty, and as a consequence the region allocated to the Free Territory remained under military occupation and was provisionally governed until 1954. In that year the powers concerned abrogated the treaty and divided the region between Italy and Yugoslavia (see *History*, below). The region is situated at the N.E. extremity of the Adriatic Sea, varies from about 1 to 15 miles in width, and extends along the coast of the Istrian Peninsula from the Gulf of Panzano to the mouth of the Quieto R. Manufacturing is an important industry in the urban areas, particularly Trieste (q.v.), the projected capital, and farming is carried on in the hinterland. Fishing, bauxite mining, and marble quarrying are other leading industries. Besides Trieste, the larger communities include Pirano, Capodistria (qq.v.), and Muggia (pop., about 12,000). Area of the projected Territory, 293 sq.m.; pop. (1953 est.) 383,000.

History. (For an account of the early history of the Trieste area, see TRIESTE.) Yugoslav and British forces occupied Italian Venezia Giulia e Zara, which included the Trieste area, in April–May, 1945, shortly before the close of World War II in Europe. Pending final disposition of Venezia Giulia e Zara, claimed in its entirety by Yugoslavia, the region was divided into Anglo-American and Yugoslav zones of occupation. The former included the Trieste area.

Basic disagreements regarding the disposition of Venezia Giulia e Zara developed among the Big Four Powers (Great Britain, France, the U.S., and the U.S.S.R.) during their discussions (1946) on peace terms for Italy. Yugoslav claims to the entire region received support only from the Soviet Union. The deadlock on how to partition the region was resolved by compromise. Under the terms of the agreement, which was incorporated into the peace treaty and became effective on Sept. 16, 1947, the Trieste area was internationalized, neutralized, and placed under the protection of the United Nations. The agreement contained provisions for the appointment by the U.N. Security Council of a governor, for the establishment of a legislative and executive authority "on democratic lines", and for the creation of two temporary occupation zones. The agreement provided also that the N. part of the Territory, known as Zone A and including the city of Trieste, would be garrisoned by 5000 British and 5000 U.S. troops; that Zone B, the remainder of the Territory, would be garrisoned by 5000 Yugoslav troops; and that all troops were to be withdrawn within forty-five days after the governor assumed office unless he advised to the contrary.

Efforts by the Security Council during the second half of 1947 to agree on the selection of a governor were unsuccessful. The impasse persisted during the early months of 1948, and in March the Big Three Powers, convinced that the treaty provisions relating to Trieste were impracticable, addressed a note to the Soviet Union proposing a treaty revision under which the Territory would be returned to Italian sovereignty. The Soviet Union rejected this proposal on April 13. During 1948 and 1949 Yugoslavia, in defiance of the treaty, introduced various economic and social reforms into Zone B.

In April, 1950, the Soviet Union accused the Big Three of preventing the implementation of the treaty provisions for Trieste. The Big Three, in reply, renewed their proposals for the return of Trieste to Italy. Yugoslavia, meanwhile, had withdrawn from the Soviet bloc of states and forged friendlier relations with the West. On May 10, 1952, the U.S., British, and Italian governments, in a memorandum of understanding, revealed plans for granting Italy a share in the administration of Zone A. The Soviet government strongly denounced (June 24) the memorandum, charging that the U.S. and Great Britain wanted to perpetuate their military occupation of Zone A.

The Yugoslav government proposed in May, 1953, certain exchanges of territory between Zones A and B as a means of settling its claims to Trieste. Late in August the Italian government accused Yugoslavia of plans to annex Zone B and alerted Italian military and naval forces. Yugoslavia protested against Italian attempts to create a "war atmosphere" over the Trieste issue. On Sept. 15 Italy formally proposed that the inhabitants of the Territory determine their future status by means of a Big Three-supervised plebiscite. The U.S. and British govern-

ments announced on Oct. 8, 1953, that their occupation forces would be withdrawn from Zone A and that administrative authority in the zone would be transferred to Italy "at the earliest practicable date". The Anglo-American declaration, joyfully received in Italy, brought vigorous denunciations from the Soviet Union and Yugoslavia. On Oct. 12 Yugoslavia warned the United Nations that it "would consider the entering of Italian armies into Zone A . . . as an act of aggression". Both governments deployed reinforcements along their frontiers during the next two weeks, but tensions gradually subsided after Oct. 27, when U.S. Secretary of State John Foster Dulles indicated that execution of the Oct. 8 decision would be deferred pending agreement among the powers concerned. Subsequent negotiations among Italy, Yugoslavia, the United States, and the United Kingdom culminated in a compromise settlement of the dispute. By the provisions of an agreement signed by the four powers in London on Oct. 5, 1954, Zone B and a small section of Zone A were awarded to Yugoslavia and the remainder of Zone A, including the city of Trieste, was awarded to Italy. The agreement stipulated in addition that Trieste should be a free port and guaranteed "equality of rights and treatment" for ethnic minorities in the respective areas.

TRIFOLIUM. See CLOVER.

TRIGONOMETRY, the branch of mathematics which treats of the relationships between the sides and angles of triangles and the relations between the various *trigonometric,* or periodic, functions of angles. Plane trigonometry, which deals with figures lying wholly in a single plane, is of great practical importance in all types of measuring work, especially in surveying, in which the curved surface of the earth may be treated essentially as a plane; spherical trigonometry, dealing with triangles having three dimensions and lying on the surface of a sphere, is employed extensively in such fields as navigation and astronomy.

Plane Trigonometry. Any problem involving distance and direction in two dimensions can be stated in terms of the unknown sides and angles of a triangle. Thus in Fig. 1, the apex of the triangle at A represents the viewpoint of an observer looking at a tall building represented by the line BC. In this case the line AC represents the distance of the observer from the building and the angle CAB represents the angular distance that the observer must move his eyes when turning

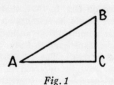

Fig. 1

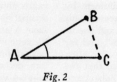

Fig. 2

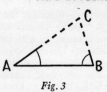

Fig. 3

his gaze from the foot of the building to its top. The same figure might also be employed to calculate the path of a boat being rowed across a swiftly flowing stream. In this case *A* would represent the original position of the boat, *AC* a vector quantity equivalent to the distance and direction that the boat would travel in a given time if the water were still, and *CB* the distance and direction that the water in the stream flowed during the same period of time. The line *AB* would then indicate the actual path traveled by the boat and the point *B* would be the actual position of the boat after the stated time interval.

From the elementary study of geometry (q.v.) it is apparent that any triangle is completely defined when certain of its sides or angles are given. Thus in the illustration, the triangle is defined if the sides *AB* and *AC* and the angle *BAC* between them are given. As can be seen from Fig. 2 one straight line and one only can be drawn between the points *B* and *C*, to complete the triangle. Similarly the triangle is defined if one side and the two angles adjacent to that side are known. In Fig. 3 it is evident that the lines *AC* and *BC* can meet at only one point, the point *C*, defining the third apex of the triangle. In like manner three segments of straight line may define a triangle, provided one segment is not longer than the sum of the other two. To sum up: a triangle can be defined by (1) two sides and the included angle, (2) a single side and the adjacent angles, and (3) the three sides. Given any one of these three groups of data, the other sides and angles of

the triangle can be found. The three angles of a triangle alone are not enough to define it, as seen in Fig. 4, which shows two triangles of different sizes which have equal angles.

Trigonometric Functions. In the discussion of angles in trigonometry it is conventional to define an angle in terms of a line moving in a counterclockwise direction around a point *O*, as shown in Fig. 5. According to convention the angle is equal to zero, when the line *OA* lies along the horizontal *X* axis of the co-ordinates shown. Moving counterclockwise the amount of the angle increases to 90°, when the line *OA* lies along the vertical *Y* axis; to 180°, when it lies along the *X* axis, but in the opposite direction; to 270°, when it lies along the lower portion of the *Y* axis, and to 360°, when it again reaches its original position. All these angles are regarded as positive. Negative angles are generated by a line moving in a clockwise direction.

For practical work the unit of measurement of angles is usually the *degree*, which is 1/360 of a complete rotation of the generating line. The degree is subdivided into 60 *minutes* and the minutes into 60 *seconds* each. In trigonometry and in higher mathematics, angles are also measured in terms of *radians*. As shown in Fig. 6 a radian is equal to the angle subtended by the arc of a circle which has a length equal to the radius of the circle. The arc *r*, through which a point travels in generating an angle of 1 radian is equal in length to the radius *r*. Because of the relationship ($C = 2\pi r$) of the radius of a circle to its circumference, it is obvious that an angle of

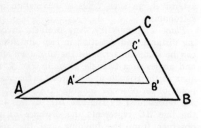

Fig. 4

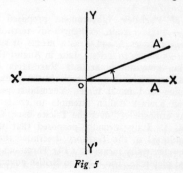

Fig. 5

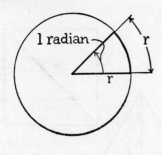

Fig. 6

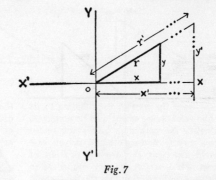

Fig. 7

360° is equal to 2π radians. Similarly an angle of 180° equals π radians, a 90° angle, $\frac{\pi}{2}$ radians, and a 45° angle, $\frac{\pi}{4}$ radians.

Trigonometric functions are defined with reference to a pair of perpendicular co-ordiate axes, and a line which rotates about the origin O from the initial line OA, generating an angle. The functions of the angle are immutable ratios which exist in a triangle between the angles and the sides. Thus in Fig. 7 the ratios between y and x and between y' and x', and between y and r and y' and r' are equal; they are independent of the lengths of the lines involved.

Six elementary trigonometric functions are recognized; they are related to each other as described below. Referring to Fig. 8, the functions of the angle a shown are as follows:

sine A (abbreviated *sin A*) $\frac{y}{r}$

cosine A (*cos A*) $\frac{x}{r}$

tangent A (*tan A*) $\frac{y}{x}$

cosecant A (*csc A*) $\frac{r}{y}$

secant A (*sec A*) $\frac{r}{x}$

cotangent A (*cot A*) $\frac{x}{y}$

The numerical values of the various functions vary within certain limits. In the case of the sine the value at 0° is zero and increases to 1 when the angle is equal to 90° or $\frac{\pi}{2}$ radians; for angles between 90° and 180° the value of the sine decreases from 1 to 0, being 0 at 180°. Between 180° and 360° the value of the sine is negative as y represents a nega-

tive number. The sine decreases from 0 to —1 at 270° and increases again to 0 at 360°.

The value of the cosine begins at 1 for an angle of 0° and runs through the same set of values as the sine, but in a different order. *Cos* 90° equals 0, *cos* 180° equals —1, and *cos* 270° equals 0. The value of the tangent is broader in its range and goes from an infinitely large negative number to an infinitely large positive number. *Tan* 0° equals 0, *tan* 90° equals an infinitely large positive number, *tan* 180° equals 0, *tan* 270° equals an infinitely large negative number, and *tan* 360° equals zero. The cotangent varies in the same range, being infinitely large and positive at 0°, 0 at 90°, infinitely large and negative at 180°, 0 at 270° and infinitely large and positive at 360°. The secant and the cosecant assume all positive and negative values except for the range between 1 and —1. *Sec* 0° equals 1, *sec* 90° is infinitely large and negative, *sec* 180° equals —1, *sec* 270° is infinitely large and positive. Corresponding values for the cosecant are: *csc* 0° is infinitely large and positive, *csc* 90° equals 1, *csc* 180° is infinitely large and negative, and *csc* 270° equals —1. Sine and cosine functions are said to be continuous in that they assume a continuous series of values as the angle increases. The other functions are said to be discontinuous in that they do not assume such a regular sequence of values. For example at 90° the tangent "jumps" from an infinitely large positive to an infinitely large negative value. The periodic nature of trigonometric functions is an advantage in the calculation and use of tables of functions. Only values for the angles between 0° and 90° need be given because the absolute value of any function of $n\pi \pm x$, where n is an integer, is equal to that function of x.

Relationship of Functions. As can be seen from the table of functions given, certain

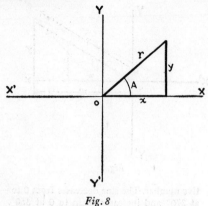

Fig. 8

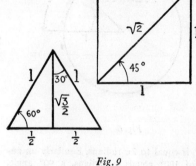

Fig. 9

obvious relations exist between the functions. The cosecant of an angle is the reciprocal of the sine, the secant is the reciprocal of the cosine, and the cotangent of the tangent. By ordinary algebraic manipulation it is possible to express any one of the functions of an angle in terms of any other function.

The most important of these relationships is that between the sine and the cosine and can be expressed as $sin\ x = \sqrt{1 - cos^2x}$, or as $cos\ x = \sqrt{1 - sin^2x}$. Other relations include $tan\ x = \dfrac{sin\ x}{cos\ x}$, $1 + tan^2x = sec^2x$, and $1 + cot^2x = csc^2x$. Relations likewise exist between the functions of two or more angles. Thus $sin\ (A + B) = sin\ A\ cos\ B + cos\ A\ sin\ B$, and $cos\ (A + B) = cos\ A\ cos\ B - sin\ A\ sin\ B$. Also $tan\ (A + B) = \dfrac{tan\ A + tan\ B}{1 - tan\ A\ tan\ B}$, and $tan\ (A-B) = \dfrac{tan\ A - tan\ B}{1 + tan\ A\ tan\ B}$. From these formulas can be derived formulas for angles equal to twice or one half of a given angle. Thus $sin\ 2A = 2\ sin\ A\ cos\ A$, and $sin\ \frac{1}{2}A$ is equal to $\pm\dfrac{\sqrt{1 - cos\ A}}{2}$.

Values of Functions. For certain specific angles the numerical values of their functions can be calculated easily. For example, simple algebraic calculation suffices to find the values of the functions of the angles 30°, 45°, and 60°, which can be derived from an equilateral triangle, or a square, with sides equal to 1.

(See Fig. 9.) The sine of 60° is $\dfrac{\sqrt{3}}{2}$, the cosine is ½, and the tangent is $\sqrt{3}$. Similarly

the sine of 30° is ½, the cosine is $\dfrac{\sqrt{3}}{2}$ and the tangent is $\dfrac{\sqrt{3}}{3}$. Sin 45° and cos 45° are equal and have the value of $\dfrac{\sqrt{2}}{2}$. Tan 45° equals 1.

In the practical application of trigonometric functions, the numerical values of the functions are usually taken from tables of values which have been compiled by more advanced methods. Such tables usually give values of angles to the nearest minute and in some cases to the nearest second, and usually also give the values of logarithms (q.v.) of the functions for ease of computation. In tables of this type the true numerical values are often called "natural functions."

Use of Functions. The simplest use of the trigonometric functions is for the solution of right-triangle problems of the type illustrated in Fig. 1. If in that figure the distance of the observer is taken as 500 ft. and the angle of elevation is 10° 30′, the height of the building can be derived from the formula for the tangent of an angle, in this case $tan\ A = \dfrac{BC}{AB}$, or, BC (the height of building) $= tan$ 10° 30′ $\times$ 500. A table of natural tangents gives the tangent of 10° 30′ as 0.1853 and therefore the length of BC is 0.1853 $\times$ 500, or 92.65 feet.

Because of the nature of a right-angled triangle, all the angles of the triangle are known if one of the acute angles is known, and thus all the elements of the triangle can be determined if one acute angle and one side are known. The simple trigonometric ratios can be applied easily to other tri-

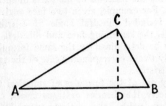 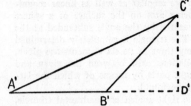

Fig. 10

angles by forming two right triangles with the appropriate altitude. Thus, in Fig. 10, the triangles ABC and $A'B'C'$ can be obtained by means of the altitudes DC and $D'C'$ which form in each case two right triangles, ADC and DBC, and $A'D'C'$ and $D'B'C'$. Moreover, by means of such constructions, the simple ratios of the right triangle can be developed to obtain formulae for obtaining the elements of any kind of triangle. The most important of such formulae are the Law of Sines, the Law of Cosines, and the Law of Tangents. In any triangle ABC, in which A, B, and C are the angles and a, b, and c are respectively the sides opposite those angles, the law of sines is expressed $a : sin A = b : sin B = c : sin C$; that is, the ratio of any side to the sine of the opposite angle equals the ratio of either of the other sides to its opposite angle. In a similarly lettered triangle the law of cosines is expressed $a^2 = b^2 + c^2 - 2bc \cos A$. In like manner, the law of tangents is $(a + b) : (a - b) = tan \frac{1}{2} (A + B) : tan \frac{1}{2} (A - B)$. In solving a triangle the formula used is selected on the basis of the elements known; for example, the law of sines is more convenient to use when two angles and a side are given, and the law of cosines is more appropriate when two sides and the included angle are known.

For an example of the application of such formulæ, (Fig. 11) let it be required to find the distance between two points A and B separated by an impassable swamp, the line AC, as represented in Fig. 10, being 15 chains; angle A is 40° 15′, and angle C is 110° 32′. By difference (B = 180° − A − C) angle B is 29° 13′. The length of the line AB is given by the law of sines: $AB : sin C = AC : sin B$. Substitution of known values in the formula gives $AB : sin 110° 32′ = 15 : sin 29° 13′$; or, obtaining the values of the sines from a table of natural functions, $AB = \dfrac{15 \times 0.9365}{0.4881} = 28.5$ chains.

From the relations of e^x, to $sin x$, and $cos x$ (see SERIES), it can be shown that $e^{ix} = cos$

$x + i \, sin \, x$, and that $e^{-ix} = cos \, x - i \, sin \, x$; whence by adding and subtracting, $cos \, x = \frac{1}{2}(e^{ix} + e^{-ix})$ and $sin \, x = \frac{1}{2}i \, (e^{ix} - e^{-ix})$. Similarly the other functions may be expressed in terms of e^{ix} and e^{-ix}. These are the exponential expressions for the circular functions of x. If i is omitted from these exponentials, the resulting functions are called the hyperbolic cosine, hyperbolic sine of the angle x. Hyperbolic functions are so called because they have geometric relations with the equilateral hyperbola analogous to those between the circular functions and the circle. The common notation for such functions is *sinh x, cosh x, tanh x,* corresponding to the circular function *sin x, cos x, tan x.* The values of these functions have been tabulated and are often used in analytic trigonometry and in spherical trigonometry (see below) dealing with pseudospheres, that is, spheres of negative radius.

Spherical Trigonometry. The spherical triangle, like the plane triangle, has six elements, the three sides a, b, c, and the angles A, B, C. But the three sides of the spherical

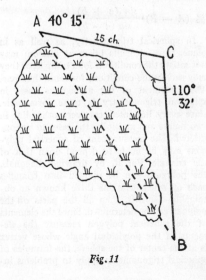

Fig. 11

triangle are angular as well as linear magnitudes being arcs on the surface of a sphere and measured by the angle subtended at the center. The triangle is completely determined when any three of its six elements are given, since relations exist between the given and the sought parts by means of which the latter may be found.

In the right-angled or quadrantal triangle, however, as in the case of the right-angled plane triangle, only two elements are necessary to determine the remaining parts. Thus, given c, A, in the right-angled triangle, ABC, the remaining parts are given by the formulas $sin\ a = sin\ c\ sin\ A$; $tan\ b = tan\ c\ cos\ A$; $cot\ B = cos\ c\ tan\ A$. The corresponding formulas when any other two parts are given may be obtained by Napier's rules concerning the relations of the five circular parts, viz., a, b, c, complement of A, complement of B, complement of C. With respect to any particular part, the remaining parts are classified as adjacent and opposite; the sine of any part is equal to the product of the tangents of the adjacent parts and also to the product of the cosines of the opposite parts.

In the case of oblique triangles no simple rules have been found, but each case is dependent upon the appropriate formula. Thus in the oblique triangle ABC, given a, b, and A, the formulas for the remaining parts are

$$sin\ B = \frac{sin\ A\ sin\ b}{sin\ a}; \quad tan\ \tfrac{1}{2}c = tan\ \tfrac{1}{2}$$

$$(a - b) \cdot \frac{sin\ \tfrac{1}{2}\ (A + B)}{sin\ \tfrac{1}{2}\ (A - B)}; \quad cot\ \tfrac{1}{2}c = tan$$

$$\tfrac{1}{2}\ (A - B) \cdot \frac{sin\ (a + b)}{sin\ (a - b)}.$$

In spherical trigonometry, as well as in plane, three elements taken at random may not satisfy the conditions for a triangle, or they may satisfy the conditions for more than one. The treatment of the ambiguous cases in spherical trigonometry is quite formidable, since every line intersects every other line in two points and multiplies the cases to be considered. The measurement of spherical polygons may be made to depend upon that of the triangle. For if, by drawing diagonals, the polygons can be divided into triangles each of which contains three known or obtainable elements, then all the parts of the polygon can be determined. Since the elements of the spherical polygon measure the elements of the polyhedral angle whose vertex is at the center of the sphere, the formulas of spherical trigonometry apply to problems involving the relations of the parts of such figures. For example, given two face angles and the included dihedral angle of a trihedral angle, the remaining face and dihedral angle may be determined by the same formulas as apply to the corresponding case of the spherical triangle.

By aid of the formulas of spherical trigonometry the theories of transversals, coaxal circles, poles, and polars may be developed for the figures of the sphere. Spherical trigonometry is of great importance also in the theory of power circles, in stereographic projection, and in geodesy. It is also the basis of the chief calculations of astronomy; for example, the solution of the so-called astronomical triangle is involved in finding the latitude and longitude of a place, the time of day, the azimuth of a star, and various other data.

History. Some traces of trigonometry exist in the earliest known writings on mathematics. In the Papyrus of Ahmose a ratio mentioned is called a *seqt,* and because of its relation to the methods of measuring the pyramids, this ratio seems to correspond to the cosine of the tangent of an angle. The first scientific trigonometric investigations, however, are due to the Greeks. The sexagesimal division of the circle was imperfectly known to the Babylonians, and Hipparchus was the first to complete a table of chords. Heron computed the values of $cot\ \dfrac{2}{n}$, for n $= 3, 4, \ldots 11, 12$, and calculated the areas of regular polygons. Thirteen books of Ptolemy's *Almagest* were given to trigonometry and astronomy. The Hindus contributed an important advance by introducing the half chord for the whole chord as used in the Greek calculations. They were familiar with the sine and calculated ratios corresponding to the versine (i.e., $1 - sine$) and cosine. The sine, however, first appears with a special name (*jaib*) in the works of the Arab Al Battani, and to his influence is due the final substitution of the half for the whole chord. Al Battani knew the theory of the right-angled triangle and gave the relation $cos\ a = cos\ b\ cos\ c + sin\ b\ sin\ c\ cos\ A$ for the spherical triangle. With another Arab writer, Abul Wefa (940–98), begins the first systematic arrangement of the theorems and proofs of trigonometry, the use of the unit radius, and the use of the secant. Nasir Eddin (born 1201) wrote the first work in which plane and spherical trigonometry appears as a science by itself, distinct from astronomy. The celebrated astronomer Jabir ibn Aflah, or Geber, of the 11th century, wrote a work confined chiefly to spherical trigonometry and rigorous in its proofs; the work was translated into Latin by Gherardo of Cremona. Regiomontanus (1436–76) wrote a complete plane and spherical trigonometry, the *De Triangulis Omnimodis Libri Quinque* (first printed at Nuremberg in 1533), a work which had great influence upon the study of the subject. Viète (1540–1603) made an important advance in the introduction of the idea of the reciprocal spherical triangle. Rhæticus (1514–76) made a great advance by considering the functions as ratios instead of lines. To John Napier are due the formulas since called the analogies. Edmund Gunter introduced the term "cosine", and Finck (1583) introduced "secant" and "tangent". Growing out of the desire to construct more accurate tables and to simplify the methods of calculation for astronomical purposes, John Napier and Justus Byrgius developed the logarithm. To Leonhard Euler much is due for simplifying and classifying the treatment of the whole subject. Joseph Louis Lagrange, Adrien Legendre, Nicolas Carnot, Karl Friedrich Gauss, and others expanded the theory of polygonometry and polyhedrometry.

TRIISODON, a fossil creodont mammal from the Puerco beds of New Mexico. The skull is the oldest known mammalian skull. See CREODONTA.

TRILLIUM, common name applied to hardy, perennial herbs belonging to the family Trilliaceae, and common and scientific name of its principal genus. The genus contains approximately thirty species native to North America and Asia. The solitary violet, white, or green flowers have three sepals, three petals, six stamens, and a solitary pistil. The fruit is a many-seeded, indehiscent berry. The painted trillium, *T. undulatum,* is native to wooded areas of Nova Scotia and E. United States; it bears white flowers and reaches a length of 18 inches. *T. erectum,* commonly known as wake robin, is similar in size to *T. undulatum.* It bears purplish-red flowers and has an extremely disagreeable odor. *T. grandiflorum,* found in E. Canada and E. United States, reaches a height of 12 inches. Its large, pure-white flowers change to pink or green when faded. The dwarf white, or snow trillium, *T. nivale,* native to Pennsylvania and Kentucky, bears white flowers and reaches a height of 5 inches. The nodding trillium, *T. cernuum,* is native to Newfoundland and bears small. white. drooping flowers;

it averages 10 inches in height. Other common names applied to trillium are birthroot and ground lily; compare LILIACEAE.

TRILOBITE, common name for any of numerous, extinct, marine arthropods belonging to the family Phacopidae of the class Trilobita, and found in fossil form throughout the Cambrian and Silurian rocks of the Paleozoic era (q.v.). Approximately 200 genera, containing more than 2000 species, have thus far been identified by paleontologists. Most species were between 1 and 2 inches in length, but several attained lengths as great as 2 feet. Trilobites were characterized by a single pair of antennae and a hard, three-lobed, chitinous shell or crust, which surrounded the dorsal surface of the body. The eyes, usually compound and attached by stalks, consisted of aggregations of facets, covered by a thin cornea. Many of the trilobites have been classified according to their former mode of existence. Some, such as the *Dalmanites,* were ocean-bottom crawlers. Others, belonging to genera *Harpes, Cryptolithus, Triarthus,* and *Trinucleus,* often buried themselves in the mud of the ocean bottom, and eventually developed vestigial eyes and specialized digging apparatus. Trilobites of the genus *Aeglina* were large-eyed and free-swimming, and their remains are often found imbedded in coral masses.

TRIMÚRTI, the Hindu triad, or the gods Brahma (masculine), Vishnu, and Siva, when thought of as an inseparable unity, although three in form.

TRINCOMALI, a seaport, naval station, and magnificent harbor on the N.E. coast of Ceylon, 110 miles N.E. of Kandy. The town is built on a bold peninsula, which divides the inner and outward harbors. Here the Malabar invaders of Ceylon built the "Temple of a Thousand Columns", to which pilgrims flocked from all parts of India. The town was held by the Dutch, and subsequently by them and the French alternately, until the capture of Ceylon by the British in 1795. Pop., about 30,000.

TRINIDAD, county seat of Las Animas Co., Colo., situated on the Purgatoire R., 10 miles N. of the New Mexico boundary and about 85 miles S. of Pueblo. It is served by four railroads, and is the center and shipping point of a stock-raising and coal-mining area. Coal, cattle, and wool are the chief products shipped. The principal industries in the city are the manufacture of dairy products, brick and tile. lumber, and coke. Trinidad is the site

Canad. Nat. S.S.; Alcoa S.S. Co.

ON THE ISLAND OF TRINIDAD

Above: A scene along one of the quays. Right: Hindus performing religious rites, praying for rain. Below: Street in the city of Port-of-Spain.

of Trinidad State Junior College, established in 1925. The city lies in the midst of picturesque scenery, at an elevation of 5963 ft. above sea level. The municipal water supply is derived from the perpetual snow on the Sangre de Cristo Range. Nearby is Fisher's Peak (9586 ft.), highest peak of the Raton Mountains. Places of interest in the city include Kit Carson Park and Museum. Trinidad was incorporated as a town in 1876 and as a city in 1879. Pop. (1950) 12,204.

TRINIDAD AND TOBAGO, a British crown colony comprising the islands of Trinidad and Tobago, and adjacent islets, lying in the Atlantic Ocean off the coast of Venezuela. Trinidad is situated N. of and opposite the mouth of the Orinoco R., and is separated from the South American coast by the Gulf of Paria. The capital of the colony is Port-of-Spain (q.v.) on Trinidad. Trinidad is traversed, roughly from E. to W., by three ranges of hills. The highest point is 3085 ft. above sea level. The island possesses only one good natural harbor, at Chaguaramas on the W. coast, but the whole of the Gulf of Paria provides safe anchorage. The N. coast is rockbound, the S. coast is steep, and the E. coast is exposed to heavy surf. In the S.W. portion of Trinidad is the famous Pitch Lake (104 acres) which yields large quantities of asphalt. The island is about 50 m. long and 37 m. wide. Area, 1864 sq.m.; pop. (1955 est.) 721,000.

The principal industry of Trinidad is agriculture. The most important crop is sugar cane; cacao, coconuts, citrus fruits, tonka beans, vegetables, rubber trees, and coffee are also cultivated. In addition to asphalt, crude oil is produced; in a recent year oil production amounted to more than 20,500,000 barrels. Coal, iron, gypsum, and graphite are found, but in such small quantities as to be economically unimportant. The chief manufactures are rum and bitters. Trinidad exports a large portion of its mineral, agricultural, and manufactured products and imports foodstuffs, tobacco products, raw materials, and manufactured goods. Trade is carried on chiefly with Canada, the United Kingdom, and the United States. The inhabitants of the island are composed chiefly of West Indians of African descent. In addition, there are more than 200,000 East Indians and a number of Chinese. Persons of European descent include English, French, Spanish, and Portuguese. English is the principal language spoken. Education on Trinidad is provided by more than 300 primary and intermediate schools, most of which are supported or assisted by the government. There are 13 secondary schools and 3 teachers' training colleges.

The island of Tobago, 20 miles N.E. of Trinidad, is of volcanic origin and is, in actuality, a single mountain mass which reaches an elevation of 1800 ft. above sea level at its summit. The chief town is Scarborough (pop., about 1200). The chief products of Tobago are cacao, copra, coconuts, livestock, poultry, and limes. The population is comprised of the same elements as that of Trinidad. Tobago has over 30 primary and intermediate schools. Area, 116 sq.m.; pop. (1951 est.) 31,000.

The colony of Trinidad and Tobago is governed according to the terms of the constitution of Jan. 19, 1949, providing for a legislative council of 18 elected members, 5 nominated members, and 3 *ex officio* members, all presided over by a speaker who is not a member of the council and who is appointed by the governor. In addition, the constitution provides for an executive council consisting of 5 members who are elected by the legislative council, 3 *ex officio* members, and one nominated member. The governor is appointed by the government of the United Kingdom.

History. Trinidad was discovered by Christopher Columbus on July 31, 1498, and in 1532 Spain appointed a governor for the island. During the 17th century the island suffered from raids by the Dutch and French. During the French Revolutionary period, many French families came to Trinidad from Haiti and other islands of the West Indies. In Feb., 1797, during the Napoleonic wars, Trinidad capitulated to a British force and in 1802 was formally ceded to Great Britain by the Treaty of Amiens (see AMIENS, TREATY OF). Tobago, also discovered in 1498 by Columbus, was successively a Spanish, British, Dutch, and French possession until 1814, when the British, at the end of the Napoleonic wars, were ceded the island by the French. Until 1899 Tobago formed a part of the Windward Islands Colony, but in that year was joined to Trinidad. In 1941, during World War II, the U.S. received a 99-year lease on military bases on Trinidad.

TRINITARIANS, the name most commonly applied in English to the members of the Order of the Holy Trinity for the Redemption of Captives, a Roman Catholic religious society founded by St. John de Matha (1160–1213) and St. Felix of Valois (1127–1212).

TRINITROTOLUENES, nitro substitution compounds produced by the substitution of nitro (NO_2) groups for hydrogen atoms in toluene ($C_6H_5CH_3$). Toluene is also known

British Information Services

The Great Court of Trinity College, Cambridge University, England

as methyl benzene. Because hydrogen atoms can be replaced not only in the C_6H_5 group but also in the CH_3 group, it becomes possible, through the different positions these three NO_2 groups may occupy in the molecules as regards one another, to produce twelve different trinitrotoluenes, each of which exhibits its individual characteristics, such as melting point, boiling point, specific gravity, solubility, sensitiveness to detonation, and the like. All are produced by nitration of the hydrocarbon or its products or by indirect reactions. Alpha-trinitrotoluene (TNT) is that trinitrotoluene which, as obtained in reaction, is at ordinary temperatures a white to pale-yellow crystalline solid having a melting point of 80.9° C. It is now widely adopted as the bursting charge for armor-piercing projectiles and for torpedoes and mines. It is a very stable body, does not attack metals, is nonhygroscopic, and practically insoluble in water. Under the influence of detonating mercury fulminate it explodes with great violence. It is loaded in shells in the molten condition and by cooling under pressure attains a density of 1.7. Its detonation arouses a higher activity in detonating explosives, such as the dynamites and permissible explosives, than mercury fulminate does; hence its frequent use in detonators and fuzes. See also EXPLOSIVES.

TRINITY COLLEGE. See DUBLIN, UNIVERSITY OF.

TRINITY COLLEGE, the largest college of Cambridge University, England, founded in 1546 by King Henry VIII. The numerous buildings of the college include three well-known gateways, the Gothic Hall, and the library; the last named was designed by the English architect Sir Christopher Wren. In a recent year, over 600 fellows were in residence at the college, the majority of whom were required to take holy orders within seven years after receiving the degree of M.A. For a description of the courses of study, see CAMBRIDGE UNIVERSITY. Among distinguished graduates of Trinity College were the mathematician and physicist Isaac Newton, the writer and statesman Thomas Babington Macaulay, the geologist Adam Sedgwick, and the poets George Gordon Byron and Alfred Tennyson.

TRINITY COLLEGE, a college of Oxford University, England, founded in 1555 by Sir Thomas Pope, privy councilor to King Henry VIII. It is situated on the site of an earlier Benedictine school for monks, established in 1290 by Richard de Hoton, prior of Durham. The college buildings include a fine Renaissance chapel, built in 1694. The faculty is composed of a president, twelve fellows, thirty scholars, and various honorary fellows and lecturers. For a description of the courses of study and degrees conferred, see OXFORD UNIVERSITY. Among distinguished graduates of the college are the English statesmen William Pitt, Frederick North, 2nd Earl of Guilford, and James Bryce; the religious leader and writer Cardinal John Henry Newman; and the poet Walter Savage Landor. In a recent year the enrollment was about 200.

TRINITY, DOCTRINE OF THE, a doctrine of theology which declares that there are three persons in the Godhead, or divine nature—the Father, the Son, and the Holy Ghost—and that "these three are one true eternal God, the same in substance, equal in power and glory—although distinguished by their personal properties". The most elaborate statement of the doctrine is to be found in the Athanasian Creed, which asserts that "the Catholic faith is this: That we worship one God in Trinity, and Trinity in Unity—neither confounding the persons nor dividing the substance—for there is one person of the Father, another of the Son, and another of the Holy Ghost. But the Godhead of the Father, and of the Son, and of the Holy Ghost is all one; the glory equal; the majesty coeternal."

The term *Trinitas* was first used by Tertullian, but the concept took form only in the debates of Christology. It was not until the progress of opposing parties sought, on the one hand, to degrade the divine dignity of Christ (Ebionitism in its various forms and Arianism), or, on the other hand, to confound the personality of Christ with God the Father, that the church was led to define in the Nicene Creed the relation of the Son to the Father, and further, in the Nicæno-Constantinopolitan Creed, the relation of the Spirit to the Father.

TRINITY HALL, a college of Cambridge University (q.v.), England, founded in 1350 by William Bateman, bishop of Norwich, for the study of canon and civil law. The full original name was College of the Scholars of the Holy Trinity of Norwich. In accordance with university statutes in force since 1882, Trinity Hall remains the college of the university devoted to legal studies. The members of the college consisted in a recent year of a master, eighteen fellows, two law students, twelve scholars and exhibitioners, and about a hundred and fifty undergraduates.

TRINITY RIVER, a river of Texas, formed by a network of small streams in Montague, Jack, Wise, Denton, and Parker counties, Tex. Above Dallas the stream frequently runs dry. It flows southeast through a fertile and well-timbered region and empties into Galveston Bay about 40 miles N. of the city of Galveston. It is over 550 miles long and navigable at high water for 300 miles.

TRIPLE ALLIANCE, the name given to several international coalitions, of which the following are the most important.

1. The first Triple Alliance, concluded between England, France, and Holland in 1596

by a pact pledging the signatories to aid each other against Spain. This treaty was notable in that it constituted the first formal recognition by France and England of the rise to national independence of Holland, which had declared its independence from Spanish rule in 1581.

2. The second Triple Alliance, concluded in 1668 by a pact between England, Holland, and Sweden, designed to check the aggressive expansionism of King Louis XIV (q.v.) of France. The treaty lost its force when King Charles II (q.v.) of England negotiated a secret agreement with Louis XIV in 1670, whereby England consented to assist France against the Dutch.

3. The third Triple Alliance, negotiated in 1717 by England, France, and Holland. The signatories to the pact announcing the coalition pledged themselves to uphold those clauses of the Peace of Utrecht (see UTRECHT, PEACE OF) guaranteeing the succession of the reigning monarchs in their respective countries. In 1718, Austria also became a signatory to the treaty, and the coalition thereupon became known as the Quadruple Alliance (q.v.).

4. The most famous of the Triple Alliances, concluded by Germany, Austria-Hungary, and Italy in the latter part of the 19th century. The groundwork for this alliance was laid in 1879, when the German diplomat Prince Otto von Bismarck (q.v.) negotiated a secret defensive pact with Austria-Hungary. This alliance served a double purpose: it strengthened Germany in her relations with France, which had reached a new peak of animosity in consequence of the Franco-German War (q.v.) of 1870–71; and it gave Austria-Hungary a powerful ally in her resistance to the developing expansionism of Russia. Italy, angered at France because of the latter's occupation of Tunis in North Africa, joined the two allies in 1882, making the Triple Alliance a reality. The existing rivalry between Italy and Austria-Hungary in the Balkans and the Adriatic area, however, prevented the former from becoming completely integrated into the alliance.

During the ensuing three decades, Europe was the scene of a steady heightening of the tensions between the nations of the Triple Alliance and the other major European powers. France, England, and Russia, alarmed by the threat to their security posed by the powerful combination of the Triple Alliance, concluded a rival pact known as the Triple Entente (q.v.). The resulting division of Europe into two armed camps led eventually to the outbreak of World War I in 1914. For some years prior to 1914, the relations between Italy and her allies had been strained, and as a result Italy did not carry out her obligations under the Triple Alliance by entering the war on the side of Germany and Austria-Hungary. Instead, after considerable secret negotiation in which the Entente powers promised Italy substantial territorial gains, Italy in 1915 declared war upon her erstwhile allies, thereby openly dissolving the Triple Alliance.

TRIPLE ENTENTE, the name given to the diplomatic and military alliance which developed between England, France, and Russia in the late 19th and early 20th centuries. It was designed primarily to counterbalance the military coalition known as the Triple Alliance (q.v.), which had been concluded earlier by Germany, Austria-Hungary, and Italy. The negotiations leading to the formation of the Triple Entente were initiated by France, whose traditional enmity for Germany had been aggravated by the disastrous defeat of the French armies in the Franco-German War (q.v.) of 1870-71. The French government first approached Russia, and in the late 1880's the existence of a diplomatic understanding between the two powers was indicated by the granting of substantial French loans to stimulate the development of Russian transport and industry. A Franco-Russian military pact was concluded in 1893, and two years later public acknowledgment was made of the conclusion of a comprehensive alliance.

Under the leadership of the statesman Théophile Delcassé (q.v.), the French government then began negotiations aimed at an alliance with Great Britain. These negotiations were hampered at first by the rivalry between France and Great Britain, both of whom were engaged in expanding and consolidating their colonial possessions, particularly in Africa and the Far East. The potential danger embodied in the military power of the Triple Alliance, however, caused the two nations to realize the necessity of forming a coalition as a measure of self-protection, and in 1904 France and Great Britain concluded several diplomatic conventions. Although no formal military alliance was ever negotiated, an *Entente Cordiale* or "friendly understanding" was reached. With the arrangement of a similar agreement between Great Britain and Russia in 1907, the system of alliances known as the Triple Entente was complete. Thereafter, the tension between the nations of the Triple Entente and those of the Triple Alliance became increasingly severe, culminating in 1914 in the out-

break of World War I; see EUROPE: *History, Modern.*

TRIPOLI or **DIATOMITE,** in mineralogy. See DIATOMACEOUS EARTH.

TRIPOLI (Ar. *Tarabulus esh Sham*; anc. *Tripolis*), the second-largest city of the Near East republic of Lebanon. The city is situated 40 miles N.N.E. of Beirut, and about 2 miles inland from its port, El-Mina, to which it is connected by electric railway. Tripoli is a major railway terminal on the Turkish-Egyptian line, and is also the terminal of an oil pipe line. The chief industries are the manufacture of soap, the cultivation of tobacco, sponge fishing, and fruitgrowing. Oranges are a principal export. The city contains a number of churches and mosques, a monastery of dancing dervishes, and a castle. Tripoli was founded after 700 B.C., and as Tripolis it was the capital of a Phenician federation. In 638 A.D. the city was taken by the Saracens. In 1109, after a siege of five years, it was captured by Crusaders. The city, which had occupied a site on the coast, was destroyed in warfare with the Egyptians in 1289, and later rebuilt on its present site. Pop. (1949 est.) 65,137.

TRIPOLI (anc. *Tripolis*), a part of Libya, North Africa, formerly a Barbary state (see BARBARY COAST) within the Ottoman Empire, and later a part of the Italian colony of Tripolitania. The coast of Tripoli is low and sandy, except in the N.E., where it is mountainous; the interior is elevated. The inhabitants are chiefly Arabs. The principal products are wheat, dates, grapes, and olives; sheep are raised on a large scale. In ancient times Tripoli formed a portion of the territory of the Carthaginians. Following the Punic Wars, it passed to the Romans, who included it within the Province of Africa. The region later passed into the hands of the Vandals, and in the 7th century was conquered by the Arabs. During the 12th century, the Normans of Sicily sacked the region, and in 1510 the city of Tripoli (q.v.) was captured by Ferdinand the Catholic, King of Spain. The region was controlled by the knights of St. John from 1528 to 1553, when Turkish corsairs (see CORSAIR) ousted them. From 1553 to 1912 Tripoli formed part of the Turkish Ottoman Empire, though the authority of the sultan until 1835 was almost negligible. During that period Tripoli was a piratical stronghold. In consequence, it was attacked by successive expeditions of European countries, notably England and France, whose vessels and citizens had been victims of Barbary piracy.

At the beginning of the 19th century, the

Ewing Galloway

An old Turkish castle in the city of Tripoli, capital of Libya

piratical practices of Tripoli caused two conflicts with the United States, the government
of which, since 1796, had been paying the
Tripolitan dey, or ruler, for protection from
piracy. In 1801 an additional sum for purposes of "protection" was demanded from the
United States. The U.S. refused and countered
with a naval blockade of Tripoli. During the
war the American frigate *Philadelphia* was
captured by the pirates, but a daring expedition led by Stephen Decatur (q.v.) succeeded
in recapturing and burning the ship to prevent
its use by the Tripolitans. An expedition consisting of 500 men, led by William Eaton,
succeeded in capturing the Tripolitan city of
Derna in 1805. In that year the war ended
when the Tripolitan dey acceded to the U.S.
demands to prevent future depredations on
U.S. shipping, and abandoned his demands for
"protection money". However, the U.S. was
compelled to pay the dey a ransom of $60,000
for the prisoners who had been captured
aboard the *Philadelphia*. In 1815 the U.S. was
again forced to send an expedition to Tripoli
to halt renewed outrages by the pirates.

Turkish rule of Tripoli was reasserted in
1835 and the region was made a vilayet of
the Ottoman Empire. Rebellions by the Arabs

against the Turks occurred in 1842 and 1844,
but were suppressed. In 1911 the Italo-Turk-
ish war broke out and according to the terms
of the Treaty of Lausanne, which ended the
war in 1912, Italian sovereignty in Tripoli
was recognized (see also CYRENAICA). In 1923
Tripoli was made a part of the Italian colony
of Tripolitania. However, the Italians were
unable completely to subdue the inland tribes
of the region until 1928. In 1943, during World
War II, following the expulsion of Italian and
German forces, Tripoli was placed under British administration. See LIBYA, UNITED KING-
DOM OF.

TRIPOLI (Ar. *Tarabulus el Gharb*; anc.
Œa), chief city and one of the two capitals
of the United Kingdom of Libya. The city is
situated on a small bay of the Mediterranean Sea, nearly 100 m. from the N.W.
border of Libya. The city is an important
trading center, and possesses a protected harbor. The chief manufactures include artillery,
carpets, scarfs, Spanish leather, tobacco products, beer, and salt. To the w. of Tripoli is a
desert which almost touches the city, and to
the E. is the oasis of Meshia. The city is surrounded by partially demolished walls. It is
typically Oriental in appearance, with slender

minarets and domed mosques. Some of the streets possess arcades. Of architectural interest is a Roman triumphal arch of white marble erected in 163 A.D. to Marcus Aurelius, and the Gurgi mosque (1833), the most beautiful of the Arabic places of worship in Tripoli. The city is connected to Sicily and Tunisia by regular steamship service, to Rome by regular air-line service, and by rail to nearby Libyan towns. Tripoli was founded as Œe, probably by Phenicians from Sicily. Following the conquest of Carthage, it became a Roman colony. It was an important Arabic city in the Middle Ages, and later became a piratical stronghold. Stephen Decatur (q.v.), during the conflict (1801–04) between the United States and the Barbary states (see BARBARY COAST), succeeded in recapturing the American frigate *Philadelphia* from the Tripolitans in Tripoli harbor, and burning it. In 1919 the city became the capital of Tripolitania, which was a separate Italian colony until 1934, when it was incorporated with Libya. In Jan., 1943, during World War II, Tripoli was occupied by the British. Pop. (1950 est.) 140,000.

TRIPOLITANIA. See LIBYA.

TRIPOLITAN WAR, the war waged by the United States against the pirate state of Tripoli, North Africa, from 1801 to 1805. The pirates of Tripoli had been preying upon European commerce in the Mediterranean Sea for two centuries, and many of the European governments had adopted the custom of paying tribute to the pirates in order to avoid their depredations. The United States began to follow this practice in 1796, immediately upon becoming a nation after the American Revolution. When Thomas Jefferson became President in 1801, he determined to subdue the Tripolitan pirates, and dispatched several naval expeditions against them. After 1802 the U.S. naval squadron which fought the pirates was commanded by Isaac Chauncey (q.v.). William Eaton, the U.S. naval agent to the Barbary States, also carried out land operations which culminated in the capture of the seaport of Derna. The pirates sued for peace, and on June 3, 1805, agreed to forego their accustomed tribute and to allow U.S. vessels to ply the Mediterranean unmolested.

TRIPTOLEMUS, in Greek mythology, the inventor of the plow and the bestower of grain upon mankind. In the Homeric *Hymn to Demeter,* Triptolemus was merely one of the princes of Eleusis to whom Demeter (q.v.), the goddess of agriculture, taught her sacred rites when she finally left her temple for Olympus. According to a later version, Trip-

tolemus was the son of Celeus, King of Eleusis, and Metaneira, and to him Demeter gave a winged chariot, or one drawn by winged dragons, and sent him forth to bear the knowledge of agriculture to all men.

TRISECTION OF AN ANGLE, one of the three classical construction problems proposed by the geometers of ancient Greece, that of dividing any angle into three equal parts by the use of ruler and compass alone. For many centuries mathematicians vainly endeavored to find a method of construction applicable to all angles. The development of analytical geometry by the French mathematician René Descartes brought an end to the search, as analytical methods proved that the construction is impossible. Solution of the problem requires the extraction of cube roots, an operation which cannot be performed with ruler and compass alone. Despite this well-known mathematical fact, amateurs have not ceased to find "solutions" to this problem and to the two other classical problems: squaring the circle and duplicating or doubling the volume of the cube.

Certain specific angles, such as the angle of 90°, may be trisected without difficulty, and several curves (which, however, are not constructable with ruler and compass) have been discovered which make possible the trisection of any angle. The simplest of these curves is the quadratrix, discovered by the Greek mathematician Hippias in the 5th century B.C. The quadratrix is the curve generated by the point P in the accompanying diagram. This point is the intersection of the lines OX and MN as OX swings from OA to OB through an arc of a quarter of a circle and MN simultaneously moves from AC to OB. To trisect the angle AOX, the distance AM is divided into three

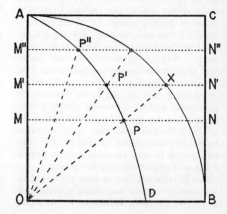

equal parts AM″, M″M′, and M′M. The points P″ and P′ on the quadratrix are then points on the two lines OP″ and OP′ which trisect the angle.

TRISSINO, Giovanni Giorgio (1478–1550), Italian critic and author, born in Vicenza. Excluded for imperialistic affiliations from his native territory by the Signoria of Venice in 1509, he spent some time in Germany, in Ferrara, and in Florence, and in 1514 went to Rome, where he was received with favor by Pope Leo X, who sent him on missions to Emperor Maximilian and to the Signoria of Venice. At the instance of Leo X the ban of proscription was removed. Trissino enjoyed the esteem of popes Clement VII and Paul III and passed some time in Venice as nuncio of the former pontiff. Between 1532 and 1545 he lived in Venice and Padua, maintaining a splendid literary hospitality in his villa at Cricoli. In 1545 he returned to Rome, where he died. Trissino, a man of less than ordinary artistic vision, is an immensely important figure in literary history. His conversations in Florence (1514) gave rise to the Italian writer and diplomat Niccolò Machiavelli's *Dialogo Intorno alla Lingua* and thereafter to the violent polemics of the following decades on the "question of the Italian language" (see ITALIAN LANGUAGE). His *Epistola* to Pope Clement VII (1527) and his *Grammatichetta* and *Dubbj Grammaticali* (1529) advocated an orthographical reform of the Italian language which he applied in his own works. In his edition of the poet Dante Alighieri's *De Vulgari Eloquentia* (1523) and in his dialogue *Il Castellano* (1528) Trissino propounded the theory of the "Italian Language", before then referred to as "Tuscan", "Florentine", or simply "vulgar", which aimed at the construction of an Italian dictionary and grammar based on a synthesis of the Italian dialects. This theory triumphed in northern Italy, where Trissino's principal follower was the Italian writer and diplomat Girolamo Muzio.

In literary theory Trissino was an enthusiastic follower of neo-Aristotelian doctrine and an illustrator of the methods of its application to creative work. Thus, his *Italia Liberata dai Goti* (1547–48) is the first "regular" epic poem, and his *Sofonisba* (1515) the first regular tragedy in modern literature, though not even this sole distinction of priority clings to his *Simillimi*, based on the *Menæchmi* of the ancient Roman playwright Titus Maccius Plautus. These works illustrate such Renaissance principles as the unities of time, place, and action, the relations of the episodic to the main themes; the use of the supernatural; and realism in manners and customs. Trissino's selection of the unrhymed hendecasyllabic verse for epic and tragedy was a permanent acquisition for the Italian classic stage; though in the epic it was crowded out by the popular Italian octave stanza used by such poets as Ludovico Ariosto and Torquato Tasso. Only an erudite curiosity attaches to Trissino's ideas and experiments in the adaptation of Greek and Latin meters to Italian lyric verse.

TRISTAN DA CUNHA, group of four small volcanic islands in the South Atlantic Ocean, 1500 miles s.w. of St. Helena, of which it is a dependency. The largest and only inhabited island consists of an extinct volcano 8500 feet high. The climate is equable and healthful. The inhabitants are chiefly descendants of British soldiers stationed there during Napoleon's captivity of St. Helena and of settlers from whaling ships. They are supported by agriculture and have a considerable number of cattle. Since 1942 the island has been a British radio and meteorological station. Until 1948 it had no organized form of government. The islands were discovered in 1506 by the Portuguese navigator Tristan da Cunha and were taken by Great Britain in 1816. Area, 44 sq.m.; pop. (1950) 267.

TRISTRAM, TRISTREM, or **TRISTAN,** the hero of a Welsh or Armorican romance originally distinct from the Arthurian cycle, but early incorporated with it. Tristram, nephew of Mark, King of Cornwall, was sent to Ireland to fetch Iseult for the king's bride, but during the voyage they unknowingly drank a love potion and forever loved each other. On discovery by the king, Tristram fled to Wales and later to Brittany, where he married another Iseult, but never forgot Iseult of Ireland. Later he sent for Iseult of Ireland to heal his wounds. When his jealous wife falsely tells him that Iseult refuses to aid him, he dies of grief; Iseult, hearing later, dies also. The theme was used as a subject by Malory, Tennyson, Matthew Arnold, Swinburne, and, as an opera, by Wagner.

TRITIUM, radioactive hydrogen isotope of mass number 3 and symbol $_1H^3$ or T. It has an atomic weight of 3.01695, decays by beta emission, and has a half life (q.v.) of 12.5 years. The nucleus of the tritium atom, called the triton, contains one proton and two neutrons. Tritium may be produced synthetically in nuclear reactors by deuteron bombardment of light elements (see DEUTERIUM). Conversely, the triton combines readily with the deuteron by nuclear fusion, forming a helium nucleus and liberating a neutron; the resulting loss of mass is converted into energy 7 times greater than that released by the fission of uranium. According to authoritative reports the thermonuclear device exploded (1952) by the United States at Eniwetok was composed of deuterium and tritium in liquefied form. Although the devices exploded in March and April, 1954, are believed to have consisted mainly of lithium-six deuteride, tritium is generally considered to have played a fundamental role, either directly as part of the core of the device, or indirectly in the transmutation of the lithium. See ATOMIC ENERGY AND ATOMIC BOMB: *Fusion;* HYDROGEN BOMB.

TRITON, an extensive genus of newts, efts, or salamanders, named by Laurenti (1768). The name applies chiefly to the aquatic species of the Old World family Salamandridae, but extends to others of similar habit in America.

TRITON, in Greek mythology, a son of Poseidon and Amphitrite, who, with his parents, dwells in a golden palace at the bottom of the sea. He is represented as a man in his upper parts, with a dolphin's tail; he calmed the billows by blowing on a conch shell. In later mythology, Triton is one of a race of marine deities attendant upon the greater sea gods, human to the waist in form, but having the lower part similar to that of a fish.

TRIUMPHAL ARCH. See ARCH, MEMORIAL OR TRIUMPHAL.

TRIUMVIRATE, in ancient Rome, a board or commission composed of three men known as *triumviri* or *tresviri.* Examples of this type of commission include the *tresviri capitales* ("police magistrates") and the *tresviri monetales* ("masters of the mint"). The term "triumvirate" is more specifically applied, however, to the political alliance made in 60 B.C. by Pompey, Gaius Julius Cæsar, and Marcus Licinius Crassus (qq.v.), designed to carry out their schemes of political aggrandizement against the opposition of the senate (see ROME: *History*). This compact, generally called the "first triumvirate", was not a triumvirate in the proper sense of the term because it had no legally constituted existence. The name is also applied to the division of the government of Rome made between Octavian (later the emperor Augustus, q.v.), Mark Antony (see ANTONIUS, MARCUS), and Marcus Æmilius Lepidus (d. 13 B.C.) in 43 B.C., following the murder of Cæsar. Their joint administration, which was sanctioned by the senate, is generally known as the "second triumvirate".

TRIVANDRUM, or TREVANDRUM, capital of Travancore-Cochin, Union of India, situated 2 m. from the W. coast and 50 miles N.W of Cape Comorin. The chief objects of interest are a large temple of Vishnu, a mint, an observatory, and the maharaja's palace and college. Pop. (1951) 186,931.

TRIVIUM. See SEVEN LIBERAL ARTS.

TROELS-LUND, TROELS FREDERIK (1840–1921), Danish historian, born in Copenhagen, and educated at Copenhagen University. For several years he was connected with the Royal Archives. He was professor at the Military School of Frederiksberg (1874–1900). His publications include an important work on Scandinavian history, *Danmarks og Norges Historie i Slutningen af det 16te Aarhundrede* ("History of Denmark and Norway at the End of the Sixteenth Century") (14 vols., 1879–1901); *Sundhedsbegreberne i Norden i 16de Aarhundrede* (1900); *De Tre Nordiske Brödrefolk* (1906); *Peder Oxe* (1906); and *Historiske Fortællinger, Tider og Tanker* (8 vols.). Troels-Lund's writings, notable for a brilliant narrative style, brought him a reputation not only as one of the most distinguished figures among Danish writers of his time, but as an author of international importance.

TROGLODYTES, name given by the ancient Greeks to various tribes or races of uncivilized men, who dwelt either in natural caverns or in holes which they had dug for themselves in the earth. The chief occupation of the Troglodytes was herding cattle, but some of them were hunters and robbers. Their habits of life were rude and debased; their drink was a mixture of milk and blood; they had a community of wives; and they killed the old men when unfit to tend cattle. Troglodytes are mentioned by Herodotus, Aristotle, and Diodorus. See CAVE DWELLERS.

TROGON, a bird of the family Trogonidae, including about fifty species, all remarkable for their beautiful plumage. Trogons have the bill short, broad, notched, or serrated, and with a wide gape; the feet small and weak, with the toes in pairs; but the first and second toes are turned backward, instead of the first and fourth, an arrangement unique among birds. The wings are short and somewhat pointed; and the tail is long and broad, often overhung by long tail coverts. The plumage is soft, lax, and loosely attached to the very delicate skin; it is very beautifully colored, some species being excelled in brilliancy only by the humming birds. These birds inhabit the tropics of the Old and New worlds; they are most numerous in South America, and are represented in Africa by two species only. The quetzal, the most gorgeous of trogons, is found in Central America.

TROGONIFORMES, an order of birds constituted by the trogon (q.v.) of the family Trogonidae.

TROILUS, in Greek legend, a Trojan hero, the son of Priam and Hecuba, or, according to a different version, the son of the god Apollo. He was slain by the Greek hero Achilles. The famous story of his love for Cressida, daughter of the Trojan high priest Calchas, was the subject of the poem *Troylus and Criseyde* by Geoffrey Chaucer and the play *Troilus and Cressida* (1603?) by William Shakespeare. The tale of Troilus and Cressida is a medieval development of the Troilus legend, however, and was unknown to the writers of antiquity.

TROJAN HORSE, in Greek legend, a huge, hollow wooden horse which enabled the Greeks to destroy Troy (q.v.; see also TROJAN WAR). Unable to capture the city after a siege of ten years, the Greeks resorted to stratagem; they sailed away and left the horse, filled with armed warriors, on the shore. Sinon (q.v.), a Greek spy, persuaded the Trojans to take the horse into the city, convincing them that to do so would mysteriously make Troy invulnerable. That night Sinon let out the armed troops; killing the guards, they opened the gates to the returning Greeks, and the city was captured and burned.

TROJAN WAR, in Greek legend, a famous war waged by the Greeks against the city of Troy (q.v.). The tradition is believed to reflect a real war between the Greeks of the late Mycenæan period and the inhabitants of the Troad or Troas. Modern archeological excavations have shown that Troy was destroyed by fire in the early 12th century B.C., the traditional date of the war, and the war may actually have resulted either from the desire to plunder the wealthy city or to put an end to Troy's commercial control of the Dardanelles. The legendary accounts traced the origin of the war to a golden apple, inscribed "To the Fairest" and thrown by Eris, goddess of discord, among the heavenly guests at the wedding of Peleus and Thetis (qq.v.). The award of the apple to Aphrodite, goddess of love, by Paris (q.v.), son of King Priam of Troy, secured for Paris the favor of the goddess and the love of Helen (see HELEN OF TROY), wife of King Menelaus of Sparta. Helen went with Paris to Troy, and an expe-

Female (left) and male elegant trogons

dition to avenge the injury to Menelaus was placed under the command of Agamemnon, king of Mycenæ. Agamemnon's force included many famous Greek heroes, the most noted being Achilles, Patroclus, the two Ajaxes, Teucer, Nestor, Odysseus, Diomedes, and Idomeneus.

The warriors assembled at the bay of Aulis with 100,000 men and 1186 ships and proceeded to Troy, where their demand for the return of Helen was refused. The siege lasted ten years, the first nine of which were uneventful. In the tenth year Achilles' withdrawal from battle because of his wrath at Agamemnon, which provides the theme of the *Iliad* (q.v.) of Homer, led to the death of Patroclus. Achilles then returned to battle, and slew Hector, the principal warrior of the Trojans. Subsequent events, described in later epic poems (see EPIC CYCLE), included Achilles' victories over Penthesilea, Queen of the Amazons, and Memnon, King of Ethiopia, and the death of Achilles at the hands of Paris. The

Anthony Trollope

city was at last captured by treachery, when the Greek warriors were introduced into Troy in the interior of a great wooden horse (see TROJAN HORSE), and subsequently sacked and burned the city. Only a few Trojans escaped from the burning city, the most famous being Æneas (q.v.; see also VERGIL), who led the other survivors to Italy. The return of the Greek warriors to Greece also provided themes for epic poems; the most celebrated story of a return is that of Odysseus, whose wanderings and arrival in Ithaca ten years later were related by Homer in his *Odyssey* (q.v.).

TROLAND, LEONARD THOMPSON (1889–1932), American engineer and psychologist, born in Norwich, Conn., and educated at the Massachusetts Institute of Technology and Harvard University. From 1916 to 1929 he was assistant professor of psychology at Harvard University, and after 1929 he served as lecturer at the same institution. He experimented with the physical and psychological aspects of vision, and was co-inventor of a process for making motion pictures in natural colors; the process was given the trade-mark name of Technicolor. After 1925 he served as director of research and process control for the Technicolor Motion-Picture Corporation, which owned the patents for the process. During World War I he developed submarine listening devices for the United States Navy. He wrote *The Mastery of Mind* (1926) and *Principles of Psychophysiology* (1929–30).

TROLLEY, a grooved, metal wheel for rolling in contact with an electric conductor (the trolley wire), usually overhead, to convey the current to a railway car. The term also denotes the trolley system, a road operated on that system, or a car belonging to such a road.

TROLLOPE, ANTHONY (1815–82), English novelist, third son of Frances Trollope, born in London, and educated at Winchester and at Harrow. While filling responsible official situations in the post office, he amused the public with a long series of novels, many of them of remarkable merit. *The Kellys and the O'Kellys* (1848) was one of the earliest novels he wrote. The first work, however, which decisively drew attention, *The Warden* (1855), was followed by a continuation, *Barchester Towers,* which remains, perhaps, the cleverest of all his books. In rapid succession to these came *Doctor Thorne, The Bertrans, The Three Clerks, Castle Richmond, Framley Parsonage, Orley Farm, The Small House at Allington, Rachel Ray, Miss Mackenzie, Can You Forgive Her?, The Claverings,* and *The Last Chronicle of Barset.* He resigned from the post office in 1867. Among novels written subsequent to his resignation are *Phineas Finn, Ralph the Heir, The Golden Lion of Granpère, Phineas Redux, John Caldigate, Ayala's Angel, The Fixed Period,* and *An Old Man's Love.* In 1883 appeared his *Autobiography* (edited by his son, H.M. Trollope).

TROLLS, in Teutonic mythology, misshapen dwarfs. They inhabited hills and mounds, had abnormal thieving propensities, and stole children and substituted their own offspring. They were peculiarly sensitive to noise, which was their special aversion, as it reminded them of the hammer of Thor, which he was accustomed to throw after them. They were called "the hill people". Although strong, they were easily outwitted by men. They had the power to make themselves invisible, to confer health and prosperity, and to foresee the future. See also DEMON.

TROMBONE, a musical instrument of the trumpet family, the tones of which are produced by means of a slide mechanism. In its present form it was known as early as the beginning of the 16th century. Today the trombone is made in four different sizes, known as the alto, tenor, bass, and contrabass trombone. The compass of the alto trombone is from A to e♭², that of the tenor trombone from E to b♭¹, that of the bass trombone from ₁B to f¹, and that of the contrabass trombone from ₁E to d¹. Besides this regular compass each trombone is capable of producing seven pedal tones, descending chromatically and beginning a tritone below the lowest tone of the compass of the instrument. The intermediate tones between the highest pedal tone and the lowest regular tone are wanting. The trombones are nontransposing instruments, and the notes all sound as written. Trombones have been constructed in which the sliding mechanism is replaced by piston or rotary valves. These instruments permit more rapid execution than the sliding trombones, but are inferior in purity of intonation.

TROMP, MAARTEN HARPERTSZOON (1597–1653), Dutch admiral, born in Briel. He went to sea as a child with his father, a commander in the Dutch navy, and was captured off the coast of Guinea by an English cruiser and compelled to serve as a cabin boy. In 1624, he was placed in command of a Dutch frigate; in 1637 he was created lieutenant admiral, with command of a squadron of eleven ships, with which he defeated a vastly superior Spanish fleet off Gravelines (1639). In the following October he defeated another fleet off the Downs, and captured thirteen galleons. But it was his conduct in the struggle with England that was to make the name of Tromp immortal. In 1652 he encountered an English fleet under Blake, and was defeated. In the same year he again encountered Blake in the Strait of Dover, and this time success was decidedly with the Dutch. The English fleet drew off, and it is said that Tromp sailed up the Channel with a broom at his masthead, to denote that he had swept the enemy from the seas. In 1653 Blake, together with Monk and Deane, engaged Tromp near Portland, and defeated him. The battle lasted three days, at the close of which Blake had taken or destroyed nine ships of war and thirty merchantmen. Tromp fought with desperate courage, and brought off in safety the remainder of his convoy of two hundred merchantmen. On June 2 and 3 another terrific battle between Tromp and Deane took place off North Foreland, in which six Dutch vessels were captured, eleven sunk, and the remainder driven into Calais Roads. The final struggle of the war was his desperate battle with Monk, July 31, 1653, off the coast of Holland. The Dutch lost thirty men-of-war, but their greatest loss was the heroic Admiral Tromp, the victor in thirty-three sea fights, killed by a bullet through the heart.

TROMSÖ, a city on the N.W. coast of Norway, in the county of Tromsö Amt, and an episcopal city in the diocese of Tromsö Stift. It is situated on a fertile island, and owing to the mildness of the Gulf Stream, its mean temperature is 36.4°F. It has a town hall, fire department, water works, electric lighting, three hospitals, schools, a seminary for teachers, a navigation school, a school for machinists, an arctic museum, boatbuilding and shipbuilding establishments, fish-oil refineries, net and rope factories, and dairies. All coast steamers call. Tromsö has also very productive fisheries in the Atlantic (near Iceland) and in the Arctic Ocean. Imports are grain, flour, coal, textiles, and salt. Pop., about 11,000.

TRONDHJEM. See NIDAROS.

TROPACOCAINE, an alkaloid, $C_{15}H_{19}$-NO_2, having the general anesthetic and mydriatic qualities of cocaine (q.v.). It is extracted from a small-leaved variety of coca growing in Java or is prepared synthetically. It is used as tropacocaine hydrochloride, and is about one half as toxic as cocaine.

TROPAEOLUM, common name applied to annual and perennial climbing herbs belonging to the family Tropaeolaceae, and common and scientific name of its principal genus. The genus, which contains approximately 45 species, is native to South America. Many of the tropaeolums are widely cultivated as ornamental plants and are commonly known as nasturtiums or Indian cress. The solitary red, orange, or yellow flowers have five sepals, five petals, eight stamens, and a solitary pistil. The fruit is a single-seeded, indehiscent carpel. The common garden nasturtium, *T. majus,* is an annual herb native to Peru, Colombia, and Brazil, and bears yellow and orange flowers. Its principal variety, *T. majus* var. *nanum,* commonly known as the Tom-Thumb nasturtium, is a dwarf strain which bears reddish-purple, dark-rose, or pure-yellow flowers.

TROPIC BIRD, common name applied to any of several pelecaniform birds belonging to the genus *Phaëthon* of the family Phaëthontidae. The birds are native to tropical waters of the Atlantic, Pacific, and Indian oceans, and are often observed on islands hundreds of miles from the nearest mainland. They have webbed feet, powerful, long, rapid-stroking wings, forked tails, and long, sharply pointed beaks. The plumage is mainly white with several black markings. During the breeding season the birds congregate in colonies on various isolated tropical islands. The female lays one white or reddish-brown egg, usually spotted with purple or gray, and deposits it in a crevice among the rock or trees. The yellow-billed tropic bird, *P. lepturus,* is commonly found throughout the Bermuda Islands. The adult birds are colored white above and below, exhibit black marking around the eyes and wings, and have long, salmon-tinged tail feathers. They reach a length of 30 inches, more than half of which comprises the long tail. *P. aethereus,* the red-billed tropic bird, bears a series of black bars along the back. It is found on Atlantic waters from Newfoundland to Bermuda. The red-tailed tropic bird, *P. rubricaudus,* has a yellow bill and black-shafted, bright-red tail feathers, and is found near Guadalupe Island. These and many other species of tropic birds are often commonly referred to as boatswains (q.v.).

TROPICS, two parallels of latitude on the terrestrial globe, passing through the most northerly and southerly points on the earth's surface at which the sun is vertical. The tropics include between them all those points on the earth's surface over which the sun is vertical. The tropic north of the equator is called the Tropic of Cancer, because the sun at the summer solstice (at which time it is vertically over the tropic) enters the constellation of Cancer; and the southern one is, for a similar reason, denominated the Tropic of Capricorn. This belt of the earth's surface is known as the Torrid Zone. See ZONE.

TROPISM (Gr. *tropē,* "a turning"), the orientative movements of entire plant and animal organisms or parts of organisms in response to the action of specific environmental stimuli. Movement toward the source of stimulation is known as positive tropism; movement away from the source of stimulation is known as negative tropism. Most knowledge concerning tropisms is derived from the work of the German-American physiologist Jacques Loeb (q.v.), whose experimental results have been used by many physiologists and psychologists to explain certain instincts and behavior patterns of plants and animals (see PSYCHOLOGY, COMPARATIVE), and to account for seemingly instinctive group movements such as mass migrations; see MIGRATION OF ANIMALS. Similar parts of symmetrical organisms usually respond equally to external stimuli. An individual organism may, however, exhibit a positive or negative tropism to the same stimulus at different times, depending on the strength of the stimulation and the internal physiological condition of the organism. Among the higher animals, the responses are also influenced greatly by psychical factors.

All tropisms are named according to the type of stimulus by which they are induced. Thus, phototropism refers to the movement of organisms toward or away from rays of artificial or natural light, and heliotropism to movements in response to the rays of the sun.

Most plants and many animals exhibit positive phototropism and positive heliotropism. The bending of plant stems and branches toward a source of illumination is explained partly by the fact that auxin, the plant chemical responsible for cell elongation, is displaced laterally away from the side of more intense illumination. The additional concentration of auxin on the weakly illuminated side of the plant causes that side to elongate more than the strongly illuminated side, and results in a bending toward the light. Some plants turn the edges of their leaves toward the sun, thus reducing the amount of exposure. Actions such as this are known as paraheliotropism. The response of organisms to internal or external chemical phenomena is known as chemotropism. Flies and other insects, attracted to certain odors emanating from the chemical decomposition of meat and cheese, are induced to lay their eggs in that medium. The same insects, however, react negatively to certain smokes and fumes, which are often used to repel them. In some organisms, chemical attraction often causes isolated cells and cell masses to move toward or away from each other. This characteristic of cells is known as cytotropism; see PHAGOCYTE. Other commonly observed tropisms include galvanotropism or electrotropism, movement in response to an electric current; hydrotropism, or movement in response to the presence of water; rheotropism, or orientation in response to the direction of a current of water; anemotropism, or movement with respect to the wind; geotropism, or orientation with respect to the gravitational pull of the earth; thermotropism, or movement in relation to unequal conditions of temperature; and thigmotropism or stereotropism, movement in response to touch or contact; see IRRITABILITY. Thigmotropism in many lower animals enables them to seek out specific crevices and to differentiate between rough and smooth areas. Positive thigmotropism is commonly known as haptotropism. Neurotropism, a characteristic of the human nervous system (q.v.), is the attraction or repulsion which certain substances exercise upon regenerating nerve fibers. A substance is positively neurotropic when regenerating nerve fibers tend to grow toward and into it; it is negatively neurotropic when the nerve fibers avoid it.

The term "tropism" was formerly applied only to the responsive movements of fixed organisms such as rooted plants and attached animals, orientative movements among free-swimming or freely locomoted animals being known as "taxis". Although today, both terms are usually used interchangeably, taxis is preferred in describing movements of such free-swimming bodies as zoospores and sperm cells. The behavior of internally administered drugs which have a greater affinity for parasites than have the white blood cells of the body is often described as parasitotropism. Many multicolored organic and inorganic salts and dyes undergo slow or spontaneous color changes in response to environmental stimuli, the transformations being known as chromotropism. See also CHEMICAL SENSE IN ANIMALS; INSTINCT.

TROSSACHS, a wooded valley of Perthshire, Scotland, situated about 8 miles w. by s. of Callander. It extends 1 m. eastward between lochs Katrine and Achray, and is overlooked to the N. by Ben A'an (1851 ft.) and to the s.w. by Benvenue (2393 ft.). The valley figures prominently in Sir Walter Scott's *Lady of the Lake* and *Rob Roy*.

TROTSKY, LEON, assumed name of LEV DAVIDOVICH BRONSTEIN (1879–1940), Russian revolutionist, organizer of the Bolshevik revolution of November, 1917, and creator of the Soviet Red Army, born in Yanovka, southern Russia, and educated at the University of Odessa. Abandoning his university studies at seventeen, Bronstein became a revolutionist, ardently dedicated to the overthrow of the czar. Because of his illegal organization of a factory workers' union, he was arrested in 1898 and exiled to Siberia. While in exile he received copies of a Russian-language periodical called *Iskra* ("The Spark") published in London by Nikolai Lenin (q.v.) and having as its purpose the creation of a disciplined group of professional Marxian revolutionists. With a forged passport in the name of Leon Trotsky, Bronstein escaped from Siberia in 1902 and joined Lenin in London; he used his assumed name thereafter. In London he became a contributing editor of *Iskra*; subsequently he made a speaking tour of the leading capitals of Europe, revealing an extraordinary gift as an orator. At the second congress of the Social Democratic Party in 1903 Trotsky opposed Lenin's demand for the centralization of power in the party. His opposition placed him temporarily in the ranks of the minority, Menshevik, faction, which split off from Lenin's Bolshevik majority; see BOLSHEVISM. Subsequently Trotsky endeavored to effect a union between the two factions.

In 1905 Trotsky returned to Russia, where he helped organize the revolution of 1905, and as chairman of the St. Petersburg Soviet of

Brown Brothers

Leon Trotsky

Workers was widely regarded as the leader of the revolution; see RUSSIA. When the revolution failed, he was arrested with the other leaders of the Soviet and again banished to Siberia. He escaped while on his way to his place of exile and fled to Vienna; there he published a Russian revolutionary paper *Pravda* ("The Truth"). At the outbreak of World War I he was compelled to leave Vienna and seek refuge first in Switzerland and later in Paris, where he published a Russian revolutionary paper, *Nashe Slovo* ("Our Word"). Because of his extreme antiwar policy he was expelled from France in 1916. He went to Spain, whence he was also expelled, and from Spain to America. He had just settled in New York City as editor of a Russian journal, *Novy Mir* ("The New World"), when news came from Russia in March, 1917, of the overthrow of the czar and the establishment of a provisional republican government. Trotsky returned to Russia immediately and soon joined the forces of the Bolshevik Party in its insurrection against the politically moderate provisional government. He was the head of the Petrograd Soviet of Workers' and Soldiers' Deputies in whose name the Bolsheviks seized power in November, 1917. He was also chairman of the

Military Revolutionary Committee which organized the insurrection of November 7.

As commissar of foreign affairs in the new government he negotiated a treaty of peace with the Central Powers at Brest-Litovsk, withdrawing Russia from participation in World War I and granting to Austria and Germany considerable territory belonging to the former Russian Empire. Shortly after the signing of the treaty on March 3, 1918, Trotsky was named commissar of war at the instance of Lenin, then head of the Soviet of People's Commissars. In this post he organized the Red Army and went into the field as its commander in chief throughout the two and a half years of civil war which followed the Bolshevik *coup d'état*. During this period he was frequently in opposition to Joseph Stalin (q.v.), then a member of the Revolutionary Military Council, over matters both of strategy and policy. This opposition marked the beginning of an intraparty contest that broke into open conflict after the death of Lenin in January, 1924. The principal issues in this contest, aside from the succession to Lenin's place of leadership, were the location of power in the Soviet state and the future of the revolutionary movement. Trotsky defended Lenin's program of "Workers' Democracy", an effort to restore power to the rank-and-file members of the Communist Party and the Soviets as against the growing dominance of a bureaucratic caste. Trotsky also advocated a world communist revolution while Stalin defended the program of "socialism in one country".

Although Trotsky was clearly, by Lenin's expressed preference, in line to succeed him, Stalin gained the ascendancy, and by 1925 had so secured his personal power in the Communist Party that he was able with impunity to demote Trotsky from the high office of Commissar of War to various minor posts. In 1927 Trotsky was expelled from the party and exiled to Alma-Ata in Asia. Finally, in January, 1929, he was accused of counterrevolutionary activities and deported to Constantinople (now Istanbul). From his exile in Constantinople and later in France Trotsky continued to agitate for a world communist revolution and to denounce Stalin as a betrayer of the true purpose and aims of the Bolshevik Party led by Lenin.

The assassination of the Soviet official Sergei Mironovich Kirov (1888–1934), in December, 1934, again unleashed the controversy between Trotsky and Stalin; the Soviet government claimed that their investigations of the assassination revealed a widespread subversive conspiracy with Trotsky at its head. In the famous Moscow purge trials (1936–38), a number of prominent Bolsheviks were accused of plotting with Trotsky to assassinate Stalin, betray the Soviet government to Germany and Japan, and commit various other acts of treason (see UNION OF SOVIET SOCIALIST REPUBLICS: *History*). Most of the accused were sentenced to death and shot. The popular agitation raised by French communist and left-wing elements over these events led to Trotsky's expulsion from France. After a brief period of asylum in Norway, Trotsky settled in Mexico City, upon the invitation of the Mexican government, in January, 1937. Soon after his arrival in Mexico he appeared in his own defense at an investigation conducted by a privately organized international commission of noncommunists presided over by the American philosopher and psychologist, John Dewey, to determine whether or not he was guilty of the charges brought against him in the Moscow trials. The report of the Dewey Investigating Committee cleared Trotsky of these charges and declared that the Moscow trials represented a perversion of judicial procedure. The conflict continued, however, and three years later, on August 20, 1940, Trotsky was assassinated in his home in a suburb of Mexico City by a young man said by the Mexican police to be a secret agent of Stalin.

Trotsky was a well-known journalist and author. His works include *Lenin* (1924), *Literature and Revolution* (1925), *The Real Situation in Russia* (1928), *My Life* (1929), *The History of the Russian Revolution* (1932), *The Revolution Betrayed* (1937), *The Stalin School of Falsification* (1937), and *Stalin* (posthumously published, 1941).

TROUBADOURS (Provençal, *trobar*, "to find or invent"), a group of lyric poets and poet-musicians, who flourished in Provence, southern France, and northern Italy during the 12th and 13th centuries. The troubadours took their inspiration from a revival in the 11th century of the ancient Greek conception of the lyric poem as a vocal composition. Their lyrics were the first to be composed in the languages of the common people rather than in Latin, the literary language of the Middle Ages. These poems incorporated new stanzaic forms and rhythms either original or borrowed from the informal music of the people. The earliest troubadour whose works have been preserved was the Provençal poet William IX (1071–1127), Duke of Aquitaine and Count of Poitou. Like William, most troubadours were

The Great Lake trout (Cristovomer namaycush)

of noble rank. Of the 460 troubadours known to have lived during the 12th and 13th centuries, the majority were nobles, and 23 were reigning princes. Troubadour music gradually disappeared during the 13th century as the courts of southern France were destroyed in the defeat of the Albigenses (q.v.) by the papal power. The last of the French troubadours died in exile in 1294, at the Spanish court of King Alfonso X.

Originally, the troubadours sang their own poems to their assembled courts; later, they engaged itinerant musicians, called jongleurs, to perform for them. The subjects of the troubadour songs were diverse; they included love, religion, politics, notable persons of the time, occasions such as funerals, and subjects derived from nature, such as morning songs and spring songs. The musical accompaniments were generally played on stringed instruments. The notation of the songs was primitive and simple, indicating pitch, but not time value or rhythm; see MUSICAL NOTATION. The music of the troubadours is generally considered one of the major factors in the development of medieval secular music. See also PROVENÇAL LANGUAGE AND LITERATURE; TROUVÈRES.

TROUT, any of many fishes of the family Salmonidae. Some are partly anadromous, but most of the species live exclusively in fresh waters, and occur in most of the lakes and streams of northern regions. They are all voracious and more or less gamy. Their food consists of almost any sort of fresh animal matter—smaller fishes, crustaceans, insect larvae, and the like. The trout, like the salmon, spawn during the colder months of the year, varying with the latitude and the species. The most widely distributed species is the common brook trout or speckled trout, *Salvelinus fontinalis,* which corresponds roughly to the brown trout of Europe, *Salmo fario.* It is rec-

ognized by its large mouth, violet mantle, dark mottlings, and red lateral spots, the general coloring being dark gray or green. In the male there is a reddish band running along the side of the body. They are found from the Alleghenies in Georgia to the Arctic Ocean, varying in size according to the extent of water and the amount of food they procure, the average weight being about 2 lb. The spawning season begins in September and lasts till December, when the female with her tail scrapes out a hole in the gravel, where she deposits her eggs, the male afterward dropping the milt upon them. Only about 5 percent of these become fertilized in the natural state, the rest being generally washed out and devoured by other fish; but as many as 90 percent can be hatched by artificial means.

West of the Rocky Mountains, ranging from the Sacramento to Montana, we find the Dolly Varden, *Salvelinus malma,* a highly colored fish having prominent spots on the body. It is large and peculiar to the west, being the only char or salmonoid fish that occurs there. It does not, however, afford good game to sportsmen, its disposition being sluggish.

The largest of all the chars is the Mackinaw or Great Lake trout, *Cristovomer namaycush,* which is known in Maine as the togue and in Vermont as the longe. Specimens weighing 30 lbs. are often caught, and some occasionally scale as much as 125 lbs. Its color is gray or black, with lightish spots which sometimes become red. It has a large mouth with strong teeth, and is as gluttonous in its feeding as the pike, often descending to deep water. It is found abundantly in the Great Lakes, Hudson Bay, Alaska, Labrador, New Brunswick, Vermont, and Maine.

Among those fish which, though not properly belonging to the trout genus, still have certain affinities to it, may be mentioned the whitefish, alewife, or menhaden, a salt-water fish now much eaten in America, though formerly used chiefly for making oil and manuring crops; the grayling, which is intermediate between the whitefish and the trout; the squeteague, gray trout, or weakfish, another salt-water fish in great demand for the table; the black bass and the sea bass. All these are sometimes classed by the uninitiated as sea or ocean trout, though their zoological connections are entirely distinct from those of the true trout.

TROUT, SALMON. See SALMON.

TROUVÈRES (OF. *trouver,* "to find or invent"), a group of court poet-musicians who flourished in northern France during the 12th and 13th centuries, corresponding to the troubadours (q.v.) of southern France. Their songs were strongly influenced by those of the troubadours, a group of whom were first brought to northern France about 1137 by Eleanor of Aquitaine, granddaughter of the earliest known troubadour, William IX, Duke of Aquitaine. Eleanor came to the court of France, at Paris, as the queen of King Louis VII, and brought with her a number of creators of the poetry and music characteristic of her region in southern France. The northern poet-musicians copied and adapted the works of the troubadours, and ultimately developed their own original *genre,* which was similar in subject and musical form to that of the troubadours, but placed more emphasis on narrative and epic poetry.

TROUVILLE, a fishing town and seaside resort of the department of Calvados, France, at the mouth of the Touques, 136 m. by rail w.n.w. of Paris, and 9 miles s. of Havre. Its equable climate, agreeable situation, remarkably fine beach, and many handsome villas make it an ideal resort during the summer and autumn months. The port is shared with Deauville, a small but well-known sea-bathing resort, a short distance s.w., with a casino. The August races here are attended by leading members of Parisian society. Pop., about 7000.

TROY, county seat of Rensselaer Co., N.Y., situated on the E. bank of the Hudson R., at the mouth of the Mohawk R., 7 miles N. of Albany and 148 miles N. of New York City. Transportation facilities include three railroads, a municipal airport, river steamers, and barges on the New York State Barge Canal. The city lies at the head of navigation on the Hudson and is an important commercial and manufacturing center, with excellent water power provided by two rapid streams, the Poestenkill and the Wynantskill. Troy has a developed water front of 7 miles. The

city is especially noted for the manufacture of men's shirts, collars, and cuffs. Other important industries are the manufacture of men's clothing, knit goods, laundry machinery, surveying instruments, automobile parts, valves, bells, chains, hydrants, brushes, abrasives, pig and bar iron, and coke. Among the educational institutions in the city are Rensselaer Polytechnic Institute (q.v.), the oldest engineering school in the U.S.; Russell Sage College for women, established in 1916; the Emma Willard School for girls, founded in 1814; St. Joseph's Seminary (Roman Catholic); and La Salle Institute (Roman Catholic) for boys, founded in 1847. The municipal park system includes 10 parks, covering about 300 acres.

The site of the present city was originally a part of the extensive lands of the Van Rensselaer family, Dutch settlers who were granted their lands in 1629. During the American Revolution the region was the site of American military installations under the command of Gen. Philip Schuyler and later of Gen. Horatio Gates. The town was founded after the close of the Revolution by a group of settlers from New England. It was named Troy in 1789, became the county seat in 1793, and was incorporated as a village in 1794. The city of Troy was chartered in 1816. The development of Troy as a commercial and industrial center commenced early in the 19th century. A steamboat line between Troy and Albany was established in 1812; and during the War of 1812 large quantities of provisions for the American army were produced in Troy. Development was also aided by the ingenuity of Hannah Lord Montague, a Troy housewife, who invented detachable collars for her husband's shirts in 1819, thus beginning the leading industry of present-day Troy. From 1839 to about 1896 Troy was one of the chief iron and steel manufacturing centers in New York. During the Civil War vast quantities of armaments and munitions were manufactured at Troy, including part of the equipment of the famous ironclad, the *Monitor.* Pop. (1950) 72,311.

TROY, also called ILION or ILIUM, the most famous city of Greek legend, situated on the N.W. corner of Asia Minor. The legendary founder of the city was Ilus, the son of Tros, from whom the name "Troy" was derived. The son and successor of Ilus was Laomedon (q.v.), who was slain by the hero Hercules when the latter captured the city. During the reign of Laomedon's son Priam (q.v.) occurred the celebrated Trojan War (q.v.; see also ILIAD; ODYSSEY), which resulted in the capture and destruction of the city.

The Troy which appears in the Homeric poems was long regarded as a purely legendary city, but in 1870 Heinrich Schliemann (q.v.) began excavations which brought to light the actual stone walls and battlements of an ancient city on the mound called Hissarlik, 3½ m. from the Ægean Sea and 3¾ m. from the Dardanelles. Schliemann's excavations were continued after his death by his assistant, Wilhelm Dörpfeld (1853–1940), whose work in 1893 and 1894 threw new and important light upon Schliemann's discoveries. Since 1932, new excavations have been carried on at the site by the University of Cincinnati, under the direction of the American archeologist Carl William Blegen (1887–). On the mound of Hissarlik the following successive settlements have been determined: *Troy I,* an early settlement with a wall built of small stones and clay, its date being perhaps 3000 to 2500 B.C.; *Troy II,* a prehistoric fortress, with strong ramparts and large brick houses, dating from 2500 to 2000 B.C.; *Troy III, IV,* and *V,* prehistoric villages successively built on the debris of *Troy II* during the period from 2000 to 1500 B.C.; *Troy VI,* a Mycenæan fortress, including a larger area than any of the preceding settlements, with huge walls, towers, and houses of wrought stones, dating from 1500 to 1200 B.C., or later; *Troy VIIA,* a reconstruction of *Troy VI,* built in the latter part of this period after the city had been destroyed by an earthquake; *Troy VIIB* and *VIII,* Greek villages, of simple stone houses containing nearly every kind of Greek pottery, dating from about 1000 B.C. to the 1st century B.C.; *Troy IX,* the acropolis (q.v.) of the Graeco-Roman city of Ilion, or New Ilion, possessing a famous temple of Athena and magnificent buildings of marble, and existing from the 1st century B.C. to about 500 A.D. Of these various settlements Schliemann discovered only the first five, and identified Troy II with the Homeric Troy. Dörpfeld's discoveries, however, made it certain that the Homeric Troy must be identified with Troy VIIA, which was destroyed by fire about the traditional date of the Trojan War. Attempts by some modern scholars to locate the Homeric city at the ruins near Bunarbashi on the Bali Dagh, a steep cliff above the Scamander R., have not been successful, since the earliest remains on the site date from about 800 B.C.

TROYES, a town of France, capital of the department of Aube, on the left bank of the river Seine, 104 miles E.S.E. of Paris. The principal buildings are the cathedral, founded in 872, and rebuilt between the 13th and 16th centuries, and the church of St. Urban. Troyes has cotton, linen, and woolen manufactures, and, as the center of a rich agricultural region, has a large transit trade. Pop. (1946) 58,805.

TROYON, CONSTANT (1810–65), French landscape painter, born in Sèvres. Many of his best works are in the United States; these paintings include "Holland Cattle and Landscape", in the Metropolitan Museum of Art, New York City, and "The Return from Market" in the Art Institute of Chicago.

TROY WEIGHT, a system of weight commonly employed in England and the United States and used chiefly for weighing such precious metals as silver and gold. The name is derived from the city of Troyes, on the Seine River in France. The Scotch Troy weight, commonly known as Dutch weight, is a similar system formerly used in France, Scotland, and the Netherlands; see WEIGHTS AND MEASURES.

TRUCE OF GOD. In the Middle Ages private warfare was very common, and the church synods, in order to limit what they could not wholly repress, in the 11th century and later, frequently passed decrees that there should be no such warfare during certain holy seasons, from Advent to Epiphany, and from Septuagesima to one week after Pentecost. In addition the time from Wednesday night to Monday morning of each week and all saints' days were included.

TRUDEAU, EDWARD LIVINGSTON (1848–1915), American physician, born in New York. Forced by ill-health to go to the Adirondack Mountains, he founded there the Adirondack Cottage Sanatorium (1884) for the treatment of incipient tuberculosis in workingmen and women. He also founded the Saranac Laboratory for the study of tuberculosis (1894) in New York, the first of its kind.

TRUFFLE. See FUNGI: *Edible Fungi.*

TRUJILLO, the capital of the province of Libertad, Peru, 320 miles N.W. of Callao. It was founded by Pizarro (1535) and was formerly an important commercial center. It contains a cathedral, a university, and a theological seminary. Pop. (1950 est.) 47,728.

TRUJILLO MOLINA, RAFAEL LEONIDAS (1891–), Dominican military and political leader, born in San Cristóbal, and edu-

Democratic State Committee

President Harry S. Truman

cated at the Military Academy of Jaina. He entered the Dominican army as a cadet in 1918, won several successive promotions, and in 1927 was elevated to the rank of brigadier general and appointed commander in chief of the army. Trujillo Molina also became the head of the Dominican Party, the most powerful political party in the Dominican Republic. He was elected to the presidency in 1930, and immediately instituted a regime notable for ruthless, often illegal measures designed to eliminate all vestiges of opposition. His term of office was also marked by a policy of strengthening the diplomatic and economic ties between his own country and the United States. Trujillo was re-elected in 1934; in 1938 he temporarily relinquished the office in favor of one of his lieutenants in the Dominican Party, which by then had become the only legal party in the nation. He was re-elected to the presidency in 1942 and again in 1947. He refused re-election in 1952, however, and nominated his brother Hector Trujillo Molina to succeed him. Hector was subsequently elected, and in 1953 appointed Rafael foreign minister.

TRUMAN, HARRY S. (1884–), thirty-third President of the United States, born in Lamar, Mo., and educated in the public schools of that city and at the Kansas City School of Law. From 1906 to 1917 he managed a farm belonging to his family. During World War I he served in the field artillery of the U.S. Army in France, attaining the rank of captain. Upon his return from overseas he conducted a retail haberdashery store in Kansas City, Mo., for a brief period. In 1922 Truman entered local politics as a member of the Democratic Party; his loyal service in the party State machine won him the sponsorship of its leader, Thomas Pendergast (1870–1945). In 1922 he was appointed a judge of the Jackson County Court; he held this office until 1924, and in 1926 was appointed presiding judge. He held the latter office until 1934, when he was elected U.S. senator from Missouri. His first term in the Senate was characterized by his unswerving support of the New Deal measures of President Franklin Delano Roosevelt. Re-elected to the Senate in 1940. Truman was named chairman of the Special Committee to Investigate the National Defense Program, known as the Truman Committee. As committee chairman he acquired a national reputation for the ability, courage, and integrity which he displayed in investigating the operations of many of the largest corporations in the nation, and in ensuring the equitable distribution of government contracts among both small and large corporations. At the Democratic national convention in July, 1944, President Roosevelt, yielding to the opposition of Democratic leaders to the renomination of Henry Agard Wallace for Vice-President, gave the delegates a choice of Harry S. Truman or Supreme Court Justice William Orville Douglas in his stead. Truman received the nomination.

Following the election of the Democratic candidates in the 1944 election, Truman took office on January 20, 1945. Three months later, on April 12, 1945, upon the sudden death of Roosevelt, Truman became the thirty-third President of the United States. The surrender of Germany to the Allied powers on May 7, ending World War II in Europe, precipitated the new President into the problems of a peace settlement. In June he attended and addressed the international conference in San Francisco for the founding and organization of the United Nations (q.v.). He went to Potsdam, Germany, in July to meet Premier Joseph Stalin and Prime Minister Winston Churchill (replaced during the conference by the newly elected prime minister, Clement Attlee) to discuss the occupation and organization of the defeated country; see POTSDAM CONFERENCE. At the conference the three heads of state drew up the Potsdam Declaration demanding immediate and unconditional surrender by Japan. Soon afterward, atomic bombs were employed for the first time in warfare on the Japanese cities of Hiroshima and Nagasaki, and on August 14, Japan announced her acceptance of the Declaration.

With the war at an end, the chief task of the President became the formulation of the postwar foreign policy of the United States. In an address to Congress on March 12, 1947, President Truman enunciated the policy known as the Truman Doctrine, aimed at checking the further spread of communism, particularly in Europe and the Near East, by giving economic, financial, and military aid to free countries threatened by political or military subjugation. As a first step in implementing the new policy, the President requested an immediate grant of $400,000,000 for economic and military aid to Greece and Turkey, then threatened by communist-led armed forces. The sum was provided in a bill passed by Congress in May. Truman also directed the formulation of the European Recovery Program (q.v.), under which substantial economic aid was rendered by the United States to those European nations whose economies were still faltering because of the devastation wrought by World War II. In domestic affairs the President did not receive the cooperation which Congress accorded to his foreign policy. Democrats in both houses withdrew their support of the New Deal program to which President Truman, as Roosevelt's successor, was committed. The President's proposal to halt rising prices by retention of the government's wartime system of price controls was rejected by Congress, which refused any further appropriation for price control agencies; see OFFICE OF PRICE ADMINISTRATION. The dissension between the President and Congress reached a crisis over the issue of revised labor legislation. A conservative Labor Management Relations Act called the Taft-Hartley bill was drafted as an amendment to the National Labor Relations Act (q.v.), and passed by Congress over the President's veto. Intraparty strife was heightened when, in February, 1948, the President proposed the adoption of a civil-rights program, having as one of its primary purposes the protection of the social and political rights of Negroes; see RIGHTS, CIVIL. The program was denounced bitterly by Southern Democratic leaders, and the proposed legislative measure was not passed.

When the Democratic national convention met in 1948, Truman won the Presidential nomination despite vehement Southern protest. Several Southern delegations withdrew and formed a States' Rights Party, called popularly the "Dixiecrats"; see POLITICAL PARTIES IN THE UNITED STATES. Despite the split within his own party, the opposition of almost all of the newspapers in the country, and a general forecast in all public-opinion polls of failure, Truman conducted a sweeping campaign with energy and self-confidence. He championed New Deal measures, calling his program the "Fair Deal", and promised repeal of the Taft-Hartley law and continued agitation for civil-rights legislation. His election over his chief Republican opponent, Governor Thomas E. Dewey of New York, by an electoral vote of 304 to 189, came as a surprise to a large part of the country and was generally regarded as a personal triumph.

Truman's second administration was marked by important developments in foreign affairs, brought about mainly by continually deteriorating relations between the United States and the Soviet Union and its satellites. In July, 1949, he signed the North Atlantic Treaty (q.v.), designed to counteract the threat of Russian expansion in western Europe, and later in the year he requested and obtained Congressional authorization to provide military assistance to noncommunist countries of Europe. Events in the Far East during the following year compelled Truman to adapt American foreign policy to radically changed conditions. In June, 1950, when the Republic of South Korea was attacked by the Soviet-sponsored Republic of North Korea, he promptly acted to rally the military support of the United Nations for the South Koreans, and formulated a new United States policy of providing troops as well as arms to assist democratic nations invaded by communist aggressors. In November of that year, when a new phase of the Korean war was ushered in by the large-scale participation of Chinese communist forces, Truman was forced to increase American commitments in the region.

At the same time, America's role in European defense plans steadily increased in scope. The planning of combined military strategy for U.S.-west European defense culminated in December, 1950, with the approval by the Atlantic Pact nations of an integrated international military force, and the Atlantic Council and President Truman jointly named the

N.Y. Philharmonic-Symphony
Playing the modern trumpet

American general Dwight D. Eisenhower as its commander. On the home front, during the same month, the President issued a proclamation declaring a national emergency.

During 1951 a hostile Congressional coalition of Republicans and conservative Democrats stymied Truman's efforts to secure enactment of his "Fair Deal" program. The same coalition reduced his proposed budget by nearly $5 billion, and Congressional investigating committees unearthed evidence of corruption in various executive agencies, notably the Reconstruction Finance Corporation and the Bureau of Internal Revenue. In his most forceful action of the year the President summarily removed (April) General Douglas MacArthur as commander in chief in the Far East. The outstanding event of Truman's final year in the White House was Federal seizure, at his direction, of the steel industry. This move, taken to avert an impending industry-wide strike, was subsequently voided as unconstitutional by the Supreme Court. Relations between the President and Congress showed no improvement during the year, the stalemate in the Korean war continued, and additional exposures of wrong-doing in Federal agencies further damaged the prestige of his administration. In March, meanwhile, Truman had revealed that he would not be a candidate for re-election. He was influential in obtaining the Democratic Presidential nomination for Adlai Ewing Stevenson, and during the election campaign he energetically stumped the country for his party, making over two hundred speeches.

In May, 1955, Truman broke ground in Independence, Mo., for the Harry S. Truman Library, which will house official and personal papers he accumulated while President. Two volumes of Truman's memoirs, *Year of Decisions* and *Years of Trial and Hope,* were published in 1955 and 1956, respectively.

TRUMBULL, JOHN (1750–1831), American lawyer and littérateur, born in Westbury (now Watertown), Conn. He was judge of the Supreme Court of Connecticut (1801–19), and from 1808 was also judge of the Supreme Court of Errors. Among his works are *The Progress of Dulness,* a satire on contemporary methods of education; and the *Anarchiad* (1786–87), a series of satirical papers written in collaboration with the famous group of early American humorists known as the "Hartford Wits".

TRUMBULL, JOHN (1756–1843), American historical and portrait painter, born in Lebanon, Conn. In 1780 he went to London, where he studied art under Benjamin West. In 1794 he served as secretary of legation in London, and from 1816 to 1825 was president of the New York Academy of Fine Arts. His paintings include "The Signing of the Declaration of Independence" (in the Capitol, Washington). Among his most noted portraits are those of Washington, Clinton, Hay, Hamilton, and Jay in the New York City Hall.

TRUMBULL, JONATHAN (1710–85), American patriot, born in Lebanon, Conn. He was successively judge, deputy governor, and governor (1769–83) of Connecticut, and took a prominent part in forwarding the War of Independence. Washington relied greatly on him, and frequently consulted him by the name of "Brother Jonathan".

TRUMPET, a musical instrument consisting usually of a long tube (often coiled to facilitate handling) with a cup-shaped mouthpiece. The sounds are modified by the player's lips, and may be varied also by the addition of slides, valves, and keys. It antedates other musical instruments. It appeared on the Egyptian bas-relief at Thebes, and was used by the Israelites.

TRUMPET FLOWER, popular name of various plants having large, trumpet-shaped flowers. They include plants of the genera *Solandra* (Solanaceae family) and *Bignonia* and *Tecoma* (both Bignoniaceae family).

TRUNKFISH, or BOXFISH, common name for fishes of the order Ostracodermi, and family Ostraciidae. They have a short, cuboid body, covered by a carapace formed of firmly united polygonal bony scutes, leaving only the jaws, fins, and caudal peduncle free.

TRUOG, EMIL (1884–), American agronomist, born in Independence, Wisconsin, and educated at the University of Wisconsin.

He taught in the department of soils of the University of Wisconsin beginning 1909, becoming professor in 1921, and head of the department in 1939. He received many academic honors, and was member of numerous scientific and agricultural societies. Among his works is *"Plowman's Folly" Refuted* (1944).

TRUST, in industry and commerce, a type of corporate monopoly (see MONOPOLY), developed in the United States in the latter part of the 19th century, and formed principally for the purposes of eliminating competition within a specific branch of trade or industry (usually the latter), and of establishing complete or dominant control over the production, supply, and price of a commodity or service.

Two principal factors, one organizational and the other purposive, are common to all forms of trusts. The first is the factor of corporate combination; the bringing of a number of corporate enterprises under centralized control distinguishes the trust from other types of monopoly, particularly that established and exercised by a single corporation in a given industry. Secondly, trusts are invariably concerned with the establishment of more or less exclusive control over the market for a commodity or service. Thereby, the trust is differentiated from those types of large-scale corporate organization which are formed for a purpose other than that of securing market control.

Development of the Trusts. The immediate forerunners of the trusts were the industrial pools which were formed in a number of fields of industry during the decade following the Civil War (1865–75). Most of the pools were simply agreements among the producers of commodities, notably salt, sugar, coal, petroleum, and iron and steel, under which production was limited, prices were fixed, and market territories and sales quotas were allocated among the participants. This type of corporate combination proved inadequate to meet the needs of the producers, however. The pools were declared illegal in several States in accordance with the common-law principle prohibiting unreasonable restraint of trade. Moreover, the parties to the agreements were not contractually bound to the pools, but were in effect free agents. In many instances, parties to pooling agreements utilized their freedom of action in a manner detrimental to the interests of the other parties, eventually destroying the pool. After some experimentation, the trust form of organization was found to be the most suitable for

the achievement of the desired monopolistic objectives. The principal advantages of the trust over the pool lay in the binding nature of trust agreements, and in the apparent legality of the methods whereby corporations "voluntarily" gave up their sovereignty to the "trustees".

The first trust was formed in 1882, when John D. Rockefeller (q.v.) and his associates merged various oil-refining and related enterprises into the Standard Oil Trust; the component companies assigned all of their stock to the central organization. The success of this trust in driving out almost all of its competitors and in cornering the petroleum market was such as to inspire a number of imitators in other industries. During the 1880's trusts modeled on or similar to Standard Oil were formed in iron-and-steel production, whisky distilling, white-lead manufacturing, sugar refining, and various other branches of industrial production.

The rapid spread of the trusts, and the monopolization of the industries in which they appeared, soon gave rise to widespread public protest. Civil suits were brought against them in various State courts, and the resulting verdicts were generally adverse to the trusts. Two principal reasons were advanced for the illegalization of the trusts: that any corporation entering into a trust and transferring control to another corporate organization had thereby exceeded the powers granted to it under its State charter; and that the practice of corporate combination for monopolistic purposes was contrary to the public interest, and at variance with the common law. The success of the early antitrust cases in the State courts led several State legislatures to enact antitrust laws in the late 1880's. The actual, total effectiveness of these State actions was necessarily limited, however, by the fact that the holdings and operations of almost all of the great trust organizations were interstate and even national in character. While the State antitrust laws and civil suits hampered and in some respects restricted the formation and activities of the trusts, Federal legislation was the only means of dealing with the trusts on a sufficiently broad scale.

Congress, taking cognizance of the imperative need for curtailment of the burgeoning trusts, enacted the Sherman Antitrust Act (q.v.) of 1890. This law declared illegal "every contract, combination, . . . or conspiracy, in restraint of trade or commerce among the several States". It defined as a misdemeanor the action of any individual "who shall monopolize, or attempt to monopolize, or combine or conspire with any other person or persons, to monopolize any part of the trade or commerce among the several States". The law provided both civil and criminal penalties for violations of its provisions. Several additional important antitrust laws were subsequently enacted by Congress, but the Sherman Act remains the basic statement of the public policy of the United States in regard to the trusts. Fundamentally, it was designed to prevent the great industrial combinations from destroying the free competitive system in U.S. industry.

One of the most notable Sherman Act cases was the suit filed jointly by the Federal government and the State of Minnesota against the Northern Securities Company in 1902. Northern Securities was a holding company which, by acquiring control of a large majority of the stock of the Northern Pacific and Great Northern railways, had come into possession of a virtual monopoly over railway transportation in the northwestern areas of the United States. After two years of litigation, the Northern Securities Company was ordered dissolved by the U.S. Supreme Court for illegal restraint of interstate commerce.

Despite this and several other successful actions undertaken by the Federal and State governments, corporate combinations continued to develop at an alarming rate, assuming new forms designed to evade the explicit provisions of the law. Thus, in 1904, the same year in which the Northern Securities Company was dissolved, seven huge industrial trusts in the United States, with an aggregate capitalization in securities of various kinds of almost $2,700,000,000, controlled more than 1500 industrial establishments. Also in 1904, about 300 smaller trusts capitalized at more than $4,00,000,000 were in control of approximately 3400 subsidiary organizations. The largest single trust was the United States Steel Corporation, formed in 1901 and capitalized at more than $1,700,000,000.

To deal with this threat to the competitive system, the Federal government, during the early 1900's, launched an unprecedented number of "trust-busting" actions. Among the giant trusts dissolved or curbed by these prosecutions were Swift and Company, the great meat-packing trust of Chicago, enjoined from suppressing competition in 1905; the Standard Oil Company of New Jersey, dissolved as an illegal combination in 1911; the American Tobacco Company, dissolved in 1911; the Du Pont de Nemours Company, an explosive-powder trust, dissolved in 1911;

and the American Sugar Refining Company, dissolved in 1911. Even while these victories were being won, however, corporate combinations in the form of trusts were multiplying, necessitating new and stronger Federal action.

The Federal government took two important steps in the field of antitrust activity in 1914. The first was the passage of the Clayton Act (q.v.), curbing the use of interlocking directorates, the acquisition by any company of stock in another engaged in the same industry, and various other trust devices, and enabling persons aggrieved by the formation of a trust in violation of the Sherman Act to recover three times the amount of damages sustained. The second notable Federal action was the establishment of the Federal Trade Commission (q.v.) a governmental agency endowed with broad regulatory powers relating to corporate organizations. These actions, and the continuing pressure exercised against the trusts by the Federal government in the courts, produced a new, far less predatory mode of behavior on the part of the trusts. Finding themselves confronted with growing public opposition and legal restriction, the trusts were compelled in some measure to forego their former ruthlessness toward their competitors. When sued for violation of the antitrust laws, the trusts adopted new tactics; instead of contesting the evidence of monopoly or disputing the right of the government to interfere with trust organization, they presented evidence of high standards of probity in commercial dealings, of technological and other improvements in productivity and efficiency, and of general benefit to industry and to the public, as bases of justification for their existence. In two significant cases (United States vs. United Shoe Machinery Company, 1918; and United States vs. United States Steel Corporation, 1920), the U.S. Supreme Court found these grounds sufficient to render legal the existence of even those trusts which were admitted to have secured a virtual monopoly in their respective industries through the amalgamation of several corporations.

The 1920's were characterized by a general relaxation of the formerly intransigeant antitrust attitude of the Federal government. Under three successive Republican Presidents (Warren G. Harding, Calvin Coolidge, and Herbert C. Hoover), few major antitrust actions were instituted. Students of this era have advanced two possible reasons for the lapse of antitrust activity. First, the comparatively prosperous economic conditions which prevailed until 1929 were widely viewed as the product of the high industrial productivity attained by the giant industrial trusts, and hence opponents of antitrust actions insisted that prosecution of the trusts would seriously damage the national economy. Secondly, the belief was widely held that corporate combination was a necessary and beneficial concomitant of technological advancement, which could best be accomplished through the construction of vast industrial complexes under centralized corporate management. As a consequence of the governmental attitude of leniency, the trusts grew and multiplied more rapidly in the 1920's than ever before.

The foregoing theoretical justifications for the development of trusts with a minimum of governmental interference were brought into serious question as a consequence of the onset of the economic crisis of 1929, and of the protracted depression which ensued. Many economists and political scientists viewed the concentration of wealth which had resulted from the growth of the trusts as a basic cause of the crisis. This view was supported by President Franklin D. Roosevelt, under whose sponsorship Congress passed the Monopoly Inquiry Act in 1938 establishing a Temporary National Economic Committee to investigate the workings of U.S. corporations and by its inquiries to lay the basis for the prosecution of "conspiracies to violate the antitrust laws". The investigations of the Committee revealed an alarming spread of trust formation and in ensuing years the Federal government, under both Roosevelt and his successor Harry S. Truman, conducted prosecutions of many of the greatest trusts in the nation. The corporations were able, however, to cause the litigation to extend over long periods of time, vitiating to some extent the effect of the Federal actions. Recent studies of U.S. industry indicate that the trend toward corporate combination has become more pronounced, and that a steadily increasing proportion of all industrial activity in the United States has come under the control of the trusts.

See also CARTEL.

TRUST, in law in England and the United States, the relationship existing between two or more parties in which one party holds the legal title to real or personal property subject to an obligation imposed by a court of equity or expressly undertaken by him to keep or use the property for the benefit of the other party or parties. The party who thus gains control of the property is called the trustee; the party

for whose benefit the property is held is known as the beneficiary of the trust, or the cestui que trust; and the property held by the trustee is known as trust property. The party who creates a trust is known as the settlor; the settlor may make himself either trustee or beneficiary.

Trusts may be classified, according to the manner in which they are created, as express, resulting, and constructive trusts. An express trust is one that is created by the settlor's conveyance of property by will or deed to a party with the intention that the property is to be held in trust for others. No consideration is necessary to create a trust and no writing or other formal document is required, except that trusts of real estate are required by the Statute of Frauds to be in writing.

A resulting trust is one which is created, not as a consequence of an actual statement of intention, but when the intention is inferred or presumed by a court of equity from the terms of the disposition of the property or from the circumstances accompanying such disposition. Thus, if a purchaser of real estate pays the purchase price, but takes title to the property in the name of a third party, a court of equity would hold that a resulting trust is created in favor of the purchaser, who is held by the court to be the real owner of the property. A constructive trust is one resulting from a conveyance of property in which no intention to create a trust can be inferred, yet a court of equity will compel the person having legal title to hold it for the benefit of another. Thus, whenever the legal title to property has been fraudulently acquired, the person guilty of the fraud will be treated by the court as a trustee and compelled to turn the property over to the defrauded party who is a constructive cestui que trust. Since neither resulting nor constructive trusts are created by intention of the interested parties, neither is within the Statute of Frauds requiring the trust to be evidenced by writing.

TRUST COMPANIES, institutions chartered by the several States of the United States for the purpose of performing, as corporations, the general acts and assuming the general responsibilities imposed upon individuals under the law of trusts. The trust company in the United States exists in various forms, and combines with its trustee business numerous other lines of banking; as, for instance, the private savings bank business, mortgage investment, title guarantee and other insurance; and of recent years a general banking business similar in most respects to that of the ordinary deposit bank. The general trust company law of New York State as it now stands authorizes the companies to perform the following functions: (1) to act as the fiscal agent or transfer agent of any State, municipality, body politic, or corporation; (2) to receive deposits of trust moneys, securities, and other personal property from any person or corporation, and to loan money on real or personal securities; (3) to lease, hold, purchase, and convey any and all real property necessary in the transaction of its business, or which the purposes of the corporation may require, or which it shall acquire in satisfaction or partial satisfaction of debts; (4) to act as trustee under any mortgage bond issued by any municipality, body politic, or corporation; (5) to accept trusts from and execute trusts for married women, in respect to their separate property, and to be their agent in the management of such property; (6) to act under the order or appointment of any court of record as guardian, receiver, or trustee of the estate of minors; (7) to take, accept, and execute any and all such legal trusts, duties, and powers in regard to the holding, management, and disposition of any estate, real or personal, and the rents and profits thereof, or the sale thereof, as may be granted or confided to it by any court of record, or by any person, corporation, municipality, or other authority; (8) to take, accept, and execute any and all such trusts and powers of whatever nature or description as may be conferred upon or intrusted or committed to it by any person or persons, or any body politic, corporation, or other authority; (9) to purchase, invest in, and sell stocks, bills of exchange, bonds and mortgages, and other securities; and (10) to be appointed and to accept the appointment of executor or of trustee under the last will and testament, or administrator with or without the will annexed, of the estate of any deceased person, and to be appointed and to act as the committee of the estates of lunatics, idiots, persons of unsound mind, and habitual drunkards.

These functions make plain both the nature of the trust company's business as contemplated by the legislators, and its difference from the banking business as conducted by an ordinary deposit bank. It will be observed that the act above quoted does not specifically in any place authorize the trust company to transact a general deposit banking business. But the statute does not deny such powers, and in Section 8 it provides that a company incorporated under the act may accept "any and all such trusts and powers, of what-

ever nature or description, as may be conferred upon or intrusted or committed to it by any person or persons". This is a sufficiently sweeping proviso to cover the doing of banking business in any deposits intrusted to the company by individuals, and on that basis a great part of the trust company business as now understood has been built up.

TRUSTEE PROCESS. See ATTACHMENT; GARNISHMENT.

TRUSTEESHIP COUNCIL, one of the principal organs of the United Nations (q.v.), established in December, 1946, for the purpose of carrying out those provisions of the Charter of the United Nations relating to the creation and administration of an international trusteeship system. As described in the Charter, the function of the international trusteeship system is to safeguard the interests of the inhabitants of territories which are not yet self-governing; such areas are classified as "trust territories" and include territories formerly held under mandate (see MANDATES), territories detached from any of the Axis Powers as a consequence of World War II, and territories voluntarily placed under the system by nations responsible for their administration. The Charter vests the General Assembly (q.v.) with authority to exercise the functions of the United Nations relating to the administration of all trust territories except those classified as "strategic areas"; the administration of the strategic areas is a responsibility of the Security Council (q.v.). The Trusteeship Council operates under the general authority of the General Assembly, and is empowered to assist the General Assembly and the Security Council in the exercise of these functions.

Three categories of members of the United Nations are included in the composition of the Trusteeship Council: members administering trust territories; permanent members of the Security Council not administering trust territories; and as many other members elected for a three-year term by the General Assembly as will ensure that the membership of the Council is equally divided between members which administer trust territories and members which do not. Each member of the Council has one vote, and decisions are made by a majority of the members present and voting. The specific powers of the Council may be listed as follows. It may consider reports submitted by nations administering trust territories; these nations are termed "administering authorities". In consultation with the administering authorities, it may examine petitions

Unations

Delegates at a session of the Trusteeship Council of the United Nations

submitted by the inhabitants of trust territories. The Council may arrange periodic visits to trust territories at times agreed upon with the administering authority. It may formulate a questionnaire on the political, economic, social, and educational advancement of the inhabitants of each trust territory; the administering authorities are required to use these questionnaires as the basis of annual reports to the General Assembly on the status of all trust territories except those classified as strategic areas.

When the Trusteeship Council was established, the following trust territories were placed under its jurisdiction: New Guinea (administered by Australia), Ruanda-Urundi (Belgium), Cameroons and Togo (France), Western Samoa (New Zealand), Tanganyika, Cameroons, and Togoland (United Kingdom), the Pacific islands formerly under Japanese mandate (United States), and Nauru (administered jointly by the United Kingdom, Australia, and New Zealand).

The Council sent an investigating mission to Western Samoa in 1947 and missions to Ruanda-Urundi and Tanganyika in 1948. Missions were sent to the trust territories at regular intervals thereafter. In 1948 the Council prepared a governing statute for Jerusalem (q.v.), which under the terms of the abortive plan for the partition of Palestine was to have been internationalized, and, at the request of the General Assembly, began consideration of the dispute with the Union of South Africa regarding a trusteeship arrangement for South-West Africa (q.v.), a League of Nations mandate administered by the Union. In 1949 the Council prepared the draft of a trusteeship agreement for Italian Somaliland. The agreement, providing for Italian administration of the territory, was approved by the General Assembly in 1950. During 1950, 1951, and 1952 the Council considered numerous complaints from various nonself-governing peoples of the African trust territories. The Council "expressed regret" (1952) over the British alienation of Meru tribal lands in Tanganyika.

TRUXTUN, THOMAS (1755–1822), American naval officer, born on Long Island, N.Y. Coming to Philadelphia late in 1775, he was made captain of the *Congress,* the first American privateer sent out during the Revolution. He held successive commands with uniform success. On the organization of the United States Navy (1798), he was put in command of the *Constellation,* and won several triumphs over French privateers in the West Indies. Subsequently, he commanded the West India Squadron as commodore. He retired in 1802.

TRYON, DWIGHT WILLIAM (1849–1925), American landscape painter, born in Hartford, Conn., and trained in Paris under the French landscape painter Charles François Daubigny and others. In 1886 he became professor of art at Smith College, Northampton, Mass., and later settled in New York City. Tryon received medals and prizes at many im-

A tsetse fly giving birth to a larva

portant exhibitions in Europe and America for his landscapes, which include "Moonlight", "Evening in Early Spring", and "Autumn", all in the Metropolitan Museum of Art, New York City.

TRYPANOSOMA. See SLEEPING SICKNESS.

TSARITSYN. See STALINGRAD.

TSCHAIKOVSKY, PETER ILITCH. See TCHAIKOVSKY, PËTR ILICH.

TSERCLAES, JOHAN. See TILLY.

TSETSE, or TSETSE FLY, common name applied to any of several blood-sucking, dipterous insects belonging to the genus *Glossina* of the family Muscidae. Tsetses are found abundantly in forests and along the edges of lakes and rivers in central and southern Africa. Several species are common to heavily wooded islands off the African mainland. The adult flies, which are about one inch long, are colored brown above and brown with yellow stripes or spots below. They have biting mouth parts, and are characterized by a large proboscis extending horizontally from the tip of the head. The heavily veined wings, in contrast to those of other blood-sucking flies, lie flat when not in use. The female periodically produces one full-sized larva and buries it in the ground or among decayed leaves; there it undergoes complete metamorphosis and develops into the adult.

The common South African tsetse fly, *G. palpalis,* transmits the parasitic flagellate, *Trypanosoma gambiense,* known to produce the often fatal sleeping sickness (q.v.). The parasites are drawn into the body of the fly in the blood sucked from an infected person and, after a period of development, are ready to be conveyed to the blood stream of healthy victims. Rhodesian sleeping sickness, a local form of the disease restricted to the region of Rhodes, is transmitted by the species *G. palpalis.* Tsetse fly disease, or *nagana,* which affects many cattle, horses, and goats throughout southern and central Africa, is caused by the trypanosome *T. brucei,* and is transmitted through the bite of *G. morsitans.* Animals constantly subjected to this disease often become immune.

TSINAN, TSINANFU, or CHI-NAN-FU, capital of the province of Shantung, China, 3 miles s. of the Yellow River, and about 175 miles w. of Kiaochow. It is noted for its silk brocades and trade in precious stones; in the vicinity are important iron mines. The Tsingtao-Tsinanfu Railway, built by Germany, operated by Japan, and sold by her to China in the Shantung Treaty (1922), is an ever-recurring source of contention between China and Japan. Two thousand Japanese live along this railway, and fifteen hundred more are in Tsinan. Clashes between the Japanese and Nationalist troops at Tsinan (May 3–4, 1928) were caused, according to the Chinese, by the dispatch of Japanese troops to Shantung. The incident, commemorated by "humiliation monuments" throughout Shantung, has since fostered anti-Japanese sentiment in the province. Pop., about 621,000. See also TSINGTAO.

TSINGTAO or **TSINGTAU,** a fortified seaport in Shantung Province, N.E. China, formerly principal city of the German protectorate of Kiaochow (q.v.). On Nov. 7, 1914, Tsingtao was taken by the Japanese, but later (1922) was restored to China. The Japanese have enormous property interests to protect in Tsingtao, and a dispute over fishing rights on the Shantung coast caused anti-Japanese riots in the city (Aug. 19, 1931). See also TSINAN. Pop. (1946 est.) 756,000.

TSINGYUAN, now **PAOTING,** capital of Hopeh Province, China. The city is located about 75 miles s.w. of Peiping, with which it is connected by rail, and about the same distance w. of Tientsin. It has a number of old temples and a Mohammedan mosque, and is the seat of a university. In 1900 it was one of the centers of the Chinese armed uprising, the Boxer Rebellion, against economic domination by foreign nationals. Pop. (1947 est.) 130,000.

TSITSIHAR or **LUNGKIANG,** capital of Heilungkiang Province, China, situated on the Nonni R., about 500 miles N.W. of Vladivostok. The city is served by the Chinese Changchun Railway and is an important commercial center, with a large trade in agricultural products, especially grain. Pop., about 80,000.

TSONECAN or **TSONEKAN,** name sometimes applied to the Patagonian natives, now used to designate the linguistic stock to which the Tehuelches (q.v.) belong.

TSU, maritime town and administrative center of Mie Prefecture, Honshu I., Japan, situated 37 miles s.s.w. of Nagoya. It is a religious center. Pop., about 59,000.

TSUNAMI, a Japanese name used as the scientific term for *seismic sea waves,* the large ocean waves generated by undersea earthquakes. Tsunami are commonly but erroneously called tidal waves, but bear no relation to tides. Tsunamis are most common in the Pacific and Indian oceans and are frequently of enormous size. In midocean the crests of the waves are many miles apart and move at speeds of hundreds of miles per hour. The waves are only a few inches high and are therefore imperceptible in midocean. When a tsunami strikes a coastline, particularly a coastline with a gradually shelving bottom, the great force of the wave piles up tremendous amounts of water, inundating the coast and causing tremendous damage. See EARTHQUAKE.

TSUTSUGAMUSHI FEVER (Japanese, *tsutsugamushi,* "dangerous insect"), an acute, febrile disease of man caused by a rickettsia (q.v.), *Rickettsia orientalis,* and transmitted by any of a number of mites or chiggers (q.v.) of the genus *Trombicula.* Until the end of the first decade of the 20th century, this disease was believed to be confined to the river valleys of Honshu province, Japan. Tsutsugamushi fever had a mortality rate in that region of from thirty to sixty percent, but excited little medical interest until World War II, when numerous American soldiers in the Pacific theatre of operations contracted the disease. The mortality rate of these American troops was ten to thirty percent.

Tsutsugamushi fever is transmitted by the larval form of various chiggers which inhabit open, extremely moist, sandy terrain supporting only such vegetation as grass, brush, and dwarf trees. The adult form of these mites is free-living. The larval mites parasitize such vertebrates as rats and voles, subsisting on their blood, and attack man only incidentally. Infestation of rodents with the microorganisms causing tsutsugamushi fever rarely results in their death; such rodents, therefore, serve as reservoirs of infection, mites unable to transmit the disease becoming active carriers after feeding on rodent blood. Because of the nature of the terrain which the transmitting mites inhabit, few persons are normally exposed to tsutsugamushi fever, also known as "rural typhus" or "scrub typhus"; during military operations, however, such terrain is often the only available site for setting up camp.

Shortly after being bitten by the larva of the causative mite, the human victim develops a shallow ulcer at the site of the bite, which is usually in the region of the groin, on the genitalia, or in the armpit. Five to eighteen days after being bitten the victim suddenly loses appetite and develops headache and muscular aches and pains. The patient first feels chill and then gradually develops a fever of about 104°F. (40°C). Abdominal pain with nausea and vomiting occasionally occur. About the fifth day after the first appearance of constitutional symptoms, a dull-red rash appears on the trunk, sometimes extending to the extremities. The rash becomes intense in three to five days, and then gradually disappears. During the second week of the disease, the victim becomes apathetic and develops conjunctivitis and extremely severe headaches. In more than half the cases, inflammation of the lungs occurs. Invasion of the central nervous system by the rickettsiae is very common and is manifested by mental confusion and disorientation, by twitching and tremors of various portions of the body, and often by delirium. In severe cases, convulsions and maniacal excitement occur. In uncomplicated cases, the fever begins to subside rapidly at the end of the second week and few aftereffects result. Common complications, which are often fatal, include blood poisoning, pneumonia, damage to the heart, and damage to the blood vessels of the brain.

Until 1948, no treatment was known for tsutsugamushi fever. Before this time, the prognosis of the disease was contingent upon the age of the patient (the older the patient, the smaller the chance of recovery). In 1948, however, with the discovery of the new antibiotic chloromycetin, physicians for the first time had a tool for the therapy of this disease. The antirickettsial antibiotic, aureomycin, discovered in 1949, provided a cure for tsutsugamushi fever.

Prior to the introduction of antirickettsial antibiotics, scientists were working on methods of prevention of the disease. Toward the end of World War II, soldiers stationed in Pacific areas in which the tsutsugamushi mites were prevalent were given a mite poison, dimethylphthalate, to smear over their socks and trouser legs. The use of such mite poisons is advocated by public health officers for the use of persons living in areas endemic for the disease.

Tsutsugamushi fever occurs not only in Japan but also in Korea, China, Indo-China, Burma, Malaya, Sumatra, India, Pakistan, Ceylon, the Philippine Islands, New Britain, and North Queensland. In regions having a subtropical or temperate climate, the mite carriers are active only in the summer months;

Two Tuareg women making camel-skin jars, in Algeria

in countries nearer the equator, the disease occurs throughout the year.

Other names applied to tsutsugamushi fever include "mite-borne typhus", "kedani fever", "flood fever", "Sumatran fever", and "Japanese river fever". The disease, which closely resembles true typhus fever, is differentiated from true typhus by a serological test. Compare TYPHUS.

TUAREG, or TUAREK, a Berber nomad of middle Sahara. Tuaregs number some 300,000. A common article of their dress is the litham, a cloth wrapped about the face for protection from the dust of the desert. The Amoshagh or Noble Tuaregs wear a black litham and the Imghad or servile a white one, hence the epithets Black Tuaregs and White Tuaregs.

TUATHA DE DANANN, a prehistoric people of tall stature and blond type, who, according to the ancient annals of Ireland, invaded the island from the north several centuries before the Christian era, and by defeating the Firbolgs in the battle of Moytura became masters of the country until in turn overcome by the Milesians (q.v.). They were probably of Scandinavian origin.

TUBA, name given to bass instruments of the saxhorn (q.v.) species, also called bom-

bardons. The most usual sizes are the bass tuba in F or E♭ and the contrabass tuba in C or B♭. Their introduction into the orchestra is due to Wagner. The helicon (q.v.) is a form of tuba.

TUBER, a short, swollen, underground, food-storing stem produced by many perennial plants. Tubers reproduce by means of small, scale-covered buds, or "eyes". Young plants developing from tuber buds derive their nourishment from starch stored in the tubers until they are mature enough to develop root systems. Many tubers such as the "Irish" potato and the Jerusalem artichoke, are staple foods. The name tuber is also erroneously applied to tuber-shaped galls (see GALL).

TUBERCLE, term applied to various rounded nodules or prominences found in or on animal and plant organisms. Tubercles located along the surfaces of bones serve as points of articulation between bones, and as points of attachment for muscles and ligaments. The tubercles located in the central nervous system (q.v.) act as nuclei for various nerves. In plants, tubercles occur as small tubers (q.v.), as roots of leguminous plants, and as tuberlike roots. In medicine, the morbid growth often found on the skin or viscera, especially those growths resulting from tuberculosis (q.v.), are known as tubercles.

TUBERCULOSIS, or WHITE PLAGUE, name applied to an infectious, contagious, chronic disease of many vertebrate animals, caused by the tubercle bacillus, *Mycobacterium tuberculosis,* which belongs to the same genus as the organism causing leprosy, and which was isolated in 1890 by the German bacteriologist Robert Koch. Tuberculosis is so called after the small, pearl-gray tubercles which develop late in the course of the disease in the internal organs of afflicted animals and humans. The tubercles are composed of modified body cells and sometimes include many tubercle bacilli. At least three subspecies of the tubercle bacillus are known: the subspecies producing most of the tuberculosis of humans; the subspecies producing bovine tuberculosis in domesticated cattle; and the subspecies producing avian tuberculosis in wild and domesticated birds. Scientists believe that two other subspecies exist, producing disease in fish and reptiles respectively. Swine are often attacked by bovine and avian tubercle bacilli. Domestic cats, dogs, horses, and sheep are rarely, if ever, attacked by the disease. Compare JOHNE'S DISEASE.

Tuberculosis is found in most temperate parts of the world, and until recent years was the seventh greatest cause of human death in the United States. The disease, which may be transmitted to humans by sprays from the respiratory tracts of infected persons, by contact with sputum from infected persons, and by ingestion of unpasteurized milk from infected cows, attacks most persons living in crowded, urban areas at some time during their lives; however, most cases of tuberculosis are not serious, the tubercle bacilli being walled off by calcified body cells from the attacked tissues. Walled-off tubercles containing dead tubercle bacilli are known as *healed lesions*; walled-off tubercles containing live tubercle bacilli are known as *quiescent* or *arrested lesions*; bacilli not walled-off form *active lesions* which spread locally or which may metastasize throughout the body. Active tuberculosis is therefore either *local* or *general* (also called miliary tuberculosis).

About one in every three hundred persons in the United States has an active case of tuberculosis. The human tubercle bacillus chiefly attacks persons between the ages of five to thirty years, and is responsible for about ninety-three percent of all cases of human tuberculosis; the bovine tubercle bacillus, which chiefly attacks children under the age of five, is responsible for about seven percent of all human cases. The incidence of tuberculosis in the United States is particularly high among Negroes, in whom resistance to the disease seems to be lower than in other people. Susceptibility to tuberculosis is increased by any influence which reduces the resistance of the body; crowded and unsanitary living conditions, unhealthy working conditions, especially in such occupations as mining in which dust constantly irritates the lungs, and constant emotional upset tend to make the individual more susceptible to tuberculosis. Tuberculosis is not commonly contracted after a single contact with an infected person; most cases occur in crowded family groups as a result of extended contact with one or more infected persons. The tubercle bacilli are extremely long-lived and are capable of producing disease in man for as long as six months after leaving their initial host; unless utensils used by tubercular individuals are carefully sterilized, foci of infection for other members of the household may persist over a long period of time. Predisposition toward the contraction of tuberculosis seems to be hereditary.

Pulmonary tuberculosis, or tuberculosis of the lungs, which is also known as *phthisis* and *consumption,* is the most common form of the disease and is the form usually thought of by laymen when the term "tuberculosis" is used. The lungs are the primary site of infection in human tuberculosis; secondary sites of infection include the larynx, intestines, joints, peritoneum, kidneys, bladder, spleen, liver, heart, reproductive organs, eyes, meninges, spinal cord, and brain. Secondary infection of the skin produces a condition known as *lupus vulgaris*. The intestines are the primary site of infection by bovine tubercle bacillus; secondary sites of infection include the lymph nodes (causing scrofula; q.v.) and the bones. The initial symptoms of all forms of tuberculosis include fever, progressive loss of weight, night sweats, and constant fatigue. In the most common form of the disease, pulmonary tuberculosis, these symptoms are accompanied by a persistent cough, husky voice, and pains in the chest, and are later followed by the expectoration of large amounts of sputum sometimes containing blood; see SPUTUM. In active cases of tuberculosis the lesions and the tissue about the lesions become cheesy, and, when emptied by coughing, form cavities in the affected organs. Tuberculosis may spread rapidly, causing death within a few months after onset, or it may persist for many years.

The diagnosis of tuberculosis has been made relatively simple by the introduction of various laboratory tests. In cases of pulmonary tuberculosis, the sputum is smeared on a glass slide and is stained to color the tubercle bacilli red that they may be identified under the microscope. In children under three years of age a skin test is employed in which *tuberculin* (an extract of dead tubercle bacilli) is injected into the skin. If tuberculosis is present, a pink to red swelling will develop at the site of injection, and slight fever will ensue. The tuberculin test is rarely used in testing for tuberculosis in adults because most adults give a false positive reaction to the test. Injection of sputum into guinea pigs is also commonly used; whereas two hundred tubercle bacilli are required to initiate active tuberculosis in man only ten bacilli are needed to produce the disease in guinea pigs. Six to ten weeks after being injected, the guinea pigs, if still alive, are killed and examined for tubercle formation in their internal organs. Chest X-ray pictures usually reveal lung lesions; healed, arrested, and active lesions may be differentiated by judicious interpretation of X-ray photographs. For forms of tuberculosis other than pulmonary tuberculosis special diagnostic measures are available; tuberculosis of the kidney or of the bladder, for example, may be confirmed by injections of concentrated urine into guinea pigs, by cystoscopic examinations, or by microscopic examination of the urine for tubercle bacilli; tuberculous meningitis (see MENINGITIS) may often be diagnosed by the findings of various laboratory tests on the cerebrospinal fluid of the diseased individual.

Early diagnosis of tuberculosis is especially important because rest, fresh air and sunshine, and proper diet administered to individuals during the early stages of the disease can effect healing of lesions in almost eighty percent of all cases. Rest sanitariums, modeled after the one organized by the American physician Edward Livingston Trudeau (q.v.), at the end of the 19th century, have provided the healthful environments necessary for recovery to thousands of early cases of tuberculosis.

Toward the close of the first half of the 20th century, several new antibiotic and chemotherapeutic agents (see ANTIBIOTIC; CHEMOTHERAPY) were developed for the treatment of tuberculosis. One of these, streptomycin (q.v.), has proven effective in many cases of the disease, especially in general or miliary tuberculosis. Streptomycin has one chief disadvantage: tubercle bacilli develop a

tolerance to the drug and, if not destroyed by the initial doses, continue to multiply despite streptomycin treatment. Para-amino-salicylic acid, isoniazid, and viomycin have recently come into use as adjuncts to streptomycin therapy; these drugs inhibit the development of bacillary tolerance to streptomycin. Tibione (TB-1), a coal-tar derivative developed by the German biochemist Gerhard Domagk, the discoverer of sulfanilamide, has proven effective in many cases of local tuberculosis in Germany, and is presently being tested in the United States. A new antibiotic called cycloserine, or Seromycin, was in experimental use in 1955 at U.S. veterans' hospitals. In preliminary tests, cycloserine showed good results in cases resistant to other drugs. Advanced tuberculosis is now treated by administration of these agents, by rest, and by any of a number of surgical procedures adapted to the site of infection. Pulmonary tuberculosis, for example, may be treated by *pneumothorax,* which consists of injecting air between the body wall and the lung to collapse the lung and allow it to rest; after a period of time, the injected air is absorbed by the body cells, and the lung reinflates spontaneously. Often pneumothorax is performed repeatedly to allow for a sufficient period of lung rest. When a lung is extensively infected, it may be collapsed permanently by the surgical removal of part of the ribs, or the lung itself may be removed to prevent spread of infection to the other lung and to other parts of the body; other infected organs and tissues, such as a kidney or sections of bone, are often removed surgically to prevent spread of infection.

The greatest difficulty encountered by public health officials attempting to control tuberculosis is the reluctance of many persons infected with the disease to present themselves for examination and treatment. Prevention of tuberculosis is the most effective method of control. Milk cows are regularly tested for tuberculosis; pasteurization of milk further reduces chances of being infected with the bovine tubercle bacillus. The human tubercle bacillus, however, is much more important as the cause of the disease. Attempts have therefore been made to develop an antitubercle-bacillus vaccine which can be injected into children routinely at the time they are inoculated against diphtheria, smallpox, whooping cough, and other such preventable diseases. Such a vaccine was developed by the French bacteriologists Albert Léon Charles Calmette and Alphonse Guerin from tubercle bacilli cultured over a long period of time on ox bile; the tubercle bacilli remain alive but become so weakened that they are unable to produce disease when injected. The vaccine, known as *Calmette's vaccine, Bacillus- Calmette-Guérin vaccine,* or *BCG,* has been tested in several countries for a period of about twenty years and was first accepted as being effective and safe in 1949. Programs of BCG inoculation are presently being set up in many States in the United States.

Preventive vaccination against tuberculosis will reduce the incidence of the disease in coming generations. Control of established tuberculosis today, however, requires extensive education of the general populace to the symptoms, dangers, and method of spread of the disease. Such an educational program is being conducted by the U.S. Public Health Service and State and municipal public-health departments. Free chest X-ray examinations are offered to the populace by many health organizations in an attempt to obtain the recognition of as many active, untreated cases as possible. Most schools and colleges require and provide facilities for periodic X-ray examination for tuberculosis. Because individuals with active tuberculosis constitute a menace to the health of their close relatives, and because the large number of such individuals makes it almost impossible to isolate each case of tuberculosis, programs of education in personal hygiene have been instituted to reduce the chances of contagion. Sterilization of utensils, burning of sputum, and avoidance of close physical contacts are essential measures to prevent the spread of the disease. Tuberculosis education by government agencies is supplemented by the work of private societies, financed by contributions.

TUBEROSE, common name applied to an annual herb, *Polianthes tuberosa,* belonging to the Amaryllis family. The plant is characterized by possession of fleshy, bulblike rootstocks, or tubers. Tuberoses are native to various parts of Mexico, and cultivated extensively in North Carolina and surrounding States in the United States. The white, waxy, funnel-shaped flowers, borne in pairs in a loose spike, have three sepals, numerous petals, six stamens, and a solitary pistil. The fruit is a many-seeded capsule. Because of their sweet fragrance, the flowers are often used in funeral decorations. The plant is commonly raised from the tubers, and grows to a height of 3 feet.

TÜBINGEN, town of Baden-Württemberg, West Germany, 18 miles s.s.w. of Stuttgart. It

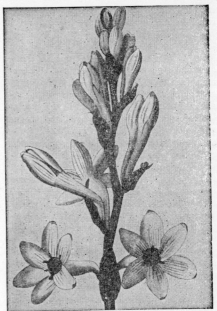

Narcissus-flowered tuberose

is the seat of Tübingen University (1477), made famous by the Protestant seminary (1536). Book printing, the making of surgical and scientific instruments, and cultivation of hops and the vine are the leading industries. Pop. (1950) 37,506.

TUBULIDENTATA, an order of mammals constituted by the aardvarks (q.v.) of Africa, and formerly included within the order Edentata (see MAMMALS).

TUCANO, a tribe residing upon the Uaupés River, on the Brazil-Colombia border, supposed to be remotely related to the Arawaks (q.v.). They take their name from the toucan bird. The Tucano tattoo three lines upon each cheek, build circular houses of poles covered with palm leaves, are good canoemen, and are noted for their skill with the blowgun.

TUCKER, SOPHIE, *nee* ABUZA (1884–), American actress, born in Russia of American parents. Starting her vaudeville career in her father's café, she subsequently appeared on the New York stage and in cabarets in the U.S. and abroad. She has also been known as a radio singer; her program was entitled *Sophie Tucker and Her Show* (1938–39).

TUCSON, county seat of Pima Co., Ariz., situated on the Santa Cruz R., 125 miles s.e. of Phoenix and about 60 miles from the Mexican border. It is a division point of the Southern Pacific Railroad, the N. terminus of a Mexican railroad, and is also served by a major transcontinental air line. The city is a famous winter resort, and the trading center and shipping point of an agricultural and mining area. Cotton, livestock, honey, and copper are the chief products of the surrounding region. Industrial establishments in the city include extensive railroad repair shops and yards. The principal industry in Tucson is the accommodation of the numerous visitors who come there for purposes of health or recreation. Tucson lies at an altitude of about 2400 ft. above sea level and is surrounded by mountains rising to a height of 9000 ft. The climate is mild and dry; sunshine is almost perpetual. The city contains a large U.S. veterans hospital, the Southern Pacific Railroad Hospital, the Arizona State Elks Hospital, and numerous private sanitariums for persons suffering from tuberculosis. Also in the city and vicinity are many hotels, dude ranches, and mountain lodges. Tucson is the site of the University of Arizona, a coeducational and nonsectarian institution, founded in 1885; the Arizona School for the Deaf and Blind; the State museum, containing archeological and natural-history collections; the Southwest Experiment Station of the U.S. Bureau of Mines; the Desert Botanical Laboratory of the Carnegie Institution; a large U.S. Air Force Base; an annual festival and rodeo; and a National Livestock Show. The city is an episcopal see of the Roman Catholic Church, and the headquarters of the Coronado National Forest. Places of interest nearby include several ruined villages of ancient Indian tribes; Tucson Mountain Park, covering about 30,000 acres in the Tucson Mountains and containing examples of Indian pictographs; Saguaro National Monument; the Yaqui Indian Village, site of a picturesque Easter festival; and the Mission San Xavier del Bac, built between 1783 and 1797 by Franciscan missionaries to replace an earlier mission constructed by the Jesuits about 1720 and abandoned by them in 1767.

The first European settlement on the site of the present city was established in 1776 by the Spanish. From 1867 to 1877 Tucson was the Territorial capital of Arizona. The Southern Pacific Railroad reached Tucson in 1880 and the Mexican railroad in 1910. Tucson was chartered as a city in 1883. Pop. (1950) 45,454.

TUCUMÁN, the capital of the province of Tucumán, Argentina, on the river Tala or Sali, 690 miles N.w. of Buenos Aires. It is the seat of a university (1912). Pop. (1950 est.) 172,000.

TUDOR (Welsh, *Tewdr,* "Theodore"), the family name of the dynasty which occupied the throne of England from 1485 to 1603. Owen Tudor, first of the race known in history, was the father of Edmund, Earl of Richmond, who married Margaret, heiress of the Beauforts, and their son ascended the throne of England as Henry VII. The Tudor monarchs were Henry VII (1485–1509), Henry VIII (1509–47), Edward VI (1547–53), Mary (1553–58), and Elizabeth I (1558–1603). See articles on individual rulers.

TUFA. See CALCAREOUS ROCKS.

TUFTS UNIVERSITY, privately controlled, nonsectarian, coeducational institution of higher learning, located in Medford, Mass., and in Boston, Mass. The institution was founded as Tufts College in 1852 by a group of members of the Universalist Church and opened for instruction in 1855. It was designated a university in 1955. Divisions of the university include the College of Liberal Arts, for men; Jackson College, a co-ordinate women's school of liberal arts; and schools of dentistry, medicine, engineering, religion, and graduate study. The Fletcher School of Law and Diplomacy is administered in co-operation with Harvard University. Numerous specialized institutions in the Boston metropolitan area are affiliated with Tufts. The university confers the bachelor's, master's, and doctor's degrees. The library contains 250,000 bound volumes. In the spring of 1956 student enrollment totaled 3374 full-time and 615 part-time students and the faculty numbered 619. The endowment was $12,088,819.

TU FU (712–70), Chinese poet, born in Siangyangfu, in the present province of Hupeh, according to one authority, or in Tuling in Shensi, according to another. Through failure in literary examinations he lost official chances, but became a professional poet, and produced three descriptive poems (742–55) which gained him favor from the reigning emperor, and a position at court. This emperor fled from rebels, but Tu Fu fell into their hands, escaping in 757. He was recalled by the new emperor, and became a censor. Having defended an official who had incurred the displeasure of the emperor, he fell into disgrace, was banished, and given the position of a subprefect in a small town of Shensi. This he promptly resigned and retired to Sze-chuen. In 761 a post was provided for him in connection with the Board of Works. This he held for six years, after which he resumed his wandering life. The edition of his poems published in 1059 contained 1405 compositions. He is the most frequently quoted poet in China.

TUGWELL, REXFORD GUY (1891–), American economist and government official, born in Sinclairville, N.Y., and educated at the University of Pennsylvania. In 1920 he became a member of the faculty of Columbia University, and from 1931 to 1937 he was professor of economics at that institution. During the last four years of his professorship Tugwell was on leave in government service, having been summoned to Washington, D.C., in 1933 by President Franklin Delano Roosevelt as his economic adviser, with the post of assistant secretary of agriculture. He was coauthor of the Agricultural Adjustment Act of 1933, and in 1934 was appointed to the newly created office of undersecretary of agriculture. He returned to New York in 1938 to head the New York City Planning Commission. Three years later President Roosevelt appointed him governor of Puerto Rico. In 1946 Tugwell joined the staff of the University of Chicago as a professor of political science and director of the university's Institute of Planning. In the Presidential election campaign of 1948 he supported Henry A. Wallace for President and was a member of the Progressive Party. His works include *Industry's Coming of Age* (1927), *The Industrial Discipline* (1933), *Battle for Democracy* (1935), *The Stricken Land* (1946), and *Chronicle of Jeopardy, 1945-55* (1955).

TUILERIES, a former royal palace situated on the right bank of the Seine R., in a locality originally occupied by tile works (*tuileries*). The erection was begun in 1563, by Catherine de Médicis, under the direction of Philibert de l'Orme. It was stormed by the Revolutionists (Aug. 10, 1792), but following the creation of the empire it was the residence of the reigning sovereigns. With the fall of Napoleon III it was burned by the Commune in 1871. The gardens, first laid out by Le Nôtre in the time of Louis XIV, are a popular resort of Parisians.

TUKEY, HAROLD BRADFORD (1896–), American horticulturist, born in Berwyn, Illinois, and educated at the universities of Illinois and Chicago. After serving in various horticultural positions in several agricultural agencies and experiment stations of New York State, he became professor of pomology at Cornell University in 1927. He served in that position until 1945, when he became head of the department of horticulture at Michigan State College. He was editor or contributing editor for several agricultural journals.

TULA, capital of a Region of the same name in Soviet Russia. The province belongs to the Black Soil belt of Russia and is watered chiefly by the Oka and the Don. The town, on the Upa River, 110 miles s. of Moscow, is in a rich iron-mining region and has extensive metal works and arms factories. It dates from the end of the 11th century. Area of province, about 11,960 sq.m.; pop., about 178,000. Pop. of town, about 272,000.

TULALIP, a tribe of Salishan stock (see SALISH) occupying a reservation of 36 square miles on Tulalip Bay, an eastern inlet of Puget Sound, Washington.

TULANE UNIVERSITY OF LOUISIANA, a coeducational, privately controlled institution of higher learning, located in New Orleans, La. It was founded in 1834 as a school for men under the name Medical College of Louisiana; the present name was adopted in 1882, when Paul Tulane, a merchant of New Orleans, donated a million dollars to the college. In the last-named year, by legislative enactment, the university absorbed the State University of Louisiana (est. 1845) and was granted exemption from taxation on its property. In 1886 a fund was raised for the foundation of a women's college at the university; this fund became the original endowment of the H. Sophie Newcomb Memorial College for Women, the women's division of the university. The university includes departments of the arts and sciences, engineering, law, commerce and business administration, social work, architecture, and medicine. Courses are offered leading to undergraduate and graduate degrees. In 1953 the enrollment of the University was 5763, including 3661 full-time students; the faculty numbered 1001; and the endowment was $18,000,000.

TULAREMIA, an acute, infectious, febrile disease which in mankind is apparently derived from infected food or game animals. It made its first appearance in 1924 and is mostly confined to the United States, although cases have been reported from Japan and Russia. The disease was believed originally to be transmitted by the deer fly, the carrier of deer-fly fever. Recent investigation has disclosed that most infections are acquired through handling or eating rabbits. The first symptom is an ulcer in the hand followed by enlarged glands at the elbow or in the arm pit. Fever readily sets in and lasts for two or three weeks. The malady is named after Tulare, Calif., where it was first recognized.

TULIP (Turk. *tülbend,* "turban"), common name for any of numerous hardy, spring-flowering, bulbous herbs belonging to the genus *Tulipa* of the Lily family, and so called from the inverted-turban shape of the flowers. The genus contains approximately one hundred species native to many temperate regions of Europe and Asia, and is widely cultivated as an ornamental plant throughout the world. The satin-textured flowers, usually occurring singly or in groups of two to five, vary in color from pure white, yellow, orange, crimson, red, or purple to various combinations of several hues. They have three petallike sepals, three petals, six stamens, and a solitary pistil. The fruit is a many-seeded capsule. The plants arise directly from bulbs, and are characterized by long, broad, and pointed leaves.

Tulips have received considerable attention in the botanical records of the past, and were cultivated by the Turks prior to the 16th century. In the year 1554, the Flemish diplomat Augier Chislain de Busbecq, then ambassador to Turkey for Holy Roman Emperor Ferdinand I, procured several tulip seeds from a garden in Constantinople and introduced them in Vienna, where they immediately became popular. Five years later, the Swiss naturalist Konrad von Gesner also visited Turkey and brought back several tulip seeds to Germany. Soon afterward tulip growing became a great fad in most of western Europe, and was further encouraged when, in 1591, the French physician Charles de Lecluse introduced the flower to Holland. The popularity of the flower became so great that, in 1634, there developed in Holland the famous *tulipomania,* a craze for acquiring and developing many varieties of tulip. Wild speculation in tulip stock ensued, with the equivalent of as much as $5200 being paid for a single bulb. The crisis was finally ended by government intervention, but only after many families and individuals had been bankrupted. The incident, although disastrous, helped to establish Holland as the principal tulip-bulb center of the world. Later, tulip growing also became an important industry of Belgium, and is now also practiced widely in the United States, particularly in the States of Washington and Michigan.

Classification. For purposes of general identification, tulips are grouped into several major classes according to their approximate flowering dates. The early flowering, or Duc Van Thol, class consists of small, short-stemmed varieties that bloom in very early spring. Tulips of this class bear solid or many-colored, single or double flowers. The later-flowering or cottage tulips are characterized by long, slender stems, narrow foliage, and pointed petals. The cottage tulips include more than half of the species of tulip, and bear flowers in midspring. The third main group, the Darwins, also bloom in midspring. Most of the flowers in this class are long stemmed and globular, and are solid crimsons, reds, pinks, purples, and whites; yellows are conspicuously absent from this group. Early-blooming, cottage, and Darwin tulips are in turn subdivided into various other categories, according to their respective coloration. Tulips bearing solid-colored flowers are commonly known as "self"; those bearing flowers with yellow ground colors and orange, red, or brown markings as "bizarres"; and those bearing flowers with white ground colors and purple, maroon, brown, or black markings as "bybloemens", or "bybloems". Bizarres and bybloemens are further classified as "feathered" and "flamed", depending on whether the various floral colors are mingled in narrow or in broad stripes, respectively. The term bybloemen is often extended to include those solid-colored tulips which bear only lilac or purple flowers; yellow-flowered selfs are often included among the bizarres. The tulips commonly called "breeders" are selected hybrids which produce very large blooms, long stems, and "art-color" flowers.

Species and Varieties. Although the original identities of most tulips have been lost through constant hybridization, it is still possible to recognize several basic species. The parent of the modern Duc Van Thol, or early-blooming tulip, is generally believed to be *Tulipa suaveolens,* a fragrant variety native to southern parts of Europe and Asia. It bears pointed, bright red, yellow, or vari-colored flowers, and grows to a height of 6 inches. Today, the numerous early bloomers descended from *T. suaveolens* are found both wild and under cultivation. The lady tulip or candy-stick tulip, *T. clusiana,* is the hardiest of the early bloomers, growing well in both north-temperate and south-temperate regions, and found wild in Persia and the Mediterranean areas of Europe. The long, slender stems, which attain a height of 18 inches, bear deep-white or rose-colored flowers. *T. kaufmanniana,* commonly known as the water-lily tulip, is native to Turkestan, where it grows to a height of 12 inches. The flowers vary in color from yellow to red, the cultivated varieties often being creamy white with yellow basal blotches. *T. greigii,* also native to Turkestan, bears bright-crimson flowers with yellow-margined blotches at the base, and reaches a height of 8 inches. A smaller variety, *T. biflora,* is found in the Caucasus and other mountain areas of central Asia. Its small, white or pale-yellow flowers, borne on long, branching stalks, are tinged with green, red, or purple. *T. praestans,* native to Bokhara, bears light-scarlet to red flowers, and attains a height of 18 inches. The tall Red Emperor, *T. fosteriana,* also native to Bokhara, bears red flowers which are probably brighter and larger than those of any other red-flowered tulips. *T. eichleri,* native to Asia, bears large, crimson-scarlet flowers.

The ancestor of the Darwins, *T. gesneriana,* also known as the common garden tulip or late tulip, is the type originally introduced from Turkey. It bears cup-shaped, bright-red or multicolored flowers, and grows to a height of 24 inches. Several varieties exist, all of which are late-season bloomers. Var. *dracontia,* commonly called the parrot tulip, bears flowers with ragged-edged, somewhat twisted petals covered with various combinations of stripes and splotches. Var. *spathulata,* native to parts of Italy, is probably the largest of the wild tulips. It has brilliant red flowers blotched with blackish purple at the base. Var. *strangewaysiana,* a large, dark-scarlet variety, is native to fields near Florence, Italy. Var. *albo-oculata,* noted for its slightly sweet odor, has dark-scarlet flowers blotched with purple at the base.

Existing species of the cottage or mid-season bloomers are mostly hybrids derived from crosses between the Darwins, *T. gesneriana,* and the early bloomers, *T. suaveolens.* The common hybrid species, *T. elegans,* bears scarlet and yellow flowers, and grows to a height of 18 inches. Its principal variety, *T. elegans* var. *picotee,* has larger, white flowers edged with light red. Other common garden hybrids include *T. retroflexa,* bearing flowers of variegated shades of yellow, and *T. macrospeila,* with crimson or cherry-red flowers. Of the hundreds of tulip varieties listed in bulb-growers catalogues, only a few of the more important types can be noted here. The most popular single early varieties are the Keiserskroon, bearing red flowers broadly edged with yellow; and the De Wet, bearing orange-scarlet flowers. Common double-early varieties include the Murillo, bearing white-flushed, rose-pink flowers; the Golden Murillo, bearing golden-yellow flowers; and the Peachblossom, bearing rose-pink flowers. Darwins are always self, or solid-colored and occur in a wide range of colors. The more popular, single-flowered Darwins are the Clara Butt, bearing salmon-pink flowers; the Farncombe Sanders, bearing geranium-scarlet flowers; La Tulipe Noire, with dark maroon flowers; the Zwanenburg, with white flowers; and the Reverend H. Ewbank, with lavender or violet flowers. The double-flowered Darwins, which are among the most recently developed garden tulips, include: the Mount Tacoma, bearing white flowers; the Uncle Tom, bearing mahogany-red flowers; and the Eros, bearing salmon-pink flowers. Popular varieties of cottage tulips are the Inglescombe Yellow, with yellow flowers; the Dido, with salmon-orange flowers; the Mrs. Moon, with deep-yellow flowers; and the Rosabella, bearing rose flowers with lighter edges. The long, slender-stemmed, lily-flowering tulips, usually recognized as a variety of cottage tulips, are noted for their reflexing petals, and include the Picotee, bearing pointed, rose-colored flowers; the Alaska, bearing yellow flowers; and the White Dutchess, bearing white flowers. More popular varieties of breeder tulips include the Louis XIV, colored in purple and brown; the Prince of Orange, bearing terra-cotta flowers edged with orange yellow; and the Dillenburg, colored salmon orange and shaded with rose.

Cultivation of Tulips. Because of their form and color variation, tulips are popular and extensively grown garden flowers. For outdoor cultivation, the bulbs are planted in sandy loams enriched with manure and spaded to a depth of about 12 inches. They are placed from 4 to 9 inches apart and from 4 to 6 inches deep, depending on the particular varieties being used. For spring bloom, bulbs are planted from September to December, before the winter frosts set in. Bulbs may remain in the ground and bear flowers for several years, but those of the second and succeeding years are poorer in quality than the first-year growth. Many growers remove tulip bulbs from the ground in summer, after the foliage has died down; the bulbs are then dried and are replanted in late fall. New bulbs are usually not planted in the spaces formerly occupied by other bulbs, unless the ground is sufficiently enriched following previous planting. Greenhouse tulips, grown for midwinter and early-spring bloom, provide most of the pot-plant and cut-flower varieties. Greenhouse bulbs are first allowed to take root in hard, freezing soils before being brought indoors.

Flowers of the tulip tree

Diseases and Pests. The most common and destructive tulip disease is the tulip blight, or tulip fire, caused by the fungus *Botrytis tulipae*. The disease is often prevalent in moist weather, when the characteristic, grayish-brown lesions appear on the leaves, bulbs, and flowers of some tulip plants, and are spread to healthy plants by wind, rain, and garden tools. Periodic spring spraying with a weak Bordeaux mixture, or soil disinfection with formalin, often controls the disease. The bulbs of tulips are frequently attacked by the minute, whitish bulb mite, *Rhizoglyphus hyacinthi*, which lays numerous eggs on the bulb surface. The young, after emerging from the eggs, burrow into the bulb and subsist on bulb and root tissue. They may burrow through the ground and attack other, healthy bulbs. Diseased bulbs are either burned or immersed in a solution of nicotine sulfate or formaldehyde.

The name "tulip" is also commonly and incorrectly applied to various other plants belonging to the genus *Calochortus* (q.v.) of the Lily family. These include the Mariposa lily, Mariposa tulip, or star tulip; the globe tulip; the meadow tulip; and the butterfly tulip. The tulip tree (q.v.), *Liriodendron tulipifera*, belongs to the magnolia family.

TULIP TREE, common name applied to a deciduous tree, *Liriodendron tulipifera*, belonging to the Magnolia family. The tree is native to E. United States and, when fully grown, attains a height of 150 to 190 feet; the trunk averages 10 feet in diameter. The solitary, tulip-shaped, greenish-yellow flowers have three sepals, six petals, numerous stamens, and many pistils arranged in a narrow column. The fruit is a cone-shaped cluster of one-seeded or two-seeded nutlets. Well-known cultivated varieties are *L. tulipifera* var. *aureomarginatum,* having yellow-edged leaves; and var. *integrifolium,* having lobeless, rounded leaves. In the United States, tulip-tree timber is sometimes called whitewood, poplar, yellow poplar, or tulip poplar. The timber is used extensively in cabinetmaking and in other woodworking processes. Various insects periodically attack tulip trees, often causing considerable damage to the leaves. Common pests are the homopterous tuliptree scale insects of the family Coccidae, and the green aphids of the family Aphididae. Insect enemies are usually controlled by spraying the trees with nicotine sulfate, soap, or miscible oils. The name "tulip tree" is sometimes extended to other trees having tulip-shaped flowers, including the majagua tree, *Pariti tiliaceum;* the portia tree or bendy tree, *Thespesia populnea*; and the banana shrub or Chinese evergreen, *Michelia fuscata*.

TULL, JETHRO (1674–1741), English agriculturist and inventor, born in Basildon, Berkshire, and educated at Oxford University. He was admitted to the bar in 1699, but never practiced law. Ill health caused him to relinquish a career in politics, and he turned to the scientific study of agriculture. He invented a machine drill for sowing seed; the rotary mechanism in the invention was the foundation of all subsequent sowing implements. He placed great emphasis on the importance of pulverizing soil so that air and moisture could reach the roots of growing plants, and he introduced the system of planting seeds in rows which were sufficiently separated from each other to allow the hoeing or ploughing of the soil after the plants had grown to maturity. His ideas about farming were incorporated in two books, *Horse-Hoeing Husbandry* (1731) and *Horse-Hoeing Husbandry, or An Essay on the Principles of Tillage and Vegetation* (1773), which exerted a long-lasting influence on farming in England.

TULLY, the name by which many English writers, particularly in the 18th and 19th centuries, referred to the famous Roman orator Marcus Tullius Cicero (q.v.).

TULSA, county seat of Tulsa Co., Okla., situated on the Arkansas R., 120 miles N.E. of Oklahoma City. Transportation facilities include six railroads and a municipal airport. Tulsa, often called the "Oil Capital of the World", is the second-largest city in the State and the metropolis of a vast oil-producing and agricultural area. It contains the headquarters of numerous large oil companies and companies associated in various ways with the oil industry. The surrounding region produces approximately 400,000 barrels of crude oil daily and contains extensive refineries. Other important products of the area are natural gas, coal, zinc, and livestock, poultry, cotton, winter wheat, corn, oats, rye, barley, peanuts, and grain sorghums. In addition to the manufacture of oil-well equipment, the principal industries in the city are meat packing, flour milling, cottonseed-oil milling, lumber milling, and the manufacture of cotton textiles, clothing, furniture, corrugated boxes, paint, building materials, machine-shop equipment, farm machinery, airplanes, and glass.

Tulsa is the site of the University of Tulsa, founded at Muskogee in 1894 and moved to Tulsa in 1907, and of Monte Cassino Junior College. The university contains the chief school of petroleum engineering in the U.S. The city is also the site of the International Petroleum Exposition, held biennially, in which various oil-producing nations of the world present exhibits. Tulsa maintains an extensive system of parks, including Mohawk Park, containing Mohawk Lake and zoological gardens in a timbered area covering 2000 acres. Of interest in the city is the large elm which once served as the council tree of the Creek Indians when Tulsa was the headquarters of their nation. The first permanent white settlement on the site of the present city developed after 1882, when the Saint Louis and San Francisco Railroad reached the Indian trading post there which was then called "Tulsi" or "Tulsey Town". Tulsa was incorporated as a town in 1898 and chartered as a city in 1902. Development of the oil industry began in 1901. Pop. (1950) 182,740.

TULUS, one of the civilized or half-civilized Dravidian (q.v.) peoples of southern India. They inhabit the coast region about Mangalore, and their language is closely related to ancient Kanarese (q.v.). See also INDIAN LANGUAGES.

TUMACACORI NATIONAL MONUMENT, a national monument in s. Arizona, established in 1908 to preserve the ruins of an ancient Spanish mission said to have been founded about 1691. The monument covers an area of 10 acres, about 18 miles N.N.W. of Nogales, and contains the ruins of the church, tower, and courtyard walls of the Mission San José de Tumacacori, established by the Jesuit missionary and explorer, Eusebio Francisco Kino. When the Jesuits were expelled from the Spanish possessions in America in 1767 the mission was taken over by Franciscan priests, who remained there until about 1828.

TUMBLEWEED, common name for any plant which habitually spreads its seed by breaking off its roots in the autumn and driving before the wind across the fields or prairies, rolling and tumbling from place to place. Among the best-known tumbleweeds of the United States are the bugseed, *Corispermum hyssopfolium,* the Russian thistle, *Salsola pestifera,* and the tumbling pigweed, *Amaranthus retroflexus.*

TUMOR, in medicine, an abnormal increase in size of an area of tissue or of an organ; a swelling, excluding swellings occurring in the course of simple inflammation. In pathology, a tumor is an overgrowth or hypertrophy, deviating in size and shape from the normal, with an inherent power and method of growth, this growth being independent of the rest of the body. Tumors are distinctly pathological, subserving no useful physiological purposes; they usually grow at the expense of useful tissues and organs. See CANCER; NEOPLASM.

TUNA. See TUNNY.

TUNBRIDGE WELLS, municipal borough of Kent, England, on the Sussex border, about 34 miles S.E. of London. Its chalybeate springs have rendered it a fashionable resort since the 17th century. In 1909 the borough prefixed the word Royal to its name. Pop. (1951) 38,397.

TUNDRA, a level, treeless region of lakes, marshes, and bogs found extensively in the arctic lowlands of North America and Eurasia. Throughout the year, the solidly frozen tundra subsoil prevents the escape of water by seepage; ice and snow which melt during summer produce numerous lakes and ponds. Land areas are usually covered with mosses, lichens, low herbs, and dwarf shrubs during the short summer, which lasts from the middle of June to the middle of August. At this time, too, migratory birds and animals travel into the tundra regions, taking advantage of the seasonal food supply.

TUNG, common name applied to perennial, tropical trees of the genus *Aleurites,* belonging to the Spurge family. The genus, which contains four species, is native to E. Asia and many Pacific Islands, and is cultivated in Europe and the United States. The inconspicuous white flowers, which are arranged in drooping, terminal cymes, have two or three sepals, three petals, eight to twenty stamens, and a solitary pistil. The fruit is a thick-seeded, drupaceous capsule. The candlenut or candle-berry tung tree, *A. moluccana,* also known as Belgaum walnut and *kukui,* is native to the Malay Peninsula. It bears large, spreading leaves and reaches a height of 15 feet. The seeds yield a valuable oil, known as *kekuna, kelum, bankul,* and *tung oil,* which is used in the manufacture of varnish. The Japan wood oil tree *A. cordata,* is native to Japan and Formosa and reaches a height of 30 feet. Oils expressed from its seeds are used in the manufacture of soap and linoleum. The China wood oil tree, *A. fordii,* is native to central Asia and is cultivated in s. United States; it grows to a height of 25 feet. Its seeds are roasted, powdered, and pressed to yield the crude, dark-brown oil called "black tung oil", which is used by the Chinese in varnishes. The pale-yellow "white-tung oil", produced in China for export and now increasingly produced in the United States, is obtained by pressing the seeds while they are cold. It is the most powerful drying agent known for paints and varnishes, and is also used for the waterproofing of paper. The banucalag, *A. trisperma,* is native to the Philippine Islands and reaches a height of 15 feet.

TUNG OIL, WOOD OIL, or NUT OIL. See TUNG.

TUNGSTEN. See WOLFRAM.

TUNGUS or **TUNGUZ,** a Mongoloid people of eastern Siberia, belonging to the Ural-Altaic (q.v.) family of Asian peoples, and numbering in a recent year about 100,000 persons. The majority of the Tungus tribesmen are nomadic hunters of fur-bearing animals; a few have settled on the land and become farmers. In common with most of the Ural-Altaic peoples, the Tungus practice the Shamanist religion (see SHAMANISM), although a minority have adopted Christianity. Exogamy (q.v.) is the prevailing marriage system of the Tungus; polygamy occurs in some groups.

TUNGUSKA, LOWER, the northernmost of the three chief tributaries of the Yenisei River, in Siberia, U.S.S.R. It rises on the Vitim Plateau in Irkutsk, about 200 miles N.W. of Lake Baikal, and within 14 miles of the Lena River, and flows first north, then northwest, joining the Yenisei not far from the Arctic Circle, after a course of 1600 miles. Its upper

course flows between low banks covered with pine forests, but lower down the banks become higher and rocky, and the river penetrates a range of mountains in a series of rapids. The river is navigable about 450 miles, but it is frozen in its lower course for seven months in the year. The ice blocks the upper waters in the spring, causing extensive inundations.

TUNICATA. See ASCIDIANS.

TUNIS (anc. *Tunes*), capital of Tunisia, situated on the western bank of the Lake of Tunis, an inlet of the Gulf of Tunis, the Mediterranean Sea. The principal industries in the city are the manufacture of silk, woolen goods, jewelry, mantles and shawls, leather, soap, wax, and olive oil. Tunis is the commercial center of Tunisia, and carries on an important trade with Europe and Central Africa. The chief exports include, in addition to the above mentioned products, grain, fruits, cattle, fish, ivory, and gold dust. The city occupies an elevated isthmus and is surrounded by walls. The streets of the inner town are narrow and winding, the bazaars are well furnished, and many of the mosques are splendid, particularly the Mosque of Yussuf. One of the finest buildings in the city is the palace of the Bey, the native ruler. The newer French, or foreign quarter, has a European aspect. Tunis contains a Mohammedan university which was founded in 732, and a national museum of arts and antiquities. As Tunes, the city belonged to Carthage. It became important under the Arabs, and at one time during the period of Islamic dominance the city is said to have rivaled Cairo. Pop. (1946) 364,592, including 189,393 Moslems, 66,422 French, 46,629 Italians, 34,193 Jews, and 4312 Maltese.

TUNISIA (Fr. *Tunisie*), a French protectorate in North Africa, bounded on the N. and E. by the Mediterranean Sea, on the s. by Libya, and on the w. by Algeria. The capital, largest city, and chief port is Tunis (q.v.); other important cities include Sfax, Bizerte (qq.v.), and Sousse. The country is mountainous in the N., except on the N.E. coast, which is a low plain about 60 m. wide. The s. half of Tunisia is part of the Sahara Desert. The country is predominantly agricultural, and about a third of the total area is arable. Farming is chiefly done on large estates. Crops include citrus fruits, olives, grapes, figs, wheat, barley, and oats. The principal mineral resource is phosphate rock, and other minerals mined include zinc, lead, iron, salt, and marble. Other industries are commercial fishing, wool weaving, carpet weaving, leather embroidery, and the manufacture of olive oil, pottery, and

Haljaouine Street in the city of Tunis, capital of Tunisia

slippers. The largest population group is composed of Moslem Arabs and Bedouins; the next-largest groups are the French and Italian, and there is a large Jewish community. Communications include 1350 m. of railroad, of which 1053 are state owned, and 5350 m. of roads of all types. The protectorate is administered under the French Foreign office by a minister resident-general and a thirteen-member ministry. Area, about 48,300 sq.m.; pop. (1956 prelim.) 3,782,480.

The ancient history of Tunisia is connected with that of Carthage (q.v.). Later, the area came successively under the control of Rome, the Vandals, and the Byzantine Empire. In the 7th century the territory was conquered by Arabs and, under Mohammedan rule, received its greatest development. For centuries thereafter Tunisia changed masters under successive Arab and Berber dynasties, and became the home of notorious corsairs (q.v.), Moslem pirates who preyed in the Mediterranean. In 1574–75 the Turkish sultan Selim II conquered the country and incorporated it into the Ottoman Empire. Some years later a military re-

volt led the sultan to establish a government headed by a dey, with limited authority. The deys ruled until 1702, when the power was taken by beys, originally tax collectors, who became the most powerful Turkish officers of Tunisia and obtained a hereditary sovereignty. In 1881 France, ostensibly to punish Tunisian pirates, sent an expedition into the country and succeeded in acquiring a protectorate over it in a short time.

The protectorate adhered to the pro-Axis Vichy government after the collapse of France in World War II. Anglo-American forces routed the Axis armies in Tunisia early in 1943, and the protectorate was restored to Free French control. The reigning bey was deposed and replaced by his cousin Sidi Mohammed al-Monsif (1881–   ). Beginning in 1947 Tunisian nationalists, led chiefly by the Neo-Destour Party, became increasingly vocal in their demands for self-government. This development was accompanied by the growth of militant trade unionism. The French introduced a number of governmental reforms in 1950 and 1951, without, however, satisfying Tunisian de-

IN TUNISIA, NORTH AFRICA. *Above: Arabs at a well in a Sahara Desert oasis. Left: Water carrier in the city of Tunis. Below: Street in Kairouan, a city in east-central Tunisia.*

Port of New York Authority

Cutaway drawing showing huge ventilating unit serving the Lincoln Tunnel

mands. During 1952 anti-French riots and terrorist acts occurred in various centers, the French arrested and interned several thousand nationalists, and the Tunisian question, at the insistence of African and Asian states, became an issue in the United Nations. The French, proceeding with their reform program despite the refusal of the bey to sign the necessary decrees, held nationwide elections for district governmental posts in April, 1953. Both the Neo-Destour Party and the Tunisian Trade Union Federation boycotted the

elections. Sporadic nationalist outbreaks occurred during the ensuing year. In September, 1954, French and Tunisian leaders began negotiations on a French plan to grant Tunisia autonomy over its internal affairs.

On April 22, 1955, they concluded an accord embodying the principle of home rule for the protectorate. The accord included provisions for the establishment of a French-Tunisian monetary and customs union and for French control over foreign affairs and defense. The French Parliament completed ratification of

Port of New York Authority

TUNNEL CONSTRUCTION. *Top: Mechanical erector arm places steel segments in position in the Lincoln Tunnel, under Hudson River between N.Y.C. and New Jersey. Bottom: Laying concrete.*

the agreement on Aug. 3; it was approved by the bey on Aug. 27.

TUNNEL, an artificial gallery, passage, or roadway beneath the ground, under the bed of a stream, or through a hill or mountain.

Tunnels through lofty mountains, or below rivers or arms of the sea, are usually worked from the two ends, and from the experience gained in recent years in tunnels of great length, and with improved boring and drilling machinery driven by compressed air, combined with the use of more powerful blasting materials, it is probable that the older methods of constructing tunnels from vertical shafts will be superseded in the future, the comparative progress under equal conditions being in favor of the new machinery by as much as three and four to one.

Modern progress in tunnel boring is due in large measure to the new type of borer, consisting of a ram armed with cutting faces operated by compressed air. Following are some of the world's greatest tunnels.

Arlberg, through the Arl Mountains in the Alps from Lenglen to St. Anton; 6¾ m. (1884).

Baltimore, under Howard Street, Baltimore, Md.; 7000 ft.

Bitterroot, under Bitterroot Range in Montana and Idaho; 10,100 ft.

Busk-Ivanhoe, under the Continental Divide, Colorado; 9600 ft.

Cascade Mountain, in Washington. It is the longest in the Western Hemisphere. 7.79 miles.

Connaught, under Rogers Pass, Selkirk Mountains, Canada; 5 m.

Cumberland, in Tennessee, under Cumberland Mountains; 8000 ft.

Detroit, under the Detroit River; 2668 feet (1910).

Gallitzin, in the Allegheny Mountains at Gallitzin, Pa.; 3600 ft. (1854).

Gunnison, through southwestern Colorado; 6 m. (1909).

Hoosac, in Massachusetts, through Hoosac Mountain; 4¾ m. (1873).

Loetschberg or *Lötschberg,* in the Alps at Oberland, Switzerland; 9¼ m. (1913).

Mont Cenis, under the Col de Fréjus, Italy to France; 8 m. (1871).

Mont d'Or, in the Jura Mountains between France and Switzerland; 3¾ m. (1913).

Mt. Roberts, at Juneau, Alaska; 1⅓ m.

New York City. Eleven rapid-transit tunnels under the East and Harlem rivers; three railroad tunnels under the East and Hudson rivers; and four vehicular tunnels, including the Holland and Lincoln tunnels under the Hudson R., the Queens-Midtown under the East R., and the Brooklyn-Battery tunnel under New York Bay. All are over 1 m. in length.

Otira, in New Zealand; 5½ m.

St. Clair, from Sarnia, Ontario, to Port Huron, Mich., under the St. Clair River; 2 m. (1891).

St. Gotthard, from Goschenen to Airolo, Switzerland, in the Alps; 9⅓ m. (1882).

Severn, in England, from Monmouthshire to Gloucestershire; 4½ m. (1886).

Simplon, in the Alps; 12⅓ m. (1905). Twin tunnel opened (1921).

Spiral. The Canadian Pacific Railway constructed two spiral tubes between Hector and Fields, British Columbia. The westerly tunnel, 3255 ft., was bored through Cathedral Mountain; the easterly tube, 2921 ft., was built through Mt. Ogden.

Trans-Andine, between Valparaiso and Buenos Aires; 5 m. (1910). The tunnel has an average height of 10,512 feet above sea level.

Wasserfluh, between Bunnadern and Lichtensteig, Switzerland, in the Alps; 2 m. (1909). See SAINT GOTTHARD; SIMPLON; see also AQUEDUCT.

TUNNEY, JAMES JOSEPH, known as GENE TUNNEY (1898–   ), American heavyweight boxing champion, born in New York City. He enlisted in the U.S. Marines and was sent to France, where he won the light-heavyweight championship of the American Expeditionary Force. Returning to the U.S., he won the light-heavyweight championship from Battling Levinsky, lost it in 1922 to Harry Greb, and rewon it from Greb in 1923. He succeeded to the heavyweight championship by defeating Jack Dempsey in a ten-round bout at Philadelphia, Sept. 23, 1926. In 1928 he retired from the ring and married; in 1938 he became chairman of the board of the American Distilling Company. He was commissioned (1941) lieutenant commander in the U.S. Naval Reserve, in charge of the athletic and physical fitness program of the U.S. Navy.

TUNNY, or HORSE MACKEREL, common name for any of several large, edible, acanthopterygian fishes of *Thunnus* and related genera belonging to the family Scombridae. Tunnies are found in all warm-temperate seas of Europe, Asia, Africa, and America, and have long been used as food fish because of their coarse, tasty flesh. They are glistening-blue above, gray, spotted with silver, below, and resemble the mackerel (q.v.) in general structure. When caught on a hook they offer great resistance, and are therefore often taken with harpoons. During August and September

U.S. Forest Service

Black tupelo, or black gum, tree

tunnies approach the coastal areas to spawn, returning to deep water at the beginning of winter. The largest and most prized tunny, *T. thunnus,* commonly known as the "great tunny", reaches a length of 10 feet and weighs up to 1500 pounds. It is native to the Mediterranean Sea. *T. saliens,* the tunny more commonly known as "tuna", is similar to the great tunny, and is found in the Pacific waters off California. The Atlantic tuna, *Neothunnus allisoni,* is caught in large numbers near Florida and Rhode Island. *Auxis thozard* and *A. rockei,* found in the South Seas and the North Atlantic, respectively, are both commonly known as "frigate mackerel" or *bonito,* and rarely exceed 18 inches in length. The little tunny, *Gymnosarda alleterata,* and the long-finned tunny, or albacore, *Germo alalunga,* are native to the Mediterranean and Atlantic, and attain a length of 2 feet. In 1953, about 313,-000,000 pounds of tunny, mainly tuna, were caught off the Atlantic and Pacific coasts of the United States and Alaska. Of this amount, approximately 188,704,000 pounds were used for canning. The liver of most tunnies yields an oil which is often employed in the processing of leather.

TUNSTALL. See STOKE ON TRENT.

TUPELO, or GUM TREE, common name applied to large, deciduous trees of the genus *Nyssa* belonging to the Heath family. The genus, which contains five species, is native to swamplands of North America and Asia, and is cultivated in many areas for its handsome foliage and brilliant autumn colors. The small, greenish-white flowers, arranged in slender, clustered peduncles, have a five-parted calyx, five petals, and either five to twelve stamens or a solitary pistil. The fruit is a blue or purple drupe. The sour gum, black gum, or pepperidge, *N. sylvatica,* native to E. United States and E. Canada, grows to a height of 60 to 100 feet. The cotton gum, *N. aquatica,* native to swamplands of S. United States, grows 60 to 90 feet high. Tupelo wood is used in the manufacture of boxes, crates, baskets, barrel staves, and railroad ties. See LIQUIDAMBAR.

TUPIAN STOCK, or TUPI-GUARANI, the most widespread and important linguistic stock of South America. When the Portuguese took possession of Brazil the Tupian tribes held the greater portion of the territory from the Río de la Plata (Paraguay or Paraná) on the south to the Amazon on the north, and extended far inland. The two principal tribes were the Tupi, situated around the mouth of the Amazon, and the Guarani, on the Lower Paraguay. Of numerous other cognate tribes, the most important were the Chiriguano, Guarayo, Mundurucu, Mura, and Omagua. Many of the eastern tribes were gathered into missions by the Jesuits at an early period, the Guarani missions in particular at one time containing more than 300,000 Indians. Through slave-hunting raids and the subsequent expulsion of the Jesuits the missions were broken up, the more civilized Indians remaining to be incorporated with the Spanish settlements, while others retired into the unexplored western wilderness. In general culture the Tupian tribes as a rule were superior to other aborigines of Brazil, though much inferior to the Quechua of Peru. They practiced agriculture to some extent, raising corn, manioc, and tobacco, and were expert stone-workers, hammock weavers, and makers of pottery. They kept monkeys and peccaries for food, but their main dependence was upon hunting and fishing. Their houses were light structures, usually communal, and most of the natives wore no clothing. With the exception of the Omagua, who had acquired considerable of the Quechua culture, they had no metals. The Tupian languages have been extensively cultivated, the Guarani having been adopted by the Jesuits for use in all the missions of the Paraguay, while the Tupi, in its corrupted form, is still the trade medium throughout the Amazon region. See GUARANI.

TUPPER, SIR CHARLES (1821–1915), Canadian statesman, born in Nova Scotia. A member of the Nova Scotian parliament for thirty years, he was premier at the Confederation (1867) and president of the privy council (1870–72). Appointed high commissioner for Canada in England (1883–87, 1888–96), he was minister of finance (1887–88), one of the British plenipotentiaries on the Fishery Commission, Washington (1887–88), and a plenipotentiary for negotiating a treaty between France and Canada (1893). Tupper became prime minister of Canada (1896). He died in England.

TURA, COSIMO (about 1430–95), Italian painter of the early Renaissance, the founder and most important master of the Ferrarese School. He was born in Ferrara, studied at Squarcione's school in Padua, and was influenced by Donatello and the early works of Mantegna. His powerful, realistic figures are hard in color, but well drawn and modeled. He delighted in the symbolic and the grotesque. His most important paintings include the impressive "Pietà" (Museo Civico, Venice); "Annunciation" in the cathedral at Ferrara; "Dead Christ Upheld by Angels" (Vienna); "Christ on the Cross" (Brera, Milan); and the altarpiece "Madonna with Saints" (Berlin Museum). Panels of saints are in Dresden, London, in the Uffizi (Florence), and in Modena and Paris.

TURACOU. See TOURACO.

TURBERVILLE or **TUBERVILLE,** GEORGE (about 1540–about 1610), English poet, born in Whitchurch, in Dorsetshire, and educated at New College, Oxford University. Leaving Oxford in 1562 without a degree, he studied law at one of the inns of court in London. In 1568 he accompanied Thomas Randolph, a special ambassador of the queen, to Russia, where he wrote verses describing the manners of the people. Of his later life nothing is known. Turberville occupies an interesting place in English literature as a translator from the Latin and the Italian and as one of the first among English poets to make use of the ottava rima and blank verse (q.v.). Chief among his works are *Epitaphs, Epigrams, Songs, and Sonnets* (1567); *The Booke of Faulconrie, or Hawking,* with which is bound *The Noble Art of Venerie, or Hunting,* generally ascribed to Turberville (1575; enlarged 1611); *Tragical Tales,* from the Italian, with original epitaphs and sonnets (1587); and *The Herocycall Epistles of Ovidius in English* (1567). To Turberville have been doubtfully ascribed two English versions of the Italian poet Torquato Tasso's *Jerusalem Delivered.*

TURBINE, a rotary motor consisting of a series of vanes or buckets rotating on a spindle in a casing having suitable openings for the admission and escape of water which serves as the motive fluid.

Unlike the ordinary type of water wheel, the turbine relies for its efficiency upon the kinetic energy and even distribution of the water upon the vanes rather than on the pressure of the water supply. Turbines are divided into two general classes: *impulse turbines* (in which rotation is effected by the direct action of the water impinging upon the vanes or buckets, as in the Pelton wheel), and *reaction turbines* (in which the water enters axially and is discharged tangentially through buckets that move by its reaction, as in the Fourneyron turbine). Turbines propelled by steam admit of the same general classification.

Many modern turbines take the names of their inventors; as, the *Curtis turbine* (an impulse turbine having usually a vertical axis and diaphragms with communicating nozzles between the rotating elements. The steam supply is admitted through expanding nozzles and is regulated by valves which are actuated by cams and levers under the control of a governor). See STEAM AND STEAM ENGINEERING: *Steam Turbines.*

TURBOJET, a form of aircraft jet-combustion engine which relies for its propulsive force upon the expansion of compressed gases. In a typical turbojet, air is admitted to the front of the engine cowling by the forward motion of the engine through the air. It is led into a rotary compressor of either the turbine or axial-flow type and its pressure is increased. From the compressor the air is forced to a set of combustion chambers in which it is mixed with fuel and burned. The gases from the combustion of the fuel, which is usually kerosene, expand partially in exhaust pipes behind the combustion chamber and drive the compressor. The remaining energy, in the form of kinetic energy of velocity and positive pressure, is used to drive the engine by expanding the gas through a suitably shaped nozzle in the rear. The turbine used in a turbojet engine of conventional design does not contribute to the thrust of the engine, as it merely operates the compressor. However, in the type of engine known as the *turboprop,* part of the turbine energy is employed to drive an air propeller

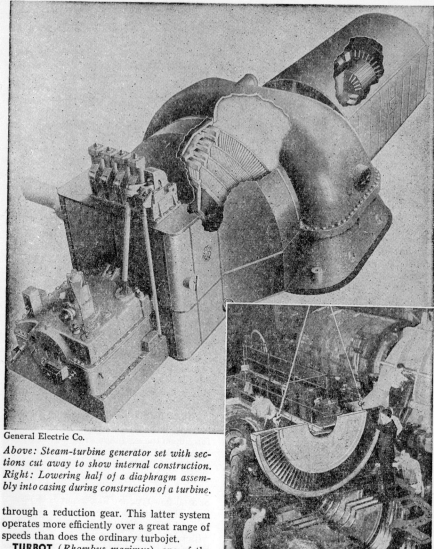

General Electric Co.

Above: Steam-turbine generator set with sections cut away to show internal construction. Right: Lowering half of a diaphragm assembly into casing during construction of a turbine.

through a reduction gear. This latter system operates more efficiently over a great range of speeds than does the ordinary turbojet.

TURBOT (*Rhombus maximus*), one of the Pleuronectidae or flatfishes (q.v.). The turbot is distinguished from the brill by the fact that it has no scales, but on the upper side bony plates in the skin from which blunt tubercles project; it is also broader in proportion than the brill. The adult turbot is about 2 ft. long, and it has been known to reach a weight of more than 30 lbs.

TURENNE, HENRI DE LA TOUR D'AUVERGNE, VICOMTE DE (1611–75), French general, grandson of William (I) of Orange, born in Sedan. For his services in the Thirty Years' War he was made a marshal of France (1644). In the civil wars of the Fronde Turenne joined the party of the *frondeurs*, but after being defeated at Rethel (1650) he withdrew to Flanders, returning on Mazarin's retirement. On the minister's return Turenne joined his party, while Condé deserted to the *frondeurs*, and Turenne triumphed over his former chief at Gien and the Faubourg St. Antoine (1652), and ultimately forced him to retire from France. Afterward Turenne subdued the revolted cities, crossed the northern frontier, and conquered much of the Spanish Netherlands. His defeat of Condé at the Dunes (1658), with the help of Cromwell's 6000, closed their long struggle. In 1660 Turenne was created marshal general of France. Turenne fought also in Holland (1672) and Germany. He was killed by a cannon ball at Sasbach.

TURGENEV, IVAN SERGEEVITCH (1818–83), Russian novelist and short-story writer, born in Orel, and educated at the University of St. Petersburg (now Leningrad). Upon graduation Turgenev went abroad to continue his studies at Berlin, Germany; he returned to St. Petersburg in 1840. Soon thereafter he left his parents' home in protest against his mother's harsh treatment of the serfs on the family estate. To support himself he obtained a position as a government clerk, but presently relinquished it to devote all his time to writing. His first important work was *Memoirs of a Sportsman* (1847–51), a volume of prose sketches pervaded by a liberal spirit and a sincere compassion for the oppressed Russian peasantry. When Turgenev's mother died in 1850, he immediately set free all the serfs on his family estate. A large inheritance made him financially independent, and five years later he left Russia to live abroad, returning to his homeland only for a few brief visits. He died at his villa in Bougival, near Paris, and was buried at St. Petersburg.

In addition to *Memoirs of a Sportsman,* Turgenev is best remembered for the play *A Month in the Country* (1850), which served as a model for the dramas of the Russian author Anton Pavlovitch Chekhov (q.v.); the short stories *Asya* (1858) and *First Love* (1860); and the novels *A House of Gentlefolk* (1858), *On the Eve* (1860), *Fathers and Sons* (1862), *Smoke* (1867), *Virgin Soil* (1876), *A Lear of the Steppes* (1880), and *Clara Milich* (1882). In *Fathers and Sons* Turgenev introduced the term *nihilist* as a designation for the young student Bazarov, employing the word to signify "a man who looks at everything from a critical point of view". Throughout his literary career Turgenev was a leading advocate of the Westernization of Russian manners and institutions, in opposition to such of his countrymen as the novelist Fedor Mikhailovich Dostoevski (q.v.), who profoundly distrusted the values of Western civilization and exhorted his countrymen to shun Western culture and return to Byzantine and Old Russian ideals.

TURGOT, ANNE ROBERT JACQUES, BARON DE L'AULNE (1727–81), French economist and statesman, born in Paris, and educated at the University of Paris. He was trained for the Church, but at the age of twenty-three abandoned the priestly calling for the government service. After holding several minor posts in the parlement, or legislature, of Paris, he was appointed in 1761 intendant, or chief executive officer, of the district of Limoges. He had earlier become an exponent of the economic theories advanced by François Quesnay, Jean de Gournay (qq.v.), and other leaders of the physiocratic school of economists (see ECONOMICS: *History*), and attempted to apply these theories in administering the finances of Limoges. Among the reforms instituted by Turgot was the substitution of a money tax for the *corvée,* under which the people of the district had formerly been required to contribute free labor to the construction and maintenance of roads. He also carried out a survey of the quantity, ownership, and value of real estate in the district, in order to provide a sound basis for the computation of tax assessments on land and other property, and secured a substantial reduction in the amount of taxes contributed by Limoges to the national government.

Turgot wrote several works dealing with economic theory and practice during his in-

Ivan Sergeevitch Turgenev

tendancy. Among these are *Mémoire sur les Prêts à Intérêt* (1769), one of the first scientific analyses of the practice of usury; and *Lettres sur la Liberté du Commerce des Grains* (1770), a series of letters addressed to the controller general of finance, advocating freedom of trade in grain among the provinces of France. His most significant work, however, is *Réflexions sur la Formation et la Distribution des Richesses* (1766), a treatise regarded by many scholars as one of the foundations of the science of political economy. In this work Turgot asserted that the sole source of wealth is land, and that therefore only agricultural produce should be taxed. Like the other physiocrats, he insisted upon the complete freedom of commerce and industry from governmental interference.

In July, 1774, Turgot was appointed minister of marine under King Louis XVI, and shortly thereafter he became controller general of finance. He immediately instituted a policy of strict economy in government expenditures, and drafted thoroughgoing reforms of the national system of taxation. Early in 1776 he submitted his famous "Six Edicts" to the Royal Council, urging among other reforms the complete abolition of the *corvée*, the suppression of commercial monopolies in the interest of free trade, and the taxation of the nobility. His advocacy of these measures incurred the open hostility of many powerful nobles, wealthy entrepreneurs, and of Queen Marie Antoinette, who particularly resented his opposition to her granting of lucrative sinecures, estates, and similar favors to various privileged individuals. Turgot was compelled to resign in May, 1776. He devoted the remainder of his life to scientific and literary studies, and in 1777 was chosen vice-president of the Académie des Inscriptions et Belles-Lettres.

TURIN (It. *Torino*), city of N. Italy, formerly capital of Piedmont, and for a time of the kingdom of Italy. It is situated near the confluence of the Po and the Dora Riparia, 80 miles N.w. of Genoa. Among the numerous churches the principal are the cathedral of San Giovanni, originally built in the 7th century, and San Filippo. On the summit of a hill near the town is La Suporga, a basilica, raised by Victor Amadeus to fulfill a vow, and now the mausoleum of the House of Savoy. Among the "palaces" are the royal palace, designed by Castellamonte, and the Carignano Palace. The University of Turin was founded in 1405.

The principal products manufactured in Turin are cotton, woolen, and silk fabrics, carpets, velvet hats, paper, iron, pottery, leather, gloves, bijouterie, furniture, wax matches, tobacco, and liqueurs. Pop. (1950) 730,570.

Turin was originally inhabited by the Taurini, a tribe of Ligurians. It became a Roman colony under Augustus. On the fall of the empire it passed to the Lombards, and became the capital of one of the thirty Lombard duchies. Charlemagne made it the residence of the Duke of Susa, whose line ruled till 1060, when the House of Savoy succeeded it. During the 16th and 17th centuries it was alternately under France and Savoy. In 1815 restored to the House of Savoy, it was the capital of Sardinia till 1860, and from 1860 to 1865 the capital of the kingdom of Italy.

TURIN, UNIVERSITY OF, an Italian university founded in 1405 by Louis of Savoy. It became at once a refuge for the professors at the universities of Pavia and Piacenza, then suffering from civil wars. Toward the latter part of the 15th century it shared the general reputation and prosperity of the Italian universities of that period. It comprised two colleges, one founded in 1457 and one in 1482. The university was reorganized in 1632, and in 1713 the present building was erected. The university has faculties of law, medicine and surgery, philosophy and letters, and physical, natural, and mathematical sciences, and a school of pharmacy.

TURKESTAN, in physical geography, a region of Central Asia, including Russian Turkestan, Eastern or Chinese Turkestan, and Afghan Turkestan. In contemporary political geography Russian Turkestan comprises part of the Kazakh, Kirghiz, Tadzhik, Turkmen, and Uzbek (qq.v.) soviet socialist republics in Soviet Central Asia; Eastern Turkestan forms the s. and central parts of the Chinese province of Sinkiang (q.v.); and Afghan Turkestan is included in the province of Mazar, in N. Afghanistan.

The history of Eastern Turkestan can be traced to the late 2nd century B.C., when the Chinese brought the region under their rule. It was conquered by Tibet in the 8th century, and in succeeding centuries was subdued by various other Asiatic peoples, including the Mongol forces of Genghis Khan in the 13th century. From about the 19th century Mohammedanism has been the prevailing religion. Eastern Turkestan was reconquered by China in the 18th century; in the 19th century occurred a series of Mohammedan uprisings against Chinese rule, none of which was permanently successful. The region was incorporated in the province of Sinkiang when that province was created by the Chinese government in 1881.

The Afghan portion of Turkestan was first brought under Afghan control in the 18th century, when it was made a part of the Afghan kingdom established in 1747 by Ahmad Shah Durrani. Following the death of Ahmad Shah's son, Timur Shah, in 1793, the region was divided among various Uzbek chiefs, who were dominated by the khanate of Bokhara. Afghan sovereignty was re-established in the middle of the 19th century by Dost Mohammed Khan, ruler of Afghanistan.

Incursions were made into the w. part of Turkestan by the Russians as early as the 16th century, but the conquest of present Russian Turkestan was not complete until the latter part of the 19th century, when Tashkent, Samarkand, and other territories were occupied and the emirate of Bokhara and the khanate of Khiva were subjected to Russian suzerainty. All of Russian Turkestan, or Russian Central Asia, as it became known, except the khanate and the emirate, were administered until 1917 by the governor general of Turkestan. In 1887 the boundary between Russian and Afghan Turkestan was demarcated by the Russo-Afghan Boundary Commission. During the Russian Revolution, Bolshevik authority was established in Russian Central Asia. In 1920 the khan of Khiva and the emir of Bokhara were deposed, and in both the khanate and the emirate soviet republics were established. In the following year the former governor-generalship of Turkestan became an autonomous soviet socialist republic in the Russian S.F.S.R. The territories in the Bokhara and Khiva soviet republics and in the Turkestan A.S.S.R. were redistributed in 1924 to form the Uzbek, Turkmen, and Tajik soviet socialist republics and several autonomous regions, among them Kirghizia, which in 1936 became the Kirghiz S.S.R. At that time also the districts of the Turkestan A.S.S.R. which were populated by Kazaks were incorporated in the Kazak S.S.R.

TURKEY, large American game bird of the genus *Meleagris,* belonging to the Pheasant family. The bird is characterized by a naked head, erectile wattles on the head and neck, and hind toes elevated above the front toes. In the male, the hind toes are equipped with spurs, and the tail feathers can be raised to form a vertical fan. The genus includes two species, native to North and Central America. Like the other members of the Pheasant family, turkeys are polygamous in their mating habits. The cocks fight fiercely among themselves for access to the hens. Wild turkeys build their nests of dried leaves and grasses, in concealed places on the ground. Nine to eighteen creamy-white eggs with red-brown speckles are laid in a clutch.

The common turkey, *Meleagris gallopavo,* native to the plateaus of N. Mexico and E. United States, is the species from which all domesticated breeds have been developed. The bird has buff-colored feathers on the tips of the wing coverts and on the tail. The male possesses a prominent tuft of bristles resembling a beard projecting downward from its chest. This turkey is still found in the wild state in the thickly wooded mountainous portions of its range. The common turkey was originally domesticated in Mexico by the Indians and became known to Europeans in the year 1498 when Mexico was discovered. It was brought into Europe early in the 16th century. Since that time turkeys have been extensively raised because of the excellent quality of their meat and eggs. Some of the most common breeds of turkey in the United States are the Bronze, Narragansett, White Holland, and Bourbon Red. About 45,000,000 turkeys are raised each year, with California, Texas, and Minnesota leading in production.

The ocellated turkey, *M. ocellata,* is an ornate bird native to Guatemala, the Mexican State of Yucatan, and British Honduras. The tail feathers of the bird are ornamented with green-blue eye spots and have an iridescent purple cast. The body feathers have a metallic golden, bronze-green sheen. The skin of the head and neck is blue, covered with red, wartlike growths.

TURKEY (Turk. *Türkiye Cümhuriyeti*), an independent republic, comprising territory in both Europe and Asia. The European territory, often called Turkey in Europe, is approximately one thirtieth the size of the Asiatic territory, frequently designated Turkey in Asia and constituting the greater part of the region known as Asia Minor. Turkey in Europe, with an area of 9254 sq.m., is separated from Turkey in Asia, with an area of 285,162 sq.m., by the Dardanelles, the Sea of Marmara, and the Bosporus. Considered as a single political entity, Turkey is bounded on the E. by the Armenian Soviet Socialist Republic of the Soviet Union and by Iran; on the S. by Iraq, Syria, and the Mediterranean Sea; on the W. by the Ægean Sea, Greece, and Bulgaria; and on the N. by Bulgaria, the Black Sea, and the Georgian S.S.R. The pos-

N.Y. Zool. Soc.; U.S.D.A., Agric. Res. Admin.
Above: The common turkey (Meleagris gallo-pavo), the species from which all domesticated breeds have been developed. Left: A small white turkey, bred to meet demand of con-sumers. This bird weighs about one-third less than normal-size turkeys.

sessions of Turkey include the islands of Imroz Adaya and Bozcaada in the Ægean Sea. Turkey is composed of sixty-three major political divisions known as ils. The ils are Afyon Karahisar, Ağri, Amasya, Ankara, Antalya, Aydin, Balikesir, Bilecik, Bingöl, Bitlis, Bolu, Burdur, Bursa, Çanak-kale, Çankiri, Çoruh, Čorum, Denizli, Diyar-bekir, Edirne, Elâziz, Erzincan, Erzurum, Es-kişehir, Gaziantep, Giresun, Gümüşane,

Hakâri, Hatay, İçel, İsparta, İstanbul, İzmir, Kars, Kastamonu, Kayseri, Kirklareli, Kirşehir, Kocaeli, Konya, Kütahya, Malatya, Manisa, Maraş, Mardin, Muğla, Muş, Niğde, Ordu, Rize, Samsun, Seyhan, Siirt, Sinop, Sivas, Tekirdağ, Tokat, Trabzon, Tunceli, Urfa, Van, Yozgat, and Zonguldak. The capital of Turkey is Ankara (q.v.) ; other important cities are İstanbul, İzmir, Adana, Bursa, Eskişehir, Gaziantep, Kayseri, Konya, and Erzurum (qq.v.). The total land area of Turkey is 296,185 sq.m.; pop. (1956 est.) 24,797,000.

Turkey in Europe, an area approximately the size of the State of New Hampshire, consists for the most part of gently undulating moorland, which rises from the Ægean and Marmara coasts in the s. and ascends to the foothills of the Istranja Dagh mountain range which skirts the Black Sea in the n. The better part of this region is drained by the Maritsa R. (q.v.) and its affluents. Turkey in Asia, roughly rectangular in shape and having an area comparable to that of the State of Texas, constitutes the western prolongation of the high tableland of Armenia. The interior consists of a broad, barren plateau, attaining an average altitude of about 3000 ft. and interspersed with treeless steppes, marshes, and lakes. The region contains several volcanic mountains, of which Erjias Dagh, with two craters, is the highest peak in Asia Minor, rising some 10,000 ft. above the plain of Kaisaria, which has itself an elevation of between 2000 and 3000 ft. The plateau is bounded on the n. and s. by parallel ranges of mountains. On the n. the Pontic chain, extending along the Black Sea from the frontier of the U.S.S.R. to the Bosporus, rises precipitously from the water except where small littoral tracts have been created by the Kizil Irmak, Yesil Irmak, and Sakarya rivers. On the s. the towering peaks of the Taurus range skirt the Mediterranean Sea, shutting in the fertile plains of Antalya and Cilicia (q.v.). The Taurus mountains are intersected by a number of natural passes, the most important one being the Gölek-Boghaz, or Cilician Gates, thirty miles n. of Tarsus (q.v.). For centuries the Gölek-Boghaz served as the pathway of armies, traders, and travelers, and as the principal route to and from the Euphrates valley. The western border of Turkey in Asia is broken up by numerous valleys opening upon the Ægean Sea through the highlands of the ancient Caria, Lydia, and Mysia (qq.v.). The coast is fringed by the multitudinous islands of the Ægean. The

chief rivers of Asiatic Turkey, in addition to those previously mentioned, are the Gediz, the Menderes, and the Küchük Menderes rivers, which empty into the Ægean Sea, and the Ceyhan, Göksu, and Seyhan rivers, which flow into the Mediterranean Sea. None of these streams is commercially navigable. The largest lakes of Turkey, all of which are salt, are Eğridir, Tuz Gölü, and Van; freshwater lakes include Apulyont, Iznik, and Manyas Gölü.

The meteorological conditions of Turkey exhibit great variation. Coastwise, from the town of Antioch on the s. to the Dardanelles on the w., the climate is Mediterranean in character, with dry summers and rainy winters. From the Dardanelles northward to the Bosporus the prevailing weather gradually verges into the type characterized by consistently heavy rainfall the year round. The region beyond Trabzon on the Black Sea, protected from severe northern winds by the massive Pontic range, is fit for the cultivation of tea and semitropical fruits. The central plateau, virtually destitute of water and trees, has hot summers and cold winters. Along the eastern plateau the climate is transitional from the steppe to the alpine type.

The natural resources of Turkey are rich, though as yet but little exploited. Almost 12% of the total land area of Turkey is forested; of this area approximately 88% is state-owned, 6% is privately owned, and the remaining 6% is apportioned among communes and religious or charitable establishments. A new forest law, enacted on February 8, 1937, makes provision for state control of all forest lands, including those privately owned. This law includes measures for reforestation and for the protection of forests against fire, insects, and marauders, and stipulates penalties for violation of any of its clauses. The most densely forested ils of Turkey are Aydin, Balikesir, Bolu, Bursa, Kastamonu, Konya, and Trabzon. The commonest trees are the beech, cedar, oak, and pine, with pines constituting 37% and oaks 14% of the total forest reserves. Turkey's mineral deposits include antimony, asphalt, chrome, coal, copper, emery, lignite, magnesite, manganese ore, meerschaum, mercury, and sulfur. Of these minerals, coal, copper, and meerschaum are the most important. The fisheries of Turkey constitute another important feature of the country's economy. Large quantities of anchovy, mullet, sturgeon, swordfish, and tunny pass annually from the Black Sea through the Bosporus, the relatively narrow confines of which afford excellent fishing. Lobsters, mussels, oysters, and shrimp are taken along the shores of the Sea of Marmara.

Agriculture, which occupies 20% of the total land area and engages approximately 65% of the population, is the chief industry of Turkey. Although farming methods are still comparatively primitive, the Turkish government has made large appropriations for the development of arable areas, the establishment of agricultural training schools and experiment stations, and the introduction of modern agricultural techniques. Tobacco, the most valuable crop, is raised in both European and Asiatic Turkey. The finest quality tobacco is cultivated near Samsun on the Black Sea coast; other important tobacco-producing regions are Bafra, Izmir, Sinop, and Trabzon. Opium poppies are cultivated in Afyon Karahisar and Konya, figs in Izmir, nuts in the wooded foothills of the Pontic mountains, and olives in the Bursa district and along the Ionian littoral. Cotton is grown for the most part in s. Asia Minor. Cereals, including barley, corn, oats, rice, rye, and wheat, come chiefly from Ankara, Kastamonu, Konya, and Sivas. Other agricultural products are fruits, gums, licorice root, linseed, sesame, and sugar cane. Livestock in Turkey in a recent year included 23,083,000 sheep, 14,577,000 ordinary goats, 3,966,000 mohair goats, 10,-216,000 cattle, 1,633,000 asses, 1,140,000 horses, 932,000 buffaloes, 110,000 camels, and 109,000 mules. Turkish machine industry, though still largely undeveloped, has been given considerable impetus through a series of state-sponsored five-year plans resulting in the establishment of seven staple industries, namely, iron and steel, textiles, mining, paper, cement, glass, and sugar. In a recent year Turkey had over one thousand industrial establishments. The country's unexploited hydroelectric power is estimated to be approximately 2.2 million kilowatts.

Turkey's post-World War II balance of trade has been unfavorable, exhibiting a preponderance of imports over exports. Exports in a recent year, valued at about $2,462,000,-000 were chiefly to Germany, the United States, the United Kingdom, and Italy, and included cotton, tobacco, fruits and nuts, and nonferrous metals and manufactures. Imports, valued at about $3,150,000,000, were principally from Germany, the United Kingdom, the United States, and France, and included machines and vehicles, iron and steel and manufactures, cotton yarn and fabrics, and petroleum. About 25 percent of both the import and the export trade of Turkey is carried on with Germany.

In a recent year the gross tonnage of the Turkish merchant marine exceeded 465,000, and over 3500 foreign-flag vessels totaling about 4,300,000 tons entered and cleared the ports of Turkey, chiefly at İçel, İstanbul, İzmir, and Samsun. The country's motorable roads covered about 13,600 m., of which approximately 9100 m. were in good condition and the remainder in need of repair. The combined railroad mileage of both European and Asiatic Turkey totaled about 4900 m. A regular Turkish air service links Ankara with İstanbul and Seyhan.

The population of Turkey is composed predominantly of native Turks, with minority elements of Circassians, Kurds (qq.v.), and Lazes. The principal established foreign groups include Greeks, Italians, Iranians, Bulgarians, Germans, French, and Hungarians. The Turkish language is spoken by the vast majority of the inhabitants; minority tongues include Arabic, Armenian, Bulgarian, Circassian, and Greek. Turkish has largely been substituted for Arabic as the liturgical language of Mohammedan worship. On April 10, 1928, a law of the Turkish Grand National Assembly disestablished Islam (q.v.) as the state religion of Turkey. Nevertheless, the Mohammedan faith is professed by more than 98 percent of the population. Other religious denominations represented are the Orthodox Church, Armenian Church, and Roman Catholic Church, Uniates of the Eastern Rite (see EASTERN RITE, CHURCHES OF THE), and the Jewish Synagogue. A Turkish law of December, 1934, applicable to both native and foreign clergy, prohibits the wearing of clerical attire except in places of worship and on the occasion of divine service.

The rate of literacy in Turkey is exceedingly low; in a recent year, only 44 percent of the male and 17 percent of the female population were able to read or write. Primary education is theoretically mandatory for all children between the ages of seven and sixteen. Such instruction is furnished in state-operated schools, in private schools, and, subject to periodic examinations, in the home. State schools, comprehending primary, secondary, and college preparatory schools, in addition to various lycées or special secondary schools, are under the direct supervision of the Ministry of Public Instruction. Other institutions of learning include normal schools, advanced technical schools, and professional schools. The University of İstanbul was founded in

IN ISTANBUL, TURKEY. *Above: Galata Bridge crossing the Golden Horn. The older section of the city is seen in background. Right: A ferry unloading passengers at Galata Bridge.*

1900 and reorganized in 1933; the University of Ankara was founded in 1935. Schools maintained by non-Moslem communities are also under the authority of the Ministry of Public Instruction. On Dec. 1, 1928, a Turkish law became effective prescribing the substitution of Latin for Arabic Letters; a subsequent law (Jan. 1, 1929) prohibits the publication of Turkish books in Arabic characters.

In January, 1921, the Turkish Grand National Assembly enacted a law vesting complete sovereignty in the people and assigning to the National Assembly both executive and legislative power. Three years later, in consequence of new legislation, Turkey was proclaimed a republic. According to the Turkish constitution, the chief governmental body is the National Assembly, composed of 485 members, or deputies, elected by popular vote for a period of four years. The National Assembly exercises executive power through a president, elected from the deputies of the Assembly, and a council of ministers, appointed by the president. The president holds office for the duration of the Assembly electing him. Turkish citizens of both sexes are eligible to vote at the age of twenty-two and to stand for election to the National Assembly at the age of thirty. The chief political party in Turkey is the Republican People's Party; the principles of this party, namely, evolutionism (modification of the structure and functions of the government as necessitated by changing circumstances), laicism (separation of the religious establishment and the state), nationalism, and statism (state ownership and control of the basic industries and utilities), were incorporated into the constitution of the Turkish republic on February 5, 1937. Prior to the election of July, 1946, permission was granted by the government for the organization of a number of other political parties, the most important one being the Democratic Party. For administrative purposes the sixty-three ils are divided into ilces, which in turn are subdivided into bucaks. The bucak is an autonomous commune possessing an elective council vested with the authority to administer all matters not coming under the jurisdiction of the state.

History. For the history of Turkey prior to the establishment of the Ottoman power, the reader is referred to the history section of the article on ASIA MINOR. In the first half of the 13th century, a small body of Mohammedan Turks, driven before the conquering Mongol (see MONGOLS) hordes under Genghis Khan, moved westward from their home in Iran and made their way into Asia Minor. Under the leadership of their chieftain, Ertogrul (d. 1288), they entered the service of Ala-ad-Din, the Sultan of Iconium (Konia), the last remnant of the great empire established by the Seljuk (see SELJUKS) Turks in western Asia. Ala-ad-Din granted his Turkish retainers some land in Phrygia, whence Osman, the son of Ertogrul, extended the power of his tribe (to which his name became thenceforth attached) by numerous conquests in Asia Minor. Orkhan (1279–1359), the son and successor of Osman, and the true organizer of the Ottoman power, carried on the aggressive policy of his father. He established his residence at Brusa (Bursa), the ancient capital of Bithynia, which he had annexed from the Byzantine Empire, and gained a foothold in Europe by taking the *Chersonesus Thracica* (Gallipoli Peninsula) in 1354. From the conquered Christian peoples of Europe Orkhan exacted a tribute of male children, who, reared as Mohammedans and trained under rigid military discipline, formed the nucleus of the highly efficient fighting force known as the Janizaries (q.v.).

Orkhan was succeeded by Murad I, under whom the Ottoman power in Europe was expanded and consolidated. At this time, side by side with the declining Byzantine Empire, stood the expanding Kingdom of Serbia. Eastward to the Black Sea, and s. of the Danube R., the Czar of Bulgaria held sway, and beyond the Danube the principalities of Moldavia (q.v.) and Walachia were each struggling toward independent existence. The Italian city states of Venice and Genoa, meanwhile, had extended their respective dominions into the E. Mediterranean region. In 1361 Murad I conquered Adrianople (Edirne) in s.E. Europe, and made it his capital. The Turks then began systematically to reduce the decadent Byzantine Empire. Murad I greatly enlarged the Turkish possessions in Asia Minor, and in 1389 broke the power of Serbia in the fierce battle of Kosovo. The sultan was slain in this battle, however, and was succeeded by his son Bajazet I. During his reign, Bajazet conquered Bulgaria, warred against Walachia, and, at Nicopolis (Nikopol), Bulgaria, in 1396, inflicted a crushing defeat upon a combined Christian army of French, Hungarians, and Poles under the command of Sigismund, King of Hungary (later Holy Roman Emperor). In 1402 Bajazet was defeated and taken captive near Angora (Ankara) by the invading Mongol warrior Tamerlane (q.v.).

On the fall of the Turkish sultan, a struggle for dominion ensued among his sons which lasted for a decade. At length, in 1413, the youngest son, Mohammed I (1387–1421), gained undisputed possession of the whole Ottoman Empire. Murad II extended the Turkish dominion over Macedonia, conquered part of Greece, waged a series of wars with the Hungarians, and attacked the Albanians, although without success. The most notable event of his reign was his victory over the Hungarians led by Ladislas III (1424–47) and János Hunyadi at Varna in 1444. Mohammed II, son of Murad II, immediately upon his accession, prepared to conquer Constantinople (Istanbul). The city fell on May 29, 1453, thus bringing the Byzantine Empire to an end. The capital of the Ottoman Empire was then transferred from Adrianople to Constantinople. In 1456 Mohammed II laid siege to Belgrade, the capture of which would greatly have facilitated his subjugation of Hungary, but the siege was lifted by the memorable victory of Hunyadi. A few years later, however, Serbia was at last annexed to the Turkish dominions and Bosnia was defeated. The Empire of Trebizond, an offshoot of the defunct Byzantine Empire, was conquered in 1461, about which time the conquest of the Peloponnesus was likewise effected. In 1470 the large Greek island of Negropont (Eubœa) was taken from Venice, and in 1475 the Tatar Khan of the Crimea was forced into vassalage to the Ottoman sultan. Albania, which under the heroic leadership of the Albanian chieftain and national hero Scanderbeg had long held out against the Turks, was subjugated. A Turkish attack against the Mediterranean island of Rhodes was successfully repulsed by the Knights of St. John of Jerusalem, a Christian military and religious order. At this time the Turks obtained a temporary foothold in Italy by the conquest of Otranto at the s.e. extremity of the Italian Peninsula.

The reign of Bajazet II, the successor of Mohammed II, was uneventful, but under Selim I the Ottoman conquests were extended both eastward and southward. Selim annexed parts of Persia (1515), conquered Syria (1516) and Egypt (1517), and assumed the guardianship of the tomb of Mohammed at Mecca, thereby proclaiming himself the successor to the Arabian caliphs (see CALIPH; MOHAMMEDANISM). About this time Moldavia, like Walachia at an earlier date, became tributary to the Ottoman sultan. At the close of Selim's reign the famous corsair Barbarossa II, who is better known as Khair ed-Din, placed himself under Turkish suzerainty. During the reign of Suleiman I, called the Magnificent, the Ottoman Empire reached the zenith of its power and splendor. Belgrade was taken in 1521 and Rhodes was conquered in the following year. The Turkish victory over the army of Louis II of Hungary at Mohács in 1526 broke up the Hungarian empire. This triumph was followed by a succession of campaigns against the Hapsburgs, in one of which Vienna itself was besieged. The heart of Hungary, including the capital, Buda, was converted into a Turkish province (see HUNGARY: *History*). Ottoman conquests were also launched from Persia (Iran). On the Mediterranean Sea the Turks were the undisputed masters. Venice had been progressively stripped of its rich possessions in the Pelo-

ponnesus and the Ægean Sea. Tripoli became subject to Turkey in 1551. Malta, however, was saved by a band of heroic Christian defenders who repelled a vast Turkish force in 1565.

The campaign of Selim II, son and successor of Suleiman the Magnificent, to take the Mediterranean island of Cyprus from the Venetians impelled Venice to form a Holy League with Spain and the Papal States, the combined fleets of which inflicted a disastrous defeat upon the Turks in the battle of Lepanto (1571). Cyprus, nevertheless, was taken by the Turks, the subjugation of Yemen was completed, and (about the time of the death of Selim II) the Spaniards were driven from Tunis in North Africa, which then became subject to Turkey. Despite these successes, the Turkish defeat at Lepanto marked the turning point of the Ottoman fortunes. Under Murad III a war with Persia, in which Turkish conquests were made in Armenia, was followed by a struggle with Austria, which continued under Mohammed III (1566–1603) and extended into the reign of Ahmed I. About this time Persia rose to a high state of power under Abbas I, known as the Great, who won a notable victory over the Turks at Basra, s. Iraq, in 1605, and who annexed extensive Turkish possessions, even making himself master of Baghdad in 1623. Murad IV, a cruel, able, and energetic ruler, largely redressed the losses of Turkey in the East, retaking Baghdad in 1638. After his death, however, maladministration and internal disorders accelerated the decline of the Ottoman Empire.

In 1656 the Venetians, on whom the Turks had made war for the possession of the Mediterranean island of Crete, gained entrance to the Dardanelles and inflicted a serious defeat upon the Turkish fleet. The Ottoman power was temporarily resuscitated through the efforts of the Albanian nobleman Mohammed Kuprili or Köprülü (1586?–1661) and his son Fazil Ahmed (1635–76), who successively held the influential post of grand vizier during part of the reign of Mohammed IV (1641–91). They revitalized the internal administration of the Ottoman Empire and to some extent enabled the Turkish military power to reassert itself. A war with Austria, in which the Turks were severely defeated by the Austrian general Count Raimund Montecuccoli (1609–80) at St. Gotthard on the banks of the Raab R. (1664), was terminated through the exertions of Fazil Ahmed Kuprili by a peace slightly advantageous to Turkey. In 1669 the Turks finally wrested Crete from the Venetians. In the region N. of the Black Sea the Turks fought with varying success against the Poles; there also they first came into conflict with the rising power of Russia. In 1683 Mohammed IV espoused the cause of Count Imre Thököly (1657–1705), the leader of the Hungarians in their revolt against Austrian rule, and once more the tide of Moslem invasion advanced to the gates of Vienna. Kara Mustafa (d. 1683), the brother-in-law and successor of Fazil Ahmed Kuprili, proceeded with a large army and laid siege to the Hapsburg capital. After a siege of two months the Turks were finally routed by Polish forces under John III Sobieski and an army under Charles of Lorraine.

This defeat signalized the end of Turkey as an aggressive power. Thereafter Austria, Poland, and Venice commenced a great onslaught upon the Ottoman Empire. The Austrians drove the Turks before them in Hungary, capturing city after city. Buda, over which the flag of Islam had flown for a century and a half, came once more into the possession of Austria in 1686. At the same time John III Sobieski scored notable successes in Moldavia and Walachia and the Venetians invaded the Peloponnesus. In 1695 Peter I of Russia took up arms against the Turks, wresting Azov from them in the following year. Under Eugene, Prince of Savoy, the Austrians utterly defeated the Turkish army opposed to them in the battle of Senta (1697). By the Treaty of Karlowitz, negotiated in 1699, Turkey was compelled to relinquish all of Hungary between the Danube and Tisza rivers; to restore to Poland a great part of the Ukraine, acquired in 1672; and to surrender the entire Peloponnesus to the Venetians.

Early in the 18th century, however, Turkey reasserted its power in Moldavia and Walachia, which were placed under the rule of the Ottoman Greeks called Phanariots. In 1711 Ahmed III (q.v.), who had offered refuge to Charles XII of Sweden after the latter's defeat by the Russian czar Peter I at Poltava, took up arms against Russia on behalf of the Swedish monarch. Peter I thereupon invaded Moldavia, but being hemmed in by Turks on the banks of the Prut R., was obliged to make peace by surrendering Azov. In 1715 the Turks reconquered the Peloponnesus from the Venetians. The struggle with Austria was renewed in the following year, when Austrian forces under Prince Eugene gained a great victory at Peterwardein on the s. bank of the Danube R.; in 1717 the Austrians captured Belgrade. By the Treaty of Passarowitz (1718) the

Turks were compelled to cede to Austria the rich agricultural region of Banat, part of Serbia, and parts of Bosnia and Walachia. The Peloponnesus remained under Ottoman control. In 1736 Russia began its greatest assault upon the Ottoman Empire with the seizure of Azov and the invasion of the Crimea, followed by the capture of Ochakov (1737) and a victorious advance into Bessarabia and Moldavia. Austria entered into an alliance with Russia in 1737, but a scheme for the partition of Turkey between the two powers was thwarted by the defeats inflicted upon the Austrian armies by the Turks. By the Treaty of Belgrade, negotiated in 1739, Austria relinquished the Serbian and Walachian territories acquired in 1718; Russia, for its part, concluded a peace of negligible advantage to itself.

Alarmed at the aggressive intervention of the Russian empress Catherine II in the affairs of Poland, and believing the security of the Ottoman Empire to be endangered by Russian intrigues, Sultan Mustafa III (1717–74), in 1768, ventured on a war with Russia which proved disastrous for Turkey. The Russians advanced victoriously through Moldavia and Walachia, defeated the Tatar khan of the Crimea (the vassal of the sultan), won a victory on the Kagal R. in Bessarabia, stormed Bandar Abbas in s. Persia, broke into the Crimea, and (1773–74) advanced into Bulgaria, where, however, the Turkish fortresses withstood the Russian attacks. In 1770 the Russians burned the Turkish fleet at Çeşme. Peace was concluded at Küchük Kainarja in 1774, with Turkey renouncing its suzerainty over the Crimea and other Tatar territories in the region of the Black Sea, and granting to Russia a quasi protectorate over Moldavia and Walachia and the free navigation of the waters around Turkey. During this war the effectiveness of the Ottoman arms had been largely reduced by the revolt against Turkish hegemony of Ali Bey (1728–73), the Mameluke (see MAMELUKES) subject-ruler of Egypt. In 1787 Abdul-Hamid I (1725–89) plunged Turkey into a fresh war with Russia. Joseph II of Austria took advantage of this new crisis to make a sudden onslaught on the Turkish territories, and the Ottoman armies met with new reverses. Grigori Aleksandrovich Potëmkin (q.v.), commander in chief of the Russian armies, stormed Ochakov in 1788; Austria and Russia obtained a notable victory at Focsani in 1789; Belgrade and Bandar Abbas were captured in the same year; and Ismail was stormed by the Russian commander Count

Turkish Information Office

Station Boulevard in Ankara, capital of Turkey

Aleksandr Vasilievich Suvorov (q.v.) at the close of 1790. Austria, through pressure from Prussia, withdrew from the struggle in 1791 without deriving any benefit from it, and Catherine II in 1792 concluded with Sultan Selim III (1761–1808) the Treaty of Jassy, which specified the Dniester R. as the boundary between the Russian and the Ottoman dominions.

Weakened by internal disorders, Turkey was unable to offer effective resistance to Napoleon Bonaparte, later Napoleon I of France, when, in 1798, he suddenly attacked Egypt, which, under its refractory Mameluke rulers, was already almost severed from the Ottoman Empire. The advance of the French in Syria, however, was checked by the spirited defenders of Acre. Napoleon returned to France, and in 1801 the British drove the French from Egypt. Three years later the Serbians, under their patriotic leader Karageorge (1766?–1817), rose in revolt against the oppressive Turkish rule. Selim III, meanwhile, under the influence of the social and political reforms effected in France by the French revolutionary government, endeavored to put a number of these advanced ideas into operation in his own realm upon his accession to the throne. His innovations were premature, however, and he aroused the hostility of the Janizaries by his attempt to reorganize the Turkish military es-

tablishment along European lines. A revolt forced Selim III to abdicate in 1807, and brought his nephew Mustafa IV (1779–1808) to the throne. Mustafa was in turn deposed, and his brother Mahmud II (q.v.) was made sultan.

A war between Turkey and Russia begun in 1806 was terminated in 1812 by the Treaty of Bucharest, by which the country between the Dniester and Prut rivers was ceded to Russia. Although the authority of the sultan was reestablished in Serbia, the Serbian patriot Prince Miloš Obrenovich (1771–1825) led his people in a war of liberation, as a result of which Serbia achieved partial independence in 1817 (see SERBIA: *History*). A Greek revolt against Turkish rule, begun in 1821, led to the espousal of the Greek cause by France, Great Britain, and Russia, and culminated in the achievement of complete independence for Greece under the Treaty of Adrianople. This treaty also provided for the surrender by Turkey to Russia of the N.E. coast of the Black Sea; the transfer to Russia of the Ottoman suzerainty over the tribes of the Caucasus; and the establishment of a Russian protectorate over Moldavia and Walachia.

In 1831 Mehemet Ali (q.v.), the viceroy of Egypt, who had elevated himself to a position of virtual independence, made war on his suzerain, the sultan of Turkey. The victories of the Egyptian general Ibrahim Pasha (q.v.) secured for Mehemet Ali the Turkish possession of Syria and Cilicia. Russia, meanwhile, took advantage of the desperate state of Turkey to enforce upon the sultan the Treaty of Unkiar-Skelessi (1833), which provided for the closing of the Black Sea to the vessels of all nations except Russia. In 1839 Mahmud II declared war against Mehemet Ali. The Turkish army was utterly defeated by Egyptian forces under Ibrahim Pasha at Nisib on June 24. Only the intervention of England, Austria, Prussia, and Russia, in 1840 prevented the downfall of the Ottoman power. Mehemet Ali was forced to relinquish Syria and other territories; he was recognized as hereditary, though tributary, ruler of Egypt. Soon after the beginning of this war Mahmud II died. His son, Abdul-Medjid I (1823–61), continued the reforms begun in the reign of Selim III. Russia's truculent attitude toward Turkey precipitated a war between the two powers in 1853, in which Turkey would have suffered severely but for the effective intervention in 1854 of England and France, soon joined by Sardinia, all bent on humbling Russia. The allies of the sultan made the Crimea the scene of their land operations, and in 1855 the strategic Russian stronghold of Sevastopol (q.v.) fell (see CRIMEAN WAR). By the Treaty of Paris (1856) the command of both sides of the lower Danube R. was restored to Turkey; Russia was excluded from its assumed protectorate over Moldavia and Walachia; and the Black Sea was closed to all warships. Moldavia and Walachia secured almost complete independence and were soon united into the principality of Romania (see ROMANIA: *History*).

Consequent upon Turkey's adoption into the family of European nations, the sultan issued a proclamation of equal civil rights to all races and creeds within the Turkish dominions. A massacre of Christians in Lebanon and Syria, however, provoked the intervention of the Western powers in 1860. The following year Abdul-Medjid I was succeeded by his brother Abdul-Aziz. The Treaty of Paris was supposed to have settled the so-called Eastern Question by guaranteeing the integrity of Turkey, but Russia was merely awaiting an opportunity to resume its old policy of aggression against the Ottoman Empire. The opportunity came in the form of war between Germany and France (see FRANCO-GERMAN WAR). With the accord among the Western powers destroyed, the Russian government declared that it felt itself no longer bound by that provision of the Paris treaty which barred all warships from the Black Sea. This stroke of Russian diplomacy was sanctioned by a conference of the major powers at London. The security of the Ottoman realm was further jeopardized by an insurrection against Turkish rule in Crete (1866–68), which was suppressed with great difficulty. In 1875 an uprising in Herzegovina, skillfully encouraged by Russian agents, served to stir up all the neighboring Slavic peoples. In May, 1876, bloody massacres of Christians took place in the Ottoman province of Bulgaria. At the close of that month Abdul-Aziz was deposed and soon after was found dead. Murad V, nephew of Abdul-Aziz and son of Abdul-Medjid I, reigned only three months when, suspected of liberalism by the influential conservative elements of his court, he was declared insane and deposed, his brother Abdul-Hamid II (1842–1918) succeeding to the throne.

In July, 1876, Serbia and Montenegro declared war against Turkey. Before the end of the year the Serbians were utterly defeated, despite the help of many Russian volunteers. The disturbed state of affairs in the Turkish provinces resulted, however, in a conference of the major powers at Constantinople. The recommendations made at this conference for the more humane government of the Christian subjects within the Turkish dominions were rejected by the Grand Council of the Ottoman Empire. Nevertheless, the Turkish government did take the extraordinary step of drafting, adopting, and bestowing upon the Ottoman Empire the parliamentary constitution of 1876. Although the parliament assembled in March, 1877, the ostensible remodeling of the political structure of the Ottoman Empire was not seriously undertaken. Russia then assumed the initiative of enforcing upon Turkey the demands made by the European powers at the Constantinople conference, and declared war on April 24, 1877. The Turks made a valiant stand, but at last succumbed, and at the close of January, 1878, the Russians, aided by the Romanians, had advanced almost to the walls of Constantinople. By the Treaty of San Stefano, signed on March 3, 1878, Turkey was stripped of most of its possessions in Europe. The European powers intervened, however, and readjusted the whole issue at the Congress of Berlin (see BERLIN, CONGRESS OF), Russia being forced to content itself with a much less radical disruption of the Ottoman Empire in Europe than had been envisaged by the Russian strategy.

For a few years, in consequence of the settlement effected at Berlin, comparative tranquillity prevailed in the Ottoman dominions. In 1883, however, as a result of disturbances in Egypt, and the bad condition of the finances in that province, Great Britain established a control there which virtually nullified what little was left of the Ottoman sovereignty. Two years later, after a revolutionary uprising against Turkish domination at Philippopolis (Plovdiv), s. Bulgaria, Prince Alexander of Bulgaria proclaimed the separation of Eastern Rumelia from Turkish control. After the lapse of ten years the Ottoman sultan was finally compelled to recognize the change, which deprived him of his richest remaining province in Europe.

In 1895 and 1896 massacres of tens of thousands of Christians in Armenia took place with the connivance of the local officials of the Ottoman government. The protests of Europe were of no avail, however, for Abdul-Hamid II was skillful in playing off the major powers against one another so as to prevent any effective intervention on their part. A rising of the Christians against the Moslems on the Turkish-controlled island of Crete followed, and was the signal for the outbreak of long-repressed anti-Moslem hostilities in Greece, which recklessly entered upon war with Turkey in April, 1897 (see GREECE: *History*). After a few weeks the Greeks were forced to sue for peace, the terms of which provided for the payment to the Ottoman government of an indemnity of $18,000,000, and the rectification of the Greco-Turkish frontier in favor of Turkey. Crete was placed under the joint trusteeship of Great Britain, Russia, France, and Italy, and in 1898 a settlement was effected by which the suzerainty of Turkey was renewed, although for an interim period of three years the island was given an autonomous government, with Prince George of Greece (1869–   ), its executive head, acting as the high commissioner of the four powers. This settlement was renewed indefinitely upon its expiration in December, 1901.

In the first decade of the 20th century the Ottoman Empire seemed on the verge of collapse. Arabia was in constant revolt. Open anarchy prevailed in Albania, where the sultan's officials found it virtually impossible to enforce law or to collect taxes. The gravest situation, however, existed in Macedonia, where Greeks, Serbians, and Bulgarians were constantly engaged in rival nationalist agitations which kept the district in turmoil. An especially violent insurrection in Macedonia, precipitated by the Bulgarians in 1903 and involving massacres on the part of the Turks, led to the intervention of the European powers. In consequence, the sultan reluctantly consented to the introduction of new reforms, which, however, were never fully implemented. Meanwhile, the state of the Ottoman finances was steadily deteriorating: railways, mines, and banks were being taken over by foreign capitalists; and the European powers were covetously regarding the Turkish provinces.

At this critical juncture, however, when the "Sick Man of Europe", as European Turkey had often been called, was apparently tottering to his end, appeared the Young Turks, a group of politicians and patriots who dreamed of rejuvenating their country. Many of these Young Turks had studied in the universities of western Europe; imbued with the liberal political ideas of the time, they looked forward to the establishment of a genuine parliamentary government in their homeland. They contemplated the transformation of Turkey into a modern, European-type state, progressive in education, science, and industry. Above all, they hoped to induce their compatriots to submerge religious differences in a spirit of common national patriotism. The Young Turk movement was the counterpart in Turkey of the militant patriotic movements which had already produced national integration and autonomy in Greece, Serbia, Romania, and Bulgaria. With great prudence, the leaders of the Young Turks avoided any decisive move until they were absolutely sure that the Turkish army would support them. Then, on July 23, 1908, the central body of the Young Turk movement, the so-called Committee of Union and Progress, with Enver Pasha (q.v.) at its head, proclaimed at Saloniki the restoration of the constitution of 1876. At the same time, the Young Turks threatened to dispatch two army corps to Constantinople. The terrified Abdul-Hamid II thereupon hastily issued an imperial decree officially restoring parliamentary government. A few conservative opponents of the *coup d'état* were assassinated, the press was freed from the close censorship under which it had formerly operated, and a liberal statesman, Kiamil Pasha, was appointed grand vizier.

Thus was Turkey transformed into a moderate constitutional monarchy. Taking advantage of the disturbed conditions in the Ottoman Empire, Austria-Hungary in October, 1908, formally annexed Bosnia and Herzegovina; simultaneously, Ferdinand I of Bulgaria proclaimed the complete independence of his state (including Eastern Rumelia) and assumed the title of king. The new Turkish government helplessly acquiesced in what it could not prevent, and in 1909, in return for financial indemnities, recognized the independence of Bulgaria and the annexation of Bosnia and Herzegovina by Austria-Hungary. The constitutional government of Kiamil Pasha was subjected to new stresses in the spring of 1909, when the insurrectionist agitation in Albania became more violent, mutiny broke out in Arabia, and the strife among rival nationalities in Macedonia was intensified. Under these circumstances a counterrevolution was begun in Constantinople and received the approval of Abdul-Hamid II. The Committee of Union and Progress, which had its headquarters at Saloniki, responded promptly by sending an army under Mahmud Shevket Pasha (1855 or 1858–1913) against Constantinople. After less than a day's fighting Shevket Pasha was in command of the Turkish capital (April 25, 1909). At the behest of the triumphant Young Turks, the parliament, now calling itself a national assembly, deposed Abdul-Hamid II, placed him under surveillance near Saloniki, and elevated his brother Mohammed V (1844–1918) to the throne.

The new parliamentary regime, under Young Turk influence, proceeded forthwith to contravene systematically all of the liberal policies previously enunciated by the movement, making the Turkish language official throughout the Ottoman dominions, planting Moslem colonies in Macedonia, employing violence and bribery in elections, forbidding public assembly, repressing anti-Ottoman agitation, and disarming the Christian villagers of Macedonia. Bitterly resentful over this turn of affairs, Bulgarians, Greeks, and Serbians in Macedonia put aside their quarrels with each other and banded together in a common front against the Turks. At the same time Bulgaria, Greece, and Serbia began to draw more closely together with the common aim of protecting the Christians in Macedonia. On September 28, 1911, Italy announced its intention of seizing the Ottoman possessions of Tripoli and Cyrenaica (see ITALY: *History*). The war that ensued was confined for the most part to irregular but fierce hostilities between the Italian expeditionary armies on the one hand, and Turkish garrisons and Arab tribesmen in Africa on the other. During the course of the war, Italian troops occupied twelve of the Turkish-controlled islands in the Ægean Sea;

and when peace was finally concluded in October, 1912, Italy not only gained Tripoli and Cyrenaica, but also acquired the right to retain the twelve Ægean islands should Turkey fail to grant to their inhabitants complete amnesty, local autonomy, and civil liberties.

During the summer of 1912, meanwhile, when Turkey was still harassed by the war with Italy, the Balkan states concluded treaties of alliance with each other and began to press Turkey more insistently for radical reforms in Macedonia. At the same time, mutinous outbreaks occurred in Albania. In October, 1912, Bulgaria, Greece, Serbia, and Montenegro mobilized their armies and presented joint ultimatums to the Turkish government demanding autonomy for Macedonia under European governors. Despite the efforts of the major powers to avert hostilities, the peremptory refusal of Turkey to comply with the ultimatums precipitated the Balkan Wars (q.v.), which lasted from October, 1912, to September, 1913. This struggle resulted in the loss to Turkey of all of its possession in Europe with the exception of Constantinople, Adrianople, and a little adjacent territory.

In the middle of the 19th century Great Britain and France had labored to bolster up the Ottoman Empire and to safeguard it against Russian aggression. By the time of the Balkan War, however, British and French interests in the Near East appeared to be menaced less by Russia than by Austria-Hungary and Germany. The latter powers were working together in the closest collaboration, with Germany arming and training the Turkish military establishment and securing the major share of new concessions in the Ottoman Empire, notably control of the Baghdad railway, and with Austria-Hungary repressing the Serbians and increasing its political and economic influence in Macedonia. In the course of the Balkan War, therefore, Great Britain and France, in conjunction with Russia, tended in the main to sympathize with the Balkan states against Turkey. Accordingly, soon after the outbreak of World War I in 1914, with Great Britain, France, Russia, and Serbia aligned against Austria-Hungary and Germany, the Turkish government threw in its lot with the Central Powers (q.v.). Behind this move was the hope on the part of the Young Turk leaders that if they were unable to recover the territory which had recently been taken from them in Europe, they might at least, through the support of their allies, maintain Ottoman sovereignty over Egypt and extend Turkish frontiers into Persia at the eventual expense

Turkish Information Office

TURKISH INDUSTRY. *Above: Paper factory in the town of Izmit. Right: A girl copying from old tapestry to produce design for new textiles. Below: In a tobacco factory at Izmir, Turkey.*

Pan American Airways
A peasant's house in Turkey

of Russia and Great Britain. The Turks unsuccessfully attacked the British forces defending Egypt along the Suez Canal (1915), but were successful in repulsing British attempts to penetrate the Dardanelles or to achieve their objectives on the Gallipoli Peninsula. British troops had been landed at the head of the Persian Gulf, and the Turks were unable to hinder their advance up the Shatt-al-Arab R. Meanwhile, Russian forces made headway in Transcaucasia, capturing Ardahan and repulsing the Turks in the coastal region.

In 1916 the Turks were driven back across the Sinai Peninsula, and faced a British invasion of Palestine; in Mesopotamia, however, they succeeded in capturing Kut-el-Amara and 12,000 Allied troops. Military operations had spread into Persia, where the Turks contended with the Russians for key positions in the north. Meanwhile such British agents as Colonel Thomas Edward Lawrence (q.v.) had incited the Arabs to revolt against their Turkish overlords, and in June they proclaimed their independence, capturing the holy city of Mecca and the seaport of Jidda on the Red Sea. In 1917 Turkey began to meet with serious reverses; the British overran s. Palestine, capturing Jerusalem, and at the same time also conquered Mesopotamia. The Turks soon lost all Arabia; upon the collapse of Russian resistance, the Russian positions in Persia were taken over by the British, the Turks withdrawing in the middle of the year. The new Bolshevik (see BOLSHEVISM) government in Russia, acting in conformity with its policy of relinquishing all former possessions of the Russian Empire, restored Kars and Ardalan (in N.W. Persia) to Turkey in March, 1918, according to the provisions of the Treaty of Brest Litovsk (see BREST LITOVSK, TREATY OF).

These restorations were of no avail, however, for Turkey's military strength was broken. British forces from Mesopotamia overran Mosul and Persia, and advanced up to the Caspian Sea; at the same time, all of Palestine was taken and Syria invaded. With its military situation thus hopeless on all sides, Turkey was compelled to sue for an armistice, which became effective October 31, 1918. The Treaty of Sèvres, negotiated on August 10, 1920, between the Ottoman government on the one hand and the Allied powers on the other, deprived Turkey of Thrace, the islands of Imbros (Imroz Adaya) and Tenedos (Bozcaada), the Dodecanese, Smyrna, the Mediterranean island of Cyprus, Egypt, Armenia, Mesopotamia, Syria, Palestine, and the Hejaz.

This drastic dismemberment of the Turkish Empire served to rally the people to the Nationalist Party of Mustafa Kemal, better known as Kemal Atatürk (q.v.), who repudiated the Treaty of Sèvres and took energetic steps to clear Turkey of foreigners. On November 20, 1922 a fresh treaty was signed at Lausanne, Switzerland, between the new Turkish government, headed by Kemal Atatürk, and the late Allies, by the provisions of which eastern Thrace and Anatolia, including Smyrna, were returned to the Turks. A Turkish republic was proclaimed on October 29, 1923, with its capital at Ankara; Kemal Atatürk became the first president. Soon thereafter the Turkish caliphate (see CALIPH) was abolished and the abandonment of Islam as the state religion was decreed. The program of revolutionary reforms inaugurated by Atatürk also included the suppression of polygamy, the abolition of the ancient Mohammedan code of law and the adoption of a Western legal system, the prohibition against wearing the fez, and the adoption of the Gregorian calendar in place of the Mohammedan calendar (see CALENDAR). Following the death of Atatürk in 1938, Ismet Inönü (q.v.) was unanimously elected president. Meanwhile, in 1936, Turkey was granted the right of remilitarizing the Dardanelles.

In World War II Turkey adopted a position of nonbelligerency, but maintained strong commercial ties with Germany until 1944. Despite this fact, Turkey was declared eligible for United States lend-lease (q.v.) assistance late in 1941, although shipments to that country were halted in the spring of 1944 when the advantage of Turkey to Allied strategy became dubious. In August of the same year, however, Turkey severed diplomatic relations with Germany and vouchsafed the Allies free passage of supplies through the Dardanelles. On February 23, 1945, the Turkish National Assembly unanimously voted a declaration of war on the Axis powers.

At the conclusion of the war consultations were held between Turkey on the one hand and the United States and Great Britain on the other, in consequence of which extensive plans were formulated for the modernization and expansion of Turkey's industry and communications facilities. Railway equipment and other machinery were purchased in England, and the construction of a new and modern port was begun at Eregli on the Black Sea. In the social sphere, a pervasive reform was enacted by the Turkish National Assembly when it passed a land-reform bill in June, 1945. Under the terms of this bill large estates were to be broken up into smaller lots, varying from 12 to 1200 acres, for distribution among about 1,000,000 families, or one third of the rural population of the country. Owners of expropriated land were to be reimbursed with government bonds. On June 26, 1945, Turkey became a charter member of the United Nations.

Soon afterward the relations between Turkey and the U.S.S.R. were severely strained in consequence of the denunciation by the Soviet Union of the 1925 treaty of friendship and neutrality between the two countries. This move was followed by the presentation to Turkey of a number of Soviet territorial demands, including the return to the U.S.S.R. of Kars and Ardelan; the granting to the U.S.S.R. of bases in the Dardanelles and Bosporus, thus providing for their joint Soviet-Turkish defense; and the cession by Turkey of a large coastal region adjoining the Georgian S.S.R. These claims were vehemently rejected by the Turks. In 1946 Turkey inaugurated a policy of diplomatic and cultural rapprochement with Iraq and Iran.

The most significant development for Turkey in 1947 was the extension of U.S. military and political support under the so-called Truman Doctrine (see TRUMAN, HARRY S.). Early in 1948 Turkey reaffirmed its friendship pacts with Great Britain and Greece. Turkish relations with the Soviet Union continued to be strained. In May, 1950, following a decisive election victory by the Democratic Party, the Democratic leader Celâl Bayar (1884–   ), was elected president.

In July, 1950, the Turkish government offered to furnish a brigade of troops to the U.N. forces fighting in defense of South Korea. The Turkish brigade went into action on November 29. Turkey was invited (September, 1951) to become a signatory of the North Atlantic Treaty (q.v.), a mutual-defense pact among the U.S., Canada, and ten West European democracies. Turkey signed the treaty in February, 1952. Headquarters of the N.A.T.O. land forces in southeastern Europe were established at İzmir later in the year.

The Turkish economy had been vastly strengthened meanwhile, largely as a result of U.S. financial and military help, which totaled over $1 billion by the close of 1952. In May, 1953, Turkey concluded a five-year friendship and collaboration treaty with Greece and Yugoslavia. More than 1000 persons were killed by an earthquake in northwestern Turkey on March 18, 1953. By the terms of a note delivered to the Turkish government in June, 1953, the Soviet Union offered to relinquish its territorial claims on Turkey in exchange for an agreement on joint control of the Dardanelles. Later in 1953 the Soviet Union withdrew the offer. The two countries

Turkish Information Office

Turkish fort which once sheltered the Crusaders, at Anamur near Antalya

subsequently settled various border issues. Celâl Bayar was re-elected president May 1, 1954. During 1954 Turkey concluded mutual-defense treaties with Greece and Yugoslavia and with Pakistan.

Work began in 1955 on the first Turkish hydroelectric project, a dam near İzmir. In February, 1955, Turkey and Iraq established a mutual-security alliance. The other Arab League states, Great Britain, the United States, Pakistan, and Iran were invited to join the alliance. Great Britain became a signatory in April. Turkey was one of the 29 nations represented at the Asian-African Conference held in Bandoeng, Indonesia, in April, 1955.

Early in September, 1955, violent anti-Greek riots took place in İstanbul, Ankara, İzmir, and other Turkish cities. The riots were provoked by Greek demands for control of Cyprus, where there is a large Turkish minority. As a result of these disorders, the minister of the Interior was forced to resign, three generals who had held key positions in İstanbul were dismissed, and thousands were arrested on charges of violence and looting.

On Nov. 29 all members of the cabinet resigned, blaming the government's policies for commodity shortages and high prices. A new cabinet was installed on Dec. 9, and a week later the government's policies were overwhelmingly approved by Parliament. Though these policies called for the curbing of inflation and the easing of press censorship, prices continued to rise in 1956 and censorship was intensified. The government continued to affirm the rights of opposition parties, but applied legal harassment to obstruct them.

On June 9, 1956, the Turkish government notified Great Britain that it opposed self-government for Cyprus and demanded British assurances that the Turkish minority in Cyprus would not be placed under Greek rule.

TURKISH LANGUAGE AND LITERATURE, the language and literature of the Turks in general, and especially of the Osmanli. Within the Ural-Altaic family the Turkish group stands somewhere nearer to the Samoyedic and Finno-Ugric than to the Tungusian and Mongolian. Among the languages or dialects comprised within the Turkish group the Osmanli has the closest affinities to the Anadoli, Krimmi, Azerbaijani, and Turkmani, though the latter two already begin to show characteristic differences. The Jagatai and Taranji, and even more the northern dialects, Kirghiz, Bashkir, Irtysh, and Volga in the west, and Altai, Baraba, Lebed, Tuba, Abakan, Kuarik, Soyon Karagass, and Ulghur in the east, have a much broader and harsher vocalization.

The onrush of the Turks from the Far East into all civilized lands, including China, which continued from the 10th century to the end of the 17th, enlarged the meager Turkish vocabulary. The tribes which invaded India, now known under the name of Moguls, lost their language; but those which conquered Persia (now Iran) and overthrew the Byzantine Empire came under the literary influence of Persian at first, then of Arabic, and finally of Greek and the European languages. The consequence was that the Ottoman Turkish (Osmanli), as the Western branch of the language is called, adopted into its literary vocabulary Persian words of poetry and history, Arabic words for religious and legal writings, Greek words for the winds and currents and fishes of the sea, Italian words for all that relates to sailing vessels, and, later, English terms for steam, and French words for many of the terms of diplomacy.

Literature. Turkish poetry is full of the subtle esoteric ideas which are characteristic of its Persian exemplars. Ottoman poetry begins soon after the establishment of the Ottoman empire. Already in the beginning of the 15th century Ahmed Da'i's "gay and flowing songs of love and wine" delighted the court of Prince Suleyman in Adrianople, and poems had been indited by Ghazi Fazil. Of the thirty-four sultans of Turkey twenty-one were poets of a sort, and the unhappy Prince Jem was especially noted for his poetic talent.

To the age of Suleiman and his predecessor Selim belong Mesihi (d. 1512), Lami'i (d. 1531), Ghazali (d. 1534), Fuzuli (d. 1562), Fazli (d. 1563), and Baki (d. 1600). The best Turkish poetry is chiefly included in this epoch, which partly corresponds in time with our Elizabethan era. Lami'i's works include poems on old Persian romances, besides many *ghazals* and other short pieces. Fuzuli, on the whole the greatest of Turkish poets, in spite of his provincial idiom, is best known by his *Leyli and Mejnun* and his charming odes. Baki was the most famous of Turkish lyricists. His famous elegy on Suleiman the Great is unsurpassed in Ottoman literature. The appreciation of nature which is shown in such poems as Mesihi's *Ode to Spring* and Baki's and Lami'i's odes to *Autumn,* and which is characteristic of their period, forms one of the best features of Turkish poetry.

Nef'i of Erzerum (d. 1635), the most renowned of Turkish satirists, wrote in the time of Murad IV; Nabi (d. 1712) wrote thousands of couplets of a didactic tendency; and Nedim

(d. about 1717), perhaps the most finished, and certainly the most blithe of Turkish singers, belongs to the time of Åhmed III. He was the last of the old classical school of Ottoman poets, although Sheykh Ghalib (d. 1795), the author of *Beauty and Love* (*Husn-u-Ashk*), was little inferior to any of the older writers.

The aim of the modern school of writers has been to free the Turkish language from the incubus of Arabic grammatical purism. The writers who have perhaps done the most toward accomplishing this object are Ahmed Vefik Pasha (d. 1893), who wrote a dictionary of Turkish in two volumes, and Ahmed Mithad Effendi, noted for his novels, essays, and historical studies. Of far greater weight was Kemal Bey (d. 1878). Jevdet Pasha, noted historian; Ziya Pasha, essayist and poet; and Jevad Pasha, who wrote a history of the Turkish military organization, are other examples of this school. Other notable names of this period are Muallim Naji, poet and essayist; Ebuzzia Tewfik, literary critic; and Sezayi Bey, Husain, Rahmi, Ahmed Rasim, and Aliyè Hanum, daughter of the historian Jevdet Pasha, all of whom are novelists, dealing with current life in a realistic style. Hamid Bey became well known as a playwright.

After the establishment of the republic the westernizing movement continued, the most important material change being the substitution of the Roman alphabet for the Arabic in 1930.

TURKMEN SOVIET SOCIALIST REPUBLIC, or TURKMENISTAN, constituent republic of the U.S.S.R., situated in Soviet Central Asia, and bounded on the N. by the Kara-Kalpak A.S.S.R., on the E. by the Uzbek S.S.R., on the S. by Iran and Afghanistan, and on the W. by the Caspian Sea. It is divided administratively into the Ashkhabad, Marysk, Chardzhou, and Tashauz districts. The capital is Ashkhabad (q.v.); other important cities are Krasnovodsk (pop., about 30,000), Chardzhou (about 55,000), Mary (about 37,000), and Kerki (about 14,000).

Most of the surface is covered by the Kara Kum desert, which extends from the Caspian Sea in the W. to the Amu Darya R. in the E., and from the S. part of the republic to Lake Aral in the Kara-Kalpak and Kazakh republics. Highlands running along the S. border are separated from the desert by a series of mountain chains varying in height from 2000 to 9000 ft. above sea level. The principal river is the Amu Darya, which flows roughly along the N.E. border. Agriculture, the leading occupation, is largely dependent upon irrigation.

Long-staple cotton, wheat, fruits, and vegetables are the chief crops, and silkworms are raised, especially in the Merv oasis and around Ashkhabad. In the republic are bred the Turkoman horse and the karakul sheep, from the latter of which astrakhan fur is obtained. Livestock in a recent year numbered about 260,000 cattle, 2,800,000 sheep and goats, 75,000 camels, and 24,000 pigs. Among the principal minerals mined are salt, sulfur, ozocerite, oil, coal, and magnesium. Manufacturing industries include the refining of oil and magnesium, and the production of textiles, carpets, agricultural implements, cement, and chemicals.

About 75% of the population are Turkomans; Uzbeks, Kazakhs, Kara-Kalpaks, Kirghiz, Great Russians, White Russians, Ukrainians, Armenians, Iranians, and Jews constitute the remainder. The Turkomans are Mohammedans of the Sunnite sect. The Turkmen S.S.R. is served by an air line, connecting the cities of Leninsk and Tashauz. The railway system consists of about 1100 miles of trackage, and the total length of motor roads is more than 6200 miles.

Prior to the formation of the Turkmen S.S.R. on October 27, 1924, most of the territory in the republic formed the Transcaspian Region of the Turkestan Autonomous Soviet Socialist Republic; the remainder formed part of the Kiva and the Bokhara people's soviet republics. See TURKESTAN. Area, 189,370 sq.m.; pop., about 1,250,000.

TURKOMANS, a people whose principal home is in the great plains between the Caspian Sea on the west and the Sea of Aral and the Amu Darya on the east—the western part of Turkestan in the broader sense. Some of them are to be found in Iran, Afghanistan, and other regions. They belong by language, and largely by blood, to the Turkic stock. The Turkomans are now the chief constituent stock of the Turkmen Soviet Socialist Republic.

TURKS AND CAICOS ISLANDS, a group of British islands in the West Indies, comprising a political dependency of Jamaica (q.v.), but geographically belonging to the Bahamas (q.v.). The Turks and Caicos islands are situated in the Atlantic Ocean, 150 to 200 miles N. of Hispaniola, and comprise the two southeastern groups of the Bahamas. Including the Turks and Caicos islands, there are approximately thirty small cays in the group, of which only eight are inhabited. The Turks Islands, which derive their name from a turban-like cactus indigenous to the Bahamas, number nine, the two largest being Grand Turk (10 sq.m.) and Salt City (5.5 sq.m.). The town of Grand Turk (pop., about 1500), on the island of the same name, is the seat of the dependency's government. The Caicos Islands are situated immediately N.W. of the Turks Islands, number seven, and include the largest island in the dependency, Grand Caicos (25 m. long and 12 m. wide).

The islands possess a healthful climate. Rainfall is relatively scarce (about 28 inches yearly), and hurricanes are not infrequent. The principal industry is the production of salt, which is gathered by raking. In a recent year the value of salt exported totaled over $45,000. Tinned lobster, fibers, sponges, and conches comprise the remainder of the exports. The principal imports include flour, sugar, rice, and rum. Education in the eleven government elementary schools is free and compulsory. There are two private elementary schools and a secondary school. The government consists of a commissioner and a seven-member legislative board, all crown appointees.

In 1678 the islands were visited by Bermudians, who began to develop the salt industry. In 1710, during the War of the Spanish Succession, the Spanish expelled the British from the islands for a short time. Although the British suffered repeated attacks by the Spanish and the French after the islands were regained, they succeeded in maintaining the salt trade, principally with the North American colonies. In 1799 the Turks and Caicos islands were given representation in the assembly of the Bahamas. On petition of the inhabitants, the islands were made a separate colony under Jamaica in 1848, and in 1873 they were formally annexed to Jamaica. Area, 165.5 sq.m.; pop. (1950 est.) 6500, including 80 Whites.

TURKU (Swedish, *Åbo*), oldest city and former capital of Finland, and present capital of Turku-Pori Department. It is situated on the Aurjoki R., 170 m. by rail W.N.W. of Helsinki, and has a considerable trade in timber and bar and cast iron. Following a disastrous fire in 1827 the university in the city was transferred to Helsinki. Pop. (1950) 101,239.

TURMERIC, common name applied to the dried, tuberous rhizomes of an erect, perennial herb, *Curcuma longa,* belonging to the Ginger family, and to its dried rhizomes. The herb is native to various parts of India. The pale-yellow flowers, borne in spikes, have a three-parted calyx, a five-lobed corolla, one fertile stamen, two sterile stamens, and a solitary pistil. The fruit is a capsule. Turmeric is widely used as a yellow dye and as a seasoning for food, especially as a constituent of curry powders.

TURNER, FREDERICK JACKSON (1861–1932), American educator, born in Portage, Wis., and educated at the University of Wisconsin. He was professor of history at Harvard until 1924, then becoming professor emeritus. He wrote *Rise of the New West* (1906) and *Frontier in American History* (1920).

TURNER, JOSEPH MALLORD WILLIAM (1775–1851), English landscape painter, born in Maiden Lane, London. He was early recognized as an artist; at twenty-four he was elected an associate of the Royal Academy, at twenty-eight an academician, and at thirty-three professor of perspective. Turner ranks as one of the three most famous landscape painters (Claude, Turner, Corot). In knowledge of nature he was far superior to the other two, and in the sense of elegance at least their equal. Among his best-known works, many of which he bequeathed to the National Gallery, are "Sun Rising in Mist" (1807); "Apollo and the Python" (1811); "The Frosty Morning" (1813); "Crossing the Brook" (1815); "Dido Building Carthage" (1815); "Bay of Baiæ" (1823); "Ulysses Deriding Polyphemus" (1829); "Childe Harold's Pilgrimage" (1832); "The Golden Bough" (1834); "Phryne Going to the Bath as Venus" (1838); "The Téméraire" (1839); "Walhalla", "The Approach to Venice", and "The Sun of Venice" (1843); and "Rain, Steam, and Speed" (1844). His drawings for the series *England and Wales* appeared in 1827–38 and *The Rivers of France* in 1833–35.

TURNIP, common name applied to a hardy, annual or biennial herb, *Brassica rapa,* belonging to the Mustard family, and grown for its edible, tuberous rootstocks. Turnips are native to Europe and parts of Asia, and are cultivated in temperate and subarctic regions throughout the world. The yellow flowers, arranged in erect racemes, have four sepals, four petals, four stamens, and a solitary pistil. The fruit is a long, slender, many-seeded pod. The turnip differs from the rutabaga (q.v.), yellow turnip, or Swede, in having densely grouped stems and elongated, white-fleshed roots. Turnips are grown extensively on farms and in gardens for food and to provide feed for livestock, but are not important in domestic or international trade. Serious diseases affecting the turnip crops include "clubroot", a swelling caused by the slime mold *Plasmodiophora brassicae,* and black rot, a discoloration caused by fungi of the genus *Phytomonas.* Insect diseases are commonly spread by the turnip

"Peace—Burial At Sea," painting by Joseph Mallord William Turner

aphid, or turnip louse, *Rhopalosiphum pseudobrassicae,* and by numerous flea beetles of the family *Chrysomelidae.*

TURNSTONE (*Arenaria*), a small genus of birds of the Plover family, Charadriidae, intermediate between the true plovers and the sandpipers. In winter the turnstone is found on the seashore all over the world. *A. interpres* visits Greenland and Alaska; *A. morinella* is found in the eastern States; and *A. melanocephala* or black turnstone may be seen on the Pacific coast. The turnstone is also called calicoback or calico bird.

TURPENTINE, name applied to numerous semifluid, yellow or brownish oleoresins obtained from various coniferous trees in Asia, Europe, and America. Formerly, all turpentine was derived as a transparent exudate from the terebinth (pistacia or pistachio) tree, *Pistacia terebinthus,* in the Cashew family, and native to the shores of the Mediterranean and Central Asia. The exudate was known as *Chian* turpentine, and became hard, dry, and brittle when exposed to the air. Today, the crude or common turpentines of commerce are derived principally from conifers of the genus *Pinus,* and are usually named after the locality from which they are obtained. In the United States, the principal sources of turpentine are the longleaf pine, *Pinus palustris;* the slash pine, *P. caribaea;* and the mountain pine, *P. pumilo,* all common to various States

along the Atlantic coast. In France, the exudate known as Bordeaux turpentine is obtained from the cluster pine, *P. pinaster.* Other European varieties include the Scotch turpentine, from the Scotch fir, *P. sylvestris;* Corsican turpentine from the larch pine, *P. larico;* Strassburg turpentine, from the bark of fir of the genus *Abies;* Swiss turpentine, from the stone pine, *P. cembra;* and Venetian turpentine, obtained from *Larix europa,* the European larch. Canadian balsam, considered a true turpentine, is derived from the bark of *Abies balsamea.*

The substance obtained from the above trees consists of 75 to 90 percent resin and 25 to 10 percent oil. Upon distillation, it yields *oil of turpentine,* or *turps,* $C_{10}H_{16}$, a colorless, oily liquid consisting of a mixture of terpenes and essential oils. The liquid is insoluble in water, slightly soluble in aqueous alcohol, and insoluble in absolute alcohol and ether. It has a specific gravity of .86 to .88, and boils at 1550°C. (2822°F.). It is the principal product of turpentine, and is used in the arts to give consistency and drying properties to various oil paints and varnishes. Medically, oil of turpentine acts as a powerful stimulant, and is often used as an antispasmodic and astringent. It is also capable of destroying various intestinal parasites, and exhibits powerful diuretic properties.

Crude, commercial turpentine is valuable

mainly as a source of resins (q.v.). See also ROSIN.

TURQUOISE, an opaque, cryptocrystalline mineral composed chiefly of hydrated aluminum phosphate, $Al_2(OH)_3PO_4 \cdot H_2O$, and prized throughout the world as a gem stone; see GEM. It has a hardness of 6, a specific gravity of 2.60 to 2.83, and, in the unpolished state, shines with a feeble, waxy luster. The color ranges from blue and blue green to greenish gray according to the various amounts of copper usually present. The sky-blue variety, commonly referred to as "robin's egg", is the form most desired for jewelry. When excessively exposed to sunlight or heat, this variety may become dehydrated and turn green. The mineral has been valued for its ornamental properties since very ancient times, and is often found in neckwear and bracelets recovered from old Egyptian tombs. The Aztecs of Mexico commonly used turquoise for their fine, mosaic art, and introduced the stone to the surrounding areas, where it became known as *chalchihuitl*. It occurs mostly in the form of kidney-shaped masses in the seams of igneous rocks; as incrustations on the surface of various slates; or as nodules in red sandstone. Principal deposits of finer, blue turquoise are located in Nishapur, a town near Teheran, Iran. Other varieties are found abundantly throughout Turkestan, the Sinai Peninsula, and Mexico. In the United States, the mineral is worked extensively in the area of Santa Fé, New Mexico, and in parts of California, Nevada, and Arizona. When cut, the stones are usually egg-shaped or globular, the facets being low and convex. In this form, they are used today for numerous types of jewelry. The name "turquoise" is sometimes loosely applied to the "occidental turquoise", "bone turquoise", or odontolite, a fossil ivory which is colored blue by the action of copper solutions.

TURTLE. See TORTOISES AND TURTLES.

TURTLEDOVE. See DOVE.

TUSCALOOSA, county seat of Tuscaloosa Co., Ala., situated on the Warrior R., 58 miles s.w. of Birmingham. It is served by three railroads, and by river barges to the Gulf of Mexico, and maintains a municipal airport. The city is the center of an area yielding cotton, livestock, timber, coal, iron ore, limestone, dolomite, and fire clay. Industrial establishments in the city and vicinity include iron foundries, pipe foundries, blast furnaces, coke ovens, railroad shops, paper mills, wood-veneer mills, sawmills, cotton and cottonseed-oil mills, meat-packing plants, creameries, bakeries, a milk condensery, and factories manufacturing rubber tires, chemicals, and brick. Tuscaloosa is the site of the University of Alabama (see ALABAMA, UNIVERSITY OF); Stillman Institute (Presbyterian), for Negroes; the Alabama Institute for Aeronautics; a U.S. veterans hospital; and Bryce Hospital for the insane. The city is noted for the old oak trees which border its streets and for its ante-bellum mansions.

Tuscaloosa, a combination of two Indian words meaning "Black Warrior", was named in honor of a Choctaw Indian chief of that name who was defeated in battle by the Spanish explorer Hernando de Soto in 1540. The first European settlement on the site was established in 1816 and the town was incorporated in 1819. From 1826 to 1846 it was the capital of the State, and the remains of the old capitol, which was destroyed by fire in 1923, are preserved in the city's Capitol Park. Pop. (1950) 46,396.

TUSCANY, formerly a sovereign grand duchy, now a district on the west coast of Italy. It comprises the maritime provinces of Grosseto, Livorno (Leghorn), Lucca, and Pisa, the inland provinces of Arezzo, Florence, and Siena, and the province of Massa e Carrara, extending from the sea northward between Liguria and the Apennines. Chiefly mountainous, the Apuan Alps attain 6385 feet and Mount Amiata 5655 feet. The rivers are the Arno, Cecina, Ombrone, and Serchio; all flow into the Mediterranean. Except in the Maremma, a marshy region in the south, the climate is mild and healthful. Mineral deposits include iron, mercury, borax, copper, and salt; there are many mineral and thermal springs. Agricultural products are wheat, maize, wine grapes, olives, and tobacco. Area, 8876 sq.m.; pop. (1950) 3,097,403.

Tuscany corresponds nearly to ancient Etruria (q.v.). The Etrurians or Tuscans were conquered by the Romans, who called the land *Tuscia*. It was held in turn by the Ostrogoths, the emperors of Constantinople, and the Lombards. The last were conquered by Charlemagne and placed under a Frankish duke, with Lucca as his capital. In 1030 Boniface II, of the house of Canossa, became Duke of Tuscany. He was also Count of Modena, Reggio, Mantua, and Ferrara. His granddaughter, Countess Matilda, known as "the Great Countess", a friend of Pope Gregory VII, was a supporter of the papal party during the investiture struggle. At her death, in 1115, she bequeathed all of her wide dominions to the papacy; but the German emperors claimed

Countryside near Florence in Tuscany, Italy

the duchy as an imperial fief, and for more than a century "the property of Matilda" was the cause of strife between the popes and the emperors. During this period the principal cities became independent and prosperous. Pisa had risen to independence long before this, and was then a great maritime republic.

For several centuries the history of Florence (q.v.) was the history of Tuscany. At the close of the 12th century Florence was at the head of the Tuscan league formed to resist the Hohenstaufen. This brought her into alliance with the papacy, and usually Florence remained a firm adherent of the Guelph party.

In the 14th century Dante, Giotto, Petrarch, and Boccaccio made Tuscany pre-eminent in the revival of letters and arts. The Tuscan dialect became the literary language of Italy. In 1406 Pisa submitted to Florence, and soon she became mistress of Livorno (Leghorn). Dissensions in Florence led to the predominance of the Medici (q.v.). Cosimo de' Medici gained control in 1434 and made the supreme power in Florence the hereditary possession of his house. In 1532, through the emperor Charles V, Alessandro de' Medici was created Duke of Florence. He was assassinated in 1537; Cosimo the Great became duke, and added to the territories of the duchy by re-

ceiving Siena from Charles V. This gift bound him to Spain, and for nearly two hundred years Tuscany was under the influence of Spain. In 1569 the Florentine dominions were erected into the grand duchy of Tuscany. The house of Medici became extinct in the male line in 1737. By the terms of the Treaty of Vienna, which had been concluded in 1735, the grand duchy was given to Francis of Lorraine, the husband of Maria Theresa of Austria. Grand Duke Ferdinand III was dispossessed by the French in 1799. By the Treaty of Madrid between France and Spain, in 1801, Tuscany was erected into the kingdom of Etruria and given to the son of the Duke of Parma. In 1807 Napoleon took the country, which was united with France. Elisa Baciocchi, the sister of Napoleon, received the title of Grand Duchess of Tuscany. In 1814 Ferdinand III was reinstated and ruled until 1824. His successor, Leopold II, did much to promote the prosperity of Tuscany. In 1847 Lucca was annexed to the grand duchy. In February, 1848, Leopold granted a liberal constitution to his subjects, but the tide of revolution carried everything before it, and early in 1849 the grand duke fled from his country. A counterrevolution was started and in a few months Leopold was restored to his throne. In 1850 he entered into a convention with Austria by which Austrian troops were to occupy Tuscany, and, thus supported, he reinstituted a regime of absolutism. In 1859 his pro-Austrian policy obliged him to leave his state, which was occupied by the forces of Victor Emmanuel. On March 15, 1860, the people by a plebiscite voted the union of Tuscany with Italy.

TUSCARORAS, a tribe of Indians forming a southern branch of the Iroquoian family (q.v.). They were driven out of North Carolina in 1715, and joined the Iroquois. They then united with the Five Nations, which then became Six Nations, being located on the Six Nations Reservation, Ontario, and with the Six Nations, New York. See IROQUOIS.

TUSKEGEE INSTITUTE, a nonsectarian normal and industrial school for the higher education of Negro men and women in Tuskegee, Ala., founded as the Tuskegee Normal and Industrial Institute in 1881 by Booker T. Washington. In 1953 the total enrollment was 1847, including 1748 full-time students, and the members of the faculty numbered 225. In the same year the endowment of the Institute was $8,859,237, and there were 100,000 volumes in the library.

TUSSAUD, MARIE, *nee* GRESHOLTZ or GROSHOLTZ, known as MADAME TUSSAUD (1760–1850), Swiss modeler in wax, born in Bern. She learned the art of wax modeling in Paris. After a three months' imprisonment during the French Revolution, she brought her collection to London and founded Madame Tussaud's Exhibition on Baker Street (1838).

TUSSOCK GRASS, or TUSSAC GRASS, common name applied to any of several large, perennial, broad-leaved grasses belonging to the family Gramineae. Falkland Islands tussock grass, *Poa flabellata,* is native to the Falkland Islands. It often grows as high as 8 feet, and is commonly used for forage. European tussock grass, *P. caespitosa,* is a similar plant native to Austria. West Indian tussock or smut grass, *Sporobolus elongatus,* native to the West Indies, is often found in southern parts of the United States, and is characterized by wiry stems and narrow panicles of flowers. Water tussock grass or great bulrush, *Scirpus lacustris,* is found in shallow, still waters throughout North America, Europe, and Asia, and is widely used as a border plant in aquatic gardens. It grows to a height of 9 feet. The tussock sedge, *Carex stricta,* is a low, tufted species, found abundantly in north-temperate regions of North America. It is used to edge aquatic and rock gardens,

and is often employed in the production of matting.

TUSSOCK MOTH, common name for any of several dull-colored moths (q.v.) belonging to the family Lymantriidae, and characterized by thick tufts of hair in the caterpillar stage. The insects are inconspicuously colored grayish white or brown, and usually attain a length of 1 inch. The female tussock moth, wingless and slightly larger than the male, lays from 200 to 300 minute eggs and deposits them beneath the outer leaves of shade and fruit trees. The tufted caterpillar larvae appear in from two to three weeks, and proceed to strip the trees of leaves, bark, and fruit. In late September the caterpillars spin a cocoon of silk and caterpillar hair, into which they retreat for the winter. They emerge in the spring to feed on the young leaf buds, flowers, and fruits, and usually pupate in June. The white-marked tussock moth, *Hemerocampa leucostigma,* is a well-known enemy of shade and fruit trees in eastern United States. It produces two or three generations each year from white, frothy, glistening masses of eggs. Other common species include the gypsy moth and the brown-tail moth (qq.v.). Measures are constantly taken to eliminate tussock moths in parks and gardens and along tree-shaded thoroughfares. Cocoons are often destroyed in winter by removing them from trees or by applying strong insecticides. The larvae may be controlled by arsenite spray in summer.

TUTANKHAMEN or **TUTENKHAMON** (fl. about 1358 B.C.), one of the last kings of the XVIIIth (Diospolite) dynasty of Egypt. His tomb was discovered by Lord Carnarvon (d. 1923) and Howard Carter in 1922. He was the husband of the third daughter of Akhenaten, or Amenhotep, the famous heretic king, and came to the throne a short time before or after the death of his father-in-law. Many treasures were found in his tomb. See EGYPTIAN ARCHEOLOGY.

TUTELO or **TOTERO,** a North American Indian tribe of Siouan stock (q.v.), living formerly on the upper Roanoke and Dan rivers in Virginia and North Carolina. They were first visited in 1670 by the German traveler John Lederer. In 1701 they were found near central North Carolina, preparing to move to the settlements for protection against the Iroquois (q.v.), who had driven them from villages on the Roanoke. They were much reduced in number and unable any longer to stand against their enemies. The refugee tribes were afterward settled by Governor Alexander Spotswood of Virginia near Fort Christanna, in what is now Brunswick Co., Va., where they remained until about 1740, when, finally at peace with the Iroquois, they removed to the north and settled on the Susquehanna River at Shamokin, now Sunbury, Pa. Later they were adopted by the Cayuga (q.v.), thus becoming a component part of the Iroquois league. Their village near Cayuga Lake was destroyed in 1779, and they fled to Canada and found their final home with the Iroquois on the Grand River Reservation, in Ontario, locating on Tutelo Heights, near Brantford. They are practically extinct.

TUTUILA. See SAMOA: *American Samoa.*

TUVA AUTONOMOUS REGION, an autonomous Region of Soviet Russia, situated in the Siberian area of the U.S.S.R., N.W. of the Mongolian People's Republic. Kizilkhoto, or Krasny (pop., about 10,000), is the capital. Topographically, the region is an elevated plateau, enclosed by the Sayan and Tannu mountains. It is traversed by several rivers, including a headstream of the Yenisei. Dense forests of coniferous and deciduous trees are found in the N., but most of the area is rich prairie land. About 75% of the population are Tuvinians, a nomadic Turkic people. Herding and the raising of cattle are their principal occupations. The Russians, who comprise about 20% of the population, engage in trading, farming, and prospecting for gold. Chinese and Mongols form the remainder of the population.

Until the early 20th century the area was known as the Uriankhai territory of Outer Mongolia (see MONGOLIA). Russian penetrations began about 1870. During the Mongolian revolt against China in 1911, when Outer Mongolia won autonomy, Russia made claims upon Uriankhai, which was detached from Outer Mongolia and made nominally independent. At the beginning of World War I, in 1914, it was made a protectorate of Russia and virtually included in the Altai Province of Siberia. During the Russian Civil War of 1917 it became an independent republic, known as Tannu Tuva, or the Tuvinian People's Republic. Because of subsequent protests made by the governments of China and of the Mongolian People's Republic (formerly Outer Mongolia) over its separation from the rest of Outer Mongolia, a commission was set up to determine the status of Tannu Tuva. Following the report of the commission, Tannu Tuva was recognized by the Mongolian People's Republic in a treaty of friendship signed by the two states in 1926.

In 1944 the republic was incorporated into the Russian R.F.S.R. as the Tuva Autonomous Region. Area, about 64,000 sq.m.; pop., about 65,000.

TUZIGOOT NATIONAL MONUMENT, a national monument in central Arizona, created in 1938 to preserve several prehistoric Indian ruins. The monument, situated about 2 miles E. of Clarkdale, covers an area of 43 acres and includes the remains of three large pueblos, believed to date from between 1000 and 1400 A.D. The pueblos are large enough to have housed approximately 400 persons. Numerous interesting artifacts, including stone implements, jewelry, and pottery, have been found in the ruins, and are now contained in a museum on the reservation.

TVER, city of Moscow Territory, U.S.S.R., situated at the confluence of the Volga and Tvertsa rivers, 100 miles N.W. of Moscow by rail. It has large textile, leather, metal, and wagon factories. The city was formerly the capital of Tver Government (since 1929 merged in Moscow Territory). Pop., about 216,000.

TWACHTMAN, JOHN HENRY (1853–1902), American painter, born in Cincinnati, Ohio, and trained at the Cincinnati School of Design under the American painter Frank Duveneck, in Munich under Duveneck and the German painter Ludwig Löfftz, and at the Académie Jullian in Paris. After 1890 Twachtman lived in Connecticut, painting there and teaching in New York City and in Newport, R.I. He is one of the outstanding American impressionists. His paintings are chiefly landscapes in oils and pastel, executed with simplicity, technical ease, and a delicate and subtle color sense. He excelled in winter scenes, employing extremely sensitive white, gray, and blue tones. Among the museums in which his work is represented are the Metropolitan Museum of Art, New York City; the Museum of Fine Arts, Boston, Mass.; and the National Gallery, Washington, D. C.

TWAIN, MARK. See CLEMENS, SAMUEL LANGHORNE.

TWEED, river of Scotland. It rises in Peebles and flows eastward, emptying into the North Sea at Berwick. It is 97 miles long, but unnavigable. For 18 miles of its lower course it forms the boundary between England and Scotland.

TWEED, WILLIAM MARCY (1823–78), American politician, leader of the so-called Tweed Ring, born in New York City. He was appointed deputy street commissioner of New York in 1861, and when in 1870 that department was changed to the department of public works, he was the commissioner at its head, a position which enabled him to initiate, it was believed, the combination known as the Tammany Ring, or Tweed Ring; see TAMMANY SOCIETY. The ring elected its candidate for mayor in 1865, and its candidate for governor in 1868, and schemes of city improvement involving heavy speculations were put under way.

Its exposure was made largely by *The New York Times* in 1871; investigation and prosecution were undertaken by a committee of seventy citizens, under the lead of Samuel J. Tilden. Tweed was indicted for forgery and grand larceny. Convicted, and sentenced to twelve years' confinement in the penitentiary and to pay a fine of $12,300, he was confined on Blackwell's Island until 1875, when he was released by a decision of the Court of Appeals, but was immediately rearrested on a warrant issued in a civil suit for $6,198,957, and sent to Ludlow Street Jail. He escaped, and fled to Spain. He was returned in November, 1876, and placed in Ludlow Street Jail until he died.

TWEEDMOUTH. See BERWICK UPON TWEED.

TWEED RING. See TWEED, WILLIAM MARCY.

TWELVE TABLES, LAW OF THE (Lat. *Lex Duodecim Tabularum*), the earliest code of Roman law, civil, criminal and religious, drawn up by the group of ten magistrates known as decemvirs in 451–450 B.C., and engraved or painted in the Roman forum on tablets of bronze or wood. According to tradition, the code was drawn up to appease the plebs (q.v.), who complained that the unwritten law as interpreted and applied by the patricians (q.v.) gave no adequate protection to their liberties. In 451 B.C. ten tables of laws were submitted to and accepted by the popular assembly; two supplementary tables were adopted later. The original tablets on which the laws were written are believed to have perished in the sack of Rome by the Gauls in 390 B.C.; copies of them stood in the forum in the 2nd century A.D. The Twelve Tables dealt mainly with the law of family, property, crimes, torts, and civil procedure, and provided the basis for the development of Roman law. They have been preserved only in fragmentary form, being quoted or paraphrased by later legal or historical writers. In this form about a third of the laws are extant. Attempts to reconstruct the code of the decemvirs have been made in modern times.

TWELVE-TONE SYSTEM or TECHNIQUE, in music, a theory of harmony developed in the first quarter of the 20th century by Arnold Schönberg (q.v.). As described by Schönberg, the twelve-tone system follows the principle of atonality (q.v.), under which a central keynote and all key relationships are abandoned; it is based on the chromatic scale of twelve equidistant semitones rather than the traditional seven-tone diatonic scale; see SCALE. Prior to Schönberg's time, the French impressionist composer Claude Debussy (see IMPRESSIONISM, in music) had begun the breakdown of diatonic harmony by using simultaneously two whole-tone scales of six steps, one scale beginning on C and the other on C♯. A combination of these whole-tone scales produced a twelve-tone chromatic scale, a new method of modulation, and a system of chord construction based upon intervals (see INTERVAL) of fourths. Schönberg carried his experiments much further; he expanded the possibilities of chords in fourths, and freely used successions of fourths in his contrapuntal texture, a practice considered dissonant in the diatonic system. In his developed twelve-tone system the standard scales are replaced by arbitrary series or "rows" of notes, in which the notes of the chromatic scale are arranged in such a way as to contain all the twelve tones. These "rows" recur throughout the compositions in which they are used in a variety of forms and groupings, providing a measure of melodic and harmonic unity.

The twelve-tone system was adopted by a number of Schönberg's pupils, notably Alban Berg, Anton von Webern, and Ernst Krenek (qq.v.), both as an approach to the teaching and study of music and as a method of practical composition. Though attacked by many critics as doctrinaire and overintellectual, the system is generally considered one of the major contributions made during the 20th century to the evolution of musical theory.

TWICKENHAM, municipal borough of Middlesex, England, situated on the Thames R., 10 miles s.w. of London. It is a residential district, and contains the international Rugby football ground of London. Alexander Pope had his estate here, and the town contains also Walpole's villa, called Strawberry Hill. It is famous for a ferry across the Thames that has been celebrated in a ballad "Twickenham Ferry". Pop. (1951 prelim.) 105,645.

TWIG PRUNER, any of several species of longicorn beetles of the genus *Elaphidion,* the females of which lay their eggs in the twigs of several kinds of trees. The eggs hatch and the larva when nearly full grown severs its twig, transforming to pupa within the twig after it has fallen. The common oak pruner, *E. villosum,* is a slender, long-horned beetle, dark brown in color, and covered with grayish pubescence. It feeds in twigs of oak, hickory, chestnut, maple, apple, plum, peach, and other trees. The purpose of the amputation of the twig by the larva seems not primarily to make the twig fall, but to penetrate the wood to the bark for an easy exit. *E. subpubescens* works in the same way in shoots of white oak, while *E. mucronatum* is found in twigs of live oak and other trees. The larva of *E. unicolor* amputates the twigs of the redbud, *Cervis canadensis.* A few other insects have similar habits. For example, certain horntails, notably the willowshoot horntail, *Phyllaecus integer,* live, in the larval stage, in twigs of willow, which they cause to wilt and break.

TWILIGHT, the diffused illumination of the sky which immediately precedes sunrise and follows sunset. When the sun sets below the horizon, we are not at once plunged into the darkness of night. There is an intermediate period of partial and slowly increasing darkness which we call twilight. It is caused by the reflection of the sunlight by dust and particles of water vapor in the upper atmosphere. The same phenomenon occurs just before sunrise, and, to distinguish it from the evening twilight, is called dawn. Dawn begins and twilight ends when the sun is about 18° below the horizon, and consequently their duration varies with the latitude and with the season of the year. In the tropics twilight rarely lasts longer than thirty minutes, while in the latitude of the north of Scotland it lasts so long that about midsummer it sometimes fills the entire interval between sunset and sunrise.

TWIN FALLS, county seat of Twin Falls Co., Idaho, near the Snake R., 40 miles N. of the Nevada boundary and about 145 miles s.w. of Boise. It is served by a railroad, and is the commercial center and shipping point of a rich, irrigated agricultural area. The diversified products of the surrounding region include grains, sugar beets, potatoes, dairy products, and livestock. Among the industrial establishments in the city are flour mills, creameries, plants dehydrating fruits, and other plants processing and packing agricultural products. Twin Falls also contains extensive wholesale houses, warehouses, and farmers' co-operative associations. The Twin Falls-Jerome Bridge, a cantilever bridge crossing the Snake R. about 2 miles N. of the city, is one of the highest bridges of its kind in the world, more than 475 ft. above the river at its center span. Places of interest nearby are Shoshone Falls of the

Snake R., falling in a drop of 212 ft. between the black lava walls of a canyon, and the Magic Mountain Winter Sports Area. Pop. (1950) 17,600.

TWINFLOWER, common name applied to a hardy evergreen shrub, *Linneae borealis,* belonging to the Honeysuckle family. The plant is native to the temperate forests of Europe and North America, and is cultivated in many areas as an ornamental shrub. The pink or purple flowers, arranged in pairs on erect peduncles, have a five-parted calyx, a five-lobed, bell-shaped corolla, four stamens, and a solitary pistil. The fruit is a single-seeded, indehiscent pod. Twinflowers are used mainly in rock gardens of cool, moist areas, and require peaty, acid soil. The principal American variety, *L. borealis* var. *americana,* native to N. U.S., Canada, and Alaska, bears tubular flowers. Mexican twinflower, *Bravoa geminiflora,* is an unrelated herb belonging to the Amaryllis family.

TWINS, in astronomy, the Gemini, Castor and Pollux (qq.v.). For twinning in biology, see TERATOLOGY: *Twinning.*

TWO-FOUR-D or **2,4-D,** popular name first given to a plant-growth regulator, 2, 4-dichlorophenoxyacetic acid, but now used to designate the acid, its salts, or its esters. These substances belong to a large group of organic compounds often called "plant hormones". External application of 2,4-D to many kinds of plants results in cessation of leaf growth, increased rate of respiration, and consequent breakdown and rapid use of reserve foods. The chemical has relatively little effect on grasses, including ornamental kinds and valuable cereal grains, when applied properly in amounts which result in destruction or stunting of many kinds of weeds. Its popular designation, "weed killer", stems from its effectiveness in freeing lawns and crops of cereal grains from certain weeds, but as a herbicide, 2,4-D does not distinguish between plants considered useful and those considered weeds (q.v.) ; it does not affect maturing crab and quack grasses, which are weeds, but when misused it destroys useful broader-leaved crops such as grapes, cotton, and tomato plants.

Great care must therefore be exercised in the use of 2,4-D, because it can injure valuable and ornamental crops. Application is usually made by spraying or dusting, in volumes and concentrations determined experimentally by the manufacturer. Use of greater volumes or concentrations results in destruction of grasses as well as broader-leaved plants. Application must be made after grass has become well established, as grass seedlings are destroyed by even moderate concentrations. Dry soil will retain 2,4-D in a state of high effectiveness, killing young grass seedlings which replace destroyed broad-leaved plants; therefore best results are obtained from applications made when the ground is moist.

TWORT, FREDERICK WILLIAM (1877–1950), English bacteriologist, born in Camberley, Surrey, and educated at St. Thomas' Hospital and Medical School. He was assistant bacteriologist at London Hospital between 1902 and 1909, and was superintendent of the Brown Institution from 1909 until 1944, when the building was destroyed by bombs. After 1931 he served as professor of bacteriology at the University of London. He studied various bacteria and viruses and in 1915 discovered the existence of bacteriophages. In addition to his work in bacteriology he invented a short-wave coil for reception of long-distance short-wave radio transmission. He was elected a member of the Royal College of Surgeons and a fellow of the Royal Society.

TWO SICILIES, KINGDOM OF THE, the name commonly given to a former kingdom embracing Sicily and southern Italy, and known often as the Kingdom of Naples. In the Middle Ages the southern part of the Italian mainland came to be known as "Sicily on this side of the Faro" (the Strait of Messina). From the earliest times both island and mainland were subject to settlement and conquest by peoples of widely different stock, producing a complicated admixture of races. At the dawn of history the Phenicians had trading settlements there. In the 8th century B.C. numerous Greek colonies were founded in both Sicily and southern Italy and became powerful and wealthy states. A new Phenician element was introduced when Carthage disputed the supremacy of Sicily with the Greeks. The Roman conquest followed. In the middle of the 5th century, at the time of the fall of the Roman Empire, Sicily was ravaged by the Vandals. Toward the close of the century the Ostrogoths made themselves masters of Italy and Sicily. In the 6th century their realm was conquered by the Byzantines. Soon afterward the Lombards established their sway over part of southern Italy. The Lombard duchy of Benevento was founded, out of which in the 9th century arose the three principalities of Benevento, Salerno, and Capua. By the side of these was the duchy of Naples, a Byzantine creation. Apulia and Calabria were held by the Byzantines until the 11th century. In the years from 827 to 878 the island of Sicily was conquered by the Saracens, and they also obtained a foothold on the mainland.

About 1037 the sons of a Norman knight, Tancred de Hauteville, setting out with a few followers, entered southern Italy in the service of the Byzantine governor, but soon seized and divided Apulia and were able to hold the country against every effort by the Greeks to dislodge them. Robert Guiscard, one of these brothers, became Count of Apulia in 1057, and in 1059 he was recognized by Pope Nicholas II as Duke of Apulia and Calabria. In 1061 his younger brother, Roger, with a few hundred Norman knights, began the conquest of the island of Sicily, which became a county and a fief of Robert's duchy, though the total subjugation of the island was not accomplished until 1090, after Robert's death. In 1127 Roger II, son of the first Roger, united Apulia, Calabria, and Sicily, and in 1130 assumed the title of King of Sicily.

He ruled over the Abruzzi, made himself master of Capua, and received the submission of Naples. The marriage of Frederick Barbarossa's son, later the emperor Henry VI, to Constance, heiress of the Two Sicilies, in 1186, united the destinies of the Norman kingdom with those of the house of Hohenstaufen, whose rule began in 1194. The child of this marriage, the emperor Frederick II (q.v.), was the most remarkable prince in the Europe of his day. He reorganized the government of the Sicilian kingdom on essentially modern lines, founded the University of Naples, and made his court a brilliant center of high culture and learning. His death in 1250 was followed by the downfall of the Hohenstaufens. In 1266 Charles of Anjou, brother of Louis IX of France, at the instance of the pope, undertook the conquest of the Two Sicilies. He vanquished Manfred, son of Frederick II, at Benevento, and in 1268 captured and executed Conradin, the last of the Hohenstaufens. Charles of Anjou made Naples his residence.

The year 1282 witnessed the fearful popular uprising against the French in Sicily known as the Sicilian Vespers (q.v.). The people shook off the yoke of Anjou and placed their island under the rule of Pedro III of Aragon. The house of Anjou continued to rule in south Italy, which thus became the kingdom of Naples. In 1296 Sicily was separated from Aragon, but continued under the rule of the Aragonese house, and in 1412 was reunited with that kingdom. Robert I of Naples (1309–43) made himself the champion of the Guelph (q.v.) party and extended his influence throughout Italy. He was succeeded by his granddaughter Joanna I, and an anarchic period began and continued for many years, the heirs of the elder Neapolitan line, which had also acquired the throne of Hungary, contending with new aspirants from Anjou. In 1399 the Neapolitan line triumphed in the person of the crafty and unprincipled Ladislas. He died in 1414, leaving the kingdom to his sister, Joanna II. During her reign disorder was renewed. After her death in 1435 Alfonso V, King of Aragon and Sicily, conquered Naples in 1442 and reigned until his death in 1458.

He left Aragon and Sicily to his eldest son, John, and Naples to his illegitimate son, Ferdinand, under whose rapacious and cruel rule new troubles arose. In 1495 Charles VIII of France invaded Naples, and although he was compelled to withdraw in the same year, his successor, Louis XII, jointly with Ferdinand of Spain, conquered the country in 1501. The Spaniards under Hernández Gonzalo de Córdoba (q.v.) drove out the French in 1503 and made Naples a Spanish province.

The country was now subjected to the oppression of Spanish viceroys. Rebellion at Naples broke out in 1647. In 1707 the Neapolitan dominions were wrested from Spain by Austria during the War of the Spanish Succession. (See SPANISH SUCCESSION, WAR OF THE.) Naples was confirmed to Austria by the Treaty of Utrecht (1713) and Sicily was given to Savoy. In 1720 Sicily was transferred by Savoy to Austria in exchange for Sardinia. In 1734 Don Carlos, second son of Philip V of Spain, of the house of Bourbon, invaded the Two Sicilies, and in 1735 he was crowned and was recognized by the Treaty of Vienna as King Charles IV. After the Peace of Aix-la-Chapelle (1748) Italy enjoyed almost fifty years of peace, and these years witnessed in the Two Sicilies progress along many lines, but the upheaval of the French Revolution brought new troubles. The coalition against the French Republic was joined by Ferdinand, the second Bourbon king of the Two Sicilies. (See FERDINAND I.)

In December, 1798, the Neapolitans attempted to drive the French out of the Papal States. They were thrown back, Naples was taken (January, 1799), and the Parthenopean Republic was created. In the same year Ferdinand was reinstated with the assistance of the English fleet. In 1796 Napoleon conquered the Kingdom of Naples and placed his brother Joseph Bonaparte on the throne, Ferdinand continuing to reign in Sicily. In 1808 Joseph was succeeded by Joachim Murat (q.v.). After the fall of Murat in 1815 Ferdinand was restored in Naples. At the close of 1816 Ferdinand united the kingdoms of Naples and Sicily into the single kingdom of the Two Sicilies and changed his title from Ferdinand IV to Ferdinand I.

In 1820 there was a military rising in the Neapolitan dominions, joined by the Carbonari (q.v.), under the leadership of General Pepe, to secure a constitutional government. The king yielded to the demand, notwithstanding his agreement with Austria to make no constitutional concessions. At the same time a revolutionary movement aiming at autonomy for the island took place in Sicily. The congress of the Great Powers at Laibach (1821) charged Austria with the restoration of Ferdinand's absolute power. The patriots made an ineffectual resistance and Ferdinand resumed his tyrannical sway under the protection of Austrian bayonets. Ferdinand died in 1825 and was succeeded by his son, Francis I, who in 1830 was succeeded by his son Ferdinand II (q.v.). The change of rulers brought about no change in the despotic policy of the government. After 1843 the republican propaganda of Mazzini took a strong hold in southern Italy. At the beginning of 1848 Sicily rose in insurrection to secure an autonomous and constitutional government. Ferdinand II was forced to grant a representative constitution to his subjects. This did not satisfy the Sicilians. The deposition of Ferdinand was declared, a provisional government organized, and the Duke of Genoa, son of the king of Sardinia, was elected king of the Sicilians (June, 1848), a dignity which he declined. In his Neapolitan dominions Ferdinand, with the aid of reactionary elements, was enabled successfully to combat the revolutionary movement now sweeping through Italy. In September, 1848, his forces entered upon a Sicilian campaign. In May, 1849, Palermo capitulated and the revolution in the island ended. Ferdinand, once more the despot, wreaked a fearful vengeance upon the champions of liberty in his dominions. His atrocities were finally checked by the intervention of England. In 1859 Ferdinand II was succeeded by his son, Francis II. The emancipation of northern Italy (except Venetia) from the rule of Austria and the tyrants upheld by her (1859–60) was speedily followed by the liberation of the Two Sicilies from the Bourbons, accomplished through the efforts of Garibaldi, and by their incorporation in the new Kingdom of Italy (1860–61). See GARIBALDI, GIUSEPPE; ITALY; VICTOR EMMANUEL II.

President John Tyler (from a painting)

TYLER, county seat of Smith Co., Tex., situated between the Neches and Sabine rivers, 98 miles S.E. of Dallas. It is served by two railroads, and contains railroad repair shops. The city is the center and shipping point of a rich agricultural and mineral-producing area, and is especially noted as a leading center of the rose-growing industry in the U.S. The diversified products of the surrounding region include cotton, corn, forage crops, tomatoes, sweet potatoes, watermelons, strawberries, blackberries, dewberries, peaches, pecans, peppers, peas, squash, livestock, oil, natural gas, clay, iron ore, lignite, and timber. Among the industrial establishments in the city are oil refineries, foundries, machine shops, fruit canneries, cottonseed-oil mills, pecanshelling plants, milk-processing plants, lumber mills, and factories manufacturing tile, pottery and other clay products, gas heaters, floor furnaces, hot-water heaters, battery cases, soil pipe, toys, prefabricated houses, crates and baskets, and clothing. In addition, the city contains the headquarters of several oil companies and oil-well supply houses. The extensive rose nurseries cover a radius of more than 10 miles around the city, and the municipal rose gardens cover 3 acres. An annual rose festival is held at Tyler, and the city is also the site of the annual East Texas Fair. Educational institutions in the city include Tyler Junior College, established in 1926, Texas College (1894), for Negroes, Butler Junior College (1905), for Negroes, and Tyler Commercial College. Tyler was settled in 1844 and incorporated as a city in 1875. Pop. (1950) 38,968.

TYLER, JOHN (1790–1862), tenth President of the United States, born in Greenway, Va., and educated at William and Mary College. He served in the State legislature (1811–16); in Congress (1816–23); was governor of Virginia (1826–28); and U.S. senator (1828–36). He was elected Vice-President on the Whig ticket in 1840 and succeeded to the Presidency when William Henry Harrison died (Apr. 4, 1841).

Shortly after taking office, Tyler broke with the Whig Party and most of his cabinet resigned. The chief accomplishments of his administration were the Webster-Ashburton Treaty with Great Britain and the annexation of Texas. He retired in 1845. In 1861 he presided over the Peace Convention at Washington, but later voted for secession in the Virginia Convention and served in the Confederate Provisional Congress.

TYLER, MOSES COIT (1835–1900), American literary historian and educator, born in Griswold, Conn., and educated at Yale University and at Andover College. He held congregational pastorates in Owego and Poughkeepsie, N.Y. successively. He resigned the latter charge in 1862, due to ill-health, and went to England, where he spent four years of rest, studying, lecturing, and writing. In 1867 he became professor of English at the University of Michigan, and in 1881 was called to the chair of American history at Cornell University, holding this post until his death. In 1881 he was ordained deacon in the Protestant Episcopal Church and was advanced to the priesthood in 1883. He wrote his *History of American Literature during the Colonial Time* (2 vols.) in 1878, and immediately won a wide reputation for scholarship. This history, which was continued in the two volumes entitled *A Literary History of the American Revolution* (1897) and, in a measure, in the essays entitled *Three Men of Letters* (1895), constitutes Tyler's chief claim to remembrance. It hardly carries the story of American literature beyond the year 1783, but within its limits is characterized by such accuracy and breadth of scholarship that it is not likely to be superseded, and fully entitles its author to a high place among literary historians. It is somewhat diffuse and fails to apply standards rigorously. Besides this history, Tyler's most important work is a biography of Patrick Henry in the *American Statesmen Series* (1888). He also wrote *The Brawnville Papers* (1868), devoted to the claims of physical culture; *Memorial of E. K. Apgar* (privately printed, 1886); and *Glimpses of England* (1898), a collection of letters from England.

TYLER, WAT or WALTER (d. 1381), leader of the English peasant revolt of 1381. His birthplace was probably in Colchester, Essex. See TYLER'S REBELLION.

TYLER'S REBELLION, or PEASANTS' REVOLT, English social revolt of 1381 led by Wat Tyler. Its immediate cause was popular resentment over the poll tax. The insurgents, mostly from Essex, Middlesex, Sussex, and Kent, stormed London and forced King Richard II to remove the poll taxes. The revolt led also to the liberation of John Ball (q.v.) from prison, where he had been confined for seditious utterances, and to the abolition of villeinage.

TYLOR, SIR EDWARD BURNETT (1832-1917), British anthropologist, born in Camberwell, England. Meeting the ethnologist Henry Christy in Cuba in 1856, he accompanied him on a scientific journey through Mexico, one result of which was his *Anahuac, or Mexico and the Mexicans* (1861). Tyler's other works include *Researches into the Early History of Mankind* (1865) and *Primitive Culture* (2 vols., 1871).

TYMPANUM. See EAR.

TYNDALE, WILLIAM (about 1490-1536), English translator of the Bible, born in Gloucestershire. At Cambridge he came under the influence of Erasmus. In 1525, in Cologne, he began the printing of his English version of the New Testament which was completed in Worms. His translation was vigorously combated by ecclesiastical authorities in England. Tyndale's combined translations were published as Matthew's Bible. He was taken into custody in Antwerp, and, after fifteen months' imprisonment, was tried in 1536, and on October 6 was burned at the stake.

TYNDALL, JOHN (1820-93), Irish physicist, born in Leighlin-Bridge, County Carlow, Ireland. In 1847 he became teacher of physics at Queenwood College, Hampshire, England, where he began original researches. In 1848 he and his colleague, Dr. Frankland, went to Germany and studied at Marburg (under Bunsen); there, in Berlin and elsewhere, he made investigations into diamagnetism and the magneto-optic properties of crystals. In

1859 he began his researches on radiation; a later subject was the acoustic properties of the atmosphere. The proceeds of a successful lecturing tour of the United States (1872) he devoted to founding scholarships for original research at Harvard and Columbia universities. His works comprise *Heat Considered as a Mode of Motion* (1863), *Contributions to Molecular Physics in the Domain of Radian' Heat* (1872), and *New Fragments* (1892).

TYNE, river of north England, formed by the North and the South Tyne in Northumberland Hills. It flows eastward and empties into the North Sea at Tynemouth. One of the principal coal-mining and manufacturing regions of England, and the cities of Newcastle, Gateshead, and South Shields lie on its banks. Its length is 80 m.; it is navigable to Blaydon, about 18 m.

TYNEMOUTH, watering place of Northumberland, England, 9 miles E. of Newcastle. The municipal and parliamentary borough comprises the townships of Tynemouth, North Shields, Chirton, Cullercoats, and Preston. There are remains of an ancient castle and priory. Pop. (1951 prelim.) 66,544.

TYPE (Gr. *typos,* "an impression" or "stamp"), piece of metal, wood, or other material, on one end of which is cast or engraved a character or sign. The word "type" is held to include many characters which are not letters, such as punctuational signs, astronomical signs, ornaments, pieces of borders, and musical characters. A necessary complement to types are the spaces which divide words and fill up openings in composed *forms.* See PRINTING.

In the United States types are designated according to the number of *points* of which the body consists. The point is 1/12 of a pica. The following specimen lines show the usual bodies used in the text of books and newspapers being set in (1) Pica, or 12 point; (2) Small pica, or 11 point; (3) Long primer, or 10 point; (4) Bourgeois, or 9 point; (5) Brevier, or 8 point; (6) Minion, or 7 point; (7) Nonpareil, or 6 point; (8) Pearl, or 5 point; (9) Diamond, or 4½ point; and (10) Brilliant, or 4 point.

(1) Encyclopedia.

(2) Encyclopedia.

(3) Encyclopedia.

(4) Encyclopedia.

(5) Encyclopedia.

(6) Encyclopedia.

(7) Encyclopedia.

(8) Encyclopedia.

(9) Encyclopedia.

(10) Encyclopedia.

Type metal is composed of tin, antimony, copper, and lead. For resisting great tear and wear brass types are made to a limited extent. Large wooden types, which are cheaper, lighter, and not so easily fractured by a fall, are cut or engraved either by hand or by a machine.

In 1838 David Bruce of New York invented the type-casting machine which has revolutionized the art of type founding, or casting. In 1862 J. R. Johnson and J. S. Atkinson of London patented a machine in which all operations subsequent to punch-cutting and matrix-justifying were performed automatically; this was later improved by P. M. Shanks. Later machines are those of Barth, which casts, finishes, and puts the type in line at a rate of over 120 types a minute, and the Wicks rotary type-casting machine. (See also TYPE-SETTING MACHINES.)

The first English founder who was really able to compete with foreign rivals was William Caslon (1692–1766). His types were not novel in design, but their merit consisted in their technical excellence—their careful cutting and good founding. They were especially readable. The style retained its supremacy in Great Britain for more than half a century. Baskerville of Birmingham (1706–75) was another eminent founder. Jackson, a pupil of Caslon, introduced a new style, shown in the Bible printed by Bensley for Macklin.

The two styles—the "modern" after that of Jackson and the "old" style after that of Caslon—are those in which nearly all present-day books are printed in Great Britain. In the United States the first attempts at typefounding were made by Christopher Saur about 1735 in Germantown, Pa. Binny and Ronaldson's type foundry was started in Philadelphia about the end of the century, and D.G. Bruce's foundry was established in New York City in 1813. In 1892 most of the large American type foundries were amalgamated as the American Type Founders' Company.

TYPESETTING MACHINES, machines designed to expedite the setting or composition of metallic type for printing (q.v.). Although the term "typesetting machines" should properly be applied only to those machines which place already cast pieces of type in the proper sequence and position for printing, the term is generally used to apply to any type-composing machine. A number of different systems have been employed for setting type by machine, but in modern printing practice only two classes of machine are in general use.

One of these is exemplified in the linotype, which casts a metal slug comprising a single line of type matter, and the other is exemplified in the monotype, which casts type for individual letters and places these letters in order in a galley. Both machines are extensively used in commercial printing and have largely supplanted the hand setting of type (q.v.).

Linotype. The general working principles of all machines which cast type in a one-line slug are similar, although different in detail, and the description which follows is based on the linotype. Other machines are manufactured and sold under such names as Intertype.

The linotype machine is provided with one or more sectioned magazines containing a supply of negative molds or matrices from which the type is cast. In the simpler forms of the machine, having a single magazine, matrices for 180 separate letters and characters are supplied. In the most elaborate machines, which have four magazines, the operator has a choice of 720 separate characters and letters, permitting him to incorporate several different fonts or styles of type into the work he is composing.

A keyboard, somewhat similar to that of a typewriter, controls the matrices. When one of the keys on the keyboard is depressed the appropriate matrix slides out of the magazine by gravity and through a vertical channel to an endless belt which conveys it to a frame called the assembler. The length of this frame can be set to the proper width for the type column being set. The linotype keyboard is also provided with special keys for spaces and quads. The quads are fixed spaces such as those used to indent a line at the beginning of a paragraph. The spaces consist of double wedges placed parallel to each other with their thin edges at opposite ends. They are used for the spaces between words and sentences and can be varied in width automatically by the action of the two wedges sliding against each other. When no pressure is applied, the spacers are at maximum width and when they are compressed, the spacers slide against each other and provide a narrower space. The use of such spacers makes it possible for the linotype to "justify" lines automatically, producing lines of identical length although containing different numbers of characters.

After the operator of the machine has filled the assembler with the appropriate matrices, quads, and spacers, the entire contents of the assembler is transferred mechanically to a position in front of a mold wheel on

Mergenthaler Linotype Co.

TYPESETTING MACHINES. *Top: Paige compositor with justifier, 1887, often called the "Mark Twain machine" because Twain invested heavily in it. Bottom, left: 1911 Polytype, a linecasting machine. Bottom, right: Linotype machine of the design widely used today.*

Lanston Monotype Machine Co.

MONOTYPE MACHINE

Top: Composing machine, one of the two separate units of a monotype system. This mechanism contains a keyboard of 225 keys and devices for counting and justifying. Left: The casting machine, the other of the two units. On it individual type slugs are cast.

which the actual line of type is cast. The matrices are held in position in front of a slot in this wheel, and molten type metal from a melting pot is forced into the hollows of the matrices by a pump. This operation forms the linotype slug, a narrow metal strip within the slot, with the letters and characters cast on one edge. After casting, the mold wheel revolves and as it travels, the slug is automatically trimmed by knives to the proper width and thickness. Finally the slug is expelled from the mold wheel into its proper position in a metal tray or galley.

When the casting operation is complete, the spacers and matrices which make up the line of type are automatically picked up and transferred to a distributor box at the top of the magazine. Each matrix is made with a series of serrations at its upper edge. The teeth on each matrix are different and act like the wards of a key to permit the matrix to fall into the proper bin in the magazine as it is conveyed through the distribution box across the top of the magazine. One of the chief virtues of the linotype machine is that the three functions of the machine, assembly, casting, and distribution, are carried out simultaneously by a single apparatus run by a single operator. Machines of this type also obviate the necessity of the redistribution of type after use, because the type slugs can be melted again after printing.

Monotype. The general principle of monotype machines is the casting of one character at a time from a single master matrix. The machines are arranged to assemble the type in galleys, but can also be used to cast type for hand setting. Special attachments permit the use of the monotype to cast rulings as well as type.

A monotype system consists of two machines, a composing machine and a separate casting machine. In some other composing devices the functions of both machines are combined into a single piece of apparatus. The monotype-composing machine contains a keyboard of 225 keys which produces coded punch marks on a paper strip. In addition to the key and perforation mechanisms, the keyboard has a counting and justifying mechanism. The counting arrangement counts the width of each character as struck and adds it to the width of the characters previously struck in the line, so that the operator can tell at a glance how much type has been put into the line and how much space remains. The justifying mechanism consists of a pointer which rises a short distance each time the

® Intertype Corp.

The Fotosetter, photographic line-composing machine, a new development in typesetting

space key of the machine is struck, to put a justifying space between words, and a cylinder called the justifying scale, which revolves automatically when the operator has put enough characters and spaces in the line to bring it within a specified distance from the end of the line. By reference to the surface of this scale the operator can find the appropriate keys to punch which will produce a code mark controlling the action of the casting machine to make spaces of the proper width to justify the line.

The casting machine is entirely automatic in its operation and is controlled by the paper ribbon perforated in the composing machine. A square matrix case contains 225 matrices in the simplest model of the machine, and these matrices are automatically moved into position over a hollow body mold under the control of the perforations of the ribbon. Type metal is forced into the mold and against the matrix face under pressure, casting an individual type slug. These slugs are automatically transported and assembled in a galley.

Photographic Typesetting. The great improvement in the apparatus used for offset lithographic printing (see PHOTOMECHANICAL PROCESSES: *Photolithography*) and the subsequent increase in the use of this process have led to the development of many machines used to produce by photographic means type copy which can be used for lithographic reproduction. In general such machines operate in a manner somewhat similar to the monotype casting machine, using a photographic negative instead of a metal matrix, and printing the completed line of type on photographic paper. None of the photographic typesetting machines introduced commercially has been widely adopted.

History. The first efforts at mechanizing the composition of printed matter were directed toward the development of true typesetting machines which actually put precast type in place in a galley. The first of such machines was patented in 1822 by the American inventor William Church. In the next fifty years a large number of similar machines were patented, but none of them achieved substantial commercial success. In almost all of these machines the justification of the line of type was accomplished by hand rather than automatically, and two or more men were needed to operate the machine. Typesetting machines patented during the 19th century included not only true typesetting machines but also machines that cast type and set it, and machines that used positive dies to make an impression on some soft substance such as wood, from which matrix a line of type could be cast.

The linotype was patented in 1885 by the German-American inventor Ottmar Mergenthaler and was the first typesetting machine to combine type casting and automatic justification. The monotype was the invention of the American Tolbert Lanston. It was patented in 1887 and introduced commercially in 1897.

TYPEWRITER, a machine designed to print or impress written characters on paper, as a speedier and more legible substitute for handwriting. Since the introduction of practical typewriters in the 1870's, the machines have come into universal use and have played an important part in the development of modern business and in the great increase of the dissemination of written and printed information which has characterized the 20th century.

The first recorded attempt to produce a writing machine was made by the English inventor Henry Mill, who obtained a British patent on such a machine in 1714, but no picture of the machine exists and the patent describes it simply as "an Artificial Machine or Method for the Impressing or Transcribing of Letters Singly or Progressively one after another, as in Writing, whereby all Writing whatever may be Engrossed in Paper or Parchment so Neat and Exact as not to be distinguished from Print".

The next patent issued for a typewriter was granted to the American inventor William Austin Burt in 1829, but details of Burt's machine are also lacking and the model of the machine required by the U.S. patent law of the period was destroyed by fire.

In 1833 a French patent was given to the French inventor Xavier Progin for a machine which embodied for the first time one of the principles employed in modern typewriters: the use for each letter or symbol of separate type bars, actuated by separate lever keys. Progin's machine, which he called a *Ktypographic machine* or *Ktypographic pen,* was so arranged that the type bars struck the paper at the same point and the paper was moved between letters to produce words and lines of writing.

The system used for moving the paper between letters and between lines on almost all modern typewriters is a cylindrical platen against which the paper is held firmly. The platen moves horizontally to produce the spacing betwen letters and revolves to produce the spacing between lines. The first machine to use this method of spacing was invented in 1843 by an American, Charles Thurber. The printing portion of Thurber's typewriter consisted of a metal ring which revolved horizontally above the platen and which was equipped with a series of vertical keys or plungers having pieces of type at the bottom. The machine was operated by revolving the wheel until the correct letter was centered over the printing position on the platen, and then striking the key. Although Thurber made several improvements to his typewriter, it was never commercially practical.

Several other inventors attempted to produce machines similar to the typewriter but intended to make embossed impressions, which could be read by the blind, rather than inked impressions. One such machine, developed by the American inventor Alfred Ely Beach in 1856, resembled modern typewriters to a great extent in the arrangement of its keys and type bars but embossed its letters on a narrow paper strip instead of a sheet. A similar machine invented by the American Samuel W. Francis, and patented by him in 1856, had a circular arrangement of type bars, a moving paper holder, and a bell which rang to signal the end of a line, as in modern machines. The keyboard arrangement of Francis' machine resembled the black and white keys of a piano.

During the 1850's and 1860's a number of inventors endeavored to produce a workable typewriter, but none succeeded until 1868, when three American inventors, Christopher Latham Sholes, Carlos Glidden, and Samuel

Milwauk. Pub. Mus.; I.B.M.

THE TYPEWRITER. *Above: A Sholes and Glidden model of 1874. Right, top: A Sholes and Glidden model of 1873. At right: A modern electric typewriter.*

W. Soule, patented an experimental writing machine; after making several other models the inventors marketed the first practical typewriter in 1873. In the following year manufacture of the typewriter was taken over by the firm of E. Remington and Sons of Ilion, N.Y., and sold under the trade-mark name of Sholes and Glidden.

The typewriter of 1874, called the Remington, incorporated almost all of the essential features of the modern machine. The paper was held in a carriage between a rubber platen and a smaller rubber cylinder set parallel to one another. The carriage was moved from right to left as the letters were struck by means of a spring, and regulated by an escapement mechanism which allowed the carriage to move the distance of one space for each letter. The carriage was returned to the right by a lever, which also served to revolve the platen for a space of one line by means of a ratchet and pawl. The type bars were arranged in a radial arc; when any one of the keys, which were arranged in a banked keyboard at the front of the machine, was depressed, the corresponding type bar struck against the platen by lever action. An inked cloth ribbon ran between the type bar and the platen, and the type struck this ribbon to make an inked impression on the underlying paper. The ribbon was carried on a pair of spools and was moved automatically after each impression to present a fresh portion of ribbon for the next letter.

The early typewriters produced under the Remington name wrote only in capital letters, but in 1878 the carriage shift, an important feature on all modern machines, was introduced. This shift consisted of a special lever which moved either the carriage or the type sector a small vertical distance; when the lever was depressed a second series of letter mounted on the same type bars was impressed on the paper. The introduction of the shift permitted the addition of numbers, lower-case letters, and other symbols without increase in the size of the keyboard. Certain other typewriters invented in the 1880's and 1890's employed double or even triple keyboards to achieve the same result, but fell into disuse with the increase of the technique of "touch typing". This system of operating a typewriter without looking at the keyboard is most efficient on the compact keyboards of shift machines.

Type bars of early commercial typewriters were adjusted to strike at the bottom of the platen; the line being written was thus not visible to the operator unless he turned the platen by hand. Beginning in the early 1880's this disadvantage was obviated by the so-called "visible" typewriters, in which the type struck the top of the platen. The system still in general use, in which the type segments strike the platen at the front, was first introduced in 1897.

Following the success of the Sholes-Glidden-Remington machine, many new models of typewriters were invented and many minor improvements were made on existing machines. Although more than 100 new typewriter designs were marketed between 1890 and 1905, few of them proved to be of any enduring worth, and most were discarded. Among the typewriters which proved successful in America were the Underwood, L.C. Smith, Royal, and Woodstock. Minor improvements included the use of multicolored ribbons and the introduction of tabulating keys by which the carriage could be moved a predetermined distance to the left for the purpose of automatically spacing or tabulating.

Two entirely different designs of typewriter which did not use the type-bar system were also introduced in America during the 1880's and 1890's. One of these was the so-called type-wheel typewriter, typified by the Blickensderfer machine. In this typewriter all the type faces were mounted on the outside of a single small cylinder which was revolved and moved up and down by the action of the keys to place in position the proper letter in the typing space. The Hammond typewriter, first introduced in 1880, worked on a somewhat similar principle and carried its type on interchangeable, curved shuttles fixed to the outside of a metal ring. In both of these machines no platens were used and the type did not strike against the paper to make an impression. Instead, the paper was held in a vertical position, unsupported by a platen, and the impression was made by a hammer which struck the back of the paper, forcing it against the ribbon and the type. The advantage of the Hammond machine was the interchange-

ability of type shuttles, making possible the use of a variety of type face on the same machine. In a modified form, the Hammond principle is still extensively used in machines such as the Varityper, employed for producing typewritten copy which can be reproduced by lithography.

Recent Developments. Developments in the typewriter field since 1900 have greatly extended the over-all usefulness of these machines. From the point of view of the businessman, the most important advance has been the development of the bookkeeping machine which combines the functions of the typewriter and the adding machine. Such machines are usually arranged to handle large flat sheets such as ledger pages or the heavy cardboard sheets used for filing accounting records. Machines of this type are made by most of the leading manufacturers of typewriters and business machinery and are adaptable to a variety of accounting operations, including inventory control and the issuing of bills or statements. Use of such machines has greatly speeded accounting procedures in businesses of many types.

Small portable typewriters working on the type bar principle were first introduced in 1912. They are used extensively not only by travelers but also in the home, in which their light weight and small size make them more convenient for occasional use. The smallest of modern portable typewriters are no larger than an unabridged dictionary, and offer most of the features of full-sized office machines.

Noiseless typewriters, which came into general use after World War I, use a lever system for actuating the type bars, but rely on pressure rather than a sharp striking motion to make the type impression. Because the type strikes the ribbon with a pressing rather than a percussive action, the noise of operation is much reduced.

Electric typewriters have been in extensive use since the late 1930's. In these machines a motor-driven mechanism performs the actual work of lifting the type bar and striking it against the ribbon and also of returning the carriage to the right and turning the platen at the end of the line. Since the keys are used only to start the electric mechanism, the pressure used by the operator is much less than on conventional mechanical typewriters and as a result the operator can write faster and with less fatigue. Another important advantage of the electric machines is that pressure of each stroke is automatically controlled, rendering the impress of each letter completely uniform.

Milwaukee Public Museum

THE TYPEWRITER. *Top, left: Crandall, 1879, first type-wheel typewriter. Top, right: The Cali-graph No. 1, 1880. Middle: Crary typewriter, 1894. Bottom, left: The Daugherty, 1890. Bottom, right: Williams, 1891, with rows of type bars on front and back.*

Typewriters which automatically "justify" the lines of copy so that all lines are of uniform length, as in a printed book, are used for typewritten copy which can be reproduced directly by lithography or other means. Justification is accomplished by automatic or manually adjusted devices which vary the spacing between individual words. Machines for this purpose are often equipped with ribbons of carbon tissue, instead of ink-impregnated cloth, to give uniform blackness to all parts of each letter typed.

TYPHACEAE. See CAT-TAIL.

TYPHOID FEVER, ENTERIC FEVER, or ABDOMINAL TYPHUS, term applied to an acute infectious disease of man caused by the typhoid bacillus *Eberthella typhi*. The typhoid bacillus, which is world-wide in distribution, was discovered in 1880 by the German pathologist Karl Joseph Eberth (1835–1926) and was designated the cause of typhoid fever by the German bacteriologist Georg Theodor August Gaffky (1850–1918) in 1884. The gram-negative organism is actively motile. It is transmitted by milk, water, or solid food contaminated by feces of typhoid victims. The incubation period of typhoid fever lasts eight to fourteen days. During the incubation period the typhoid bacilli travel through the alimentary tract to the ileum of the small intestine, in which they localize in a group of masses of lymphatic tissue known as *Peyer's patches.* From Peyer's patches the bacilli enter the lymphatics (q.v.) and are carried into the blood stream. The symptoms of typhoid fever begin as the bacilli enter the blood stream, and include chills followed by diarrhea, high persistent fever, and prostration. The mucous membrane lining the intestinal tract becomes inflamed and the spleen is enlarged. During the first week of the disease, the relative distribution of white blood cells in the blood changes, and monocytes, which normally constitute about four percent of the total number of white blood cells, increase to comprise fifteen percent or more of the total number. At the end of the first week of the disease, a characteristic rose-colored eruption usually breaks out on the chest and abdomen. In uncomplicated cases, the fever and rash persist for several weeks and then gradually subside. In ten to thirty percent of all cases, complications such as pneumonia, inflammation of the gall bladder, formation of blood clots in the blood vessels, and hemorrhage or perforation of the intestine occur; most of such cases of typhoid fever result in death.

There was no specific treatment for typhoid fever until 1954. In that year medical authorities announced the development of a new antibiotic, called synnematin, which is a specific for the disease. In tests conducted in Mexico, the new drug is reported to have produced complete cures.

The disease is gradually disappearing from the United States because of the prevalence of preventive measures. Compulsory inspection of milk and water supplies to detect typhoid bacilli has resulted in preventing typhoid-fever transmission through milk and water supplies; pasteurization of milk has been particularly effective in eradicating one route of transmission of the disease. Attention was called to typhoid "carriers" by the case of "typhoid Mary", a housemaid who harbored typhoid bacilli and who, because of her unsanitary habits, caused the infection of members of almost every household in which she was employed.

Recognition that some individuals harbor typhoid bacilli without presenting symptoms of typhoid fever and that such individuals may serve as foci of infection for others has resulted in the passage of laws, in most States and municipalities of the U.S., requiring medical inspection of persons handling food. Improvement of sewage facilities in the U.S. has also reduced the incidence of typhoid fever. The most important single factor in the control of typhoid fever is typhoid inoculation. In 1898, one fifth of all American troops in the Spanish-American War were stricken with typhoid fever; by 1913, inoculation of troops with typhoid vaccine resulted in a decrease in incidence to one case of typhoid fever for every 40,000 American soldiers in the Mexican War. Preventive inoculation against typhoid fever, however, has only recently been applied to the general populace. Immunity (q.v.) against typhoid fever conferred by inoculation lasts for two to three years.

TYPHOON, a tropical cyclone similar to a hurricane, and occurring in the Indian Ocean and the East China Sea. The typhoon is characterized by a central area of extremely low pressure, known as the eye, surrounded by a vortex of winds of high velocity which blow counterclockwise in the Northern Hemisphere and clockwise in the Southern Hemisphere. The speeds of the winds near the center of the storm are commonly 100 miles per hour and may reach speeds of as much as 175 miles per hour. Typhoons are accompanied by extensive rainfall, which may amount to as much as 50 inches, in the areas over which the storm passes. Typhoons originate at sea and are extremely dangerous to ships. They also cause great damage in coastal areas which they strike with great speed, driving large, humplike waves of water before them.

TYPHUS, common name applied to any number of acute infectious diseases, but especially applied to two diseases of humans caused by Rickettsial bodies; see RICKETTSIA. Epidemic or European typhus is the more virulent of the two diseases, occurring in widespread epidemics during wartime or other periods when sanitation is not strictly observed. Epidemic typhus is caused by *Rickettsia prowazeki,* which is transmitted to man by the body louse; see LOUSE. The disease, which occurs chiefly in temperate countries, has many alternate popular names, most of which reflect the conditions under which it flourishes; these names include "louse-borne typhus", "jail fever", "famine fever", "putrid fever", "hospital fever", "camp fever", and "ship fever". Symptoms of epidemic typhus occur abruptly; they include high fever, pain in the muscles and joints, stiffness, headache, and cerebral disturbance. About the fifth day of the disease, a dark-red rash of elevated spots breaks out over the body. During the second week of the disease, the patient often becomes delirious. After two to three weeks, patients who eventually recover from the disease undergo a sudden remission of fever with prompt recovery; in severe epidemics, however, the mortality rate is often as high as fifty to seventy percent, most individuals dying within the first two weeks of being afflicted with the disease. During the first six months of World War I, 150,000 soldiers died of epidemic typhus. During World War II, protective vaccination and control of lice with D.D.T. resulted in much lower incidence of typhus among military personnel than in previous wars; however, the incidence of typhus among civilians in war-ravaged areas was very high. The discovery of the antibiotics chloromycetin and aureomycin in 1948 and 1949, respectively, for the first time gave physicians specific drugs to cure epidemic typhus.

Endemic or tropical typhus is the milder of the two diseases known as typhus. This condition, which is caused by *Rickettsia mooseri,* occurs in tropical and semitropical countries, and is found in several of the southernmost States of the United States. Unlike epidemic typhus, endemic typhus is transmitted by the rat flea, *Xenopsylla cheopis.* Rat fleas, which also spread plague (q.v.), attack man secondarily, the primary host being the brown rat. The symptoms of endemic typhus chiefly differ from those of epidemic typhus in being much less severe; the two diseases are differentiated diagnostically by a serological test called the *Weil-Felix* test. Among other names given to endemic typhus are "flea-borne typhus", "murine typhus", "urban typhus", and "shop typhus". The disease seems to be identical with a Mexican disease known as "tabardillo".

Among other conditions commonly called typhus are mite-borne or scrub typhus (see TSUTSUGAMUSHI FEVER), abdominal typhus (see TYPHOID FEVER), and amarillic typhus (see YELLOW FEVER).

TYPOGRAPHICAL UNION OF NORTH AMERICA, THE INTERNATIONAL, the labor organization of the printers and those engaged in kindred trades, the oldest national trade union in the United States. It was organized in 1850 as the National Convention of Journeymen Printers, but assumed the name National Typographical Union in 1852, and the present name in 1869 when Canadian unions were admitted. For many years prior to 1850 there had been in existence organizations of printers' societies formed for betterment of wages and working conditions in their respective localities. The International regulates the maximum hours of labor of all members, the number of days' work per week, the method of securing work and the discharge of employees (through foremen, who must belong to the union) and the employment of substitutes. In a recent year the International Typographical Union had a total membership of about 96,000. The organization conducts a pension system for members. It also pays a mortuary benefit based on continuity of membership. The Union Printers Home in Colorado Springs, Colo., is maintained for aged and incapacitated members. Headquarters of the organization are in Indianapolis, Ind.

TYRANNOSAURUS, a genus of gigantic, extinct dinosaurs (see DINOSAURIA) excavated from the Upper Cretaceous rocks of Montana, Wyoming, and other areas of w. United States. The only known species, *T. rex,* reached a height of 20 feet at the shoulder and was 47 feet long. The large teeth, nearly 12 inches long, indicate that the animal was carnivorous. The narrow, very deep body was supported by a thick, heavy tail. The animal had very short forelegs which were unsuitable for walking; its hind legs, used for walking, were very thick and strong. Two similar genera, *Megalosaurus* and *Allosaurus,* have been found in the Lower Jurassic rocks of England and in Upper

American Museum of Natural History
Museum painting of a Tyrannosaurus

Jurassic rocks of North America, respectively.

TYRANT FLYCATCHER. See FLYCATCHER.

TYRE (Lat. *Tyrus,* from Gr. Tυρός Aramaic *Tur,* from Phenician *Sûr,* "rock"), town of Lebanon, on the Mediterranean coast about 50 miles s. of Beirut. Its name comes from the double rock just off the coast, the site of the earliest settlement. Tyre was the most important city of ancient Phenicia. Herodotus records a tradition which traced the settlement to Tyre back to the 28th century B.C. In the 7th century it came under the dominion of the Saracens, and so remained until taken by the Crusaders, who defended it till 1291. After the settlement of the Metâweleh or Persian schismatics, in 1766, the town began to be rebuilt. Pop., about 5000.

TYROL. See TIROL.

TYRONE, inland county of Northern Ireland. The principal rivers are the Blackwater, the Foyle, and the Mourne. The northwestern mountains rise in Slieve Sawel to a height of 2236 feet. Linens, coarse woolens, and earthenware are manufactured. The capital is Omagh. Area, 1260 sq.m.; pop. (1951 prelim.) 132,049.

TYRONE, HUGH O'NEILL, EARL OF (1540–1616), Irish revolutionist, grandson of Conn O'Neill, 1st Earl of Tyrone. In 1597 he assumed the ancient title of "The O'Neill", and defied the English power. He met at first with some success, but was defeated by Lord Mountjoy in spite of help from Spain. After Kinsale fell Tyrone made his submission at Mellefont and was reinstated in his earldom. But under James I he intrigued anew with Spain, and in 1607 was forced to flee. His lands were confiscated, and he died in Rome.

TYRRHENIAN SEA (It. *Mare Tirreno*), a portion of the Mediterranean Sea situated off the s.w. coast of Italy, and partially enclosed by the Italian peninsula and the islands of Sicily, Sardinia, and Corsica.

TYRTÆUS (fl. middle 7th century B.C.), Greek poet. According to Athenian tradition, he was a lame schoolmaster of Attica, sent to Sparta when the Spartans asked the Athenians for assistance against the Messenians; this story, however, seems to have been the invention of a later period. Tyrtæus is now generally believed to have been a Spartan. He served as a general in the Second Messenian War (685–668 B.C.), and by his poems aroused the Spartans and led them to victory over their foes. Extant fragments of his poems include exhortations to battle, and lines on courage and on the nature of the brave warrior. Tyrtæus' poetry contains many echoes of the language and style of Homer.

TYUMEN, city in the Ural area of the Russian Soviet Federated Socialist Republic, situated on the Tura R. It is noted for the manufacture of carpets, and also contains dyeing plants, tanneries, sawmills, and a shipbuilding yard. Tyumen stands at the junction of several trade routes, and is a commercial center. The town was the oldest Russian colony in Siberia, having been founded as a fort by the cossack Ermak Timofeev in 1585. Pop., about 75,000.

TZANA, TANA, or DEMBEA, a great freshwater lake on the high plateau of Ethiopia, s. of Gondar. The greatest length is 60 m.; the breadth varies from 30 to 40 m. It is fed by numerous streams and is the main reservoir of the Blue Nile.

TZENTAL, an ancient nation of Mayan stock, occupying a large part of the States of Tabasco and northern Chiapas, in Mexico. Their traditional culture hero was Votan, who was said to have built the great ruins at Palenque, in Chiapas, and their general civilization resembled that of the Maya and other cognate tribes. They still constitute an important part of the population of their ancient territory.

TZU HSI, TZE-HSI, or **TZI-HI** (1835–1908), Chinese empress, known as the Great Empress Dowager, and virtually the ruler of China for almost half a century. She was born in Peking of a Manchu family named Hweicheng, and belonged to the historic Nara or Nala clan. In her sixteenth year Tzu Hsi was selected for the imperial harem of the emperor Hien-fung. She started as a *kwei-jen,* or concubine of the fifth rank. Because of her beauty and talents she was promoted to the fourth rank in 1854; in 1856 she was advanced to the third rank, and by 1858 she was second only to the first concubine, who became imperial consort on the death of Hien-fung's legal wife. Practically uneducated when she entered the palace, she applied herself diligently to a thorough course in Chinese history, calligraphy, and classics, and became known as a fine scholar of the old school. On April 27, 1856, she gave birth to a son, afterward the emperor Tung-chih; this greatly increased Tzu Hsi's influence. She was now known as the Empress of the Western Palace. It was her almost unerring judgment of people

and events which enabled her eventually to reach absolute power. On the death of Hien-fung she frustrated a conspiracy to put her out of the way, and together with the emperor's consort, known as the Empress of the Eastern Palace, and Prince Kung she secured the overthrow of her enemies. She was then twenty-six years of age.

From that time she was the real ruler of China, remaining so during the reigns of Tung-chih (1861–75) and Kwang-sü (1875–1908). Tzu Hsi kept her country in fairly good standing among the nations of the world until the Sino-Japanese War (1894–95) revealed the weakness of China and the inability of the Chinese government to prevent territorial aggression. The result is found in the most critical period of Chinese history, from 1895 to 1902. First came the seizures, leases, and concessions of the powers, which Tzu Hsi was powerless to withstand. Then came the short-lived era of reform of the emperor Kwang-sü in 1908, which Tzu Hsi believed to be premature and therefore crushed, through her agents Jung-lu and Yuan Shih-kai. But she was not able to prevent the Boxer Rebellion (q.v.), and although she at first disapproved of it, she later gave the Boxers encouragement and imperial support. The tragic results of the Rebellion having taught Tzu Hsi that the old order in China must be eradicated, from 1901 to 1908 she distinctly encouraged the modernizing of China, and also was in favor of constitutional government, which she promised should be granted in 1916.

Tzu Hsi was ambitious and arbitrary, but, like Queen Elizabeth I of England, was able to surround herself with good advisers and the ablest of her subjects. Remarkably patriotic, she never spared herself the grinding toil necessary to rule the Chinese world. Her character has been much maligned, especially by her enemies in south China, and as much overpraised by her admirers. She is one of the few women who have profoundly influenced the world's history.

U, the twenty-first letter in our alphabet. The Semitic alphabet ended with *t*, which is now followed by the four new letters *u, v, w,* and *y,* which have been placed at the end because they are differentiated forms, developed at various periods out of the Semitic letter *vau,* whose direct descendant is *F,* which retains its original place as the sixth letter of our alphabet. The letter *vau* was derived from the Egyptian hieroglyphic picture of the cerastes or horned asp which had the value of *f.* From the Phenician symbol, whose form was intermediate between F and Y, the Greeks evolved two characters— one was the digamma, which survives as our letter F. The other was a sign called *upsilon,* which had the value of *u.* The form V was carried to Italy, where it represented the sound *u* as well as that of our *w.* From V, the lapidary and capital form, the cursive and uncial forms U and u were developed. The history of the characters is represented as follows.

U	ΥΓ	Υ	◡	ఠ·
Ro-man.	Early Greek.	Pheni-.cian.	Egyptian Hieratic.	Hiero-glyphic Asp.

The two forms *u* and *v* were differentiated about the 15th century A.D., when V was limited to representing the consonant sound. In English *u* represents a variety of sounds besides its original value, which is that of a rounded back vowel, the *u* in *rude.* It stands also for the sound *yoo,* as *educate, mule, value.*

It is pronounced like *ŏŏ* in *full, pull, push*; *û in Turk, turnip, urge*; *ŭ* (unrounded) in *tub, up, muff.* A *u* is always written after *q.* In this case it has the consonantal value of *w,* which it has also often after other consonants, especially *g* and *s,* as in *quick, quartz, quote*; *language, anguish*; *suave, dissuade.* It is silent in *guard, tongue, build.* In chemistry U stands for *uranium.* In the international code of signals for ships, the letter is denoted by a red-and-white flag.

UARAYCU, a South American tribe on the lower Jurua and Jutay rivers, and the adjacent portion of the Amazon, western Brazil. As tests of fortitude they whip their youths, and suspend their maidens over smoking fires. Girls are betrothed in childhood, and the young man must hunt game for his bride long before he is permitted to marry her. Their dead they burn and bury the ashes in their huts.

UAUPÉ, an extensive group of tribes, probably remotely of Arawakan stock, residing on the Uaupés River, a head stream of the Río Negro, in southeastern Colombia. They cultivate corn, tobacco, manioc, cane, and bananas, are experts with the bow, lance, and blowgun, and are great fishermen. They live in large communal houses, sometimes nearly 100 feet square, with a roof nearly 40 feet high supported by columns hewn from tree trunks. They make pottery and baskets and use canoes hollowed out from logs. The men wear the G-string, feather headdresses, and amulets. The women go naked. Those of the same clan are not allowed to intermarry. Each communal household has its hereditary chief. In physique they are tall, stout, and well built. They are reputed to be very industrious.

UAUPÉS, a large tributary of the Río Negro, considered by some geographers as the true headstream of that river. It rises in the Eastern Cordillera of the Colombian Andes, descends in falls and rapids, and flows southeastward to its confluence with the main stream in northwest Brazil. It is over 700 miles long, and navigable in its lower course.

UBANGI, a river of Central Africa, the largest northern tributary of the Congo. It is known also as the Mobangi (near its mouth), the Dua, the Koyu, and the Makua and Welle (in its upper course). The river rises in the extreme northeastern corner of Belgian Congo, not far from the Nile, and flows westward, then southward just above the Zongo rapids, and finally joins the Congo near the equator after a course of about 1500 m. From its mouth to its confluence with the Mbomu at Yakoma, the Ubangi forms the boundary between French Equatorial Africa and the Belgian Congo.

UBANGI-SHARI (Fr. *Oubangui-Chari*), second largest of the Territories in French Equatorial Africa (q.v.), bounded on the N. by the Territory of Chad, on the E. by the Sudan, on the S. by the Ubangi and Mbomu rivers and the Territory of Middle Congo, and on the W. by Cameroun. Bangui is the capital. The surface of Ubangi-Shari is predominantly savanna, or grassland. The S. part, which is traversed by a parallel series of rivers, is covered with dense virgin forest. Cotton is the principal agricultural crop. Area 238,767 sq.m.; pop. (1950) 1,067,400, including 4391 Whites.

UBIQUITY (from Lat. *ubique,* "everywhere", from *ubi,* "where"), a term applied in theology to the doctrine that the Lord's body, in consequence of its personal union with the divine, by a "communication of properties", is everywhere present. This use of the word has its origin in the teachings of Luther, who, to defend the real presence of the entire Christ in the elements of the Lord's Supper, taught that Christ's body could be everywhere, although he called this presence "illocal". A small sect, followers of John Brentius, in 1560 accepted this tenet, and were known as *Ubiquitarians,* or *Ubiquarians.*

U-BOATS, the common name for German submarines during World War I. See SUB-MARINE; WORLD WAR I: *The War at Sea.*

UCAYALI, a river of Peru, one of the head waters of the Amazon. It is formed by the confluence of the Apurimac and Urubamba and winds more than 1500 miles N. to join the Marañon opposite Nauta.

UCCELLO, PAOLO, assumed name of PAOLO DE DONO (1397–1475), Florentine painter, born in Florence, and apprenticed at an early age to the artist Lorenzo Ghiberti (q.v.). In 1425 he went to Venice to design mosaics for the façade of the Church of St. Mark's. He returned to Florence around 1434 and painted a famous equestrian fresco of the English soldier of fortune Sir John de Hawkwood for the Duomo (Cathedral Santa Maria del Fiore). Later he executed a series of windows for the Duomo, of which one, on the subject of the Resurrection, is still in place in the Cathedral. Fragments also remain of a group of frescoes painted by Uccello in the cloisters of the church of Santa Maria Novella in Florence, and depicting the Biblical stories of the Creation and the Flood. Little of his other work is extant.

Uccello's paintings are notable for their exact representation of the costumes of his period, and for their accurate studies of animals and birds. He kept a small private menagerie and aviary, and his assumed name "Uccello" (It., "bird") was adopted not only because of his love for these creatures, but because of his habit of introducing representations of them into so many of his paintings. He is also well known for his portraiture, which is particularly well represented by his paintings of Giotto, Donatello, and Brunelleschi, and by a self-portrait (all now in the Louvre, Paris). Among his other works are three paintings of the "Battle of San Romano" (Uffizi Gallery, Florence; the Louvre, Paris; and the National Gallery, London), and "Man and Woman of the Portinari Family" (Metropolitan Museum of Art, New York City).

UDALL, NICHOLAS (about 1505–56), English schoolmaster, author of *Ralph Roister Doister* the earliest English comedy, born in Hampshire. It seems to have been composed for the boys of Eton before 1551, though not published until 1566.

UDINE, capital of Friuli-Venezia Giulia Region and Udine Province, Italy, 85 miles N.E. of Venice. It contains a Romanesque cathedral, an archbishop's palace, a beautiful campo santo, and, in the midst of the city, a castle, formerly the residence of the patriarchs of Aquileia. Udine has manufactures of silk, leather, gloves, and hats. During World War I the general headquarters of the Italian army was established at Udine, but it fell into Aus-

British Information Services

NATIVES IN UGANDA

Boys and girls of the Northern province. Their lips are pierced by metal pins.

trian hands following the disaster at Caporetto in October, 1917, and was not recovered until November 3, 1918. Pop., about 66,000.

UFA, the capital of the Autonomous Bashkir Republic, on the Belaya River, at the junction of the Ufa and Belaya rivers. It is situated on the western slope of the Ural, the center of an agricultural, timber, and mining region, 326 miles N.E. of Samara. It was the first (1596) Russian town and fortress in Bashkiria. In 1918 the Czechoslovakian forces seized the town. The Soviet government was established in 1919, and Ufa became the capital of the Bashkir Republic in 1922. Pop., about 246,000.

UFFIZI, PALAZZO DEGLI, a celebrated Florentine palace, containing one of the finest collections of sculpture and painting in the world. It was erected in 1560–76, after the designs of Giorgio Vasari, for the government offices of the grand duchy of Tuscany. The ground story is one of the most beautiful open halls of Italy. The top story, now containing the gallery, was originally an open loggia. In the vestibule and court are many statues of celebrated Tuscans. The nucleus of the gallery was a part of the celebrated collections made by the Medici in the 15th century. Additions were acquired or inherited by many of the Medicean dukes, and the collection was bequeathed to the state by the last representative of the line in 1737. It is especially rich in antique statuary.

UGANDA, a British protectorate in East Africa, bounded on the N. by the Anglo-Egyptian Sudan, on the E. by Kenya Colony, on the S. by Tanganyika Territory, and on the W. by the Belgian Congo. Administratively, the protectorate is divided into four provinces, the Eastern, Western, Northern, and Buganda. Buganda is recognized as a native kingdom ruled by a hereditary chief, assisted by three native ministers and a native assembly. Entebbe (pop., about 7320) is the capital of the protectorate. The area of Uganda includes all the waters of lakes George, Kioga, and Salisbury; parts of lakes Victoria Nyanza, Edward, and Albert; and the Nile R. from its exit out of Lake Victoria Nyanza at Ripon Falls to Nimule on the Sudan frontier. The land surface is remarkably diversified, with snow-capped peaks, the highest being Ruwenzori (16,787 ft.), elevated plains, vast forests, low swamps, and arid depressions. Farming and the raising of livestock are the chief occupations of the people. Cotton is the main crop. Other products of Uganda are coffee, sugar cane, oilseed, sisal, tobacco, hides, ivory, and tin. The bulk of the population is African, principally Bantus; the Bagada tribe is the most numerous. The Kenya and Uganda Railway reaches Kampala (pop., about 40,000), the commercial center of the protectorate, and the railroad maintains steamer services on lakes Victoria, Kioga, and Albert. A governor is the chief British representative; assisted by legislative and executive councils, he makes ordinances for raising revenue and for the administration of justice. Native kings or chiefs, their rights regulated in several instances by treaty, are encouraged to conduct their own administration.

The Uganda protectorate was originally formed of the once-powerful native kingdom of Uganda, or more properly, Buganda, in the British sphere of influence since 1890. The protectorate was established formally in 1894. Area, 93,981 sq.m. (including 13,680 sq.m. of water surface); pop. (1956 est.) 5,593,000, including about 50,000 Indians and 7000 Europeans.

UHDE, FRITZ VON (1848–1911), German historical and genre painter, born in Wolkenburg, Saxony, and trained at the Dresden Academy. He followed a military career until 1877, then took up painting in Munich, giving his attention especially to the old Dutch masters. In 1879 he removed to Paris, where he principally studied from nature and Dutch models. A result of these combined influences was the "Family Concert" (1881, Cologne Museum). The new coloristic principles which he in the meanwhile adopted are apparent in the "Arrival of the Organ Grinder" (1883), and, turning now to religious subjects, he created the remarkable and pathetic masterpieces "Suffer the Little Children to Come unto Me" (1884, Leipzig Museum) and "Come, Lord Jesus, and Be Our Guest" (1885, National Gallery, Berlin), both scenes in a workingman's cottage. He next produced "Christ with the Disciples at Emmaus" (1885, Städel Institute, Frankfort), "The Sermon on the Mount" (1887), the triptych of the "Nativity" (1889, Dresden Gallery), and "The Walk to Bethlehem" (1890, New Pinakothek, Munich), the last a bold modern conception of the subject. Uhde brought about a complete change in German art, counting among his followers most of the younger generation. His later productions include "Noli Me Tangere" (1894, New Pinakothek, Munich), "The Wise Men from the East" (1896, Magdeburg Museum), "The Last Supper" (1897, Stuttgart Museum), "Richard III" and "Ascension" (1898, New Pinakothek, Munich), "Woman,

Why Weepest Thou?" (1900, Vienna Museum), the altarpiece of the Lutherkirche, Ziorchan (1905), and "Going Home" (1908). Uhde is known for his attempt to bring back German art to its ancient religious ideals. Like the primitive painters, he depicts with deep religious feeling, yet with powerful naturalism and highly poetic treatment of light and atmosphere, the personages of the New Testament in the lowly garb of the German working classes. He also portrays the woes of laboring people.

UHLAND, JOHANN LUDWIG (1787–1862), German poet and philologist, born in Tübingen. His ballads and romances rank among the treasures of German literature. Of his songs the most widely popular are *Der Wirtin Töchterlein* and *Der Gute Kamerad*. Although poetically effective, his glorifications of German faith, the dramas *Ernst, Herzog von Schwaben* (1817), and *Ludwig der Bayer* (1819) lack dramatic action and had only moderate success. He was a founder of Germanic and Romance philology. Besides the treatise *Ueber das Altfranzösische Epos* (1812), and an essay *Zur Geschichte der Freischiessen* (1828), there are to be especially mentioned *Walther von der Vogelweide, ein Altdeutscher Dichter* (1822); *Der Mythus von Thôr* (1836), the result of painstaking original investigation; and the masterly collection *Alte hoch- und Niederdeutsche Volkslieder* (1844–45).

UHLENBECK, GEORGE EUGENE (1900–), Dutch-American physicist, born in Batavia, Java, and educated at the University of Leiden. While still a graduate student, he discovered, in collaboration with the Dutch-American physicist Samuel Goudsmit, the phenomenon of electron spin; see SPIN. Uhlenbeck emigrated to the United States in 1927, and taught physics at the University of Michigan from that year until 1935. During the next four years he was professor of theoretical physics at the University of Utrecht in Holland and in 1939 he returned to the University of Michigan, at which he served as professor of physics. During World War II he was a staff member of the Radiation Laboratory at Massachusetts Institute of Technology, and contributed to research on radar.

UIGURS, a people of East Turkestan, and of Turkic stock. They founded the powerful kingdom of Hiong-Nu, which reached its zenith in the 1st century A.D., when it was divided into a northern and a southern empire. The latter was destroyed by the Tunguses in the 3rd century, whereupon the southern Uigurs retreated to the west and founded the empire of the Huns. In the 8th century the northern Uigurs founded a kingdom which was destroyed by the Kirghizes. In the 5th century A.D. their culture, developed on the slopes of the Tian Shan, was in a flourishing condition, and about this time they underwent considerable Buddhistic and Chinese influence, their religion having already been modified to some extent by Nestorian Christians, from whom they adopted the traces of Zoroastrianism present among them. But they finally adopted the faith of Islam, and have been modified in blood and other characteristics by more recent Mongol-Chinese, Arab, and Turkic elements. Probably from Uigur influence the Mongols and Manchus have adopted the Syrian system of writing, and other advances in the culture of the numerous tribes of central Asia and Siberia are, perhaps, from the Uigurs.

UJIYAMADA, city of Honshu I., Japan, situated in Mie Prefecture, near Ise Bay, 75 miles E. of Osaka. It lies in an agricultural area producing tea and oranges. Lacquer ware, umbrellas, and paper goods are the leading manufactures. The city, which consists of the once separate communities of Uji and Yamada, has a famous museum and library and is noted as the site of the holiest Shinto shrines in Japan, namely the Great Shrine of Ise, of Naiku, and of Geku. Every year thousands of people visit these ancient holy places. Pop. (1947) 65,970.

UJJAIN, or OOJEIN, a walled town of central India, one of the seven sacred cities of the Hindus, on the river Sipra, 30 miles N. of Indore. Pop., about 53,000.

UJPEST, city of Hungary, situated on the Danube R., and forming a northern suburb of Budapest. A shipping and industrial center, it has factories engaged in the production of iron and steel, machinery, textiles, leather goods, and chemicals. The city was formerly known as Neupest. Pop., about 90,000.

UKIYOYE SCHOOL. See JAPANESE ART AND ARCHITECTURE.

UKRAINIAN SOVIET SOCIALIST REPUBLIC, or UKRAINE, a constituent republic of the Union of Soviet Socialist Republics (q.v.), bounded on the N. by the Byelorussian S.S.R. and the Russian Soviet Federated Socialist Republic, on the E. by the Russian S.F.S.R., on the s. by the Sea of Azov and by the Black Sea, and on the w. by Romania and Poland. For territorial modifications, see *History,* below. The republic is divided into twenty-five Regions. The capital and largest city is Kiev, and other important cities include Kharkov, Odessa, Stalino, and Dnepropetrovsk (qq.v.), all with populations of more than 100,000. The most distinctive topographical feature of the Ukraine is its wide belt of fertile steppe, crossing the republic from s.w. to N.W.; about 70,500,000 acres are arable. The Dnieper R. traverses central Ukraine from N. to s.; other important rivers are the Bug and Dniester rivers in the w. and the Donetz and Don in the E. The region is inhabited predominantly by Ukrainians, a branch of the Slavonic peoples, but distinct in language, traits, and general history from the Russian Slavs.

The Ukraine, called the "granary of Russia", is one of the most important agricultural regions of the Soviet Union, yielding wheat, buckwheat, sugar beets, cotton, flax, sunflower seeds, soybeans, hops, tobacco, fruits, and livestock. About 90% of Soviet grain exports are grown in this region. Manufacturing industries, centered in the N.W. portion, which is the most densely inhabited section of the Soviet Union, rival agriculture in importance. Manufacturing is based largely on the vast Ukrainian mineral resources, centered in the s.E. around the cities of Kharkov, Zaporozhye, and Stalino. The coal fields of the Donets (q.v.) Basin contain an estimated 60% of all Soviet coal. About 200 miles w., in Krivoi Rogg, are equally rich iron-ore mines. Other minerals include manganese, oil, salt, and fire clay. An additional natural resource is the water power available from Ukrainian rivers. The greatest Ukrainian dam, constructed in 1932 across the Dnieper R. at Zaporozhye, was destroyed by Soviet forces on Aug. 28, 1941, to prevent its capture by the invading Germans, and reconstructed in 1945; in connection with the hydroelectric project, a large aluminum plant was established. The principal manufactures in the Ukraine are iron and steel, machinery, and chemicals. Communications include over 9000 m. of railroad and 1782 m. of navigable rivers, as well as ports on the Black Sea. Area, 225,000 sq.m.; pop., about 40,000,000.

History. The early history of the Ukraine is that of Russia (q.v.) itself. Kiev was the center of a Rus principality in the 11th and 12th centuries, and is still known as the "Mother of Russia". The Ukrainian principality of Galicia (q.v.), founded in the 12th century, was annexed by Poland in the 14th century. At the same time Kiev and Ukrainian Volhynia (q.v.) were conquered by

Sovfoto

Threshing wheat by machine on a collective farm in the Ukrainian S.S.R

Lithuania and later came, with the latter country, into the possession of Poland. However, Poland could not subjugate the Ukrainian Cossacks (q.v.), who allied themselves with Russia. The lands E. of the Dnieper R. were ceded to Russia in 1667, and the remainder of the Ukraine, except for Galicia, was incorporated into the Russian Empire after the 1793 partition of Poland.

Though many Ukrainians remained under Austria, in Galicia and Bucovina (see RUTHENIANS) and in a region of Hungary known as the Carpatho-Ukraine, they preserved their identity as a separate group and engendered a forceful nationalist movement; in 1917, during World War I, the Russian Ukrainians established an independent republic following the military collapse of Russia. Austrian Ukraine proclaimed itself a republic in 1918; the Allies took little cognizance of Ukrainian claims for Galicia, however, and, following the war, awarded that area to Poland. In 1919 the Russian Ukrainian republic, under the leader Simon Petlyura, declared war on Poland. In the same year Ukrainian communists established a second government, as the Ukrainian Soviet Socialist Republic. In 1920 the advance of the Russian Bolshevik armies caused the Petlyura government and Poland to become allies; but they were powerless before the communist drive, and the Soviet government obtained control of the country. In 1922 communist Ukrainian delegates joined with other Soviet republics in the formation of the U.S.S.R.

In the period between 1922 and 1939 drastic efforts were made by the Soviet Union to suppress Ukrainian nationalism. The ultimate goal of Ukrainian nationalism was the independence of a Greater Ukraine, embracing the Russian Ukraine, Polish Galicia, and Czechoslovakian Carpatho-Ukraine. Following the Soviet seizure of E. Poland in September, 1939, Polish Galicia, comprising nearly 24,000 sq.m., was incorporated into the Ukrainian S.S.R. When the Germans invaded the Ukraine in 1941, during World War II, it was hoped by the nationalists that an autonomous or independent Ukrainian republic would be set up under German protection. Much to their disappointment, the Germans not only divided Russian Ukraine and West Ukraine (Galicia), but came as hostile conquerors. The Ukraine was retaken by Russia in 1944. In the same year parts of Bessarabia and N. Bucovina, formerly Romanian, were added to the Ukraine, and the Carpatho-Ukraine region of Czechoslovakia was added in 1945. The Ukrainian S.S.R. became a charter member of the United Nations in 1945. The Crimean Region of the Russian S.F.S.R. was transferred to the Ukraine in 1954.

UKULELE, musical instrument of Portuguese origin, closely related to the guitar. It has four strings and a long neck, and is played by strumming or plucking the strings with the fingers. The ukulele attained popularity in Hawaii in the latter part of the 19th century. Subsequently it became a favorite instrument in the United States for the playing of popular songs and jazz.

ULAN BATOR, formerly URGA, city and capital of the Mongolian People's Republic, situated on the Tola R., 165 miles s. of Kyakhta, Buryat-Mongol A.S.S.R., and 720 miles N.W. of Peking. It is a caravan trading junction and has rail and air service to Siberian cities. Points of interest include the Monastery of the Living Buddha, the sanctuary of a greatly revered Lamaist saint, and the university, with an enrollment of approximately 1000 students. The movement for Outer Mongolian independence, which began early in the 20th century, had its center in the city. Its name was changed to Ulan Bator in 1924. Pop., about 80,000.

ULAN UDE, formerly VERKHNEUDINSK, city and capital of Buryat-Mongol A.S.S.R., situated at the confluence of the Uda and Selenga rivers, about 50 miles E. of Laka Baikal, with which it is connected by steamer, and about 150 miles E. of Irkutsk. The city lies in a live-stock raising and grain-growing region, is served by the Trans-Siberian Railway, and is an important industrial center. One of the largest railway car and locomotive works in the Soviet Union is located in Ulan Ude. Other industrial establishments include meat canneries, tanneries, chemical and metallurgical works, a foundry, and plants engaged in the manufacture of glass and bricks. In the vicinity are coal and tungsten mines.

Russian Cossacks founded a fur-trading camp on the site of present-day Ulan Ude in 1666. The camp was fortified early in the 18th century; eventually, as the city of Verkhneudinsk, it became the administrative center of the Baikal region. With the construction of the Trans-Siberian Railway, the city grew in importance after the middle of the 19th century. In 1923 the city became the capital of the newly formed Buryat-Mongol A.S.S.R. It received its present name about 1935. Pop. (1946 est.) 150,000.

ULCER, a shallow sore produced by the destruction of skin or mucous membrane, occurring spontaneously in the course of disease or as a result of injury. Ulcers occur in association with a large number of chronic illnesses, such as diabetes, kidney and heart ailments, varicose veins, chronic gastritis, ulcerative colitis, syphilis, typhoid fever, leprosy, tuberculosis, and cancer. Local physiological disturbances, such as the reduction of blood supply to an affected area arising from arteriosclerosis or arterial embolism, also are common causes of ulcers. The edges of an ulcer are generally slightly elevated above the level of the surrounding healthy tissues, and the floor of the ulcer is usually concave and moist with serum or pus. When the ulcer is healing, the base is granular, and fibrous tissue forms; the lesion is then replaced by permanent scar tissue, and covered by epithelium. When the ulcer is enlarging, the floor is composed of fluid secretions and dead tissues which, in such diseases as tuberculosis and syphilis, may contain the causative organism. Complete rest of the affected part is the first requisite in the treatment of any kind of ulcer, and further steps generally depend on the eradication of the underlying cause. Cancerous ulcers are usually treated by surgery or electrocoagulation, or by radiations of X rays, radium, or radioactive isotopes.

Peptic Ulcer. Ulcers of the gastrointestinal tract, caused by digestion of the walls of the stomach or small intestines by the enzymes of the stomach, are classified according to their position as gastric, gastroduodenal, or duodenal ulcers. In addition to the distress caused by the ulcer itself, peptic ulcers give rise to such complications as hemorrhage, from the erosion of a major blood vessel; perforation of the wall of the stomach or intestine, with resultant peritonitis; and contractures, causing obstruction. The various causes of peptic ulcer may be classified as *chemical,* arising from excessive secretion of gastric enzymes and hydrochloric acid; *neurogenic,* caused by the muscular and secretory disorders associated with emotional and psychic strain; *infective,* arising from focal infection in another part of the body; *nutritional,* caused by deficiencies in the diet, especially of proteins and vitamins, and by lack of certain gastric hormones; and *traumatic,* from local injury caused by a foreign body. Peptic ulcers are treated by diet, medication, or surgery. Rest is of great therapeutic importance, as is the avoidance of mental and physical fatigue and psychic tension. The combination of psychotherapy with physical therapy has recently proved to be of great importance in promoting recovery and preventing recurrence.

ULEABORG. See OULU.

ULEMA, the collective name (which cannot be used as a singular) of professional theologians and doctors of divinity, and therefore of law, in any Mohammedan country. They

The Protestant cathedral in Ulm, second-largest church in Germany

form the legal and judicial class, and interpret the Koran; they also constitute whatever there is of hierarchy in Islam. The most renowned are the ulema of Istanbul, of Mecca, and of the Azhar University in Cairo.

ULEX. See FURZE.

ULFILAS, ULPHILAS, or **WULFILA** (about 311–81), Bishop of the Goths and translator of the Bible into Gothic. For over thirty years he labored in Lower Mœsia, at the foot of the Hæmus, visited Constantinople (now Istanbul) in 360 in the interest of the Arian Party, and again in 381. He is remembered chiefly for his translation of the Bible, which marks the beginning not only of Christianity among his people, but of Germanic literature. See GOTHIC VERSION OF THE BIBLE.

ULLSWATER, the largest of the English lakes, after Windermere, lying between Cumberland and Westmoreland, 10 miles E. of Keswick. Length, 8½ miles; breadth, ¼ to ¾ mile. Its scenery is rugged and grand, and one of its chief features is Helvellyn.

ULM, city of Baden-Württemberg, West Germany, 58 miles S.E. of Stuttgart, on the left bank of the Danube. On the Bavarian side of the river is New Ulm. Its fortifications (1842–66) have since been greatly extended. The Protestant cathedral is remarkable for architectural beauty, and is, next to the cathedral of Cologne, the largest church in Germany. Leading industries are the manufacture of cotton, woolen, and other textiles, leather, and beer. Ulm is famed, moreover, for ornamental pipe bowls and pastry called Ulmer bread. By the Treaty of Ulm (1620) Frederick V lost Bohemia. Ulm was in October, 1805, the scene of the defeat by Ney of General Mack, and of his surrender with 28,000 Austrians. In 1931 there was found in a cave near Ulm the skull of a man of the Aurignacian period, some twenty to fifty thousand years ago. The cave was a neolithic burial place and contained bones of mammoths and other species of prehistoric animals. Pop. (1950 prelim.) 69,941. See SWABIAN LEAGUE.

ULPHILAS. See ULFILAS.

ULRICH VON LICHTENSTEIN (about 1200–76), German minnesinger (q.v.), born in Styria, of an ancient noble race. He was *landeshauptmann* of Styria in 1245, headed the refractory Styrian nobility, and went through a terrible imprisonment in his own castle of Frauenburg. His chief work, *Frauendienst* (1255), is valuable for the history of contemporary civilization. It describes many tournaments and foolish adventures, which he, a married man and an otherwise sensible gentleman of good reputation, claims to have undertaken in the service of a high-born mistress.

ULSTER, the most northern of the four provinces of Ireland. It comprises nine counties: Antrim, Armagh, Cavan, Donegal, Down, Fermanagh, Londonderry, Monaghan, and Tyrone. See BELFAST; IRELAND, REPUBLIC OF; NORTHERN IRELAND.

ULSTER REBELLION, a revolution that took place in Ireland between 1641 and 1649, and in which Roger More, Phelim O'Neill, and other Irish leaders participated. The attempt to seize Dublin Castle was made but failed. A general uprising throughout Ulster took place and the country was wasted, towns were taken, and many settlers were put to death and thousands of lives lost. Then, in 1649, Cromwell arrived as lord lieutenant and commander in chief and by drastic methods suppressed the movement.

ULTRAMONTANISM, in the Roman Catholic Church, the doctrine of those who recognize the papal claim of supremacy over all national churches and sovereigns. Since 1870 it has been used also as a designation of all who accept the decrees of the Vatican Council, and in a broader sense it has been applied to the most conservative element in the Roman Catholic Church. In a purely political sense it has come to be used to designate the extreme Catholic party in almost every nation of northern Europe. The Ultramontanists as a Church party first appeared in the papacy of Gregory VII, who maintained that the pope had the power to depose and absolve temporal rulers.

ULTRASONICS, branch of physics dealing with high-frequency sound waves, usually in the range above 20,000 cycles per second. In contradistinction to supersonics (q.v.), which deals with phenomena arising when the velocity of a solid body exceeds the speed of sound, ultrasonics deals with acoustical sound waves too high-pitched to be heard. The two words were formerly used interchangeably. Modern ultrasonic generators can produce frequencies up to about 500,000 cycles per second by transforming alternating electric currents into mechanical oscillations. Detection and measurement of ultrasonic waves are accomplished mainly through the use of a piezoelectric receiver (see CRYSTAL) or by optical means. The latter method is based on the fact that ultrasonic waves are rendered visible by the diffraction of light.

The science of ultrasonics has numerous applications in various fields of physics, chemistry, technology, and medicine. Applied originally after World War I as a means of underwater signalling, ultrasonic waves were later used for detection and communication devices called sonar (q.v.), of great importance in present-day navigation, and especially in submarine warfare. Applications in physics include determination of such properties of matter as compressibility, specific heat ratios, and elasticity. Ultrasonics is employed in the production of emulsions, such as homogenized milk and photographic film, for dispersion and coagulation processes, and for the detection of flaws in industrial materials. Strong screen illumination in television is accomplished through the use of ultrasonic waves modulated by diffraction of light. The newest applications of ultrasonics are in the field of medicine. Ultrasonic devices are employed diagnostically for such pathologies as gallstones, and in the mid-1950's the therapeutic possibilities of ultrasonic diathermy were being investigated.

V